BRITISH WARSHIPS

1914-1919

British Warships
1914-1919

F. J. DITTMAR & J. J. COLLEDGE

LONDON
IAN ALLAN

First published 1972

SBN 7110 0380 7

All rights reserved. No part of this book may be reproduced or transmitted in any form or by any means, electronic or mechanical, including photo-copying, recording or by any information storage and retrieval system, without permission from the Publisher in writing.

> London Borough
> of Enfield
> Public Libraries
>
> K56072
>
> 623.8'25
>
> Mly E337

© F. J. Dittmar and J. J. Colledge 1972

Published by Ian Allan Ltd, Shepperton, Surrey and printed in the United Kingdom by The Press at Coombelands Ltd, Addlestone, Surrey

CONTENTS

Introduction .. ..page	6
Abbreviations	8
Ship particulars	9
Pendant numbers	10
Signal Flags and Pendants	11
Wartime alterations and colour of HM Ships	13
Nominal strength of Fleets and Squadrons	14
Fleet distribution	15
Home and Foreign Stations	28
Pre-Dreadnought Battleships ..	29
Dreadnought Battleships	32
Battlecruisers	35
Light Battlecruisers	37
Cruisers	38
Light Cruisers	47
Aircraft Carriers	51
Destroyers and Leaders..	56
Torpedo Boats	78
Ex-coastal Destroyers	81
Submarines	82
Escorts	92
Monitors	102
Gunboats	105
Minesweepers	107
Screw Minesweepers	108
Paddle Minesweepers	109
Minelayers	117
Armed Merchant Cruisers	119
Commissioned Escort Ships	122
Armed Boarding Steamers	123
Patrol Paddle Vessels	124
Coastguard and Fishery Protection ..	125
Q Ships	126
Motor Boats	134
Motor Launches	136
Coastal Motor Boats	137
The Auxiliary Patrol	141
Auxiliary Patrol Areas	143
Home Waters-Patrol Areas	144
Mediterranean-Patrol Zones	145
Numbers in the Auxiliary Patrol page	146
Hired Yachts	149
Admiralty Trawlers	153
Canadian Trawlers	170
Indian Trawlers	173
Prize Trawlers	174
Hired Trawlers and Drifters	177
Fishery Trawlers	214
Admiralty Whalers	218
Whalers	219
Admiralty Drifters	220
Canadian-built Admiralty Wood Drifters	224
Admiralty Steel Drifters	227
Hired Drifters	232
Motor Drifters	263
Miscellaneous Patrol Vessels ..	267
Tugs	271
Rescue Tugs	282
Salvage Vessels	287
Lifting Craft	287
Boom Defence Vessels..	288
Blockships..	290
Mooring Vessels	291
Depot and Repair Ships	292
Fuel Ships	296
Water Tank Vessels	302
Store Carriers	304
Mercantile Fleet Auxiliaries	305
Landing Craft	313
Lighters and Barges	314
Aircraft Lighters	315
Special Service Vessels	316
Survey Vessels	319
Hospital Ships	320
Troopships	321
Harbour Service	322
Harbour Identification Pendants ..	325
Pendant members of USN Warships	326
Warship Builders	327
Ship Breakers	330
Renamed Ships	331

INTRODUCTION

In 1914 the Royal Navy was as well prepared for a major surface war as prewar operations, planning and established concepts could predict. The decade previous to the outbreak of war had seen Britain's naval dockyards and commercial shipbuilding industry out-produce those of Germany to such an extent that the nation had a larger fleet of big-gun capital ships than either its potential enemy or any other nation could boast. In respect to cruisers and smaller warships, in spite of vast world-wide commitments, she could feel as secure. The auxiliary support vessels, depot ships, and lesser craft numbered more than any other power and would be capable of serving the combatant units efficiently in time of war. In addition, the Royal Navy had the world's largest merchant navy and fishing fleet from which to draw reserve strength As a nation heavily dependent upon the sea, there was no shortage of experienced and capable seamen to man the ships. For some years work had been underway on new bases and improvement of the facilities of the well established Royal Dockyards. Despite these numerous strong points, the ensuing hard years of war taxed all of these resources to the limit and naval losses were higher than in any previous war.

As the land war was settling into a long and costly stalemate in the trenches of France, the sea war rapidly developed in directions other than had been expected. It had been anticipated that the big, expensive fleets of battleships and battle-cruisers would soon come into action with the enemy and produce a favourable decision at sea. In addition to naval thinking, public opinion and pride lent credibility to this belief, which was later proven correct to a certain extent. The situation was not as simple as this; the several large naval battles that took place during the next few years produced final success more from a strategic outcome than from direct and overwhelming victory in battle.

It was generally accepted that mine warfare would be of increased importance in the war, but the mine threat was underestimated and far greater loss and effort was involved. An even more dangerous threat also came from beneath the surface of the sea in the form of the submarine. Germany, although not among the original developers of this type of warship, with quite a limited number of U-boats soon caused extreme concern as underwater successes against both warships and merchant shipping alike made their vulnerability all too obvious. Initial U-boat successes resulted to a high degree on a total lack of countermeasure weapons and detection devices. By 1917 the anti-submarine warfare and weapons were vastly improved, but by that time the shipping losses reached their peak because the number of U-boats on sea patrol had risen greatly. As later repeated in World War II, Germany made every effort to pursue the U-boat advantage. Utmost priority was given to U-boat construction in an effort to win the war by this means. A very large number of submarines were built as minelayers and these U-boats carried on where the earlier surface minelayers left off. Shipping losses rose to staggering heights and even the most powerful battleships were in need of protection.

Aircraft were used more and more as the war progressed, but the numbers employed were not sufficient to directly influence tactics and the general conduct of the war. Certainly the future potential of the aircraft as a weapon was recognised to a degree and had the development been more advanced and proven at this date it may have come into its own a war earlier. Heavy and concentrated strategic air bombing attacks were beyond the capabilities of these aircraft because of their very limited bomb load. Nevertheless they did scouting, intercept, and a number of air attacks on warships of small size were successful.

The task of maintaining supply lines, by no means new to a long-standing world power such as Britain, was even more critical as the war continued. Increased efficiency in detection and destruction of submarines was essential. The convoy system must take a great deal of credit for the defeat of the German submarine campaign, though in order to be successful they had to be large, well disciplined and provided with an adequate escort.

Wireless equipment, although primitive, was rapidly being improved upon and its use helped the stronger of the naval powers to maintain a firmer hold on the seaways since detection of the presence of naval forces was now more probable. Dazzle camouflage was introduced during the war with some proven advantage, its intention being to obscure features and confuse speed and direction of steaming rather than prevent sighting of a vessel by the enemy. Various other innovations and inventions saw light during these years including listening hydrophones followed by echo-ranging equipment, but these mentioned were perhaps the most noteworthy.

It is the intention of this book to include a basic record of essentially all of the wide range of vessel types, both large and small, existing in 1914 and conceived or projected as a direct result of the war. The number of heavy units in the RN 1914–1919 exceeded the number involved in World War II, and except for the landing craft of the 1939–45 period, the grand total involved in World War I also must have been greater. Abbreviations and tabular form for classes of ships has been employed in order that maximum coverage could be possible. Each vessel made a contribution to the over all effort, however small or routine, and it is intended that recognition be given to these vessels, their designers and builders, and to the thousands of seamen of the regular navy, the merchant navy, and the fishing fleet who participated in the war.

Acknowledgments
Grateful appreciation is extended to the following museums whose facilities have been used extensively in the preparation of this book: The Admiralty Library, London (now Naval Historical Library, Ministry of Defence); The National Maritime Museum, Greenwich; The Public Record Office, London; and the Science Museum, London. Recognition of the following persons whose interest and effort made important contributions include Lt-Cdr F. W. Denny RN, G. Ransome, A. Preston, L. Moore, I. Buxton, G. Osbon, D. Lyon, K. Macpherson, Miss V. Riley (Naval Library), Miss Farrow (Naval Historical Branch, M.O.D.) and R. Robinson.

References
Admiralty Pink Lists, Admiralty Red Lists, Navy Lists, Service Lists, Signal Books, Official Loss Lists, Records of War Construction, Admiralty Fleet Orders, Technical Histories, Ships Covers, Ships Histories, Naval Estimates, Lloyds Registers, Lloyds Registers of Yachts, Mercantile Navy List & Maritime Directories, World Ship Society Records, Olsen's Almanacks, British Battleships, British Destroyers, Warships of World War I, Belgian Shiplovers, Brassey's Annuals, German Submarine War, Naval Operations, The Merchant Navy, The Dover Patrol, War Monographs, Janes Fighting Ships, Ships of the Royal Navy, Warships of World War II, Warship International, British Standard Ships, Q Ships and Their Story, Phantom Fleet and many others.

Photographs
Acknowledgment to the National Maritime Museum, Imperial War Museum, P. A. Vicary, Kestins, and the Ministry of Defence for photos used.

ABBREVIATIONS

AA	anti-aircraft (high angle guns)		LH	light house
ABS	armed boarding steamer		LV	light vessel
A/C	aircraft			
Accom	accommodation ship		MB	motor boat
Adty	Admiralty		MG	machine gun
AMC	armed merchant cruiser		ML	motor launch
A/P	armed patrol		M/L	minelayer
A/S	anti-submarine		mm	millimetre
aux	auxiliary		M/S	minesweeper
avg	average			
			oa	over-all
BCS	battlecruiser squadron			
BDV	boom defence vessel		PB	patrol boat
bhp	brake horsepower		pdr	pounder
BS	battle squadron		PMS	paddle minesweeper
BT	bomb thrower (A/S howitzer)		pp	between perpendiculars
BU	broken up			
			Q ship	submarine decoy vessel
c	circa (precedes dates)			
CMB	coastal motor boat		RAN	Royal Australian Navy
comp	compound (steam)		RCN	Royal Canadian Navy
CS	cruiser squadron		RIM	Royal Indian Marine
CTL	constructional total loss		RN	Royal Navy
			RNZN	Royal New Zealand Navy
DF	destroyer flotilla			
dhd	depth of hold		SAN	South African Navy
D/S	depot ship		shp	shaft horsepower
DY	H.M. Dockyard		sqdn	squadron
exam	examination vessel		S/M	submarine
			SS	steam ship (red ensign)
F/O	fitted out		SSV	special service vessel
FT	fishery trawler			
ft	feet		TB	torpedo boat
			TE	triple-expansion (steam)
GF	Grand Fleet		TG	tons gross
govt	government		TGB	torpedo gunboat
			T/S	training ship
HS	harbour service		TT	torpedo tube (s)
Hydro	equipped with listening hydrophones		USN	United States Navy
			USS	United States Ship
ihp	indicated horsepower			
in	inch; inches		WW I	First World War
			WW II	Second World War
kts	knots			
			Yr	year built
LCS	light cruiser squadron			
LDF	local defence flotilla		=	equals; later became

SHIP PARTICULARS

Displacement tonnage is the Navy-list figure (pre-1926 rules). Dimensions are length over-all (oa), length between perpendiculars (pp) ×maximum beam× mean draught. Engines: triple-expansion (TE), Compound (comp), steam turbines (turbine), etc. Horsepower: indicated horsepower (ihp), shaft horsepower (shp), or brake horsepower (bhp)=maximum original designed speed.

Armour: figures given are for the maximum thickness of side armour (usually tapered towards the ship's ends), maximum thickness of deck armour and heaviest armour protection of the main guns.

Pendant numbers: (see special notes).

Ships' names: normally one previous non-naval name-change is given for vessels acquired by the RN. Vessels returning to commercial management are assumed to revert to their former non-naval name unless otherwise noted. After disposal following the war, navy-built vessels that were renamed have at least one change of name noted. The term "=in WW II" signifies that the vessel began service in World War II under the same name borne while last on the World War I list. Many naval names of former mercantile vessels had neither record nor application of this outside the RN and nearly all of the Roman numerals I–VIII were added commencing or during naval service to avoid confusing the name with that of an existing warship. Periods of service where only the month and year (or year alone) is shown indicates when the vessel was first found in the Red List (minor war vessels) or Pink List (major war vessels) and is therefore not the precise date of requisition. The exact dates of most fishing vessels, for example, are not recorded in available references. The demobilisation period was extended over several months and the lists are indistinctive for extracting a month of discharge, hence the year "1919" appears consistently.

Dates are given as day-month-year (ie. 1.12.17 means 1st December 1917).

The photographs as far as is known, are all of war-time origin, except where otherwise stated.

Renaming dates: It is not always clear from Admiralty records whether a renaming date is that of the actual name change or of the Admiralty order to rename; hence in most cases a date has been restricted to month/year only. The same applies to sale dates.

PENDANT NUMBERS

By the year 1914 various identification features for warships had already been in use for several hundred years. Simple signals and flags date back to the first employment of ships together as a fleet. In the 18th century HM ships used signal codebooks with numerous combinations of flags, most of which represented numbers, to send messages to other ships and stations by visual means. In these books each warship was assigned an identification number; other combinations represented phrases such as "engage the enemy more closely" to avoid laboriously spelling it out letter by letter.

From the 19th century onwards the British Navy always consisted of well in excess of 1000 vessels counting from the largest battleship to the smallest auxiliary. Small navies certainly had little difficulty differentiating between one and another of their vessels, but the huge RN was confronted with problems of identification of the highest magnitude. It became common practice after 1880 for numerous warships to be built closely to the same plan and similar vessels were, whenever possible, formed into homogeneous squadrons in order that the group could function as a single, more efficient unit. These factors increased individual identity problems. Smaller warships, in particular, were built in great numbers to standard designs during the war and operated together in force.

Means of individual ship identification varied widely from having names painted up, to the use of funnel bands, etc., and finally combinations of letters and numbers. Numbers provided the simplest and most straightforward means, and in addition, were easy to record. Using a very limited number of pendants (or painted-up digits), normally two, provide 100 different identities from 00 to 99. In 1914, the first-line battleships, battlecruisers and modern cruisers used two numbers only. The pendant number series could be considerably expanded by using different letter flags superior (that is, hoisted first or above) to two number pendants. Each flag superior, as they are called, using a letter or special flag can increase by 100 the different identities possible. Three number pendants can provide 1000 combinations (000–999) while one letter and two number pendants can create 2600 (A.00 to Z.99). Older battleships, and all smaller warships were included in various flag superiors. Further expansion yet, was possible if one of several special pendants were used inferior with one of the number pendants, creating what in effect are new numbers. Each special pendant inferior to each letter group increases the group coverage by 20 units. Destroyers grouped together in December 1914, for example, under H flag superior contained H.00 to H.99, H.0A to H.9A, H.A0 to H.A9, H.C0 to HC.9, and H.0C to H.9C for a total of 140 vessels. When painted-up, Answer became A, Code became C, Numeral became N and Oblique became /. In the example given, H.9C signifies: H flag superior with number 9 pendant and code pendant inferior. Number 13 was not used after late 1917 and in modern pendant lists, with one exception, thus reducing the coverage to 99 units. Special wartime and night signals for recognition purposes were also used by HM ships of highly secretive, complicated and temporary nature.

The pendant numbers supplied in this book were those assigned by the Admiralty Pendant Board for use by warships in Home Waters only. Ships on foreign stations were not assigned pendants by the board unless it was expected that they might enter home waters. American warships operating with the RN also received British pendant numbers while stationed in home waters and the North Sea. Admirals commanding foreign stations were expected to assign pendants to vessels under their command. It was possible for ships to have more than one number in effect for use with alternate organisational units. Destroyers and smaller warships had their pendant numbers painted-up in immediate concurrence with effected changes after mid 1916. Many

SIGNAL FLAGS & PENDANTS W.W. I

A	N	1	1	Answer	
B	O	2	2	Code	
C	P	3	3	Numeral	
D	Q	4	4	Oblique	
E	R	5	5	Interrog.	
F	S	6	6	Guard	
G	T	7	7	Equal Speed	
H	U	8	8	Compass	
I	V	9	9	Blue	
J	W	0	0	Yellow	
K	X	Prep	Blue Burgee	Church	
L	Y	Red Flag	Red Burgee	Fishery Flag	
M	Z	Green Flag	M int.	Red Affirm.	
				Blue Affirm.	
				Negat.	

trawlers and drifters retained their fishing numbers for identification along with their naval numbers. Non-commissioned fishing vessels retained their fishing numbers as their sole identification feature in this respect. When it was considered that no possible confusion would arise, the flag superior was sometimes not painted-up. This applies in particular to destroyers who occasionally omitted flag superiors D and H.

Pendant number alterations could have taken place for security reasons but it is far more likely that re-organisation of squadrons and flotillas, with additions of new vessels made many of the changes necessary. Change of flotilla leader numbers frequently caused other vessels which were commonly in alphabetical order to shift by one number.

Most of the regular combatant ships that were in continuous service from 8.14 to 1.19 had at least three different pendant numbers as a result of major changes put into effect 1.9.15, 1.1.18 and 31.3.18. Pendants given in this book are arranged in dated columns to indicate as closely as possible when a number originated. Stressing that changes are indicated, it should be assumed that a number is not altered until a new one is listed or a cancellation noted. Therefore, the dates given for each number confirms its use by that date but since a few of the signal books containing routine or minor alterations have not been located, some of the 1.18 pendants could have been put into effect earlier. Quite possibly, the 6.10.17 list which is missing could have contained the major changes which were indicated 1.1.18. A total of 21 pendant lists have been located, perhaps six more existed but have not been found. Because most of the lists merely repeated existing assignments and that other pendants have been taken from photographs, at least 90 per cent of the assignments are known. Prewar signal books were completely revised in late 1913 and the first combined pendant list must have been that of 6.12.14 since it was the only issue not cancelling a previously issued list. The normal issuing frequency of the lists was quarterly, although nearly a year elapsed between late war issues. Changes of individual pendants were circulated in Admiralty Fleet Orders which were issued on a daily basis when necessary.

Pendant numbers with a flag superior have a decimal point inserted between the superior and inferior portions when written in this book. The pendant numbers of vessels delivered to the navy after 1.1.19 have their first number recorded while the coverage of older vessels ceases at this date. Except for harbour pendants, which consisted of a single flag, all other pendants were borne by one ship only at a particular time. Some significance of N (Nore), P (Portsmouth) and D (Devonport) flag superiors early in the war is apparent. The use of G and F flag superiors for the new Grand Fleet destroyers (where G was created first) presents more speculation of early selections.

The appearance of flags and pendants commonly used for signalling purposes between 1914 and 1920 is shown in the illustration following where colour of the flags was less important than shades and shapes.

WARTIME ALTERATIONS AND COLOUR OF H.M. SHIPS

The general modifications effected during the 1914–20 period included the reduction of rigging top hamper, shortening of upper masts, removal of anti-torpedo booms and nets, the change from coal to oil fuel, heightened fore funnels to keep bridgework clear of smoke and gases, fitting of anti-torpedo bulges (free-flooding at first), the addition of winged aircraft and balloons, and anti-aircraft guns. Various means of obscuring ship features to confuse the silhouette and make coincidence rangefinding more difficult were employed. Since the Germans did not use this type of range finder, these efforts were ineffective. Depth charges and anti-submarine howitzers originated during this period. Hydrophones for underwater listening purposes appeared, and these led to the development of asdic (sonar) equipment which in June 1920 was experimentally fitted aboard HMSs CACHALOT, ICEWHALE, P.31, P.38 and P.59. This equipment used a hand-keyed oscillator (20KCS to 50KCS) employing piezo-electric effect with an effective range of 2500 to 3000 yards. Although quite primitive, this equipment could transmit and receive using a tilting searchlight type transducer for sounding and detection.

COLOUR OF HM SHIPS: CHRONOLOGICAL NOTES

- **8. 9.14** Flotilla leader FAULKNOR has been painted grey
- **19.11.14** Hulls and weather work of all H M ships in home waters except torpedo craft to become light grey. Mixture to be 1 part black to 20 parts white by weight.
- **27. 3.15** Destroyers of the 6th Flotilla experimentally patchy grey.
- **6. 4.15** Destroyers to remain dead black but masts to become a very light grey.
- **6. 4.15** A false bow wave to be painted on all ships.
- **7. 5.15** False bow wave not to be painted on destroyers and torpedo boats.
- **1. 6.15** No bow wave on any ships.
- **13. 7.15** Paint flotilla leaders grey, destroyers remain black.
- **18. 8.15** Armed trawlers to be painted in their original fishing colours with their commercial fishing numbers.
- **1916** The cruiser CARYSFORT temporarily painted blue.
- **15. 4.16** Approval given to paint destroyers of the 2nd DF grey while with that command.
- **23. 5.16** Commander-in-Chief Rosyth's proposal to paint his torpedo craft grey approved—to be done during the summer months.
- **7. 7.16** All torpedo craft hitherto black to be painted grey. Hull 1 part black to 20 parts white (by weight), upper works to use mixture 1 part black to 23 parts white.
- **14. 7.16** Boats of destroyers to be painted grey, 1 part black to 23 parts white.
- **1. 8.16** H M ships and armed patrol yachts to be painted grey (formula 1:20 black and white). Destroyers to remain dead black with masts very light grey.
- **4. 8.16** Upper works of destroyers and leaders painted grey.
- **22. 8.16** Suggested that submarines be painted black on horizontal parts, vertical parts grey. Colour depends upon decision of Senior Officer of each area.
- **19. 4.17** Topmasts of H M ships to paint 1 part black to 250 parts white (by weight) mixture by order of Commander-in-Chief, Grand Fleet.
- **10. 8.18** Dazzle camouflage painting ordered for merchant ships and armed merchant cruisers of the 10th CS.
- **8. 2.19** All light cruisers on East Indies and China stations to be painted white.
- **1. 3.19** Survey ships to be painted white.

Notes: In spite of the confusion generated in painting orders concerning destroyers and torpedo boats, it can be concluded that order of 7.7.16 did become effective by 15.8.16 and from that date the pendant numbers were painted up. An order from 1914 specified that two ensigns were to be flown by H M ships in order that confusion resulting from distant similarities between the white ensign and the German ensign could be reduced. An order dated 19.11.14 put into effect a system of markings on the after two funnels to denote divisional status; this system was a repetition of earlier ones and did not remain in effect for long. The colour notes above all originated from Admiralty fleet orders of that date and were effective when received.

NOMINAL STRENGTH OF FLEETS AND SQUADRONS

GRAND FLEET	8.14	1.16	11.18
Dreadnoughts	21	27	36*
Pre-dreadnoughts	15	7	—
Battlecruisers	4	10	10
Armrd. cruisers	11	13	4
Cruisers	13	31	44
A/C Carriers	—	2	5
Destroyers	94	120	200

*includes 5 USN

MEDITERRANEAN			
Dreadnoughts	—	—	2
Pre-dreadnoughts	—	21	3
Battlecruisers	3	—	—
Armrd. cruisers	4	2	—
Cruisers	4	23	22
A/C Carriers	—	4	6
Monitors	—	22	16
Destroyers	16	29	65*
Torpedo boats	8	19	16
Submarines	6	13	18

*includes 14 Japanese.

CHINA, E. INDIES, E. AFRICA			
Pre-dreadnoughts	2	—	—
Armrd. cruisers	2	1	3
Cruisers	3	6	9
Destroyers	8	3	3
Torpedo boats	4	4	4
Submarines	3	3	3

OTHER UK-based SHIPS, ships paid off etc.	8.14	1.16	11.18
Dreadnoughts	—	—	3(USN)
Pre-dreadnoughts	22	3	18
Armrd. cruisers	11	3	1
Cruisers	38	7	10
A/C Carriers	—	4	—
Monitors	—	12	16
Destroyers	95	90	215*
Torpedo boats	79	76	45
Submarines	65	76	118**

*includes 24 USN. **includes 7 USN.

ATLANTIC, WEST INDIES			
Pre-dreadnoughts	1	1	—
Armrd. cruisers	10	8	11
Cruisers	4	4	4

CAPE, WEST AFRICA			
Pre-dreadnoughts	—	1	—
Armrd. cruisers	—	—	1
Cruisers	3	3	4
Torpedo boats	2	2	2

PACIFIC			
Battlecruisers	1	—	—
Armrd. cruisers	—	1	1
Cruisers	9	2	5
Destroyers	3	3	—
Submarines	2	—	—

FLEET DISTRIBUTION

(Excluding depot ships, ships on harbour service etc; 'old Ds' implies the destroyers of the A to E classes; 'det' implies 'detached')

5 August 1914

Grand Fleet

Fleet flagship: IRON DUKE

1st BS	2nd BS	3rd BS	4th BS	9th BS (Grimsby)
MARLBOROUGH	K. GEORGE V	K. EDWARD VII	DREADNOUGHT	HANNIBAL
COLLINGWOOD	AJAX	AFRICA	BELLEROPHON	MAGNIFICENT
COLOSSUS	AUDACIOUS	BRITANNIA	TEMERAIRE	MARS
HERCULES	CENTURION	COMMONWEALTH	AGINCOURT	VICTORIOUS
NEPTUNE	CONQUEROR	DOMINION	(on Tyne)	
ST VINCENT	MONARCH	HIBERNIA		
SUPERB	ORION	HINDUSTAN		
VANGUARD	THUNDERER	ZEALANDIA		

Attached	1st BCS	2nd CS	3rd CS	6th CS
BELLONA	LION	SHANNON	ANTRIM	DRAKE
BLANCHE	NEW ZEALAND	ACHILLES	ARGYLL	LEVIATHAN
BLONDE	PSS ROYAL	COCHRANE	DEVONSHIRE	GOOD HOPE
BOADICEA	QUEEN MARY	NATAL	ROXBURGH	KING ALFRED (later)
SAPPHO				
OAK				

Destroyer Cmd: AMETHYST

1st LCS	1st DF	2nd DF	3rd DF (Harwich)	4th DF
SOUTHAMPTON	FEARLESS	ACTIVE	AMPHION	SWIFT
BIRMINGHAM	20 I class	20 H class	16 L class (4 to join)	20 K class
FALMOUTH				
LIVERPOOL	Local defence	Minelayers	Minesweepers	Miscellaneous
LOWESTOFT	FORWARD	7 cruisers (at Sheerness)	10 TGBs (2 det)	1 Armed yacht
NOTTINGHAM	16 old Ds			2 ABSs

Other forces in UK waters

5th BS (Portland)	6th BS (Portland)	7th BS (Devonport)	8th BS (Devonport)	Cruiser Force 'F' (Sheerness)
P OF WALES	LORD NELSON*	PRINCE GEORGE	ALBION	HOGUE
BULWARK	RUSSELL	CAESAR	CANOPUS	SUTLEJ
IMPLACABLE	AGAMEMNON*	ILLUSTRIOUS	GLORY	
IRRESISTIBLE	ALBEMARLE	MAJESTIC	GOLIATH	5th CS
FORMIDABLE	CORNWALLIS	SAPPHIRE	JUPITER	CARNARVON
LONDON	DUNCAN		OCEAN	CORNWALL
QUEEN	EXMOUTH		PROSERPINE	CUMBERLAND
VENERABLE	VENGEANCE		(GLORY to W.	MONMOUTH
TOPAZE	DIAMOND*		Atlantic,	(all to W Africa)
	*to 5th BS		others to 7th BS)	

7th CS (Southern North Sea)	9th CS (Portland)	10th CS (Northern Patrol)	11th CS	12th CS
BACCHANTE	AMPHITRITE	CRESCENT	DORIS	CHARYBDIS
ABOUKIR	ARGONAUT	EDGAR	ISIS	DIANA
CRESSY	EUROPA	ENDYMION	JUNO	ECLIPSE
EURYALUS	HIGHFLYER	GIBRALTAR	MINERVA	TALBOT
	VINDICTIVE	GRAFTON	VENUS	
	CHALLENGER (in Bristol Channel)	HAWKE		
		ROYAL ARTHUR		
		THESEUS		

6th DF (Dover)	7th DF (Humber)	Patrol Flotillas 8th DF (Forth)	9th DF (Tyne)	Downs Boarding Flotilla
ATTENTIVE ADVENTURE FORESIGHT SENTINEL 12 F class 12 old Ds	SKIRMISHER 22 old Ds 12 TBs	PATHFINDER 9 old Ds 12 TBs	PATROL 19 old Ds	6 Armed tugs 2 TGBs

3rd (Devonport)	4th (Dover)	Submarine Flotillas 5th (Nore)	7th (Forth)	8th (Harwich)
3 B class 3 C class (det to Dover)	7 C class D.I, S.1	6 C class 6th (Humber) 6 C class	12 C class 9th (Ardrossan) 1 destroyer 3 A class	2 destroyers 8 D class 9 E class

Nore	Portsmouth	Local Defence Flotillas Devonport	Pembroke	Home Ports
12 old Ds 20 TBs	6 old Ds 13 TBs 4 old S/Ms	4 TBs	4 TBs Queenstown 4 TBs	13 Adm. Trawlers 13 Hired Trawlers

		Fitting-out in the UK		
Q ELIZABETH	ARETHUSA AURORA CORDELIA	DONEGAL HERMES KENT	SIRIUS TERRIBLE	5 AMCs 4 A/C carriers

Mediterranean	W Atlantic	Cape & W Africa	Australia	China
2nd BCS INFLEXIBLE INDEFATIGABLE INDOMITABLE 1st CS DEFENCE BLACK PRINCE D OF EDINBURGH WARRIOR	4th CS SUFFOLK BERWICK BRISTOL ESSEX LANCASTER GLORY NIOBE 1 AMC	HYACINTH ASTRAEA PEGASUS (det) 1 gunboat Pacific NEWCASTLE RAINBOW 2 sloops	AUSTRALIA ENCOUNTER MELBOURNE SYDNEY PIONEER 3 destroyers 2 E class S/Ms	MINOTAUR HAMPSHIRE YARMOUTH TRIUMPH 8 old Ds 4 TBs 3 old S/Ms 6 sloops 4 AMCS (fitting out)

Cruisers	S Atlantic	New Zealand	E Indies	
CHATHAM DUBLIN GLOUCESTER WEYMOUTH 16 G class Ds 1 TGB 1 AMC	GLASGOW	PSYCHE PHILOMEL PYRAMUS 1 sloop	SWIFTSURE DARTMOUTH FOX 3 sloops 5 RIM ships	

January 1915

Grand Fleet
Fleet flagship: IRON DUKE

1st BS	2nd BS	3rd BS	4th BS	1st BCS
MARLBOROUGH COLLINGWOOD COLOSSUS HERCULES NEPTUNE ST VINCENT SUPERB VANGUARD	CENTURION AJAX AUDACIOUS CONQUEROR K GEORGE V MONARCH ORION THUNDERER	K EDWARD VII AFRICA BRITANNIA COMMONWEALTH DOMINION HIBERNIA HINDUSTAN ZEALANDIA	BENBOW AGINCOURT BELLEROPHON DREADNOUGHT E OF INDIA ERIN TEMERAIRE	LION INDOMITABLE NEW ZEALAND PRINCESS ROYAL QUEEN MARY TIGER

Attached	1st CS	2nd CS	3rd CS	6th CS
BELLONA BLANCHE BLONDE BOADICEA SAPPHIRE SAPPHO OAK	LEVIATHAN BLACK PRINCE DUKE OF EDINBURGH WARRIOR	SHANNON ACHILLES COCHRANE NATAL	ANTRIM ARGYLL DEVONSHIRE ROXBURGH	DRAKE CUMBERLAND DONEGAL HAMPSHIRE

Dest. Cmd.	1st LCS	2nd LCS	A/C Carriers (at Harwich)	Minesweepers
ARETHUSA	SOUTHAMPTON	FALMOUTH	EMPRESS	8 TGBs
AURORA	BIRMINGHAM	GLOUCESTER	ENGADINE	8 Hired vessels
(at Chatham)	LOWESTOFT	LIVERPOOL	RIVIERA	
	NOTTINGHAM	YARMOUTH		
		DARTMOUTH (det)		

1st DF	2nd DF	3rd DF (Harwich)	4th DF	Local defence
FEARLESS	ACTIVE	UNDAUNTED	CAROLINE	29 old Ds
METEOR	GALATEA	30 L & M classes	FAULKNOR	
20 I class	BROKE		SWIFT	Miscellaneous
	21 H class		22 K class	8 ABSs

Other forces in UK waters

5th BS (Channel)	6th BS (Nore)	10th CS (Northern Patrol)	11th CS (Irish Ports)	12th CS (Atlantic Convoys)
LORD NELSON	ALBEMARLE	23 AMCs	SUTLEJ	EURYALUS
AGAMEMNON	CORNWALLIS		ISIS	BACCHANTE
FORMIDABLE	DUNCAN		JUNO	CHARYBDIS
IMPLACABLE	EXMOUTH		VENUS	DIANA
IRRESISTIBLE	RUSSELL		4 ABSs	ECLIPSE
LONDON	REVENGE			TALBOT
P OF WALES	(at Dover)			4 ABSs
QUEEN				
VENERABLE				
DIAMOND				
TOPAZE				

Patrol Flotillas

6th DF (Dover)	7th DF (Humber)	8th DF (Forth)	9th DF (Tyne)	Downs Boarding Flot.
ATTENTIVE	SKIRMISHER	SENTINEL	PATROL	4 ABSs
ADVENTURE	FORWARD	7 old Ds	14 old Ds	8 Armed Tugs
FORESIGHT	10 old Ds	14 TBs	4 TBs	
12 F class	8 TBs			
12 old Ds				
2 monitors				

Submarine Flotillas

1st (Devonport)	2nd (Portsmouth)	3rd (Yarmouth)	4th (Dover)	5th (Sheerness)
2 A class	2 A class	1 C class	3 B class	6 C class
	1 B class		9 C class	

6th (Tyne)	7th (Forth)	8th (Harwich)	9th (Clyde)	10th (Humber)
7 C class	6 C class	2 destroyers	3 A class	5 C class
		4 D class		
		10 E class		
		1 S class		

	Local Defence etc		Guardships, refits etc	
Nore	Portsmouth	Devonport	Q ELIZABETH	BRILLIANT
12 old Ds	8 old Ds	4 old Ds	HANNIBAL	CORDELIA
20 TBs	17 TBs	8 TBs	ILLUSTRIOUS	DIADEM
7 minelayers	6 G class (to		JUPITER	HERMIONE
1 monitor	10th DF)		MAGNIFICENT	SIRIUS
1 sloop	1 sloop		MAJESTIC	WALLAROO
			VICTORIOUS	

Portland	Pembroke	Queenstown
6 TBs	4 TBs	4 TBs

Mediterranean	E Indies & Egypt	China	Australia	Pacific
INDEFATIGABLE	SWIFTSURE	TRIUMPH	ENCOUNTER	AUSTRALIA
DUBLIN	OCEAN	3 old Ds	PIONEER	NEWCASTLE
PELORUS	DORIS	4 TBs	3 destroyers	PSYCHE
PHILOMEL	MINERVA	3 submarines	1 submarine	RAINBOW
9 destroyers	PROSERPINE	1 AMC	2 sloops	1 sloop
11 TBs	PYRAMUS			
5 submarines	7 old Ds			
	6 TBs			
	3 sloops			
	3 AMCs			
	6 RIM ships			

N America & W Indies	SE Coast of America	Cape & W Africa	Cape Verde	Off W Africa 9th CS
GLORY	CANOPUS	ALBION	VENGEANCE	ARGONAUT
BERWICK	BRISTOL	GOLIATH	HIGHFLYER	AMPHITRITE
DARTMOUTH	CARNARVON	ASTRAEA	2 AMCs	VINDICTIVE
ESSEX	CORNWALL	DEFENCE		EUROPA (at Portsmouth)
LANCASTER	GLASGOW	HYACINTH		PRINCE GEORGE (at Lisbon)
MELBOURNE	KENT	MINOTAUR		3 AMCs
NIOBE	5 AMCs	2 TBs		
SUFFOLK		2 AMCs		
SYDNEY		CHALLENGER		
2 AMCs		1 gunboat		

January 1916
Grand Fleet
Fleet flagship: IRON DUKE
BC Force flagship: LION

1st BS	2nd BS	3rd BS	4th BS	5th BS
MARLBOROUGH	K GEORGE V	K EDWARD VII	BENBOW	BARHAM
AGINCOURT	AJAX	AFRICA	BELLEROPHON	Q ELIZABETH
COLLINGWOOD	CENTURION	ALBEMARLE	CANADA	WARSPITE
COLOSSUS	CONQUEROR	BRITANNIA	DREADNOUGHT	
HERCULES	ERIN	COMMONWEALTH	E OF INDIA	
NEPTUNE	MONARCH	DOMINION	SUPERB	
ST VINCENT	ORION	HINDUSTAN	TEMERAIRE	
VANGUARD	THUNDERER			Attached ships
				BELLONA
				BLANCHE
1st BCS	2nd BCS	3rd BCS		BOADICEA
PSS ROYAL	AUSTRALIA	INVINCIBLE		DIAMOND
QUEEN MARY	INDEFATIGABLE	INDOMITABLE		SAPPHO
TIGER	NEW ZEALAND	INFLEXIBLE		OAK

1st CS	2nd CS	3rd CS	7th CS	A/C carriers
DEFENCE	SHANNON	ANTRIM	MINOTAUR	CAMPANIA
BLACK PRINCE	ACHILLES	DEVONSHIRE	DONEGAL	EMPRESS
DK OF EDINBURGH	COCHRANE	ROXBURGH	HAMPSHIRE	ENGADINE (Forth)
WARRIOR				VINDEX (Harwich)

1st LCS	2nd LCS	3rd LCS	4th LCS	5th LCS (Harwich)
GALATEA	SOUTHAMPTON	FALMOUTH	CALLIOPE	ARETHUSA
CORDELIA	BIRMINGHAM	BIRKENHEAD	CAROLINE	CLEOPATRA
INCONSTANT	LOWESTOFT	GLOUCESTER	COMUS	CONQUEST
PHAETON	NOTTINGHAM	YARMOUTH		PENELOPE
	CHAMPION			

1st DF	2nd DF (Cromarty)	4th DF	9th DF (Harwich)	10th DF (Harwich)
FEARLESS	BROKE	CARYSFORT	UNDAUNTED	AURORA
BOTHA	2 M class	FAULKNOR	LIGHTFOOT	NIMROD
20 I class		19 K class	18 L class	16 M class

11th DF (Cromarty)	12th DF	Local Defence	Minesweepers	10th CS (Northern Patrol)
CASTOR	ROYALIST	15 old Ds	6 TGBs	23 AMCs
KEMPENFELT	MARKSMAN	Miscellaneous	9 sloops	
15 M class	5 M class	9 ABSs		

Patrol Flotillas

6th DF (Dover)	7th DF (Humber)	8th DF (Rosyth)	North Channel (Larne)	Downs Boarding Flotilla
ATTENTIVE	PATROL	7 old Ds	2 old Ds	5 ABSs
SWIFT	20 old Ds	10 TBs	**(Liverpool)**	10 Armed Tugs
11 F class			2 old Ds	
13 old Ds				

Submarine Flotillas

1st (Devonport)	2nd (Portsmouth)	4th (Dover)	5th (Sheerness)	6th (Tyne)
2 A class	1 A class	2 A class	6 C class	8 C class
	2 B class	6 C class		
7th (Leith)	1 G class	1 F class	8th (Harwich)	
8 C class		2 V class	2 destroyers	
			4 D class	
9th (Ardrossan)	10th (Humber)	11th (Blyth)	9 E class	
1 destroyer	3 C class	1 destroyer	5 E class (detached)	
1 A class	2 W class	2 D class	2 H class	
2 B class		2 E class	4 H class (at Yarmouth)	

Local Defence etc

Nore	Portsmouth	Devonport	Queenstown	Minesweepers (North Sea)
10 old Ds	18 old Ds	6 old Ds	4 TBs	4 TGBs
17 TBs	21 TBs	8 TBs	12 sloops	4 sloops
4 minelayers				
	Portland	Part 2nd DF	Dover	
	6 TBs	TIPPERARY	12 monitors	
		9 H class	1 A/C Carrier	

Ships paid-off, refits etc

ILLUSTRIOUS	ACTIVE	ARIADNE	DRAKE	LANCASTER
REDOUBTABLE	AMPHITRITE	BERWICK	DUBLIN	NAIAD
VICTORIOUS	ANDROMACHE	BRISTOL	ECLIPSE	SUTLEJ
	APOLLO	CRESCENT	HERMIONE	THETIS
	ARGONAUT	DIADEM	INTREPID	WALLAROO

Mediterranean

Battleships	Battleships	Cruisers	Cruisers	Destroyers
HIBERNIA	GLORY	BACCHANTE	FORWARD	3 L class
AGAMEMNON	LORD NELSON	CHATHAM	GRAFTON	4 H class
ALBION	PRINCE GEORGE	DORIS	PELORUS	13 G class
CANOPUS	P OF WALES	EDGAR	SENTINEL	9 old Ds
CORNWALLIS	RUSSELL	ENDYMION	SKIRMISHER	
EXMOUTH	SWIFTSURE	EURYALUS	TALBOT	19 TBs
	ZEALANDIA	FORESIGHT	THESEUS	11 submarines
Trooping				2 A/C carriers
MAGNIFICENT				19 monitors
MARS				2 minelayers
TERRIBLE				13 ABSs

Attached Italian Fleet

QUEEN	DUNCAN	DARTMOUTH	TOPAZE	5 B class S/Ms
LONDON	VENERABLE	LIVERPOOL	WEYMOUTH	
		SAPPHIRE		

Egyptian Waters

HANNIBAL (D/S)	IMPLACABLE	FOX	2 A/C carriers	6 sloops
	JUPITER	MINERVA	2 monitors	4 RIM ships
		PROSERPINE		
		VENUS		

Persian Gulf	China	China	Pacific	Australia
JUNO	CORNWALL	3 old Ds	KENT	3 destroyers
PHILOMEL	DIANA	4 TBs	NEWCASTLE	1 sloop
PYRAMUS	ENCOUNTER	3 C class S/Ms	RAINBOW (D/S)	
5 sloops	PSYCHE	2 sloops	1 AMC	
2 RIM ships		1 AMC		

E Africa	Cape	W Africa	Off W Africa	N America & W Indies
CHALLENGER	HYACINTH	ASTRAEA	HIGHFLYER	LEVIATHAN
PIONEER	VENGEANCE	SIRIUS	1 AMC	CARNARVON
1 AMC	2 AMCs	2 sloops		CUMBERLAND
2 monitors	2 TBs		9th CS	ISIS
1 gunboat			KING ALFRED	MELBOURNE
			ESSEX	SYDNEY
	White Sea		2 AMCs	SUFFOLK
	IPHIGENIA			CAESAR
				2 AMCs

January 1917

Grand Fleet
Fleet flagship: IRON DUKE
BC Force flagship: LION

1st BS	2nd BS	3rd BS	4th BS	5th BS
MARLBOROUGH	K GEORGE V	DREADNOUGHT	HERCULES	BARHAM
AGINCOURT	AJAX	COMMONWEALTH	BELLEROPHON	MALAYA
BENBOW	CENTURION	DOMINION	COLLINGWOOD	Q ELIZABETH
CANADA	CONQUEROR	HIBERNIA	COLOSSUS	VALIANT
E OF INDIA	ERIN	HINDUSTAN	NEPTUNE	WARSPITE
REVENGE	MONARCH	ZEALANDIA	ST VINCENT	
ROYAL OAK	ORION		SUPERB	
R SOVEREIGN	THUNDERER		TEMERAIRE	
			VANGUARD	

Attached	1st BCS	2nd BCS	2nd CS	A/C carriers
BELLONA	PSS ROYAL	NEW ZEALAND	COCHRANE	CAMPANIA
BLONDE	TIGER	AUSTRALIA	ACHILLES	VINDEX (Harwich)
BOADICEA	REPULSE	INDOMITABLE	MINOTAUR	
DIAMOND	RENOWN (later)	INFLEXIBLE	SHANNON	Destroyer Cmd
ABDIEL			DK OF	CASTOR
OAK			EDINBURGH	
			(detached)	

1st LCS	2nd LCS	3rd LCS	4th LCS	5th LCS (Harwich)
GALATEA	SOUTHAMPTON	BIRKENHEAD	CALLIOPE	CENTAUR
CORDELIA	DUBLIN	CHESTER	CAROLINE	AURORA
INCONSTANT	MELBOURNE	CHATHAM	CAMBRIAN	CANTERBURY
PHAETON	SYDNEY	YARMOUTH	COMUS	CARYSFORT
		COURAGEOUS	CONSTANCE	CLEOPATRA
6th LCS			ROYALIST	CONCORD
WEYMOUTH (det)				CONQUEST
				PENELOPE

1st DF (Harwich)	9th DF (Harwich)	10th DF (Harwich)	11th DF	12th DF
8 I class	UNDAUNTED	8 M class	SEYMOUR	SAUMAREZ
	LIGHTFOOT	NIMROD and	KEMPENFELT	MARKSMAN
	20 L class	6 M class det to Dover	16 M class 2 R class	18 M class

13th DF	14th DF	15th DF	Local Defence	
CHAMPION	BOTHA	PARKER	15 old Ds	
GABRIEL	ITHURIEL	GRENVILLE		
25 M class	17 M class	5 M class		
	1 R class	13 R class		

10th CS (Clyde)	1st M/S Flot	2nd M/S Flot	3rd M/S Flot	Miscellaneous
26 AMCs	10 sloops	4 sloops	12 paddle M/S	8 ABSs
		6 TGBs		

		Patrol Flotillas etc		
Dover	**Humber**	**Forth**	**N Channel**	**Queenstown**
6th DF	ALBION	**8th DF**	4 old Ds	ADVENTURE
ATTENTIVE	**7th DF**	6 old Ds		4 TBs
BROKE	PATROL	10 TBs		**1st Sloop Flot**
SWIFT	20 old Ds	2 A/C carriers		19 sloops
FAULKNOR	1 P boat			
11 F class		**Lowestoft**	**Tyne**	**Pembroke**
7 I & K classes	**Harwich**	1 monitor	**10th Sloop Flot**	4 TBs
11 old Ds	2 TGBs	2 TGBs	6 sloops	
3 TBs	2 P boats	4 P boats		
12 monitors		6 paddle M/S		
1 A/C carrier				
5 P boats	**Nore**	**Portsmouth**	**Devonport**	**Portland**
6 paddle M/S	3 minelayers	**LD Flotilla**	**LD Flotilla**	4 TBs
		8 old Ds	6 old Ds	
Downs Brdg Flot		22 TBs	8 TBs	
5 ABSs				
10 Armed tugs	**LD Flotilla**	**Escort Flot**	**2nd DF**	**Newhaven**
	9 old Ds	10 old Ds	14 H, I classes	4 TBs
	14 TBs	3 H, I classes		
	10 P boats	4 P boats		
		4th DF		
		ACTIVE		
		10 K class		

Submarine Flotillas

1st (Leith)	**2nd (Tyne)**	**3rd (Humber)**	**4th (Medway)**	**5th (Dover)**
4 B,C classes	1 destroyer	6 D class	6 C class	8 C class
	8 C class			

6th (Portsmouth)	**8th (Yarmouth)**	**9th (Harwich)**	**10th (Tees)**	**11th (Blyth)**
2 C class	2 F class	3 destroyers	2 destroyers	2 destroyers
1 S class	4 V class	18 E class	3 E class	6 G class
	5 H class		7 G class	6 J class

12th (Grand Fleet)
FEARLESS
1 K class
3 K class (later)

Ships paid-off, refits etc

ALBEMARLE	MAGNIFICENT	AMPHITRITE	BIRMINGHAM	SAPPHO
CANOPUS	PRINCE GEORGE	APOLLO	BLANCHE	SUFFOLK
JUPITER	REDOUBTABLE	ARGONAUT	CUMBERLAND	TERRIBLE
LONDON	VENERABLE	ARIADNE	ECLIPSE	WALLAROO
		BACCHANTE	ESSEX	

Mediterranean

Battleships	**Cruisers**	**Cruisers**	**Destroyers**	13 Monitors
AFRICA	ANDROMACHE	GRAFTON	16 G class	2 A/C carriers
AGAMEMNON	(H/S)	LOWESTOFT	8 H class	3 minelayers
CORNWALLIS	DARTMOUTH	NEWCASTLE	10 old Ds	26 sloops
EXMOUTH	DORIS	PELORUS	18 TBs	10 ABSs
IMPLACABLE	EDGAR	SENTINEL	5 B class S/Ms	
LORD NELSON	ENDYMION	SKIRMISHER	8 E class S/Ms	
	FORESIGHT	THESEUS		
	FORWARD			

Attached Italian Fleet

QUEEN		BRISTOL	4 destroyers
BRITANNIA		GLOUCESTER	3 H class S/Ms
DUNCAN		LIVERPOOL	1 monitor
PRINCE OF WALES		TOPAZE	

Egypt & East Indies

HANNIBAL (D/S)	EURYALUS	PHILOMEL	4 monitors
VENGEANCE	FOX	PROSERPINE	3 A/C carriers
	JUNO	PYRAMUS	16 sloops
	MINERVA	SAPPHIRE	6 RIM ships

China	Pacific	East Africa	West Africa	N America & W Indies
CORNWALL	LANCASTER	CHALLENGER	ASTRAEA	LEVIATHAN
DIANA	3 AMCs	TALBOT	SIRIUS	ANTRIM
PSYCHE		4 AMCs		BERWICK
VENUS	Australia	2 monitors	9th CS	CARNARVON
3 Old Ds	BRISBANE	2 sloops	KING ALFRED	DEVONSHIRE
4 TBs	ENCOUNTER		DONEGAL	DRAKE
3 C class S/Ms	PIONEER	Cape	SUTLEJ	ISIS
2 sloops	6 destroyers	KENT	2 AMCs	ROXBURGH
	1 sloop	HYACINTH	SWIFTSURE	2 AMCs
SE Coast of S America		2 TBs	HIGHFLYER	CAESAR
AMETHYST		White Sea		
GLASGOW		VINDICTIVE		
3 AMCs		INTREPID (at Chatham)		
		IPHIGENIA (at Chatham)		
		GLORY (D/S)		

January 1918

Grand Fleet
Fleet flagship: QUEEN ELIZABETH

1st BS	2nd BS	3rd BS	4th BS	5th BS
RESOLUTION	K GEORGE V	DREADNOUGHT	HERCULES	BARHAM
BENBOW	AGINCOURT	COMMONWEALTH	BELLEROPHON	MALAYA
CANADA	AJAX	DOMINION	COLLINGWOOD	VALIANT
E OF INDIA	CENTURION	HINDUSTAN	COLOSSUS	WARSPITE
IRON DUKE	CONQUEROR	ZEALANDIA	NEPTUNE	
MARLBOROUGH	ERIN		ST VINCENT	6th BS
RAMILLIES	MONARCH		SUPERB	USS NEW YORK
REVENGE	ORION		TEMERAIRE	USS DELAWARE
ROYAL OAK	THUNDERER			USS FLORIDA
R SOVEREIGN				USS WYOMING

Attached	2nd CS	4th LCS	6th LCS	A/C carriers
BELLONA	MINOTAUR	CALLIOPE	CARDIFF	CAMPANIA
BLANCHE	SHANNON	CAMBRIAN	CALYPSO	NAIRANA
BLONDE	3 AMCs	CAROLINE	CARADOC	PEGASUS
BOADICEA		COMUS	CASSANDRA	
DIAMOND		CONSTANCE	CERES	
ABDIEL		CORDELIA		
OAK				

11th DF	12th DF	14th DF	15th DF	LD Flotilla
SEYMOUR	SAUMAREZ	VAMPIRE	PARKER	10 old Ds
VALOROUS	VALHALLA	ANZAC	GRENVILLE	Lerwick Force
9 M class	18 M class	16 M class	10 R & mod	8 R class
8 R class		1 R class	R classes	
1 V class				

1st M/S Flot.	2nd M/S Flot.	3rd M/S Flot.	Hydrophone Flotilla	Miscellaneous
10 sloops	4 sloops	12 Hunts	5 sloops	1 ABS
	4 Hunts			

Battlecruiser Force
Flagship: LION

1st BCS	2nd BCS	1st CS	1st LCS	2nd LCS
RENOWN	AUSTRALIA	COURAGEOUS	CALEDON	BIRMINGHAM
REPULSE	INDOMITABLE	GLORIOUS	GALATEA (M/L)	DUBLIN
PSS ROYAL	INFLEXIBLE	FURIOUS	INCONSTANT (M/L)	MELBOURNE
TIGER	NEW ZEALAND		PHAETON (M/L)	SOUTHAMPTON
			ROYALIST (M/L)	SYDNEY

	3rd LCS	13th DF		
	CHATHAM	CHAMPION	12 M class	
	CHESTER	GABRIEL	8 R & Mod.R classes	
	BIRKENHEAD	VALENTINE	7 V/W class	
	YARMOUTH		7 V class (M/Ls)	

Harwich Force

5th LCS		10th DF		A/C carrier
AURORA	CENTAUR	UNDAUNTED	NIMROD	VINDEX
CARYSFORT	CONCORD	SPENSER	SHAKESPEARE	
CLEOPATRA	CURLEW	VALKYRIE	21 R & Mod. R classes	
CONQUEST	PENELOPE			
CANTERBURY				

Patrol Flotillas etc

Dover	Humber	N Channel	Queenstown	Lowestoft
6th DF	7th DF	6 old Ds	ACTIVE	2 old Ds
ATTENTIVE	PATROL	11 sloops	ADVENTURE	1 monitor
BOTHA	29 old Ds		1 A/C carrier	2 TGB M/S
BROKE	4 P boats	N Ireland	37 US destroyers	
FAULKNOR	ALBION	2nd DF	4 TBs	
KEMPENFELT	WALLAROO	10 G class	9 Hunt M/S	
LIGHTFOOT	2 M/L dest	3 H, I classes		
MARKSMAN	1 minelayer	11 M class		
SWIFT	4 paddle M/S			
7 F class				
10 old Ds	Nore	Portsmouth	Devonport	Pembroke
17 M class	AMPHITRITE	LD Flotilla	LD Flotilla	4 TBs
2 R class	(M/L)	9 destroyers	4 old Ds	12 P boats
2 TBs	4 boarding tugs	25 TBs	8 TBs	Portland
1 A/C carrier				1 old D
15 monitors	LD Flotilla	1st DF	4th DF	6 TBs
6 P boats	12 old Ds	6 L class	APOLLO	
7 paddle M/S	13 TBs	SWORDFISH	21 I, K classes	W Scotland
Downs Brdg Flot		31 P boats	18 L, M classes	7 TGB M/S
3 ABSs		1 minelayer		3 Paddle M/S
5 A tugs				
White Sea		Tyne	Yarmouth	Tees
GLORY (D/S)		ILLUSTRIOUS	1 monitor	1 monitor
INTREPID (Chatham)		NAIAD		
IPHIGENIA (Lerwick)				
VINDICTIVE (Liverpool)				
2 ABSs				

Submarine Flotillas

1st (Rosyth)	2nd (Tyne)	3rd (Humber)	5th (Dover)	8th (Yarmouth)
1 B class	1 destroyer	4 C class	5 C class	4 H class
	4 C class			4 V class
1st (Portsmouth)	9th (Harwich)	10th (Tees)	11th (G. Fleet)	12th (G. Fleet)
N.I	3 destroyers	2 destroyers	2 destroyers	7 K class
3 C class	8 C class	3 E class	5 G class	13th (G. Fleet)
2 D class	17 E class	8 G class	7 J class	ITHURIEL
3 F class				6 K class

Ships paid-off, refits etc

ALBEMARLE	HIBERNIA	P OF WALES	ARGONAUT	ESSEX
CANOPUS	IMPLACABLE	REDOUBTABLE	DIADEM	SAPPHO
DUNCAN	JUPITER	SWIFTSURE	ECLIPSE	TERRIBLE
EXMOUTH	LONDON	VENERABLE		
	PRINCE GEORGE	VENGEANCE		

Mediterranean

Battleships	Cruisers	Cruisers	Destroyers	6 E class S/Ms
LORD NELSON	EDGAR	LATONA (D/S)	9 old Ds	2 A/C carriers
AGAMEMNON	ENDYMION	LOWESTOFT	5 G class	12 monitors
	EUROPA (D/S)	PELORUS	15 H class	30 sloops
	FORESIGHT	SENTINEL	5 I class	18 TBs
	FORWARD	SKIRMISHER	2 M class	2 minelayers
		THESEUS	6 Australian	13 ABSs
			14 Japanese	

Battleship	Adriatic Force				Egypt & Red Sea
QUEEN	8th LCS	2 Monitors			GRAFTON
	BRISTOL	3 H class S/Ms			FOX
	DARTMOUTH	4 patrol boats			PYRAMUS
	GLOUCESTER	(ex-B class S/Ms)			TOPAZE
	LIVERPOOL				2 A/C carriers
	WEYMOUTH				2 monitors
					14 sloops

East Indies	China	Pacific	Australia	Cape
DIANA	SUFFOLK	LANCASTER	BRISBANE	HYACINTH
DORIS	EURYALUS (po)	3 AMCs	ENCOUNTER	KENT
JUNO	3 old Ds		PHILOMEL	2 TBs
PROSERPINE	4 TBs		PIONEER (po)	1 AMC
SAPPHIRE	3 C class S/Ms		PSYCHE	
VENUS			1 sloop	
4 RIM ships				

East Africa	West Africa	SE Coast	Atlantic Convoys	
CHALLENGER	ASTRAEA	NEWCASTLE	9th CS	20 ACMs
MINERVA	SIRIUS	AMETHYST	BACCHANTE	8 Escort ships
TALBOT	1 gunboat	GLASGOW	AFRICA	
2 monitors		2 AMCs	BRITANNIA	
2 sloops			4 AMCs	

		N America & W Indies		
LEVIATHAN	CARNARVON	DEVONSHIRE	ISIS	1 AMC
ACHILLES	COCHRANE	DONEGAL	KING ALFRED	1 sloop
ANTRIM	CORNWALL	D OF EDINBURGH	ROXBURGH	2 submarines
BERWICK	CUMBERLAND	HIGHFLYER	CAESAR	

11 November 1918

Grand Fleet
Fleet flagship: QUEEN ELIZABETH

1st BS	2nd BS	4th BS	5th BS	6th BS
REVENGE	K GEORGE V	HERCULES	BARHAM	USS NEW YORK
BENBOW	AGINCOURT	BELLEROPHON	MALAYA	USS ARKANSAS
CANADA	AJAX	COLLINGWOOD	VALIANT	USS FLORIDA
E OF INDIA	CENTURION	COLOSSUS	WARSPITE	USS TEXAS
IRON DUKE	CONQUEROR	DREADNOUGHT		USS WYOMING
MARLBOROUGH	ERIN	NEPTUNE		
RAMILLIES	ORION	ST VINCENT		
RESOLUTION	MONARCH			
ROYAL OAK	THUNDERER			
R SOVEREIGN				

Attached	2nd CS	4th LCS	7th LCS	Flying Sqdn.
BELLONA	MINOTAUR	CALLIOPE	CARYSFORT	FURIOUS
BLANCHE	ACHILLES (det)	CAMBRIAN	AURORA	ARGUS
BLONDE	COCHRANE	CAROLINE	CLEOPATRA	NAIRANA
BOADICEA	SHANNON	COMUS	PENELOPE	PEGASUS
OAK		CONSTANCE	UNDAUNTED	VINDICTIVE
		CORDELIA		CANNING
				(K/B ship)

Destroyer Command	21st DF	3rd DF	11th DF	12th DF
CASTOR	BOTHA	NIMROD	SEYMOUR	SAUMAREZ
	DOUGLAS	TALISMAN	KEMPENFELT	VALHALLA
	SWIFT	12 M class	VALOROUS	13 S class
	8 M class		5 R class	4 V/W class
			12 V/W class	

13th DF	14th DF	15th DF	Temporarily Attached	Miscellaneous
CHAMPION	VAMPIRE	PARKER	16 L, M classes	1 sloop
VALENTINE	ANZAC	GRENVILLE		1 ABS
VALKYRIE	14 M class	18 R class		
7 Mod.R class	5 R/S classes			
21 V/W class	3 V/W class			

Minesweepers (based at Granton)

1st Flotilla	2nd Flotilla	3rd Flotilla
8 sloops	7 sloops	14 Hunts
2 Hunts	2 Hunts	

Battlecruiser Force
Flagship: LION

1st BCS	2nd BCS	1st CS	1st LCS	2nd LCS
REPULSE	NEW ZEALAND	COURAGEOUS	INCONSTANT	BIRMINGHAM
RENOWN	AUSTRALIA	GLORIOUS	CALEDON	DUBLIN
PSS ROYAL	INDOMITABLE		GALATEA	MELBOURNE
TIGER	INFLEXIBLE		PHAETON	SYDNEY
			ROYALIST	YARMOUTH

	6th LCS		3rd LCS	
CARDIFF	CALYPSO	CHATHAM	CHESTER	
CARADOC	CASSANDRA	BIRKENHEAD	SOUTHAMPTON	
	CERES			

Harwich Force

	5th LCS	10th DF	6th M/S Flotilla	
CURACOA	CENTAUR	SPENSER	4 Hunts	15 CMBs
CONCORD	CONQUEST	SHAKESPEARE		
COVENTRY	CURLEW	BRUCE		
DANAE	DRAGON	MONTROSE		
		24 R class		

Minelayers

Methil Convoy DF
6 L class

20th DF (Humber)	1st M/L Sqdn (Grangemouth)	2nd M/L Sqdn 10 US ships
ABDIEL	LONDON	
GABRIEL	AMPHITRITE	
9 destroyers	ANGORA	
	PSS MARGARET	
	WAHINE	

3rd Sloop Flotilla (Dundee)
20 sloops

Nthrn Patrol (Dundee)	Sthrn Patrol (Granton)	E Coast Convoys 7th DF (Humber)	8th DF (Forth)	Lowestoft
MARKSMAN	4th Sloop Flot	28 old Ds	10 TBs	2 old Ds
3 destroyers	LIGHTFOOT	3 TBs		
	6 sloops			

Dover 6th DF	Nore LDF	Portsmouth 1st DF	Devonport 4th DF	Queenstown 1st Sloop Flot
BROKE	6 old Ds	8 old Ds	6 G class	8 sloops
FAULKNOR	13 TBs		20 K, L classes	
6 F class	Pembroke	Escort Flot	12 M class	Holyhead
8 old Ds	19 PC boats	30 P boats		6 old Ds
9 M class			LDF	
12 P boats		Portland	3 old Ds	
9 monitors		1 old D	8 TBs	
23 CMBs		5 TBs		
		6 CMBs		

Berehaven Battleships	Kingstown Irish Sea Hunting Flot	N Channel Patrol	N Coast of Ireland 2nd DF	2nd Sloop Flot
USS UTAH	5 old Ds	6 old Ds	6 G class	8 sloops
USS NEVADA			14 M class	
USS OKLAHOMA				
24 US destroyers				

Submarine Flotillas

3rd (Humber)	6th (Portsmouth)	8th (Yarmouth)	9th (Harwich)	10th (Tees)
3 C class	8 C class	2 V class	3 destroyers	2 destroyers
	3 D class	4 H class	3 C class	6 E class
	1 G class		11 E class	3 G class
	N.1		4 L class	3 L class

11th (Blyth)	12th Grand Fleet	13th Grand Fleet	14th (Blyth)	Berehaven
2 destroyers	FEARLESS	ITHURIEL	1 destroyer	7 US boats
8 G class	7 K class	7 K class	7 H class	
5 J class			1 L class	
			1 R class	

Killybegs	Falmouth	Training (Forth/Clyde)	Training (Campbeltown)
2 E class	7 L class	1 B class	3 F class
4 R class		4 C class	2 V class

Minesweeping Flotillas

7th (Grimsby)	8th (Queenstown)	9th (Granton)	10th (Dover)	11th (Liverpool)
9 Hunts	4 Hunts	4 paddle	5 paddle	4 Hunts

12th (Clyde)	13th (Oban)	14th (Oban)	15th (Falmouth)	16th (Granton)
4 Hunts	6 TGBS	4 paddle	4 Hunts	5 paddle

17th (Portland)	18th (Plymouth)	19th (Swansea)	20th (Felixstowe)
6 Hired paddle	4 paddle	4 Hunts	4 Hunts

Ships paid-off, refits etc

ALBEMARLE	DOMINION	JUPITER	AMETHYST	SAPPHO
ALBION	DUNCAN	P OF WALES	ARGONAUT	TERRIBLE
AFRICA	EXMOUTH	REDOUBTABLE	DIADEM	WALLAROO
CANOPUS	HIBERNIA	SWIFTSURE	ECLIPSE	
COMMON- WEALTH	HINDUSTAN ILLUSTRIOUS	VENGEANCE	ESSEX	8 monitors

Mediterranean

Battleships	Cruisers	Cruisers	Destroyers	A/C carriers
LORD NELSON	ACTIVE (in UK)	FORESIGHT	8 old Ds	ARK ROYAL
AGAMEMNON	ADVENTURE	FORWARD	15 H class	EMPRESS
SUPERB	CANTERBURY	GRAFTON	15 I class	ENGADINE
TEMERAIRE	DIAMOND	LIVERPOOL	2 M class	MANXMAN
	EDGAR (in UK)	SENTINEL	5 S class	RIVIERA
	ENDYMION	SKIRMISHER	6 Australian	VINDEX
		THESEUS	14 Japanese	

Submarines	9th Sloop Flotilla	11th Sloop Flotilla	12th Sloop Flotilla	
6 E class	5 sloops	17 sloops	9 sloops	13 monitors
3 H class				12 TBs
J.1, M.1				1 minelayer
				5 Hunt M/S
				12 ABSs

Adriatic Force

Battleship	8th LCS	Submarines	10th Sloop Flotilla	Miscellaneous
QUEEN	LOWESTOFT	1 C class	6 sloops	4 TBs
	DARTMOUTH	4 E class		2 ABSs
	GLASGOW	2 H class		
	GLOUCESTER			
	WEYMOUTH			

Egypt/Red Sea	East Indies	China	Australia	Pacific
FOX	EURYALUS (po)	SUFFOLK	BRISBANE	LANCASTER
PROSERPINE	DIANA	KENT	ENCOUNTER	1 AMC
SAPPHIRE	DORIS	3 old Ds	PHILOMEL	
TOPAZE	JUNO	4 TBs	PIONEER(po)	SE Coast of S America
3 old sloops	VENUS	3 old S/Ms	PSYCHE(po)	NEWCASTLE
	4 RIM ships	2 sloops	2 sloops	BRISTOL
13th Sl.Flot	4 gunboats			
11 sloops				

East Africa	Cape	West Africa	N America & W Indies	
CHALLENGER	HYACINTH	ASTRAEA	ANTRIM	DEVONSHIRE
1 gunboat	MINERVA	1 gunboat	BERWICK	DONEGAL
	TALBOT		CARNARVON	D OF EDINBURGH
	1 sloop	**9th CS**	CORNWALL	HIGHFLYER
	2 TBs	BACCHANTE	CUMBERLAND	ISIS
			KING ALFRED	LEVIATHAN
White Sea		**Atlantic Convoys**	ROXBURGH	1 sloop
GLORY (D/S)	ATTENTIVE	30 AMCs	1 AMC	
2 monitors	GLORY IV	9 Escort ships		

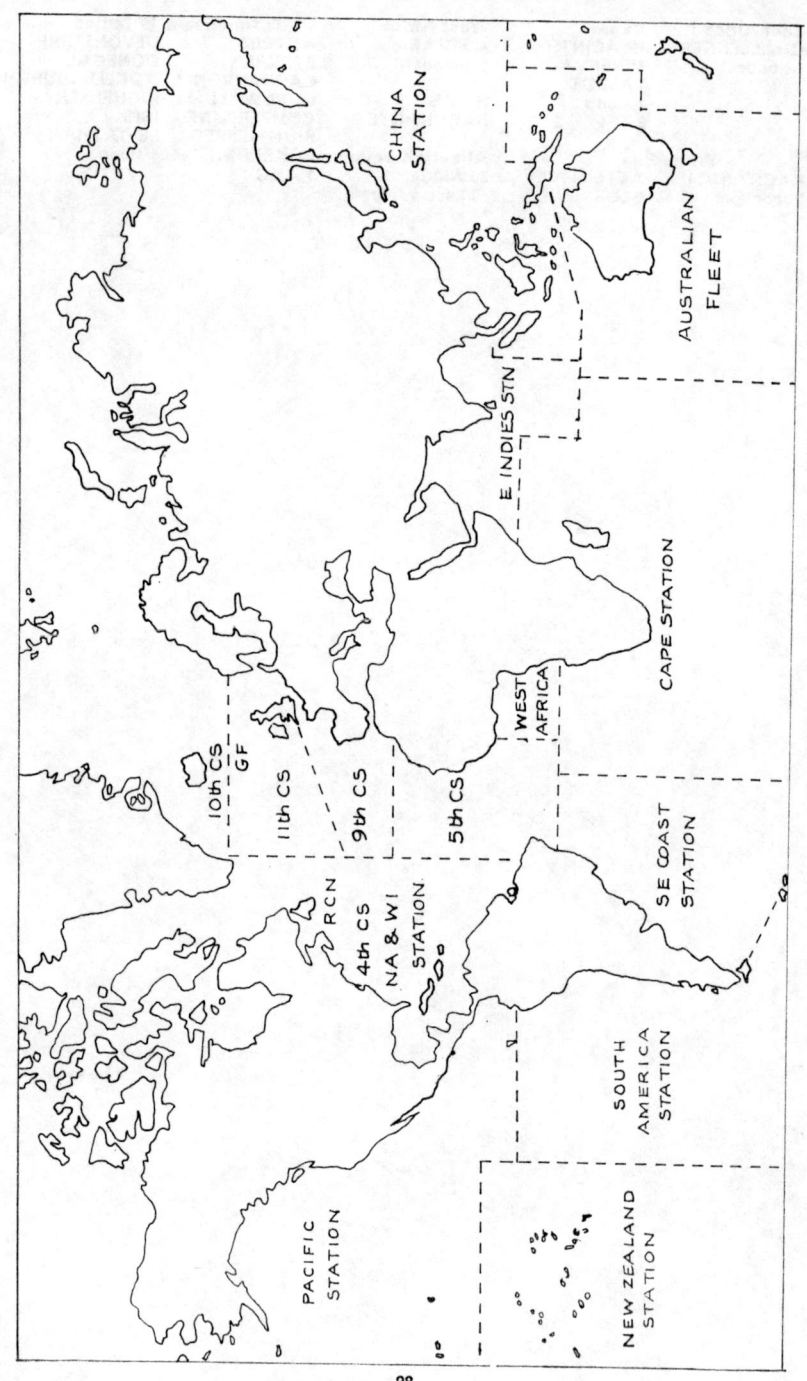

PRE-DREADNOUGHT BATTLESHIPS

ROYAL SOVEREIGN (OLD) CLASS

14150 tons.   410½ (oa), 380 (pp) ×75×27 ft.   TE 13000 ihp=17½ kts.
Armament: 4–13.5 in (relined to 12 in 1914), 10–6 in, 7–18 in TT.
Armour: (compound) 18 in sides, 3 in deck, 18 in guns.

Pendant Nos. 1914 9.15 1.18			Name	Launched	Builder—Fate
P.55	N.12	N.84	REVENGE =REDOUBTABLE 8.15	3.11.92	Palmer. Laid up 1913; Bombarding ship 10.14. Sold 6.11.19 Ward, Briton Ferry.

Notes: One similar ship, HOOD (Chatham DY 30.6.91), was on the sale list in 8.14 and sunk 4.11.14 as a blockship at the southern entrance to Portland harbour. Six sister ships; EMPRESS OF INDIA, RAMILLIES, REPULSE, RESOLUTION, ROYAL OAK and ROYAL SOVEREIGN were deleted between 7.1911 and 4.14. REVENGE served at Dover until 10.15 and was then laid up at Portsmouth.

MAJESTIC CLASS

14900 tons.   421 (oa), 390 (pp) ×75×27½ ft.   TE 12000 ihp=17½ kts.
Armament: 4–12 in, 12–6 in, 18–12 pdr, 5–18 in TT.
Armour: 9 in sides, 4 in deck, 14 in guns.

1914	9.15	1.18	Name	Launched	Builder—Fate
D.27	P.02	P.10	CAESAR	2. 9.96	Portsmouth DY. Sold 8.11.21 Slough T.C.; BU in Germany.
D.36	P.45	N.54	HANNIBAL	28. 4.96	Pembroke DY. Sold 28.1.20 M. Yates; BU in Italy.
D.40	P.40	P.97	ILLUSTRIOUS	17. 9.96	Chatham DY. Sold 18.6.20 Ward, Barrow.
D.50	P.50	N.64	JUPITER	18.11.95	Thomson. Sold 15.1.20 Hughes Bolckow, Tyne.
D.13	P.83	P.3A	MAGNIFICENT	19.12.94	Chatham DY. Sold 9.5.21 Ward, Inverkeithing.
D.04			MAJESTIC	31. 1.95	Portsmouth DY. Sunk 27.5.15 by U.21 off Cape Helles.
D.42	P.01	P.6A	MARS	3. 3.96	Laird. Sold 9.5.21 Ward, Briton Ferry.
D.46	P.86	P.9A	PRINCE GEORGE =VICTORIOUS II 7.18 =PRINCE GEORGE 2.19	22. 8.95	Portsmouth DY. Sold 21.9.21 Cohen; resold and foundered 30.12.21 off Kamperduin on passage to Germany to BU.
D.48	P.65	P.3C	VICTORIOUS =INDUS II 1920	19.10.95	Chatham DY. Sold 19.12.22 A. J. Purves; resold 4.23 Stanlee, Dover.

Notes: Part of the 7th and 9th Battle Squadrons in the Channel at the outbreak of war. Later in the year they were dispersed abroad, most of them going to the Mediterranean. Four vessels, ILLUSTRIOUS, MAGNIFICENT, MARS and VICTORIOUS. were disarmed during 1915 providing guns for the LORD CLIVE class monitors. VICTORIOUS became a repair ship 3.16. HANNIBAL and PRINCE GEORGE were also disarmed later leaving CAESAR and JUPITER actively employed on foreign stations for some time. The disarmed ships became depots or unarmed transport, etc. In 11.18 CAESAR had become a depot at Malta and JUPITER was in use as an accommodation ship at Devonport.

CANOPUS CLASS

12950 tons. 421½ (oa), 390 (pp) × 74 × 26 ft. TE 13500 ihp = 18 kts.
Armament: 4–12 in, 12–6 in, 12–12 pdr, 4–18 in TT.
Armour: 6 in sides, 2½ in deck, 9 in guns.

Pendant Nos. 1914	1.18	Name	Launched	Builder—Fate
N.48	N.00	ALBION	21. 6.98	Thames IW. Sold 11.12.19 Ward, Morecambe.
N.29	N.17	CANOPUS	13.10.97	Portsmouth DY. Sold 18.2.20 Stanlee.
P.08	P.92	GLORY =CRESCENT 4.20	11. 3.99	Laird. Sold 19.12.22 Granton S.Bkg. Co.
N.54		GOLIATH	23. 3.98	Chatham DY. Torpedoed 15.5.15 by Turkish TB MAUVENET off Cape Helles.
N.56		OCEAN	5. 7.98	Devonport DY. Mined 18.3.15 in the Dardanelles.
N.57	N.1A	VENGEANCE	25. 7.99	Vickers. Sold 1.12.21 Stanlee.

Notes: These six ships along with the MAJESTIC and her sisters formed the 7th and 9th Battle Squadrons in 1914. These ships were also scattered abroad later. GLORY became the depot ship CRESCENT in 4.20 after late war service in N. Russia.

FORMIDABLE AND LONDON CLASSES

15000 tons. 431¾ (oa), 400 (pp) × 75 × 27 ft. TE 15000 ihp = 18 kts.
Armament: 4–12 in, 12–6 in, 16–12 pdr, 4–18 in TT.
Armour: 9 in sides, 3 in deck, 12 in guns.

1914	1.18	4.18	Name	Launched	Builder—Fate
95			BULWARK	18.10.99	Devonport DY. Sunk 26.11.14 by internal explosion in the Medway.
50			FORMIDABLE	17.11.98	Portsmouth DY. Sunk 1.1.15 by U.24 off Portland Bill.
63	72	N.48	IMPLACABLE	11. 3.99	Devonport DY. Sold 8.11.21 Slough T.C.; BU in Germany.
64			IRRESISTIBLE	15.12.98	Chatham DY. Mined 18.3.15 in the Dardanelles.
70	81	N.41	LONDON	21. 9.99	Portsmouth DY. Sold 4.6.20 Stanlee; resold Slough T.C.; BU in Germany.
81	94	N.46	PRINCE OF WALES	25. 3.02	Chatham DY. Sold 12.4.20 Ward, Milford Haven.
82	96		QUEEN	8. 3.02	Devonport DY. Sold 4.11.20 Ward, Birkenhead and Preston.
96	A8	N.36	VENERABLE	2.11.99	Chatham DY. Sold 4.6.20 Stanlee; resold Slough T.C.; BU in Germany.

Notes: FORMIDABLE, IMPLACABLE and IRRESISTIBLE were from the 1897 programme, while the others were provided for by the 1898 and 1900 estimates. Differences between classes were confined to minor features. These formed the 5th BS Channel Fleet in 8.14 and in the Grand Fleet at the end of the year. In 1915 all surviving vessels were in the Mediterranean where QUEEN remained until the end of the war. LONDON was converted to a minelayer (3–6 in, 1–4 in and 240 mines) completed 5.18 at Rosyth. The remainder were on harbour service 1917–19.

DUNCAN CLASS

14000 tons. 432 (oa), 405 (pp) × 75½ × 27 ft. TE 18000 ihp = 19 kts.
Armament: 4–12 in, 12–6 in, 12–12 pdr, 4–18 in TT.
Armour: 7 in sides, 2½ in deck, 11 in guns.

1914	1.18	4.18	Name	Launched	Builder—Fate
07	06	N.39	ALBEMARLE	5. 3.01	Chatham DY. Sold 19.11.19 Cohen, Swansea; arrived 11.22 after stranding.
33			CORNWALLIS	13. 7.01	Thames IW. Sunk 9.1.17 by U.32 east of Malta.
43	59	N.53	DUNCAN	21. 3.01	Thames IW. Sold 18.2.20 Stanlee.
12	63	N.44	EXMOUTH	31. 8.01	Laird. Sold 15.1.20 Forth S.Bkg. Co, Bo'ness; resold and BU in Holland.
23			RUSSELL	19. 2.01	Palmer. Mined 27.4.16 off Malta.

Notes: A sixth unit of this class, MONTAGU (ex-Montague) was wrecked 30.5.06 on Lundy Island. At the outbreak of war they formed part of the 3rd BS and later the 6th BS at the Nore. All surviving ships were on harbour service from 1917 after a few months spent in the Mediterranean.

PURCHASED SHIPS

11800 and 11985 tons respectively. 479¾ (oa), 436 (pp) ×71×24 ft. TE 14000 ihp=20 kts.
Armament: 4–10 in, 14–7.5 in, 14–14 pdr, 2–18 in TT.
Armour: 7 in sides, 3 in deck, 10 in guns.

1.18	Name	Launched	Builder—Fate
P.05	SWIFTSURE	12. 1.03	Armstrong. Sold 18.6.20 Stanlee.
	TRIUMPH	15. 1.03	Vickers. Sunk 25.5.15 by U.21 off Gaba Tepe, Dardanelles.

Notes: Originally ex-Chilean *Constitucion* and *Libertad* respectively, they were purchased 3.12.03 and differed radically in appearance from contemporary British ships. SWIFTSURE was in the E. Indies until 1915 and then went to the Mediterranean. Converted into a blockship at Chatham in 1918 but not so used. TRIUMPH was in China until 1915, then to the Mediterranean. At the time of her loss, TRIUMPH had her protective nets out but they failed to stop the torpedo.

KING EDWARD VII CLASS

16350 tons. 457 (oa), 425 (pp) ×78×26½ ft. TE 18000 ihp=19 kts.
Armament: 4–12 in, 4–9.2 in, 10–6 in, 12–12 pdr, 5–18 in TT.
Armour: 9 in sides, 2 in deck, 12 in guns.

1914	1.18	4.18	Name	Launched	Builder—Fate
25	02	N.07	AFRICA	20. 5.05	Chatham DY. Sold 30.6.20 Ellis, Newcastle.
27	21	N.40	BRITANNIA	10.12.04	Portsmouth DY. Sunk 9.11.18 by UB.50 off Cape Trafalgar.
31	44	31 N.88 (6.18)	COMMONWEALTH	13. 5.03	Fairfield. Sold 18.11.21 Slough T.C.; BU in Germany.
41	54	41 N.90 (6.18)	DOMINION	25. 8.03	Vickers. Sold 9.5.21 Ward; arrived Preston 28.10.24 after laying up at Belfast.
60	70	N.66	HIBERNIA	17. 6.05	Devonport DY. Sold 8.11.21 Stanlee; re-sold Slough T.C.; BU in Germany.
62	71	N.67	HINDUSTAN	19.12.03	John Brown. Sold 9.5.21 Ward; arrived 14.10.23 after laying up at Belfast.
66			KING EDWARD VII	23. 7.03	Devonport DY. Mined 6.1.16 off Cape Wrath.
73	2C N.89 (6.18)	19	ZEALANDIA	4. 2.04	Portsmouth DY. Sold 8.11.21 Stanlee; resold Slough T.C.; BU in Germany.

Notes: ZEALANDIA (*ex-New Zealand*) was renamed 1.11.11. These were the only pre-dreadnoughts to remain for any length of time with the Grand Fleet, forming the 3rd BS; four were still there in 1918. AFRICA and BRITANNIA were in the Mediterranean during 1916–17.

LORD NELSON CLASS

16500 tons. 443½ (oa), 410 (pp) ×79½×27 ft. TE 16750 ihp=18½ kts.
Armament: 4–12 in, 10–9.2 in, 24–12 pdr, 5–18 in TT.
Armour: 12 in sides, 3 in deck, 12 in guns.

1914	1.18*	Name	Launched	Builder—Fate
01	03	AGAMEMNON	23. 6.06	Beardmore. Sold 24.1.27 Cashmore.
04	82	LORD NELSON	4. 9.06	Palmer. Sold 4.6.20 Stanlee; resold Slough T.C.; BU in Germany.

*Pendants cancelled 4.18

Notes: Design and armament was influenced by DREADNOUGHT laid down five months after these ships were commenced. Possessing better protection and an exceptionally heavy secondary armament along with an increased number of anti-torpedo boat guns these ships were the peak of mixed calibre gunned battleship design. After a year in the 5th BS in the Channel and Grand Fleet both ships served in the Mediterranean until 1919. AGAMEMNON was converted to radio-controlled target ship at Chatham 6.19 to 7.21.

DREADNOUGHT BATTLESHIPS

DREADNOUGHT

17900 tons. 526 (oa), 490 (pp) ×82×27 ft. Turbine 23000 shp=21 kts.
Armament: 10–12 in, 27–12 pdr, 5–18 in TT.
Armour: 11 in sides, 2¾ in deck, 11 in guns.

1914	1.18	4.18	Name	Launched	Builder—Fate
00	56	73	DREADNOUGHT	10. 2.06	Portsmouth DY. Sold 9.5.21 Ward, Inverkeithing.

Notes: The first "all big gun" ship completed and the pattern for all succeeding battleships. Laid down 2.10.05 and completed 12.06, her construction was given full priority by the Admiralty. Served in the Grand Fleet throughout the war, 4th BS until 1916, 3rd BS to 1918, then in the 4th BS again.

BELLEROPHON CLASS

18600 tons. 526 (oa), 490 (pp) ×82½×27 ft. Turbine 23000 shp=21 kts.
Armament: 10–12 in, 16–4 in, 3–18 in TT.
Armour: 11 in sides, 4 in deck, 11 in guns.

1914	1.18	4.18	Name	Launched	Builder—Fate
72	11	63	BELLEROPHON	27. 7.07	Portsmouth DY. Sold 8.11.21 Slough T.C.; BU in Germany.
49	A0	49	SUPERB	7.11.07	Armstrong. Sold 12.12.22 Stanlee.
48	A2	92	TEMERAIRE	24. 8.07	Devonport DY. Sold 7.12.21 Stanlee.

Notes: BELLEROPHON 4th BS 1914–18; SUPERB 1st BS 1914–15, then 4th BS to 1918; TEMERAIRE 4th BS 1914–18. Both SUPERB and TEMERAIRE went to the Mediterranean in 1918.

ST. VINCENT CLASS

19250 tons. 536 (oa), 500 (pp) ×84×27 ft. Turbine 24500 shp=21 kts.
Armament: 10–12 in, 20–4 in, 2–18 in TT.
Armour: 10 in sides, 3 in deck, 11 in guns.

1914	1.18	4.18	Name	Launched	Builder—Fate
26	42	03	COLLINGWOOD	7.11.08	Devonport DY. Sold 12.12.22 Cashmore.
16	7A	85	ST. VINCENT	10. 9.08	Portsmouth DY. Sold 1.12.21 Stanlee.
39			VANGUARD	22. 2.09	Vickers. Sunk 9.7.17 by internal explosion at Scapa Flow.

Notes: VANGUARD was originally to have been named RODNEY. All three served in the 1st BS of the Grand Fleet 1914–16, then to the 4th BS.

NEPTUNE AND COLOSSUS CLASS

20000 tons (NEPTUNE 19900). 546 (oa), 510 (pp) ×86×27 ft. Turbine 25000 shp=21 kts.
Armament: 10–12 in, 16–4 in, 3–21 in TT.
Armour: 11 in sides (NEPTUNE 10 in), 3 in deck, 11 in guns.

1914	1.18	4.18	Name	Launched	Builder—Fate
93	43	24	COLOSSUS	9. 4.10	Scotts. Sold 7.28 Alloa S.Bkg. Co, Rosyth.
47	69	54	HERCULES	10. 5.10	Palmer. Sold 8.11.21 Slough T.C.; BU in Germany.
02	89	79	NEPTUNE	30. 9.09	Portsmouth DY. Sold 9.22 Hughes Bolckow.

Notes: NEPTUNE was originally to have been named FOUDROYANT. In all ships, four 4 in guns were replaced by 2–3 in AA. All three served in the 1st BS until 1916, then to the 4th BS.

ORION CLASS

22500 tons. 581 (oa), 545 (pp) × 88½ × 27½ ft. Turbine 27000 shp = 21 kts.
Armament: 10–13.5 in, 16–4 in, 3–21 in TT.
Armour: 12 in sides, 3 in deck, 11 in guns.

1914	1.18	4.18	Name	Launched	Builder—Fate
06	47	95	CONQUEROR	1. 5.11	Beardmore. Sold 19.12.22 Cox & Danks, Upnor.
55	88	60	MONARCH	30. 3.11	Armstrong. Sunk 20.1.25 as target off Scilly.
52	91	86	ORION	20. 8.10	Portsmouth DY. Sold 19.12.22 Cox & Danks, Upnor.
32	A3	36	THUNDERER	1. 2.11	Thames IW. Sold 12.26 Hughes Bolckow.

Notes: MONARCH was originally to have been named KING GEORGE V. Two AA guns were added to all ships during the war. All four served in the 2nd BS of the Grand Fleet 1914–18.

KING GEORGE V CLASS

23000 tons. 597½ (oa), 555 (pp) × 89 × 28 ft. Turbine 27000 shp = 21 kts.
Armament: 10–13.5 in, 16–4 in. 3–21 in TT.
Armour: 12 in sides, 3 in deck, 11 in guns.

1914	1.18	4.18	Name	Launched	Builder—Fate
40	05	46	AJAX	21. 3.12	Scotts. Sold 9.11.26 Alloa, Rosyth.
54			AUDACIOUS	14. 9.12	Cammell Laird. Mined 27.10.14 off Tory Island.
21	35	83	CENTURION	18.11.11	Devonport DY. Sunk 9.6.44 as blockship at Arromanches.
61	77	70	KING GEORGE V	9.10.11	Portsmouth DY. Sold 12.26 Alloa, Rosyth.

Notes: KING GEORGE V was originally to have been named ROYAL GEORGE. Two 4 in AA guns added in all ships. All four served in the 2nd BS. CENTURION converted to target ship at Chatham DY 4.26 to 8.27 and became dummy battleship ANSON in 1941.

IRON DUKE CLASS

25000 tons: 623 (oa), 580 (pp) × 89½ × 29 ft. Turbine 29000 shp = 21 kts.
Armament: 10–13.5 in, 12–6 in, 2–3 in AA, 4–21 in TT.
Armour: 12 in sides, 2½ in deck, 11 in guns.

1914	1.18	4.18	Name	Launched	Builder—Fate
75	14	51	BENBOW	12.11.13	Beardmore. Sold 3.31 Metal Ind, Rosyth.
11	60	16	EMPEROR OF INDIA	27.11.13	Vickers. Sunk 1.7.31 as target, raised. Sold 6.2.32 Metal Ind, Rosyth.
94	76	14	IRON DUKE	12.10.12	Portsmouth DY. Sold 2.3.46, BU by Metal Ind, Rosyth.
79	85	66	MARLBOROUGH	24.10.12	Devonport DY. Sold 27.6.32 Metal Ind, Rosyth.

Notes: EMPEROR OF INDIA was (ex-*Delhi*), renamed 10.13. IRON DUKE was fleet flagship of the Grand Fleet 1914–17, then 1st BS. BENBOW and EMPEROR OF INDIA in 4th BS to 1916, then to 1st BS. MARLBOROUGH in 1st BS 1914–18. IRON DUKE became gunnery ship 1931; depot ship 1939.

THREE SHIPS REQUISITIONED IN 8.14

27500 tons. 672 (oa), 632 (pp) × 89 × 27 ft. Turbine 34000 shp = 22 kts.
Armament: 14–12 in, 20–6 in, 6–3 in, 2–3 in AA.
Armour: 9 in sides, 2½ in deck, 9 in guns.

1914	1.18	4.18	Name	Launched	Builder—Fate
53	04	09	AGINCOURT	22. 1.13	Armstrong. Sold 19.12.22 Rosyth S.Bkg. Co.

Notes: Ex-Turkish SULTAN OSMAN I seized 2.8.14 (ex-*Rio de Janeiro*) ordered for Brazil and sold to Turkey 1.14. Unusually high standard of personnel accommodation causing protection qualities to be suspect when compared with British contemporaries. She was the longest battleship of the period and carried the most heavy guns. In the 4th BS to 1915, then 1st BS to 1918 and 2nd BS in late 1918.

23000 tons. 559½ (oa), 525 (pp) ×91½×28 ft. Turbine 26500 shp=21 kts.
Armament: 10–13.5 in, 16–6 in, 2–12 pdrAA, 4–21 in TT.
Armour: 12 in sides, 1½ in deck, 11 in guns.

1914	1.18	4.18	Name	Launched	Builder—Fate
56	61	76	ERIN	3. 9.13	Vickers. Sold 19.12.22 Cox & Danks, Queenborough.

Notes: Ex-Turkish RESHADIEH seized 8.14. Served in the 4th BS 1914–15, and 2nd BS 1915–18. The Turkish FATIH (24700 tons) laid down by Vickers 11.6.14, was cleared from the slip in 8.14.

28000 tons. 661 (oa), 625 (pp) ×103×28 ft. Turbine 37000 shp=22¼ kts.
Armament: 10–14 in, 12–6 in, 2–3 in AA, 4–21 in TT.
Armour: 10 in sides, 4 in deck, 16 in guns.

1914	1.18	4.18	Name	Launched	Builder—Fate
28	26	01	CANADA	27.11.13	Armstrong. Resold 4.20 to Chilean Navy = ALMIRANTE LATORRE.

Notes: Ex-Chilean ALMIRANTE LATORRE (ex-Valparaiso) purchased 9.9.14. In 4th BS to 1916, then 1st BS. A sister ship, ALMIRANTE COCHRANE, also purchased was converted and launched as aircraft carrier EAGLE in 1918.

QUEEN ELIZABETH CLASS

27500 tons. 640 (oa), 600 (pp) ×90½×30 ft. Turbine 75000 shp=25 kts.
Armament: 8–15 in, 14–6 in, 2–3 inAA, 4–21 in TT.
Armour: 13 in sides, 3 in deck, 11 in guns.

1914	1.18	4.18	Name	Launched	Builder—Fate
97	10	34	BARHAM	31.12.14	John Brown. Sunk 25.11.41 by U.331 in the central Mediterranean.
3A	84	06	MALAYA	18. 3.15	Armstrong. Sold 20.2.48, BU Metal Ind, Faslane.
10	97	00	QUEEN ELIZABETH	16.10.13	Portsmouth DY. Sold 19. 3.48, BU Arnott Young, Dalmuir.
34	A6	43	VALIANT	4.11.14	Fairfield. Sold 19.3.48, BU Arnott Young, Cairnryan.
57	A9	12	WARSPITE	26.11.13	Devonport DY. Sold 12.7.46 for Metal Ind, Faslane. Wrecked in tow 23.4.47 in Mounts Bay. Wreck sold 6.49 R. H. Bennett, Bristol.

Notes: A sixth ship, AGINCOURT ordered at Portsmouth DY was cancelled 26.8.14. All served in the 5th BS attached to the Battlecruiser Force, Grand Fleet from completion. QUEEN ELIZABETH was Fleet Flagship from 1917. Considered the most successful design of their time, they were the first British oil burners and had geared cruising turbines.

ROYAL SOVEREIGN CLASS

25750 tons. 624 (oa), 580 (pp) ×88½ (102 over bulges) ×28½ ft. Turbine 40000 shp=23 kts.
(REVENGE 628 (oa)).
Armament: 8–15 in, 14–6 in, 2–3 in AA, 4–21 in TT.
Armour: 13 in sides, 5½ in deck, 13 in guns. (RAMILLIES built with bulges).

1914	1.18	4.18	Name	Launched	Builder—Fate
74	98	21	RAMILLIES	12. 9.16	Beardmore. Sold 20.2.48, BU Arnott Young, Cairnryan and Troon.
8A	1A	57	RESOLUTION	14. 1.15	Palmer. Sold 5.5.48, BU Metal Ind, Faslane.
98	2A	29	REVENGE	29. 5.15	Vickers. Arrived 5.9.48 Ward, Inverkeithing to BU.
67	4A	38	ROYAL OAK	17.11.14	Devonport DY. Sunk 14.10.39 by U.47 in Scapa Flow.
59	5A	89	ROYAL SOVEREIGN	29. 4.15	Portsmouth DY. Lent Russia 30.5.44 to 9.2.49 as ARCHANGELSK. Sold 5.4.49, BU Ward, Inverkeithing.

Notes: Two further ships of this class were completed as battlecruisers RENOWN and REPULSE (qv) and an eighth ship, RESISTANCE, ordered at Devonport DY was cancelled 26.8.14. REVENGE was originally named RENOWN. All served in the 1st BS from completion. These ships were coal burners and had lower freeboard than the previous class. In the postwar years all of the 15 in gun battleships were modernised to various degrees during refits in the late 1920s and in the 1930s.

BATTLECRUISERS

The first six ships of this type were originally designated Armoured Cruisers. All were essentially vessels of this type, armour protection not being up to battleship standard, though mounting battleship guns.

INVINCIBLE CLASS

17250 tons. 567 (oa), 530 (pp) × 78½ × 26 ft. Turbine 41000 shp = 25½ kts.
Armament: 8–12 in, 16–4 in, 4–18 in TT.
Armour: 6 in sides, 2 in deck, 7 in guns.

Pendant Nos.			Name	Launched	Builder—Fate
1914	1.18	4.18			
77	74	05	INDOMITABLE	16. 3.07	Fairfield. Sold 1.12.21 Stanlee.
83	75	47	INFLEXIBLE	26. 6.07	John Brown. Sold 1.12.21 Stanlee; resold BU in Germany.
85			INVINCIBLE	13. 4.07	Armstrong. Sunk 31.5.16 at Jutland.

Notes. INDOMITABLE and INFLEXIBLE in the Mediterranean in 8.14, INVINCIBLE at Queenstown, then to Humber area. INFLEXIBLE and INVINCIBLE detached 1914 to the S. Atlantic (Falklands battle). All three joined the GF Battlecruiser Force late in the year, remaining two still there to 1918.

INDEFATIGABLE CLASS

18800 tons. (INDEFATIGABLE 18750). 590 (oa), 555 (pp) × 80 × 26½ ft. Turbine 43000 shp = 25½ kts.
Armament: 8–12 in, 16–4 in, 3–21 in TT.
Armour: 6 in sides, 2 in deck, 7 in guns.

1914	1.18	4.18	Name	Launched	Builder—Fate
C6*	09	81	AUSTRALIA (RAN)	25.10.11	John Brown. Sunk 12.4.24 as target off Sydney.
13			INDEFATIGABLE	28.10.09	Devonport DY. Sunk 31.5.16 at Jutland.
08	90	53	NEW ZEALAND	1. 7.11	Fairfield. Sold 19.12.22 Rosyth S.Bkg. Co.

*Pendant dates from 2.15.
Notes: AUSTRALIA joined the 2nd BCS from the Pacific in 1915. INDEFATIGABLE from the Mediterranean to 2nd BCS in 1915. NEW ZEALAND served in the 1st BCS 1914–15 and 2nd BCS 1915–18.

LION CLASS

26350 tons. 700 (oa), 660 (pp) × 88½ × 28 ft. Turbine 70000 shp = 28 kts.
Armament: 8–13.5 in, 16–4 in, 2–21 in TT.
Armour: 9 in sides, 2½ in deck, 9 in guns.

1914	1.18	4.18	Name	Launched	Builder—Fate
22	79	67	LION	6. 8.10	Devonport DY. Sold 31.1.24 Hughes Bolckow, Jarrow.
29	95	68	PRINCESS ROYAL	29. 4.11	Vickers. Sold 19.12.22 Rosyth S.Bkg. Co.

As LION; except 26500 tons. 704 (oa) ft. 75000 shp.

1914	1.18	4.18	Name	Launched	Builder—Fate
14			QUEEN MARY	20. 3.12	Palmer. Sunk 31.5.16 at Jutland.

Notes: All served in the 1st BCS, Grand Fleet. LION was Battlecruiser Force flagship from 1915.

TIGER

28500 tons. 704 (oa), 660 (pp) × 90½ × 28½ ft. Turbine 85000 shp = 28 kts.
Armament: 8–13.5 in, 12–6 in, 4–3 pdr, 4–21 in TT.
Armour: 9 in sides, 3 in deck, 9 in guns.

1914	1.18	4.18	Name	Launched	Builder—Fate
42	A4	91	TIGER	15.12.13	John Brown. Sold 2.32 Ward, Inverkeithing.

Notes: Influenced heavily by the Japanese KONGO, this ship was a distinct improvement of the LION design. Later the shp was increased to 108000 which increased the maximum speed to 29 knots. Served in the 1st BCS, GF from completion.

RENOWN CLASS

26500 tons. 794 (oa), 750 (pp) × 90 × 27 ft. Turbine 112000 shp = 31½ kts.
Armament: 6–15 in, 17–4 in, 2–3 in AA, 2–21 in TT.
Armour: 6 in sides, 3 in deck, 11 in guns.

1.16	1.18	4.18	Name	Launched	Builder—Fate
64	99	23	RENOWN	4. 3.16	Fairfield. Sold 19.3.48; BU Metal Ind, Faslane.
54	OA	26	REPULSE	8. 1.16	John Brown. Sunk 10.12.41 by Japanese A/C off Malaya.

Notes: Laid down as Royal Sovereign class battleships, altered on stocks. RENOWN was originally ordered from Palmer, contract was reassigned when design increase in length exceeded Palmer's slip lengths. They were designed to carry 25 mines but no record indicating actual provision for mines has been found. Both ships served in the 1st BCS from completion.

HOOD CLASS

41200 tons. 860½ (oa), 810 (pp) × 104 × 28½ ft. Turbine 144000 shp = 31 kts.
Armament: 8–15 in. 12–5.5 in, 4–4 in AA, 4–3 pdr, 6–21 in TT.
Armour: 12 in sides, 3 in deck, 15 in guns.

3.20	Name	Launched	Builder—Fate
51	HOOD	22. 8.18	John Brown. Sunk 24.5.41 by gunfire of BISMARCK, Greenland Passage.

Notes: Three ships were ordered 7.4.16; a fourth ship, ANSON, was ordered in 7.16. At least eighteen designs were under consideration, including one with 18 in guns and another with triple turrets before the final plan emerged. Work was suspended 9.3.17 on ANSON (Armstrong), HOWE (Cammell Laird) and RODNEY (Fairfield) following a War Cabinet decision on 8.2.17 to proceed with HOOD alone. The three ships were cancelled 10.18, disposal of machinery, etc. continued until 8.19. When suspended, between 1330 and 1626 tons of material had been assembled on the slips for the cancelled trio. The designed displacement of HOOD, originally 36300 tons, was increased to 40600 tons in 9.16. HOOD, completed in 3.20, was the last of the British battlecruisers and the longest ship ever built for the RN.

1st class CRUISERS (LIGHT BATTLECRUISERS)

GLORIOUS CLASS

18600 tons.   786 (oa), 735 (pp) ×81 ×24 ft.   Turbine 90000 shp=31 kts.
Armament: 4–15 in, 18–4 in, 2–3 in AA, 2–(later 14) 21 in TT.
Armour: 3 in sides, 3 in deck, 7 in guns.

Pendant Nos. 1.18	4.18	Name	Launched	Builder—Fate
51	94	COURAGEOUS	5. 2.16	Armstrong. Sunk 17.9.39 by U.29, S.W. Approaches.
67	56	GLORIOUS	20. 4.16	Harland & Wolff. Sunk 8.6.40 by German battlecruisers off Narvik.

Notes: Both served in 1st CS, Grand Fleet 1917–18. COURAGEOUS converted to A/C carrier 6.24–5.28. GLORIOUS completed conversion to A/C carrier 3.30.

FURIOUS

19513 tons.   786½ (oa), 750 (pp) ×88 ×24 ft.   Turbine 94000 shp=31¼ kts.
Armament: 1–18, in 11–5.5 in, 4–3 in AA, 18–(later 6) 21 in TT.
Armour: 3 in sides, 3 in deck, 7 in guns.

1.18	4.18	Name	Launched	Builder—Fate
65	40	FURIOUS	15. 8.16	Armstrong. Sold 23.1.48, BU Dalmuir and Troon.

Notes: Designed to mount 2–18 in guns, she completed with a flight deck forward and one gun aft in 7.17. On 1.9.17 she was ordered to remove the gun and add an additional flight deck aft which was completed in 1918. Served 1918 in the Flying Squadron, GF. She underwent extensive alterations during 1921–25, receiving a full flight deck and having her island removed.

CRUISERS

In 1913 all armoured and 1st class protected cruisers had been reclassified Cruisers and the 2nd and 3rd class protected cruisers became Light Cruisers. In the following lists, the original designation is used.

PEARL CLASS: 3rd CLASS CRUISERS

2575 tons. 278 (oa), 265 (pp) ×41 ×15½ ft. TE 7500 ihp=19 kts.
Armament: 8–4.7 in, 8–3 pdr.
Armour: 2½ in deck, 2 in guns.

Pendant Nos. 1914 1.18	Name	Launched	Builder—Fate
	PHILOMEL	28. 8.90	Devonport DY. To New Zealand Govt. 1914. Depot ship 3.21. Sold 17.1.47 Strongman & Co NZ; hull scuttled 6.8.49 off E. coast of New Zealand.
N.82 N.6A	WALLAROO =D/S WALLINGTON 3.19	5. 2.90	Armstrong. Harbour service 1906; commissioned as guardship 11.14; Sold 27.2.20 G. Sharpe.

Notes: WALLAROO was originally PERSIAN, renamed 4.90. Seven others of this class were sold in 1906. PHILOMEL served in the Pacific 1914, Mediterranean and Persian Gulf 1914–17, RAN 1917–18. WALLAROO was guardship in the Gunfleet 1914–15, then became a depot ship.

EDGAR CLASS: 1st CLASS CRUISERS

7350 tons. (last three 7700). 387¼ (oa), 360 (pp) ×60½ ×24 ft. TE 12000 ihp=20 kts.
Armament: 2–9.2 in, 10–6 in, (last three 1–9.2 in, 12–6 in) 12–6 pdr, 4–18 in TT.
Armour: 5 in deck, 6 in guns.

Pendant Nos. 1914 9.15 1.18	Name	Launched	Builder—Fate
A5 N.05 N.38	EDGAR	24.11.90	Devonport DY. Sold 9.5.21 Ward, Morecambe.
A6 N.17 N.41	ENDYMION	22. 7.91	Earle. Sold 16.3.20 Evans, Cardiff.
A8 N.23 N.53	GRAFTON	30. 1.92	Thames IW. Sold 1.7.20 Castle, Plymouth.
A9	HAWKE	11. 3.91	Chatham DY. Sunk 15.10.14 by U.9 in the North Sea.
2A N.14 N.98	THESEUS	8. 9.92	Thames IW. Sold 1921 Stanlee; resold 8.11.21 Slough T.C., BU in Germany.
A4 N.04 N.29	CRESCENT	30. 3.92	Portsmouth DY. Guardship (4–6 in guns) 2.15. Sold 22.9.21, BU in Germany.
A7 N.19 N.49	GIBRALTAR	27. 4.92	Napier. Depot ship 6.15. Sold 9.23 Cashmore.
AO N.10 N.86	ROYAL ARTHUR	26. 2.91	Portsmouth DY. Depot ship 2.15. Sold 22.9.21 Cohen, BU in Germany.

Notes: For ST. GEORGE of this class, see under depot ships. ROYAL ARTHUR was laid down as CENTAUR. All of these ships formed the 10th CS, N. Atlantic until late 1914. EDGAR, ENDYMION, GRAFTON, fitted with bulges, served in the Mediterranean 1915–18. CRESCENT, GIBRALTAR and ROYAL ARTHUR became depot ships in Scapa/Rosyth area 1915.

APOLLO CLASS: 2nd CLASS CRUISERS

3600 tons (SAPPHO 3400). 314½ (oa), 300 (pp) ×43½×16½ ft. TE 9000 ihp=20 kts.
Armament: 2–6 in, 6–4.7 in, 8–6 pdr, 4–14 in TT.
Armour: 2 in deck, 4½ in guns.

1914	1.18	Name	Launched	Builder—Fate
N.16	N.14	BRILLIANT	24. 6.91	Sheerness DY. Sunk 23.4.18 as blockship at Zeebrugge.
		RAINBOW (RCN)	25. 3.91	Palmer. To RCN 8.10; depot ship; sold 1920.
P.41	P.A1	SAPPHO	9. 5.91	Samuda. Sold 3.21 Castle, Plymouth.
N.20	N.94	SIRIUS	27.10.90	Armstrong. Sunk 23.4.18 as blockship at Ostend.

Notes: For seven ships of this class, see under minelayers and for SPARTAN see under harbour service. One ship of this class was wrecked in 1901 and eight others were sold between 1910 and 1914. BRILLIANT served as depot ship in the Tyne 1914–15 and Lerwick 1915–18. RAINBOW served in the Pacific, based at Esquimalt. SAPPHO was in the GF as flagship tender 1914–16 and was then laid up. SIRIUS in the Nore command until 1915 then in West Africa until 1918.

ASTRAEA CLASS: 2nd CLASS CRUISERS

4360 tons. 339½ (oa), 320 (pp) ×49½×17 ft. TE 9000 ihp=19¼ kts.
Armament: 2–6 in, 8–4.7 in, 8–6 pdr, 3–18 in TT.
Armour: 2 in deck, 4½ in guns.

1914	9.15	1.18	Name	Launched	Builder—Fate
			ASTRAEA	17. 3.93	Devonport DY. Sold 1.7.20 Castle, BU in Germany.
			CAMBRIAN =HARLECH 3.16 =VIVID 9.21	31. 1.93	Pembrock DY. Depot ship 3.16; Sold 21.2.23 Young, Sunderland.
D.56	P.56	N.21	CHARYBDIS	15. 6.93	Sheerness DY. Laid up at Bermuda 1914 after collision damage; completed 3.18 as cargo carrier on loan to 12.19. Sold 27.1.22 in Bermuda; resold 10.23 BU in Holland.
			FOX	15. 6.93	Portsmouth DY. Sold 14.7.20 Cardiff Marine Stores.
P.17	N.32	N.57	HERMIONE	7.11.93	Devonport DY. Sold 25.10.21 Multilocular S.Bkg. Co; resold 18.12.22 and became training ship WARSPITE. BU 9.40 Ward, Grays.

Notes: For BONAVENTURE and FLORA of this class see under Depot ships and Harbour service respectively. The eighth ship, FORTE, was sold 2.4.14. ASTRAEA spent the war years on the Cape and West Africa stations. CHARYBDIS was in the 12th CS until laid up. FOX served in the East Indies 1914, East Africa and Egypt 1915–17, Red Sea 1917–18. HERMIONE was guardship then depot ship at Southampton 1914–18.

POWERFUL CLASS: 1st CLASS CRUISERS

14200 tons. 538 (oa), 500 (pp) ×71×27 ft. TE 25000 ihp=22 kts.
Armament: 2–9.2 in, 16–6 in, 16–12 pdr, 4–18 in TT.
Armour: 6 in deck, 6 in guns.

1914	1.18	Name	Launched	Builder—Fate
P.70	P.A9	TERRIBLE =FISGARD III 8.20	27. 5.95	Thomson. Harbour service 1.18; Sold 7.32 Cashmore.

Notes: For POWERFUL, see Harbour service list. TERRIBLE on transport and trooping service, Mediterranean 1915–16 then accommodation ship at Portsmouth.

ECLIPSE CLASS: 2nd CLASS CRUISERS

5600 tons. 373 (oa), 350 (pp) ×53½×19 ft. TE 9600 ihp=19½ kts.
Armament: 11–6 in, 8–12 pdr, 3–18 in TT.
Armour: 2½ in deck, 3 in guns.

Pendant Nos. 1914 9.15 1.18			Name	Launched	Builder—Fate
D.18	P.58	N.34	DIANA	5.12.95	Fairfield. Sold 1.7.20 Castle, Plymouth.
D.59	P.47	*	DORIS	3. 3.96	Vickers. Sold 20.2.19 at Bombay.
D.58	*		ECLIPSE	19. 7.94	Portsmouth DY. Depot ship 1916; Sold 8.21 Cohen.
D.60	P.60	N.61	ISIS	27. 6.96	London & Glasgow. Sold 26.2.20 Granton S.Bkg. Co.
N.37		N.65	JUNO	16.11.95	Vickers. Sold 24.9.20 Earle & Co.; Resold and BU in Denmark
P.32	P.1A	P7A	MINERVA	23. 9.95	Chatham DY. Sold 5.10.20 Auten Ltd.
D.61	P.61	P.A7	TALBOT	25. 4.95	Devonport DY. Sold 6.12.21 Multilocular S.Bkg. Co.
P.36		P.2C	VENUS	5. 9.95	Fairfield. Sold 22.9.21 Cohen; BU in Germany.

*No pendants assigned. ECLIPSE assigned Oblique pendant at Portsmouth 3.16.

Notes: Originally the class was armed with 5–6 in, 6–4.7 in guns, altered by 1905. For DIDO see under depot ships. DIANA, ECLIPSE and TALBOT 12th CS 1914–15. DIANA to China and East Indies until 1918. ECLIPSE accommodation ship 1915–18 and TALBOT to Mediterranean and E. Africa from 1915. Others were in 11th CS to 1915, then DORIS went to Mediterranean and E. Indies, ISIS to N. America and W. Indies, JUNO to E. Indies, MINERVA to E. Mediterranean and E. Africa, and VENUS to E. Mediterranean, China and E. Indies.

ARROGANT CLASS: 2nd CLASS CRUISERS

5750 tons. 342 (oa), 320 (pp) ×57½×20 ft. TE 10000 ihp=19 kts.
Armament: 10–6 in, 9–12 pdr, 3–18 in TT.
Armour: 2 in sides (bow), 1½ in deck, 4½ in guns.

1914	9.15	1.18	Name	Launched	Builder—Fate
7C	P.75	P.4C	VINDICTIVE	9.12.97	Chatham DY. Sunk 10.5.18 as Blockship at Ostend.

Notes: GLADIATOR of this class was lost in collision 25.4.08. For ARROGANT see under depot ships and for FURIOUS see under harbour service. VINDICTIVE was in 9th CS 1914–15, then S.E. coast of America to 1916 and in White Sea 1916–17. In early 1918 she was converted to an assault ship for the Zeebrugge action.

DIADEM CLASS: 1st CLASS CRUISERS

11000 tons. 466 (oa), 435 (pp) ×69×26 ft. TE 16500 ihp=20½ kts.
Armament: 16–6 in, 12–12 pdr, 4–3 pdr, 2–18 in TT.
Armour: 4 in deck, 4½ in guns.

Pendant Nos. 1914 9.15 1.18			Name	Launched	Builder—Fate
D.52*		P.7C	AMPHITRITE	5. 1.98	Vickers. M/L 1917; Sold 12.4.20 Ward, Milford Haven.
P.78		P.04	ARGONAUT	24. 1.98	Fairfield. Sold 18.5.20 Ward, Milford Haven.
P.69			ARIADNE	22. 4.98	Thomson. M/L 1917; Sunk 26.7.17 by UC.65 off Beachy Head.
P.20	N.50	N.32	DIADEM	21.10.96	Fairfield. Sold 9.5.21 Ward, Morecambe.
P.06		P.91	EUROPA	20.3.97	John Brown. Depot ship 1915; Sold 15.9.20 G. F. Bletto, Malta.
			NIOBE (RCN)	20. 2.97	Vickers. RCN 6.9.10; BU 1922 at Philadelphia.

*Assigned Compass pendant at Portsmouth 9.15.

Notes: For ANDROMEDA and SPARTIATE of this class see under Harbour service. AMPHITRITE and ARGONAUT 9th CS to 1915, then harbour service. AMPHITRITE converting to M/L Portsmouth in 1917. ARIADNE was laid up at Devonport and converted to M/L 1917. DIADEM was stokers' training ship at Portsmouth 1914–18. EUROPA 9th CS to 1915, then depot ship in the Mediterranean. NIOBE at Halifax in 1914 was disarmed for harbour service in 10.15.

P CLASS: 3rd CLASS CRUISERS

2135 tons. 313½ (oa), 300 (pp) ×36½ × 16 ft. TE 7000 ihp=20 kts.
Armament: 8–4 in, 8–3 pdr, 2–18 in TT. (PSYCHE: 2–4.7 in, 2–3 pdr in 1918).
Armour: 2 in deck.

1914	1.18	Name	Launched	Builder—Fate
		PEGASUS	4. 3.97	Palmer. Sunk 20.9.14 by the German KONIGSBERG at Zanzibar.
		PELORUS	15.12.96	Sheerness DY. D/S 1916; Sold 6.5.20 Ward, Grays.
N.84*		PROSERPINE	5.12.96	Sheerness DY. Sold 30.11.19, BU at Genoa.
		PSYCHE	19. 7.98	Devonport DY. RAN 1.7.15; Sold 6.22 at Melbourne.
		PYRAMUS	15. 5.97	Palmer. Sold 21.4.20 T.C. Pas, Holland.

2200 tons. 318¾ (oa), 305 (pp). Guns reduced to 4–3 pdr in 1916.

		PIONEER (RAN)	28. 6.99	Chatham DY. RAN 28.12.12; Sold 1924 at Sydney.

*No pendant 1.18.

Notes: PANDORA, PERSEUS and PROMETHEUS sold 1913–14. For PACTOLUS and POMONE see under depot ships and harbour service respectively. PEGASUS on Cape Station 1914. PELORUS on Bristol Channel patrol 1914, then Mediterranean. PIONEER was in Australian waters to 1915, E. Africa 1915–16, then paid off at Sydney. PROSPERINE served in the 7th CS in the Channel 1914, then to Egypt and Mesopotamia to 1918. PSYCHE and PYRAMUS in New Zealand 1914, the former going to China and the latter to the Persian Gulf and E. Indies in 1915–18.

HIGHFLYER CLASS: 2nd CLASS CRUISERS

5650 tons. 373 (oa), 350 (pp) ×54 ×20 ft. TE 10000 ihp=20 kts.
Armament: 11–6 in, 9–12 pdr, 6–3 pdr, 2–18 in TT.
Armour: 3 in deck, 3 in guns.

1914	9.15	1.18	Name	Launched	Builder—Fate
			HERMES	7. 4.98	Fairfield. Sunk 31.10.14 by U.27 off the Ruylingen Bank.
D.22	N.69	N.58	HIGHFLYER	4. 6.98	Fairfield. Sold 6.21 at Bombay.
*N.85 (9.18)					
			HYACINTH	27.10.98	London & Glasgow. Sold 11.23 Cohen, Swansea.

*No pendant from 4.18–9.18.

Notes: HERMES was fitted to carry a seaplane 1913. She was attached to Nore Command 1914. HIGHFLYER was 9th CS and 5th CS 1914, based on Cape Verde Is. 1914–15 then W. Africa 1916–17 and W. Indies 1917–18. HYACINTH on Cape and E. Africa station 1914–18.

CRESSY CLASS: ARMOURED CRUISERS

12000 tons. 472 (oa), 440 (pp) ×69½ ×25 ft. TE 21000 ihp=21 kts.
Armament: 2–9.2 in, 12–6 in, 14–12 pdr, 2–18 in TT. (4–6 in removed 1916).
Armour: 6 in sides, 3 in deck, 6 in guns.

Pendant Nos. 1914	1.18	4.18	Name	Launched	Builder—Fate
N.00			ABOUKIR	16. 5.00	Fairfield. Sunk 22.9.14 by U.9 in North Sea.
N.39	N.09		BACCHANTE	21. 2.01	John Brown. Sold 1.7.20 Castle, Plymouth.
N.40			CRESSY	4.12.99	Fairfield. Sunk 22.9.14 by U.9 in North Sea.
N.51	N.44		EURYALUS	20. 5.01	Vickers. Sold 1.7.20 Castle; resold and BU 1922 in Germany.
N.59			HOGUE	13. 8.00	Vickers. Sunk 22.9.14 by U.9 in North Sea.
N.74*		N.65	SUTLEJ =CRESCENT c1920	18.11.99	John Brown. Sold 9.5.21 Ward, Preston.

*No pendant from 1.18–4.18.

Notes: The first cruisers built with side armour since the Orlando class of 1886. The first five named above were in the 7th CS 1914 and the two survivors in the 12th CS 1914–15, then to the Mediterranean until 1916. BACCHANTE in 9th CS W. Africa 1917–18 and EURYALUS to the E. Indies. EURYALUS started conversion to M/L at Hong Kong in 11.17 but not completed. SUTLEJ was 9th CS 1914 and 11th CS 1914–15. Under repair at Devonport 1916, 9th CS W. Africa 1916–17 and accommodation ship at Rosyth 1917–18, later D/S.

DRAKE CLASS: ARMOURED CRUISERS

14100 tons. 533½ (oa), 500 (pp) ×71×25 ft. TE 30000 ihp=24 kts.
Armament: 2–9.2 in, 16–6 in, 14–12 pdr, 2–18 in TT.
Armour: 6 in sides, 3 in deck, 6 in guns.

1914	9.15	1.18	Name	Launched	Builder—F/te
P.09			DRAKE	5. 3.01	Pembroke DY. Capsized 2.10.17 in Rathlin Sound after being torpedoed by U.79 in the North Channel.
P.16			GOOD HOPE	21. 2.01	Fairfield. Sunk 1.11.14 at the Battle of Coronel.
P.10	P.98		KING ALFRED	28.10.01	Vickers. Sold 30.1.20 F. Rijsdijk, Holland.
P.28	P.73	P.1A	LEVIATHAN	3. 7.01	John Brown. Sold 3.3.20 Hughes, Bolckow.

Notes: GOOD HOPE laid down as AFRICA, renamed 2.10.99. All were in the 6th CS, GF 1914, DRAKE until 1915, detached to N. America & W. Indies 1916–17. GOOD HOPE 4th CS N. America & W. Indies 1914. KING ALFRED 9th CS/W. Africa 1915–17. LEVIATHAN 1st CS, GF 1914-15, then N. America & W. Indies 1915-18.

KENT CLASS: ARMOURED CRUISERS

9800 tons. 463½ (oa), 440 (pp) ×66×23 ft. TE 21000 ihp=23 kts.
Armament: 14–6 in, 10–12 pdr, 2–18 in TT.
Armour: 4 in sides, 2 in deck, 5 in guns.

1914	9.15	1.18	Name	Launched	Builder—Fate
36	P.74	P.08	BERWICK	20. 9.02	Beardmore. Sold 1.7.20 Castle; BU in Germany 1922.
D.31	P.04	P.84	CORNWALL	29.10.02	Pembroke DY. Sold 7.6.20 Ward, Briton Ferry.
D.37	P.76	P.86	CUMBERLAND	16.12.02	London & Glasgow. Sold 9.5.21 Ward, Briton Ferry.
9C N.28	55 (4.18)		DONEGAL	4. 9.02	Fairfield. Sold 1.7.20 Castle; resold Granton S.Bkg. Co.
51 N.38	62 (4.18)		ESSEX	29. 8.01	Pembroke DY. Sold 8.11.21 Slough T.C. BU in Germany.
P.27	P.80	P.99	KENT	6. 3.01	Portsmouth DY. Sold 6.20 at Hong Kong.
71		78	LANCASTER	22. 3.02	Armstrong. Sold 3.3.20 Ward, Preston.
D.28			MONMOUTH	13.11.01	London & Glasgow. Sunk 1.11.14 at Coronel.
20	P.87	P.A5	SUFFOLK	15. 1.03	Portsmouth DY. Sold 1.7.20 Castle; resold, BU 1922 in Germany.

Notes: BEDFORD of this class wrecked 21.8.10. BERWICK, ESSEX, LANCASTER and SUFFOLK 4th CS W. Indies 1914, North America & W. Indies station 1914–15 (BERWICK to 1918, SUFFOLK to 1916). ESSEX 9th CS Atlantic 1915–16, accommodation ship Devonport 1917–18. LANCASTER in Pacific 1916–18, SUFFOLK China 1917–18. CORNWALL 5th CS W. Africa 1914, S. America 1914–15, Mediterranean 1915, China 1916–17, N. America & W. Indies 1917–18. CUMBERLAND 5th CS W. Africa 1914, 6th CS GF 1914–15, N. America & W. Indies 1918–18. DONEGAL 6th CS GF 1915, 7th CS GF 1915–16, 9th CS W. Africa 1916–17, N. America & W. Indies 1916–18, China 1918. MONMOUTH 5th CS W. Africa 1914, S. America 1914.

CHALLENGER CLASS: 2nd CLASS CRUISERS

5650 tons. 373 (oa), 350 (pp) ×54×20 ft. TE 10000 ihp=20 kts.
Armament: 11–6 in, 9–12 pdr, 6–3 pdr, 2–18 in TT.
Armour: 3 in deck, 3 in guns.

1914	9.15	1.18	Name	Launched	Builder—Fate
D.33	P.07	P.81	CHALLENGER	27. 5.02	Chatham DY. Sold 31.5.20 Ward, Preston.
			ENCOUNTER (RAN) =PENGUIN 5.23 D/S	18. 6.02	Devonport DY. RAN 7.12; Dismantled 10.29, hulk scuttled 9.32 off Sydney.

Notes: CHALLENGER 9th CS 1914, W. Africa 1914–15, E. Africa 1915–18. ENCOUNTER in Pacific 1914–15, China 1915–16, Pacific 1916–18.

DEVONSHIRE CLASS: ARMOURED CRUISERS

10850 tons. 473½ (oa), 450 (pp) × 68½ × 23 ft. TE 21000 ihp = 22 kts.
Armament: 4–7.5 in, 6–6 in, 2–12 pdr, 2–18 in TT.
Armour: 6 in sides, 2 in deck, 6 in guns.

1914	1.18	4.18	Name	Launched	Builder—Fate
09	07	N.58	ANTRIM	8.10.03	John Brown. Sold 19.12.22 Hughes Bolckow, Derwenthaugh.
80			ARGYLL	3. 4.04	Scotts. Wrecked 28.10.15 on Bell Rock.
30	P.3A	(9.15)	CARNARVON	7.10.03	Beardmore. Sold 8.11.21 Slough T.C.; BU in Germany.
	P.80				
38	53	N.19	DEVONSHIRE	30. 4.04	Chatham DY. Sold 9.5.21 Ward, Preston and Barrow.
50	(2.15)		HAMPSHIRE	4. 9.03	Armstrong. Mined 5.6.16 off the Orkneys.
86	3A	N.34	ROXBURGH	19. 1.04	London & Glasgow. Sold 8.11.21 Slough T.C.; BU in Germany.

Notes: ANTRIM, ARGYLL, DEVONSHIRE and ROXBURGH 3rd CS GF 1914–16, remaining three N. America & W. Indies 1916–18. CARNARVON 5th CS W. Africa 1914, S. America 1914–15, N. America & W. Indies 1915–18. HAMPSHIRE in China 1914, 6th CS and 7th CS GF 1915–16.

GEM CLASS: 3rd CLASS CRUISERS

3000 tons. 373¾ (oa), 360 (pp) × 40 × 14 ft. TE 9800 ihp = 22 kts.
   (AMETHYST: Turbine 12000 shp = 23¼ kts.)
Armament: 12–4 in, 11–3 pdr, 2–18 in TT. (AMETHYST 2–6 in, 8–4 in from 1918).
Armour: 2 in deck.

1914	9.15	1.18	Name	Launched	Builder—Fate
P.00		P.02	AMETHYST	5.11.03	Armstrong. Sold 1.10.20 J. W. Towers, Milford Haven.
N.61		N.33	DIAMOND	6. 1.04	Laird. Sold 9.5.21 Ward, Grays.
32	(4.19)	N.70*			
N.78		N.89	SAPPHIRE	17. 3.04	Palmer. Sold 9.5.21 Ward, Grays.
P.29	P.2A	P.1C	TOPAZE	23. 7.03	Laird Sold 22.9.21 Cohen; BU in Germany.

*Pendant from 6.18.

Notes: AMETHYST 1st LCS GF 1914, Mediterranean 1915, S. America 1916–18. DIAMOND attached 5th BS 1914, and 3rd BS 1915–18 ,Mediterranean 1918. DIAMOND converted to CMB carrier 1918, fitted to carry 6–40 foot CMBs. SAPPHIRE attached 7th BS Channel Fleet 1914, 4th BS 1914–15, Mediterranean 1915–16, E. Indies 1916–18. TOPAZE attached 5th BS 1914–15, Mediterranean 1915–17, Red Sea 1917–18.

ADVENTURE CLASS: SCOUTS

2670 tons. 395 (oa), 374 (pp) × 38½ × 13 ft. TE 15000 ihp = 25¼ kts.
Armament: 9–4 in, 1–3 in AA, 2–14 in TT. (ATTENTIVE: 2–6 in, 6–4 in, 1–3 in AA 1918).
Armour: 2 in deck.

1914	9.15	1.18	Name	Launched	Builder—Fate
D.10	P.64	P.01	ADVENTURE	8. 9.04	Armstrong. Sold 3.3.20 Ward, Morecambe.
	P.03	P.06	ATTENTIVE	24.11.04	Armstrong. Sold 12.4.20 Ward, Preston.

Notes: ADVENTURE originally to have been named EDDYSTONE. ADVENTURE was 6th DF leader at Dover 1914–15, then at Queenstown 1915–18 when she joined the Mediterranean Fleet. ATTENTIVE was 6th DF leader 1914–18, then to White Sea.

FORWARD CLASS: SCOUTS

2850 tons. 379 (oa), 370 (pp) × 38½ × 13 ft. TE avg. 14500 ihp = 25½ kts.
Armament: 9–4 in, 1–3 in AA, 2–14 in TT.
Armour: 2 in deck.

1914	9.15	1.18	Name	Launched	Builder—Fate
D.38	N.26	N.46	FORESIGHT	8.10.04	Fairfield. Sold 3.3.20 Granton S.Bkg. Co.
N.53		N.48	FORWARD	27. 8.04	Fairfield. Sold 27.7.21 Fryer, Sunderland.

Notes: FORWARD was originally to have been named NORE. FORESIGHT was 6th DF leader at Dover 1914–15, then to the Mediterranean. FORWARD was Shetlands Patrol 1914, 7th DF leader in the Humber 1914–15, then to the Mediterranean.

PATHFINDER CLASS: SCOUTS

2940 tons. 379 (oa), 370 (pp) ×38½×13 ft. TE avg. 17000 ihp=25¼ kts.
Armament: 9–4 in, 1–3 in AA, 2–14 in TT.
Armour: 2 in deck.

1914	1.18	Name	Launched	Builder—Fate
		PATHFINDER	16. 7.04	Cammell Laird. Sunk 5.9.14 by U.21 in the North Sea.
N.24	N.80	PATROL	13.10.04	Cammell Laird. Sold 21.4.20 Machine-handel Co; BU in Holland.

Notes: PATHFINDER originally to have been named FASTNET. She was 8th DF leader, Forth 1914. PATROL was 9th DF leader, Forth and Tyne 1914–15; 7th DF leader, Humber 1915–18.

SENTINEL CLASS: SCOUTS

2895 tons. 381 (oa), 360 (pp) ×40×13 ft. TE avg. 17000 ihp=25¼ kts.
Armament: 9–4 in, 1–3 in AA, 2–14 in TT.
Armour: 2 in deck.

1914	9.15	1.18	Name	Launched	Builder—Fate
N.73		N.92	SENTINEL	19. 4.04	Vickers. Sold 18.1.23 Young, Sunderland.
D.55	P.55	N.95	SKIRMISHER	7. 2.05	Vickers. Sold 3.3.20 Ward, Preston.

Notes: SENTINEL originally to have been named INCHKEITH. She was 6th DF leader at Dover 1914; 8th DF leader, Forth 1914–15; then to the Mediterranean. SKIRMISHER was 7th DF leader, Humber 1914–18. All eight of the above scouts were originally armed with 10–12 pdr and 8–3 pdr guns.

DUKE OF EDINBURGH AND WARRIOR CLASSES: ARMOURED CRUISERS

13550 tons: 505½ (oa), 480 (pp) ×73½×26 ft. TE avg. 23000 ihp=23 kts.
Armament: 6–9.2 in, 10–6 in, 23–3 pdr, 3–18 in TT. (1st two).
6–9.2 in, 4–7.5 in, 1–12 pdr, 29–3 pdr, 3–18 in TT. (others).
Armour: 6 in sides, 1 in deck, 6 in guns.

Pendant Nos. 1914	1.18	4.18	Name	Launched	Builder—Fate
65			BLACK PRINCE	8.11.04	Thames IW. Sunk 31.5.16 at Jutland.
15	58	N.33*	DUKE OF EDINBURGH	11. 6.04	Pembroke DY. Sold 12.4.20 Hughes Bolckow.
24	00	N.03	ACHILLES	17. 6.05	Armstrong. Sold 9.5.21 Ward, Briton Ferry.
19	41	N.10	COCHRANE	20. 5.05	Fairfield. Stranded 14.11.18 in the Mersey.
69			NATAL	30. 9.05	Vickers. Sunk 30.12.15 by internal explosion, Cromarty Firth.
18			WARRIOR	25.11.05	Pembroke DY. Foundered in tow 1.6.16 after damage at Jutland.

*No pendant 4.18, assigned N.33 in 6.18.

Notes: ACHILLES, COCHRANE, NATAL all 2nd CS GF 1914–17, first two to N. America and W. Indies 1917–18, then 2nd CS again later. BLACK PRINCE and WARRIOR were in the Mediterranean 1914, then 1st CS GF 1914–16. DUKE OF EDINBURGH in Mediterranean 1914, 1st CS 1914–16, then N. America and W. Indies 1916–18.

MINOTAUR CLASS: ARMOURED CRUISERS

14600 tons. 519 (oa), 490 (pp) ×75½×25 ft. TE 27000 ihp=22¼ kts.
Armament: 4–9.2 in, 10–7.5 in, 16–12 pdr, 5–18 in TT.
Armour: 6 in sides, 1½ in deck, 8 in guns.

1914	1.18	4.18	Name	Launched	Builder—Fate
05			DEFENCE	24. 4.07	Pembroke DY. Sunk 31.5.16 at Jutland.
91*	87	71	MINOTAUR	6. 6.06	Devonport DY. Sold 12.4.20 Ward, Milford Haven.
	N.73	(6.18)			
92	8A	74	SHANNON	20. 9.06	Chatham DY. Sold 12.12.22 McLellan.
	N.25	(6.18)			

*Assigned pendant 91 in 2.15.

Notes: A fourth ship, ORION, was cancelled. DEFENCE in Mediterranean 1914, in 1st CS GF 1915–16. MINOTAUR in China 1914, 7th CS GF 1915–16, then 2nd CS GF 1916–18. SHANNON 2nd CS GF 1914–18.

BOADICEA AND ACTIVE CLASSES: SCOUTS

3300 tons. (BOADICEA), 3350 tons (others in class), 3440 tons (ACTIVE, etc.).
405 (oa), 385 (pp) ×41×14 ft. Turbine 18000 shp=25½ kts.
Armament: 6–4 in (1st two), 10–4 in (others), 4–3 pdr, 2– TT.
Armour: 1 in deck.

1914	1.18	4.18	Name	Launched	Builder—Fate
1C	12	87	BELLONA	20. 3.09	Pembroke DY. Sold 9.5.21 Ward, Lelant.
4C	19	11	BOADICEA	14. 5.08	Pembroke DY. Sold 13.7.26 Alloa, Rosyth.
6C	17	84	BLANCHE	25.11.09	Pembroke DY. Sold 27.7.21 Fryer, Sunderland.
C7	18	64	BLONDE	22. 7.10	Pembroke DY. Sold 6.5.20 T. C. Pas, Holland.
A2	01	N.06	ACTIVE	14. 3.11	Pembroke DY. Sold 21.4.20; BU in Norway.
			AMPHION	4.12.11	Pembroke DY. Mined 6.8.14 North Sea.
46	64	27	FEARLESS	12. 6.12	Pembroke DY. Sold 8.11.21 Slough T.C.; BU in Germany.

Notes: The first two had 18 in TT, others 21 in. All had 10–4 in in 1916 with the addition of 1–3 in AA in BELLONA, BOADICEA and ACTIVE. In 1918, ACTIVE and FEARLESS had 8–4 in, 1–3 in AA; BLANCHE and BLONDE 10–4 in; BELLONA and BOADICEA 10–4 in, 1–4 in AA. BOADICEA and class attached to GF battle squadrons 1914–19. BOADICEA, while on harbour service, was to have been named POMONE in 4.20, the order was cancelled in 7.20. ACTIVE was 2nd DF leader, Harwich 1914–15 and GF 1915; then 4th DF leader Portsmouth 1916–17, at Queenstown 1917–18, Mediterranean 1918. AMPHION was 3rd DF leader, Harwich 1914. FEARLESS was 1st DF leader Harwich 1914–16, then 12th S/M flotilla GF to 1918.

BRISTOL CLASS: 2nd CLASS CRUISERS

4800 tons. 453 (oa), 430 (pp) ×47×15½ ft. Turbine 22000 shp=25 kts.
Armament: 2–6 in, 10–4 in, 1–3 in AA, 2–18 in TT.
Armour: 2 in deck.

1914	1.18	Name	Launched	Builder—Fate
99	20	BRISTOL	23. 2.10	John Brown. Sold 9.5.21 Ward, Hayle.
		GLASGOW	30. 9.09	Fairfield. Sold 29.4.27 Ward, Morecambe.
58	68	GLOUCESTER	28.10.09	Beardmore. Sold 9.5.21 Ward, Briton Ferry.
44	80	LIVERPOOL	30.10.09	Vickers. Sold 8.11.21 Slough T.C.; BU in Germany.
		NEWCASTLE	25.11.09	Armstrong. Sold 9.5.21 Ward, Lelant.

Notes: BRISTOL in West Indies and South America 1914–15, Mediterranean 1915–18, South America 1918. GLASGOW in S. America 1914–18, Mediterranean 1918. GLOUCESTER in Mediterranean 1914, 2nd LCS GF 1914–15, 3rd LCS 1915–16, Mediterranean 1916–18. LIVERPOOL in 1st LCS GF 1914, 2nd LCS 1914–15, Mediterranean 1915–18. NEWCASTLE in Pacific 1914–16, Mediterranean 1916–17, S. America 1917–18.

WEYMOUTH CLASS: 2nd CLASS CRUISERS

5250 tons. 453 (oa), 430 (pp) ×48½×15½ ft. Turbine 22000 shp=25 kts.
Armament: 8–6 in, 1–3 in AA, 2–21 in TT.
Armour: 2 in deck.

1914	2.15	1.18	Name	Launched	Builder—Fate
	A9	52	DARTMOUTH	14.12.10	Vickers. Sold 13.12.30 Alloa, Rosyth.
90			FALMOUTH	20. 9.10	Beardmore. Sunk 19.8.16 by U.63 in the North Sea.
03		0C	WEYMOUTH	18.11.10	Armstrong. Sold 2.10.28 Hughes Bolckow.
	95	1C	YARMOUTH	12. 4.11	London & Glasgow. Sold 2.7.29 Alloa, Rosyth.
72 (in 4.18)					

Notes: DARTMOUTH in E. Indies 1914, 2nd LCS GF 1914–15, Mediterranean 1915–18. FALMOUTH in 1st LCS 1914, 2nd LCS 1914–15, 3rd LCS 1915–16. WEYMOUTH in Mediterranean 1914, E. Africa 1914–15, Mediterranean 1915–16, 6th LCS GF 1916–17, Mediterranean 1917–18. YARMOUTH in China 1914, 2nd LCS 1914–15, 3rd LCS 1915–18, 2nd LCS 1918.

CHATHAM CLASS: 2nd CLASS CRUISERS

5400 tons. 458 (oa), 430 (pp) × 49 × 16 ft. Turbine 25000 shp = 25¼ kts.
Armament: 8–6 in, 1–3 in AA, 2–21 in TT.
Armour: 3 in sides, 2 in deck.

1914	1.18	4.18	Name	Launched	Builder—Fate
			BRISBANE (RAN)	30. 9.15	Cockatoo DY. Sold 13.6.36 Ward, Briton Ferry.
37	38	18	CHATHAM	19.11.11	Chatham DY. To RNZN 10.20; Sold 13.7.26 Ward, Pembroke Dock.
68	57	42	DUBLIN	30. 4.12	Beardmore. Sold 7.26 King, Troon.
	86	93	MELBOURNE (RAN)	30. 5.12	Cammell Laird. Sold 8.12.28 Alloa, Rosyth.
89	9A	35	SOUTHAMPTON	16. 5.12	John Brown. Sold 13.7.26 Ward, Pembroke Dock.
	A1	52	SYDNEY (RAN)	29. 8.12	London & Glasgow. BU 4.29 Cockatoo DY.

Notes: BRISBANE in Pacific 1916–18. CHATHAM in Red Sea/E. Africa 1914–15, Mediterranean 1915–16, 3rd LCS GF 1916–18. DUBLIN in Mediterranean 1914–15, 2nd LCS GF 1916–18. MELBOURNE and SYDNEY in Pacific 1914, N. America and W. Indies 1914–16, 2nd LCS GF 1916–18. SOUTHAMPTON in 1st LCS GF 1914–15, 2nd LCS 1915–18, 3rd LCS 1918.

BIRMINGHAM CLASS: 2nd CLASS CRUISERS

5440 tons. 457 (oa), 430 (pp) × 50 × 16 ft. Turbine 25000 shp = 25¼ kts.
Armament: 9–6 in, 1–3 in AA, 2–21 in TT.
Armour: 3 in sides, 2 in deck.

1914	1.18	4.18	Name	Launched	Builder—Fate
45	16	28	BIRMINGHAM	7. 5.13	Armstrong. Sold 5.2.31 Ward, Pembroke Dock.
17	83	*	LOWESTOFT	23. 4.13	Chatham DY. Sold 8.1.31 Ward, Milford Haven.
35			NOTTINGHAM	18. 4.13	Pembroke DY. Sunk 19.8.16 by U.52 in the North Sea.

5500 tons. 462¾ (oa).

			ADELAIDE (RAN)	27. 7.18	Cockatoo DY. Sold 1.49 Australian Iron & Steel Co, Port Kembla.

*No pendant from 4.18.
Notes: BIRMINGHAM in 1st LCS 1914–15, 2nd LCS 1915–18. LOWESTOFT and NOTTINGHAM in 1st LCS 1914–15, 2nd LCS 1915–16. LOWESTOFT to Mediterranean 1916–18. ADELAIDE completed in 8.22.

LIGHT CRUISERS

ARETHUSA CLASS

3500 tons.   436 (oa), 410 (pp) × 39 × 14 ft.   Turbine 40000 shp = 29 kts.
Armament: 2–6 in, 6–4 in (altered to 3–6 in, 4–4 in, 2–3 in AA), 8–21 in TT.
Armour: 3 in sides, 1 in deck.

Pendant Nos. 1914	1.18	4.18	Name	Launched	Builder—Fate
3C			ARETHUSA	25.10.13	Chatham DY. Wrecked 11.2.16 near Harwich after mine damage.
C1	08	*	AURORA	30. 9.13	Devonport DY. To RCN 11.20; Sold 8.27 Lasseque, Sorel, PQ.
0C	66	33	GALATEA	14. 5.14	Beardmore. Sold 25.10.21 Multilocular S.Bkg. Co.
5A	73	77	INCONSTANT	6. 7.14	Beardmore. Sold 9.6.22 Cashmore.
8A	92	17	PENELOPE	25. 8.14	Vickers. Sold 10.24 Stanlee.
6A	93	45	PHAETON	21.10.14	Vickers. Sold 16.1.23 King, Troon.
4A	6A	75	ROYALIST	14. 1.15	Beardmore. Sold 24.8.22 Cashmore.
2C	A5	80	UNDAUNTED	28. 4.14	Fairfield. Sold 9.4.23 Cashmore.

*No pendant from 4.18.
Notes: Ordered 9.12. A torpedo cruiser described as "of ARETHUSA type" to be named POLY-PHEMUS with a main armament of torpedo tubes and having three conning positions was projected in 1915. She was never ordered. ARETHUSA and PENELOPE served in the 5th LCS, Harwich, the latter joining the 7th LCS GF in 1918. AURORA was 10th DF leader, Harwich 1915–16, 5th LCS 1916–18, then 7th LCS. GALATEA, after a short time as 2nd DF leader, Harwich, served in the 1st LCS GF 1915–18. INCONSTANT was 1st LCS 1915–18. PHAETON 4th LCS 1915, 1st LCS 1915–18. UNDAUNTED was 3rd DF leader, Harwich 1914–15, then 9th DF leader, Harwich 1915–17, 10th DF leader at Harwich 1917–18, 7th LCS GF 1918. ROYALIST in 4th LCS 1915, 12th DF GF 1915–16, 4th LCS 1916–17, 1st LCS 1917–18.

BIRKENHEAD CLASS

5235 and 5185 tons.   446 (oa), 430 (pp) × 50 × 16 ft.   Turbine 25000 shp = 25½ kts.
(CHESTER 31000 shp = 26½ kts).
Armament: 10–5.5 in, 1–3 in AA, 2–21 in TT.
Armour: 3 in sides.

9.15	1.18	4.18	Name	Launched	Builder—Fate
9A	15	07	BIRKENHEAD	18. 1.15	Cammell Laird. Sold 26.10.21 Cashmore.
C9	39	50	CHESTER	8.12.15	Cammell Laird. Sold 9.11.21 Rees, Llanelly.

Notes: Laid down as the Greek ANTINARKOS CONDOUROTIS and LAMBROS KATSONIS respectively and purchased on the stocks. Both served in the 3rd LCS GF from completion to 1918.

CAROLINE CLASS

3750 tons.   446 (oa), 420 (pp) × 41½ × 14 ft.   Turbine 40000 shp = 29 kts.
Armament: 2–6 in, 8–4 in (4–6 in 1918), 8–21 in TT.
Armour: 3 in sides, 1 in deck.

1914	1.18	4.18	Name	Launched	Builder—Fate
87	30	44	CAROLINE	29. 9.14	Cammell Laird. RNVR drill ship 4.24. (still in service).
88	31	22	CARYSFORT	14.11.14	Pembroke DY. Sold 1931 McLellan.
1A	40	88	CLEOPATRA	14. 1.15	Devonport DY. Sold 1931 Hughes Bolckow.
5C	A7 45	(3.16) 02	COMUS	16.12.14	Swan Hunter. Sold 28.7.34 Ward, Barrow
C0	48	37	CONQUEST	20. 1.15	Chatham DY. Sold 29.8.30 Metal Ind, Rosyth.
78	50	69	CORDELIA	23. 2.14	Pembroke DY. Sold 31.7.23 Cashmore.

Notes: Ordered during 7/8.13. CAROLINE, COMUS and CORDELIA in GF 1915–18. CARYSFORT in GF 1915–16, Harwich 1916–17, GF 1918. CLEOPATRA at Harwich 1915–18, then to GF. CONQUEST at Harwich 1915–18.

47

CALLIOPE CLASS

3750 tons. 446 (oa), 420 (pp) × 41½ × 14 ft. Turbine 40000 shp = 29 kts.
Armament: (1st two) 2–6 in, 8–4 in (changed to 4–6 in, 2–3 in AA in 1918).
(others) 4–6 in, 1–4 in AA.
Armour: 4 in sides (1st two), 3 in sides (others), 1 in deck.

Pendant Nos.*			Name	Launched	Builder—Fate
1914	1.18	4.18			
76	23	78	CALLIOPE	17.12.14	Chatham DY. Sold 28.8.31 Ward, Inverkeithing.
C8	37	25	CHAMPION	29. 5.15	Hawthorn Leslie. Sold 28.7.34 Metal Ind, Rosyth.
A3	25	30	CAMBRIAN	3. 3.16	Pembroke DY. Sold 28.7.34 Metal Ind, Rosyth.
0A	27	59	CANTERBURY	21.12.15	John Brown. Sold 28.7.34 Metal Ind, Rosyth.
C4	33	20	CASTOR	28. 7.15	Cammell Laird. Sold 30.7.36 Metal Ind, Rosyth.
C5	49	90	CONSTANCE	12. 9.15	Cammell Laird. Sold 8.6.36 Arnott Young.

*Pendants were normally assigned well in advance of completion. Only pendants still effective at completion are recorded for this class and others built during the war.

Notes: First two ordered 7/8.13, last four ordered 9.14. CANTERBURY in Harwich Force 1916–18, then to Mediterranean. All others were in the Grand Fleet from completion. These vessels and following light cruisers were oil burners.

CENTAUR CLASS

3750 tons. 446 (oa), 420 (pp) × 42 × 14½ ft. Turbine 40000 shp = 28¼ kts.
Armament: 5–6 in, 2–3 in AA.
Armour: 3 in sides, 1 in deck.

9.15	1.18	4.18	Name	Launched	Builder—Fate
36	34	10	CENTAUR	6. 1.16	Armstrong. Sold 2.34 King, Troon.
2A	46	15	CONCORD	1. 4.16	Armstrong. Sold 8.35 Metal Ind, Rosyth.

Notes: Ordered in 12.14, these vessels replaced orders and used material originally intended for two scouts to be built for Turkey. Both vessels served in the Harwich Force from completion.

CALEDON CLASS

4120 tons. 450 (oa), 425 (pp) × 43 × 14½ ft. Turbine 40000 shp = 29 kts.
Armament: 5–6 in, 2–3 in AA, 8–21 in TT.
Armour: 3 in sides, 1 in deck.

4.17	1.18	4.18	Name	Launched	Builder—Fate
69	22	65	CALEDON	25.11.16	Cammell Laird. AA ship 12.43; Sold 22.1.48, BU at Dover.
	24	82	CALYPSO	24. 1.17	Hawthorn Leslie. Sunk 12.6.40 by Italian S/M BAGNOLINI South of Crete.
A0*	28	55	CARADOC	23.12.16	Scotts. Base ship 4.44; BU 5.46 Ward, Briton Ferry.
3C*	32	04	CASSANDRA	25.11.16	Vickers. Mined 5.12.18 in the Baltic.

*Pendants from 6.17.

Notes: Ordered 12.15. All served in the Grand Fleet from completion.

The battleship REDOUBTABLE. Old 'Royal Sovereign' class /*Imperial War Museum*

The battleship PRINCE GEORGE. 'Majestic' class /*Imperial War Museum*/

TOP: The battleship GLORY. 'Canopus' class /*National Maritime Museum*
ABOVE: The battleship SWIFTSURE /*National Maritime Museum*

The battleship HINDUSTAN. 'King Edward VII' class /*National Maritime Museum*/

The battleship LORD NELSON. 'Lord Nelson' class /National Maritime Museum

The battleship DREADNOUGHT /National Maritime Museum

The battleship THUNDERER. 'Orion' class /*National Maritime Museum*

The battleship EMPEROR OF INDIA. 'Iron Duke' class

TOP: The battleship ERIN /*National Maritime Museum*
ABOVE: The battleship CANADA /*National Maritime Museum*

The battleship BARHAM. 'Queen Elizabeth' class /*National Maritime Museum*

The battleship ROYAL OAK. 'Royal Sovereign' class /*National Maritime Museum*

The battlecruiser **INDEFATIGABLE**. 'Indefatigable' class

The battlecruiser QUEEN MARY /National Maritime Museum

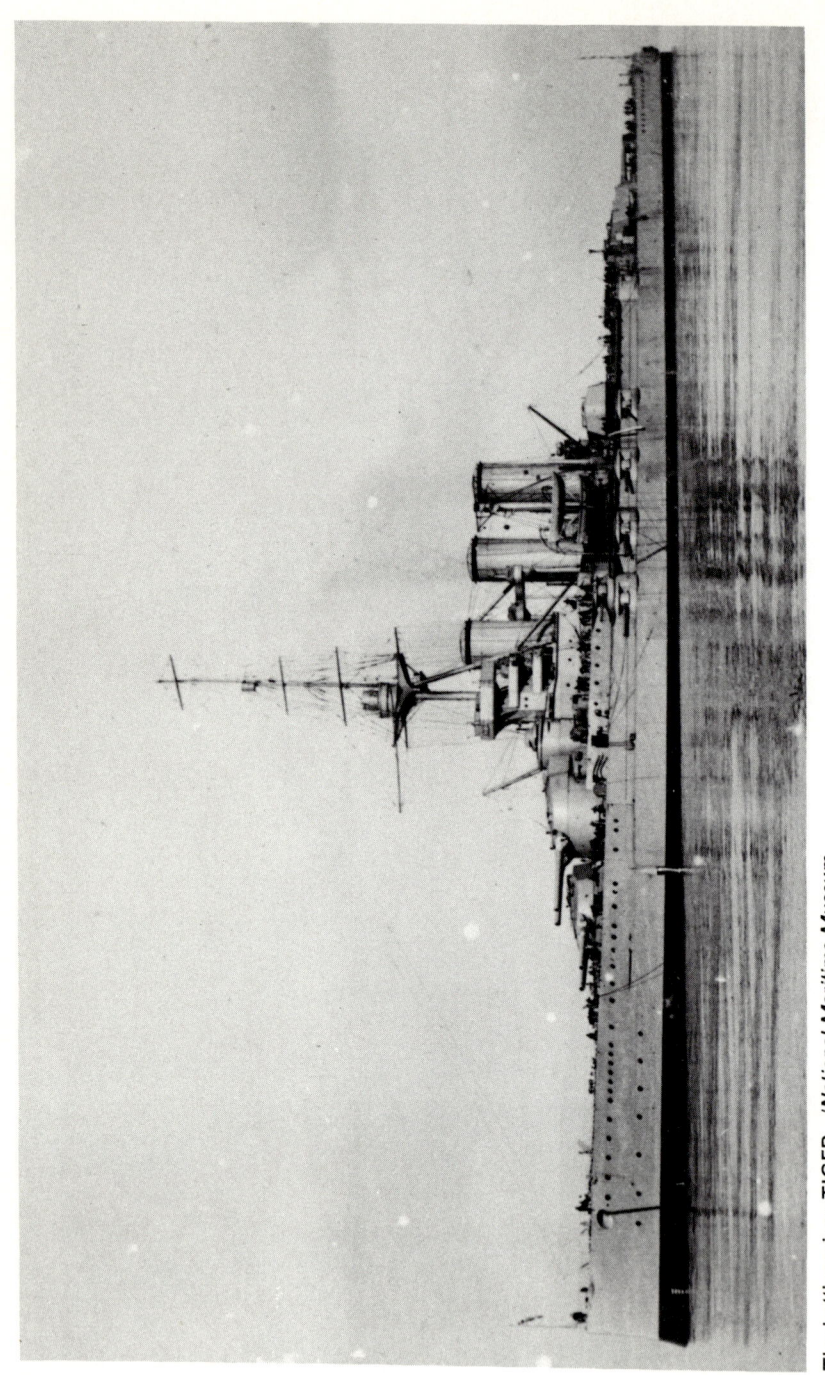

The battlecruiser TIGER /National Maritime Museum

The battlecruiser HOOD /*National Maritime Museum*

TOP: The light battlecruiser COURAGEOUS /*National Maritime Museum*
ABOVE: The light battlecruiser FURIOUS as completed with flight deck.
/*National Maritime Museum*

CERES AND CARLISLE CLASSES

4190 tons. 450 (oa), 425 (pp) × 43½ × 14½ ft. Turbine 40000 shp=29 kts.
Armament: 5–6 in, 2–3 in AA, 8–21 in TT.
Armour: 3 in sides, 1 in deck.

6.17	1.18	4.18	Name	Launched	Builder—Fate
	29	39	CARDIFF	12. 4.17	Fairfield. Sold 23.1.46, BU at Troon.
66	36	58	CERES	24. 3.17	John Brown. Sold 5.4.46, BU Hughes Bolckow.
	4C	61	COVENTRY	6. 7.17	Swan Hunter. AA ship 1937; Sunk 14.9.42 by A/C in the Mediterranean.
	A7	62	CURACOA	5. 5.17	Pembroke DY. AA ship 1939; Sunk 2.10.42 in collision with QUEEN MARY North of Ireland.
80*	3C	48	CURLEW	5. 7.17	Vickers. AA ship 1938; Sunk 26.5.40 by A/C, Ofot Fjord, Norway.

451½ (oa) Trawler bows.

97	(9.19)		CAIRO	19.11.18	Cammell Laird. AA ship 1939; Sunk 12.8.42 by Italian S/M AXUM off Bizerta.
74	(8.19)		CALCUTTA	9. 7.18	Vickers. AA ship 1939; Sunk 1.6.41 by A/C off Crete.
88	(11.19)		CAPETOWN	28. 6.19	Cammell Laird. Sold 5.4.46; BU Ward, Preston.
41	(11.18)		CARLISLE	9. 7.18	Fairfield. AA ship 1939; Base ship 1944; Sold 1948 at Alexandria.
7A	(6.19)		COLOMBO	18.12.18	Fairfield. AA ship 1943; Sold 22.1.48 BU Cashmore.

*Pendant from 8.17.
Notes: First five ordered 3/4.16, others ordered 6/7.17. Original name chosen for CARDIFF was CAPRICE; for COVENTRY, CORSAIR; and for CARLISLE, CAWNPORE. CARDIFF and CERES in GF 1917–18; COVENTRY, CURLEW and CURACOA in Harwich Force from completion to 1918. CAPETOWN was towed to Pembroke DY and completed 2.22.

EX-RUSSIAN CRUISER

5905 tons. 444 (oa), 426½ (pp) × 49¼ × 20¾ ft. TE 19500 ihp=23 kts.
Armament: 12–6 in, 12–12 pdr, 8–3 pdr, 6–18 in TT.
Armour: 3 in deck.

	Name	Launched	Builder—Fate
	GLORY IV	3.00	Krupp, Kiel. Returned to Russia 1919.

Notes: Former Russian cruiser ASKOLD seized and commissioned 3.8.18. Operated as a cruiser in the White Sea. Very distinctive appearance with five tall funnels.

HAWKINS CLASS

9750 tons. 605 (oa), 565 (pp) × 65 × 17½ ft. Turbine 60000 shp=30 kts.
(first two 70000 shp=31 kts)
Armament: 7–7.5 in, 6–12 pdr, 4–3 in AA, 6–21 in TT.
Armour: 3 in sides, 1½ in deck.

Pendant Nos.		Name	Launched	Builder—Fate
98	(7.25)	EFFINGHAM	8. 6.21	Portsmouth DY. Wrecked 18.5.40 near Harstad, Norway.
81	(9.24)	FROBISHER	20. 3.20	Devonport DY. T/S 9.44; Sold 26.3.49, BU Cashmore.
8A	(7.19)	HAWKINS	1.10.17	Chatham DY. Sold 26.8.47, BU Arnott Young.
96	(9.20)	RALEIGH	28. 8.19	Beardmore. Wrecked 8.8.22 in Belle Isle Strait, Labrador.

Notes: Ordered in 12.15. A fifth ship, CAVENDISH, ordered in 4.16 was renamed VINDICTIVE in 6.18 and completed during the war as an aircraft carrier. For this vessel, see A/C carriers. None of the light cruisers were completed in time for any war service.

D CLASS

4650 tons. 472 (oa), 445 (pp) ×46×14½ ft. Turbine 40000 shp=29 kts.
Armament: 6–6 in, 2–3 in AA, 12–21 in TT.
Armour: 3 in sides, 1 in deck.

Pendant Nos.		Name	Launched	Builder—Fate
32	(7.18)	DANAE	26. 1.18	Armstrong.=Polish CONRAD 10.44–46; Sold 22.1.48, BU Ward, Barrow.
71	(11.18)	DAUNTLESS	10. 4.18	Palmer. T/S 3.44; Sold 13.2.46, BU by Ward, Inverkeithing.
19	(9.18)	DRAGON	29.12.17	Scotts. Sunk 8.7.44 as breakwater at Arromanches.
Trawler bows. (last two 4765 tons).				
6A	(11.18)	DELHI	23. 8.18	Armstrong. AA ship 1943; Sold 22.1.48, BU Cashmore.
96	(8.19)	DUNEDIN	19.11.18	Armstrong. To RNZN 1925; Sunk 24.11.41 by U.124 in the S Atlantic.
99	(9.21)	DURBAN	29. 5.19	Scotts. Sunk 9.6.44 as breakwater at Normandy.
30	(6.22)	DESPATCH	24. 9.19	Fairfield. Sold 5.4.46, BU Dalmuir by Arnott Young.
92	(4.22)	DIOMEDE	29. 4.19	Vickers. To RNZN 1925; T/S 2.44; Sold 5.4.46, BU Dalmuir by Arnott Young.

Notes: First three ordered 9.16, next three ordered 7.17, last two 3.18. Four others; DAEDALUS (Armstrong), DARING (Beardmore), DESPERATE (Hawthorn Leslie), DRYAD (Vickers) were ordered in 3.18 and cancelled 26.11.18. DURBAN was completed by Devonport DY, DESPATCH completed by Chatham DY and DIOMEDE completed by Portsmouth DY. DANAE and DRAGON in Harwich Force 1918.

In 1920 it was proposed to complete DESPATCH as a Royal Yacht; her armament and two boiler rooms were to have been removed (sea speed 24 knots) and focsle deck to be extended for the whole length of the ship. Her bow and stern were to have been altered to a "yacht design". This proposal was later cancelled.

E CLASS

7600 tons. 570 (oa), 535 (pp) ×54½×18½ ft. Turbine 80000 shp=33 kts.
Armament: 7–6 in, 2–4 in AA, 12–21 in TT.
Armour: 3 in sides, 1 in deck.

Pendant Nos.		Name	Launched	Builder—Fate
66	(1.26)	EMERALD	19. 5.20	Armstrong. Sold 23.6.48, BU Dalmuir by Arnott Young.
52	(4.20)	ENTERPRISE	23.12.19	John Brown Sold 11.4.46, BU by Cashmore.

Notes: Three vessels ordered in 3.18, EUPHRATES (Fairfield) was cancelled 26.11.18. EMERALD completed 1.26 at Chatham DY and ENTERPRISE completed 1.26 at Devonport DY.

AIRCRAFT CARRIERS

Aircraft experiments were conducted in early 1912 utilising temporary flying-off platforms built over the fore gun turrets of the battleships AFRICA and HIBERNIA. The success of these trials was followed by conversion of the cruiser HERMES providing permanent platforms fore and aft. She served as a "special service cruiser" until her loss in 1914. The first ship completed as a seaplane carrier was the converted oiler purchased on the stocks in 5.14 and later named ARK ROYAL. At the outbreak of war three fast cross-channel packets were requisitioned for conversion to seaplane carriers. The first aircraft carrier designed as such, HERMES, was laid down in 1.18 and completed after the war. As proper flight decks came into being and the carrier development progressed, the aircraft designed to land on water were replaced by landplanes with strengthened landing gear and much more promising potential performance.

MERCANTILE CONVERSIONS

7080 tons. 366 (oa), $352\frac{1}{2}$ (pp) $\times 51 \times 17\frac{1}{2}$ ft. TE 3000 ihp=11 kts.
Armament: 4–12 pdr, 4 seaplanes.

1914	1.18	Name	Launched	Builder—Fate
N.80	N.07	ARK ROYAL =PEGASUS 12.34	5. 9.14	Blyth SB Co. D/S 1923; Catapult ship 4.41; D/S 1944; Sold 18.10.46 =ANITA I.

Notes: Served in the Eastern Mediterranean 1915–18.

THREE SHIPS REQUISITIONED 11.8.14

1695, 1676 and 1675 tons gross respectively. Avg 316 (pp) $\times$ 41 ft. Turbine=21 kts.
Armament: 2–4 in, 1–6 pdr AA, 4 to 6 seaplanes.

1914	1.18	Name	Launched	Builder—Fate
N.38	N.39	EMPRESS	13. 4.07	Denny. Returned 11.19.
N.91	N.42	ENGADINE	23. 9.11	Denny. Returned 12.19.
N.85		RIVIERA	1. 4.11	Denny. Returned late 1919. LAIRD'S ISLE in WW II.

Notes: All converted at Chatham DY. All three at Harwich 1914–15; EMPRESS at Queenstown 1915; ENGADINE in the GF 1915–17; RIVIERA at Dover 1915–18; all to the Mediterranean 1918.

PURCHASED 27.11.14

18000 tons; 12884 tons gross. 622 (oa), 601 (pp) $\times 65 \times 26$ ft. TE 31050 ihp =23 kts.
Armament: 6–4.7 in, 1–3 in AA, 10 aircraft.

4.15	1.18	Name	Launched	Builder—Fate
P.54	N.15	CAMPANIA	8. 9.93	Fairfield. Sunk 5.11.18 in collision with GLORIOUS and ROYAL OAK during a gale in the Firth of Forth.

Notes: Purchased from shipbreakers and underwent two stages of conversion. The fore funnel was split into two tandem funnels, allowing a longer take-off deck forward. Conversion completed by Cammell Laird in 4.16.

THREE VESSELS REQUISITIONED 1915–16

3888 tons; 2651 tons gross. 375 (pp) $\times$ 46 ft. Turbine 14000 shp=$24\frac{1}{2}$ kts.
Armament: 2–4 in, 1–6 pdr AA, 4 aircraft.

1.15	Name	Launched	Builder—Fate
P.49	BEN-MY-CHREE	23. 3.08	Vickers. Sunk 11.1.17 by Turkish batteries off Kastelorizo; raised 1920 and BU.

Notes: Commissioned 2.1.15; in the Eastern Mediterranean 1915–17.

2950 tons; 1951 tons gross. 361 (oa), 350 (pp) $\times$ 42 ft. Turbine 11000 shp=23 kts.
Armament: 4–12 pdr, 1–6 pdr AA, 7 aircraft.

4.15	1.18	Name	Launched	Builder—Fate
N.00	N.3A	VINDEX	7. 3.05	Armstrong. Resold 12.2.20 Isle of Man SP Co.

Notes: *Ex Viking* requisitioned and commissioned 26.3.15, purchased 11.10.15. Served at the Nore and Harwich 1915–18, then to the Mediterranean.

2048 tons gross.   341 (oa), 334 (pp) × 43 ft.   Turbine = 21 kts.
Armament: 2–4 in, 1–6 pdr AA, 8 aircraft.

1.18	Name	Launched	Builder—Fate
N.70	MANXMAN	15. 6.04	Vickers. Returned 12.2.20. = CADUCEUS in WW II.

Notes: Converted at Chatham DY; commissioned 17.4.16—24.12.19. At Rosyth 1916–17, then to the Mediterranean.

TWO EX-GERMAN VESSELS SEIZED 8.14 AT PORT SAID

4678 tons gross.   390½ (pp) × 51½ ft.   Quad. Expansion = 10 kts.
Armament: 1–12 pdr, 2 seaplanes.

	Name	Launched	Builder—Fate
	RAVEN II = RAVENROCK 1917	1903	Swan Hunter. Sold 1923.

Notes: Was *ex-Rabenfels* commissioned 12.6.15 and renamed in 8.15. Served in the E. Mediterranean 1915–17. From 14.1.18 RAVENROCK was on various services under the red ensign (as store carrier, collier and troop ship) until 1.21.

7000 tons; 4083 tons gross.   367 (pp) × 47½ ft.   TE = 10 kts.
Armament: 1–12 pdr, 2 seaplanes.

	Name	Launched	Builder—Fate
	ANNE	1911	Rickmers, Bremerhaven. Sold 1922.

Notes: Was *Aenne Rickmers* in service under the red ensign from 1.15. Commissioned 4.8.15 and named ANNE the next day, she served in the E. Mediterranean 1915–17. Decommissioned 8.8.17, she later became a store carrier and in 1.18 a collier in government service until 1.19.

THREE VESSELS PURCHASED WHILE BUILDING

3070 tons; 3547 TG.   352 (oa), 315 (pp) × 45½ × 14 ft.   Turbine 6700 shp = 19 kts.
Armament: 2–3 in, 2–12 pdr AA, 7 aircraft.

4.17	1.18	Name	Launched	Builder—Fate
N.94	N.72	NAIRANA	.17	Denny. Sold 1921.

Notes: Commissioned 25.8.17; in GF 1917–18.

3300 tons; 2450 TG.   332 (oa), 330 (pp) × 43 × 15 ft.   Turbine 9500 shp = 20 kts.
Armament: 2–3 in, 2–12 pdr AA, 9 aircraft.

4.17	1.18	Name	Launched	Builder—Fate
N.8A	N.9A	PEGASUS	9. 6.17	John Brown. Sold 22.8.31 Ward, Morecambe.

Notes: Laid down as *Stockholm*, purchased 27.2.17 and renamed 28.8.17. Served in the GF 1917–18.

14450 tons.   566 (oa), 535 (pp) × 68 × 21 ft.   Turbine 20000 shp = 20 kts.
Armament: 6–4 in AA, 20 Sopwith torpedo planes.

1919	9.19	Name	Launched	Builder—Fate
N.96	49	ARGUS	2.12.17	Beardmore. Accom ship 12.44; Sold 5.12.46; BU Ward, Inverkeithing.

Notes: Building as the Italian CONTE ROSSO and purchased in 8.16. Completed in 9.18, she was the first aircraft carrier with a large hangar and a full-length flight deck and proved a successful design from which later carriers developed.

WARSHIP CONVERSIONS

9750 tons.   605 (oa), 565 (pp) × 65 × 17½ ft.   Turbine 60000 shp = 29 kts.
Armament: 4–7.5 in, 4–3 in, 4–12 pdr, 6–21 in TT, 6 aircraft.

10.18	9.19	Name	Launched	Builder—Fate
31	48	VINDICTIVE	17. 1.18	Harland & Wolff. Became a cruiser 1925; T/S 1937; repair ship 1940; Sold 2.46, BU Hughes Bolckow, Blyth.

Notes: Originally ordered in 4.16 as the cruiser CAVENDISH, renamed 6.18 and completed in 10.18 as an aircraft carrier. The light battlecruiser FURIOUS ordered 2.3.17 to be completed as an aircraft carrier for 16 aircraft is listed earlier.

22790 tons.   667 (oa), 625 (pp) ×94×24 ft.   Turbine 37000 shp =22¼ kts.
Armament: 9–6 in, 4–4 in, 21 aircraft.

1920	Name	Launched	Builder—Fate
94	EAGLE	8. 6.18	Armstrong. Sunk 11.8.42 by U.73 in the Western Mediterranean.

Notes: Laid down February 1913 as the Chilean battleship ALMIRANTE COCHRANE, work was suspended when the war began and resumed in 1917 completing in early 1920 as an aircraft carrier. EAGLE was commissioned in 4.20 and underwent further modifications later that year as a result of trials conducted during the summer months.

for FURIOUS see under 1st class cruisers.

HERMES

10950 tons.   598 (oa), 548 (pp) ×70¼×18½ ft.   Turbine 40000=25 kts.
Armament: 10–6 in, 4–4 in, 20 aircraft.

6.20	Name	Launched	Builder—Fate
95	HERMES	11. 9.19	Armstrong. Sunk 9.4.42 by Japanese A/C off Ceylon.

Notes: Ordered in 7.17 and completed at Devonport DY in 7.23, HERMES was the first aircraft carrier designed and built from keel up as such. She combined the more successful features of previous converted vessels. Built to cruiser hull dimensions, her design was not repeated in later carriers where much greater stowage of aircraft and performance was favoured.

PROJECTED VESSELS

In late 1916 it was proposed that 12 VINDEX type seaplane carriers should be built, but this project was not proceeded with. In early 1917 two ocean type and two North Sea/Mediterranean type aircraft carriers were in planning. A war cabinet decision on 8.2.17 specified that these four carriers were to be built. In 4.17 orders were provisionally placed with Cammell Laird and Fairfield for the two ocean type carriers, but soon thereafter they were cancelled. At the same time the smaller pair were also cancelled and the PEGASUS and NAIRANA conversions effected instead. Additionally, the purchase of one unspecified vessel for conversion and another to be built on contract as seaplane carriers were cancelled in 1917. Clearly, the question of priorities and possible length of the war led to aborting these programmes.

AIRCRAFT CARRIED BY OTHER H M SHIPS 1917–19

During June 1917, a Sopwith Pup was successfully flown off from a platform that provided a 20 foot take-off run from the forecastle of the cruiser YARMOUTH. A few weeks later an improved platform was fitted aboard YARMOUTH and aboard CALEDON, CASSANDRA, and DUBLIN as well. Although by no means the first shipboard launch of aircraft, this period began the ever increasing number of similar installations to enable warships to carry and fly off aircraft.

A revolving platform for flying off aircraft was fitted on the forecastle of the cruiser SYDNEY at Chatham Dockyard in November 1917. This installation met with success and similar platforms were soon fitted aboard BIRKENHEAD, MELBOURNE, and SOUTHAMPTON. In June and August 1918 respectively YARMOUTH and DUBLIN were fitted with revolving platforms in lieu of the fixed type. These platforms were located just above and to the rear of the forward gun and extended to the bridge structure. Some interference was encountered with guns on some early installations necessitating alterations to preserve arcs of fire.

Mention thus far has been confined to the smaller cruisers with less spacious decks available for aircraft, but all dreadnought era capital ships were being fitted with fighter and reconnaissance aircraft during this period as well. By Autumn 1918 the cruisers COURAGEOUS, GLORIOUS, the light cruisers AURORA, CALLIOPE, CAROLINE, COMUS, CORDELIA, GALATEA, INCONSTANT, PENELOPE, PHAETON, ROYALIST, UNDAUNTED and eleven others, including those previously mentioned had flying-off platforms. Included in this list were two D class and one C class cruisers, DAUNTLESS, DRAGON, and CARLISLE which were completed with hangars beneath the bridge and a fixed platform.

Interference with gun arcs of fire and wind current problems in the partially open hangars where the folding aircraft was stowed had heavy influence on later designs which found the aircraft provisions in the midship section instead of forward.

Temporary revolving standard flying-off platforms were installed aboard CALEDON, CASSANDRA, DELHI, and DUNEDIN. Success of the revolving platform caused fixed hangars and platforms to be abandoned in vessels which were being built. After the Armistice aircraft ceased to be carried aboard the light cruisers.

The following abstract of aircraft aboard H M ships in the closing days of the war is provided to indicate the ascending role of heavier-than-air aircraft at sea.

AIRCRAFT ABOARD SHIPS OF THE GRAND FLEET 11.11.18

Class	Ships	Fighters	Recon.	Total A/C	Location
DREADNOUGHT	4	6	2	8	A & Y turrets
COLLINGWOOD	2	2	2	4	A & Y turrets
HERCULES	3	4	2	6	A & Y turrets
AGINCOURT	1	2	0	2	No 2 & 3 turrets
ORION	4	6	2	8	B & X turrets
KING GEORGE V	3	4	2	6	B & X turrets
IRON DUKE	4	6	2	8	B & X turrets
ERIN	1	1	1	2	B & X turrets
CANADA	1	1	1	2	B & X turrets
QUEEN ELIZABETH	5	7	3	10	B & X turrets
ROYAL SOVEREIGN	5	8	2	10	B & X turrets
Battleships	33	47	19	66	
INDOMITABLE	2	2	2	4	P & Q turrets
AUSTRALIA	2	2	2	4	P & Q turrets
PRINCESS ROYAL	1	2	0	2	Q & X turrets
LION	1	2	0	2	Q & X turrets
TIGER	1	1	0	1	Q turret
RENOWN	2	2	2	4	B & Y turrets
Battlecruisers	9	11	6	17	
COURAGEOUS	2	2	2	4	A & Y turrets
Various Light Cruisers*	16			16	

*Aircraft had been transferred from one ship to another such that, although more vessels could stow aircraft, fewer aircraft were in fact carried at this time.

In addition to the 103 aircraft, provision was being made for 33 more (one per ship) in eleven D class cruisers, three E class, 7 AURORA class, 6 in CAMBRIAN class, and 6 in CAROLINE class. It must be noted that some monitors serving in the Mediterranean had flying-off platforms and could handle aircraft. Various other vessels including BROCKLESBY, KILLINGHOLME and various paddle mine sweepers and sloops had aircraft capabilities but very few did, in fact carry them. Lighters towed by destroyers, etc. should also be noted as having operated aircraft.

AIR SERVICE KITE BALLOON SHIPS

Pendants	Name	TG/Yr.	Service, etc.
Y4.46 N.16	CANNING	5375/96	Was a hired transport, red ensign 5.15–6.15. Purchased 28.6.15, commissioned 29.6.15–27.6.16; In the Mediterranean 1915–16, Scapa 1916–18; D/S 1917; attached to Flying Squadron in 11.18. Sold 21.1.20 to Greek owners.
Y4.50	CITY OF OXFORD	4019/82	Purchased 28.10.14 as dummy battleship (qv.) Commissioned as KBS 17.7.15–20.11.18. Served in E. Mediterranean 1917–18. Sold 1920.
Y4.20	HECTOR	4660/95	Hired as KBS, commissioned 12.5.15–24.5.16. In E. Mediterranean 1915–16. From 25.5.16 served under the red ensign as collier, troop ship and store carrier Y8.103 until 12.18.
Y4.17	MANICA	4120/00	Hired as KBS 11.3.15–19.8.17. Purchased 1915; In Mediterranean 1915, home waters 1915–16. Renamed HUNTBALL 1917, later a red ensign collier Y3.313 until 6.18.
Y4.21	MENELAUS	4672/95	Hired and commissioned as KBS 5.5.15–7.6.17. Served at Dover 1915–16, Scapa 1916–17. Served on red ensign charter as store carrier Y8.138, and troop ship from 6.17–12.19.

Notes: Pendant numbers were of Y4 (fleet messenger) series; N pendant assigned 1.18. Employed on observation work and gunfire spotting, they had their forward hold enlarged to enable a fully inflated kite balloon to be stowed below deck. Most were re-employed elsewhere as the need for special balloon ships decreased.

From mid 1916 balloon-towing trials were held using the battleship HERCULES and later the cruiser CHESTER. The number of balloon-towing winch installations increased. KING GEORGE V was fitted in 1.17 and the destroyer PATRIOT had a special winch installation in 6.17. BERBERIS and other sloops, P and PC boats, armed boarding steamers, light cruisers and many other vessels were fitted with kite balloon winches. By 11.11.18 AJAX, BARHAM, BELLEROPHON, COLOSSUS, E. OF INDIA, HERCULES, KING GEORGE V, MARLBOROUGH, MONARCH, ORION, Q. ELIZABETH, RAMILLIES, REVENGE, ST. VINCENT, COURAGEOUS, GLORIOUS, LION, REPULSE, COMMONWEALTH, ERIN, and RESOLUTION had been fitted. The trawler LYNX II, light cruiser CARDIFF as well as an experimental winch aboard RENOWN in 1917 furthered the list. For a time in 1917 the armed merchant cruiser PATUCA served as a kite balloon ship.

The dumb barge ARCTIC 88/98* completed conversion in 5.16 by C & H Crichton for experimental use as a kite balloon vessel. Eventually purchased in 11.17, ARCTIC was employed for other purposes later. (*rebuilt in 1898).

EXPERIMENTAL CATAPULT SHIP

Pendants	Name	TG/Yr.	Service, etc.
X.50 (6.17)	SLINGER	875/17	Lobnitz. Former hopper, purchased while building.
X.66 (1.18)			Sold 16.10.19 M. S. Hilton.

DESTROYERS AND LEADERS

In the year 1885 the British Admiralty, worried by the large fleet of torpedo boats in some foreign, notably the French, navies, developed as a counter-measure the "torpedo gunboat". Four classes of these vessels were built between 1886 and 1894 but none of them proved fast enough for their intended work and so the "torpedo boat destroyer" came into being with the advent of the HAVOCK, ordered in June 1892 and launched in August 1893.

By 1895, 42 boats of 27 knots speed had been launched, usually known as the "27-knotters", to be followed by 72 30-knot boats in the course of the next seven years.

Since the design of most of these craft had been left to their builders, it was difficult to group them together into classes. In September 1913, their survivors were designated as "A", "B", "C" and "D" classes; the "A" class being the 27-knotters, and "B", "C" and "D" classes the 30-knotters with respectively four, three, or two funnels. At the same time other destroyer classes were redesignated as the E to K classes (no "J" class) and a class then under construction had their names changed to new ones beginning with the letter "L".

Generally speaking, the older A to E classes in 1914 formed the coastal Patrol Flotillas or Local Defence Flotillas and used scouts and the large destroyer SWIFT as leaders. A flotilla leader needed to be only slightly larger than common destroyers in order to accommodate the commanding officer and his staff. The four purchased Chilean boats were ideal for this purpose. The first RN-built leaders were the MARKSMAN and her sisters, two of which were laid down in 6.14 in place of three destroyers cancelled from the 1913 "M" programme.

A CLASS   27-KNOTTERS

280 to 350 tons.   Avg 200 (pp) $\times 20 \times 5\frac{1}{2}$ ft.   TE 3500 to 4500 ihp=27 kts.
Armament: 1–12 pdr, 5–6 pdr, 2–18 in TT.

| Pendant Nos. | | | Name | Launched | Builder—Fate |
1914	9.15	1.18			
H.4C*		D.16	BOXER	28.11.94	Thornycroft. Sunk 8.2.18 in collision with SS ST. PATRICK in the Channel.
P.24	D.96*	D.18	CONFLICT	13.12.94	White. Sold 20.5.20 Ward, Milford Haven.
N.17	D.97	D.39	FERVENT	28. 3.95	Hanna, Donald. Sold 29.4.20 Ward, Rainham.
N.23			LIGHTNING	10. 4.95	Palmer. Mined 30.6.15 in North Sea.
D.12	D.99	D.62	OPOSSUM	9. 8.95	Hawthorn Leslie. Sold 29.7.20 Ward, Preston.
N.19	D.0A	D.69	PORCUPINE	19. 9.95	Palmer. Sold 29.4.20 Ward, Rainham.
	D.1A*		RANGER	4.10.95	Hawthorn Leslie. Sold 20.5.20 Riddle & Co.
D.47	D.2A	D.81	SUNFISH	23. 5.95	Hawthorn Leslie. Sold 7.6.20 J. Kelly.
P.30	D.3A	D.82	SURLY	10.11.94	Thomson. Sold 23.3.20 Ward, Milford Haven.
H.3C*		H.7A	WIZARD	26. 2.95	White. Sold 20.5.20 Ward, Milford Haven.
N.86	D.4A	D.98	ZEPHYR	10. 5.95	Hanna, Donald. Sold 10.2.20 Ward, Rainham.

*Pendants cancelled 4.17. D.98 assigned LIGHTNING 9.15 but not extant then.
Notes: 30 were BU between 1907 and 1914 and one (DECOY) lost 13.8.04. HANDY was on sale list 1914 and sold at Hong Kong by 1916. ZEBRA had been sold as recently as 30.7.14. BOXER, CONFLICT, RANGER, SURLY and WIZARD in Portsmouth LDF. FERVENT, LIGHTNING, PORCUPINE and ZEPHYR in Nore LDF.

B CLASS

355 to 400 tons. (ARAB 470, EXPRESS 499). Avg 215 (pp) ×21 ×6 ft. TE Avg 6000 ihp=30 kts.
Armament: 1–12 pdr, 5–6 pdr, 2–18 in TT.

1914	9.15	1.18	4.18	Name	Launched	Builder—Fate
D.01	D.77	D.05	H.08	ARAB	9. 2.01	Thomson. Sold 23.7.19 Fryer, Sunderland.
D.05	D.79	D.29		EARNEST	7.11.96	Laird. Sold 1.7.20 Castle, Plymouth.
D.84	D.80	D.34		EXPRESS	11.12.97	Laird. Sold 17.3.21 Clarkson, Whitby.
D.39	D.81	D.45		GRIFFON	21.11.96	Laird. Sold 1.7.20 Castle, Plymouth.
P.02	D.82	D.48		KANGAROO	8. 9.00	Palmer. Sold 23.3.20 M. Yates; resold 1920 Ward, Milford Haven.
D.91	D.83	D.53		LIVELY	14. 7.00	Laird. Sold 1.7.20 Castle, Plymouth.
D.29	D.84	D.54	H.02	LOCUST	8.12.96	Laird. Sold 10.6.19 J. Jackson.
P.83	D.85			MYRMIDON	26. 5.00	Palmer. Sunk 26.3.17 in collision with SS HAMBORN in the Channel.
D.49	D.86	D.63		ORWELL	29. 9.98	Laird. Sold 1.7.20 Castle, Plymouth; BU 10.22.
D.69	D.87	D.67		PANTHER	21. 1.97	Laird. Sold 7.6.20 J. Kelly.
P.74	D.88	D.68	H.54*	PETEREL	30. 3.99	Palmer. Sold 30.8.19 T. R. Sales.
D.85	D.89	D.70	H.32*	QUAIL	24. 9.95	Laird. Sold 23.7.19 Ward, New Holland.
D.77	D.90	D.75		SEAL	6. 3.97	Laird. Sold 17.3.21 Ward, Rainham.
P.73	D.91	D.76		SPITEFUL	11. 1.99	Palmer. Sold 14.9.20 Hayes, Porthcawl.
D.62	D.92	D.77		SPRIGHTLY	25. 9.00	Laird. Sold 1.7.21 Castle, Plymouth.
D.24				SUCCESS	21. 3.01	Doxford. Wrecked 27.12.14 off Fife Ness.
P.72	D.93	D.85		SYREN	20.12.00	Palmer. Sold 14.9.20 Hayes, Porthcawl.
D.79	D.94	D.90		THRASHER	5.11.95	Laird. Sold 4.11.19 Fryer, Sunderland.
				VIRAGO	19.11.95	Laird. Sold 10.10.19 at Hong Kong.
D.98	D.95	D.97		WOLF	2. 6. 97	Laird. Sold 1.7.21 Castle, Plymouth.

*Pendants assigned 9.18.
Notes: COBRA (turbine) wrecked 19.9.01 and SPARROWHAWK wrecked 17.6.04. ARAB, GRIFFON, LIVELY, LOCUST and SPRIGHTLY in Scapa LDF; KANGAROO, MYRMIDON and SYREN at Dover; VIRAGO in China; the others in Patrol Flotillas Forth or Grimsby.

C CLASS

350 to 400 tons. (ALBATROSS 430, VELOX 420). Avg 215 (pp) ×21 ×6 ft. TE Avg 6000 ihp=30 kts.
Armament: 1–12 pdr, 5–6 pdr, 2–18 in TT.

1914	9.15	1.18	9.18	Name	Launched	Builder—Fate
D.32	D.44	D.02		ALBATROSS	19. 7.98	Thornycroft. Sold 7.6.20 J. Houston.
D.02	D.45	D.08		AVON	10.10.96	Vickers. Sold 1.7.20 Castle, Plymouth; BU 10.22.
P.97	D.46	D.09	H.87	BAT	7.10.96	Palmer. Sold 30.8.19 Hayes, Porthcawl.
D.03	D.5A	D.10		BITTERN	1. 2.97	Vickers. Sunk 4.4.18 in collision with SS KENILWORTH in the Channel.
N.11	D.47	D.14		BRAZEN	3. 7.96	Thomson. Sold 4.11.19 J. H. Lee.
D.17	D.48	D.15	H.04*	BULLFINCH	10. 2.98	Earle. Sold 10.6.19 Young, Sunderland.
P.13	D.49			CHEERFUL	14. 7.97	Hawthorn Leslie. Mined 30.6.17 off the Shetlands.
P.26	D.50	D.20	H.72	CRANE	17.12.96	Palmer. Sold 10.6.19 Ward, New Holland.
D.34	D.51	D.28		DOVE	21. 3.98	Earle. Sold 27.1.20 Maden & McKee.
N.55	D.52	D.31		ELECTRA	14. 7.96	Thomson. Sold 29.4.20 Barking S. Bkg Co.
P.40	D.53	D.35		FAIRY	29. 5.97	Fairfield. Foundered 31.5.18 after ramming UC.75 in the North Sea.
P.31	D.54	D.36		FALCON	29.12.99	Fairfield. Sunk 1.4.18 in collision with trawler JOHN FITZGERALD in N. Sea.
P.94	D.55	D.38	H.38	FAWN	13. 4.97	Palmer. Sold 23.7.19 Ward, New Holland.
P.87	D.56			FLIRT	15. 5.97	Palmer. Sunk 27.10.16 in action in the Straits of Dover.
P.86	D.57	D.40	H.69	FLYING FISH	4. 3.97	Palmer. Sold 30.8.19 T. R. Sales.
P.23	D.58	D.43		GIPSY	9. 3.97	Fairfield. Sold 17.3.21 C. A. Beard, Teignmouth (hull still at Dartmouth as a jetty).
P.01	D.59	D.44	H.43	GREYHOUND	6.10.00	Hawthorn Leslie. Sold 10.6.19 Clarkson, Whitby.
N.47	D.60	D.49		KESTREL	25. 3.98	Thomson. Sold 17.3.21 Ward, Rainham.
D.75	D.61	D.50	H.06*	LEOPARD	20. 3.97	Vickers. Sold 10.6.19 J. Jackson.
P.33	D.62	D.51		LEVEN	28. 6.98	Fairfield. Sold 14.9.20 Hayes, Porthcawl.
P.35	D.63	D.56	H.85	MERMAID	22. 2.98	Hawthorn Leslie. Sold 23.7.19 Ward, New Holland.
P.80	D.64			OSPREY	17. 4.97	Fairfield. Sold 4.11.19 J. H. Lee.

1914	9.15	1.18	9.18	Name	Launched	Builder—Fate
P.56	D.65			OSTRICH	22. 3.00	Fairfield. Sold 29.4.20 Barking S.Bkg Co.
				OTTER	23.11.96	Vickers. Sold 26.10.16 at Hong Kong.
P.15	D.66	D.71		RACEHORSE	8.11.00	Hawthorn Leslie. Sold 23.3.20 M. Yates; resold Ward, Milford Haven.
N.60				RECRUIT	22. 8.96	Thomson. Sunk 1.5.15 by UB.16 off the Galloper LV.
D.53	D.67	D.72		ROEBUCK	4. 1.01	Hawthorn Leslie. BU 1919 at Portsmouth DY.
P.07	D.68	D.79	H.07	STAR	11. 8.96	Palmer. Sold 10.6.19 Ward, New Holland.
D.23	D.69	D.84	H.03*	SYLVIA	3. 7.97	Doxford. Sold 23.7.19 Ward, New Holland.
D.57	D.70	D.89		THORN	17. 3.00	Thomson. BU 1919 at Portsmouth DY.
P.45	D.71			VELOX	11. 2.02	Hawthorn Leslie. Mined 25.10.15 off the Nab.
D.43	D.72	D.92		VIGILANT	16. 8.00	Thomson. Sold 10.2.20 South Alloa S. Bkg Co.
D.09	D.73	D.94		VIOLET	3. 5.97	Doxford. Sold 7.6.20 J. Houston, Montrose.
D.44	D.74	D.95		VIXEN	29. 3.00	Vickers. Sold 17.3.21 Ward, Grays.
N.50	D.75**			VULTURE	22. 3.98	Thomson. Sold 27.5.19 Hayes, Porthcawl.
				WHITING	26. 8.96	Palmer. Sold 27.11.19 at Hong Kong.

*Pendants assigned 4.18. **No Pendant 1.18.
Notes: Also of this group were CHAMOIS, foundered 26.9.04; LEE, wrecked 5.10.09; TIGER, in collision 2.4.08 and VIPER (turbine), lost 3.8.01. VELOX (turbine) was launched as PYTHON and purchased 7.6.02 from her builder. VIGILANT was purchased 31.3.00 from her builder. Ten served on patrol, GF area; nine at Dover; fifteen on Patrol or LDF and two (OTTER and WHITING) in China, OTTER being in commission for a few months only.

D CLASS

Avg 340 tons. 210 (pp) ×19½×7 ft. TE 5800 ihp=30 kts.
Armament: 1–12 pdr, 5–6 pdr, 2–18 in TT.

1914	9.15	1.18	Name	Launched	Builder—Fate
P.25	D.36	D.04	ANGLER	2. 2.97	Thornycroft. Sold 20.5.20 Ward, Milford Haven.
N.21	D.37		COQUETTE	25.11.97	Thornycroft. Mined 7.3.16 off E. Coast.
N.49	D.38	D.22	CYGNET	8. 1.98	Thornycroft. Sold 29.4.20 Ward, Rainham.
N.09	D.39	D.23	CYNTHIA	3. 9.98	Thornycroft. Sold 29.4.20 Ward, Rainham.
P.50	D.40	D.26	DESPERATE	15. 2.96	Thornycroft. Sold 20.5.20 Ward, Milford Haven.
	D.41	D.37	FAME	15. 4.96	Thornycroft. Sold 31.8.21 at Hong Kong.
D.26	D.42	D.55	MALLARD	19.11.96	Thornycroft. Sold 10.2.20 South Alloa S. Bkg Co.
P.34	D.43	D.78	STAG	18.11.99	Thornycroft. Sold 17.3.21 Ward, Grays.

Notes: One vessel, ARIEL, lost 19.4.07. ANGLER and DESPERATE in Portsmouth LDF; COQUETTE, CYGNET and CYNTHIA in Nore LDF; MALLARD and STAG in Patrol Flotillas; and FAME in China.

EX-CHINESE: D CLASS

305 tons. 193½ (pp) ×20×5 ft. TE 6000 ihp=32 kts.
Armament: 6–3 pdr, 3–14 in TT.

Name	Launched	Builder—Fate
TAKU	1898	Schichau. Sold 25.10.16 at Hong Kong.

Notes: Formerly the Chinese HAI-NJU captured 17.6.00.

PURCHASED B CLASS

440 tons. 215 (pp) ×21 ×7 ft. Turbine 7000 shp=26½ kts.
Armament: 3–12 pdr, 2–18 in TT.

1914	9.15	1.18	Name	Launched	Builder—Fate
P.14	D.76	D.01	ALBACORE	19. 9.06	Palmer. Sold 1.8.19 T. R. Sales.
D.15	D.78	D.11	BONETTA	14. 1.07	Palmer. Sold 7.6.20 Ward, Hayle; then Briton Ferry.

Notes: Built on speculation and purchased in 3.09. ALBACORE in GF Local Patrol; BONETTA was S/M tender on the Clyde and later the Tyne.

E. (RIVER) CLASS

545 to 560 tons. (Yarrow boats 590). Avg 222 (pp) ×23½×9¼ ft. TE Avg 7500 ihp=25½ kts.
Armament: 4–12 pdr, 2–18 in TT. (EDEN—Turbine)

Pendant Nos.				Name	Launched	Builder—Fate
1914	9.15	1.18	9.18			
N.04	D.11	D.07		ARUN	30. 4.03	Laird. Sold 30.6.20 Ward, Hayle.
N.44	D.20			FOYLE	25. 2.03	Laird. Mined 15.3.17 in Dover Straits.
N.06	D.22			ITCHEN	17. 3.03	Laird. Sunk 6.7.17 by U.99 in N. Sea.
N.07	D.24	D.52		LIFFEY	24. 9.04	Laird. Sold 23.6.19 Ward, Grays.
N.02	D.25	D.58	H.76	MOY	10.11.04	Laird. Sold 27.5.19 T. Oakley.
N.81	D.26	D.59	H.77	NESS	5. 1.05	White. Sold 27.5.19 T. R. Sales.
N.77	D.27	D.60	H.78	NITH	7. 3.05	White. Sold 23.6.19 Ward, Preston.
N.69	D.28	D.66	H.80	OUSE	7. 1.05	Laird. Sold 22.10.19 J. H. Lee.
N.68	D.12		H.23	BOYNE	12. 9.04	Hawthorn Leslie. Sold 30.8.19 Hayes, Porthcawl.
N.25	D.15			DERWENT	14. 2.03	Hawthorn Leslie. Mined 2.5.17 off Le Havre.
N.14	D.16	D.27	H.41	DOON	8.11.04	Hawthorn Leslie. Sold 27.5.19 Ward, Rainham.
N.42	D.17			EDEN	14. 3.03	Hawthorn Leslie. Sunk 18.6.16 in collision with SS FRANCE in the Channel.
N.45	D.23	D.47		KALE	8.11.04	Hawthorn Leslie. Mined 27.3.18 in North Sea.
N.79	D.35	D.96	H.86	WAVENEY	16. 4.03	Hawthorn Leslie. Sold 10.2.20 Ward, Grays.
				CHELMER	8.12.04	Thornycroft. Sold 30.6.20 Ward, Hayle.
				COLNE	21. 2.05	Thornycroft. Sold 4.11.19 J. H. Lee, Dover.
				JED	16. 2.04	Thornycroft. Sold 29. 7.20 Purves, Teignmouth.
				KENNET	4. 12.03	Thornycroft. Sold 11.12.19 J. H. Lee, Dover.
N.90	D.13	D.17		CHERWELL	25. 7.03	Palmer. Sold 23.6.19 Ward, Rainham.
N.95	D.14	D.24	H.31	DEE	10. 9.03	Palmer. Sold 23.7.19 Ward, Briton Ferry.
N.58				ERNE	14. 1.03	Palmer. Wrecked 6.2.15, Rattray Head.
N.01	D.18	D.32		ETTRICK	28. 2.03	Palmer. Sold 27.5.19 James Dredging Co.
N.05	D.19	D.33	H.70	EXE	27. 4.03	Palmer. Sold 10.2.20 Ward, Rainham.
N.32	D.29	D.73		ROTHER	5. 1.04	Palmer. Sold 23.6.19 Ward, Briton Ferry.
N.03	D.31	D.83		SWALE	20. 3.05	Palmer. Sold 23.6.19 Ward, Preston.
N.12	D.34	D.91		URE	25.10.04	Palmer. Sold 27.5.19 T. R. Sales.
N.92*				WEAR	21. 1.05	Palmer. Sold 4.11.19 Ward, Grays.
N.10	D.21	D.41	H.73	GARRY	21. 3.05	Yarrow. Sold 22.10.19 J. H. Lee.
				RIBBLE	19. 3.04	Yarrow. Sold 29.7.20 Ward, Preston.
N.26	D.33	D.88		TEVIOT	7.11.03	Yarrow. Sold 23.6.19 Ward, Morecambe.
				USK	25. 7.03	Yarrow. Sold 29.7.20 Ward, Morecambe.
				WELLAND	14. 4.04	Yarrow. Sold 30.6.20 Ward, Preston.

*No Pendant 9.15.

PURCHASED 12.09

570 tons. 220 (pp) ×24×8 ft. Turbine 7000 shp=25½ kts.
Armament: 4–12 pdr, 2–18 in TT.

N.08	D.30	D.80	H.83	STOUR	3. 6.05	Laird. Sold 30.8.19 J. Smith.
N 34	D.32	D.87	H.84	TEST	6. 5.05	Laird. Sold 30.8.19 Loveridge & Co.

Notes: ARUN group had two medium funnels; BOYNE group, two short funnels; CHELMER group, two high funnels; CHERWELL group, four funnels closely paired; GARRY group, four funnels in open pairs. BLACKWATER (Laird 25.7.03) lost 6.4.09 and GALA (Yarrow 7.1.05) lost 27.4.08; both by collisions. CHELMER, COLNE, JED, KENNET, RIBBLE, USK and WELLAND in China 1914, Mediterranean 1914–18. The others served in Patrol Flotillas.

F (TRIBAL) CLASS
1st GROUP:

865 to 885 tons. Avg 260 (pp) ×25½×8 ft. Turbine Avg 14250 shp=34 kts.
Armament: 5–12 pdr, 2–18 in TT.

1914	9.15	1.18	Name	Launched	Builder—Fate
H.40	D.00		AFRIDI	8. 5.07	Armstrong. Sold 9.12.19 F. Wilkinson.
H.09	D.02	D.19	COSSACK	16. 2.07	Cammell Laird. Sold 12.12.19 Ward, Preston.
H.52	D.04		GHURKA	29. 4.07	Hawthorn Leslie. Mined 8.2.17 off Dungeness.
H.19	D.05	D.57	MOHAWK	15. 3.07	White. Sold 27.5.19 Hughes Bolckow.
H.29	D.08	D.86	TARTAR	25. 6.07	Thornycroft. Sold 9.5.21 Ward, Hayle.

2nd GROUP

970 to 1090 tons. Avg 280 (pp) ×26½×9 ft. Turbine 15500 shp=34 kts.
Armament: 2–4 in, 2–18 in TT.

1914	9.15	1.18	Name	Launched	Builder—Fate
H.37	D.01	D.03	AMAZON	29. 7.08	Thornycroft. Sold 22.10.19 Ward, Preston.
H.66	D.03	D.21	CRUSADER	20. 3.09	White. Sold 30.6.20 Ward, Preston.
H.16			MAORI	24. 5.09	Denny. Mined 7.5.15 off Belgian coast.
H.70	D.06		NUBIAN	20. 4.09	Thornycroft. Disabled 27.10.16 by torpedo off the Belgian coast.
H.38	D.07	D.74	SARACEN	31. 3.08	White. Sold 22.10.19 Ward, Preston.
H.90	D.09	D.93	VIKING	14. 9.09	Palmer. Sold 12.12.19 Ward, Briton Ferry.
H.86	D.10		ZULU	16. 9.09	Hawthorn Leslie. Disabled 8.11.16 by mine off Dover.

Notes: AFRIDI, COSSACK and GHURKA had three funnels, VIKING had six (the only one in the RN) and the others had four. They burned oil fuel only. All served at Dover throughout the war, with one exception. MOHAWK spent the last year of the war with the 10th S/M Flotilla. The bow section of ZULU was joined to the stern portion of NUBIAN (between 3rd & 4th funnels) and a new ship of 1050 tons named ZUBIAN emerged 7.6.17.

8.17	1.18	Name	Completed	Dockyard—Fate
D.20	D.99	ZUBIAN	2. 7.17	Chatham DY. Sold 9.12.19 Fryer, Sunderland.

EXPERIMENTAL DESTROYER

2170 tons. 353¾ (oa), 345 (pp) ×34×10½ ft. Turbine 30000 shp=36 kts.
Armament: 4–4 in (changed to 1–6 in, 2–4 in 1918), 2–18 in TT.

1914	1.18	9.18	Name	Launched	Builder—Fate
H.64	H.3A	D.60	SWIFT	7.12.07	Cammell Laird. Sold 9.11.21 Rees, Llanelly.

Notes: Oil fuel only. Served as destroyer leader GF 1914–15 and Dover 1915–18.

G (BEAGLE) CLASS

916 to 975 tons. Avg 270 (pp) ×27½×8½ ft. Turbine 12500 shp=27½ kts.
Armament: 1–4 in, 3–12 pdr (designed for 5–12 pdr), 2–18 in TT.

Pendant Nos.			Name	Launched	Builder—Fate
2.15	1.18	6.18			
D.89		H.C8*	BASILISK	9. 2.10	White. Sold 1.11.21 Fryer, Sunderland.
	H.C5		BEAGLE	16.10.09	John Brown. Sold 1.11.21 Fryer, Sunderland.
	H.C7	H.C4*	BULLDOG	13.11.09	John Brown. Sold 21.9.20 Ward, Rainham.
	H.16	H.58**	FOXHOUND	11.12.09	John Brown. Sold 1.11.21 Fryer, Sunderland.
H.07†	H.38	H.A7	GRAMPUS	30. 3.10	Thames IW. Sold 21.9.20 Ward, Rainham.
	H.17	H.60	GRASSHOPPER	22.10.09	Fairfield. Sold 1.11.21 Fryer, Sunderland.
D.88	H.19	H.71	HARPY	27.11.09	White. Sold 1.11.21 Fryer, Sunderland.
	H.A3		MOSQUITO	27. 1.10	Fairfield. Sold 31.8.20 Ward, Rainham.
D.87		H.C2**	PINCHER	15. 3.10	Denny. Wrecked 24.7.18 on the 7 Stones.
	H.A7		RACOON	15. 2.10	Cammell Laird. Wrecked 9.1.18 on West Coast of Ireland.
D.94		H.C7*	RATTLESNAKE	14. 3.10	Harland & Wolff, Govan. Sold. 9.5.21 Ward, Milford Haven.
		H.99††	RENARD	13.11.09	Cammell Laird. Sold 31.8.20 Ward, New Holland.

Pendant Nos.			Name	Launched	Builder—Fate
2.15	1.18	6.18			
D.92	H.A9		SAVAGE	10. 3.10	Thornycroft. Sold 9.5.21 Ward, Portishead.
D.90		H.C3	SCORPION	19. 2.10	Fairfield. Sold 26.10.21 Barking S. Bkg Co.
D.96	H.8A†††		SCOURGE	11. 2.10	Hawthorn Leslie. Sold 9.5.21 Ward, Briton Ferry.
	H.18***		WOLVERINE	15. 1.10	Cammell Laird. Sunk 12.12.17 in collision with sloop ROSEMARY off NW coast of Ireland.

*Pendants from 9.18; **from 4.18; ***from 1917; †from 1916; ††from 11.18; †††from 10.17. The D pendants were all cancelled 9.15. GRAMPUS had no pendant from 4.18 to 6.18.
Notes: GRAMPUS was launched as NAUTILUS and renamed in 12.13. These were the last coal-burners of the British destroyers. No home pendants for 1914, all ships being in the Mediterranean. Six vessels were in the UK from late 1914 and all again in the Mediterranean 1915–17 returning to the UK 1917–18 in 2nd DF.

H (ACORN) CLASS

720 to 760 tons. 246 (oa), 240 (pp) $\times 25\frac{1}{2} \times 8\frac{1}{2}$ ft. Turbine 13500 shp=27 kts.
Armament: 2–4 in, 2–12 pdr, 2–21 in TT.

1914	9.15	1.18	Name	Launched	Builder—Fate
H.02		H.03	ACORN	1. 7.10	John Brown. Sold 29.11.21 Marple & Gillott, Saltash.
H.05		H.04	ALARM	29. 8.10	John Brown. Sold 9.5.21 Ward, Hayle.
H.18	H.70	H.22	BRISK	20. 9.10	John Brown. Sold 15.11.21 Distin, Devonport.
H.21		H.24	CAMELEON	2. 6.10	Fairfield. Sold 15.11.21 Devonport.
H.25	*		COMET	23. 6.10	Fairfield. Sunk 6.8.18 by Austrian S/M in the Mediterranean.
H.42		H.35	FURY	25. 4.11	Inglis. Sold 4.11.21 Rees, Llanelly.
H.44			GOLDFINCH	12. 7.10	Fairfield. Wrecked 19.2.15 in the Orkneys.
H.48		H.41	HOPE	6. 9.10	Swan Hunter. Sold 2.20 at Malta.
H.57		H.50	LARNE	23. 8.10	Thornycroft. Sold 9.5.21 Ward, Lelant; BU 10.22
H.60		H.67	LYRA	4.10.10	Thornycroft. Sold 9.5.21 Ward, Milford Haven.
H.65		H.71	MARTIN	15.12.10	Thornycroft. Sold 21.8.20 at Malta.
H.69		H.82	MINSTREL	2. 2.11	Thornycroft. Sold 1.12.21 Stanlee.
H.72		H.88	NEMESIS	9. 8.10	Hawthorn Leslie. Sold 26.11.21 British Legion, Plymouth.
H.74		H.89	NEREIDE	6. 9.10	Hawthorn Leslie. Sold 1.12.21 Stanlee.
H.83		D.25	NYMPHE	31. 1.11	Hawthorn Leslie. Sold 9.5.21 Ward, Hayle.
H.77		H.96	REDPOLE	24. 6.10	White. Sold 9.5.21 Ward, Milford Haven.
H.82		H.97	RIFLEMAN	22. 8.10	White. Sold 9.5.21 Ward, Briton Ferry.
H.85		H.98	RUBY	4.11.10	White. Sold 9.5.21 Ward, Grays.
H.88		H.0A	SHELDRAKE	18. 1.11	Denny. Sold 9.5.21 Ward, Grays.
H.89	H.2A**		STAUNCH	29.10.10	Denny. Sunk 11.11.17 by UC38 off the Coast of Palestine.

*Pendant cancelled 1916. **Assigned 1917. All pendants cancelled 4.18; except NYMPHE D.25 cancelled 6.18 and BRISK H.22 cancelled 9.18.
Notes: These and all succeeding destroyers were oil-burners. MINSTREL & NEMESIS on loan to the Japanese in the Mediterranean 6.17–1919 as SENDAN and KANRAN respectively. The whole class formed the 2nd DF, GF 1914–15; six returned to the Mediterranean in 1915 and five more in 1916. All were there by 1918.

I (ACHERON) CLASS

745 to 810 tons. Avg 246 (oa), 240 (pp) ×25½×9 ft. Turbine 16000 shp=28 kts.
Armament: 2–4 in, 2–12 pdr, 2–21 in TT.

1914	9.15	1.18	Name	Launched	Builder—Fate
H.00		H.02	ACHERON	27. 6.11	Thornycroft. Sold 9.5.21 Ward.
H.10	H.29	H.06	ARCHER	21.10.11	Yarrow. Sold 9.5.21 Ward, Rainham; BU 10.22.
H.11	H.37	H.07	ARIEL	26. 9.11	Thornycroft. Mined 2.8.18 in North Sea.
H.14	H.86*	H.08	ATTACK	21.12.11	Yarrow. Mined 30.12.17 off Alexandria.
H.15	H.52	H.09	BADGER	11. 7.11	Denny. Sold 9.5.21 Ward, Hayle.
H.17	H.66	H.20	BEAVER	6.10.11	Denny. Sold 9.5.21 Ward, Hayle.
H.28		H.29	DEFENDER	30. 8.11	Denny. Sold 4.11.21 Rees, Llanelly.
H.33		H.30	DRUID	4.12.11	Denny. Sold 9.5.21 Ward, Briton Ferry.
H.35		H.32 F.93**	FERRET	12. 4.11	White. Sold 9.5.21 Ward, Milfrod Haven.
H.39		H.34	FORESTER	1. 6.11	White. Sold 4.11.21 Rees, Llanelly.
H.45		H.37	GOSHAWK	18.10.11	Beardmore. Sold 4.11.21 Rees, Llanelly.
H.47		H.40	HIND	28. 7.11	John Brown. Sold 9.5.21 Ward, Preston; BU 6.24.
H.49		H.42	HORNET	20.12.11	John Brown. Sold 9.5.21 Ward, Rainham; BU 10.22.
H.50		H.43	HYDRA	19. 2.12	John Brown. Sold 9.5.21 Ward, Portishead,
H.55		H.44	JACKAL	9. 9.11	Hawthorn Leslie. Sold 28.9.20 J. Smith.
H.56		H.48	LAPWING	29. 7.11	Cammell Laird. Sold 26.10.21 Barking S. Bkg Co.
H.58		H.60	LIZARD	10.10.11	Cammell Laird. Sold 4.11.21 Rees, Llanelly.
H.75		H.94	PHOENIX	9.10.11	Vickers. Sunk 14.5.18 by Austrian S/M in the Adriatic.
H.87		H.99 F.95**	SANDFLY	26. 7.11	Swan Hunter. Sold 9.5.21 Ward, Milford Haven.
H.92		H.4A	TIGRESS	20.12.11	Hawthorn Leslie. Sold 9.5.21 Ward, Milford Haven.

*Pendant from 1.16; **from 9.18. Pendants of ACHERON, ARCHER, HYDRA, JACKAL, LAPWING, LAPWING, LIZARD, PHOENIX and TIGRESS cancelled 4.18.

Notes: Fore funnels ordered 29.9.16 to be heightened by six feet. All formed the 1st DF, GF 1914–16; Devonport, Harwich or Dover 1916–17. All were in the Mediterranean by 1918 except ARIEL, FERRET and SANDFLY fitted as minelayers, 20th DF in the North Sea.

AUSTRALIAN I CLASS

700 tons. 246 (oa) (last three 251 oa), ×24½×8 ft. Turbine 13000 shp=27 kts.
Armament: 1–4 in, 3–12 pdr, 3–18 in TT.

Name	Launched	Builder—Fate
PARRAMATTA	9. 2.10	Fairfield. Dismantled from 10.29 at Cockatoo DY.
WARREGO	4. 4.11	Fairfield & Cockatoo DY. Dismantled from 10.29 at Cockatoo DY.
YARRA	8. 4.10	Denny. Dismantled from 10.29 at Cockatoo DY.
HUON	19.12.14	Cockatoo DY. Sunk 9.4.30 as target, Jervis Bay.
SWAN	11.12.15	Cockatoo DY. BU 9.29.
TORRENS	28. 8.15	Cockatoo DY. Sunk 24.11.30 as target off Sydney.

Notes: HUON *ex-Derwent* renamed 12.14. All served in the Pacific from completion to 1917, then to the Mediterranean.

SPECIAL BOATS: I CLASS

765 tons. 262 (oa), (255 pp)×25½×9½ ft. Turbine 20000 shp=32 kts.
Armament: 2–4 in, 2–12 pdr, 2–21 in TT.

1914	9.15	1.18	Name	Launched	Builder—Fate
H.97		H.33	FIREDRAKE	9. 4.12	Yarrow. Sold 10.10.21 J. Smith.
H.01		H.65	LURCHER	1. 6.12	Yarrow. Sold 9.6.22 Cashmore.
H.12	H.38	H.92	OAK	5. 9.12	Yarrow. Sold 9.5.21 Ward, Hayle; BU 9.22.

Notes: The first two served with Harwich S/M Flotillas 1914–18 and OAK was tender to the GF Flagship.

K (ACASTA) CLASS

935 to 957 tons. 267½ (oa), 260 (pp) × 26½ × 9¼ ft. Turbine 24500 shp = 30 kts.
Armament: 3–4 in, 2–21 in TT.

1914	9.15	1.18	Name	Launched	Builder—Fate
H.59		H.00	ACASTA	10. 9.12	John Brown. Sold 9.5.21 Ward, Hayle
H.46		H.01	ACHATES	14.11.12	John Brown. Sold 9.5.21 Ward, Rainham.
H.62		H.05	AMBUSCADE	25. 1.13	John Brown. Sold 6.9.21 Petersen & Albeck, Denmark.
H.51		H.25	CHRISTOPHER	29. 8.12	Hawthorn Leslie. Sold 9.5.21 Ward; resold 10.23 King, Garston.
H.73		H.26	COCKATRICE	8.11.12	Hawthorn Leslie. Sold 9.5.21 Ward, Hayle.
H.63	H.28*		CONTEST	7. 1.13	Hawthorn Leslie. Sunk 18.9.17 by S/M in the Channel.
H.71			LYNX	20. 3.13	Harland & Wolff, Govan. Mined 9.8.15 in Moray Firth.
H.13	H.40	H.79	MIDGE	22. 5.13	Harland & Wolff, Govan. Sold 5.11.21 Granton S. Bkg Co.
H.31		H.93	OWL	7. 7.13	Harland & Wolff, Govan. Sold 5.11.21 Granton S. Bkg Co.
H.04			SHARK	30. 7.12	Swan Hunter. Sunk 31.5.16 at Jutland.
H.61			SPARROWHAWK	12.10.12	Swan Hunter. Sunk 1.6.16 at Jutland.
H.41		H.1A	SPITFIRE	23.12.12	Swan Hunter. Sold 9.5.21 Ward, Hayle.

SPECIAL BOATS

898 to 1000 tons. Avg 265 (oa), 257 (pp) × 26½ × 9½ ft. Turbine 22500 shp = 30 kts.

1914	9.15	1.18	Name	Launched	Builder—Fate
H.78			ARDENT	8. 9.13	Denny. Sunk 1.6.16 at Jutland.
H.30			FORTUNE	17. 3.13	Fairfield. Sunk 31.5.16 at Jutland.
H.32		H.36	GARLAND	23. 4.13	Cammell Laird. Sold 6.9.21 Petersen & Albeck, Denmark.
H.67		H.39	HARDY	10.10.12	Thornycroft. Sold 9.5.21 Ward, Briton Ferry.
H.26			PARAGON	21. 2.13	Thornycroft. Sunk 18.3.17 by destroyer torpedo in Dover Straits action.
H.27		H.95	PORPOISE	21. 7.13	Thornycroft. Sold 23.2.20 Thornycroft for resale to Brazil = ALEXANDRINO DEALENCA, later MARANHAO.
H.68		H.5A	UNITY	18. 9.13	Thornycroft. Sold 25.10.22 Rees, Llanelly.
H.36		H.6A	VICTOR	28.11.13	Thornycroft. Sold 20.1.23 King, Garston.

*Pendant from 1917.

Notes: These vessels were to have been named KING, KNIGHT, KEITH, KITE, KINGFISHER, KITTIWAKE, KOODOO, KEITLOA, KILLER, KESTREL, KINGSMILL, KEPPEL, KENRIC, KISMET, KENWULF, KELPIE, KATRINE, KENNINGTON, KINSALE, and KINGSTON in 9.13, but these K names were not used. All formed the 4th DF, GF 1914–16, then the 4th and 6th DF Portsmouth, Devonport or Dover.

L CLASS

965 to 994 tons. 269 (oa), 260 (pp) × 27¾ × 10½ ft. Turbine 24500 shp = 29 kts.
Armament: 3–4 in, 1–2 pdr, 4–21 in TT. (LEONIDAS & LUCIFER 22500)

1914	1.18	Name	Launched	Builder—Fate
H.54	H.47	LANDRAIL (ex-Hotspur)	7. 2.14	Yarrow. Sold 1.12.21 Stanlee.
H.34	H.49	LARK (ex-Haughty)	26. 5.13	Yarrow. Sold 20.1.23 Hayes, Porthcawl.
H.91	H.51	LAUREL (ex-Redgauntlet)	6. 5.13	White. Sold 1.11.21 Fryer, Sunderland.
H.53	H.53	LAVEROCK (ex-Hereward)	19.11.13	Yarrow. Sold 9.5.21 Ward, Grays.
H.81	H.57	LIBERTY (ex-Rosalind)	15. 9.13	White. Sold 5.11.21 Granton S. Bkg Co.
H.43	H.59	LINNET (ex-Havock)	16. 8.13	Yarrow. Sold 4.11.21 Rees, Llanelly.

965 to 1010 tons

1914	1.18	Name	Launched	Builder—Fate
H.94	H.45	LAERTES (ex-Sarpedon)	6. 6.13	Swan Hunter. Sold 1.12.21 Stanlee.
H.03		LAFOREY (ex-Florizel)	22. 8.13	Fairfield. Sunk 25.3.17 by RN mine in the Channel.
H.23	H.46	LANCE (ex-Daring)	25. 2.14	Thornycroft. Sold 5.11.21 Granton S. Bkg Co.
H.06	H.53	LAWFORD (ex-Ivanhoe)	30.10.13	Fairfield. Sold 24.8.22 Hayes, Porthcawl.
H.79	H.54 F.94*	LEGION (ex-Viola)	3. 2.14	Denny. Sold 9.5.21 Ward, New Holland.

1914 1.18		Name	Launched	Builder—Fate
H.95	H.55	LENNOX (ex-Portia)	17. 3.14	Beardmore. Sold 26.10.21 Barking S. Bkg Co.
H.20	H.56	LEONIDAS (ex-Rob Roy)	30.10.13	Palmer. Sold 9.5.21 Ward, Hayle.
H.99	H.61	LLEWELLYN (ex-Picton)	30.10.13	Beardmore. Sold 10.3.22 J. Smith.
H.24	H.62	LOOKOUT (ex-Dragon)	27. 4.14	Thornycroft. Sold 24.8.22 Hayes, Porthcawl.
H.07		LOUIS (ex-Talisman)	30.12.13	Fairfield. Wrecked 31.10.15, Suvla Bay.
H.80	H.63	LOYAL (ex-Orlando)	10.11.13	Denny. Sold 24.11.21 Hayes, Porthcawl.
H.22	H.64	LUCIFER (ex-Rocket)	29.12.13	Palmer. Sold 1.12.21 Stanlee.
H.08	H.66	LYDIARD (ex-Waverley)	26. 2.14	Fairfield. Sold 5.11.21 Granton S. Bkg Co.
H.93	H.68	LYSANDER (ex-Ulysses)	18. 8.13	Swan Hunter. Sold 9.6.22 Cashmore.
9.15	1916			
G.01	F.41	LASSOO (ex-Magic)	24. 8.15	Beardmore. Mined 13.8.16 in North Sea.
G.06	F.42 F.52**	LOCHINVAR (ex-Malice)	9.10.15	Beardmore. Sold 25.11.21 Hayes, Porthcawl.

*Pendant assigned 9.18; **Assigned 1.18.

Notes: The first six vessels had two funnels, others three funnels. Seven vessels were launched under their original names; Renamed by Admiralty Order 30.9.13 except LASSOO and LOCHINVAR (war programme renamed 2.15). All served at Harwich 1914–17, then at Devonport or Portsmouth. LAFOREY, LAWFORD, LOUIS and LYDIARD in Mediterranean 1915–16. LAWFORD and LEGION were minelayers from 1917.

1913 PROGRAMME M CLASS

1010 tons. 272 (oa), 265 (pp) × 26½ × 8½ ft. Turbine 25000 = 34 kts.
883 tons.   270 (oa), 260 (pp) × 25½ × 9½ ft. Turbine 23000 = 35 kts. (Yarrow)
985–1070 tons. 271 (oa), 265 (pp) × 27½ × 10 ft. Turbine 26500 = 35 kts. (Thorny)
1055 tons. 271 (oa), 265 (pp) × 27 × 10½ ft. Turbine 27000 = 35 kts. (Hawthorn)
Armament: 3–4 in, 1–2 pdr, 4–21 in TT.

1914 1.18	9.18	Name	Launched	Builder—Fate
H.0A H.69	D.20	MANLY	12.10.14	Yarrow. Sold 26.10.21 Barking S. Bkg Co.
H.1A H.70	D.37	MANSFIELD	3.12.14	Hawthorn Leslie. Sold 26.10.21 Barking S. Bkg Co.
H.3A H.72	D.66	MASTIFF	5. 9.14	Thornycroft. Sold 9.5.21 Ward, Briton Ferry.
H.4A H.73	D.47	MATCHLESS	5.10.14	Swan Hunter. Sold 26.10.21 Barking S. Bkg Co.
H.6A H.77	D.54	MENTOR	21. 8.14	Hawthorn Leslie. Sold 9.5.21 Ward, Hayle.
H.7A H.78	D.84	METEOR	24. 7.14	Thornycroft. Sold 9.5.21 Ward, Milford Haven.
H.8A H.80	D.12	MILNE	5.10.14	John Brown. Sold 22.9.21 Cohen; BU in Germany.
H.9A H.81		MINOS	6. 8.14	Yarrow. Sold 31.8.20 Ward, Hayle.
H.A0 H.83	D.24	MIRANDA	27. 5.14	Yarrow. Sold 26.10.21 Barking S. Bkg Co.
H.A2 H.84	D.27	MOORSOM	20.12.14	John Brown. Sold 8.11.21 Slough T.C.; BU in Germany.
H.A3 H.85	D.35	MORRIS	19.11.14	John Brown. Sold 8.11.21 Slough T.C.; BU in Germany.
H.A4 H.86	D.33	MURRAY	6. 8.14	Palmer. Sold 9.5.21 Ward, Briton Ferry.
H.A5 H.87	D.41	MYNGS	24. 9.14	Palmer. Sold 9.5.21 Ward, Rainham.

Notes: Three boats, MARKSMAN, MENACE and MONITOR were cancelled in favour of two MARKSMAN class leaders. All served at Harwich 1914–17 (MASTIFF to 11th S/M Flotilla 1915–17), five being on loan to Dover 1916–17. All went to the Mediterranean 1917–18, then to the GF or Dover Force.

PURCHASED EX-CHILEAN CLASS

1742, 1704, 1694, 1737 tons respectively. 331 (oa), 320 (pp) ×32½ ×11 ft. Turbine 30000 shp=31¼ kts.
Armament: 6–4 in (2.18: 2–4.7 in, 2–4 in), 2–2 pdr, 4–21 in TT.

1914	1.18	9.18	Name	Launched	Builder—Fate
H.5C	G.60* F.50	F.61** D.80	BOTHA	2.12.14	White. Sold 5.20 Chilean Navy, =ALMIRANTE WILLIAMS.
H.98	H.23	D.10	BROKE	25. 5.14	White. Sold 5.20 Chilean Navy, =ALMIRANTE URIBE.
H.84	H.31	D.16	FAULKNOR	26. 2.14	White. Sold 5.20 Chilean Navy, =ALMIRANTE RIVEROS.
H.6C			TIPPERARY	5. 3.15	White. Sunk 1.6.16 at Jutland.

*Pendant in 2.17; **in 4.17.
Notes: Purchased in 8.14; these were originally the Chilean ALMIRANTE WILLIAMS ROBEL-LEDO, ALMIRANTE GONI, ALMIRANTE SIMPSON and ALMIRANTE RIVEROS respectively. They were used as leaders in the GF 1915–16 (BOTHA to 1917), then at Dover.

MARKSMAN CLASS LEADERS

1604 to 1608 tons. 325 (oa), 315 (pp) ×32 ×12 ft. Turbine 36000 shp=34 kts.
Armament: 4–4 in, 2–2 pdr, 4–21 in TT. (2–14 in TT added 1917 in LIGHTFOOT & NIMROD)

1914	1917	1.18	4.18	Name	Launched	Builder—Fate
H.A1	G.10	F.87	G.12	KEMPENFELT	1. 5.15	Cammell Laird. Sold 9.5.21 Ward, Morecambe.
H.76		H.58	G.22 F.78*	LIGHTFOOT	28. 5.15	White. Sold 9.5.21 Ward, New Holland.
H.96	G.35	F.85	G.23 F.66*	MARKSMAN	28. 4.15	Hawthorn Leslie. Sold 8.11.21 Slough T.C.; BU in Germany.
H.5A		H.90		NIMROD	12. 4.15	Denny. Sold 5.11.26 Alloa S. Bkg Co, Rosyth.

*Pendants from 9.18.
Notes: LIGHTFOOT and NIMROD (1913–14 programme) at Harwich 1915–18, then to GF. KEMPENFELT and MARKSMAN (1914–15 programme) in GF 1915–17, Dover 1917–18, then GF again.

ADMIRALTY M AND REPEAT M CLASS

Avg 1025 tons. 274 (oa), 265 (pp) ×26¾ ×9 ft. Turbine 25000 shp=34 kts.
Armament: 3–4 in, 1–2 pdr, 4–21 in TT.

Ordered 9.14

1914	1.17	1.18	4.18	Name	Launched	Builder—Fate
H.A7	G.26	G.27	G.A8*	MAENAD	10. 8.15	Denny. Sold 22.9.21 Cohen; BU in Germany.
G.C0	G.01		G.0A	MAGIC (ex-Marigold)	10. 9.15	White. Sold 22.9.21 Cohen; BU in Germany.
H.A8	G.02	H.9A		MANDATE	27. 4.15	Fairfield. Sold 22.9.21 Cohen; BU in Germany.
H.A9	G.03		H.Cl*	MANNERS	15. 6.15	Fairfield. Sold 26.10.21 Barking S. Bkg Co.
H.C2	G.04			MARMION	28. 5.15	Swan Hunter. Sunk 21.10.17 in collision with TIRADE off Lerwick.
H.A6	G.05	H.A0		MARNE	29. 5.15	John Brown. Sold 29.9.21 Cohen; BU in Germany.
H.C3	G.06	F.77		MARTIAL	1. 7.15	Swan Hunter. Sold 9.5.21 Ward, Briton Ferry.
H.C4	G.29			MARY ROSE	8.10.15	Swan Hunter. Sunk 17.10.17 by BREMSE & BRUMMER in the North Sea.
H.7C	G.28	G.30	G.6A**	MENACE	9.11.15	Swan Hunter. Sold 9.5.21 Ward, Grays.
H.C5	G.07	H.A1		MICHAEL	19. 5.15	Thornycroft. Sold 22.9.21 Cohen; BU in Germany.
H.C6	G.08	H.A2		MILBROOK	12. 7.15	Thornycroft. Sold 22.9.21 Cohen; BU in Germany.
H.C7		G.09	G.14 H.82**	MINION	11. 9.15	Thornycroft. Sold 8.11.21 Slough T. C.; BU in Germany.
H.2A	G.11	G.10	G.1A H.89**	MONS	1. 5.15	John Brown. Sold 8.11.21 Slough T. C.; BU in Germany.
H.C1	F.02	H.27		MORESBY (ex-Marlion)	20.11.15	White. Sold 9.5.21 Ward, Grays.
H.8C	G.33		G.7A**	MUNSTER (ex-Monitor)	24.11.15	Thornycroft. Sold 15.11.21 Cashmore.
H.2C	G.16		G.3A	MYSTIC (ex-Myrtle)	20. 6.15	Denny. Sold 8.11.21 Slough T.C.; BU in Germany.

11.14 (1st ORDER)

9.15	1.17	1.18	4.18	Name	Launched	Builder—Fate
G.11	G.27	G.26	G.02*	MAMELUKE	14. 8.15	John Brown. Sold 22.9.21 Cohen; BU in Germany.
G.20	G.28		G.A3*	MARVEL	7.10.15	Denny. Sold 9.5.21 Ward, Hayle.
G.04		G.31	H.91**	MINDFUL	24. 8.15	Fairfield. Sold 22.9.21 Cohen; BU in Germany.
G.10	G.32		G.A4*	MISCHIEF	12.10.15	Fairfield. Sold 8.11.21 Slough T. C.; BU in Germany.
G.13				NEGRO	8. 3.16	Palmer. Sunk 21.12.16 in collision with HOSTE in North Sea.
G.18	F.03		H.44	NEPEAN	22. 1.16	Thornycroft. Sold 15.11.21 Cashmore.
G.19	F.12	F.33	H.21 H.37†	NEREUS	24. 2.16	Thornycroft. Sold 15.11.21 Cashmore.
G.00	G.37	G.36	G.5A**	NESSUS	24. 8.15	Swan Hunter. Sunk 8.9.18 in collision with AMPHITRITE in North Sea.
G.12	G.39	G.38	G.A5*	NONSUCH (ex-Narcissus)	7.12.15	Palmer. Sold 9.5.21 Ward, Milford Haven.

11.14 (2nd ORDER)

				Name	Launched	Builder—Fate
G.30				NESTOR	22.12.15	Swan Hunter. Sunk 31.5.16 at Jutland.
G.28	G.52	G.53	H.C6*	NIZAM	6. 4.16	Stephen. Sold 9.5.21 Ward, Rainham.
G.09	G.38	G.37	G.9A**	NOBLE (ex-Nisus)	25.11.15	Stephen. Sold 8.11.21 Slough T.C.
G.31				NOMAD	7. 2.16	Stephen. Sunk 31.5.16 at Jutland.
G.37	G.53	G.54	D.0A*	NONPAREIL	16. 5.16	Stephen. Sold 9.5.21 Ward, Briton Ferry.
G.14	G.54	G.55	H.0A*	NORMAN	20. 3.16	Palmer. Sold 9.5.21 Ward, Milford Haven.
G.16	F.45	F.53		NORTH STAR	9.11.16	Palmer. Sunk 23.4.18 by gunfire, Zeebrugge raid.
G.15	G.83	H.21††		NORTHESK	5. 7.16	Palmer. Sold 9.5.21 Ward, Rainham.
G.17	F.46	F.54	D.58*	NUGENT	23. 1.17	Palmer. Sold 9.5.21 Ward, Hayle.
G.26	F.06	F.07	H.50**	OBDURATE	21. 1.16	Scotts. Sold 15.11.21 Cashmore.
G.25	G.40	G.39	H.88**	OBEDIENT	6.11.15	Scotts. Sold 25.11.21 Hayes, Porthcawl.
G.51	F.07	F.09	G.71	OCTAVIA (ex-Oryx)	21. 6.16	Doxford. Sold 5.11.21 Granton S. Bkg Co.
G.22	G.41	G.40	G.8A**	ONSLAUGHT	4.12.15	Fairfield. Sold 30.10.21 W. & A. T. Burden.
G.29	F.09	F.34	H.24	ONSLOW	15. 2.16	Fairfield. Sold 26.10.21 Barking S. Bkg Co.
G.02	G.42	G.41		OPAL	11. 9.15	Doxford. Wrecked 21.1.18, Pentland Skerries.
G.03	G.57	G.58	G.A9†	OPHELIA	13.10.15	Doxford. Sold 8.11.21 Slough T. C.
G.05	G.58	G.59		OPPORTUNE	20.11.15	Doxford. Sold 7.12.23 J. J. King.
G.27	F.08	D.46		ORACLE	23.12.15	Doxford. Sold 31.10.21 W. & A. T. Burden, Milford Haven.
G.33	G.61	G.60	D.56†	ORESTES	21. 3.16	Doxford. Sold 31.10.21 W. & A. T. Burden.
G.38	G.59	G.61	D.70†	ORFORD	19. 4.16	Doxford. Sold 31.10.21 W. & A. T. Burden.
G.43	F.17	F.35	H.28 G.A9†	ORPHEUS	17. 6.16	Doxford. Sold 1.11.21 Fryer, Sunderland.
G.23	G.17	H.A5		OSSORY	9.10.15	John Brown. Sold 8.11.21 Slough T.C.

ORDERED 2.15

9.15	1.17	1.18	4.18	Name	Launched	Builder—Fate
G.34			G.A0**	NAPIER	27.11.15	John Brown. Sold 8.11.21 Slough T. C.; BU in Germany.
G.39	F.11	F.02		NARBROUGH	2. 3.16	John Brown. Wrecked 12.1.18, Pentland Skerries.
G.47	G.36	G.35	H.29**	NARWHAL	30.12.15	Denny. BU 1920 at Devonport DY after collision damage.
G.55	F.05	H.A4		NICATOR	3. 2.16	Denny. Sold 9.5.21 Ward, Milford Haven.
G.70	F.13	F.06	G.51 H.22†	NORSEMAN	15. 8.16	Doxford. Sold 9.5.21 Ward, Grays.
G.80	F.27	F.36	H.35]	OBERON	29. 9.16	Doxford. Sold 9.5.21 Ward, Rainham.
G.41	G.55	G.51	D.79†	OBSERVER	1. 5.16	Fairfield. Sold 30.10.21 W. & A. T. Burden.
G.45	G.56	G.57	D.96†	OFFA	7. 6.16	Fairfield. Sold 30.10.21 W. & A. T. Burden.
G.53	G.80	D.30		ORCADIA	26. 7.16	Fairfield. Sold 31.10.21 W. & A. T. Burden, Poole.
G.69	F.14	F.11	H.34**	ORIANA	23. 9.16	Fairfield. Sold 31.10.21 W. & A. T. Burden.
G.44	F.16	D.1A	D.06	ORIOLE	31. 7.16	Palmer. Sold 9.5.21 Ward, Grays.
G.68	F.26	F.31	G.72 H.30†	OSIRIS	28. 9.16	Palmer. Sold 9.5.21 Ward, Rainham.

9.15	1.17	1.18	4.18	Name	Launched	Builder—Fate
G.40	F.18	F.14	G.73 D.1A†	PALADIN	27. 3.16	Scotts. Sold 9.5.21 Ward, Rainham.
G.52	G.77	H.91		PARTHIAN	3. 7.16	Scotts. Sold 8.11.21 Slough T. C.; BU in Germany.
G.46	G.62			PARTRIDGE	4. 3.16	Swan Hunter. Sunk 12.12.17 by German destroyers in the North Sea.
G.54	F.22	D.42		PASLEY	15. 4.16	Swan Hunter. Sold 9.5.21 Ward, Hayle.
				ORDERED 5.15		
G.75	G.51	G.52	D.87†	MEDINA (ex-*Redmill*)	8. 3.16	White. Sold 9.5.21 Ward, Milford Haven.
G.76	F.01		G.2A	MEDWAY (ex-*Redwing*)	19. 4.16	White. Sold 9.5.21 Ward, Milford Haven.
G.58	F.10	H.A8		PELICAN	18. 3.16	Beardmore. Sold 9.5.21 Ward, Preston; BU 5.24.
G.64			H.98†	PELLEW	8. 5.16	Beardmore. Sold 9.5.21 Ward, Briton Ferry, BU 1923.
G.50	F.19	F.16	G.74	PENN	8. 4.16	John Brown. Sold 31.10.21 W. & A. T. Burden.
G.60	G.65		H.94†	PEREGRINE	29. 5.16	John Brown. Sold 15.11.21 Cashmore.
G.66	F.20	F.32	G.29 G.A7†	PETARD	24. 3.16	Denny. Sold 9.5.21 Ward, Grays; BU 10.23.
G.72	G.66		H.96†	PEYTON	2. 5.16	Denny. Sold 9.5.21 Ward, Morecambe.
G.74	G.89			PHEASANT	23.10.16	Fairfield. Mined 1.3.17 off Orkneys.
G.82	F.53	F.55	D.59*	PHOEBE	20.11.16	Fairfield. Sold 15.11.21 Cashmore.
G.59	F.21	F.18	H.67	PIGEON	3. 3.16	Hawthorn Leslie. Sold 9.5.21 Ward, New Holland.
G.65	G.67			PLOVER	3. 3.16	Hawthorn Leslie. Sold 9.5.21 Ward, Hayle.
G.67	G.68		G.A6* D.2A†	PLUCKY	21. 4.16	Scotts. Sold 9.5.21 Ward, Preston; BU 6.24.
G.73	G.84	H.A6		PORTIA	10. 8.16	Scotts. Sold 9.5.21 Ward, Milford Haven.
G.77	G.43	G.42	F.92*	PRINCE	26. 7.16	Stephen. Sold 9.5.21 Ward, Hayle.
G.78	F.28	F.19	G.62 H.97†	PYLADES	28. 9.16	Stephen. Sold 9.5.21 Ward, Hayle.

*Pendants from 9.18; **from 6.18; †from 11.18; ††no pendant from 4.18.
Notes: MARLION and MONITOR were renamed 9.14; MARIGOLD, MYRTLE and NARCISSUS during 5.15; ORYX by 9.15; and NISUS by 10.15. On 4.7.16 all three-shaft destroyers of this type were classed as Admiralty M and new two-shaft destroyers were to be known as Admiralty R class. In accordance with this directive REDMILL was renamed MEDINA and REDWING renamed MEDORA (On 18.7.16 REDWING was renamed MEDWAY instead). All of these vessels spent their war years in the GF, only four of them served elsewhere (in the Mediterranean for a few months 1917–18).

YARROW M CLASS

Avg 900 tons. 271½ (oa), 260½ (pp) ×26×9½ ft. Turbine 23000 shp=36 kts.
Armament: 3–4 in, 1–2 pdr, 4–21 in TT.

2.15	1.17	1.18	4.18	6.18	Name	Launched	Builder—Fate
H.C8	G.12	G.11	G.11	F.69	MOON	23. 4.15	Yarrow. Sold 9.5.21 Ward, Briton Ferry.
H.C9	G.13	G.12	G.18	H.48	MORNING STAR	26. 6.15	Yarrow. Sold 1.12.21 Stanlee.
H.0C	G.14		H.C0	G.1A	MOUNSEY	11. 9.15	Yarrow. Sold 8.11.21 Slough T. C.; BU in Germany.
H.1C	G.15		G.19	H.42	MUSKETEER	12.11.15	Yarrow. Sold 25.11.21 Hayes, Porthcawl.

9.15	1.17	1.18	6.18	Name	Launched	Builder—Fate
G.35	F.04	F.05	H.09	NERISSA	9. 2.16	Yarrow. Sold 15.11.21 Cashmore.
G.57	G.69			RELENTLESS	15. 4.16	Yarrow. Sold 5.11.26 Cashmore.
G.62	F.24	F.20	H.40	RIVAL	14. 6.16	Yarrow. Sold 13.7.26 Cashmore.
	G.79	G.92		SABRINA	24. 7.16	Yarrow. Sold 5.11.26 Cashmore.
	G.44			STRONGBOW	30. 9.16	Yarrow. Sunk 17.10.17 by BREMSE and BRUMMER in the North Sea.
	F.69 G.A4*	F.66		SURPRISE	25.11.16	Yarrow. Mined 23.12.17 in the North Sea.
	F.77	F.67		SYBILLE	5. 2.17	Yarrow. Sold 5.11.26 Cashmore.
	F.70	F.82		TRUCULENT	24. 3.17	Yarrow. Sold 29.4.27 Cashmore.
**F.90	G.07 G.06***	G.49		TYRANT	19. 5.17	Yarrow. Sold 4.38 Cashmore.
	F.83			ULLESWATER	4. 8.17	Yarrow. Sunk 15.8.18 by UC.17 off the Dutch Coast.

*Pendant assigned 23.1.17; **from 4.17; ***from 4.18.
Notes: M boats ordered 9.14; NERISSA ordered early 11.14; R boats in 5.15; S boats in 7.15; TU boats in 3.16. All served in the GF or Harwich Force from completion.

THORNYCROFT M CLASS

1004 tons (1033 tons last two). 274 (oa), 265 (pp) ×27½×10½ ft. Turbine 27500 shp=35 kts.
Armament: 3–4 in, 1–2 pdr, 4–21 in TT.

9.15	1.17	1.18	9.18	Name	Launched	Builder—Fate
G.48	F.23	F.15	G.A1	PATRICIAN	5. 6.16	Thornycroft. To RCN 9.20; BU 1929 at Esquimalt.
G.56	G.63		*	PATRIOT	20. 4.16	Thornycroft. To RCN 9.20; Sold 1929 Ward, Briton Ferry.
G.63	G.78	G.83		RAPID	15. 7.16	Thornycroft. Sold 20.4.27 Cohen.
G.71	G.87	G.84		READY	26. 8.16	Thornycroft. Sold 13.7.26 King, Garston.

*No pendant from 9.18.
Notes: First two ordered 2.15; others in 5.15. All served in the GF 1916–18.

EX-GREEK M CLASS

1007 tons (1040 last two). 273½ (oa), 265 (pp) ×26½×10 ft. Turbine 25000 shp=32 kts.
Armament: 3–4 in, 1–2 pdr, 4–21 in TT.

9.15	1.17	1.18	9.18	Name	Launched	Builder—Fate
H.9C	H.74			MEDEA	30. 1.15	John Brown. Sold 9.5.21 Ward, Milford Haven.
H.90				MEDUSA	27. 3.15	John Brown. Sunk 25.3.16 in collision with LAVEROCK in the North Sea.
H.44	H.75			MELAMPUS	16.12.14	Fairfield. Sold 22.9.21 Cohen; BU in Germany.
H.09		H.76	D.50	MELPOMENE	1. 2.15	Fairfield. Sold 9.5.21 Ward, New Holland.

Notes: Originally KRITI, LESVOS, CHIOS and SAMOS respectively; purchased in 8.14. All served at Harwich 1915–16; MEDEA in 10th S/M Flotilla, Tees 1916–18; MELPOMENE at Dover 1916–17, then in the Mediterranean and GF; MELAMPUS in 9th S/M Flotilla, Harwich 1916–18.

IMPROVED MARKSMAN CLASS LEADERS

1666 to 1687 tons.   325 (oa), 315 (pp) ×31¾×12 ft.   Turbine 36000 shp=34 kts.
Armament: 4–4 in, 4–21 in TT. (ABDIEL: 3–4 in, 70 mines).

9.15	1.17	1.18	4.18	Name	Launched	Builder—Fate
G.07	F.43	F.49		ABDIEL	12.10.15	Cammell Laird. Sold 7.36 Rees, Llanelly.
G.21	F.00		F.91*	GABRIEL	23.12.15	Cammell Laird. Sold 9.5.21 Ward, Lelant.
G.32	G.50	F.88		ITHURIEL	8. 3.16	Cammell Laird. Sold 8.11.21 Slough T. C.; BU in Germany.
G.61	G.85	G.75	G.95	GRENVILLE	17. 6.16	Cammell Laird. Sold 12.31 Rees, Llanelly.
G.49	G.71	G.95	G.75	PARKER	16. 8.16	Cammell Laird. Sold 5.11.21 Cashmore.
	G.90			HOSTE	16. 8.16	Cammell Laird. Sunk 21.12.16 in collision with NEGRO in the North Sea.
	G.3A	G.45	G.25	SAUMAREZ	14.10.16	Cammell Laird. Sold 8.1.31 Ward, Briton Ferry.
	G.00	G.20	G.00 D.09**	SEYMOUR	31. 8.16	Cammell Laird. Sold 7.1.30 Cashmore.
***F.61 ***G.60		G.50	G.70	ANZAC	11. 1.17	Denny. To RAN 3.19; Sold 8.8.35 Abrahams & Wilson, Redfern, NSW.

*Pendant from 9.18; **from 11.18; ***F.61 assigend 9.2.17, G.60 assigned 18.4.17.
Notes: The first three, ordered 11.14, had four funnels, others had three. GRENVILLE and PARKER ordered 2.15; next three, 7.15; ANZAC in 12.15. Original names for ABDIEL, GABRIEL, ITHURIEL and PARKER were ITHURIEL, ABDIEL, GABRIEL and FROBISHER respectively; renamed before launch. GABRIEL and SEYMOUR were used as minelayers in 8.18. ABDIEL served as minelayer GF 1916–18 and as Leader of 20th (M/L) DF, North Sea 1918. Others were leaders for GF Flotillas 1916–18; ITHURIEL attached to 13th S/M Flotilla 1917–18.

EX-PORTUGUESE

600 tons.   230 (pp)×22×7 ft.   Turbine 8000 shp=29 kts.
Armament: 4–14 pdr, 3–18 in TT.

9.15	1.18	Name	Launched	Builder—Fate
D.62	D.06	ARNO	22.12.14	Ansaldo, Genoa. Sunk 23.3.18 in collision with HOPE off the Dardanelles.

Notes: Portuguese LIZ purchased in 3.15 before completion. Served in the Mediterranean 1915–18.

TALISMAN CLASS

1098 tons.   309 (oa), 300 (pp)×28½×9½ ft.   Turbine shp=34 kts.
Armament: 5–4 in, 4–21 in TT.

9.15	1.17	1.18	6.18	Name	Launched	Builder—Fate
G.08	F.44	F.69	G.4A	TALISMAN	15. 7.15	Hawthorn Leslie. Sold 9.5.21 Ward, Grays.
G.24	F.47	F.73	D.36*	TERMAGANT	26. 8.15	Hawthorn Leslie. Sold 9.5.21 Ward, Briton Ferry.
G.36	F.50	F.81	D.38*	TRIDENT	20.11.15	Hawthorn Leslie. Sold 9.5.21 Ward, Grays.
G.42				TURBULENT	5. 1.16	Hawthorn Leslie. Sunk 1.6.16 at Jutland.

*Pendants from 9.18.
Notes: Ordered 11.14 from material prepared for four Turkish boats. Names originally chosen were NAPIER, NARBROUGH, OFFA and OGRE respectively; renamed 2.15. TURBULENT in GF 1916; others with S/M flotillas 1916–17, and Dover 1917–18.

ADMIRALTY R CLASS

Avg 1065 tons.   276 (oa), 265 (pp)×26¾×9 ft.   Turbine 27000 shp=36 kts.
Armament: 3–4 in, 1–2 pdr, 4–21 in TT.

1916	1.17	1.18	4.18	Name	Launched	Builder—Fate
G.79	G.76		G.81	RADSTOCK	3. 6.16	Swan Hunter. Sold 29.4.27 Ward, Grays.
G.81	G.86		G.82	RAIDER	17. 7.16	Swan Hunter. Sold 29.4.27 Geo. Cohen.
	F.63			RECRUIT	9.12.16	Doxford. Mined 9.8.17 in the North Sea.
F.58	F.51*	F.97		REDGAUNTLET	23.11.16	Denny. Sold 7.27 King, Garston.
	F.A4**					
	F.56	F.57		REDOUBT	28.10.16	Doxford. Sold 13.7.26 J. Smith.
	G.88	G.85		RESTLESS	12. 8.16	John Brown. Handed over 23.11.36 Ward, Briton Ferry.
	G.90	G.86		RIGOROUS	30. 9.16	John Brown. Sold 5.11.26 Cashmore.
	G.92	G.87		ROB ROY	29. 8.16	Denny. Sold 13.7.26 King, Garston.
	G.82	G.88		ROCKET	2. 7.16	Denny. Sold 16.12.26 Ward, Inverkeithing.

1916	1.17	1.18	4.18	Name	Launched	Builder—Fate
G.83		G.18	G.15	ROMOLA	14. 5.16	John Brown. Sold 13.3.30 King, Troon.
	G.81	G.90		ROWENA	1. 7.16	John Brown. Handed over 27.1.37 Ward, Milford Haven.
			G.91	SABLE	28. 6.16	White. Sold 8.27 Hughes Bolckow.
	G.94	G.93		SALMON =SABLE 12.33	7.10.16	Harland & Wolff, Govan. Handed over 28.1.37 Ward, Hayle.
	G.19		G.21 G.14†	SARPEDON	1. 6.16	Hawthorn Leslie. Sold 13.7.26 Alloa, Charlestown.
	F.79	F.60		SCEPTRE	18. 4.17	Stephen. Sold 16.12.26 Ward, Briton Ferry.
G.98	F.55			SETTER	18. 8.16	White. Sunk 17.5.17 in collision with SYLPH off Harwich.
	G.93	G.94		SORCERESS	29. 8.16	Swan Hunter. Sold 29.4.27 Ward, Inverkeithing.
	F.49	G.17	F.47	STURGEON	11. 1.17	Stephen. Sold 16.12.26 Plymouth & Devon S. Bkg Co, Plymouth.
	F.54	F.68		SYLPH	15.11.16	Harland & Wolff, Govan. Sold 16.12.26 Cashmore; stranded 28.1.27 and BU at Aberavon.
	F.51	F.59		SATYR	27.12.16	Beardmore. Sold 16.12.26 Ward, Milford Haven.
	F.48	F.61		SHARPSHOOTER	27. 2.17	Beardmore. Sold 29.4.27 Ward, Briton Ferry.
	F.57			SIMOOM	30.10.16	John Brown. Torpedoed 23.1.17 by German S.50 in the North Sea.
	F.62	G.05	F.46	SKATE	11. 1.17	John Brown. Sold 4.3.47; BU 7.47 Cashmore.
	F.78	F.62		SKILFUL	3. 2.17	Harland & Wolff, Govan. Sold 13.7.26 King, Garston.
	F.65	F.63		SPRINGBOK	9. 3.17	Harland & Wolff, Govan. Sold 16.12.26 Granton S. Bkg Co.
	F.60	F.04		STARFISH	27. 9.16	Hawthorn Leslie. Sold 21.4.28 Alloa, Charlestown.
	F.66	F.65		STORK	15.11.16	Hawthorn Leslie. Sold 7.10.27 Cashmore.
	F.85	G.08	G.07	TANCRED	30. 6.17	Beardmore. Sold 17.5.28 Cashmore; stranded and BU at Port Talbot.
	F.72	F.22	F.79†	TARPON	10. 3.17	John Brown. Sold 4.8.27 Cashmore.
	F.86	F.23	F.81†	TELEMACHUS	21. 4.17	John Brown. Sold 26.7.27 Hughes Bolckow.
	F.76	F.72		TEMPEST	26. 1.17	Fairfield. Handed over 28.1.37 Ward, Briton Ferry.
	F.96	G.02		TENACIOUS	21. 5.17	Harland & Wolff, Govan. Sold 26.6.28 Ward, Briton Ferry.
	F.87	F.74		TETRARCH	20. 4.17	Harland & Wolff, Govan. Sold 28.7.34 Metal Ind, Charlestown.
	F.82	F.75		THISBE	8. 3.17	Hawthorn Leslie. Handed over 31.8.36 Ward, Pembroke Dock.
	F.74	F.76		THRUSTER	10. 1.17	Hawthorn Leslie. Sold 1937 Ward, Grays.
	F.68	G.06	G.11	TORMENTOR	22. 5.17	Stephen. Sold 19.11.29 King, for Troon; wrecked in tow 13.12.29 off S. Wales.
	F.97	F.78		TORNADO	4. 8.17	Stephen. Mined 23.12.17 in North Sea.
	F.67	F.79		TORRENT	26.11.16	Swan Hunter. Mined 23.12.16 in N. Sea.
	F.75	F.80		TORRID	10. 2.17	Swan Hunter. Handed over 27.1.37 Ward for Hayle; wrecked 16.3.37 in tow near Falmouth.

*Pendant F.51 assigned 7.17; **F.A4 assigned 8.17; †from 9.18.

Notes: The first two were ordered in 5.15; next 17 ordered 7.15; next eight, 12.15; and TANCRED, etc. in 3.16. The Admiralty R class differed from the M type in that it had two shafts, geared turbines and the after 4 in in a bandstand. The six ships handed over to Messrs Ward were in part payment for the liner MAJESTIC which had been purchased for conversion to training ship CALEDONIA. TARPON and TELEMACHUS completed as minelayers (60 mines) per Admiralty order 12.1.17. All served with the Grand Fleet or the Harwich Force from completion.

THORNYCROFT R CLASS

1034 tons (1065 tons last two). 274 (oa), 265 (pp) ×27½×10 ft. Turbine 29000 shp=35 kts.
Armament: 3–4 in, 1–2 pdr, 4–21 in TT.

1.17	1.18	Name	Launched	Builder—Fate
F.59	F.56	RADIANT	25.11.16	Thornycroft. Sold 21.6.20 Thornycroft for resale to Siam; =PHRA RUANG 9.20.
F.64	F.58	RETRIEVER	15. 1.17	Thornycroft. Sold 26.7.27 Hughes Bolckow.
G.95	G.89	ROSALIND	14.10.16	Thornycroft. Sold 13.7.26 King, Garston.
F.71	F.70	TAURUS	10. 3.17	Thornycroft. Sold 18.2.30 Metal Ind, Charlestown.
F.93	F.71	TEAZER	21. 4.17	Thornycroft. Sold 6.2.31 Cashmore.

Notes: First three ordered 7.15; others in 12.15. ROSALIND served in GF; others in the Harwich Force.

MODIFIED R CLASS

Avg 1085 tons. 276 (oa), 265 (pp) ×27×11 ft. Turbine 27000 shp=36 kts.
Armament: 3–4 in, 1–2 pdr, 4–21 in TT.

1.17	1.18	4.18	Name	Launched	Builder—Fate
F.81	G.80		TIRADE	21. 4.17	Scotts. Sold 15.11.21 Cashmore.
F.98	F.24		TOWER	5. 4.17	Swan Hunter. Sold 17.5.28 Cashmore.
G.96	G.78		TRENCHANT	23.12.16	White. Sold 15.11.28 Plymouth & Devon S. Bkg Co.
F.89	F.25		TRISTRAM	24. 2.17	White. Sold 9.5.21 Ward, Briton Ferry.
F.91	F.17		ULSTER	10.10.17	Beardmore. Sold 4.28 Ward, Pembroke Dock.
F.80	G.96	G.77	ULYSSES	24. 3.17	Doxford. Sunk 29.10.18 in collision with SS ELLERIE in the Clyde.
F.94	F.26		UMPIRE	9. 6.17	Doxford. Sold 7.1.30 Metal Ind, Charlestown.
G.97		G.79	UNDINE	22. 3.17	Fairfield. Sold 4.28 Ward; wrecked off Horse Fort. Wreck sold 27.8.28 Middlesbrough Salvage Co.
F.95	F.04		URCHIN	7. 6.17	Palmer. Sold 7.1.30 Metal Ind, Charlestown.
	F.10		URSA	23. 7.17	Palmer. Sold 13.7.26 J. Smith.
F.88	F.84	F.01	URSULA	2. 8.17	Scotts. Sold 19.11.29 Cashmore.

Notes: Ordered in 3.16. All served in the Grand Fleet 1917–18.

SHAKESPEARE CLASS LEADERS

1750 tons. 329 (oa), 318 (pp) ×31½×12½ ft. Turbine 40000 shp=36 kts.
Armament: 5–4.7 in, 1–3 in AA, 6–21 in TT.

Pendant Nos.	Name	Launched	Builder—Fate
F.89 (1.18)	SHAKESPEARE	7. 7.17	Thornycroft. Handed over 2.9.36 Ward, Jarrow.
F.90 (1.18)	SPENSER	22. 9.17	Thornycroft. Handed over 29.9.36 Ward, Inverkeithing.
D.3A (2.19)	WALLACE	26.10.18	Thornycroft. Sold 20.3.45; BU Clayton & Davie.
D.84 (4.25)	KEPPEL	23. 4.20	Thornycroft. Sold 7.45; BU Ward, Barrow.
D.83 (12.24)	ROOKE =BROKE 4.21	16. 9.20	Thornycroft. Foundered 9.11.42 after damage at Algiers 8.11.42.

Notes: First two ordered 4.16; WALLACE, 4.17; others in 4.18. Four sisters from the final order were cancelled 12.18; BARRINGTON and HUGHES (both Cammell Laird), SAUNDERS and SPRAGGE (both Thornycroft). SHAKESPEARE and SPENSER served at Harwich 1917–18. Both vessels went to Messrs. Ward in part payment for MAJESTIC in 1936. KEPPEL and BROKE completed at Portsmouth and Pembroke DYs respectively.

SCOTT CLASS LEADERS

1800 tons. 332½ (oa), 320 (pp) ×32×12½ ft. Turbine 40000 shp=36 kts.
Armament: 5–4.7 in, 1–3 in AA, 6–21 in TT.

Pendant Nos.	Name	Launched	Builder—Fate
F.48 (6.18)	BRUCE	26. 2.18	Cammell Laird. Sunk 22.11.39 as target off the Isle of Wight.
G.76 (1.19)	CAMPBELL	21. 9.18	Cammell Laird. Sold 18.2.47; BU Metal Ind, Rosyth.
D.09 (9.18) G.00 (11.18)	DOUGLAS	8. 6.18	Cammell Laird. Sold 20.3.45; BU Ward, Inverkeithing.
F.A6 (6.19)	MACKAY	21.12.18	Cammell Laird. Sold 18.2.47; BU Metal Ind, Charlestown 6.49.
D.19 (11.19)	MALCOLM	29. 5.19	Cammell Laird. Sold 25.7.45; BU Ward, Barrow.
F.45 (9.18)	MONTROSE	10. 6.18	Hawthorn Leslie. Sold 31.1.46; BU Hughes Bolckow.
F.98 (1.18)	SCOTT	18.10.17	Cammell Laird. Sunk 15.8.18 by S/M (UC.17?) in the North Sea.
G.46 (2.19)	STUART	22. 8.18	Hawthorn Leslie. To RAN 10.33; Sold 3.2.47 T. Carr.

Notes: SCOTT ordered 4.16; BRUCE & DOUGLAS in 12.16; others 4.17. MACKAY was formerly CLAVERHOUSE, renamed by order 31.12.18. Four of these leaders served in the GF or at Harwich 1918.

ADMIRALTY V CLASS

Avg 1300 tons. 312 (oa), 300 (pp) ×29½×10½ ft. Turbine 27000=34 kts.
Armament: 4–4 in, 1–3 in AA, 4–21 in TT.

1917	1.18	4.18	Name	Launched	Builder—Fate
F.99	F.30		VALENTINE	24. 3.17	Cammell Laird. Bombed and stranded 15.5.40, mouth of the Schelde.
F.9A	G.25	G.45	VALHALLA	22. 5.17	Cammell Laird. Sold 17.12.31 Cashmore.
F.83	F.86	F.05*	VALKYRIE	13. 3.17	Denny. Handed over 24.8.36 Ward, Inverkeithing.
F.92	G.00	G.20	VALOROUS	8. 5.17	Denny. Sold 4.3.47; BU Stockton Ship & Salvage Co.
F.0A	G.70	G.50	VAMPIRE	21. 5.17	White. To RAN 10.33; Sunk 9.4.42 by A/C in Bay of Bengal.
		G.04 =VIMY 4.28	VANCOUVER	28.12.17	Beardmore. Sold 4.3.47; BU 2.48 at Charlestown.
		G.18†	VANESSA	16. 3.18	Beardmore. Sold 4.3.47; BU 2.49 at Charlestown.
	G.37†	G.19*	VANITY	3. 5.18	Beardmore. Sold 4.3.47; BU Brunton, Grangemouth.
F.8A	F.27	H.4A† F.84*	VANOC	14. 6.17	John Brown. Sold 26.7.45 for Ward, stranded 6.46 near Penryn; BU Falmouth.
F.3A	F.08	F.85* H.0A†	VANQUISHER	18. 8.17	John Brown. Sold 4.3.47; BU Metal Ind, Charlestown 1948.
F.A0	F.94	F.06	VECTIS	4. 9.17	White. Handed over 25.8.36 Ward, Inverkeithing.
F.4A	F.92	F.09	VEGA	1. 9.17	Doxford. Sold 4.3.47; BU 3.48 Clayton & Davie.
F.1A	F.12	H.2A†	VEHEMENT	6. 7.17	Denny. Mined 1.8.18 in the North Sea.
		H.43 D.40* G.65**	VELOX	17.11.17	Doxford. Sold 18.2.47; BU Metal Ind, Charlestown.
F.A3	F.29		VENDETTA	3. 9.17	Fairfield. To RAN 10.33; Scuttled 2.7.48 off Sydney.
F.9A	F.93	F.14	VENETIA	29.10.17	Fairfield. Mined 19.10.40 in the Thames estuary.
F.30	F.21	F.87*	VENTUROUS	21. 9.17	Denny. Handed over 24.8.36 Ward, Inverkeithing.
F.2A	F.91	F.16*	VERDUN	21. 8.17	Hawthorn Leslie. Sold 3.46; BU M. Brechin, Granton.
F.29	G.10		VERSATILE	31.10.17	Hawthorn Leslie. Sold 8.48; BU M. Brechin, Granton.
F.A2	F.96	F.19	VERULAM	3.10.17	Hawthorn Leslie. Mined 4.9.19 in Gulf of Finland.

1917	1.18	4.18	Name	Launched	Builder—Fate
		F.39	VESPER	15.12.17	Stephen. Sold 4.3.47; BU Ward, Inverkeithing.
		F.07†	VIDETTE	28. 2.18	Stephen. Sold 4.3.47; BU Brunton, Grangemouth.
		F.28	VIMIERA	22. 6.17	Swan Hunter. Mined 9.1.42 in the Thames estuary.
F.A1	F.95	F.31	VIOLENT	1. 9.17	Swan Hunter. Handed over 8.3.37 Ward, Inverkeithing.
	F.96	G.05 (10.18)	VITTORIA	29.10.17	Swan Hunter. Torpedoed 1.9.19 by Russian MTB in the Baltic.
F.32	G.71	G.01	VIVACIOUS	13.11.17	Yarrow. Sold 4.3.47; BU 10.48 Metal Ind, Charlestown.
		G.39†	VIVIEN	16. 2.18	Yarrow. Sold 18.2.47; BU 4.48 Metal Ind, Charlestown.
F.35	G.21	G.03	VORTIGERN	15.10.17	White. Torpedoed 15.3.42 by MTB off Cromer.

*Pendants from 9.18; **from 11.18; †from 6.18.

ADMIRALTY W CLASS

As V class, except: 6–21 in TT.

Pendant Nos.	Name	Launched	Builder—Fate
G.36 (6.18) G.16 (9.18)	VOYAGER	8. 5.18	Stephen. To RAN 10.33; Grounded 23.9.42, S. Timor and destroyed by crew.
F.37 (1.18)	WAKEFUL	6.10.17	John Brown. Torpedoed 29.5.40 by MTB off Dunkirk.
G.22 (1.18) G.08 (4.18)	WALKER	29.11.17	Denny. Sold 15.3.46; BU Arnott Young.
F.15 (9.18)	WALPOLE	12. 2.18	Doxford. Sold 8.2.45; BU Ward, Grays.
G.17 (4.18)	WALRUS	27.12.17	Fairfield. Stranded 12.2.38 in Filey Bay; Sold 5.3.38 T. Round, Scarborough; BU 10.38 Dunston.
H.38 (4.18)* G.96 (2.19)	WARWICK	28.12.17	Hawthorn Leslie. Sunk 20.2.44 by U.413 off North Cornwall.
G.23 (1.18) G.09 (4.18)	WATCHMAN	2.11.17	John Brown. Sold 23.7.45; BU Ward, Inverkeithing.
G.28 (9.18)	WATERHEN	26. 3.18	Palmer. To RAN 10.33; Foundered 30.6.41 off Sollum after bomb damage.
F.32 (6.18)	WESSEX	12. 3.18	Hawthorn Leslie. Sunk 24.5.40 by A/C off Calais.
F.03 (4.18)	WESTCOTT	14. 2.18	Denny. Sold 8.1.46; BU Arnott Young.
F.02 (4.18)	WESTMINSTER	24. 2.18	Scotts. Sold 4.3.47; BU 8.48 Metal Ind.
H.41 (4.18) D.25 (9.18) G.73 (11.18)	WHIRLWIND	15.12.17	Swan Hunter. Sunk 5.7.40 by U.34 SW of Ireland.
F.20 (11.18)	WHITLEY	13. 4.18	Doxford. Bombed and beached 19.5.40, Belgian Coast.
F.40 (4.18)	WINCHELSEA	15.12.17	White. Sold 20.3.45; BU Rosyth.
G.43 (4.18)	WINCHESTER	1. 2.18	White. Sold 5.3.46; BU Ward, Inverkeithing.
F.12 (9.18)	WINDSOR	21. 6.18	Scotts. Sold 4.3.47; BU 6.49 Metal Ind, Charlestown.
F.18 (4.18)	WOLFHOUND	14. 3.18	Fairfield. Sold 18.2.48, BU M. Brechin, Granton.
G.31 (6.18)	WRESTLER	25. 2.18	Swan Hunter. Sold 20.7.44; BU Cashmore.
G.05 (11.18)	WRYNECK	13. 5.18	Palmer. Sunk 27.4.41 by A/C off Greece.

*Pendant cancelled 9.18.

Notes, V and W classes: The first five Vs were ordered 4.16 as leaders and were originally to have been named BRUCE, DOUGLAS, MALCOLM, MONTROSE and WALLACE respectively: renamed 9.16. 23 Vs were ordered in 7.16 and 21 Ws (including VOYAGER) were ordered 12.16. WAYFARER and WOODPECKER ordered from Yarrow 12.16 were cancelled 4.17 and replaced by two S class orders. VALENTINE, VALOROUS, VANCOUVER, VANOC, VANQUISHER, VEHEMENT and VENTUROUS were fitted to carry 60 mines by Admiralty order 12.1.17. The five original Vs served as leaders in the GF 1917–18. The other Vs and Ws were in the GF or Harwich Force. The V class was fitted with 5 TT in 1921 and 6 TT from 1923. Four vessels went to Ward in part replacement of the MAJESTIC.

THORNYCROFT V & W CLASS

1325 tons. 312 (oa), 300 (pp) ×30½×11 ft. Turbine 30000 shp=35 kts.
Armament: 4–4 in, 1–3 in AA, 6–21 in TT.

F.99 (1.18)	VICEROY	17.11.17	Thornycroft. Sold 6.48; BU at Granton.
F.38 (4.18) G.24 (4.18)	VISCOUNT	29.12.17	Thornycroft. Sold 20.3.45; BU 5.47 Clayton & Davie.
G.40 (6.18)	WOLSEY	16. 3.18	Thornycroft. Sold 4.3.47; BU Young; Sunderland.
F.08 (6.18)	WOOLSTON	27. 4.18	Thornycroft. Sold 18.2.47; BU Brunton, Grangemouth.

Notes: First pair ordered 7.16; second pair 12.16. All served in the GF 1918.

ADMIRALTY S CLASS

Avg 1075 tons. 276 (oa), 265 (pp) ×27×11 ft. Turbine 27000 shp=36 kts.
Armament: 3–4 in, 1–2 pdr, 4–21 in TT. (also 2–14 in TT, removed 1918).

Pendant Nos.	Name	Launched	Builder—Fate
G.56 (11.18)	SABRE	23. 9.18	Stephen. Sold 11.45; BU Brunton, Grangemouth.
F.0A (4.19)	SALADIN	17. 2.19	Stephen. Sold 29.6.47; BU Rees, Llanelly.
G.41 (4.18)	SCIMITAR	27. 2.18	John Brown. Sold 29.6.47; BU Ward, Briton Ferry.
G.30 (6.18)	SCOTSMAN	30. 3.18	John Brown. Handed over 13.7.37 Ward, Briton Ferry.
G.35 (6.18)	SCOUT	27. 4.18	John Brown. Arrived 2.3.46 Ward, Briton Ferry to BU.
G.36 (6.18) D.44 (9.18)	SENATOR	2. 4.18	Denny. Handed over 7.9.36 Ward, Jarrow.
G.26 (9.18)	SEPOY	22. 5.18	Denny. Sold 2.7.32 Cashmore.
G.60 (12.18)	SERAPH	8. 7.18	Denny. Sold 5.34 Ward, Pembroke Dock.
F.50 (8.19)	SHAMROCK	26. 8.18	Doxford. Handed over 23.11.36 Ward, Milford Haven.
F.A1 (1919)	SHARK	9. 4.18	Swan Hunter. Sold 5.2.31 Ward, Inverkeithing.
D.85 (1924)	SHIKARI	14. 7.19	Doxford. Arrived 4.11.45 Cashmore to BU.
H.94 (6.18) D.68	SIKH	7. 5.18	Fairfield. Sold 26.7.27 Granton S. Bkg Co.
G.44 (4.18)	SIMOOM	26. 1.18	John Brown. Sold 8.1.31 Metal Ind, Charlestown.
G.27 (11.18)	SIRDAR	6. 7.18	Fairfield. Sold 4.5.34 Cashmore.
G.52 (11.18)	SOMME	10. 9.18	Fairfield. Sold 25.8.32 Ward, Pembroke Dock.
G.53 (11.18)	SPARROWHAWK	14. 5.18	Swan Hunter. Sold 5.2.31 Ward, Grays.
G.57 (11.18)	SPLENDID	10. 7.18	Swan Hunter. Sold 8.1.31 Metal Ind, Charlestown.
F.99 (3.19)	STEADFAST	8. 8.18	Palmer. Sold 28.7.34 Metal Ind, Charlestown.
F.A3 (3.19)	STERLING	8.10.18	Palmer. Sold 25.8.32 Rees, Llanelly.
F.1A (4.19)	SUCCESS	29. 6.18	Doxford. To RAN 6.19; Sold 4.6.37 Penguins Ltd, Sydney.
F.73 (11.18)	SWALLOW	1. 8.18	Scotts. Handed over 24.9.36 Ward, Inverkeithing.
F.3A (3.19)	SWORDSMAN	28.12.18	Scotts. To RAN 6.19; Sold 4.6.37. Penguins Ltd, Sydney.
F.9A (1919)	TRIBUNE	28. 3.18	White. Sold 17.12.31 Cashmore.
G.38 (9.18)	TRINIDAD	8. 4.18	White. Sold 16.2.32 Ward, Inverkeithing.
F.34 (6.19)	SARDONYX	27. 5.19	Stephen. BU 10.45 Ward, Preston.
G.32 (9.18)	SCYTHE	25. 4.18	John Brown. Sold 28.11.31 Cashmore.
G.29 (11.18)	SEABEAR	6. 7.18	John Brown. Sold 5.2.31 Ward, Grays.
G.68 (11.18)	SEAFIRE	10. 8.18	John Brown. Handed over 14.9.36 Ward, Inverkeithing.
G.72 (11.18)	SEARCHER	11. 9.18	John Brown. Sold 25.3.38 Ward, Barrow.
G.47 (2.19)	SEAWOLF	2.11.18	John Brown. Sold 23.2.31 Cashmore.
F.21 (2.19)	SERAPIS	17. 9.18	Denny. Sold 25.1.34 Rees, Llanelly.
F.7A (5.19)	SERENE	30.11.18	Denny. Handed over 14.9.36 Ward, Inverkeithing.
F.5A (4.19)	SESAME	30.12.18	Denny. Sold 4.5.34 Cashmore.
G.55 (12.18)	SPEAR	9.11.18	Fairfield. Sold 13.7.26 Alloa, Charlestown.

Pendant Nos.	Name	Launched	Builder—Fate
G.21 (4.19)	SPINDRIFT	30.12.18	Fairfield. Sold 7.36 Ward, Inverkeithing.
G.48 (1.19)	SPORTIVE	19. 9.18	Swan Hunter. Handed over 25.9.36 Ward, Inverkeithing.
F.4A (4.19)	STALWART	23.10.18	Swan Hunter. To RAN 6.19; Sold 4.6.37 Penguins Ltd, Sydney.
G.99 (8.19)	STONEHENGE	19. 3.19	Palmer. Wrecked 6.11.20 near Smyrna.
D.89 (1.20)	STORMCLOUD	30. 5.19	Palmer. Sold 28.7.34 Metal Ind, Charlestown.
G.64 (1.19)	STRENUOUS	9.11.18	Scotts. Sold 25.8.32 Alloa, Charlestown.
F.A8 (6.19)	STRONGHOLD	6. 5.19	Scotts. Sunk 4.3.42 in action South of Java.
F.96 (1919)	STURDY	25. 6.19	Scotts. Wrecked 30.10.40 on Tiree.
G.54 (11.18)	TACTICIAN	7. 8.18	Beardmore. Sold 2.31 Metal Ind, Charlestown.
G.62 (11.18)	TARA	12.10.18	Beardmore. Sold 17.12.31 Rees, Llanelly.
G.97 (2.19)	TASMANIA	22.11.18	Beardmore. To RAN 6.19; Sold 4.6.37 Penguins Ltd, Sydney.
F.2A (4.19)	TATTOO	28.12.18	Beardmore. To RAN 6.19; Sold 9.1.37 Penguins Ltd, Sydney.
F.A4 (6.19)	TENEDOS	21.10.18	Hawthorn Leslie. Sunk 5.4.42 by Japanese A/C off Colombo.
G.24 (8.19)	THANET	5.11.18	Hawthorn Leslie. Sunk 27.1.42 in action off Malaya.
G.A4 (1920)	THRACIAN	5. 3.20	Hawthorn Leslie. Run ashore 24.12.41 at Hong Kong; became Japanese No. 101 in 9.42; returned to RN 9.45; BU 1947.
G.37 (9.18)	TILBURY	13. 6.18	Swan Hunter. Sold 2.31 Rees, Llanelly.
G.51 (12.18)	TINTAGEL	9. 8.18	Swan Hunter. Sold 16.2.32 Castle Plymouth.
G.66 (11.18)	TROJAN	20. 7.18	White. Handed over 24.9.36 Ward, Inverkeithing.
G.23 (3.19)	TRUANT	18. 9.18	White. Sold 28.11.31 Rees, Llanelly.
F.A2 (5.19)	TRUSTY	6.11.18	White. Handed over 25.9.36 Ward, Inverkeithing.
F.55 (10.19)	TURBULENT	29. 5.19	Hawthorn Leslie. Handed over 25.8.36 Ward, Inverkeithing.
D.92 (11.19)			

Notes: 24 were ordered 4.17; 33 in 6.17. Two boats were cancelled from the second order, SATURN and SYCAMORE (both Stephen), in 1919. 20 of this class were completed before 11.18 and served in the GF, Harwich or in the Mediterranean. Ten vessels were given to Ward as part replacement of the MAJESTIC in 1936.

THORNYCROFT S CLASS

1087 tons. 276 (oa), 267 (pp) ×27½×10½ ft. Turbine 29000 shp=36 kts.
Armament: 3–4 in, 1–2 pdr, 4–2 1in TT.

Pendant Nos.	Name	Launched	Builder—Fate
G.36 (9.18)	SPEEDY	1. 6.18	Thornycroft. Sunk 24.9.22 in collision with a merchant ship, Sea of Marmora.
G.61 (11.18)	TOBAGO	15. 7.18	Thornycroft. Sold 9.2.22 at Malta after being mined 12.11.20.
F.35 (6.19)	TORBAY =CHAMPLAIN 3.28	6. 3.19	Thornycroft. To RCN 3.28; BU 1937.
F.6A (4.19)	TOREADOR =VANCOUVER 3.28	7.12.18	Thornycroft. To RCN 3.28; BU 1937.
D.83 (12.19)	TOURMALINE	12. 4.19	Thornycroft. Sold 28.11.31 Ward, Grays.

Notes: The first two were ordered 4.17; served in the GF 1918. Last three ordered 6.17.

YARROW S CLASS

930 tons. 273½ (oa), 260 (pp) ×26×10 ft. Turbine 23000 shp=36 kts.
Armament: 3–4 in, 1–2 pdr, 4–21 in TT.

Pendant Nos.	Name	Launched	Builder—Fate
G.34 (6.18)	TOMAHAWK	16. 5.18	Yarrow. Sold 26.6.28 Ward; resold 8.28 J. King.
G.33 (6.18)	TORCH	16. 3.18	Yarrow. Sold 19.11.29 J. King.
G.42 (11.18)	TRYPHON	22. 6.18	Yarrow. Sold 27.9.20 at Malta after stranding 4.5.19.
G.58 (11.18)	TUMULT	17. 9.18	Yarrow. Sold 3.10.28 Alloa, Charlestown.
G.22 (3.19)	TURQUOISE	9.11.18	Yarrow. Sold 1.32 Alloa, Charlestown.
F.A5 (6.19)	TUSCAN	1. 3.19	Yarrow. Sold 25.8.32 Metal Ind, Charlestown.
D.84 (12.19)	TYRIAN	2. 7.19	Yarrow. Sold 2.30 Metal Ind, Charlestown.

Notes: Ordered 4.17. TOMAHAWK and TORCH were built in place of two W class (WOODPECKER & WAYFARER) previously ordered. The first three of this class served in the GF 1918.

ADMIRALTY MODIFIED W CLASS

Avg 1325 tons. 312 (oa), 300 (pp) ×29½×11 ft. Turbine 27000 shp=34 kts.
Armament. 4–4.7 in, 2–2 pdr, 6–21 in TT.

Pendant Nos.	Name	Launched	Builder—Fate
D.64 (11.19)	VANSITTART	17. 4.19	Beardmore. Sold 25.2.46; BU Cashmore.
G.98 (6.19)	VENOMOUS (ex-Venom 4.19)	21.12.18	John Brown. Sold 4.3.47; BU Metal Ind, Charlestown.
F.36 (9.19)	VERITY	19. 3.19	John Brown. Sold 4.3.47; BU Cashmore.
D.71 (11.19)	VOLUNTEER	17. 4.19	Denny. Sold 4.3.47; BU M. Brechin, Granton 4.48.
D.74 (9.19)	WANDERER	1. 5.19	Fairfield. Sold 31.1.46; BU Hughes Bolckow.
D.94 (7.24)	WHITEHALL	11. 9.19	Swan Hunter. Sold 10.45; BU Ward, Barrow.
D.88 (2.23)	WREN	11.11.19	Yarrow. Sunk 27.7.40 by A/C off Aldeburgh.
D.72 (11.19)	VETERAN	26. 4.19	John Brown. Sunk 26.9.42 by U.404 in the North Atlantic.
F.A7 (7.19)	WHITSHED	31. 1.19	Swan Hunter. Sold 18.2.47; BU King, Gateshead 4.48.
D.62 (11.19)	WILD SWAN	17. 5.19	Swan Hunter. Sunk 17.6.42 in action, Bay of Biscay.
D.76 (10.19)	WITHERINGTON	16. 4.19	White. Sold 20.3.47 for Metal Ind; wrecked 29.4.47 in tow to Tyne.
D.66 (12.19)	WIVERN	16. 4.19	White. Sold 18.2.47; BU Metal Ind, Charlestown.
D.78 (7.20)	WOLVERINE	17. 7.19	White. Sold 1.46; BU Troon.
D 96 (9.22)	WORCESTER =YEOMAN 1945	24.10.19	White. Base ship 1945; BU 9.46 Ward, Grays.

Notes: The first seven ships above, along with cancellations marked * were ordered 1.18; 38 others in 4.18.
19 vessels were cancelled by Admiralty order 26.11.18: VASHON, VENGEFUL, VIMY (ex-Vantage 8.19)* all Beardmore; VIGO, VIRULENT, VOLAGE, VOLCANO, WISTFUL (ex-Vigorous 6.18) all John Brown; WAKE, WALDEGRAVE, WALTON, WHITAKER all Denny; WAVE, WEAZEL, WHITE BEAR all Fairfield; WELLESLEY, Hawthorn Leslie; WHIP, WHIPPET, Scotts; and WINTER, Swan Hunter.
13 cancelled by Admiralty order 12.4.19: VOTARY*, WAGER, Denny; WELCOME*, WELFARE*, Hawthorn Leslie; WESTPHAL, WESTWARD HO, White; WHELER, Scotts; WHITEHEAD*, WILLOUGHBY, Swan Hunter; and YEOMAN, ZEALOUS, ZEBRA, ZODIAC all Yarrow.
Cancelled 9.19: WARREN*, Chatham DY ex-Fairfield; WATSON, Devonport DY ex-Fairfield; WHELP, Pembroke DY ex-Scotts; WRANGLER, WEREWOLF (launched 17.7.19), both White; and WYE*, Yarrow.
Machinery of WAVE was transferred to WEREWOLF 11.18. WHITEHALL was completed at Chatham DY and WREN at Pembroke DY.
WESTPHAL, WESTWARD HO, WEREWOLF were originally ordered from Hawthorn Leslie.

THORNYCROFT MODIFIED W CLASS

1345 tons. 312 (oa), 300 (pp) ×30½×11 ft. Turbine 27000 shp=34 kts.
Armament: 4–4.7 in, 2–2 pdr, 6–21 in TT.

Pendant Nos.	Name	Launched	Builder—Fate
D.67 (11.19)	WISHART	18. 7.19	Thornycroft. Sold 20.3.45; BU Ward, Inverkeithing.
G.A6 (1920)	WITCH	11.11.19	Thornycroft. Sold 7.46; BU Rosyth.

Notes: Ordered 1.18. WITCH completed at Devonport DY in 3.24.

TORPEDO BOATS

The first torpedo boat, so called, was a slow steam vessel named VESUVIUS (see harbour service list). She was launched 24.3.1874 at Pembroke Dockyard and spent her lifetime on training duties. Following her came 117 faster vessels from 1877 (TB.1) to 1904 (TB.117). These boats were in turn followed by 36 larger boats added 1906–1909 numbered TB.1–36 and older boats which had numbers up to 79 were then renumbered, taking the cypher "O" before their old numbers; TB.79 thus becoming TB.079. The red burgee was sometimes hoisted singly to denote a torpedo boat and after 15.4.16 the red burgee hoisted superior to boat numbers served as TB pendant numbers. The size and endurance of the TBs limited their wartime activity to participation with local defence patrol flotillas where base and depot ship support was available.

CHILDERS (RAN)
65 tons.   113 (pp) × 12½ × 6ft.   TE 730 ihp = 20 kts.
Armament: 2–1 pdr.
Built by Thornycroft, Chiswick 1883; Served as tender to CERBERUS at Williamstown. Sold 5.8.18 and used as a hulk.

TB.025–027, 029
60 tons.   125¼ (pp) × 12½ × 6 ft.   TE 600 ihp = 21 kts.
Armament: 4–14 in TT.
All built by Thornycroft 1886:
TB.025, 026, 027 all sold 2.10.19 Maden & McKee.
TB.029 sold 1.7.19 Runciman Walker, Capetown.
The first three served at Portsmouth and TB.029 at the Cape.

TB.034–038
63 tons.   125 (pp) × 14½ × 4 ft.   TE 950 ihp = 20 kts.
Armament: 5–14 in TT.
All built by White 1886:
TB.034 sold 2.10.19 Maden & McKee.
TB.035, 036, 037, 038 all sold 27.11.19 at Hong Kong.
Notes: TB.034 served in the Portsmouth LD Flotilla and the others at Hong Kong.

TB.041–046, 048–050, 052, 054–055, 057–058, 060
60 tons.   127½ (pp) × 12½ × 6 ft.   TE 700 ihp = 21 kts.
Armament: 2–3 pdr, 4–14 in TT.
All built by Thornycroft 1886:
TB.041 sold 1.8.19 Multilocular S. Bkg Co, Stranraer.
TB.042, 057 sold 2.10.19 Maden & McKee.
TB.043, 044 sold 8.12.19 at Malta.
TB.045, 054 sold 1.8.19 T. R. Sales.
TB.046 wrecked in tow 27.12.15 Eastern Mediterranean; salved & BU 1920.
TB.048 sold c1915.
TB.049 sold 1.8.19 Hayes, Porthcawl.
TB.050, 055 sold 23.2.20 R. Longmate.
TB.052, 058 sold 19.12.19 Multilocular S Bkg Co, Stranraer.
TB.060 sold 1.7.19 Runciman Walker, Capetown.
Notes: TB.043 and 044 served in the Mediterranean; TB.060 at the Cape; the others were in LD Flotillas at Portsmouth, Devonport, Pembroke and Queenstown.

TB.063–068, 070–074, 076–079
75 tons.   125 (pp) × 13 × 5½ ft.   TE 700 ihp = 19½ kts.
Armament: 2–3 pdr, 5–14 in TT.   (TB.079: 1000 ihp = 22½ kts)
All built by Yarrow 1886:
TB.063, 070 sold 18.12.19 at Malta.
TB.064 wrecked 21.3.15 in the Aegean Sea.
TB.065, 078 sold 2.10.19 Maden & McKee.
TB.066, 068, 076 sold 30.6.20 Ward, Hayle.
TB.067, 074 sold 27.1.20 Willoughby (Plymouth) Ltd.
TB.071 sold 5.7.23 B. Newton.
TB.072 sold 19.12.19 Ward, Rainham.
TB.073 sold 6.2.23 L. Basso, Weymouth.
TB.077 sold 27.3.20 Stanlee.
TB.079 sold 19.12.19 Ward, Grays.
Notes: TB.063, 064 and 070 were in the Mediterranean; the others were in LD Flotillas at Portsmouth, Devonport or at the Nore.

TB.80

105 tons. 135 (pp) × 14 × 6 ft. TE 1540 ihp = 23 kts.
Armament: 4–3 pdr, 5–14 in TT.
Built by Yarrow 1887. Served at Portsmouth and Portland; Sold 1921 Stanlee; resold 22.10.21 J. E. Thomas.

TB.81

125 tons. 154 (oa) × 17½ × 6 ft.
Armament: 6–3 pdr, 3–14 in TT.
Ex-Swift, built by White 1885 and purchased. Served at Portsmouth and Portland. Sold along with TB.80.

TB.82, 83, 85–87

85 tons. 130 (pp) × 13½ × 5½ ft. TE 1100 ihp = 23 kts.
Armament: 3–3 pdr, 3–14 in TT.
All built by Yarrow 1889:
TB.82, 85, 86 all sold 1921 Stanlee; resold 22.10.21 J. E. Thomas.
TB.83 sold 13.10.19 Messrs Brand.
TB.87 sold 27.3.20 Stanlee.

COUNTESS OF HOPETOUN (RAN)

75 tons. 130 (pp) × 13½ × 6 ft. TE 1150 ihp = 23 kts.
Armament: 3–3 pdr, 3–14 in TT.
Built 1891 by Yarrow; Sold 4.24 J. Hill, Melbourne, BU 1925. Was a gunnery school tender.

TB.88–90

112 tons (TB.90; 100 tons). 142 (pp) × 14 × 4 ft.
Armament: 3–3 pdr, 3–14 in TT.
All built by Yarrow 1894–95:
TB.88, 89 both sold 13.10.19 Messrs Brand.
TB.90 Capsized 25.4.18 off Gibraltar.
Notes: All three served at Gibraltar 1914–18.

TB.91 CLASS

130 tons. 140 (pp) × 15½ × 7½ ft. TE 2400 ihp = 23½ kts.
Armament: 3–3 pdr, 3–14 in TT.

Name	Launched	Builder—Fate
TB.91	1894	Thornycroft. Sold 13.10.19 Messrs Brand.
TB.92	1894	Thornycroft. Sold 1920 at Gibraltar.
TB.93	1893	Thornycroft. Sold 13.10.19 Messrs Brand.
TB.94	27. 7.93	White. Sold 13.10.19 Messrs Brand.
TB.95	1894	White. Sold 13.10.19 Messrs Brand.
TB.96	1894	White. Sunk 1.11.15 in collision with SS TRINGA off Gibraltar.
TB.97	16. 9.93	Laird. Sold 1920 at Gibraltar.

Notes: All served at Gibraltar 1914–18.

TB.98 CLASS

178 tons. 160 (pp) × 17 × 8 ft. TE 2850 ihp = 25 kts.
Armament: 3–3 pdr, 3–14 in TT.

Name	Launched	Builder—Fate
TB.98	22. 1.01	Thornycroft. Sold 30.6.20 Ward, Preston.
TB.99	1901	Thornycroft. Sold 29.7.20 Ward, Preston.
TB.107	1901	Thornycroft. Sold 29.7.20 Ward, Morecambe.
TB.108	30. 8.01	Thornycroft. Sold 29.7.20 Willoughby (Plymouth) Ltd.

Notes: All served in LDFs at Portsmouth and Devonport.

EX-INDIAN TBs

92 tons (TB.101) 135 (oa), 130 (pp) ×14×7 ft. TE 1060 ihp=21 kts (TB.101).
95 tons (others). TE 1030 ihp=20 kts (others).
Armament: 5–14 in TT.

TB.101 (*ex-No. 7 Ghurka*)	1888	McArthur, Paisley. Sold 27.3.20 Stanlee.
TB.104 (*ex-No' 4 Mahratta*)	1889	White. Sold 29.7.20 Willoughby (Plymouth) Ltd.
TB.105 (*ex-No. 5 Sikh*)	1889	White. Sold 27.1.20 Willoughby (Plymouth) Ltd.

Notes: Survivors of a group of seven TBs formerly in the Royal Indian Marine, they were renumbered 1901 (TB.100–106 series). All served in LDFs at Portsmouth or Devonport during the war.

TB. 109 CLASS

200 tons. 166 (pp) ×17×8 ft. TE 2900 ihp=25 kts.
Armament: 3–3 pdr, 3–14 in TT.

TB.109	22. 7.02	Thornycroft. Sold 27.3.20 Stanlee.
TB.110	5. 9.02	Thornycroft. Sold 27.3.20 Stanlee.
TB.111	31.10.02	Thornycroft. Sold 10.2.20 Ward, Grays.
TB.112	15. 1.03	Thornycroft. Sold 10.2.20 Ward, Grays.
TB.113	12. 2.03	Thornycroft. Sold 19.12.19 Ward, Grays.

Notes: War service in LDFs at the Nore and Portsmouth.

TB.114 CLASS

205 tons. 165 (pp) ×17½×8½ ft. TE 2900 ihp=25 kts.
Armament: 3–3 pdr, 3–14 in TT.

TB.114	8. 6.03	White. Sold 1919 Ward, Grays, later to Rainham.
TB.115	19.11.03	White. Sold 1919 Ward, Rainham.
TB.116	21.12.03	White. Sold 22.10.21 J. E. Thomas, Newport.
TB.117	18. 2.04	White. Sunk 10.6.17 in collision with SS KAMOURASKA in the Channel.

Notes: Served in LDFs at the Nore and Portsmouth. Lighter No. 80 "*ex-TB.117*" sold 31.3.21 to W. T. Beaumont may have been the same vessel as above.

EX-COASTAL DESTROYERS

TB.1–12 CLASS

225 to 255 tons. 175 (oa), 167 (pp) × 17½ × 6 ft. Turbine 3750 shp = 26¼ kts.
Armament: 2–12 pdr, 3–18 in TT.

Name		Launched	Builder—Fate
TB.1	(ex-*Cricket*)	23. 1.06	White. Sold 7.10.20 Fowey Coaling & Ship Co.
TB.2	(ex-*Dragonfly*)	11. 3.06	White. Sold 7.10.20 Ward.
TB.3	(ex-*Firefly*)	1. 9.06	White. Sold 7.10.20 Ward.
TB.4	(ex-*Sandfly*)	30.10.06	White. Sold 7.10.20 Ward; Stranded 11.1.21 near Westward Ho; BU 1921.
TB.5	(ex-*Spider*)	15.12.06	White. Sold 7.10.20 Ward.
TB.6	(ex-*Gadfly*)	24. 6.06	Thornycroft. Sold 22.10.20 Stanlee.
TB.7	(ex-*Glowworm*)	20.12.06	Thornycroft. Sold 9.5.21 Ward, Rainham.
TB.8	(ex-*Gnat*)	1.12.06	Thornycroft. Sold 9.5.21 Ward, Rainham.
TB.9	(ex-*Grasshopper*)	18. 3.07	Thornycroft. Sunk 26.7.16 in collision, N. Sea.
TB.10	(ex-*Greenfly*)	15. 2.07	Thornycroft. Mined 10.6.15 in the North Sea.
TB.11	(ex-*Mayfly*)	29. 1.07	Yarrow. Mined 7.3.16 in the North Sea.
TB.12	(ex-*Moth*)	15. 3.07	Yarrow. Mined 10.6.15 in the North Sea.

TB.13–36 CLASS

256 to 306 tons. 185 (oa), 177 (pp) × 18 × 6½ ft. Turbine 4000 shp = 26 kts.
Armament: 2–12 pdr, 3–18 in TT.

	Launched	Builder—Fate
TB.13	10. 7.07	White. Sunk 26.1.16 in collision, North Sea.
TB.14	26. 9.07	White. Sold 7.10.20 Philip, Dartmouth (still there as a jetty).
TB.15	19.11.07	White. Sold 7.10.20 Ward.
TB.16	23.12.07	White. Sold 7.10.20 Ward.
TB.17	21.12.07	Denny. Sold 1919 at Gibraltar.
TB.18	15. 2.08	Denny. Sold 1920 at Gibraltar.
TB.19	7.12.07	Thornycroft, Chiswick. Sold 9.5.21 Ward, Grays.
TB.20	21. 1.08	Thornycroft, Chiswick. Sold 9.5.21 Ward, Grays.
TB.21	20.12.07	Hawthorn Leslie. Sold 7.10.20 Maden & McKee; resold 8.24 Hayes, Porthcawl.
TB.22	1. 2.08	Hawthorn Leslie. Sold 7.10.20 Maden & McKee; resold 8.24 Hayes, Porthcawl.
TB.23	5.12.07	Yarrow. Sold 9.5.21 Ward, Grays.
TB.24	19. 3.08	Palmer. Wrecked 28.1.17 off Dover breakwater.
TB.25	28. 7.08	White. Sold 9.5.21 Ward, Grays.
TB.26	28. 8.08	White. Sold 9.5.21 Ward, Rainham.
TB.27	29. 9.08	White. Sold 9.5.21 Ward, Rainham.
TB.28	29.10.08	White. Sold 9.5.21 Ward, Rainham.
TB.29	29. 8.08	Denny. Sold 28.11.19 at Malta.
TB.30	29. 9.08	Denny. Sold 28.11.19 at Malta.
TB.31	10.10.08	Thornycroft. Sold 9.5.21 Ward, Rainham.
TB.32	23.11.08	Thornycroft. Sold 9.5.21 Ward, Rainham.
TB.33	22. 2.09	Hawthorn Leslie. Sold 24.8.22 Cashmore.
TB.34	22. 2.09	Hawthron Leslie. Sold 9.5.21 Ward, Rainham.
TB.35	19. 4.09	Palmer. Sold 24.8.22 Cashmore
TB.36	6. 5.09	Palmer. Sold 9.5.21 Ward, Rainham.

Notes: The first twelve boats were re-classified TBs and renamed in 1906. These 36 boats were in North Sea Patrol Flotillas or in the Nore LDF 1914–18; TBs 17, 18, 29 and 30 were in the Mediterranean 1918.

SUBMARINES

The Irish-born American, John P. Holland, had built seven submarines between 1896 and 1901 for the U.S. Navy, and based on this design, five (Nos. 1–5) were built in 1901 by Messrs. Vickers for the RN. These were followed by the A class, listed below. Both surface and submerged tonnages and propulsion figures are included in class descriptions that follow. Submarines carried I flag superior pendant numbers from 1914 (last listed 24.4.15), which were replaced in mid 1915 by their class letter and number. The I pendants were painted up on conning towers omitting the flag superior. From about 9.15, when pendants matched the boat names, the full name appeared on conning towers and was used on flag hoists.

A CLASS

165/180 tons (1st two), 180/207 tons (others).
100 (oa) × 11½ × 10 ft (1st two), 94 (oa) × 13 × 10 ft (others).
Petrol motors/electric: 450/150 HP (A.2–4) = 11/7 kts, 550/150 HP (others) = 11½/7 kts.
Armament: 2–18 in TT

Pendants	Name	Launched	Builder—Fate
	A.2	16. 4.03	Vickers. Wrecked 1.20 in Bomb Ketch Lake, Portsmouth; Sold 22.10.25 Pounds, Portsmouth.
	A.4	9. 6.03	Vickers. Sold 16.1.20 J. H. Lee, Bembridge.
I.15	A.5	3. 3.04	Vickers. BU 1920 at Portsmouth DY.
I.16	A.6	3. 3.04	Vickers. Sold 16.1.20 J. H. Lee, Bembridge.
I.18	A.8	23. 1.05	Vickers. Sold 8.10.20 Philip, Dartmouth.
I.19	A.9	8. 2.05	Vickers. BU 1920.
I.10	A.10	8. 2.05	Vickers. Sold 1.4.19 Ardrossan DY Co.
I.01	A.11	8. 3.05	Vickers. BU 5.20 at Portsmouth DY.
I.02	A.12	8. 3.05	Vickers. Sold 16.1.20 J. H. Lee, Bembridge.
I.03	A.13	18. 4.05	Vickers. BU 1920.

Notes: A.1, A.3 and A.7 all lost prewar. A.2 and A.4 on harbour service at Portsmouth. A.5, A.6 in 2nd Flotilla, Portsmouth; A.8, A.9 in 1st Flotilla, Devonport; A.10–12 in 9th Flotilla, Ardrossan 1914–15. A.11, A.12 in 4th Flotilla at Dover 1915–16. All were on training duty by 1918, (except A.13 laid-up 10.14).

B CLASS

280/314 tons.   135 (oa) × 13½ × 10 ft.
Petrol motors/electric: 600/190 HP = 13/8½ kts.
Armament: 2–18 in TT.

Pendants	Name	Launched	Builder—Fate
I.21	B.1	25.10.04	Vickers. Sold 25.8.21 A. J. Andersen; resold 2.5.22 J. Smith, Poole.
I.23	B.3	31.10.05	Vickers. Sold 20.12.19 J. Jackson.
I.24	B.4	14.11.05	Vickers. Sold 1.4.19 Ardrossan DY Co.
I.25	B.5	14.11.05	Vickers. Sold 25.8.21 A. J. Andersen; resold 1.3.22 J. Smith, Poole.
I.26	B.6	30.11.05	Vickers. Sold 1919 at Malta.
I.27	B.7	30.11.05	Vickers. Sold 31.10.19 at Malta.
I.28	B.8	23. 1.06	Vickers. Sold 1919.
I.29	B.9	24. 1.06	Vickers. Sold 1919 at Malta.
I.20	B.10	23. 3.06	Vickers. Sunk 9.8.16 by A/C while under repair at Venice.
I.00	B.11	21. 2.06	Vickers. Sold 1919 at Malta.

Notes: B.2 lost 1912. B.6, B.7, B.8, B.9 and B.11 were converted to surface patrol boats in the Mediterranean 1917; motors being removed, hull raised and conning tower replaced by a wheelhouse. They were renamed S.6–11 respectively.

C CLASS

280/320 tons.   135 (oa) × 13½ × 11½ ft.
Petrol motors/electric: 600/300 HP = 13½/10 kts.
Armament: 2–18 in TT.

I.31	C.1	10. 7.06	Vickers. Sold 22.10.20 Stanlee; resold 14.11.21 Young, Sunderland.
I.32	C.2	10. 7.06	Vickers. Sold 8.10.20 Maden & McKee.
I.33	C.3	3.10.06	Vickers. Expended 23.4.18 at Zeebrugge.
I.34	C.4	18.10.06	Vickers. Sold 28.2.22 Hallamshire Metal Co.
I.35	C.5	20. 8.06	Vickers. Sold 31.10.19 at Malta.
I.36	C.6	20. 8.06	Vickers. Sold 20.11.19 J. A. Walker.
I.37	C.7	15. 2.07	Vickers. Sold 20.12.19 J. Jackson.
I.38	C.8	15. 2.07	Vickers. Sold 22.10.20 Stanlee; resold 14.11.21 Young, Sunderland.
I.39	C.9	3. 4.07	Vickers. Sold 7.22 Stanlee.
I.30	C.10	15. 4.07	Vickers. Sold 7.22 Stanlee.
I.42	C.12	9. 9.07	Vickers. Sold 2.2.20 J. H. Lee.
I.43	C.13	9.11.07	Vickers. Sold 2.2.20 J. H. Lee.
I.44	C.14	7.12.07	Vickers. Sold 5.12.21 C. A. Beard, Upnor.
I.45	C.15	21. 1.08	Vickers. Sold 28.2.22 Hallamshire Metal Co.
I.46	C.16	19. 3.08	Vickers. Sold 12.8.22 C. A. Beard, Upnor.
I.47	C.17	13. 3.08	Chatham DY. Sold 20.11.19 J. A. Walker.
I.48	C.18	10.10.08	Chatham DY. Sold 26.5.21 B. Fryer.
I.49	C.19	20. 3.09	Chatham DY. Sold 2.2.20 J. H. Lee.
I.50	C.20	27.11.09	Chatham DY. Sold 26.5.21 B. Fryer.
I.51	C.21	26. 9.08	Vickers. Sold 5.12.21 C. A. Beard, Upnor.
I.52	C.22	10.10.08	Vickers. Sold 2.2.20 J. H. Lee.
I.53	C.23	26.11.08	Vickers. Sold 5.12.21 C. A. Beard, Upnor.
I.54	C.24	26.11.08	Vickers. Sold 26.5.21 B. Fryer.
I.55	C.25	10. 3.09	Vickers. Sold 5.12.21 C. A. Beard, Upnor.
I.56	C.26	20. 3.09	Vickers. Scuttled 4.4.18 in Helsingfors Bay.
I.57	C.27	22. 4.09	Vickers. Scuttled 5.4.18 in Helsingfors Bay.
I.58	C.28	22. 4.09	Vickers. Sold 25.8.21 B. Fryer, Sunderland.
I.59	C.29	19. 6.09	Vickers. Mined 29.8.15 in the North Sea.
I.60	C.30	19. 7.09	Vickers. Sold 25.8.21 B. Fryer, Sunderland.
I.61	C.31	2. 9.09	Vickers. Sunk 4.1.15, unknown cause, Belgian coast.
I.62	C.32	29. 9.09	Vickers. Stranded 24.10.17 and destroyed, Gulf of Riga.
I.63	C.33	10. 5.10	Chatham DY. Sunk 4.8.15, unknown cause, North Sea.
I.64	C.34	8. 6.10	Chatham DY. Sunk 21.7.17 by U.52 off North Ireland.
I.65	C.35	2.11.09	Vickers. Destroyed 5.4.18 in Helsingfors Bay.
I.66	C.36	30.11.09	Vickers. Sold 25.6.19 at Hong Kong.
I.67	C.37	1. 1.10	Vickers. Sold 25.6.19 at Hong Kong.
I.68	C.38	10. 2.10	Vickers. Sold 25.6.19 at Hong Kong.

Notes: C.11 was lost in 1909. Apart from three boats who spent the war years in China and four more who served in the Baltic from 1916, all of this class operated in flotillas from Dover or East coast ports or on training duty at Portsmouth.

310/373 tons.   144 (oa) × 14 × 11½ ft (CC.1).   600/260 HP = 13/10 kts.
151½ (oa) × 15 × 11 ft (CC.2).
Armament: 5–18 in TT (CC.1), 3–18 in TT (CC.2).

CC.1 (RCN)	3. 6.13	Seattle Con. & DD Co. To sale list 1925.
CC.2 (RCN)	31.12.13	Seattle Con. & DD Co. To sale list 1925.

Notes: They were formerly the Chilean IQUIQUE and ANTOFAGASTA respectively, purchased 4.8.14.

D CLASS

550/620 tons. 150 (pp) ×22½ × 12 ft.
Petrol motors (D.1), Diesel (others)/electric; 1200/550 hp = 14/10 kts.
Armament: 3–18 in TT, 1–12 pdr.

Pendant No.	Name	Launched	Builder—Fate
I.71	D.1	16. 5.08	Vickers. Sunk 23.10.18 as target.
I.72	D.2	25. 5.10	Vickers. Sunk 25.11.14 by Germans PB off the Ems.
I.73	D.3	17.10.10	Vickers. Sunk 15.3.18 in error by French airship in the Channel.
I.74	D.4	27. 5.11	Vickers. Sold 19.12.21 H. Pounds.
I.75	D.5	28. 8.11	Vickers. Mined 3.11.14 in the North Sea.
I.76	D.6	23.10.11	Vickers. Sunk 26.6.18 by UB.73 off N. coast of Ireland.
I.77	D.7	14. 1.11	Chatham DY. Sold 19.12.21 H. Pounds.
I.78	D.8	23. 9.11	Chatham DY. Sold 19.12.21 H. Pounds.

Notes: Served mostly at Dover, Harwich or Immingham until 1917, then they were relegated to training duties.

E CLASS

660/810 tons. 176 (pp) ×22½ × 12 ft. D/E* 1600/840 hp = 15/10 kts.
Armament: 4–18 in TT, 1–12 pdr.

Pendant No.	Name	Launched	Builder—Fate
I.81	E.1	9.11.12	Chatham DY. Destroyed 8.4.18 at Helsingfors.
I.82	E.2	23.11.12	Chatham DY. Sold 7.3.21 at Malta.
I.83	E.3	29.10.12	Vickers. Sunk 18.10.14 by U.27 in the North Sea.
I.84	E.4	5. 2.12	Vickers. Sold 21.2.22 Upnor S.Bkg Co.
I.85	E.5	17. 5.12	Vickers. Sunk 7.3.16 by unknown cause, North Sea.
I.86	E.6	12.11.12	Vickers. Mined 26.12.15 in North Sea.
	AE.1	18. 6.13	Vickers. (RAN) Sunk 14.9.14 by unknown cause off Bismarck Archipelago.
	AE.2	22. 5.13	Vickers. (RAN) Scuttled after damage 30.4.15 in Sea of Marmora.

*Diesel/electric; this combination, with two screws, was normal propulsion plant for nearly all subsequent boats.

662/835 tons. 181 (oa), 180 (pp) ×22½ × 12¼ ft.
Armament: 5–18 in TT, 1–12 pdr.

Pendant No.	Name	Launched	Builder—Fate
I.87	E.7	2.10.13	Chatham DY. Sunk 5.9.15 by explosive charge from UB.14 after becoming trapped in S/M netting Dardanelles.
I.88	E.8	30.10.13	Chatham DY. Destroyed 8.4.18 at Helsingfors.
I.89	E.9	29.11.13	Vickers. Destroyed 8.4.18 at Helsingfors.
I.90	E.10	29.11.13	Vickers. Sunk 18.1.15 by unknown cause, North Sea.
I.91	E.11	23. 4.14	Vickers. Sold 7.3.21 at Malta.
I.92	E.12	5. 9.14	Chatham DY. Sold 7.3.21 at Malta.
I.93	E.13	22. 9.14	Chatham DY. Stranded 18.8.15 on coast of Denmark and interned; sold 14.12.21 Petersen & Albeck, Denmark.
I.94	E.14	7. 7.14	Vickers. Mined 27.1.18 off Kum Kale, Dardanelles.
I.95	E.15	23. 4.14	Vickers. Stranded 15.4.15 at Kephez Point, Dardanelles and destroyed.
I.96	E.16	23. 9.14	Vickers. Mined 22.8.16 in the North Sea.
I.97	E.17	16. 1.15	Vickers. Wrecked 6.1.16 off the Texel.
I.98	E.18	4. 3.15	Vickers. Sunk 24.5.16 by German decoy "K" off Bornholm.
I.99*	E.19	13. 5.15	Vickers. Destroyed 8.4.18 at Helsingfors.
I.69*	E.20	12. 6.15	Vickers. Sunk 5.11.15 by UB.14, Sea of Marmora.
I.70*	E.21	24. 7.15	Vickers. Sold 14.12.21 Petersen & Albeck.
I.79*	E.22	27. 8.15	Vickers. Sunk 25.4.16 by UB.18 in the North Sea.
	E.23	28. 9.15	Vickers. Sold 6.9.22 Young, Sunderland.
	E.24	9.12.15	Vickers. Mined 24.3.16 in the North Sea.
	E.25	23. 8.15	Beardmore. Sold 14.12.21 Petersen & Albeck.
	E.26	11.11.15	Beardmore. Sunk 6.7.16 by unknown cause, North Sea.
	E.27	9. 6.17	Yarrow. Sold 6.9.22 Cashmore.
	E.29	1. 6.15	Armstrong. Sold 21.2.22 Upnor S Bkg Co.
	E.30	29. 6.15	Armstrong. Sunk 22.11.16 by unknown cause, North Sea.
	E.31	23. 8.15	Scotts. Sold 6.9.22 Young, Sunderland.

Pendant Nos.	Name	Launched	Builder—Fate
	E.32	16. 8.16	White. Sold 6.9.22 Young, Sunderland.
	E.33	18. 4.16	Thornycroft. Sold 6.9.22 Cashmore.
	E.34	27. 1.17	Thornycroft. Mined 20.7.18 in the North Sea.
	E.35	20. 5.16	John Brown. Sold 6.9.22 Ellis & Co.
	E.36	16. 9.16	John Brown. Sunk 17.1.17 by unknown cause, North Sea.
	E.37	2. 9.15	Fairfield. Sunk 1.12.16 by unknown cause, North Sea.
	E.38	13. 6.16	Fairfield. Sold 6.9.22 Ellis & Co.
	E.39	18. 5.16	Palmer. Sold 13.10.21 S. Wales Salvage Co; foundered 9.22 in tow.
	E.40	9.11.16	Palmer. Sold 14.12.21 Petersen & Albeck.
	E.41	28. 7.15	Cammell Laird. Sold 6.9.22 Ellis & Co, Newcastle.
	E.42	22.10.15	Cammell Laird. Sold 6.9.22 J. Smith.
	E.43	11.11.15	Swan Hunter. Sold 3.1.21 S. Wales Salvage Co; stranded and lost at St. Agnes, Cornwall.
	E.44	21. 2.16	Swan Hunter. Sold 13.10.21 S. Wales Salvage Co.
	E.45	25. 1.16	Cammell Laird. Sold 6.9.22. Ellis & Co.
	E.46	4. 4.16	Cammell Laird. Sold 6.9.22 Ellis & Co.
	E.47	29. 5.16	Fairfield. Sunk 20.8.17 by unknown cause, North Sea.
	E.48	2. 8.16	Fairfield. Sold 7.28 Cashmore.
	E.49	18. 9.16	Swan Hunter. Mined 12.3.17 off the Shetlands.
	E.50	13.11.16	John Brown. Mined 1.2.18 in the North Sea.
	E.51	30.11.16	Scotts. Sold 13.10.21 S. Wales Salvage Co.
	E.52	25. 1.17	Denny. Sold 3.1.21 Brixham Marine & Eng. Co.
	E.53	.16	Beardmore. Sold 6.9.22 C. A. Beard.
	E.54	.16	Beardmore. Sold 14.12.21 Petersen & Albeck.
	E.55	5. 2.16	Denny. Sold 6.9.22 Ellis & Co.
	E.56	19. 6.16	Denny. Sold 9.6.23 Granton S Bkg Co.

*Pendants for E.19–22 were assigned 24.4.15.
Notes: E.1 and E.2 were laid down as D.9 and D.10. E.19 to E.56 were all ordered during 11.14. E.25 and E.26 were boats originally ordered for Turkish Navy. Contracts for E.27 and E.28 were cancelled 20.4.15 to allow Messrs Yarrow to concentrate on other work. Work was resumed on E.27 on 7.8.15. E.47 and E.48 were completed by Beardmore. E.51 and E.52 were originally ordered from Yarrow, contracts transferred 3.3.15. E.24, E.34, E.41, E.45, E.46 and E.51 were all minelayers (3-TT, 20 mines). The most hard-worked group of S/Ms in the war with a loss rate of almost 50%. During exercises off Harwich E.4 running submerged, collided with E.41 travelling on the surface. Both boats sank with heavy loss of life (15.8.16) and they were both salvaged by lifting craft and returned to service about 5.17. The first 15 RN boats served at Harwich until 1915, when 9 of them went to the Mediterranean or the Baltic; the other 6 remained at Harwich until 1918. The rest of the class served at Harwich or from other East Coast ports from completion until 1918, some of them later operating from the West of Ireland or in the Mediterranean.

F CLASS

353/525 tons.   151 (oa), 150 (pp) ×16×10¼ ft.   D/E 900/400 hp = 14½/8¼ kts.
Armament: 3–18 in TT.

I.AO	F.1	31. 3.15	Chatham DY. BU 1920 at Portsmouth DY.
I.A1	F.2	7. 7.17	White. Sold 7.22 C. Welton, Portsmouth.
I.A2	F.3	9. 2.16	Thornycroft. BU 1920 at Portsmouth DY.

Notes: Ordered before the war, F.4–8 were also projected but cancelled. F.1 was at Harwich 1915, Dover 1915–16, Yarmouth, Portsmouth and Campbeltown 1916–18; F.2 at Portsmouth and Campbeltown 1917–18; F.3 at Yarmouth 1916–17, then at Portsmouth and Campbeltown 1917–18.

EXPERIMENTAL BOAT

1270/1694 tons. 242½ (oa), 240 (pp) ×26 ft. D/E 3700/1000 hp=17/10 kts.
Armament: 8–18 in TT, 1–12 pdr.

Pendant Nos.	Name	Launched	Builder—Fate
I.AC	NAUTILUS	31.12.14	Vickers. Sold 9.6.22 Cashmore.
20 (9.15*)	=N.1 1918		

*Pendant cancelled 1.16.
Notes: An unsuccessful experimental vessel of large size intended as an ocean-going submarine. She spent the war years at Portsmouth, nominally in the 1st Flotilla, but never became operational.

EXPERIMENTAL STEAM SUBMARINE

932/1470 tons. 231¼ (oa) ×23×14½ ft. Turbine/electric 3750/1400 hp=18/10 kts.
Armament: 2–21 in TT, 4–18 in TT.

I.CA	SWORDFISH	18. 3.16	Scotts. Sold 7.22 Pounds; resold Hayes, Porthcawl.
30 (9.15*)	=S.1 4.16		
D.15 (6.18)	=SWORDFISH 7.17		

*Pendant cancelled 1.16.
Notes: An experimental steam-driven submarine and not a success. Nominally in the 2nd and later the 6th Flotilla. Converted to a surface patrol vessel with a built-up superstructure, wheelhouse, and 2–12 pdr guns in 7.17. During the time spent as a patrol vessel she was based at Portsmouth.

S CLASS

255/390 tons. 148¼ (oa) ×14×9½ ft. D/E 600/400 hp=13/8¼ kts.
Armament: 2–18 in TT.

I.04	S.1	28. 2.14	Scotts. Ceded to Italy 25.10.15.
I.0A	S.2	14. 4.15	Scotts. Ceded to Italy 25.10.15.
I.1A	S.3	10. 6.15	Scotts. Ceded to Italy 25.10.15.

Notes: Scott-Laurenti type of Italian design. S.1 was in 4th Flotilla at Dover 1914, 8th Flotilla at Harwich 1914–15. S.2 completed 5.15 had short RN service following trials, while S.3 (completed 9.15) was never commissioned by the RN.

V CLASS

364/486 tons. 148 (oa) ×16×11 ft. D/E 900/380 hp=14/9 kts.
Armament: 2–18 in TT, (1–12 pdr in V.2–4).

I.2A	V.1	23. 7.14	Vickers. Sold 29.11.21 J. Kelly.
I.3A	V.2	17. 2.15	Vickers. Sold 29.11.21 J. Kelly.
I.4A	V.3	1. 4.15	Vickers. Sold 8.10.20 J. W. Towers.
I.5A	V.4	25.11.15	Vickers. Sold 8.10.20 J. W. Towers.

Notes: V.I and V.2 in 4th Flotilla, Dover 1915–16; all four in 8th Flotilla, Harwich 1916–18.

W CLASS

340/500 tons. 171½ (oa) ×15½×9 ft. (W.1–2) D/E 750/480 hp=13/8 kts.
149½ (oa) ×17×9½ ft. (W.3–4)
Armament: 1–3 in AA, 2–18 in TT.

I.6A	W.1	19.11.14	Armstrong. Ceded to Italy 23.8.16.
I.7A	W.2	15. 2.15	Armstrong. Ceded to Italy 23.8.16.
I.8A	W.3	28. 7.15	Armstrong. Ceded to Italy 23.8.16.
I.9A	W.4	11. 9.15	Armstrong. Ceded to Italy 7.8.16.

Notes: W.1 and 2 were in the 10th Flotilla, Humber 1915–16. W.4 became a war loss 8.17 in Italian service and the others were discarded during 1919.

G CLASS

700/975 tons.   187 (oa), 185 (pp) ×22½×13 ft.   D/E 1600/840 hp=14/10 kts.
Armament: 1–3 in AA, 1–21 in TT, 4–18 in TT.

Pendant Nos.	Name	Launched	Builder—Fate
I.A3	G.1	14. 8.15	Chatham DY. Sold 14.2.20 Fryer, Sunderland.
I.A4	G.2	23.12.15	Chatham DY. Sold 16.1.20 Fryer, Sunderland.
I.A5	G.3	22. 1.16	Chatham DY. Sold 4.11.21 Young, Sunderland.
I.A6	G.4	23.10.15	Chatham DY. Sold 27.6.28 Cashmore.
I.A7	G.5	23.11.15	Chatham DY. Sold 25.10.22 Cashmore.
I.A8	G.6	7.12.15	Armstrong. Sold 4.11.21 Young, Sunderland.
I.A9	G.7	4. 3.16	Armstrong. Sunk 1.11.18 by unknown cause, North Sea.
I.OC	G.8	1. 5.16	Vickers. Sunk 14.1.18 by unknown cause, North Sea.
I.1C	G.9	15. 6.16	Vickers. Sunk 16.9.17 in error by PETARD off Norway.
I.2C	G.10	11. 1.16	Vickers. Sold 20.1.23 J. Smith.
I.3C	G.11	22. 2.16	Vickers. Wrecked 22.11.18 off Harwich.
I.4C	G.12	24. 3.16	Vickers. Sold 14.2.20 J. G. Potts.
I.5C	G.13	18. 7.16	Vickers. Sold 20.1.23 J. Smith.
I.6C	G.14	17. 5.17	Scotts. Sold 11.3.21 Stanlee.

Notes: Seven boats were on order by 7.14; G.8–15 were part of the huge war order placed during 11.14. G.15 being built by White was cancelled 20.4.15. G.1–6 served in the 11th Flotilla. Blyth 1916–18; G.7–14 in the 10th based on the Tees.

H.1 CLASS

364/434 tons.   150 (oa) ×15½×12½ ft.   D/E 480/320 hp=13/11 kts.
Armament: 4–18 in TT.
Built 1915 by Canadian Vickers, Montreal:

H.1		Sold 7.3.21 at Malta.
H.2		Sold 7.3.21 at Malta.
H.3		Mined 15.7.16 off Cattaro, Adriatic Sea.
H.4		Sold 30.11.21 at Malta.
H.5		Sunk 6.3.18 in collision, Irish Sea.
H.6		Stranded 8.1.16 on the Dutch coast, interned; sold 2.16 Dutch navy =0.8.
H.7		Sold 30.11.21 at Malta.
H.8		Sold 29.11.21 J. Kelly.
H.9		Sold 30.11.21 at Malta.
H.10		Sunk 19.1.18 by unknown cause, North Sea.

Built 1915 by Fore River Plant, Quincy, Mass. USA:

H.11			Sold 1921 Stanlee.
H.12			Sold 4.22 Stanlee.
H.13			Ceded to Chile 3.7.17 =H.1; =GUALCOLDA.
H.14	=CH.14	6.19	RCN; Sold 1925.
H.15	=CH.15	6.19	RCN; Sold 1925.
H.16			Ceded to Chile 3.7.17 =H.2; =TEGUALDA.
H.17			Ceded to Chile 3.7.17 =H.3; =RUCUMILLA.
H.18			Ceded to Chile 3.7.17 =H.4; =GUALE.
H.19			Ceded to Chile 3.7.17 =H.5; =QUIDORA.
H.20			Ceded to Chile 3.7.17 =H.6; =FRESIA.

Notes: H.1–4 in Mediterranean 1915–18; H.5–10 in 8th Flotilla of 1918; H.11–12 in 14th Flotilla 1918. H.13–20 were not commissioned in the RN; two went to the RCN and six went to Chile as part replacement for ships requisitioned while building in 1914. All ten boats built in USA were to be armed in Canada, but delivery was delayed until after the US declaration of war in 1917.

H.21 CLASS

440/500 tons.   171 (oa), 164½ (pp) × 16 × 11 ft.   D/E 480/320 hp = 13/10½ kts.
Armament: 1–3 in AA, 4–21 in TT.

Name	Launched	Builder—Fate
H.21	20.10.17	Vickers. Sold 13.7.26 Cashmore.
H.22	14.11.17	Vickers. Sold 19.2.29 Alloa, Charlestown.
H.23	29. 1.18	Vickers. Sold 4.5.34 Young, Sunderland.
H.24	14.11.17	Vickers. Sold 4.5.34 Young, Sunderland.
H.25	27. 4.18	Vickers. Sold 19.2.29 Alloa, Charlestown.
H.26	15.11.17	Vickers. Sold 21.4.28 Ward, Pembroke Dock.
H.27	25. 9.18	Vickers. Sold 30.8.35 Cashmore.
H 28	12. 3.18	Vickers. Sold 18.8.44 BU at Troon.
H.29	8. 6.18	Vickers. Foundered 9.8.26 at Devonport; raised, sold 7.10.27 Ward, Pembroke Dock.
H.30	9. 5.18	Vickers. Sold 30.8.35 Cashmore.
H.31	16.11.18	Vickers. Sunk 24.12.41 by unknown cause, Bay of Biscay.
H.32	19.11.18	Vickers. Sold 18.10.44; BU at Troon 11.44.
H.33	24. 8.18	Cammell Laird. Sold 1944; BU at Troon 10.44.
H.34	5.11.18	Cammell Laird. Sold 1945; BU at Troon 7.45.
H.41	26. 7.18	Armstrong. Sold 12.3.20 incomplete to Young, Sunderland.
H.42	21.10.18	Armstrong. Sunk 23.3.22 in collision with VERSATILE off Gibraltar.
H.43	3. 2.19	Armstrong. Sold 1944; BU at Troon 11.44.
H.44	17. 2.19	Armstrong. Sold 1944; BU at Troon 2.45.
H.47	19.11.18	Beardmore. Sunk 9.7.29 in collision with L.12.
H.48	31. 3.19	Beardmore. Sold 30.8.35 Rees, Llanelly.
H.49	15. 7.19	Beardmore. Sunk 27.10.40 by German patrol vessels off the Dutch coast.
H.50	25.10.19	Beardmore. Sold 1945; BU at Troon 7.45.
H.51	15.11.18	Pembroke DY. Sold 6.6.24 W. C. Keen, Bristol; resold 17.7.24 Davo S Bkg Co.
H.52	31. 3.19	Pembroke DY. Sold 9.11.27 New Era Productions.

Notes: H.21–32 were ordered during 1–2.17 and H.33–54 during 6–7.17. An improvement on the earlier H.1 (Holland) type, they were larger and carried 21 in TT. The J, K and many L boats predated this class. Cancellation of H.35–40 (Cammell Laird), H.45–46 (Armstrong) and H.53–54 (Devonport DY) was noted in a fleet order of 20.11.17. H.21–30 served in the 14th and 8th Flotillas from completion.

J CLASS

1210/1760 tons.   275 (oa), 270 (pp) × 23½ × 14 ft.   D/E 3600/1400 hp = 19/9½ kts.
Armament: 1–4 in, 6–18 in TT.

Name	Launched	Builder—Fate
J.1	6.11.15	Portsmouth DY. Sold 26.2.24 Melbourne Salvage Co.
J.2	6.11.15	Portsmouth DY. Sold 26.2.24 Melbourne Salvage Co.
J.3 (ex-J.7)	4.12.15	Pembroke DY. Sold 1.26 Hill, Melbourne.
J.4 (ex-J.8)	2. 2.16	Pembroke DY. Sold 26.2.24 Melbourne Salvage Co.
J.5	9. 9.15	Devonport DY. Sold 26.2.24 Melbourne Salvage Co.
J.6	9. 9.15	Devonport DY. Sunk 15.10.18 in error by decoy ship CYMRIC off Blyth.

1260/1820 tons.

J.7	21. 2.17	Devonport DY. Sold 11.29 Morris & Watt, Melbourne.

Notes: The first group was ordered 1.15 and J.7 in 5.16. The original J.3–4 (both Pembroke DY) were cancelled in 4.15. All served in the 11th Flotilla at Blyth from completion to 1918. On 25.3.19 the six remaining boats were transferred to the RAN.

K CLASS

1880/2650 tons.   338 (oa), 334 (pp) × 26½ × 16 ft.   GT/E 10000/1400 hp = 24/9½ kts.
Armament: 2–4 in, 1–3 in AA, 10–18 TT.

K.1	14.11.16	Portsmouth DY. Damaged in collision with K.4 off the coast of Denmark and sunk 17.11.17 by gunfire of BLONDE.
K.2	14.10.16	Portsmouth DY. Sold 13.7.26 Cashmore.
K.3	20. 5.16	Vickers. Sold 26.10.21 Barking S Bkg Co.
K.4	15. 7.16	Vickers. Sunk 31.1.18 in collision with K.6 off May Island.
K.5	16.12.16	Portsmouth DY. Sunk 20.1.21 by accident, Bay of Biscay.
K.6	31. 5.16	Devonport DY. Sold 13.7.26 Cashmore.
K.7	31. 5.16	Devonport DY. Sold 9.9.21 Fryer.
K.8	10.10.16	Vickers. Sold 11.10.23 McLellan.
K.9	8.11.16	Vickers. Sold 23.7.26 Alloa S Bkg Co, Charlestown.
K.10	27.12.16	Vickers. Sold 4.11.21 Beard; Foundered in tow 10.1.22.
K.11	16. 8.16	Armstrong. Sold 4.11.21 C. A. Beard.
K.12	23. 2.17	Armstrong. Sold 23.7.26 Alloa, Charlestown.
K.13 = K.22 3.17	11.11.16	Fairfield. Foundered 29.1.17 while on trials in the Gareloch; Salved 3.17 and renamed; Sold 16.12.26 Young, Sunderland.
K.14	8. 2.17	Fairfield. Sold 16.12.26 Granton S Bkg Co.
K.15	30.10.17	Scotts. Sold 8.24 Upnor S Bkg Co.
K.16	5.11.17	Beardmore. Sold 22.8.24 J. Hornby; resold 9.24 Alloa, Charlestown.
K.17	10. 4.17	Vickers. Sunk 31.1.18 in collision with FEARLESS off May Island.

Notes: Fleet submarines driven on the surface by steam geared turbines providing unprecedented speed. K.3–4 were the first orders placed (6.15), followed by 12 others in 8.15, K.15–18 in 2.16, K.19 in 5.16, and finally K.20–21 in 8.16. The last 4 boats (K.18–21) became M.1–4. There was some variation in armament and positioning, particularly after they were given high bulbous bows to reduce their tendency to bury their forepart in a seaway. Although capable of exercising with the fleet by virtue of their surface speed, the K boats met disaster when steaming with heavy surface units during night operations near May Island causing chaos and multiple collisions. All of this class served in the 12th or 13th Flotillas with the Grand Fleet from completion to 1918. Technical problems and some degree of unreliability led to Diesel engines being employed in standard submarines until the development of the nuclear-powered boats in the 1950s.

K.26 CLASS

2140/2770 tons.   351½ (oa), 347 (pp) × 28 × 16½ ft.   GT/E 10000/1400 hp = 23½/9 kts.
Armament: 3–4 in, 6–21 in TT (bow), 4–18 in TT (sides).

K.26	26. 8.19	Vickers. Sold 3.31 at Malta.

Notes: K.26 was completed 9.23 at Chatham DY. Others ordered in 1918 were K.23, K.24, K.25 (all Armstrong) and K.27, K.28 (both Vickers). All five were cancelled 26.11.18. Frames of K.24, K.25 and K.28 were ordered 31.12.18 to be taken to Chatham DY for completion, but this was also cancelled. K.26 was also steam-driven but achieved a lower surface speed due to an increase in hull size over the K.1–17 class.

M CLASS

1600/1950 tons.   296 (oa), 290 (pp) × 24½ × 16 ft.   D/E 2400/1600 hp = 15½/9½ kts.
303 (oa) M.3 only.
Armament: 1–12 in, 1–3 in AA, 4–18 in TT (4–21 in in M.3).

M.1 (ex-K.18)	9. 7.17	Vickers. Sunk 12.11.25 in collision off Start Point.
M.2 (ex-K.19)	19.10.18	Vickers. Sunk 26.1.32 off Portland.
M.3 (ex-K.20)	19.10.18	Armstrong. Sold 2.32 Cashmore.
M.4 (ex-K.21)	20. 7.19	Armstrong. Sold 30.11.21 Armstrong.

Notes: Described as 'submarine monitors', they mounted 12 in guns taken from old pre-dreadnoughts. The gun could be loaded only while on the surface but could be fired while the submarine was at periscope depth with only the gun muzzle and periscope visible above water. They were altered from "K" class, M.2–4 being renamed by an order dated 25.6.18. M.1 served in the Mediterranean in 1918. The completion of M.4 was cancelled and her hull sold to the builder. M.3 became a minelayer in 1927 (4–MG, 4–TT and mines); M.2 became a seaplane carrier 4.28 (1–3 in, 4–TT); she is believed to have foundered due to her hanger hatch opening while partially submerged.

L.1 CLASS

890/1070 tons.   231 (oa), 222 (pp) ×23½×14 ft.   D/E 2400/1600 hp=17½/10¼ kts.
Armament: 1–4 in, 4–21 in TT.

L.1	10. 5.17	Vickers. Sold 1930 Cashmore.
L.2	6. 7.17	Vickers. Sold 3.30 Ward, Grays.
L.3	1. 9.17	Vickers. Sold 1931 Metal Ind, Charlestown.
L.4	17.11.17	Vickers. Sold 2.34 Ward, Grays.
L.5	26. 1.18	Swan Hunter. Sold 1931 Metal Ind, Charlestown.
L.6	14. 1.18	Beardmore. Sold 1935 Cashmore.
L.7	24. 4.17	Cammell Laird. Sold 1930 Hughes Bolckow.
L.8	7. 7.17	Cammell Laird. Sold 7.10.30 Cashmore.

Notes: L.1–2 were ordered in 2.16 as E.56–57; L.3–8 in 5.16. All were based at Falmouth in 1918.

L.9 CLASS

890/1080 tons.   238½ (oa), 229 (pp) ×23½×14 ft.   D/E 2400/1600 hp=17½/10½ kts.
Armament: 1–4 in, 6–21 in TT (minelayers: 1–4 in, 4–21 in TT, 14 mines).

L.9	29. 1.18	Denny. Sold 30.6.27 at Hong Kong.
L.10	24. 1.18	Denny. Sunk 30.10.18 by German destroyers off the Texel.
L.11	26. 2.18	Vickers. Sold 16.2.32 Young, Sunderland.
L.12	16. 3.18	Vickers. Sold 16.2.32 Cashmore.
L.14	10. 6,18	Vickers. Sold 5.34 Cashmore.
L.15	16. 1.18	Fairfield. Sold 2.32 Cashmore.
L.16	9. 4.18	Fairfield. Sold 2.34 Brechin. Granton.
L.17	13. 5.18	Vickers. Sold 2.34 Ward, Pembroke Dock.
L.18	21.11.18	Vickers. Sold 10.36 Ward, Pembroke Dock.
L.19	4. 2.19	Vickers. Sold 1937 Ward, Pembroke Dock.
L.20	23. 9.18	Vickers. Sold 7.1.35 Cashmore.
L.21	11.10.19	Vickers. Sold 2.39 Arnott Young, Dalmuir.
L.22	25.10.19	Vickers. Sold 30.8.35 Cashmore.
L.23	1. 7.19	Vickers. Sank in tow 5.46 off Nova Scotia on passage to ship breakers.
L.24	19. 2.19	Vickers. Sunk 14.1.24 in collision with RESOLUTION off Portland.
L.25	13. 2.19	Vickers. Sold 1935 Cashmore.
L.26	29. 5.19	Vickers. Sold 1946.
L.27	14. 6.19	Vickers. Sold 1946.
L.33	29. 5.19	Swan Hunter. Sold 2.32 Young, Sunderland.

Notes: L.9 ordered 8.16; L.10–33 in 12.16; L.13 and L.36–49 group not ordered. L.23 was completed at Chatham DY and L.26 at Portsmouth DY. L.28–31 (all Vickers), L.34–35 (both Pembroke DY) were cancelled by Admiralty Order 12.4.19. L.32 (launched 23.8.19 by Vickers) was also cancelled; hull sold 1.3.20 to Leith Salvage Co. L.11, 12, 14, 17 and 25 were minelayers. L.9–17 served at Harwich or on the Tees 1918.

L.50 CLASS

960/1150 tons.   235 (oa), 230½ (pp) ×23½×13 ft.   D/E 960/1150 hp=17/10¼ kts.
Armament: 2–4 in, 6–21 in TT.

L.52	18.12.18	Armstrong. Sold 1935 Rees, Llanelly.
L.53	12. 8.19	Armstrong. Sold 1938 Ward, Briton Ferry.
L.54	20. 8.19	Denny. Sold 1938 Ward, Pembroke Dock.
L.55	21. 9.18	Fairfield. Sunk 9.6.19 by Russian patrol craft in the Baltic. Salved and later in Russian navy.
L.56	29. 5.19	Fairfield. Sold 25.3.38 Ward, Pembroke Dock.
L.69	6.12.18	Beardmore. Sold 2.39 Arnott Young, Dalmuir.
L.71	17. 5.19	Scotts. Sold 25.3.38 Ward, Milford Haven.

Notes: L.50–55 ordered during 1–2.17; L.56–58 and L.67–73 in 4.17; L.59–66 and L.74 in 4.18. L.50–51, L.60–61 (all Cammell Laird); L.57–58, L.62 (all Fairfield); L.59, L.70 (both Beardmore); L.63–64, L.72 (all Scotts); L.65–66 (both Swan Hunter); L.67–68 (both Armstrong); and L.73–74 (both Denny) were cancelled. L.59, 60–66 and 74 by Admiralty Order 26.11.18 and the others 12.4.19. The frames for L.67–68 were used for the Jugoslav HRABRI and NEBOJSA, both completed in 1927. L.53 was completed at Chatham DY, L.54 at Devonport DY, and L.69 at Rosyth DY.

R CLASS

420/500 tons.   163 (oa), 160 (pp) ×16×11½ ft.   D/E 240/1200 hp=9½/15 kts.
Armament: 6–18 in TT.

R.1	25. 4.18	Chatham DY. Sold 20.1.23 J. Smith.
R.2	25. 4.18	Chatham DY. Sold 21.2.23 E. Suren.
R.3	8. 6.18	Chatham DY. Sold 21.2.23 E. Suren.
R.4	8. 6.18	Chatham DY. Sold 26.5.34 Young, Sunderland.
R.7	14. 5.18	Vickers. Sold 21.2.23 E. Suren.
R.8	28. 6.18	Vickers. Sold 21.2.23 E. Suren
R.9	12. 8.18	Armstrong. Sold 21.2.23 E. Suren.
R.10	5.10.18	Armstrong. Sold 19.2.29 Cashmore.
R.11	16. 3.18	Cammell Laird. Sold 21.2.23 J. Smith.
R.12	9. 4.18	Cammell Laird. Sold 21.2.23 J. Smith.

Notes: Ordered 12.17; R.5–6 (Pembroke DY ex-Devonport DY) were cancelled by Admiralty Order 28.8.19. This class was built with a streamlined hull, single screw and high submerged speed in order to hunt U-boats. R.7, 8, 11 and 12 based at Killybegs, Donegal in 1918.

ESCORTS

Included under this heading are the old sloops and gun vessels along with the war construction programme of sloops and patrol vessels.

OLD TYPE SLOOPS, etc.

1130 tons. 220 (oa), 200 (pp) $\times 32 \times 10\frac{1}{2}$ ft. Paddle 1140 ihp$=12\frac{1}{2}$ kts.
Armament: 1–6 in, 6–4 in.

Name	Launched	Builder—Fate
SPHINX	28.11.82	Green, Blackwall. CTL by fire 2.19; Sold 27.7.19 at Calcutta.

Notes: Was a SSV with composite hull and sloop armament. Formerly employed as a despatch vessel and in coast guard service. She spent the war on the East Indies Station.

1650 tons. 275 (oa), 250 (pp) $\times 32\frac{1}{2} \times 14$ ft. Horizontal compound engines 3030 ihp = 17 kts.
Armament: 6–6 pdr.

Name	Launched	Builder—Fate
ALACRITY	17. 1.85	Palmer. Sold 1919.

Notes: Rated as *despatch vessel*, launched as SURPRISE and renamed in 1914. Served on the China Station from 1914.

960 tons. $204\frac{1}{2}$ (oa), 180 (pp) $\times 32\frac{1}{2} \times 11$ ft. TE 1400 ihp$=13\frac{1}{2}$ kts.
Armament: 6–4 in, 4–3 pdr.

Name	Launched	Builder—Fate
TORCH =FIREBRAND 8.17	28.12.94	Sheerness DY. To NZ Government 1917; Sold 7.20 in New Zealand.

Notes: Served in the Pacific, then on harbour training service in New Zealand.

1050 tons. $210\frac{1}{2}$ (oa), 185 (pp) $\times 32\frac{1}{2} \times 11\frac{1}{2}$ ft. TE 1400 ihp$=13\frac{1}{2}$ kts.
Armament: 6–4 in, 4–3 pdr.

Name	Launched	Builder—Fate
ALGERINE	6. 6.95	Devonport DY. Sold 11.4.19 mercantile.

Notes: Based at Vancouver (Esquimalt) 1914–19, harbour service from 1915.

BRAMBLE CLASS 1st CLASS GUNBOATS

710 tons. $187\frac{1}{2}$ (oa), 180 (pp) $\times 33 \times 8\frac{1}{2}$ ft. TE 1300 ihp$=13\frac{1}{2}$ kts.
Armament: 2–4 in, 4–12 pdr.

	Name	Launched	Builder—Fate
	BRAMBLE	26.11.98	Potter, Liverpool. Sold 26.1.20 at Bombay.
	BRITOMART	28. 3.99	Potter, Liverpool. Sold 10.6.20 at Bombay.
P.8C (1.18)	DWARF	15.11.98	London and Glasgow. Sold 13.7.26 Ward, Pembroke Dock.
	THISTLE	22. 6.99	London and Glasgow. Sold 13.7.26 Ward, Pembroke Dock.

Notes: The first two were in China and the East Indies 1914–18; the others, West and East Africa.

CONDOR CLASS SLOOPS

980 tons. 204 (oa), 180 (pp) $\times 33 \times 11\frac{1}{2}$ ft. TE 1400 ihp$=13$ kts.
Armament: 6–4 in, 4–3 pdr.

Name	Launched	Builder—Fate
RINALDO	29. 5.00	Laird. Sold 21.10.21 W. Thomas, Anglesey.
SHEARWATER	10. 2.00	Sheerness DY. Sold 5.22 =VEDAS.
VESTAL	10. 2.00	Sheerness DY. Sold 21.10.21 W. Thomas, Anglesey.

Notes: For MUTINE and ROSARIO of this class, see under survey and depot ships. RINALDO was guardship in the Wash to 1915, then to West and East Africa. SHEARWATER on patrol from Vancouver 1914, then became D/S for the RCN. VESTAL was a gunnery tender at Portsmouth.

ESPIEGLE CLASS SLOOPS

1070 tons. 210 (oa), 185 (pp) ×33 ×11 ft. TE 1400 ihp=13 kts.
Armament: 6–4 in, 4–3 pdr.

Name	Launched	Builder—Fate
CADMUS	29. 4.03	Sheerness DY. Sold 1.9.21 at Hong Kong.
CLIO	14. 3.03	Sheerness DY. Sold 12.11.20 at Bombay.
ESPIEGLE	8.12.00	Sheerness DY. Sold 7.9.23 at Bombay.
ODIN	30.11.01	Sheerness DY. Sold 12.11.20 at Bombay.

Notes: For FANTOME and MERLIN of this class, see under survey ships. All served in China and the East Indies during the war.

PRIZE SLOOP

1438 tons. 210 (pp) ×31 ×15 ft. TE 1300 ihp=16 kts.
Armament: 3–4 in, 2–12 pdr.

Name	Launched	Builder—Fate
UNA (RAN)	1911	Bremer Vulkan. Sold 1.25 =AKUNA.

Notes: Was the German survey ship KOMET, captured 11.10.14 in the Pacific. Served in the Pacific 1915–18.

FLOWER CLASS: FLEET SWEEPING SLOOPS
ACACIA TYPE

1200 tons. 262½ (oa), 250 (pp) ×33 ×11 ft. TE 1800 ihp=16¼ kts.
Armament: 2–12 pdr, 2–3 pdrAA.

Pendant Nos. 2.15* 9.15 1.18	Name	Launched	Builder—Fate
	Ordered 1.15:		
M.26 T.00	ACACIA	15. 4.15	Swan Hunter. Sold 6.9.22 Dornom Bros.
M.27 T.01 T.03	ANEMONE	13. 5.15	Swan Hunter. Sold 6.9.22 Marple & Gillott, Saltash.
M.28 T.02	ASTER	1. 5.15	Earle. Mined 4.7.17 in Mediterranean.
M.29 T.03 T.12	BLUEBELL	24. 7.15	Scotts. Sold 26.5.30 Cashmore.
M.31 T.05 T.27	DAFFODIL	17. 8.15	Scotts. Sold 22.2.35 Cashmore.
M.37 T.11 T.28	DAHLIA	21. 4.15	Barclay Curle. Sold 2.7.32 Metal Ind, Charlestown.
M.38 T.12 T.29	DAPHNE	19. 5.15	Barclay Curle. Sold 15.1.23 Unity S Bkg Co.
M.41 T.15 T.33	FOXGLOVE	30. 3.15	Barclay Curle. Sold 7.9.46, BU at Troon.
M.42 T.16 T.43	HOLLYHOCK	1. 5.15	Barclay Curle. Sold 7.10.30 Ward, Pembroke Dock.
M.43 T.17 T.44	HONEYSUCKLE	29. 4.15	Lobnitz. Sold 6.9.22 Distinn.
M.44 T.18 T.46	IRIS	2. 6.15	Lobnitz. Sold 26.1.20 C. W. Kellock; =PRINCIPE D'ASTURIAS.
M.46 T.20 T.48	JONQUIL	12. 5.15	Connell. Sold 5.20 Portugal; =CARVALHO ARAUJO.
M.47 T.21 T.49	LABURNUM	10. 6.15	Connell. Lost 2.42 at fall of Singapore.
M.48 T.22 T.50	LARKSPUR	11. 5.15	Napier & Miller. Sold 3.22 Ward, Inverkeithing.
M.49 T.23	LAVENDER	12. 6.15	McMillan. Sunk 4.5.17 by UC.75, Channel.
M.65 T.24 T.52	LILAC	29. 4.15	Greenock and Grangemouth. Sold 15.12.22 Batson Syndicate.
M.66 T.25 T.53	LILY =VULCAN II 10.23 =ADAMANT II 1930	16. 6.15	Barclay Curle. D/S 10.23; Sold 25.6.30 Cashmore.
M.67 T.26 T.58	MAGNOLIA	26. 6.15	Scotts. Sold 2.7.32 Metal Ind, Charlestown.
M.68 T.27 T.59	MALLOW	13. 7.15	Barclay Curle. To RAN 7.19; dismantled 7.32; sunk 1.8.35 as target off Sydney.
M.45 T.19 T.61	MARIGOLD (ex-Ivy)	27. 5.15	Bow McLachlan. Sold 26.1.20 C. W. Kellock; =PRINCIPE DE PIAMONTE.
M.95 T.28 T.62	MIMOSA	16. 7.15	Bow McLachlan. Sold 18.11.22 S. Wales Salvage Co.
M.96 T.29 T.75	PRIMROSE	29. 6.15	Simons. Sold 9.4.23 Rees, Llanelly.
M.97 T.30 T.82	SUNFLOWER	28. 5.15	Henderson. Sold 27.1.21 Rangoon Port Commissioners =LANBYA.
M.98 T.31 T.87	VERONICA	27. 5.15	Dunlop Bremner. Sold 22.2.35 Cashmore.

Flag M pendants changed 24.4.15 to flag M (International).

AZALEA TYPE

as Acacia type, except 2–4.7 in, 2–3 pdrAA (some with 2–4 in, 2–3 pdrAA)

9.15	1.18	Name	Launched	Builder—Fate
		Ordered 5.15:		
T.32	T.07	AZALEA	10. 9.15	Barclay Curle. Sold 1.2.23 J. Hornby.
T.33		BEGONIA	26. 8.15	Barclay Curle. =decoy ship from 9.8.17, (DOLCIS, JESSOP, Q.10); Sunk 2.10.17 in collision with U.151 off Casablanca.
T.34	T.15	CAMELLIA	25. 9.15	Bow McLachlan. Sold 15.1.23 Unity S Bkg Co.
T.36	T.18	CARNATION	6. 9.15	Greenock and Grangemouth. Sold 14.1.22 Stanlee.
T.35	T.22	CLEMATIS	29. 7.15	Greenock and Grangemouth. Sold 5.2.31 Young, Sunderland.
T.37	T.41	HELIOTROPE	10. 9.15	Lobnitz. Sold 7.1.35 Metal Ind, Charlestown.
T.43	T.47	JESSAMINE	9. 9.15	Swan Hunter. Sold 21.12.22 T. E. Evans, Penarth.
T.38	T.65	MYRTLE	11.10.15	Lobnitz. Mined 16.7.19 in Gulf of Finland.
T.41	T.66	NARCISSUS	22. 9.15	Napier and Miller. Sold 6.9.22 A. A. Bond.
T.39	T.71	PEONY	25. 8.15	McMillan. Sold 20.8.19 T. R. Sales; resold =ARDENA.
T.40	T.80	SNOWDROP	7.10.15	McMillan. Sold 15.1.23 Unity S Bkg Co.
T.42	T.92	ZINNIA	12. 8.15	Swan Hunter. Sold 19.4.20 Belgian navy =ZINNIA.

ARABIS TYPE

1250 tons. 268 (oa), 255 (pp) ×33½×11 ft. TE 2000 ihp=16 kts.
Armament: 2–4.7 in (2–4 in in six), 2–3 pdrAA.

1.16	1.18	Name	Launched	Builder—Fate
		Ordered 7.15:		
T.46		ALYSSUM	5.11.15	Earle. Mined 18.3.17 SW of Ireland.
T.69	T.02	AMARYLLIS	9.12.15	Earle. Sold 30.1.23 B. Fryer.
T.44		ARABIS	6.11.15	Henderson. Sunk 10.2.16 by German TBs off Dogger Bank.
T.70	T.04	ASPHODEL	21.12.15	Henderson. Sold 16.6.20 Denmark, =FYLLA.
T.60	T.09	BERBERIS	3. 2.16	Henderson. Sold 30.1.23 Stuart General Trading Co.
T.45	T.14	BUTTERCUP	24.10.15	Barclay Curle. Sold 5.2.20 Hughes & Co, =SEMPER PARATUS.
T.48	T.16	CAMPANULA	25. 12.15	Barclay Curle. Sold 6.9.22 Cove & Distinn.
T.72	T.20	CELANDINE	19. 2.16	Barclay Curle. Sold 15.1.23 Unity S Bkg Co.
T.64	T.24	CORNFLOWER	30. 3.16	Barclay Curle. Lost 19.12.41 at the fall of Hong Kong.
T.59	T.25	CROCUS	24.12.15	Lobnitz. Sold 7.30 at Bombay.
T.73	T.26	CYCLAMEN	22. 2.16	Lobnitz. Sold 2.7.32 Metal Ind, Charlestown.
T.54	T.30	DELPHINIUM	23.12.15	Napier & Miller. Sold 13.10.33 Rees, Llanelly.
T.63		GENISTA	26. 2.16	Napier & Miller. Sunk 23.10.16 by U.57 in the Atlantic.
T.49	T.36	GENTIAN	23.12.15	Greenock & Grangemouth. Mined 16.7.19 in the Gulf of Finland.
T.56	T.37	GERANIUM	8.11.15	Greenock & Grangemouth. To RAN 1919; Dismantled 6.32; Sunk 24.4.35 as target off Sydney.
T.50	T.38	GLADIOLUS	25.10.15	Connell. Sold 10.3.20 Portugal, =REPUBLICA.
T.57	T.39	GODETIA	8. 1.16	Connell. Handed over 26.2.37 Ward, Milford Haven in part payment for MAJESTIC.
T.62	T.45	HYDRANGEA	2. 3.16	Connell. Sold 7.4.20 at Hong Kong, same name.
T.74	T.54	LOBELIA	7. 3.16	Simons. Sold 3.20 to Newfoundland Govt, same name; =hulk 1924.
T.65	T.55	LUPIN	31. 5.16	Simons. Sold 22.3.46, foundered and raised; BU 1947 Pounds, Portchester.
T.51	T.60	MARGUERITE	23.11.15	Dunlop Bremner. To RAN 1919; Dismantled 9.32; Sunk 1.8.35 as target.
T.75		MIGNONETTE	26. 1.16	Dunlop Bremner. Mined 17.3.17 off Galley Head, SW Ireland.
T.68	T.64	MYOSOTIS	4. 4.16	Bow McLachlan. Sold 30.1.23 B. Fryer.
T.76		NASTURTIUM	21.12.15	McMillan. Mined 27.4.16 near Malta.
T.52	T.68	NIGELLA	10.12.15	Hamilton. Sold 29.11.22 Hallamshire Metal Co.
T.61	T.69	PANSY	1. 2.16	Hamilton. Sold 12.1.20 Calcutta Port Commissioners, same name.
T.53	T.70	PENTSTEMON	5. 2.16	Workman Clark. Sold 20.4.20 =LILA.
T.66	T.72	PETUNIA	3. 4.16	Workman Clark. Sold 15.12.22 Batson Syndicate.

1.16	1.18	Name	Launched	Builder—Fate
T.47	T.74	POPPY	9.11.15	Swan Hunter. Sold 9.4.23 Rees, Llanelly.
T.55		PRIMULA	6.12.15	Swan Hunter. Sunk 1.3.16 by U.35 in the Mediterranean.
T.58	T.77	ROSEMARY	22.11.15	Richardson Duck. Sold 17.12.47; BU Ward Milford Haven.
T.71	T.79	SNAPDRAGON	21.12.15	Ropner. Sold 4.5.34 Cashmore.
T.67	T.85	VALERIAN	21. 2.16	C. Rennoldson. Foundered 22.10.26 off Bermuda.
T.77	T.86	VERBENA	9.11.15	Blyth SB. Sold 13.10.33 Rees, Llanelly.
T.78	T.89	WALLFLOWER	8.11.15	Irvine. Sold 28.8.31 Ward, Inverkeithing.
T.79	T.91	WISTARIA	7.12.15	Irvine. Sold 18.1.31 Ward, Inverkeithing.

Notes: All Flower class sloops were built on contract along merchant ship lines to facilitate production. The 72 vessels of the Acacia, Azalea and Arabis types were similar in their warship-like appearance and differed primarily in variations of armament. The first two types were all originally fitted as minesweepers and were shared out between the Grand Fleet, Queenstown and the Mediterranean. BEGONIA was fitted out as a submarine decoy ship (note her other identities) and lost while serving as such. LABURNUM became a drill ship at Singapore in 1935. The Arabis type M/S sloops were built to three orders all placed during 7.15. In addition to serving in the areas mentioned earlier for the Acacia and Azalea types, some of the Arabis type served in the North Sea. CORNFLOWER became a drill ship 1935, was sold 1940 = TAI HING; and repurchased 9.40. Eight similar vessels; ALDEBARAN, ALGOL (both Barclay Curle); ALTAIR, ANTARES (both Hamilton); BELLATRIX, RIGEL (both Henderson) ordered 1.16 and CASSIOPE, REGULUS (both Barclay Curle) ordered 9.16 were delivered to the French during 1916–17.

FLOWER CLASS: CONVOY SLOOPS
AUBRIETIA TYPE

1250 tons. 268 (oa), 255 (pp) ×33½×11½ ft. TE 2500 ihp=17½ kts.
Armament: 2–4 in, 1–3 pdrAA (designed for 3–12 pdr, 2–3 pdrAA).

1.18	6.18	Name	Launched	Builder—Fate
		Ordered 1.16:		
T.06		AUBRIETIA	17. 6.16	Blyth SB (KAI; Q.13; WINTON; ZEBAL) Sold 25.10.22 R. H. Partridge.
T.40		HEATHER	16. 6.16	Greenock & Grangemouth. (BYWATER; Q.16; SEETRUS) Sold 16.2.32 Demellweek & Redding, Plymouth.
		SALVIA	16. 6.16	Irvine. (Q.15) Sunk 20.6.17 by U.94 off SW Ireland.
T.84		TAMARISK	2. 6.16	Lobnitz. (COMPATRIOT; FERNRIDGE; Q.11) Sold 17.10.22 B. Fryer.
		TULIP	15. 7.16	Richardson Duck. (Q.12) Sunk 30.4.17 by U.62 in the Atlantic.
T.88		VIOLA	14. 7.16	Ropner. (CRANFORD; DAMARIS; Q.14) Sold 17.12.22 B. Fryer.
		Ordered 12.16:		
T.4A	T.02	ANDROMEDA	6.17	Swan Hunter. To French navy = ANDROMEDE; later = VILLE D' YS.
T.34		GAILLARDIA	19. 5.17	Blyth SB. Mined 22.3.18 in the Northern Barrage, North Sea.
T.42		HIBISCUS	17.11.17	Greenock & Grangemouth. (PALETTE) Sold 18.1.23 Metal Ind, Charlestown.
T.56		LYCHNIS = CORNWALLIS	21. 8.17 9.21	Hamilton. (KIDNER; WILANGIL) Ro RIM 9.21; Sold 1946.
T.63		MONTBRETIA	3. 9.17	Irvine. (ROCHFORT) Sold 25.1.21 Clan Line = CHIHUAHUA.
T.73		POLYANTHUS	24. 9.17	Lobnitz. (DEVERILL) Sold 25.1.21 Clan Line = COLIMA.

Notes: The first six served in the 1st sloop Flotilla at Queenstown 1916–17, then to 3rd sloop Flotilla, North Sea. ANDROMEDA (both a flower and star name) was later delivered to the French and re-rendered ANDROMEDE. Note that she was given a new pendant number in the 6.18 list. Notes for the Anchusa type following, also apply to this type for appearance and employment.

ANCHUSA TYPE

1290 tons. 262½ (oa), 250 (pp) × 35 × 11½ ft. TE 2500 ihp = 16½ kts.
Armament: 2–4 in, 2–12 pdr.

1.18	6.18	Name	Launched	Builder—Fate
T.01		Ordered 1.17: ANCHUSA	21. 4.17	Armstrong. (CASHEL; WINSTREE) Sunk 16.7.18 by U.54 off W coast of Ireland.
T.17		BERGAMOT	5. 5.17	Armstrong. Sunk 13.8.17 by U.84, Atlantic.
		CANDYTUFT	19. 5.17	Armstrong. (PAVITT) Torpedoed 18.11.17 by S/M and stranded near Bougie, N. Africa.
T.19		CEANOTHUS	2. 6.17	Armstrong. (CAIRD; LINKSMAN) To RIM 5.22 =ELPHINSTONE; Wrecked 29.1.25 Nicobar Islands.
T.23		CONVOLVULUS	19. 5.17	Barclay Curle. (ABNEY; MANTON) Sold 1.12.21 Stanlee.
T.31		EGLANTINE	22. 6.17	Barclay Curle. (ALDWYCH; HICKORY) Sold 1.12.21 Stanlee.
T.81		SPIRAEA	1.11.17	Simons. (AIRBLAST; CALEB) Sold 6.9.22 Distinn Syndicate.
T.3A	T.83	SYRINGA	29. 9.17	Workman Clark. Sold 31.3.20 Egypt, =SOLLUM.
T.94		Ordered 2.17: ARBUTUS	8. 9.17	Armstrong. (SPRIGG) Sunk 16.12.17 by UB.65 in St. Georges Channel.
T.98		AURICULA	4.10.17	Armstrong. (HEMPSEED) Sold 1.2.23 J. Hornby.
T.96		BRYONY	27.10.17	Armstrong. (COOKCROFT) Sold 3.4.38 Cashmore.
T.98		CHRYSANTHEMUM	10.11.17	Armstrong. Target towing 5.20; To RNVR 1938; Still in service, Embankment, London.
T.93		COREOPSIS	15. 9.17	Barclay Curle. (BEARDSLEY; BIGOTT) Sold 6.9.22 Ward, Preston; BU 5.24.
T.05		COWSLIP	19.10.17	Barclay Curle. (BRIGAND) Sunk 25.4.18 by UB.105 off Cape Spartel.
		DIANTHUS	1.12.17	Barclay Curle. (DHOBY) Sold 3.6.21 Mexican State Line =GUERRERO.
T.11		GARDENIA	27.12.17	Barclay Curle. Sold 15.1.23 Richardson Westgarth.
		GILIA	15. 3.18	Barclay Curle. Sold 15.1.23 Unity S Bkg Co.
	T.03	HAREBELL	10. 5.18	Barclay Curle. Arrived 12.39 Arnott Young, Dalmuir to BU.
T.21		IVY	31.10.17	Blyth SB. Sold 2.20 Howard, Ipswich; resold 2.6.21 Clan Line =SINALOA.
T.51		MARJORAM	26.12.17	Greenock & Grangemouth. To be renamed PRESIDENT 1921, but wrecked 1.21 at Flintstone Head on passage to Haulbowline to fit out.
T.99		MISTLETOE	17.11.17	Greenock & Grangemouth. Sold 25.1.21 Clan Line =CHIAPAS.
T.0A		PELARGONIUM	18. 3.18	Hamilton. Sold 25.1.21 Clan Line =OAXACA.
T.95		RHODODENDRON	15.10.17	Irvine. Sunk 5.5.18 by U.70 in the North Sea.
T.97		SAXIFRAGE =PRESIDENT 7.22	29. 1.18	Lobnitz. =RNVR drillship 1921, Still in service, Embankment, London.
T.67		SILENE	12. 3.18	Simons. Sold 29.12.21 Stanlee.
T.83		SWEETBRIAR	5.10.17	Swan Hunter. (AYRES; BRANGWYN) Sold 7.10.27 Cashmore.
T.2A		TUBEROSE	16.11.17	Swan Hunter. (SCATLIFF) Sold 15.1.23 Unity S Bkg Co.
T.1A		WINDFLOWER	12. 4.18	Workman Clark. Sold 7.10.27 Cashmore.

Notes: Built to resemble merchant ships; there were at least 18 variations of design among the Aubrietia and Anchusa types. Each builder was permitted to complete his contracts to his own designs while still retaining class dimensions, etc. Armstrong built to at least three designs, Barclay Curle at least two. The convoy sloops were intended to provide escorts for convoys while presenting the appearance of an ordinary merchant ship. As decoy (Q ships) some had false identities (in parentheses) given in the above listing and all had their armament hidden behind false plating, etc. A light defensive weapon (or dummy) was commonly visible on the poops of some vessels. These vessels served with the Grand Fleet or in the Mediterranean.

24 CLASS FLEET SWEEPING SLOOPS

1320 tons. 267½ (oa), 258 (pp) ×35 ×10½ ft. TE 2500 ihp=17 kts.
Armament: 2–4 in, 39 depth charges.

Pendant Nos.*	Name	Launched	Builder—Fate
T.95 (9.18)	ARD PATRICK	6. 6.18	Swan Hunter. Sold 12.8.20 M. Mazza; resold 1.12.21 Stanlee.
T.N9 (1919)	BEND OR	24. 9.18	Barclay Curle. Sold 12.8.20 M. Mazza; resold C. A. Beard.
T.3N (8.18)	CICERO	26. 7.18	Swan Hunter. Sold 1.12.21 Cashmore.
N.79 (9.18)			
T./6 (11.19)	DONOVAN	27. 4.18	Greenock & Grangemouth. Sold 15.11.22 Ferguson Muir.
T.00 (6.18)	FLYING FOX	28. 3.18	Swan Hunter. To RNVR 24.3.20 (still in service).
T.11 (1919)	HARVESTER	2.11.18	Barclay Curle. Sold 8.22 C. A. Beard.
T.N2 (10.18)	IROQUOIS	24. 8.18	Barclay Curle. =Survey vessel 1922; Handed over 28.6.37 Ward, Briton Ferry.
N.1A (11.19)	ISINGLASS	5. 3.19	Greenock & Grangemouth. Sold 12.8.20 M. Mazza; resold 15.11.22 Ferguson Muir.
T.99 (1919)	LADAS	21. 9.18	Osbourne Graham. Sold 6.11.20; Repurchased as mooring hulk; Sold 8.6.36 Metal Ind, Rosyth.
T.8N (5.19)	MERRY HAMPTON =HERALD 2.23	19.12.18	Blyth SB. =Survey vessel 1923; Scuttled 2.42 at Selatar; became Japanese HEIYO 10.42; Mined 14.11.44.
N.A3 (8.19)	MINORU	6. 6.19	Swan Hunter. Sold 25.2.20 M. Mazza, =HAIM MAZZA.
T.17 (1919)	ORBY	22.10.18	Swan Hunter. Sold 15.11.22 Ferguson Muir.
N.A0 (8.19)	ORMONDE	8. 6.18	Blyth SB. =Survey vessel 3.24; Sold 6.8.37 Ward, Briton Ferry.
T.4/ (4.19)	PERSIMMON	4. 3.19	Osbourne Graham. Sold 12.8.20 M. Mazza (to =SARINA MAZZA); sale cancelled, resold 13.10.22 Dundas Simpson to BU.
N.77 (9.19)	ROCKSAND	10. 7.18	Swan Hunter. Sold 15.11.22 Ferguson Muir.
T.6N (11.18)	SANFOIN	10. 6.18	Greenock & Grangemouth. Sold 15.11.22 Ferguson Muir.
T.2N (8.18)	SEFTON	6. 7.18	Barclay Curle. Sold 8.22 Colonel J. Lithgow.
N.A1 (8.18)			
T.05 (9.18)	SILVIO =MORESBY 4.25	12. 4.18	Barclay Curle. To RAN 12.24; =Survey ship 1925; =Escort 1940; BU 1946 Newcastle, NSW.
T.93 (6.18)	SIR BEVIS =IRWELL 9.23 =EAGLET 1926	11. 5.18	Barclay Curle. To RNVR 9.23.
T.3N (5.19)	SIR HUGO	20. 9.18	Greenock & Grangemouth. =D/S 10.19; Sold 25.6.30 Cashmore.
T./3 (1919)	SIR VISTO	4.12.18	Osbourne Graham. Sold 8.20 M. Mazza, =FANNY MAZZA.
T.N7 (10.18)	SPEARMINT	23. 9.18	Swan Hunter. Sold 29.11.22 Hallamshire Metal Co.

*Inferior pendants N and I signify Numeral and Oblique pendants respectively.
Notes: Ordered between 12.16 and 4.17. Two vessels, GALTEE MORE (Osbourne Graham, transferred to Swan Hunter 7.6.18) and SUNSTAR (Swan Hunter) were cancelled 3.12.18. These ships were built with straight stems and sterns, with superstructure of symmetrical layout to give a "double-ended" appearance. Some ships had their mast before the funnel, others had the mast abaft of the funnel. Ten ships were completed in 1918 and served in sloop flotillas at Granton and Gibraltar.

P CLASS PATROL BOATS

613 tons. 244½ (oa), 230 (pp) ×23¾×8 ft. Turbine 3500 shp=20 kts.
Armament: 1–4 in, 1–2 pdr, 2–14 in TT (P.52 had 2–4 in, 1–2 pdr, no TT).

Name	Launched	Builder—Fate
P.11	14.10.15	White. Sold 1.12.21 Stanlee.
P.12	4.12.15	White. Sunk 4.11.18 in collision in the Channel.
P.13	7. 6.16	Hamilton. Sold 31.7.23 Dover S Bkg Co.
=P.75 8.17		
P.14	4. 7.16	Connell. Sold 31.7.23 Cashmore.
P.15	24. 1.16	Workman Clark. Sold 26.11.21 British Legion, Plymouth.
P.16	23. 3.16	Workman Clark. Sold 26.11.21 British Legion, Plymouth.
P.17	21.10.15	Workman Clark. Sold 26.11.21 British Legion, Plymouth.
P.18	20. 4.16	Inglis. Sold 26.11.21 British Legion, Plymouth.
P.19	21. 2.16	Northumberland SB. Sold 24.7.23 British Legion, Richborough.
P.20	3. 4.16	Northumberland SB. Sold 5.23 Richardson Westgarth, Saltash.
P.21	31. 3.16	Russell. Sold 26.11.21 British Legion, Plymouth.
P.22	22. 2.16	Caird. Sold 12.12.23 Keen, Bristol.
P.23	5. 3.16	Bartram. Sold 24.7.23 British Legion, Richborough.
P.24	24.11.15	Harland & Wolff, Govan. Sold 1.12.21 Stanlee.
P.25	15. 1.16	Harland & Wolff, Govan. Sold 1.12.21 Stanlee.
P.26	22.12.15	Tyne Iron SB. Mined 10.4.17 off Le Havre.
P.27	21.12.15	Eltringham. Sold 24.7.23 British Legion, Richborough.
P.28	6. 3.16	R. Thompson. Sold 24.7.23 British Legion, Richborough.
P.29	6.12.15	Gray. Sold 24.7.23 British Legion, Richborough.
P.30	5. 2.16	Gray. Sold 24.7.23 British Legion, Richborough.
P.31	5. 2.16	Readhead. Sold 16.12.26 Demellweek & Redding, Plymouth.
P.32	20. 1.16	Harkess. Sold 1.12.21 Stanlee.
P.33	8. 6.16	Napier & Miller. Sold 1.12.21 Stanlee
P.34	22. 3.16	Barclay Curle. Sold 1.12.21 Stanlee.
P.35	29. 1.17	Caird. Sold 15.1.23 Unity S Bkg Co.
P.36	25.10.16	Eltringham. Sold 5.23 Richardson Westgarth, Saltash.
P.37	28.10.16	Gray. Sold 18.2.24 British Legion, Ramsgate.
P.38	10. 2.17	Hamilton. Sold 7.12 37 Ward, Grays.
=SPEY 2.25		
P.39	1. 3.17	Inglis. Sold 6.9.22 Marple & Gillott.
P.40	12. 7.16	White. Sold 1937 Ward, Milford Haven.
P.41	23. 3.17	Bartram. Sold 6.9.22 Granton S Bkg Co.
P.45	24. 1.17	Gray. Sold 15.1.23 Unity S Bkg Co.
P.46	7. 2.17	Harkess. Sold 28.10.25 Cashmore.
P.47	9. 7.17	Readhead. Sold 28.10.25 Alloa S Bkg Co, Charlestown.
P.48	5. 9.17	Readhead. Sold 5.23 Dover S Bkg Co.
P.49	19. 4.17	R. Thompson. Sold 15.1.23 Unity S Bkg Co.
P.50	25.11.16	Tyne Iron SB. Sold 1.12.21 Stanlee.
P.52	28. 9.16	White. Sold 5.23 Dover S Bkg Co.
P.53	8. 2.17	Barclay Curle. Sold 18.2.24 British Legion, Ramsgate.
P.54	25. 4.17	Barclay Curle. Sold 18.2.24 British Legion, Ramsgate.
P.57	6. 8.17	Hamilton. Sold 21.5.20 Egypt =RAQIB.
P.58	9. 5.18	Hamilton. Sold 1.12.21 Stanlee.
P.59	2.11.17	White. Sold 16.6.38 Ward.
P.64	30. 8.17	Inglis. Sold 9.4.23 Cashmore.

Notes: P.1–10 did not exist within this class. P.11–34 were ordered in 5.15; P.35–40 in 2.16; P.41–54 in 3.16; P.55–62 during 4/5.16; and P.63–64 in 6.16. Missing numbers were altered on the stocks and appear as part of the PC class. In pendant lists issued from 1.9.15 onwards, the P boats carried pendants P.11–75 (the same as their name). Other P flag superior numbers, including 1–10, were assigned to old battleships, cruisers, etc. Despite their lack of freeboard, the P boats proved themselves to be successful and useful fast patrol craft. They had a very low silhouette, twin screws, and were designed with ram bows of hardened steel. Boats P.11, 17, 21, 23 ,24, 49 and 50 were at Dover to 1918. All others were in the Nore LDF or Portsmouth Escort Force to 1918. Their TTs were removed and depth charges later added. Lack of a weatherproof charthouse was a definite handicap because the P boats were very wet during adverse weather conditions. In 8.18 several vessels were fitted to tow kite balloons.

PC CLASS PATROL BOATS

682 tons (PC.42–56). 247 (oa), 233 (pp) ×25¼ ×8 ft. Turbine 3500 shp=20 kts.
694 tons (PC 60–74).
Armament: 1–4 in, 2–12 pdr.

Name	Launched	Builder—(Q ship names)—Fate
PC.42	7. 6.17	Caird. (CULLODEN; MALLORY) Sold 1.12.21 Stanlee.
PC.43	14. 8.17	Caird. (CHARING; TREGO) Sold 20.1.23 J. Smith, Poole.
PC.44	25. 4.17	Eltringham. (MORTMAIN; ROLASK) Sold 9.4.23 E. Suren.
PC.51	25.11.16	Tyne Iron SB. (COCKELYTE; MOPSWORTH) Sold 18.1.23 Alloa S Bkg Co.
PC.55 =BALUCHI 5.22	5. 5.17	Barclay Curle. (JUGGERNAUT; METHYL) Commissioned in the RIM 2.2.22; Sold 1935.
PC.56	2. 6.17	Barclay Curle. (BIRDWOOD; PANACHE) Sold 31.7.23 Dover S Bkg Co.
PC.60	4 6.17	Workman Clark. (BURLINGTON; MEREDITH) Sold 18.2.24 British Legion, Ramsgate.
PC.61	19. 6.17	Workman Clark. (CHESNEY; DOWNTON) Sold 9.4.23 E. Suren.
PC.62	7. 6.17	Harland & Wolff, Govan. (KINGSNAKE; MORNINGTON) Sold 1.12.21 Stanlee.
PC.63	2.10.17	Connell. (ORRISROOT) Sold 5.23 Cashmore.
PC.65	5. 9.17	Eltringham. (MILFOIL) Sold 18.1.23 Alloa, Charlestown; BU 3.24.
PC.66	12. 2.18	Harkess. Sold 31.7.23 Hughes Bolckow.
PC.67	7. 5.17	White. (CHINTZ; FLASHLIGHT) Sold 1.12.21 Stanlee.
PC.68	29. 6.17	White. (NAKERBY; TELFORD) Sold 1.12.21 Stanlee.
PC.69 =PATHAN 5.22	11. 3.18	Workman Clark. TO RIM 5.8.21; Sunk 23.6.40 by internal explosion off Bombay.
PC.70	12. 4.18	Workman Clarke. Sold 3.9.26 Hughes Bolckow.
PC.71	18. 3.18	White. Sold 28.10.25 Alloa; wrecked 25.11.25 off South Shields.
PC.72	8. 6.18	White Sold 28.10.25 Hayes, Porthcawl.
PC.73 =DART 4.25	1. 8.18	White. Sold 25.2.39 Ward, Briton Ferry.
PC.74	4.10.18	White. =Decoy ship CHATSGROVE 9.39–10.39; Sold 19.7.48, BU Hayes, Porthcawl.

Notes: PC.65–70 were ordered 1.17; PC.71–74 in 6.17 The PC.42 to PC.63 group was ordered as plain P boats and converted while on the stocks 12.16. PC boats were built to resemble small merchant vessels for use as decoy (Q) ships. They were also known as "PQ" boats. The earlier vessels normally used at least two other names while acting as decoys and were in service as such until 3.18. All were based at Pembroke DY from completion to 1918. PC boats carried P flag superior pendants matching their boat number.

TWO SLOOPS (RIM)

2100 tons. 270½ (oa), 240 (pp) ×38½ ×11 ft. Turbine 1700 shp=14¼ kts.
Armament: 4–3 pdr.

Name	Launched	Builder—Fate
CLIVE	10.12.19	Beardmore. On sale list 1947.

259 tons. 248½ (oa), 225 (pp) ×34 ×9½ ft. Turbine 1900 shp=15 kts.
Armament: 4–12 pdr.

Name	Launched	Builder—Fate
LAWRENCE	30. 7.19	Beardmore. On sale list 1947.

Notes: LAWRENCE was known as NEW LAWRENCE until completion.

KIL CLASS PATROL GUNBOATS

895 tons. 182 (oa), 170 (pp) × 30 × 10½ ft. TE 1400 ihp = 13 kts.
Armament: 1–4 in, 6 (or more) depth charges.

Adty No.	Name	Launched	Builder—Fate
4004	KILBEGGAN	23. 9.18	George Brown. Sold 14.2.20 Robinson, Brown & Jopli =LUCKER.
4003	KILBERRY	2. 7.18	George Brown. Sold 14.2.20 RB & J =BOLAM.
4005	KILBIRNIE	16. 5.19	George Brown. Sold 14.2.20 RB & J =HOMESTEAD foundered 6.9.20 off the Seven Stones.
4007	KILBRIDE	21. 8.18	Hall Russell. Sold 14.2.20 RB & J =SCOTSGAP.
4009	KILBURN	28. 5.18	Hall Russell. Sold 14.2.20 RB & J =TARSET.
4013	KILCHATTAN	13. 4.18	Cook, W & G. Sold 14.2.20 RB & J =BENTON.
3814	KILCHREEST	8. 6.18	Smiths Dock. Sold 14.2.20 RB & J =HARROGATE.
3805	KILCHRENAN	15. 1.18	Smiths Dock. Sold 14.2.20 RB & J =BOMBARDIER.
4014	KILCHVAN	13. 7.18	Cook, W & G. Sold 14.2.20 RB & J =BELSAY.
3804	KILCLARE	14. 1.18	Smiths Dock. 14.2.20 RB & J =STANHOPE.
4015	KILCLIEF	8.10.18	Cook, W & G. Sold 14.2.20 RB & J =TYNEHOME.
4016	KILCLOGHER	24.10.18	Cook, W & G. Sold 14.2.20 RB & J =NORTHERNER.
3810	KILCOCK	27. 4.18	Smiths Dock. Sold 14.2.20 RB & J =SPINNER.
4027	KILDALKEY	13. 3.18	Cochrane. Sold 14.2.20 RB & J =KILDALKEY.
4028	KILDANGAN	15. 3.18	Cochrane. Sold 14.2.20 RB & J =BEBSIDE.
4029	KILDARE	10. 4.18	Cochrane. Sold 14.2.20 RB & J =MITFORD.
3800	KILDARY	1.11.17	Smiths Dock. Sold 14.2.20 RB & J =SORCERER.
3806	KILDAVIN	13. 2.18	Smiths Dock. Sold 14.2.20 RB & J =LEASIDE.
3811	KILDIMO	27. 4.18	Smiths Dock. Sold 14.2.20 RB & J =SOUTHERNER.
4030	KILDONAN	11. 4.18	Cochrane. Sold 21.11.19 Thornycroft =WATKIN.
3801	KILDOROUGH	16.11.17	Smiths Dock. Sold 14.2.20 RB & J =WEARMOUTH. =HASHEMI in RIN WW II.
3807	KILDORREY	14. 2.18	Smiths Dock. Sold 14.2.20 RB & J =DEMPSTER.
4031	KILDRESS	13. 4.18	Cochrane. Sold 21.11.19 Thornycroft =GLYNARTHEN
4032	KILDWICK	27. 4.18	Cochrane. Sold 21.11.19 Thornycroft =PENGAM.
3812	KILDYSART	11. 5.18	Smiths Dock. Sold 14.2.20 RB & J =EMBLETON. =INDIRA in RIN WW II.
3802	KILFENORA	14.12.17	Smiths Dock. Sold 14.2.20 RB & J =KILFENORA.
4033	KILFINNY	10. 5.18	Cochrane. Sold 14.2.20 RB & J =KENRHOS.
4034	KILFREE	11. 5.18	Cochrane. Sold 21.11.19 Thornycroft=PORTHMINSTER
3808	KILFULLERT	15. 3.18	Smiths Dock. Sold 14.2.20 RB & J =WEARHOME.
3813	KILGARVAN	27. 5.18	Smiths Dock. Sold 14.2.20 RB & J =HEATHER KING
3803	KILGOBNET	14.12.17	Smiths Dock. Sold 14.2.20 RB & J =MAXTON.
3815	KILHAM	10. 6.18	Smiths Dock. Sold 14.2.20 RB & J =EASTERNER.
3809	KILKEEL	27. 3.18	Smiths Dock. Sold 14.2.20 RB & J =FALCONER.
4049	KILLENA	9. 7.18	Smiths Dock. Sold 14.2.20 RB & J =EDWIN DOUGLAS.
4050	KILLERIG	9. 7.18	Smiths Dock. Sold 11.20 Lindsay, Swan Hunter =KILLERIG.
4051	KILLINEY	29. 7.18	Smiths Dock. Sold 14.2.20 RB & J =THROPTON.
4052	KILLOUR	9. 8.18	Smiths Dock. Sold 14.2.20 RB & J =NAWORTH
4053	KILLOWEN	6. 9.18	Smiths Dock. Sold 14.2.20 RB & J =CURLER.
4054	KILLYBEGS	7. 9.18	Smiths Dock. Sold 14.2.20 RB & J =ALWINTON.
4055	KILLYGORDON	10.10.18	Smiths Dock. Sold 14.2.20 RB & J =HOMEFORD.
4056	KILMACOLM	3.10.18	Smiths Dock. Sold 14.2.20 RB & J =NIGRETIA.
4057	KILMACRENNAN	5.11.18	Smiths Dock. Sold 14.2.20 RB & J =SEGHILL.
4058	KILMAINE	5.11.18	Smiths Dock. Sold 14.2.20 RB & J =CROFTER.
4059	KILMALLOCK	4.12.18	Smiths Dock. Sold 14.2.20 L. Gueret =MALLOCK.
4060	KILMANAHAN	17.12.18	Smiths Dock. Sold 14.2.20 L. Gueret =MANAHAN.
4061	KILMARNOCK	31. 3.19	Smiths Dock. Sold 14.2.20 L. Gueret =KILMARNOCK
4062	KILMARTIN	31. 3.19	Smiths Dock. Sold 14.2.20 L. Gueret =MANDRAKE.
4063	KILMEAD	1. 5.19	Smiths Dock. Sold 14.2.20 L. Gueret =MEAD; =MEAD in SAN WW II.
4064	KILMELFORD	14. 5.19	Smiths Dock. Sold 14.2.20 L. Gueret =MELFORD.
4065	KILMERSDON	30. 5.19	Smiths Dock. Sold 14.2.20 L. Gueret =MERSDON.
4066	KILMINGTON	30. 5.19	Smiths Dock. Sold 14.2.20 L. Gueret =MINGTON.
4067	KILMORE	17. 7.19	Smiths Dock. Sold 14.2.20 L. Gueret =NEWTONIA.
4068	KILMUCKRIDGE	28. 7.19	Smiths Dock. Sold 14.2.20 L. Gueret =NEWTON BAY
4069	KILMUN	11.10.19	Smiths Dock. Completed 20.2.20 as cable vessel; Sol 16.9.46 =RASK; wrecked 31.1.50.

Notes: Orders for these patrol gunboats (known as "fast trawlers" until 18.1.18) were placed with with six trawler-building firms from 7.17. Financial approval for all 85 along with constructional priority over standard trawlers was given in 11.17, since this programme clashed with the Strath-Castle-Mersey effort. From mid 1917 a type of patrol and escort vessel possessing greater endurance and sea-keeping qualities than trawlers was desired. 16 projected Castles were cancelled to enable Smiths Dock to build the 3800-3815 series gunboats; other builders were similarly diverted. Smiths Dock, the parent firm, produced these vessels at an average cost of between £18550 to £20300 for each hull and £19700 for each set of machinery. A reassessment of priorities was made on 2.3.18 in favour of normal trawlers, resulting in the cancellation of 30 gunboat contracts. Four builders were instructed to send prepared materials for cancelled gunboats to Middlesbrough where Smiths Dock was to continue production of KILS alone. Smiths Dock built a further 21 gunboats and on 16.7.18 received relocation of the cancelled contracts to become their numbers 757-786.

All vessels had Fishery flag superior (to Admiralty numbers) pendants and such vessels completed in time were part of the Auxiliary Patrol. At least eleven vessels were fitted as mine sweepers. The first vessel, KILDARY, was laid down 31.7.17 and delivered 17.12.17. Selection of Kil (meaning church) names for these ships caused considerable confusion and corruption of spellings. KILCAVAN, a cancelled vessel, appears in Navy List as in commission but in fact this ship was never completed. A double-ended appearance was given these vessels in an effort to deceive the enemy as to the direction of steaming. Gunboats completed after the Armistice were unarmed and soon appeared on the sale list. Robinson, Brown & Joplin (RB & J) purchased most of them and then resold to other buyers. With the sole exception of KILMUN, all vessels were sold out by early 1920. When altered for mercantile service; bows were straightened, the ships cut in two and sections were added amidships in most instances. When re-launched these reconditioned vessels were about 45 feet longer (pp) and their gross tonnage was increased by 200 or more tons over their original 530 TG measurement.

On 6.12.18 final cancellation of 30 KILS (then building by Smiths Dock) was reported. Only KILBRACHAN, cancelled 10.12.18, was still with her original builder. Cancellations are given below with their original builder:

Builder	No.	Name	No.	Name
Cochrane:	4035	KILGLASS	4042	KILLADOON
	4036	KILGOWAN	4043	KILLAGON
	4037	KILKEE	4044	KILLALOO
	4038	KILKENNY	4045	KILLANE
	4039	KILKENZIE	4046	KILLARNEY
	4040	KILKERRIN	4047	KILLARY
	4041	KILKHAMPTON	4048	KILLEGAR
Cook, W & G:	4017	KILCOLGAN	4022	KILCOT
	4018	KILCOMMON	4023	KILCREGGAN
	4019	KILCONNELL	4024	KILCULLEN
	4020	KILCOOLE	4025	KILCURRIG
	4021	KILCORNEY	4026	KILDALE
Geo. Brown:	4006	KILBRACHAN		
Hall Russell:	4008	KILBRITTAIN	4011	KILCAR
	4010	KILBY	4012	KILCAVAN
Hawthorns:	4001	KILBANE		
	4002	KILBARCHAN		

MONITORS

This type descended from the coast-service armoured ships of the Victorian era, though none had been built after 1872. When the need arose for coastal bombardment ships mounting large guns in hulls essentially of shallow draught, construction of this warship type was resumed. Hulls were quickly built to utilise spare heavy calibre guns and weapons taken from worn out or obsolete capital ships. Considering the exposure risks involved with such bombardment operations, it was desirable to present the least valuable ship type while retaining maximum gunpower. High speed and endurance were sacrificed in the monitor design and necessary protection and stability were provided for by a very unusual hull form in the larger vessels. They were used in support of the land forces and in the important attacks on bases in Belgium that were so valuable to the enemy U-boat campaign. The first two ships listed were not actual monitors, but were used for the same purpose.

GORGON CLASS COAST DEFENCE SHIPS

5700 tons.   310 (oa), 290 (pp) × 55 (73½ over bulges) × 16½ ft.   TE 4000 ihp = 13 kts.
Armament: 2–9.2 in, 4–6 in, 2–3 in AA.   Armour: 7 in sides, 2 in deck, 8 in guns.

Pendant Nos. 9.15 1.18		Name	Launched	Builder—Fate
N.03	N.50	GLATTON	8. 8.14	Armstrong. Sunk 16.9.18 by internal explosion at Dover.
P.59	N.51	GORGON	9. 6.14	Armstrong. Sold 28.8.28 Ward, Pembroke Dock.

Notes: Originally the Norwegian BJOERGVIN and NIDAROS, construction was suspended 8.14, they were taken over 9.1.15 and purchased 31.1.15; completed 7.18 and 6.18 respectively. They lacked the important virtues of the monitor design; compared with a monitor of similar tonnage, the guns were too small and the draught too great. They operated off the Belgian coast in 1918.

ABERCROMBIE CLASS

6150 tons.   334½ (oa), 320 (pp) × 90 × 10 ft.   Quad. Expansion (1st two).
Armament: 2–14 in, 2–12 pdr, 1–3 pdr, 1–2 pdr.   TE (others) 2300 ihp = 6 kts.
        1–7.5 in added in HAVELOCK, 2–6 in to others 1916–17).
Armour: 4 in deck, 10 in guns.

4.15	9.15	1.18	Name	Launched	Builder—Fate
M.01		M.00	ABERCROMBIE	15. 4.15	Harland & Wolff, Belfast. Sold 25.6.27 Ward, Inverkeithing.
M.02		M.05	HAVELOCK	29. 4.15	Harland & Wolff, Belfast. Sold 25.6.27 Ward, Preston.
M.09	M.03	M.14	RAGLAN	29. 4.15	Harland & Wolff, Govan. Sunk 20.1.18 by BRESLAU & GOEBEN off Imbros.
M.08	M.04	M.1A	ROBERTS	15. 4.15	Swan Hunter. Sold 9.36 Ward, Preston.

Notes: These ships had many alterations of name:
(1) LD 11.14 as FARRAGUT; ADMIRAL FARRAGUT 12.14; M.1 31.5.15; GENERAL ABERCROMBIE 19.6.15; ABERCROMBIE 21.6.15.
(2) LD 11.14 as GENERAL GRANT; M.2 31.5.15; HAVELOCK 20.6.15.
(3) LD 11.14 as ROBERT E. LEE; M.3 31.5.15; LORD RAGLAN 20.6.15; RAGLAN 23.6.15.
(4) LD 11.14 as STONEWALL JACKSON; M.4 31.5.15; EARL ROBERTS 19.6.15; ROBERTS 22.6.15.

The 14 in guns had been intended for Greek battleships building in Germany. All went to the Eastern Mediterranean upon completion, remaining until 1918 except HAVELOCK and ROBERTS returned to home waters in 1916. HAVELOCK and ROBERTS were sold to Ward 9.5.21, but retained.

LORD CLIVE CLASS

5900 tons. 336½ (oa), 320 (pp) ×87×10 ft. TE avg 2300 ihp = 6¼ kts.
Armament: 2-12 in, 2-12 pdr, 1-3 pdr AA.
   1 to 4-6 in added 1916-17 (none in EARL OF PETERBOROUGH).
   4-4 in added 1918 in place of 6 in (LORD CLIVE & SIR JOHN MOORE only).
   1-18 in added 1918 (GENERAL WOLFE and LORD CLIVE only).
Armour: 6 in deck, 10½ in guns.

4.15	9.15	1.18	Name	Launched	Builder—Fate
M.04	M.09	M.01	EARL OF PETERBOROUGH	28. 8.15	Harland & Wolff. Sold 8.11.21 Slough T. C.; BU in Germany.
M.05		M.03	GENERAL CRAUFURD	8. 7.15	Harland & Wolff. Sold 9.5.21 Ward, New Holland.
M.14		M.04	GENERAL WOLFE	9. 9.15	Palmer, Hebburn. Sold 9.5.21 Ward, Hayle.
M.03	M.08	M.07	LORD CLIVE	10. 6.15	Harland & Wolff. Sold 10.27 McLellan.
M.10		M.11	PRINCE EUGENE	14. 7.15	Harland & Wolff, Govan. Sold 9.5.21 Ward, Preston.
M.07		M.12	PRINCE RUPERT =PEMBROKE 2.22	20. 5.15	Hamilton.=Base ship 2.22; Sold 5.23 Beardmore.
M.11		M.3A	SIR JOHN MOORE	31. 5.15	Scotts. Sold 8.11.21 Slough T. C.; BU 1922 in Germany.
M.06		M.4A	SIR THOMAS PICTON	30. 9.15	Harland & Wolff. Sold 8.11.21 Slough T. C.; BU in Germany.

Notes: Respectively these were *ex-M.8; ex Craufurd, ex-M.7; ex- Sir James Wolfe, ex-Wolfe, ex-M.9; ex-Clive, ex-M.6; ex-M.11; ex-M.10; ex-M.5;* and *ex-Picton, ex-M.12*. The M numbers were changed in 6.15. The 12 in guns came from disarmed battleships. Three vessels were selected in 9.17 to mount the 18 in guns (two plus one spare) built for FURIOUS. The installation abaft funnel with the big gun pointing to starboard (only 10 degrees trainable either way from central position) was effected in two ships, but the PRINCE EUGENE project was not completed. EARL OF PETERBOROUGH and SIR THOMAS PICTON were in the Mediterranean 1915-18; the others operated from Dover for most of the war.

MARSHAL NEY CLASS

6670 tons. 336 (oa), 340 (pp) ×90×10 ft. Diesel 1500 bhp = 6¼ kts.
Armament: 2-15 in, 2-12 pdr.
   2-6 in added 1916, replaced by 8-4 in 1918 (MARSHAL SOULT).
   15 in removed 1916, replaced by 1-9.2 in, 4-6 in (MARSHAL NEY).
   6-6 in, 2-3 in AA 1917 (MARSHAL NEY).
Armour: 4 in deck, 13 in guns.

4.15	1.18	Name	Launched	Builder—Fate
M.12	M.08	MARSHAL NEY =VIVID 6.22 =DRAKE 1.34 =ALAUNIA II 1947	17. 6.15	Palmer.=Base ship 6.22; arrived 6.10.57 Ward, Milford Haven.
M.13	M.09	MARSHAL SOULT	24. 8.15	Palmer.=Base ship 1940; sold 10.7.46, BU at Troon.

Notes: These were laid down as M.13 and M.14 respectively. Their engines were dangerous and unreliable. M. NEY was re-armed as a guardship and M. SOULT was often towed into action by EREBUS or TERROR. Both based at Dover 1915-18.

CANCELLED MONITORS

Four improved steam-driven "MARSHAL NEYs" with 4-15 in guns, 10 knots speed were ordered in 5.15. Two were building by Harland & Wolff, one by Swan Hunter, and one by Hamilton. Provisionally named M.34-37 respectively, they were cancelled in 6.15.

EREBUS CLASS

8000 tons. 405 (oa), 380 (pp) ×88×11 ft. TE 6000 ihp = 12 kts.
Armament: 2-15 in, 8-4 in.
Armour: 6 in sides, 5 in deck, 13 in guns.

1.18	Name	Launched	Builder—Fate
M.02	EREBUS	19. 6.16	Harland & Wolff, Govan. Arrived 7.46 Ward, Inverkeithing to BU.
M.5A	TERROR	18. 5.16	Harland & Wolff, Belfast. Sunk 24.2.41 by A/C off Derna.

Notes: Ordered in 9.15. EREBUS received the 15 in guns and barbette removed from MARSHAL NEY. The blister hull proved to be successful protection against torpedo attack and provided a very stable gun platform, making them the most successful of the monitor designs to date. Both were based at Dover 1916-18.

HUMBER CLASS RIVER MONITORS

1260 tons. 266¾ (oa), 261½ (pp) × 49 × 5 ft. TE 1450 ihp = 12 kts.
Armament: 2–6 in, 2–4.7 in howitzers, (HUMBER had 3–6 in from 1915 and others later).

1914	9.15	1.18	Name	Launched	Builder—Fate
N.15	M.00*	M.06	HUMBER	17. 6.13	Vickers. Sold 17.9.20 F. Rijsdijk; became a crane lighter.
P.62	M.1A	M.10	MERSEY	1.10.13	Vickers. Sold 9.5.21 Ward, Morecambe BU 1923.
D.70	M.2A		SEVERN	19. 8.13	Vickers. Sold 9.5.21 Ward, Preston; BU 1923.

*Pendant from 4.15.
Notes: Taken over 4.8.14 from Brazil before completion. They were *ex-Javary, ex-Madeira* (wrongly MADURA in some references), and *ex-Solimoes* respectively; listed in the RN as gunboats HUMBER at Dover 1914, then to the Mediterranean; MERSEY and SEVERN at Dover 1914, in East Africa 1915–18, then to the Mediterranean.

M CLASS COASTAL MONITORS

540 tons (M.15–27); 570 tons (M.28); 535 tons (M.29–33).   170 (pp) × 31 × 6 ft.
TE 800 ihp = 12 kts (M.15–18); 650 ihp = 12 kts (M.21–22); Bolinders oil engines 640 bhp = 12 kts (others).
Armament: 1–9.2 in, 1–12 pdr, 1–6 pdr (M.15–28); 2–6 in, 1–6 pdr (M.29–33).
        1–7.5 in, 2–3 in (M.21, M.23–26) later.
        1–6 in, 2–3 in (M.27) later; finally 3.4 in, 2–3 in.

Name and Pendant No.	Launched	Builder—Fate
M.15	28. 4.15	Gray. Sunk 11.11.17 by UC.38 off Gaza.
M.16	3. 5.15	Gray. Sold 29.1.20 = TIGA.
M.17	12. 5.15	Gray. Sold 12.5.20 = TOEDJOE.
M.18	15. 5.15	Gray. Sold 29.1.20 = ANAM.
M.19	4. 5.15	Raylton Dixon. Sold 12.5.20 = DELAPAN.
M.20	11. 5.15	Raylton Dixon. Sold 29.1.20 = LIMA.
M.21	27. 5.15	Raylton Dixon. Mined 20.10.18 off Ostend.
M.22 = MEDEA 12.25	10. 6.15	Raylton Dixon. = M/L 1919; = T/S 1.37; sold 12.38 Cashmore; Stranded 22.1.39 coast of Cornwall.
M.23 = CLAVERHOUSE 12.22	17. 6.15	Raylton Dixon. To RNVR 12.22; arrived 21.4.59 S Bkg Industries, Charlestown to BU.
M.24	9. 8.15	Raylton Dixon. Sold 29.1.20 = SATOE.
M.25	24. 7.15	Raylton Dixon. Scuttled 16.9.19 in the Dvina River.
M.26	24. 8.15	Raylton Dixon. Sold 29.1.20 = DOEWA.
M.27	8. 9.15	Raylton Dixon. Scuttled 16.9.19 in the Dvina River.
M.28	28. 6.15	Raylton Dixon. Sunk 20.1.18 by BRESLAU and GOEBEN off Imbros.
M.29 = MEDUSA 12.25 = TALBOT 9.41 = MEDWAY II 1943 = MEDUSA 9.44	22. 5.15	Harland & Wolff. = M/L 1919; = D/S 9.41; sold 9.9.46, BU 1947 at Dover.
M.30	23. 6.15	Harland & Wolff. Sunk 13.5.16 by shore batteries, Gulf of Smyrna.
M.31 = MELPOMENE 12.25 = MENELAUS 1941	24. 6.15	Harland & Wolff. = M/L 1919; BU 1948 Rees, Llanelly.
M.32	22. 5.15	Workman Clark. Sold 29.1.20 = AMPAT.
M.33 = MINERVA 12.25	22. 5.15	Workman Clark. = M/L 1919; = hulk 6.43 (C.23), still in service.

Notes: Pendant members from 4.15 were M flag superior to the boat number. M.29–33 all ordered 15.3.15 from Harland & Wolff, who subcontracted M.32–33 to Workman Clark. M.29–33 received their 6 in guns from Queen Elizabeth class battleships. M.24–27 operated from Dover 1915–18, then went to the White Sea. The rest of the class served in the Mediterranean 1915–18.

GUNBOATS

ANT CLASS (EX-HARBOUR SERVICE TENDERS)

254 tons. 89½ (oa), 85 (pp) ×26×6 ft. Horizontal engines 260 ihp=8 kts.
Armament (1914): ANT 2–4.7 in; BLAZER 2–12 pdr, 2–6 pdr; BLOODHOUND 2–6 pdr; BUSTARD, KITE each 1–6 in, 1–4.7 in; MASTIFF 2–4.7 in, 1–12 pdr.

Pendant	Name	Launched	Builder—Fate
Answer	ANT (old)	14. 8.73	Laird. =BDV 1916; =target 10.21; sold 2.6.26 Granton S Bkg Co.
5	BLAZER	7.12.70	Portsmouth DY. Sold 19.8.19 Loveridge, West Hartlepool.
	BLOODHOUND	22. 4.71	Armstrong. Sold 28.6.21 F. Bevis.
Code	BUSTARD	7. 1.71	Napier. Sold 3.23 Ward, Milford Haven.
	KITE	8. 2.71	Napier. Sold 18.5.20 Hughes Bolckow, =dredger.
	MASTIFF =SNAPPER 1914	4. 4.71	Armstrong. Sold 28.11.31 S Bkg Ltd, Thames.

Notes: These old "flatiron" ex-gunboats had been on harbour service since 1905 or earlier, and were commissioned in 1914 for service as gunboats on the Belgian coast. These iron-hulled vessels reverted to harbour service by 1916. BLOODHOUND and KITE were disarmed in 11.15; BUSTARD in 10.16. For others of this class, see under harbour service.

HERON CLASS RIVER GUNBOATS

85 tons. 108 (oa), 100 (pp) ×20×2 ft. TE 240 ihp=9 kts.
Armament: 2–6 pdr, 4 MG.

Pendant Nos. 11.19	Name	Launched	Builder—Fate
N.N8	NIGHTINGALE	27.10.97	Yarrow. Sold 20.11.19 at Hong Kong.
	ROBIN	.97	Yarrow. Sold 9.28 at Hong Kong.
	SANDPIPER	2. 7.97	Yarrow. Sold 18.10.20 at Hong Kong.
N.N5	SNIPE	.97	Yarrow. Sold 20.11.19 at Hong Kong.

Notes: Served on the China Station until 12.14 when they were paid off.

MISCELLANEOUS RIVER GUNBOATS

150 tons (1st two); 180 tons (2nd two); 195 tons (last one).
    148½ (oa), 145 (pp) ×24×2 ft. Compound 550 ihp=13 kts.
    165¼ (oa), 160 (pp) ×24½×2½ ft (WIDGEON).
Armament: 2–6 pdr, 4 MG.

11.19	Name	Launched	Builder—Fate
	WOODCOCK	*8. 4.98	Thornycroft. Sold 3.28 at Hong Kong.
N.0C	WOODLARK	*8. 4.98	Thornycroft. Sold 7.28 at Hong Kong.
N.6A	MOORHEN	13. 8.01	Yarrow. Sold 8.33 at Hong Kong.
N.72	TEAL	18. 5.01	Yarrow. Sold 10.31 at Shanghai.
N.71	WIDGEON	16. 4.04	Yarrow. Sold 10.31 at Shanghai.

Notes: The first two were built 1897 in sections and re-launched (*) in China. All were on the China Station and paid off in 12.14.

PURCHASED RIVER STEAMER

616 tons. 192 (oa), 180 (pp) ×30×6½ ft. Paddle 1200 ihp=14 kts.
Armament: 2–12 pdr.

	Name	Launched	Builder—Fate
	KINSHA	1900	Denny. Sold 30.4.21 at Shanghai.

Notes: Was *ex-Pioneer* purchased in 11.1900. China Station, paid off 12.14.

FLY CLASS RIVER GUNBOATS

98 tons.   126 (oa), 102 (pp) ×20×2 ft.   TE 175 ihp=9¼ kts. (tunnel screw).
Armament: 1–4 in, 1–12 pdr, 1–6 pdr (or 1–2 pdr).

Ordered 2.15:

Name	Date	Builder / Fate
BUTTERFLY	7.15	Yarrow. Sold 1.3.23 at Basra.
CRANEFLY	8.15	Yarrow. Sold 1.3.23 at Basra.
DRAGONFLY	7.15	Yarrow. Sold 16.2.23 at Basra.
FIREFLY	7.15	Yarrow. In Turkish hands 1.12.15 to 26.2.17; sunk 14.6.24 by Insurgents on the Euphrates.
GADFLY	8.15	Yarrow. To Air Ministry at Basra 1922.
GRAYFLY	8.15	Yarrow. To War Dept 1923.
GREENFLY	9.15	Yarrow. Sold 1.3.23 at Basra.
MAYFLY	8.15	Yarrow. Sold 1.3.23 at Basra.
SAWFLY	8.15	Yarrow. Sold 1.3.23 at Basra.
SNAKEFLY	9.15	Yarrow. Sold 1.3.23 at Basra.
STONEFLY	9.15	Yarrow. Sold 1.3.23 at Basra.
WATERFLY	9.15	Yarrow. Sold 17.2.23 Anglo-Persian Oil Co at Basra.

Ordered 12.15:

Name	Date	Builder / Fate
BLACKFLY	4.16	Yarrow. Lost 26.5.23 in collision (struck a bridge) at Baghdad while on loan to Air Ministry.
CADDISFLY	4.16	Yarrow. Sold 17.2.23 Anglo-Persian Oil Co.
HOVERFLY	4.16	Yarrow. Sold 16.2.23 Basra Port Authority.
SEDGEFLY	9.16	Yarrow. Sold 1.3.23 at Basra.

Notes: These were built in sections and re-erected on the river Tigris. The dates in what is normally the launch column are when the sections were sent out. The first date of re-erection is 11.15 (BUTTERFLY and FIREFLY). BLACKFLY, from the second order, was re-erected 22.3.17. These vessels spent their war careers in Mesopotamia in support of military operations there.

INSECT CLASS RIVER GUNBOATS

645 tons.   237½ (oa), 230 (pp) ×36×4 ft.   TE 2000 ihp=14 kts.
Armament: 2–6 in, 2–12 pdr.   (twin screws in tunnels)

1.16	1.18	Name	Launched	Builder—Fate
P.96	P.03	APHIS	15. 9.15	Ailsa SB. Sold 1947 at Singapore.
P.99	P.07	BEE	8.12.15	Ailsa SB. Sold 22.3.39 at Shanghai.
P.4A	P.82	CICALA	10.12.15	Barclay Curle. Sunk 21.12.41 by A/C, Hong Kong.
P.95	P.83	COCKCHAFER	16.12.15	Barclay Curle. Sold 1949 at Singapore.
P.82	P.85	CRICKET	16.12.15	Barclay Curle. Mined 6.41 in the Mediterranean and BU 1942.
P.94	P.93	GLOWWORM	5. 2.16	Barclay Curle. Sold 9.28 at Malta.
P.97	P.94	GNAT	3.12.15	Lobnitz. Torpedoed 21.10.41 in Mediterranean, laid up; BU 1945.
P.5A	P.0A	LADYBIRD	12. 4.16	Lobnitz. Sunk 12.5.44 by A/C off Tobruk.
P.0A	P.5A	MANTIS	14. 9.15	Sunderland SB. Sold 20.1.40 in China.
P.7A	P.8A	MOTH	9.10.15	Sunderland SB. Scuttled 21.12.41 at Hong Kong; =Japanese SUMA; Mined 19.3.45.
P.98	P.A2	SCARAB	7.10.15	Wood Skinner. BU 5.48 at Singapore.
P.6A	P.A8	TARANTULA	18.12.15	Wood Skinner. Sunk 1.5.46 as target off Ceylon.

Notes: Ordered 2.15, these "China Gunboats" were actually intended for operations on the Danube but served elsewhere. APHIS, BEE, LADYBIRD, SCARAB were in the Mediterranean 1916–18 (last 3 in Mesopotamia 1917–18); GNAT, MANTIS, MOTH, TARANTULA in Mesopotamia 1916–18. The other four in the North Sea 1916–18, then to the White Sea.

MINESWEEPERS

Despite the lessons that should have been learned from the Russo-Japanese War of 1905, little attention was paid to mine-sweeping until 1909 when some of the torpedo gunboats were fitted for this duty and half a dozen trawlers were purchased for conversion. The naval powers were slow to appreciate the warnings of future mine warfare and to admit that one offensive minelayer was capable of providing a threat that could cause employment of hundreds of sweeping vessels. At the outbreak of war in August 1914 the total minesweeping force of the Royal Navy comprised 10 torpedo gunboats and 13 trawlers, the latter being used on training duties. For details of the trawlers, see under that section. Also the minesweeping reserve which became the Auxiliary Patrol was available but this took time to put into service on a scale to become equal to the task facing them. Requisition and construction of vessels for minesweeping service soon added large numbers to the navy.

SHARPSHOOTER CLASS TORPEDO GUNBOATS; FITTED WITH SWEEPS
1909

735 tons   230 (pp) ×27×8½ ft.   TE 3600 ihp =20 kts.
Armament: 2–4.7 in, 4–3 pdr, 3–14 in TT.

Pendant Nos. 1914	1.18	9.18	Name	Launched	Builder—Fate
D.68*	N.52		GOSSAMER	9. 1.90	Sheerness DY. Sold 20.3.20 Cornish Salvage Co, Ilfracombe.
C.85	C.81	C.82	SEAGULL	31. 5.89	Chatham DY. Sunk 30.9.18 in collision with SS CORRIB in the Clyde.
P.81	P.A3		SKIPJACK	30. 4.89	Chatham DY. Sold 23.2.20 Hammond Lane Foundry, Dublin.
C.86	C.82	C.83	SPANKER	27. 2.89	Devonport DY. Sold 20.3.20 Cornish Salvage Co, Ilfracombe.
P.89	P.A4		SPEEDWELL	15. 3.89	Devonport DY. Sold 20.3.20 Cornish Salvage Co, Ilfracombe.

*Flag superior changed 9.15=N.68.
Note: For SHARPSHOOTER, see NORTHAMPTON under harbour service. Seven others of this class (not fitted for sweeping) were sold 1904–07.

ALARM CLASS TORPEDO GUNBOATS; FITTED 1909

810 tons.   230 (pp) ×27×10 ft.   TE 3500 ihp =19 kts.
Armament: 2–4.7 in, 4–3 pdr, 3–14 in TT.

1914	9.15	1.18	Name	Launched	Builder—Fate
D.81	N.81	N.26	CIRCE	14. 6.92	Sheerness DY. Sold 30.7.20 H. Auten.
N.18			JASON	14. 5.92	Vickers. Mined 7.4.17 West of Scotland.
N.28		N.69	LEDA	13. 9.92	Sheerness DY. Sold 14.7.20 Cardiff Marine Stores; BU 1922 in Germany.
			NIGER	17.12.92	Vickers. Sunk 11.11.14 by U.12 off Deal.
			SPEEDY	18. 5.93	Thornycroft. Mined 3.9.14 off the Humber.

Notes: For ANTELOPE (assigned pendants D.25 in 1914 and N.25 in 9.15), see under harbour service and for HEBE and ONYX, see depot ships. Three others (not converted) were sold 1905–07.

DRYAD CLASS TORPEDO GUNBOATS; FITTED AS SWEEPERS
1914–15

1070 tons.   262½ (oa), 250 (pp) ×30½×10½ ft.   TE 3500 ihp =18 kts.
Armament: 2–4.7 in, 4–6 pdr, 3–18 in TT.   (HALYCON 6000 ihp =20 kts)
            (HUSSAR 1–4.7 in, 2–12 pdr, 1–6 pdr)

1914	1.18	Name	Launched	Builder—Fate
P.90		DRYAD =HAMADRYAD 1.18	22.11.93	Chatham DY. On harbour service 1918; sold 24.9.20 H. Auten.
C.82	C.76	HALYCON	6. 4.94	Devonport DY. Sold 6.11.19 J. H. Lee.
P.63	P.95	HARRIER	20. 2.94	Devonport DY. Sold 23.2.20 T. R. Sales.
		HUSSAR	3. 7.94	Devonport DY. Sold 12.20; resold 13.7.21 at Malta.

Notes: DRYAD attached to 10th CS 1914–15, then M/S at Lowestoft to 1.18. HALYCON served as M/S at Lowestoft 1914–18; HARRIER was in the Downs Boarding Flotilla until 1915, then to the Mediterranean; HUSSAR spent the war in the Mediterranean, being S. O. M/S Force from 1915. For HAZARD of this class, see under depot ships.

SCREW MINESWEEPERS

Pendant Nos. 1914 9.15 1.18	Name	TG/Yr	Armament, etc.	Service
Fy.572	ATALANTA II	486/06	2–6 pdr AA.	3.12.15–26.6.19
M.30 T.04	CLACTON	820/04	2–12 pdr.	7.10.14–Sunk 3.8.16 by U.73 at Chai Aghizi.
M.33 T.07 T.32	FOLKESTONE	496/03	2–12 pdr.	9.10.14–31.1.20
M.40 T.14 T.35	GAZELLE	613/89	2–12 pdr =M/L 50 mines 5.15–11.15.	27.10.14–10.4.20
M.36 T.10	HYTHE	509/05	2–12 pdr.	18.10.14–Sunk 28.10.15 in collision with SARNIA off Cape Helles.
M.39 T.13 T.57	LYNN	609/89	(ex-*Lynx*) 2–12 pdr	27.10.14–5.3.20
M.32 T.06	NEWMARKET	833/07	2–12 pdr.	8.10.14–Sunk 16.7.17 by UC.38 in the Eastern Mediterranean.
M.34 T.08 T.76	REINDEER	1101/97	2–12 pdr.	2.10.14–30.1.20
M.35	ROEDEAN	1094/97	(ex-*Roebuck*) 2–12 pdr.	2.10.14–Sunk 13.1.15 at Longhope.
Fy.573	ST. SEIRIOL	928/14	2–6 pdr AA.	5.12.15–Mined 25.4.18 off the Shipwash LV.
M.35* T.09 T.90	WHITBY ABBEY	1188/08	2–12 pdr.	10.2.15–23.12.19

*Pendant from 22.2.15. The flag M pendants became MI (M international) 24.4.15 with the same inferior numbers. The two Fishery pendants date from 12.15.

Notes: Some accounts say ROEBUCK was added as ROEBUCK II; both LYNX and ROEBUCK were reported with their naval names on 6.11.14. CLACTON and NEWMARKET were at Sennen Cove 1.15 and the others were en route to northern waters, later in 1915 the vessels with MI pendants went to the Mediterranean.

ROEDEAN was lost after dragging her anchor in a gale and drifting on to the ram-bow of the repair hulk IMPERIEUSE (*ex-Fisgard*—see harbour service list).

PADDLE MINESWEEPERS

Adty No.	Name	TG/Yr	Armament—Service—Fate	
938	AIGLON	647/98	(ex-Eagle) 2-6 pdrAA.	22.11.15–23.7.20
587	ALBYN	363/93	(ex-Albion) 1-6 pdrAA.	26.5.15–15.3.19
583	BALMORAL	473/00	1-6 pdr. =in WW II.	15.5.15–11.6.19
842	BELLE	147/92	1-6 pdr.	26.5.17–9.1.19
506	BICKERSTAFFE	213/79		16.4.17–1.4.19
188	BOURNE	353/08	(ex-Bournemouth Queen) 2-6 pdrAA. =BOURNEMOUTH QUEEN in WW II.	5.2.15–5.5.20
181	BRIGHTON QUEEN	553/97	6.10.15 off Nieuport.	16.9.14–Mined
190	BRITAIN	459/96	(ex-Britannia) 1-6 pdrAA. =SKIDDAW in WW II.	28.1.15–13.4.19
557	CALEDONIA	244/89	1-3 pdr.	26.4.17–18.11.19
183	CAMBRIDGE	420/95	(ex-Cambria) 1-6 pdrAA, 1-3 pdrAA. =PLINLIMMON in WW II.	4.11.14–9.6.19
1238	CITY OF ROCHESTER	235/04	Fleet messenger 18.12.14; =PMS =in WW II.	17.6.17–27.11.19
930	CLACTON BELLE	458/90	2-6 pdrAA.	16.8.15–8.11.19
182	DEVONIA	520/05	1-12 pdrAA, 1-6 pdrAA. =in WW II.	16.9.14–9.6.19
533	DUCHESS	336/03	(ex-Duchess of Fife) 2-6 pdr. sold 1.23 Rees, Llanelly; =DUCHESS OF FIFE in WW II.	26.5.16–3.9.19;
590	DUCHESS OF BUCCLEUCH	450/15	1-6 pdr, 1-6 pdrAA. 1.23 E. G. Rees.	Purchased 12.7.15–Sold
531	DUCHESS OF FIFE	443/99	2-6 pdrAA.	23.3.16–9.12.19
933	DUCHESS OF HAMILTON	553/90	29.11.15 off the Longsand.	11.9.15–Mined
537	DUCHESS OF KENT	399/97	1-6 pdrAA.	20.6.16–23.9.19
585	DUCHESS OF MONTROSE	322/02	18.3.17 off Dunkirk.	15.5.15–Mined
935	DUCHESS OF ROTHESAY	385/95	1-12 pdr, 1-6 pdrAA. =in WW II.	14.10.15–29.3.20
534	EAGLE III	432/10	1-6 pdr, 1-6 pdrAA. =ORIOLE in WW II.	2.6.16–10.3.20
571	ERIN'S ISLE	633/12	1-6 pdr, 1-6 drpAA. 7.2.19 near Edinburgh LV, Nore.	21.11.15–Mined
589	FAIR MAID	432/15	9.11.16 near Cross Sand Buoy.	Purchased 12.7.15–Mined
185	GLEN AVON	509/12	1-12 pdr, 1-6 pdrAA. =in WW II.	4.11.14–5.7.19
843	GLEN CROSS	306/93	(ex-Glen Rosa) 1-6 pdr.	12.6.17–12.9.19
839	GLEN ROSA	323/77	1- pdr.	11.5.17–20.5.19
189	GLEN USK	524/14	1-6 pdrAA. =in WW II.	28.1.15–5.9.19
536	GRENADE	357/85	(ex-Grenadier) 1-6 pdrAA.	3.7.16–23.10.19
931	GREYHOUND II	542/95	2-6 pdrAA.	1.10.15–14.5.19
T.87 1246	HELPER	173/73	(ex-Sir Francis Drake tug =PMS,1.12.17–21.2.19. 1-3 pdr.	1.4.15–10.5.15;
554	HER MAJESTY	235/85	1-3 pdr.	23.4.17–24.6.19
556	ISLE OF ARRAN	313/92	1-3 pdr.	30.5.17–27.3.20
187	JUNIOR	592/98	(ex-Juno) 1-6 pdrAA.	29.1.15–27.6.19
584	JUPITER II	394/96	1-6 pdrAA.	15.5.15–29.5.20
844	KENILWORTH	390/98		18.6.17–2.5.19
576	KYLEMORE	319/97	(ex-Vulcan) 1-6 pdrAA. =in WW II.	23.11.15–20.2.20
841	LADY CLARE	234/91	1-3 pdr.	25.5.17–24.12.18
559	LADY EVELYN	320/00	1-6 pdr. =BRIGHTON BELLE in WW II.	25.4.17–6.6.19
186	LADY ISMAY	495/11	21.12.15 near the Galloper.	4.11.14–Mined

Adty No.	Name	TG/Yr	Armament—Service—Fate	
937	LADY MOYRA	519/05	(ex-Gwalia) 2-6 pdrAA. =BRIGHTON QUEEN in WW II.	21.11.15–9.7.19
1239	LADY ROWENA	332/91	Ferry at Scapa 12.4.16; =PMS	12.8.17–6.2.19
530	LONDON BELLE =HC.2 5.19	738/93	2-6 pdrAA. =hospital carrier 1.5.19.	18.3.16–9.7.20
575	LORNA DOONE	410/91	Misc Vessel 8.8.14–16.10.14; =PMS 1-6 pdrAA 13.12.15–30.12.19; =in WW II.	
558	MARCHIONESS OF BREADALBANE	246/90	=troop carrier from 21.1.19.	20.4.17–30.5.19
936	MARCHIONESS OF FIFE =HC.6 5.19	246/90	1-6 pdr, 1-6 pdrAA. 27.10.15–Purchased 23.10.17; =troop carrier 24.1.19; =hospital carrier 10.4.19; Sold 16.1.23 Ward, Inverkeithing.	
586	MARMION II	403/06	1-6 pdrAA. =in WW II.	15.5.15–27.5.20
438	MARSA	317/02	(ex-Mars) 1-6 pdr, 1-6 pdrAA. 22.9.16–Sunk 18.11.17 in collision at entrance to Harwich harbour.	
1637	MELCOMBE REGIS	253/92	(ex-Lune) 1-3 pdr. =Medway ferry from 17.5.19.	1.12.17–31.5.20
578	MERCURY	378/92	2-6 pdrAA.	21.12.15–24.1.20
560	MONARCHY	315/88	(ex-Monarch) 1-6 pdr. =EXWEY in WW II.	5.5.17–23.8.19
574	NEPAULIN	378/92	(ex-Neptune) 20.4.17 near Dyck LV.	7.12.15–Mined
555	PRINCESS BEATRICE	253/80	1-3 pdr.	23.4.17–26.6.19
934	QUEEN EMPRESS =HC.4 5.19	411/12	2-6 pdrAA. =hospital carrier 6.5.19; =in WW II.	25.10.15–30.6.20
580	QUEEN OF THE NORTH	590/95	2-6 pdrAA. 20.7.17 off Orford Ness.	29.3.16–Mined
588	RAVENSWOOD	345/91	1-6 pdrAA. =in WW II.	26.5.15–28.3.19
535	REDGAUNTLET II	278/95	4.6.16–Purchased 30.7.17; Sold 29.4.19.	
504	ROYAL PEARL	171/97	(ex-Pearl)	16.4.17–19.5.19
503	ROYAL RUBY	171/97	(ex-Ruby)	16.4.17–19.5.19
505	ROYAL SAPPHIRE	223/98	(ex-Sapphire)	16.4.17–31.10.18
582	ST. ELVIES	567/96	2-6 pdrAA.	4.3.15–8.5.19
837	ST. TRILLO	164/76	(ex-Rhos Trevor) 1-3 pdr.	22.4.17–3.6.19
581	SLIEVE BEARNAGH =HC.5 5.19	383/94	1-6 pdrAA. 24.2.15–Purchased 23.10.17; =hospital carrier 21.1.19; Sold 16.1.23 Ward.	
577	SNOWDON	338/92	1-6 pdrAA.	31.12.15–31.5.19
532	SOUTHEND BELLE	570/96	2-6 pdrAA. =LAGUNA BELLE in WW II.	2.4.16–8.11.19
845	TALLA	279/96	(ex-Talisman)	8.6.17–10.10.19
529	VERDUN VERDUN II 2.17	804/88	(ex-Paris) 1-6 pdrAA. Purchased 17.3.16; Sold 4.22.	
579	WALTON BELLE =HC.3 5.19	465/97	2-6 pdrAA. =hospital carrier 6.5.19; =ESSEX QUEEN in WW II.	22.12.15–19.5.20
932	WAVERLEY	449/99	1-6 pdr, 1-6 pdrAA. =in WW II.	21.9.15–9.7.20
840	WAY	240/85	(ex-Waverley) 1-6 pdr.	11.5.17–20.5.19
184	WESTWARD HO =WESTERN QUEEN 7.18	438/94	1-12 pdrAA, 1-6 pdrAA. =WESTWARD HO in WW II.	4.11.14–20.5.19
846	WILLIAM MUIR	412/79	1-12 pdr.	7.6.17–21.5.19
929	YARMOUTH BELLE	522/98	2-6 pdrAA. =THAMES QUEEN in WW II.	16.8.15–3.1.20

Notes: Two additional vessels were fitting as PMS 15.5.17, CLOGHMORE (ex-Greenore) 217/96 and EARL OF DUNRAVEN 174/88 but they were released shortly after. The ferries HARLEQUIN and WANDERER (qv) became PMSs in 1917 and 1918 respectively. The patrol paddlers and other vessels including BROCKLESBY and KILLINGHOLME listed with MFAs were similar vessels. WESTWARD HO was intended to be renamed WESTHOPE by order 13.6.18, instead an order of 27.6.18 specified the name WESTERN QUEEN to become effective 1.7.18. Although most vessels of this type were hired, several were purchased by the Admiralty, two of which came into the RN as soon as completed. All carried Fishery flag superior pendants and served with the Auxiliary Patrol. The shallow draught, high speed and manoevrability of these ships made them desirable for most minesweeping work but they were far less satisfactory than trawlers as all-weather sweepers.

ASCOT CLASS PADDLE MINESWEEPERS

810 tons. 245¾ (oa), 235 (pp) × 29 (58 oa) × 7 ft. Diagonal Compound engines
Armament: 2–6 pdr, 2–2 pdr. 1500 ihp = 14½ kts.

Pendant Nos. Adty. 9.18		Name	Launched	Builder—Fate
881	T.16	ASCOT	26. 1.16	Ailsa SB. Sunk 10.11.18 by UB.67 off the Faroes.
882	T.09	ATHERSTONE	4. 4.16	Ailsa SB. Sold 12.8.27; =QUEEN OF KENT in WW II.
883	T.21	CHELMSFORD	14. 6.16	Ailsa SB. Sold 25.11.27 Hughes Bolckow.
884	T.54	CHELTENHAM	12. 4.16	Ardrossan SB. Sold 7.10.27 Cashmore.
885	T.19	CHEPSTOW	29. 2.16	Ayrshire. Sold 25.11.27 Hughes Bolckow.
886	T.20	CROXTON	7. 4.16	Ayrshire. Sold 3.22 Ward, Inverkeithing.
887	T.56	DONCASTER	15. 6.16	Ayrshire. Sold 3.22 Ward, Inverkeithing.
888	T.02	EGLINTON	9. 9.16	Ayrshire. Sold 7.22 King, Garston.
889	T.59	EPSOM	4. 5.16	George Brown. Sold 3.22 Ward, Inverkeithing.
890	T.60	ERIDGE	23. 2.16	Clyde SB. Sold 3.22 Ward, Inverkeithing.
891	T.10	GATWICK	18. 4.16	Dundee SB. Sold 3.22 Ward, Inverkeithing.
892	T.22	GOODWOOD	15. 6.16	Dundee SB. Sold 7.22 Stanlee.
893	T.62	HALDON	29. 3.16	Dunlop Bremner. Sold 14.12.21 Stanlee.
894	T.66	HURST	6. 5.16	Dunlop Bremner. Sold 3.22 Ward. Inverkeithing.
895		KEMPTON	3. 6.16	Ferguson. Mined 24.6.17 off Dover.
896	T.24	LINGFIELD	29. 4.16	Fleming & Ferguson. Sold 5.23 Stanlee.
897		LUDLOW	1. 5.16	Goole SB. Mined 29.12.16 off the Shipwash.
898	T.94	MELTON	16. 3.16	Hamilton. Sold 25.11.27; =QUEEN OF THANET in WW II.
899	T.26	NEWBURY	3. 7.16	Inglis. Sold 3.22 Ward, Inverkeithing.
900	T.32	PLUMPTON	20. 3.16	McMillan. Beached on the Belgian Coast 19.10.18 after hitting a mine; later BU there.
901	T.C2	PONTEFRACT	2. 5.16	Murdoch & Murray. Sold 6.9.22 Bond.
902		REDCAR	31. 7.16	Ayrshire. Mined 24.6.17 off Dover.
903	T.68	SANDOWN	6. 7.16	Dunlop Bremner. Sold 3.22 Ward.
904	T.53	TOTNES	17. 5.16	McMillan. Sold 3.22 Ward, Inverkeithing.

820 tons. 249¾ (oa), 235 (pp) × 29½ × 7 ft.

1641	T.34	BANBURY	19.12.17	Ailsa SB. Sold 14.9.23 Hayes, Porthcawl.
3431	T.58	HARPENDEN	26. 2.18	Ailsa SB. Arrived 4.28, Charlestown to BU.
1639	T.35	HEXHAM	15.12.17	Clyde SB. Sold 14.9.23 Hayes, Porthcawl.
1646	T.37	LANARK	18.12.17	Fleming & Ferguson. Sold 5.23 Stanlee.
3433	T.85	LEWES	12. 3.18	Fleming & Ferguson. Sold 3.22 Ward, Inverkeithing.
3438	T.81	SHINCLIFFE	29. 1.18	Dundee SB. Sold 3.22 Ward, Inverkeithing.
905	T.57	SHIRLEY	28. 9.17	Dunlop Bremner. Sold 8.4.19 James Dredging Co, as a ferry.
3428	T.41	WETHERBY	2. 3.18	Murdoch & Murray. Sold 10.6.24 Alloa, Charlestown.

Notes: Named for racecourses, they were also referred to as "Racecourse class". 17 vessels were ordered 9.15; CHELTENHAM, GOODWOOD, HALDON and HURST in 10.15; the last three in 1.16. The BANBURY group was ordered in 1.17. These vessels were built as a result of the success of the hired paddlers in sweeping coastal waters and Ailsa'a GLEN USK was their prototype. Moored mines situated in areas where the range of tide was great could be swept much more safely by these types because of their shallow draught. All were given Fishery flag superior pendants using the Admiralty number and served with the Auxiliary Patrol. Later when they were in the Mine Clearance Service they still used these numbers even though the T pendants were also in use.

SEA BIRD CLASS PADDLE MINESWEEPERS

Five additional paddle sweepers were ordered in 1918 and cancelled 10.12.18. FULMAR, GADWALL and POCHARD (all Ailsa SB); STORMY PETREL and TERN (both Murdoch & Murray) were probably very similar to the previous types. No details are known and Admiralty Orders mentioned them only by name and builder indicating that very little progress had been made on them by the time of the Armistice. Two others, REDSHANK and SHRIKE, were unofficially mentioned as sisters but this pair was not ordered.

EARLY HUNT CLASS

750 tons. 231 (oa), 220 (pp) ×28×7 ft. TE 1800 ihp=16 kts.
Armament: 2–12 pdr, 2–6 pdr (some had 1–12 pdr, 1–6 pdr only).

Pendant Nos. Adty. 6.18		Name	Launched	Builder—Fate
483	T.C0	BELVOIR	8. 3.17	Ailsa SB. Sold 7.22 Stanlee.
484	T.C1	BICESTER	8. 6.17	Ailsa SB. Sold 8.1.23 Alloa, Charlestown.
485	T.C2	BLACKMOREVALE	23. 3.17	Ardrossan BS. Mined 1.5.18 off Montrose.
486	T.O7*	CATTISTOCK	21. 2.17	Clyde SB. Sold 22.2.23 Alloa, Charlestown.
487	T.C3	COTSWOLD	28.11.16	Bow McLachlan. Sold 18.1.23 Alloa, Charlestown.
488	T.6C	COTTESMORE	9. 2.17	Bow McLachlan. Sold 18.1.23 Alloa, Charlestown.
489	T.C4	CROOME	22. 5.17	Clyde SB. Sold 7.22 Stanlee.
490	T.C5	DARTMOOR	30. 3.17	Dunlop Bremner. Sold 21.2.23 Alloa, Charlestown.
491	T.C6	GARTH	9. 5.17	Dunlop Bremner. Sold 21.2.23 Alloa, Charlestown.
492	T.C7	HAMBLEDON	9. 3.17	Fleming & Ferguson. Sold 7.22 Stanlee.
493	T.C8	HEYTHROP	4. 6.17	Fleming & Ferguson. Sold 7.22 Stanlee.
494	T.C9	HOLDERNESS	9.11.16	Henderson. Sold 8.24 Ward.
495	T.7C	MEYNELL	7. 2.17	Henderson. Sold 4.11.22 Col. J. Lithgow.
496	T.0C	MUSKERRY	28.11.16	Lobnitz. Sold 22.1.23 Rees, Llanelly.
497	T.1C	OAKLEY	10. 1.17	Lobnitz. Sold 18.1.23 Alloa, Charlestown.
498	T.2C	PYTCHLEY	24. 3.17	Napier & Miller. Sold 7.22 Stanlee.
499	T.3C	QUORN	4. 6.17	Napier & Miller. Sold 18.9.22 J. Smith.
500	T.08*	SOUTHDOWN	7. 5.17	Simons. Sold 16.12.26 Granton S Bkg Co.
501	T.4C	TEDWORTH	20. 6.17	Simons. =Diving tender 8.23; sold 11.46, BU Ward, Hayle.
502	T.5C	ZETLAND	.17	Murdoch & Murray. Sold 18.1.23 North-East Salvage Co, W. Hartlepool.

*Pendants assigned 9.18.

Notes: Twin-screw fleet minesweepers, ordered during 1916. This class and other contemporary sweepers were coal-fired. ZETLAND completed in 9.17 and probably had been launched in 6.17. Most of this class formed the 2nd and 3rd Flotillas based at Granton.

LATER HUNT CLASS

800 tons. 231 (oa), 220 (pp) ×28½×7½ ft. TE 2200 ihp=16 kts.
Armament: 1–4 in, 1–12 pdrAA.

Pendant Nos. Adty. 11.19		Name	Launched	Builder—Fate
3450	T.0N	ABERDARE	29. 4.18	Ailsa SB. Sold 13.3.47 Dohmen & Habets.
3453	N.9C	ABINGDON	11. 6.18	Ailsa SB. Bombed 5.4.42 by Italian A/C off Malta, beached at Calcara; BU 1950.
T.9/ T.41	(1.19)	ALBURY	21.11.18	Ailsa SB. Sold 13.3.47 Dohmen & Habets.
T.92 T.06	(5.19)	ALRESFORD	17. 1.19	Ailsa SB. Sold 13.3.47 Dohmen & Habets.
T.00		AMBLESIDE =BEAUFORT 3.19	21. 2.19	Ailsa SB. Completed as survey vessel; sold 30.6.38 Cashmore; resold 27.7.39 Rees, Llanelly.
T.01		AMERSHAM =COLLINSON 3.19	30. 4.19	Ailsa SB. Completed as survey vessel; sold 25.10.22 McLellan.
N.7A		APPLEDORE	15. 8.19	Ailsa SB. Sold 16.10.20 =KAMLAVATI.
3458	T.N1 (10.18) T.8N	BADMINTON	18. 3.18	Ardrossan SB. Sold 19.5.28 Ward, Inverkeithing.
3452	T.15 (4.19) T.57	BAGSHOT	23. 5.18	Ardrossan SB. =D/S MEDWAY II 4.45 to 2.46; sold c1949; mined 1.9.51 in tow off Corfu.
3451	N.C0	BANCHORY	15. 5.18	Ayrshire. Sold 18.5.22 B. Zammitt, Malta.
		BARNSTAPLE	20. 3.19	Ardrossan SB. Sold 1.12.21 Stanlee; resold =LADY CYNTHIA.
		BATTLE	.19	Dundee SB. Sold 3.22 Ward, Inverkeithing.
3460	T.N8 (10.18) T.N5	BLACKBURN (ex-Burnham*)	13. 8.18	Bow McLachlan. Sold 17.10.22 Fryer.
		BLOXHAM (ex-Brixham*)	11. 9.19	Ayrshire. Sold 23.10.23 Col. J. Lithgow.
3444	T.9C (9.18) T.8C	BOOTLE (ex-Buckie*)	11. 6.18	Bow McLachlan. Sold 21.2.23 Alloa, Charlestown.

112

TOP: The cruiser BRILLIANT. 'Apollo' class
ABOVE: The cruiser VINDICTIVE. 'Arrogant' class—as assault ship 1918
/National Maritime Museum

TOP: The cruiser DIADEM. 'Diadem' class /*National Maritime Museum*
ABOVE: The cruiser PELORUS. 'P' class /*National Maritime Museum*

TOP: The cruiser CUMBERLAND. 'Kent' class   /*National Maritime Museum*
ABOVE: The cruiser ANTRIM. 'Devonshire' class   /*National Maritime Museum*

TOP: The cruiser TOPAZE. 'Gem' class /National Maritime Museum
ABOVE: The cruiser MINOTAUR. 'Minotaur' class /National Maritime Museum

TOP: The cruiser AMPHION.   'Active' class   /*National Maritime Museum*
ABOVE: The cruiser FALMOUTH.   'Weymouth' class   /*National Maritime Museum*

TOP: The cruiser **LOWESTOFT**. 'Birmingham' class /*Imperial War Museum*
ABOVE: The cruiser **UNDAUNTED**. 'Arethusa' class /*National Maritime Museum*

TOP: The cruiser CHESTER.   'Birkenhead' class   /*Imperial War Museum*
ABOVE: The cruiser CENTAUR.   'Centaur' class

TOP: The cruiser RALEIGH. 'Hawkins' class /*National Maritime Museum*
ABOVE: The cruiser DRAGON. 'D' class with hanger

TOP: The aircraft carrier EMPRESS /Vicary
ABOVE: The aircraft carrier CAMPANIA /Imperial War Museum

TOP: The aircraft carrier ARGUS   /*National Maritime Museum*
CENTRE: The aircraft carrier HERMES as completed 1923   /*National Maritime Museum*
ABOVE: The kite-balloon ship CANNING   /*Imperial War Museum*

TOP: The destroyer CONFLICT.   'A' class   /*National Maritime Museum*
CENTRE: The destroyer QUAIL.   'B' class   /*National Maritime Museum*
ABOVE: The destroyer STAR.   'C' class   /*National Maritime Museum*

TOP: The destroyer MALLARD. 'D' class   /*National Maritime Museum*
CENTRE: The destroyer DEE.   'E' class   /*National Maritime Museum*
ABOVE: The destroyer VIKING.   'F' class

TOP: The destroyer **SHELDRAKE**. 'H' class /*Imperial War Museum*
CENTRE: The destroyer **ACHERON**. 'I' class /*Imperial War Museum*
ABOVE: The destroyer **PORPOISE**. 'K' class /*National Maritime Museum*

TOP: The destroyer LANDRAIL. 'L' class, two funnels /*Imperial War Museum*/
CENTRE: The leader BROKE.   Chilean group   /*National Maritime Museum*/
ABOVE: The leader KEMPENFELT.   'Marksman' class   /*National Maritime Museum*/

TOP: The destroyer **OPAL**. 'M' class
CENTRE: The destroyer **STRONGBOW**.   Yarrow 'M' class   /*Imperial War Museum*
ABOVE: The destroyer **READY**.   Thornycroft 'M' class   /*National Maritime Museum*

TOP: The destroyer RESTLESS. 'R' class /*National Maritime Museum*
CENTRE: The leader MACKAY. 'Scott' class /*National Maritime Museum*
ABOVE: The destroyer WALRUS. 'W' class /*Imperial War Museum*

Pendant Nos. Adty 11.19		Name	Launched Builder—Fate
T.36 N.8A	(9.19)	BRADFIELD	14. 5.19 Ayrshire. Sold 10.20 =CHAMPAVATI.
3436 T.90 T.68	(6.18)	BURSLEM (ex-Blakeney*)	5. 3.18 Ayrshire. Sold 19.5.28 Ward, Inverkeithing.
		BURY	17. 5.19 Eltringham. Sold 20.1.23 J. Smith.
T.8/ T.43	(1.19)	CAERLEON	6.12.18 Bow McLachlan. Sold 4.22 Stanlee.
T./7* T.7/		CAMBERLEY	28.12.18 Bow McLachlan. Sold 7.23 C. A. Beard.
T.08		CARSTAIRS (ex-Cawsand*)	18. 4.19 Bow McLachlan. =DRYAD 1.24 to 8.24; sold 26.4.35 Ward, Grays.
T.80 T.07	(7.19)	CATERHAM	6. 3.19 Bow McLachlan. Sold 26.4.35 Cashmore.
T.60		CHEAM	2. 7.19 Eltringham. Sold 18.3.22 Coaster Construction Co.
3440 T.72 T.99	(9.18)	CLONMEL (ex-Stranraer)	14. 5.18 Simons. Sold 7.22 S. D. Harrison.
3442 T.99 T.A6	(9.18)	CRAIGIE	29. 5.18 Clyde SB. Sold 18.5.22 B. Zammitt, Malta.
3435 T.86	(9.18)	CUPAR (ex-Rosslare)	27. 3.18 McMillan. Mined 5.5.19 off the Tyne.
4352 T.N4 T.NO	(10.18)	DERBY (ex-Dawlish*)	9. 8.18 Clyde SB. Sold 7.46 at Gibraltar, BU in Spain.
4361 T.32 T.19	(12.18)	DORKING	26. 9.18 Clyde SB. Sold 6.28 Alloa, Charlestown.
T.91 T.0A	(4.19)	DUNDALK	21. 3.19 Clyde SB. Sank 17.10.40 off Harwich after mine damage the day earlier.
T.57 N.3A	(6.19)	DUNOON	21. 3.19 Clyde SB. Mined 30.4.40 in the North Sea.
T./5* T.39		ELGIN (ex-Troon)	3. 3.19 Simons. Sold 20.3.45; BU King, Gateshead.
		FAIRFIELD	30. 5.19 Clyde SB. Sold 3.3.20 =FLECHA.
3446 T.1N* T.C9		FAREHAM	7. 6.18 Dunlop Bremner. =ST. ANGELO II 44–45; Sold 24.8.48; BU Ward, Hayle.
3457 T.NO T.7N	(10.18)	FAVERSHAM	19. 7.18 Dunlop Bremner. Sold 25.11.27 Alloa, Charlestown.
N.7A N.A0	(7.19)	FERMOY	5. 2.19 Dundee SB. Sunk 4.5.41 by A/C at Malta DY; later BU.
4363 T.2/ T.N7	(12.18)	FORD (ex-Fleetwood*)	19.10.18 Dunlop Bremner. Sold 10.28 Hill, Dover; resold 8.12.28 =FORDE.
T./6* T.6/		FORFAR (ex-Fairburn)	20.11.18 Dundee SB. Sold 3.22 Ward, Inverkeithing.
T./1* T.40		FORRES (ex-Fowey)	22.11.18 Clyde SB. Sold 26.4.35 Ward, Pembroke Dock.
1638 T.43 T.78	(9.18)	GADDESDON	30.11.17 Eltringham. Sold 4.11.22 Col. J. Lithgow.
3430 T.76 T.67	(9.18)	GAINSBOROUGH (ex-Gorleston*)	12. 2.18 Eltringham. Sold 6.28 Alloa, Charlestown.
		GOOLE (ex-Bridlington) =IRWELL 9.26	12. 8.19 Ayrshire. Completed 4.26 as RNVR drillship; BU 11.62 Lacmots Ltd, Liverpool.
3441 T.8C T.38	(9.18)	GRETNA	11. 4.18 Eltringham. Sold 3.10.28 Alloa, Rosyth.
4351 T.N5 T.N1	(10.18)	HARROW	30. 7.18 Eltringham. Sold 1947 at Malta, BU at Genoa.
T./9* T.N2		HAVANT	24. 3.19 Eltringham. Sold 8.22 Thorneycroft for Siam =CHOW PHRAYA.
T.12 T.56	(4.19)	HUNTLEY (ex-Helmsdale*)	18. 1.19 Eltringham. Sunk 31.1.41 by A/C in the Eastern Mediterranean.
N.A4 N.A1	(8.19)	INSTOW (ex-Ilfracombe*)	15. 4.19 Eltringham. Sold 15.11.20 A. S. Miller, =TILAK.
1640 T.44* T.79		IRVINE	8.12.17 Fairfield. Sold 21.2.23 J. W. Houston, Montrose.
3426 T.45 T.80	(9.18)	KENDAL	9. 2.18 Fairfield. Sold 3.10.28 Alloa, Charlestown.
3449 T.5N	(8.18)	KINROSS	4. 7.18 Fairfield. Mined 16.6.19 in the Aegean.
4364 T.1/ T.N6	(12.18)	LEAMINGTOM (ex-Aldeburgh)	26. 8.18 Ailsa SB. Sold 19.5.28 Ward, Pembroke Dock.

Pendant Nos. Adty 11.19	Name	Launched	Builder—Fate
T.61 (6.19) N.A2	LONGFORD (ex-Minehead)	15. 3.19	Harkess. Sold 18.1.23 Col. J. Lithgow.
T./0 (1.19) T.44	LYDD (ex-Lydney 8.18)	4.12.18	Fairfield. Sold 13.3.47 Dohmen & Habets.
4362 T.5/ (12.18) T.N9	MALLAIG	10.10.18	Fleming & Ferguson. Sold 25.11.27 Hughes Bolckow.
T.16 (4.19) T.58	MALVERN	19. 2.19	Fleming & Ferguson. Sold 26.6.28 Alloa, Charlestown.
N.3A (6.19) N.4A	MARAZION	15. 4.19	Fleming & Ferguson. Sold 3.33 at Hong Kong.
4355 T.42 (12.18) T.77	MARLOW	7. 8.18	Harkess. Sold 21.4.28 Alloa, Charlestown.
T./4* T.3/	MISTLEY (ex-Maryport*)	19.10.18	Harkess. Sold 19.5.28 Ward, Pembroke Dock.
N.A3	MONAGHAN (ex-Mullion*)	29. 5.19	Harkess. Sold 15.11.20 A. S. Miller, =BOA VIAGEM.
3443 T.98 (9.18) T.A5	MUNLOCHY (ex-Macduff*)	12. 6.18	Fleming & Ferguson. Sold 23.11.22 J. Smith, Poole.
4356 T.A7* T.18	NAILSEA (ex-Newquay*)	7. 8.18	Inglis. Sold 25.11.27 Hughes Bolckow.
3455 T.7N* T.5N	NEWARK (ex-Newlyn*)	19. 6.18	Inglis. Sold 6. 28 Alloa, Charlestown.
4357 T.A8*	NORTHOLT	21. 6.18	Eltringham. Sold 29.2.28 Cashmore.
3432 T.79 (9.18) T.37	PANGBOURNE (ex-Padstow 5.18)	26. 3.18	Lobnitz. Sold 13.3.47 Dohmen & Habets.
3437 T.91 (6.18)	PENARTH	21. 5.18	Lobnitz. Mined 4.2.19 in the North Sea.
T./8* T.21	PETERSFIELD (ex-Portmadoc*)	3. 3.19	Lobnitz. Wrecked 11.11.31 Tung Yung Island China.
N.98 (6.19) T.03	PINNER (ex-Portreath*) =FITZROY 3.19	15. 4.19	Lobnitz. Completed as survey vessel; =M/S 1939; mined 27.5.42 off Great Yarmouth.
3445	PONTYPOOL (ex-Polperro*)	25. 6.18	Lobnitz. Sold 18.5.22 B. Zammitt.
4360 T.5N (11.18) T.2N	PRESTATYN (ex-Porlock*)	6.11.18	Lobnitz. Sold 22.1.23 Rees, Llanelly.
T.04	RADLEY =FLINDERS 3.19	26. 8.19	Lobnitz. Completed as survey vessel; =Accom ship 8.40; sold 8.45, BU at Falmouth.
T.65 (7.19)	REPTON (ex-Wicklow)	29. 5.19	Inglis. Sold 10.20 =RUPAVATI.
T.0/ (8.19) N.A4	ROSS (ex-Ramsey*)	12. 6.19	Lobnitz. Sold 13.3.47 Dohmen & Habets.
4359 T.01 (11.18) T.47	RUGBY (ex-Filey)	6. 9.18	Dunlop Bremner. Sold 25.11.27 Hughes Bolckow.
N.06 (7.19) N.A5	SALFORD (ex-Shoreham*)	3. 4.19	Murdoch & Murray. Sold 10.20 =VEGAVATI.
3456 T.9N (10.18) T.6N	SALTASH	25. 7.18	Murdoch & Murray. Sold 13.3.47 Dohmen & Habets.
4365 T.3/ (12.18) T.5/	SALTBURN	9.10.18	Murdoch & Murray. Sold 23.10.46; wrecked 12.46 in tow off Hartland Point; BU 1948.
T./2* T.1/	SELKIRK	2.12.18	Murdoch & Murray. BU 10.48.
3439 T.96 (9.18) T.36	SHERBORNE (ex-Tarbert)	27. 6.18	Simons. Sold 19.5.28 Ward, Inverkeithing.
3429 T.48 (9.18) T.81	SHREWSBURY	12. 2.18	Napier & Miller. Sold 25.11.27 Alloa, Charlestown.
3434 T.71 (9.18) T.98	SLIGO	23. 3.18	Napier & Miller. Sold 4.11.22 Col. J. Lithgow.
4367 T.7/ (7.19) T.42	STAFFORD (ex-Staithes*)	20. 9.18	C. Rennoldson. Sold 6.28 Alloa, Charlestown.
4353 T.N6 (10.18) T.N3	STOKE (ex-Southwold)	8. 7.18	C. Rennoldson. Sunk 7.5.41 by A/C at Tobruk.
3447 T.0N* T.C8	SUTTON (ex-Salcombe*)	8. 5.18	McMillan. Sold 1947.
N.91 (7.19) N.5A	SWINDON (ex-Bantry)	25.12.18	Ardrossan SB. Sold 1.12.21 Stanlee; resold =LADY CECILIA.
T.N3 (10.18) T.9N	TIVERTON	24. 9.18	Simons. Sold 12.38 Ward, Grays.
4358 T.A9*	TONBRIDGE	5.11.18	Simons. Sold 19.5.28 Ward, Briton Ferry.

Pendant Nos. Adty. 11.19	Name	Launched	Builder—Fate
4366 T.6/ (12.18) T.0/	TRALEE	17.12.18	Simons. Sold 2.7.29 A. O. Hill, Dover.
3454 T.4N (8.18)	TRING (ex-Teignmouth*)	23. 8.18	Simons. Sold 7.10.27 Alloa, Rosyth.
T.87 (4.19) T.7A	TRURO	15. 4.19	Simons. Sold 19.5.28 Ward, Milford Haven.
T.49* T.05	UPPINGHAM =KELLETT 3.19	31. 5.19	Simons. Completed as survey vessel; =M/S 1939; sold 20.3.45; BU Young, Sunderland.
T.02	VERWOOD (ex-Ventnor*) =CROZIER 3.19	12. 8.19	Simons. Completed as survey vessel; TO SAN 1921; =PROTEA 10.22; sold 10.33
T.86* N.A6	WEM (ex-Walmer*)	12. 9.19	Simons. Sold 22.4.21 =DESHALPUR.
N.A7	WEXFORD	10.10.19	Simons. Sold 1.12.21 Stanlee; resold; =DOOMBA in RAN WW II.
T.2N (5.19) T.4N	WEYBOURNE	21. 2.19	Inglis. Sold 4.10.28 Ward, Pembroke Dock.
3448 T.6N (9.18) T.1N	WIDNES (ex-Withernsea*)	28. 6.18	Napier & Miller. Damaged by A/C 20.5.41 and beached at Suda Bay; =German "12.V4" then UJ.2109; sunk 17.10.43 by RN destroyers in the Dodecanese.
4354 T.A6* T.A7	YEOVIL	27. 8.18	Napier & Miller. Sold 4.10.28 Ward, Pembroke Dock.

*Pendants assigned early 1919. Inferior pendants are: A (answer), C (code), N (numeral) and / (oblique) used to extend coverage for T flag superior.

Notes: 56 later Hunts were ordered in the first placing and by 11.18 there were 131 vessels built, building or projected. Many of the ships originally named for coastal towns were given new names (those renamed 25.6.18 are denoted *) when it was decided that confusion in signals and orders, etc. might arise from their use. The contract for FOWEY was originally placed with Dunlop Bremner as their number 330, but it was later transferred to Clyde SB and completed as FORRES. Some of them did not receive their intended armament when delivered after the war ended. These ships were slightly heavier than the early group and did not have a break in the deck aft. Only 32 vessels were in service by 10.11.18, widely distributed around home waters and five in the Mediterranean. They were employed on post war mine clearance duties and some of them remained in service to WW II.

35 vessels were cancelled 17.12.18; another, BOLTON, was cancelled later.

Ailsa SB:	ALTON (ex-Arbroath*), ASHBURTON.
Ardrossan SB:	BIDEFORD, BOLTON (ex-Beaumaris*).
Bow McLachlan:	CASHEL (ex-Cley*), CAVAN (ex-Clovelly*), CLIFTON, CREDITON (ex-Colwyn).
Clyde SB:	ATHELENEY, BALA, BATHGATE.
Dundee SB:	BECCLES, BLICKLING.
Eltringham:	CURRAGH, FLINT, FROME, GRAYS, KEW, KINGUSSIE, KNOWLE, NAAS.
Fleming & Ferguson:	two projected vessels.
Lobnitz:	NORTHREPPS, OKEHAMPTON, OUNDLE, RADNOR, READING RETFORD, RINGWOOD, RUNCORN, SHIFNAL, SMETHWICK.
Simons:	TAIN, WEMBDON, YEALMPTON.

BATTLE and BLOXHAM, in the "launched" list, were cancelled in 10.19 and sold incomplete.

DANCE CLASS TUNNEL MINESWEEPERS

290 tons (1st six). 130 (pp) ×26¼×3¾ ft. Compound 450 lhp=9½ kts (tunnel screw).
265 tons (others):
Armament: 1–12 pdr, 1–6 pdr (GAVOTTE, TARANTELLA);
1–3 pdr (COTILLION, COVERLEY, PIROUETTE, QUADRILLE, and SARABANDE);
1–6 pdr (all others).

Pendant Nos.*	Name	Launched	Builder—Fate
1240	COTILLION (ex-T.92)	4. 9.17	Day Summers. Sold 1.5.20 Crichton Thompson & Co.
1244	COVERLEY (ex-Roger de Coverley)	19. 7.17	Ferguson. Sold 1.5.20 Crichton Thompson; resold 10.26 Ward, Morecambe.
1243	HORNPIPE	25. 7.17	Murdoch & Murray. Sold 1.5.20 Crichton Thompson & Co.
1242	MAZURKA	13.10.17	Murdoch & Murray. Sold 1.5.20 Crichton Thompson & Co.
1241	MINUET (ex-T.93)	18. 9.17	Day Summers. Sold 1.5.20 Crichton Thompson & Co.
1245	QUADRILLE	21. 9.17	Ferguson. Sold 1.5.20 Crichton Thompson & Co.
1643	GAVOTTE	1. 3.18	Goole SB. Returned 1920 to War Dept.
1645	PIROUETTE	10. 9.17	Rennie Forrestt. Returned 1920 to War Dept.
1644	SARABANDE	12. 4.18	Goole SB. Returned 1920 to War Dept.
1642	TARANTELLA (ex-T.95)	22.10.17	Hamilton. Sold 1921 mercantile.
T.2N	FANDANGO (ex-T.98)	.17	Lytham SB. Mined 3.7.19 in the Dvina River.
T.0N	MORRIS DANCE (ex-T.99)	.18	Lytham SB. Sold 1.5.20 Crichton Thompson & Co.
T.1N	STEP DANCE (ex-ET.11)	.18	Lytham SB. Sold 1.5.20 Crichton Thompson & Co.
T.3N	SWORD DANCE (ex-ET.10)	.18	Lytham SB. Mined 24.6.19 in the Dvina River.

*Fishery flag superior pendants (except the last four, designated 11.6.19).
Notes: These were designed as "tunnel tugs" and were ordered by the War Department for use in Mesopotamia. The screw was in a tunnel under the hull (in same manner as many river gunboats) in order that the vessel's draught could be kept at a minimum. The first six were transferred from the War Deprtment 10.17; the next four in 12.17 and the last four in 4.19 (FANDANGO, etc. named 12.4.19). COVERLEY was known as ROGER DE COVERLEY until 1918.

MINELAYERS

APOLLO CLASS

3400 tons. 314½ (oa), 300 (pp) ×43×16½ ft. TE 9000 ihp=20 kts (designed).
Armament: 4–4.7 in, 100 mines. (ANDROMACHE 1–12 pdr only 6.18).

Pendant Nos.		Name	Launched—Bldr.	Conversion—Fate completed
1914	9.15	1.18		
N.22		N.03	ANDROMACHE	(14.8.90 Chatham DY)	13.9.09 Chatham DY. BU 8.20 Castle, Plymouth.
N.36		N.05	APOLLO	(10.2.91 Chatham DY)	4.8.09 Chatham DY. BU 8.20 Castle Plymouth.
P.51	N.49	N.67	LATONA	(22.5.90 Vickers)	6.08 Portsmouth DY. Sold 22.12.20 at Malta.
P.52		N.71	NAIAD	(29.9.90 Vickers)	23.8.10 Chatham DY. Sold 9.6.22 King, Troon.
P.85		P.0C	THETIS	(29.10.90 Thomson)	1.8.07 Portsmouth DY. Sunk 23.4.18 as blockship at Zebruggee.

3600 tons. 140 mines. (INTREPID 100.)

1914	1.18	4.18	Name	Launched—Bldr.	Conversion—Fate
N.30	N.59	N.21	INTREPID	(20.6.91 L & Glasgow)	27.9.10 Chatham DY. Sunk 23.4.18 as blockship at Zeebrugge.
N.27	N.60		IPHIGENIA	(19.11.91 L & Glasgow)	8.07 Chatham DY. Sunk 23.4.18 as blockship at Zeebrugge.

Notes: All minelayers of WW I were conversions from warships or mercantile vessels. These ships operated as minelayers from Dover and Sheerness 1914–15, then went on to subsidiary service, finishing the war as depot ships. As M/Ls, they laid nearly 8000 mines on 22 operations.

WARTIME WARSHIP CONVERSIONS

1.18	Name	Details
P.69	ARIADNE	Completed 20.3.17 at Devonport DY; 4–6 in, 1–4 in AA, 400 mines.
P.7C	AMPHITRITE	Completed 9.8.17 at Portsmouth DY; 4–6 in, 1–4 in AA, 354 mines.
N.41	LONDON	Completed 18.5.18 at Rosyth DY; 3–6 in, 1–4 in AA, 240 mines.
N.44	EURYALUS	Under conversion at Hong Kong, not completed.

Notes: For other details of this group see *cruisers* and *battleships* (for LONDON). The first three were in the 1st Mine Squadron, Grangemouth in 1917–18.

Apart from destroyers and submarines fitted for minelaying, the following cruisers were given mine rails aft, the after TTs being taken out and after guns rendered temporarily unusable. All mine rails were removed in 12.18.

Name	Fitted	Mines	M/L Operations	Mines laid
ROYALIST	2.17	74	16	1183
BLANCHE	3.17	66	16	1238
UNDAUNTED	4.17	70	—	—
AURORA	5.17	74	3	212
BELLONA	6.17	66	4	306
PHAETON	8.17	74	5	358
BLONDE	9.17	66	—	—
INCONSTANT	9.17	74	5	370
PENELOPE	11.17	70	3	210
GALATEA	11.17	74	3	220
BOADICEA	12.17	66	3	184

Also COURAGEOUS fitted 4.17 to carry 202 mines. No operations, ordered to have M/L installations removed 23.11.17. The lighter X.149, 21 CMBs, and 12 MLs were some of the other M/Ls.

MERCANTILE CONVERSIONS

Pendant Nos.	Name	Speed	TG/Yr.	Armament—Service
N.40 (4.15) N.04 (1.18)	ANGORA	17 kts	4298/11	3–4.7 in, 2–6 pdrAA, 320 mines. F/O at Blackwall; in service 27.2.15–15.11.19.
P.48 (3.15) N.10 (1.18)	BIARRITZ	23 kts	2495/15	2–12 pdr, 180 mines. F/O by Denny; in service 8.3.15–6.5.20. =in WW II.
N.62 (1.18)	OLD COLONY		4779/07	Taken over 20.5.18, fitting at Millwall in 11.18 and not completed. Sold 3.20 Walliker & Hindmarsh.
P.53 (1.15)	ORVIETO	18 kts	12130/09	4–4.7 in, 1–3 pdrAA, 600 mines. F/O at Blackwall; from 6.1.15 on 6 operations, laid 3000 mines. =Armed merchant cruiser (qv) from 27.5.16.
N.59 (1914) N.79 (1.18)	PARIS	25 kts	1774/13	1–4 in, 1–12 pdr, 1–6 pdrAA, 140 mines. F/O at Blackwall; service 14.11.14–5.11.19.
Y4.44	PERDITA	10½ kts	543/10	1–12 pdr, 1–6 pdrAA, 100 mines. Service 7.8.15–21.8.19; fitted as M/L at Mudros 1.16.
P.47 (1.15)	PRINCESS IRENE	23 kts	5934/14	2–4.7 in, 2–12 pdr, 2–6 pdrAA, 500 mines. F/O by Denny. In service 20.1.15; destroyed 27.5.15 by internal explosion at Sheerness.
P.46 (1.15) N.82 (1.18)	PRINCESS MARGARET	23 kts	5934/14	2–4.7 in, 2–12 pdr, 2–6 pdrAA, 500 mines. F/O by Denny. In service 26.12.14; purchased 14.6.19; sold 30.5.29 to BU.
Y4.51 N.5A (1.18)	WAHINE	21 kts	4436/13	2–14 pdr (Turkish), 2–6 pdrAA, 180 mines. Was fleet messenger 17.7.15–27.5.16. F/O at Blackwall as M/L, commissioned 22.7.16, listed to 17.2.20.

Notes: The screw minesweeper GAZELLE (qv) was fitted at Mudros in 5.15 (2–12 pdr, 50 mines) and continued as M/L until 11.15. KINFAUNS CASTLE, formerly a merchant cruiser and more recently a troopship, was commissed 13.7.18–15.2.19 while fitting at Millwall as a M/L. This conversion was not complete when the war ended and the project was then cancelled.

TRAWLER MINELAYERS
The following trawlers were each fitted to carry 24 mines and appear in the trawler listing: F/O 5.15 CARMANIA II, KING EMPEROR, RUSSELL II, SCOTT, SHACKLETON and WELBECK; F/O 5.16 OSTA, OSTRICH; F/O 3.18 THE NORMAN; F/O 4.18 SAVITRI; F/O 5.18 ST. MAURICE; F/O 6.18 PITFOUR; F/O 8.18 ERNA, HERO, KATE LEWIS and STRATHCOE.

CONTROLLED MINELAYERS
Six paddle vessels were fitted as controlled minelayers in early 1918: ALBERT VICTOR, QUINCE (each 8 mines); AMERICA, IRELAND, MEDLAR, and THE LADY CARMICHAEL (each 10 mines). Two other paddle vessels, FLYING FISH II (8 mines) and GOLDEN EAGLE (50 mines), were fitting in 11.18 and not completed. These vessels are included elsewhere with tugs, minesweepers, etc.

CANCELLED VESSELS
Two vessels, named ANGLESEY and SHEPPEY, were being built on contract by Messrs. Denny when the war ended. These minelayers were identified as builder's numbers 1034 and 1035, being cancelled 6.12.18 and directed to be fitted for other use. These numbers emerged in 1920 as ANGLIA 3460 TG and HIBERNIA 3458 TG.

ARMED MERCHANT CRUISERS

For some thirty years prior to the outbreak of war, surplus naval guns had been kept in store at strategic ports, many of them overseas, for the conversion of merchant liners into combatant units. The arming of some of these ships anticipated hostilities by a few days, and by the end of August 1914 a total of 18 ships had been taken up for conversion. Three of these, AQUITANIA, LUSITANIA and MAURETANIA were released after a very short time because of their exceptionally heavy fuel consumption; AQUITANIA and MAURETANIA were again requisitioned in 1918.

Pendant Nos. first*	1.18	4.18	Name	TG/Yr	Armament—Speed—Service
M.94			ALCANTARA	15831/14	8–6 in, 2–6 pdr; 16 kts. 10.3.15–Sunk 29.2.16 in action with German GREIF in the North Sea.
Ml.A0	Ml.50	Ml.28	ALMANZORA	16034/14	6–6 in; 16 kts. 23.8.15–20.12.19.
M.50	Ml.51	Ml.29	ALSATIAN	18481/13	8–4.7 in; 19½ kts. 7.8.14–4.4.19 later 8–6 in, 2–6 pdrAA. =EMPRESS OF FRANCE 1919.
M.87			AMBROSE	4595/03	8–4.7 in, 2–6 pdr; 15 kts. 20.11.14–Purchased 20.10.15 =depot ship (qv).
M.82	Ml.52	Ml.30	ANDES	15620/13	6–6 in, 2–6 pdr; 16 kts. 22.3.15–22.10.19 =ATLANTIS in WW II.
		Ml.56	AQUITANIA	45647/14	12–6 in; 24 kts. 2.8.14–5.9.14 and 1.18–1919
M.93	Ml.53	Ml.31	ARLANZA	15044/12	6–6 in, 2–6 pdr; 16 kts. 23.3.15–1.6.20.
M.63	Ml.54	Ml.32	ARMADALE CASTLE	12973/03	8–4.7 in; 17 kts. 2.8.14–11.9.19.
Ml.75			AVENGER	15000/15	8.6 in, 2–3 pdr; 18 kts. (ex-Aotearoa) 14.12.15–Sunk 14.6.17 by U.69 in the North Atlantic.
Ml.79	Ml.57	***	AVOCA	11073/07	8–6 in, 2–6 pdr; 16 kts. (ex-Avon) 14.1.16–29.10.19.
M.78			BAYANO	5948/13	2–6 in; 14 kts. 21.11.14–Sunk 11.3.15 by U.27 off Corsewall Point, near Stranraer.
			BERRIMA (RAN)	11137/13	14 kts. 11.8.14–20.10.14 =store carrier.
M.54	Ml.58		CALGARIAN	17515/14	8–6 in; 20 kts. 15.9.14–Sunk 1.3.18 by U.29 off Rathlin Island.
M.86			CALYX	2876/04	8–4.7 in, 2–3 pdr; 14 kts. (ex-Calypso) 19.11.14–26.6.15; later sunk 10.7.16 by S/M off Flamborough Head.
M.79			CARIBBEAN	5824/90	8–4.7 in, 2–6 pdr; 16 kts. (ex-Dunottar Castle) 19.11.14– =Accom ship 1.6.15; foundered 26.9.15 enroute to Scapa.
M.55			CARMANIA	19524/05	8–4.7 in; 18 kts. 8.8.14–6.7.16.
M.53			CARONIA	19687/05	8–4.7 in; 18 kts. 2.8.14–22.9.16.
M.74			CEDRIC	21040/03	8–6 in, 2–6 pdr; 17 kts. 17.11.14–20.1.16.
M.69			CELTIC	20904/01	8–6 in; 17 kts. 27.10.14–11.1.16.
M.85	Ml.63	Ml.35	CHANGUINOLA	5978/12	8–6 in, 2–3 pdr; 15½ kts. (ex-Carl Schurz) 21.11.14–17.1.20.
Ml.69	Ml.64	Ml.42	CITY OF LONDON	8917/07	8–6 in, 2–6 pdrAA; 15½ kts. 8.1.16–6.7.19.
M.81			CLAN MACNAUGHTON	4985/11	14 kts. 8–4.7 in. 19.11.14– Mined 3.2.15 in the North Atlantic.
M.89	Ml.69	Ml.36	COLUMBELLA	8292/02	6–6 in, 2–6 pdr; 18 kts. (ex-Columbia) 20.11.14–6.6.19.
M.83	Ml.55	Ml.33	DIGBY =ARTOIS 11.15	3966/13	5–6 in, 2–6 pdr; 14¼ kts. 22.11.14–6.1.19.
M.78	Ml.70	Ml.37	EBRO	8480/15	6–6 in, 2–6 pdr; 15 kts. 23.3.15–2.10.19.
M.62	Ml.71	Ml.55	EDINBURGH CASTLE	13326/10	8–6 in; 17½ kts. 4.9.14–12.7.19. =in WW II.
M.65	**		EMPRESS OF ASIA	16909/13	8–4.7 in; 19½ kts. 2.8.14–20.3.16.
M.57			EMPRESS OF BRITAIN	14189/06	8–4.7 in; 18 kts. 16.8.14–11.5.15.
M.66	**		EMPRESS OF JAPAN	5940/91	8–4.7 in; 16½ kts. 13.8.14–27.10.15.
M.68	**		EMPRESS OF RUSSIA	16810/13	8–4.7 in; 19½ kts. 24.8.14–12.2.16.
M.75			ESKIMO	3326/10	4–6 in, 2–6 pdr; 17 kts. 19.11.14– Released 18.7.15; captured 26.7.16 by Germans on mercantile service, restored 16.1.19.
Ml.87	Ml.72	Ml.38	GLOUCESTERSHIRE	8124/10	8–6 in, 2–3 pdr; 20.12.15–24.7.19.
M.90			HILARY	6239/08	6–6 in, 2–6 pdr; 15 kts. 21.11.14– Sunk 25.5.17 by U.88 west of the Shetlands.

Pendant Nos. first* 1.18 4.18	Name	TG/Yr	Armament—Speed—Service
M.91 Ml.73 Ml.39	HILDEBRAND	6991/11	8–4.7 in, 2–6 pdr; 15½ kts. Later 8–6 in, 2–6 pdr. 20.11.14–15.7.19.
M.67 ***	HIMALAYA	6929/92	8–4.7 in; 18½ kts. Later 8–6 in. 17.8.14– Purchased 1916, sold 4.22 Stelp & Leighton to BU.
M.81	INDIA	7940/96	18 kts. 13.3.15– Sunk 8.8.15 by U.22 off Norway.
Ml.74 Ml.34	KILDONAN CASTLE	9692/99	8–4.7 in; 17½ kts. Later 8–6 in. 25.3.16– 1.1.19.
M.64	KINFAUNS CASTLE	9664/99	8–4.7 in; 17½ kts. 5.8.14–16.9.15. Taken up 13.7.18 for conversion to M/L (qv).
M.70 Ml.75	LACONIA	18099/12	8–6 in; 16 kts. 27.10.14–2.8.16 =Armed storeship; sunk 25.2.17 by U.50 160 miles NW of Fastnet.
M.71	LAURENTIC	14892/08	8–6 in, 2–6 pdr; 17½ kts. 31.10.14– Mined 25.1.17 off Northern Ireland.
	LUSITANIA	30396/07	25 kts. 10.8.14– Released 1914; sunk 7.5.15 by U.20 off the Old Head of Kinsale.
M.59 Ml.76 ***	MACEDONIA	10512/04	8–4.7 in; 18 kts. Later 8–6 in. 2.8.14– 17.11.18.
M.51 Ml.77 Ml.40	MANTUA	10885/08	8–4.7 in, 2–6 pdr; 18 kts. 5.8.14–26.12.19.
M.58 Ml.78 Ml.41	MARMORA	10509/03	8–4.7 in; 18 kts. 3.8.14– Sunk 23.7.18 by UB.64 south of Ireland.
Ml.57	MAURETANIA	31938/07	25 kts. 17.8.14–1914 and 1.18–1919.
Ml.64 Ml.79 Ml.42	MOLDAVIA	9500/03	8–6 in, 2–6 pdrAA; 18½ kts. 27.11.15– Sunk 23.5.18 by UB.57 off Brighton.
Ml.80 Ml.43	MOREA	10890/08	4–6 in; 18½ kts. 28.3.16–18.10.19.
M.84 Ml.81 Ml.44	MOTAGUA	5977/12	6–6 in, 2–3 pdrAA; 15 kts. (ex-*Emil L. Boas*) 21.11.14–18.12.19.
Ml.58	NALDERA	15993/18	8–6 in, 2–6 pdrAA, 2–7.5 inBT; 18 kts. 29.5.18–14.3.19.
Ml.48	NARKUNDA	16227/20	Converting, work stopped 6.12.18.
	OCEANIC	17274/99	8–4.7 in; 20 kts. 9.8.14–Wrecked 8.9.14 on Foula, Shetlands.
Ml.26	OLYMPIC	46359/11	Taken up 1914 and released; Taken up again 31.3.17 and scheduled to complete 5.12.18; released 1919.
M.92 Ml.82	OPHIR	6942/91	8–6 in; 18 kts. 26.1.15– Purchased 26.2.15; paid off 29.7.19 and sold 8.21 to BU.
M.61	ORAMA	12927/11	8–6 in; 18½ kts. 4.9.14– Sunk 19.10.17 by U.62 south of Ireland.
Ml.A1 Ml.84 Ml.59	ORBITA	15678/15	6–6 in; 15 kts. 21.6.15–12.8.19.
M.86 Ml.85 Ml.46	ORCOMA	11571/08	6–6 in, 2–6 pdr; 15 kts. 23.3.15–11.10.19.
M.88	OROPESA =CHAMPAGNE 12.15	5364/95	6–6 in, 2–3 pdr; 14½ kts. 22.11.14– Sunk 9.10.17 by U.96 off Dundrum Bay, County Down.
M.80 Ml.86 Ml.47	OROTAVA	5980/89	5–6 in, 2–6 pdrAA; 16 kts. 19.11.14– Purchased 31.5.15, paid off 1.1.19; =troopship & BU 1923.
N.76 Ml.25	ORVIETO	12130/09	8–6 in, 2–6 pdrAA; 18 kts. Former M/L (qv) 26.5.16–19.10.19.
	OSIRIS	1728/98	21 kts. 5.8.14–9.10.14 and as depot ship 11.4.15–10.3.20.
M.60 Ml.87 ***	OTRANTO	12128/09	8–4.7 in; 18 kts. Later 8–6 in. 4.8.14– Driven ashore 5.10.18 off Islay after collision with SS KASHMIR.
M.73 Ml.88	OTWAY	12077/09	8–6 in, 2–6 pdr; 18½ kts. 11.11.14– Sunk 23.7.17 by UC.49 near Rona N. Minch.
M.76 Ml.89 Ml.48	PATIA	6103/13	6–6 in, 2–3 pdrAA; 15½ kts. 21.11.14– Sunk 13.6.18 by UC.49 in the Bristol Channel.
M.77 Ml.90 Ml.49	PATUCA	6103/13	6–6 in, 2–3 pdrAA; 15½ kts. 21.11.14– 17.7.19; =Kite balloon ship from 1917 to 13.12.18.
Ml.57 Ml.91	PRINCESS	8689/05	8–6 in, 2–6 pdrAA; 15 kts. (ex-*Kronprinzessin Cecilie*) Ex-dummy AJAX (qv); 9.1.16–10.9.17.

Pendant Nos. first* 1.18 4.18	Name	TG/Yr	Armament—Speed—Service
M.52 Ml.93 Ml.50	TEUTONIC	9984/89	8–6 in, 2–6 pdr; 19 kts. 5.9.14–Purchased 16.8.15; BU 1922 at Emden.
M.56 Ml.94 Ml.51	VICTORIAN	10635/04	8–4.7 in; 17½ kts. Later 6–6 in. 17.8.14–31.1.20.
M.82	VIKNOR	5386/88	15 kts. (ex-*The Viking*; ex-*Atrato*) 19.11.14–Mined 13.1.15 north of Ireland.
M.72 Ml.95 Ml.52	VIRGINIAN	10757/05	8–4.7 in, 2–6 pdr; 18 kts. Later 6–6 in, 2–6 pdr. 13.11.14–31.1.20; =DROTT-NINGHOLM 1920.

*Pendants in this column were assigned 1914–3.16 as the ships came into service; the flag superior of M pendants was changed 24.4.15 to MI (flag M from international code of signals) with change to the numbers inferior. ** Pendants cancelled 9.15. *** No pendant assigned; MACEDONIA's MI.76 cancelled 6.18, also OTRANTO's MI.87 gone 6.18. The pendants MI.25 (6.18), MI.42, MI.55, MI.34 (all 9.18) and MI.58, MI.48, MI.59 (after 9.18) included in the 4.18 column were later assignments.
Notes: DIGBY and OROPESA were transferred to the French flag and renamed from 24.11.15–19.7.17 and 2.12.15–27.7.17 respectively. KINFAUNS CASTLE was still converting to M/L at Millwall when the war ended. NARKUNDA was completing as a merchant cruiser, but this was not completed and this much-delayed ship was delivered in 1920. These ships were employed on patrol and convoy protection all over the world; 33 of them served for varying periods in the 10th CS based in Scotland and patrolled the German "north-about" route to the Atlantic.

COMMISSIONED ESCORT SHIPS

These ships were taken up in 1917–18 for convoy protection in the Atlantic and in addition to their gun armament, they were given a couple of 11 in anti-submarine howitzers. More aptly termed "convoy escort ships", they were an intermediate sized mercantile warship of slower speed and more economical to operate than the armed merchant cruisers.

Pendant Nos. 7.17	1.18	6.18	Name	TG/Yr	Armament—Speed—Service
		Ml.20	BAYANO	6788/17	4–6 in, 2–4 in; 14 kts. 3.12.17–3.19.
P.A1	Ml.59		BOSTONIAN	5626/96	3–6 in; 12 kts. (*ex-Cambrian*) 11.6.17–Sunk 10.10.17 by U.53 off Start Point.
		Ml.21	CAMITO	6611/15	4–6 in; 14 kts. 26.2.18–27.3.19. =in WW II.
		Ml.22	CARRIGAN HEAD	4201/01	2–6 in, 2–4 in; 3.8.17–25.2.19. Had been sqdn supply ship 4.8.14–1.4.16; Q ship 1.6.16–2.8.17 also Q.4 (1–4 in, 2–12 pdr).
		Ml.23	CORONADO	6539/15	4–6 in, 2–4 in; 14 kts. 30.9.17–20.3.19.
P.A3	Ml.96	Ml.53	DISCOVERER	5409/13	4–6 in; 13 kts. 16.6.17–1.3.19.
P.A2	Ml.97	Ml.54	KNIGHT TEMPLAR	7175/05	3–6 in; 11½ kts. 27.5.17–5.2.19.
		Ml.45*	LEPANTO	6389/15	2–6 in, 2–4 in; 10½ kts. 8.2.18–3.5.19.
P.A5	Ml.98		MECHANICIAN	9044/00	2–6 in, 2–4 in; 13 kts. 20.6.17–Sunk 20.1.18 by UB.35 off St. Catherine's Point, Channel.
		Ml.24	NANERIC	5609/95	2–6 in, 2–4 in; 10 kts. (*ex-Aotea*) 7.12.17–11.3.19.
P.A4	Ml.99		QUERNMORE	7302/98	3–6 in; 12½ kts. 29.6.17–Sunk 31.7.17 by U.82 off Tory Island.
P.A0	Ml.92		SACHEM	5354/93	3–6 in; 13 kts. 28.5.17–28.3.19.
		Ml.27	WYNCOTE	4937/07	2–6 in, 2–4 in; 10½ kts. (*ex-Den of Ruthven*) 10.8.17–12.3.19.

*Pendant assigned 9.18.

ARMED BOARDING STEAMERS

These vessels were employed on examination duties at sea for the purpose of enforcing the naval blockade. The great volume of traffic carried on by neutral ships made it necessary that constant checks be made to ensure that materials of benefit to the enemy were not allowed to slip through. The boarding vessels worked with cruiser squadrons and since they were much smaller and less valuable than the cruisers, they were exposed in the risky work of stopping at sea to perform the checks on merchant ships.

Pendant Nos. first* 1.18 6.18			Name	TG/Yr	Armament—Service
N.54	N.02		ALOUETTE	570/94	1–12 pdr. (ex-Calvados) Formerly a fleet messenger (Y4.5) 23.9.14–6.7.15; =ABS 7.7.15–21.11.19.
M.08	MI.00		AMSTERDAM	1777/94	1–4 in, 1–12 pdr; 17 kts. 31.10.14–29.9.19.
P.75			ANGLIA	1862/00	3–6 pdr. 8.8.14–24.4.15; =military hospital ship; mined 17.11.15 off Folkestone Gate.
M.12			CAESAREA	1500/10	2–12 pdr. 21.10.14–17.12.15; =BRUCE in WW II.
P.76			CAMBRIA	1842/97	3–6 pdr. 8.8.14–7.8.15; =military hospital ship; =ARVONIA 1919.
M.19	MI.01		CARRON	2351/09	2–4 .7 in; 15 kts. 22.11.14–9.10.19.
M.15	MI.02	**	CITY OF BELFAST	994/93	2–12 pdr; 16 kts. 30.10.14–3.10.19.
M.09	MI.03	MI.02	DUCHESS OF DEVONSHIRE	1200/97	2–12 pdr; 19 kts. 30.10.14–6.11.19; was a troop carrier 3.1.19–10.5.19.
M.11			DUKE OF ALBANY	1997/07	30.10.14– Sunk 25.8.16 by UB.27 east of Pentland Skerries.
MI.14	MI.04	MI.03	DUKE OF CLARENCE	1635/92	1–4 in, 1–12 pdr; 18 kts. 6.11.15–11.2.20.
M.10	MI.05		DUKE OF CORNWALL	1528/98	1–4 in, 1–12 pdr; 18 kts. 31.10.14–14.11.19.
MI.12			DUNDEE	2709/11	2–4 in; 14½ kts. 11.10.15– Sunk 3.9.17 by UC.49 in the Channel.
MI.26			FAUVETTE	2644/12	2–12 pdr. Formerly a store carrier (Y8.44) 2.15–18.3.15; =ABS 19.3.15– Mined 9.3.16 in the North Sea.
M.17	MI.07		FIONA	1611/05	1–4 in, 1–12 pdr; 17½ kts. 28.10.14– Wrecked 6.9.17 off Pentland Skerries.
M.22	MI.08	**	GRANGEMOUTH	1560/08	1–4 in, 1–12 pdr; 15 kts. 5.1.15–1.4.19.
MI.24	MI.09		GRIVE	2037/05	2–4.7 in; 13 kts. Formerly flotilla supply ship (No. 3) 5.8.14–2.8.15; =ABS 24.2.16– Foundered 24.12.17 off the Shetlands after being torpedoed by UC.40.
M.00	MI.10	**	HAZEL	1241/07	2–12 pdr; 18 kts. 11.11.14–11.5.19; =MONA 1919.
M.05	MI.11	**	HEROIC	1869/06	2–12 pdr; 18 kts. 18.11.14–6.7.20.
M.18	MI.12	MI.06	KING ORRY	1877/13	2–4 in, 21 kts. 29.10.14–5.6.19; =in WW II.
			LAMA	2198/05	3–4.7 in; 16 kts. 12.7.15–17.1.18.
M.07	MI.14		LOUVAIN	1830/97	2–12 pdr; 17 kts. (ex-Dresden) 31.10.14– Sunk 20.1.18 by UC.22 in the eastern Mediterranean.
			LUNKA	2193/05	3–4.7 in; 16 kts. 20.7.15–22.1.19.
M.03	MI.15		PARTRIDGE =PARTRIDGE II 12.15	1461/06	2–12 pdr; 16 kts. 15.11.14–12.7.20.
M.13	MI.16	MI.07	PEEL CASTLE	1474/94	2–12 pdr; 17 kts. (ex-Duke of York) 28.10.14–10.5.19.
MI.23	MI.17	**	PERTH	2502/15	3–4.7 in; 14½ kts. 27.8.15–18.9.19.
			PRINCE ABBAS	2030/92	5.6.15–29.5.16; sunk 9.7.17.
M.21	MI.18	**	RICHARD WELFORD	1349/08	2–12 pdr; 14 kts. 5.1.15–9.8.19.
M.01	MI.19	MI.08	ROWAN	1493/09	2–12 pdr, 1–3 pdr; 16 kts. 14.11.14–15.6.20.
M.16	MI.20	**	ROYAL SCOT	1726/10	1–4 in, 3–12 pdr; 17½ kts. 28.10.14–27.12.19; =troop carrier 14.1.19–10.4.19.
M.04	MI.21	**	SARNIA	1498/10	2–12 pdr; 20 kts. 14.11.14– Sunk 12.9.18 by S-M off Alexandria.
			SCOTIA	1872/02	1–12 pdr. 8.8.14–1.8.17.

Pendent Nos. first* 1.18 6.18		Name	TG/Yr	Armament—Service
M.06	MI.22	SNAEFELL	1368/10	2–12 pdr, 1–2 pdr; 18 kts. 24.11.14– Sunk 5.6.18 by UB.105 in Mediterranean.
MI.27	MI.23	STEPHEN FURNESS	1712/10	2–4.7 in; 14½ kts. Formerly squadron supply ship 1.12.14–7.3.16; =ABS 8.3.16– sunk 13.12.17 by UB.64 near Belfast Lough.
		SUVA	2229/06	3–4.7 in; 13 kts. 20.7.15–19.12.19.
		TARA	1862/00	3–6 pdr. (ex-Hibernia) 8.8.14– Sunk 5.11.15 by U.35 in the Mediterranean.
M.14		THE RAMSEY	1443/95	2–12 pdr. (ex-Duke of Lancaster) 28.10.14– Sunk 8.8.15 in action with German M/L METEOR southeast of Pentland Firth.
MI.28	MI.24	TITHONUS	3463/08	2–6 in, 2–6 pdr; 15 kts. (ex-Titania) 2.16– Sunk 28.3.18 by UB.72 in the North Sea.
P.57	N.2A	VIENNA	1767/94	2–12 pdr. Was Accom ship 29.8.14– 18.12.14; =Q ship ANTWERP 1.1.15– 28.4.15 also VIENNA; =ABS 29.4.15– 25.8.19.
M.02	MI.25 **	WOODNUT	1470/06	3–12 pdr; 16 kts. (ex-Woodcock) 15.11.14– 31.5.20.
M.20	MI.26 **	YORK	1132/07	1–4 in, 2–12 pdr; 14½ kts. 3.1.15–4.4.19.

*These pendants were assigned as the vessels began service; all M pendants became MI 24.4.15 without change of numbers inferior. **No pendant assigned.
Notes: The yachts (qv) DRAMA, MARCELLA, MLADA and SIGISMUND were also boarding steamers; also the armed store ship EL KAHIRA (qv) served for a short time during 1916. "THE RAMSEY", is in Navy Lists as "RAMSEY".

PATROL PADDLE VESSELS

Adty No.	Name	TG/Yr	Armament—Service—Fate	
0109	CLEETHORPES	273/03	1–6 pdr, 1–6 pdrAA. =PMS 20.4.19.	19.6.16–1920
0100	DUCHESS OF NORFOLK	381/11	1–6 pdrAA M/S. =PMS 20.4.19; =AMBASSADOR in WW II.	17.5.16–1920
0101	DUCHESS OF RICHMOND	354/10	1–6 pdrAA M/S. =PMS 20.4.19; mined 28.6.19 in the Aegean Sea	17.5.16–
0103	DUCHESS OF YORK	302/96	1–6 pdrAA M/S. Purchased 6.19; sold 23.6.21.	18.5.16–
0108	DUKE =DUKE II 3.19	257/96	(ex-Duke of Devonshire) 2–6 pdrAA. 23.5.16– 31.12.20 =PMS 20.4.19.	
0106	EMPEROR OF INDIA II =MAHRATTA 5.18	482/06	(ex-Princess Royal) 2–6 pdrAA. 23.5.16–1920 =PMS 20.4.19; =EMPEROR OF INDIA in WW II.	
0107	MAJESTIC II	408/01	2–6 pdrAA. Foundered 28.7.16 near Oran.	23.5.16–
0110	MARCHIONESS OF LORNE	295/91	1–6 pdr, 1–6 pdrAA. =PMS 20.4.19.	19.6.16–1920
0111	MINERVA II	315/93	1–6 pdr, 1–6 pdrAA. =PMS 20.4.19.	19.6.16–7.4.20
0103	PRINCESS MARY =PRINCESS MARY II 5.16	326/11	1–6 pdrAA M/S. 17.5.16– Sank 2.8.19 after striking the submerged wreck of MAJESTIC off Cape Helles. Was PMS from 20.4.19.	
0104	QUEEN IV	345/02	1–6 pdrAA M/S. =PMS 20.4.19.	17.5.16–25.11.20
0105	STIRLING CASTLE	271/99	2–6 pdrAA. 18.5.16– Sunk 26.9.16 by explosion off Malta, cause unknown.	

Notes: All served in the Mediterranean; Fishery pendants 0100–0105 were assigned to vessels based at Malta, 0106–0111 based at Alexandria. DUKE became a base ship 1919 in Egypt for a short time.

COASTGUARD AND FISHERY PROTECTION

The prewar duties of Coastguard vessels were anti-smuggling and fishery protection, both of which naturally lapsed in 1914. The ships were put on patrol and examination service during the war.

310 tons. 120 (pp) = 20½ × 9 ft. TE 655 ihp = 12 kts.
Armament:

1914 1.18		Name	Launched	Builder—Fate
C.80 C.77		JULIA	1897	J. P. Rennoldson. Sold 6.11.20 M. S. Hilton.

Notes: Was ex-yacht MARETANZA, purchased 1.4.01. On examination service based at Queenstown 1914–18.

380 tons. 130 (pp) × 23 × 9 ft. TE 650 ihp = 11½ kts.
Armament: 2–6 pdr.

C.75		ARGUS = ARGON 1.17	6.12.04	Bow McLachlan. Sold 5.2.20 = PENINNIS.

Notes: On examination service at Berehaven 1914–18.

230 tons. 108 (oa), 103 (pp) × 21 × 9½ ft. TE 300 ihp = 10 kts.
Armament: 2–3 pdr.

1914 1.18	9.18	Name	Launched	Builder—Fate
C.81 C.83	C.85	SQUIRREL	21.12.04	Workman Clark. = Cable ship 1914; sold 6.11.21 = yacht VEDRA.

Notes: Based at Devonport and Falmouth 1914–18.

805 tons. 177 (oa), 165 (pp) × 31 × 11½ ft. TE 1200 ihp = 13 kts.
Armament: 4–4 in (originally 6–4 in). (RINGDOVE 1–4 in 1916).

1914 3.16	1.18	Name	Launched	Builder—Fate
C.84 X.37 X.40		RINGDOVE = MELITA 12.15	30. 4.89	Devonport DY. = Salvage vessel 11.15; sold 22.1.20 = TELIMA.
C.76 X.36		THRUSH	22. 6.89	Scotts. = Cable ship 1914; = Salvage vessel 1916; wrecked 11.4.17 near Glenarm, Antrim.

Notes: Ex-1st class gunboats transferred to Coastguard in 1906. RINGDOVE on examination service Queensferry 1914–15; THRUSH based at Berehaven on cable service 1914–16.

612 tons. 154 (oa), 145¼ (pp) × 25 × 12 ft. TE 800 ihp = 11½ kts.
Armament: 2–3 pdr.

1914 1.18	9.18	Name	Launched	Builder—Fate
C.77 C.84	C.86	WATCHFUL	26. 4.11	Hall Russell. Sold 15.5.20 Newfoundland Government.

Notes: Senior Officer Minesweepers, Sheerness 1914–18.

875 tons. 160¼ (pp) × 29 × 11 ft. TE 1350 ihp = 15 kts.
Armament: 2–3 pdr.

C.78 C.80	C.81	SAFEGUARD	24. 6.14	Day Summers. Sold 13.2.20 = SAFEGUARDER.

Notes: Based at Queenstown 1914–18. Pendants C.75–86 series was used for ships, all other C flag superior numbers were Coastguard Stations.

FISHERY CRUISERS FOR SPECIAL SERVICE

The following vessels were listed from 8.14: BRENDA 174/98, FREYA 280/04, GOLDSEEKER 206/00, MINNA 281/00, NORNA 457/09 and VIGILANT 92/86.

Owned by the Scottish Fishery Board, they were employed mainly on examination service in Scottish waters.

Q SHIPS (SUBMARINE DECOY VESSELS)

Very soon after the war began, the destructive potential of the submarine made itself known. The success of U.9 sinking three large cruisers in a single day boldly illustrated how helpless and vulnerable surface warships could be when attacked by an undetected submarine. There were no special anti-submarine weapons or detection devices at that time and the advantage was all in the U-boat's favour. Fortunately, there were only a limited number of U-boats at sea and their range of action was also limited or the early naval disasters of this nature could have been far worse.

The use of special warships disguised as harmless merchant vessels began in late 1914 in what was perhaps the earliest effective attempt to destroy enemy submarines. These vessels were made to appear as routine merchant types engaged in normal traffic, usually of sloven and unkempt outward appearance, while disguising their real purpose. German submarines would, whenever possible, capture individual ships at sea, remove the crews, and then effect destruction of the ship by means of time bombs or gunfire. From the U-boat's point of view it was far more economical to destroy shipping in this manner than to expend precious torpedoes, particularly when the victim was of small size. The torpedoes were normally conserved for use against more difficult targets such as warships and large merchant ships capable of high speed. Attacking on the surface in this manner, the submarine lost its advantage of surprise and concealment, and if the target happened to be a Q ship, put itself in deadly peril.

Older vessels, colliers, small coasters, sailing vessels, and various fishing craft (including sailing smacks) were selected for conversion into decoys and they were secretly taken up and armed with hidden weapons. These ships were fully commissioned warships manned by naval crews and when in direct action with the enemy, flew the white ensign. A great deal of exhaustive effort was expended in maintaining their disguises, they altered both name and appearance frequently and posed as other commercial vessels as the opportunity arose. Special "panic parties" went to the lifeboats when the decoy was stopped by a U-boat, while other crew members remained hidden aboard, ready to man the guns when the disguise was dropped and action commenced.

Since detection of submarines was indeed the most difficult problem, the Q ship provided one means of bypassing this difficulty at a time when very few effective measures were available to counter-act the submarine offensive. Q ships proved to be most successful when there were only a few in service and when surprise was accordingly the greatest. As the U-boat campaign changed to one of unrestricted warfare, the decoy vessel had seen its better days, but nevertheless had contributed to ridding the seas of some of the dangerous enemy. While this method of warfare was used as an excuse for increasing the ferocity of submarine attacks, it must be appreciated that many otherwise unsuitable vessels saw active service as decoys and even after their success had waned they continued to cause anxiety and discomfort to the enemy.

Aside from individual vessels operating as decoys, at least ten trawler and submarine combinations were employed whereby an ordinary fishing trawler towed a submerged C class submarine at the end of its trawl cable. Once the enemy U-boat was lured into commencing an attack on the trawler, the submarine was released and proceeded in attack upon the unsuspecting U-boat.

For a short period during 1915, the decoy ships were assigned Q numbers; these were rescinded when it was concluded that this system reduced their secrecy. Although a few of these vessels appeared in pendant lists and secret disposition lists under one auxiliary guise or another, most of the others were never listed on any circulated document for fear it might fall into the hands of the enemy. The term "Special Service Vessels" was occasionally applied to them. By nature of the extreme secrecy involved and the fact that they readily created false identities has increased the difficulty in tracing their true origins. Four decoy colliers dispatched to the Mediterranean, for example, managed to prevent their true purpose from being disclosed to a port admiral in command of their operating area until after they had sailed and then he received a "most secret" signal from the Admiralty informing him that they were operating as decoys. Some sources suggest a very high number of decoy vessels, undoubtedly counting the false identities along with the proper ones. There were in fact about 215 vessels fitted as decoys, including proper warship types such as sloops and PC boats whose disguise was only acceptable at a distance. Only one vessel was designed and built purely as a Q ship, HYDERABAD of 1917.

Light weapons were purposely exposed at a later date when most merchant vessels had received some defensive armament and tactics were altered to meet the change in U-boat methods of attack. Later it was accepted that the larger decoy ships should allow themselves to be torpedoed, having their holds filled with buoyant material in an effort to remain afloat long enough to sink the submarine if it surfaced. Unfortunately several Q ships were torpedoed and sunk without ever sighting the submarine.

List (a) includes decoy vessels (and their description and other names) whose naval service was only in this capacity, while list (c) notes decoys that were regular naval ships and as such are included elsewhere in this book. Alternate identities (both legitimate name changes and some of the false names) of vessels included in lists (a) through (d) are given in the Decoy vessel operational name index in order that a cross-reference may be possible. Although the prime naval name is in many cases obvious, others were very well known by operational names and the prime name to accept is more difficult to determine.

(a) MERCANTILE CONVERSIONS

Name	TG/Yr	Type—Other names—Armament—Service
ACTON	1288/01	Cargo. (ex-Harelda) also GANDY; HARELDA; Q.34; WOFFINGTON. 1–4 in, 4–12 pdr. 15.2.17–26.3.19.
ALBERT H. WHITMAN	*94/16	Schooner (ex-A. H. Whitman) 10.7.17–22.11.17.
ALBERT J. LUTZ	*95/08	Schooner. 6.7.17–22.11.17.
AMY B. SILVER	129/12	Schooner. 17.7.17–22.11.17.
ARVONIAN	2794/05	Collier. (Y3.538) also ALASTAIR; BALFAME; BENDISH; DORINDA; GIRDLER; USS SANTEE. 3–4 in, 3–12 pdr, 4–18 in TT. 19.8.17–21.4.19 (purchased 20.11.17).
BARON ROSE	524/81	Aux schooner. (ex-Samuel S. Thorp) also SIEUX. 1–4.1 in, 2–12 pdr. 9.4.18–14.6.19.
BARRANCA	4124/06	Cargo. Also ECHUNGA; Q.3. 1–4 in, 2–12 pdr. 26.4.16–30.1.18.
BAYARD	220/08	Motor lugger. Also LEDGER No. 898; Q.20; SYREN. 1–13 pdr, 1–3 pdr. 25.1.17– sunk 29.3.17 in collision in the Channel.
BLESSING	/	Smack or large coble. Carried mined nets. 6.16–31.3.17.
BRACONDALE	2095/03	Collier. (YS.1456) also CHAGFORD. 24.5.17– sunk 7.8.17 by S/M in the Atlantic.
BRADFORD CITY	3683/10	Collier. (Y3.500) also BALLISTAN; SAROS. 16.10.15– sunk 16.8.17 by S/M in the Straits of Messina.
BREADWINNER	57/07	Smack. (LT.1095) also S.7; SEAGULL. 2.17–11.11.18.
BRIG 1	123/07	Aux barkentine. (ex-Emilia C., ex-Marguerite) also EMELIA C. 2–2 pdr, 2–Lewis MG. 10.11.17–16.10.18.
BRIG 2	227/76	Brigantine. (ex-Rosina Ferrara, ex-Emma M., ex-Mongibello, ex-Luigi F.) also ROSINA FERRARA. 1–4 in, 2–12 pdr. 8.1.18–11.11.18.
BRIG 3	155/00	Brigantine. (ex-Sant' Anna M.) also S. ANNA. 18.2.18–11.11.18.
BRIG 4	212/03	Brigantine. (ex-Vera) also MARGARET & ANNIE; VERA. 6.4.18–11.11.18.
BRIG 5	225/14	Brigantine. (ex-Salomea K.) also SALOMEA K. 28.5.18–11.11.18.
BRIG 9	*117/02	Sail. (ex-Kostoula) also KOSTOULA; Q.500; QS.9. 8.17–12.17.
BRIG 10	221/95	Brigantine. (ex-Helgoland, ex-Vooruitgang, ex-Hoogezand II) also HELGOLAND; HORLEY; Q.17. 7.6.17–8.1.19.
BRIG 11	224/98	Barkentine. (ex-Gaelic) also GAELIC; GOBO; Q.22. 6.11.16–5.3.19.
BRIG 12	/	Schooner. (ex-Vassiliki) also VASSILIKI. 17.12.17–11.11.18.
CHEVINGTON	3876/12	Collier. (Y3.2045) 10.15–27.6.16.
CHILDREN'S FRIEND	60/98	Motor smack. (LT.174) also S.6. 7.2.17–11.11.18.
CYMRIC	226/93	Schooner. Also OLIVE. 1–4 in, 2–12 pdr. 15.3.18–8.4.19.
DARGLE	253/02	Brigantine. (ex-James J. Bibby) also BIBBY; GRABBITT; J. J. BIBBY; PEGGY; Q.29. 1–4 in, 2–12 pdr. 23.2.17–9.3.20.
DJERISSA	3723/10	Collier. (Y3.231) also MALLINA; SOLAX; WOKING. 9.12.16–18.5.18.
DORANDO PIETRI	54/08	Motor ketch. (LT.295) also S.5. 7.2.17–11.11.18.
DOROTHY G. SNOW	*98/11	Schooner. 4.7.17–22.11.17.
DREADNOUGHT II	/	Smack. Also LEDGER No. 897. 6.17–11.11.18.
DUNCLUTHA	3973/10	Collier. (Y3.1335) also CHAMPNEY; STAMFORD. 23.11.16–23.6.18.
DUNRAVEN	3117/10	Collier. (Y3.283) (ex-Boverton) also BOVERTON. 1–4 in, 4–12 pdr, 2– TT. 25.6.17– foundered in tow 10.8.17 in the Channel after severe damage received 8.8.17 in prolonged gun action with UC.71 in the Atlantic.
EARLY BLOSSOM	57/08	Smack. (LT.16) also S.2. 23.11.16–11.11.18.
EILIAN	140/08	Aux 3 mast schooner. Also CHROMIUM. 2–12 pdr, 1–Lewis MG. 7.9.17–1.2.19.
ELEUTHERA	156/92	3 mast schooner. (ex-Elizabeth) also ELIZABETH. 1.5.18–12.2.19.
ENERGIC	59/12	Smack. (LT.1195) also CHEERIO; MASCOT; S.1. Carried mined nets. 20.1.16–11.11.18.
ETHEL & MILLIE	58/08	Smack. (LT.200) also BOY ALFRED; LEDGER No. 929; S.3. 1–6 pdr. 1.2.17– sunk 15.8.17 by S/M gunfire off East Anglia.
FARNBOROUGH	3207/04	Collier. (Y3.859) (ex-Sandyford) also LODORER; Q.5; SANDYFORD. 5–12 pdr, 2–6 pdr. 22.10.15–25.2.18. (purchased 22.10.17) sold 4.19 =HOLLYPARK.
FIRST PRIZE	227/01	3 mast schooner. (ex-Else) also ELSE; PRIZE; Q.21. 6.11.16– sunk 14.8.17 by S/M in the Atlantic.

Name	TG/Yr	Type—Other names—Armament—Service
FRESH HOPE	648/89	3 mast schooner. (ex-Freshhope, ex-Edith S. Cummins) also EDITH E. CUMMINS; IROQUOIS. 2–4 in, 2–12 pdr. 8.11.17– 6.6.19; wrecked 10.19.
G. & E.	61/05	Smack. (LT.649) 1–3 pdr. 8.8.15–9.15. Re-acquired 22.1.16– motor smack by 8.17. Also BIRD; EXTIRPATOR; FOAM CREST; I'LL TRY; LEDGER No. 929; NELSON; S.3. 1–13 pdr. Sunk 15.8.17 by S/M gunfire off East Anglia.
GEORGE L. MUIR	65/83	Motor ketch. (ex-George L. Munro, ex-Cholmondeley) also G. L. M.; GEORGE L. MUNRO; PADRE. 7.17–11.11.18.
GLEN	112/97	Aux schooner. (ex-Sidney) also ATHOS; SIDNEY. 1–12 pdr, 1–3 pdr. 27.2.17–18.12.18.
GLENDEVON	4169/07	Collier. (Y3.1842) 10.15–5.7.16.
GLENFOYLE	1680/13	Collier. (Y3.1235) also DONLEVON; STONECROP. 22.4.17– sunk 18.9.17 by S/M in the Atlantic.
GLENISLA	1263/78	Collier. (Y3.876) 14.10.15–20.3.16. Sunk 25.11.17 on other services.
GLORY	58/06	Smack. (LT.1027) 1–3 pdr. 2 8.15–9.15.
GOBLIN	91/12	Motor schooner. (ex-Mana) also MANA. 24.9.17–3.1.18.
GOODWIN	1928/17	Cargo. Also BALLANTRAL; MODERLEY; UNDERWING. 3–4 in. 23.5.17–2.5.19. =WW II.
GRANTLEY	1869/08	Collier. (Y3.297) Released as unsuitable.
HARMONIC	2827/05	Collier. (Y3.240) also COCKSEDGE; FAIRLIGHT; TRI-CORD. 8.8.16–21.4.18.
HARTSIDE	2740/09	Collier. (Y3.235) also DUNSANY; FAIRFAX; TRIOA. 25.8.16–2.5.18.
HELEN M. COOLEN	94/14	Aux schooner. 13.7.17–22.11.17.
HOLKAR	61/05	Motor smack. 8.16–9.16. Sunk 6.2.18 as fishing vessel.
HYANTHES	3427/99	Collier. (Y3.1349) also CRAVEN; LORIMER; OOMA. 5.12.16–9.10.18 (tonnage altered to 4355 TG 2.10.18).
IANTHE	212/10	Aux 3 mast schooner. Also MANON. 5–12 pdr, 1– Lewis MG. 15.9.17–11.3.19.
I'LL TRY	59/01	Smack. (LT.379) 21.4.16–1916. Sunk 27.7.18 as fishing vessel.
IMOGENE	189/82	Barkentine. (ex-Strathendrick) also DOROTHY; IMPEY; JEANETTE. 1–4 in, 2–12 pdr, 1–7.5 in BT. 24.2.18– sold 15.5.19 Ledger Hill.
INVERLYON	59/03	Smack. (LT.687) 1–3 pdr. 2.8.15–9.15. Sunk 30.1.17 by S/M 15 miles N by W of Trevose Head while on commercial fishing.
KEMES	57/11	Smack. (M.105) also M.105. 1–12 pdr. 4.5.16–11.16.
LADY OLIVE	701/13	Coaster. (ex-Tees Trader) also Q.18. 1–4 in, 4–12 pdr. 24.11.16– sunk 19.2.17 by S/M in the Channel.
LADY PATRICIA	1372/16	Cargo. Also PAXTON; Q.25; TOSCA SVERIGE. 1–4 in. 2–12 pdr. 6.2.17– sunk 20.5.17 by U.46 in the Atlantic.
LAGGAN	1334/07	Cargo. (ex-Pladda) also GRANMER; PLADDA; Q.24. 1–4 in, 2–12 pdr. 16.1.17–14.5.19.
LOWTYNE	3231/92	Collier. (Y3.1512) (ex-Slingsby) 7.6.18– sunk 10.6.18 by S/M 3½ miles ESE of Whitby.
MARESFIELD	4176/10	Collier. (Y3.777) also CHISWELL; SEQUAX. 8.3.17–15.5.18.
MARGARET MURRAY	184/85	Aux schooner. Also SARAH JONES. 1–4 in, 3–12 pdr. 30.4.18–18.10.19.
MARSHFORT	1988/93	Cargo. (ex-Huayna, ex-Hildebrand) also HILLCOLLOW; HUAYNA; SENLEY. 2–4 in, 2–12 pdr. 22.4.17–13.5.19.
MARY B. MITCHELL	227/92	3 mast schooner. Also AMARIS; ARIUS; BRINE; CANCALAIS; EIDER; JEANETTE; MARIE THERESE; MARY Y JOSE; MITCHELL; NEPTUN; Q.9. 1–4 in, 1–12 pdr., 1–6 pdr. 25.4.16–24.3.19.
MAVIS	1295/03	Cargo. (ex-Nyroca) also NYROCA; Q.26. 1–4 in, 2–12 pdr. 31.1.17–27.7.18.
MEROPS	313/92	Barkentine. (ex-Maracaibo) also BELLMORE; ILMA; MARACAIBO; Q.28; STEADY; TOOFA. 1–4 in, 2–12 pdr. 2.2.17– 11.2.19. =BELLMORE.
PARGUST	2914/07	Collier. (Y3.540) (ex-Vittoria) also FRISWELL; PANGLOSS; SNAIL; VITTORIA. 3.4 in, 4–12 pdr, 1–11 in BT, 4–18 in TT. 22.3.17– purchased 8.17, loaned to USN 10.17–4.18, sold 3.19.
PENHALLOW	4318/13	Collier. (Y3.301) also CENTURY. 10.15–23.5.17.
PENSHURST	1191/06	Collier. (Y3.253) also MANFORD; Q.7. 1–12 pdr, 2–6 pdr, 2–3 pdr. 9.11.15– sunk 25.12.17 by U.110 off the Bristol Channel.
PERIM	1348/77	Collier. (Y3.1568) Released as unsuitable.

Name	TG/Yr	Type—Other names—Armament—Service
PERUGIA	4348/01	Collier. (Y3.1049) also MOERAKI; Q.1. 18.4.16– sunk 3.12.16 by U.63 in the Gulf of Genoa.
PET	56/06	Smack. (LT.560) 1–3 pdr. 2.8.15–9.15.
PEVERIL	1459/04	Cargo. Also PUMA; Q.36; STEPHENSON. 18.2.15–21.4.15 and 17.2.17– sunk 6.11.17 by S/M outside the Straits of Gibraltar.
PINTA	101/93	Aux cutter. 4.7.17–22.11.17.
PREVALENT	42/13	Smack. Also HURTER. 1–12 pdr. 30.1.17–4.2.19.
PRINCE CHARLES	373/05	Collier. (Y3.402) 2–6 pdr, 2–3 pdr. 8.8.15–1.16. Sunk 5.3.16 on mercantile service.
PRIVET	803/16	Cargo. (ex-Island Queen) also ALCALA; ISLAND QUEEN; Q.19; SWISHER. 1–4 in, 2–12 pdr. 23.11.16–11.6.19.
PROBUS	179/65	Brigantine. Also ELIXIR; Q.30; READY; THIRZA. 2–12 pdr. 2–6 pdr. 30.8.15–11.11.18.
RAVENSTONE	3049/05	Collier. (Y3.440) also DONLEVON. 22.5.17–30.9.17.
RECORD REIGN	184/97	Motor schooner. 1–4 in, 4–12 pdr. 9.10.17– sunk 12.12.18.
REMEMBRANCE	3660/10	Collier. (Y3.252) also LAMMEROO. 10.15– sunk 14.8.16 by U.38 in the Mediterranean.
RESOLUTE	229/69	Barkentine, Also PAMELA; RENTOUL. 1–4 in, 2–12 pdr, 1–7.5 in BT. 27.3.18–14.3.19.
RESULT	122/93	Aux 3 mast schooner. Also CAPULET; DAG; LEDGER No. 928. 2–12 pdr, 2– TT. 29.11.16–22.12.17.
REVENGE	39/98	Aux smack. (ex-Fame) also FAME. 21.1.16– sunk 19.11.16 in collision.
RULE	1004/11	Cargo. (ex-Ouse) also BARYTA; CASSOR; OUSE; Q.35. 1–4 in, 2–12 pdr, 2–14 in TT. 19.2.17–29.5.19.
SARAH COLEBROOKE	158/13	Aux ketch. Also BALHAM; MERYL. 2–12 pdr. 3.5.17–7.10.18.
STARMOUNT	2529/05	Collier. (Y3.511) (ex-Glenmay) also GLENMAY; GRAVENY; TRING. 3.6.17–10.1.19.
STOCK FORCE	732/17	Coaster. Also CHARYCE. 2–4 in, 2–12 pdr. 14.2.17– damaged in action with U.98 in the Channel and sank in tow 30.7.18 off Bolt Head.
STRUMBLE	45/12	Smack. (M.135) also M.135. 1–12 pdf. 1.6.16– sunk 4.5.17 by U.65 off Strumble Head.
SUFFOLK COAST	870/17	Collier. (Y3.1765) 16.8.18–7.7.19.
SUPERIOR	44/96	Smack (ex-Superb) also DESMOND; SUPERB. 1–12 pdr. 30.1.17–10.2.19.
TAY & TYNE =INDUSTRY 1920	556/09	Coaster. Also CHERITON; DUNDREARY; LEDGER No. 928. 1–4 in, 2–12 pdr, 1–6 pdrAA, 1–3 pdr, 1–14 in TT. 28.6.17–11.11.18. Purchased 26.9.17, later =store carrier (X.83); sold 31.10.24.
TELESIA	59/11	Smack. (LT.1155) also C. B.; COMMODORE; HOBBY HAWK; S.4. 20.1.16–17.7.17.
THORNHILL	3848/11	Collier. (Y3.260) also MARGIT; WELLHOLME; WERRIBEE; WOGANELLA. 18.11.15–11.8.17.
VALA	1016/94	Collier. (Y3.446) also Q.8. 7.8.15– sunk 21.8.17 by UB.54 in the Atlantic.
VERA ELIZABETH	/	Schooner from Granton. Also ALMA. 21.9.17–29.4.18.
VICTORIA =SURF II 10.18	710/96	Coaster. 2–12 pdr. 28.11.14–8.1.15. Re-acquired 8.10.18–5.12.18 for other services.
VIOLA	168/72	3 mast schooner. Also VEREKER; VIOLETTA. 1–4 in, 2–12 pdr. 20.8.18–11.11.18.
WARNER	1273/11	Cargo. Also Q.27. 17.1.17– sunk 13.3.17 by U.61 west of Ireland.
WELLHOLME	113/16	Motor ketch. Also DANTON. 4.9.17– sunk 30.1.18 by S/M in the Channel.
WILLOW BRANCH	3314/92	Collier. (Y3.1042) also BOMBALA; JUGGLER; VINETROE. 28.1.17– sunk 25.4.18 by S/M east of Cape Verde Islands.
ZYLPHA	2917/94	Collier. (Y3.139) also Q.6. 19.9.15– sunk 15.6.17 by S/M southwest of Ireland.

*Registered tonnage.

Other decoys of undetermined true identity include: AMBER also REMO (trawler); DEFENDER 13.6.17–11.11.18; GOOD HOPE 1.17–2.17 (trawler); LOTHIAN 8.8.17–11.11.18 (trawler); MARGARETHA 19.9.18–11.11.18; MORNING STAR 17.8.16–24.10.16 and 3.2.17–31.3.17; SUNSHINE also STRATHALLAN 16.5.17–11.11.18 (trawler); UNION also UNION II 19.9.18–11.11.18; WADSWORTH; and WILD ROSE also STRATHEARN 16.5.17–11.11.18 (trawler).

Notes: this group includes decoys of mercantile origin used only for this purpose, others with multiple activities are indicated in group (c). The Y3 pendants were borne by colliers on Admiralty charter wearing the red ensign until altered to Q ships. Decoy activity ceased in late 1918, though the date of the Armistice is given in most records. P pendants were assigned to three vessels: FARNBOROUGH was given P.71 (1.16), WYANDRA received P.62 (1.16) followed by P.5C (1.18) and ZYLPHA had pendant P.79 (1.16).

(b) WAR CONSTRUCTION DECOY VESSEL

595 tons (light).   240½ (pp) ×36×6¾ ft.
624 tons (loaded).
Armament (hidden): 1–4 in, 2–12 pdr (tilting mounts), 4–3.5 in BT, 2–18 in TT, 4 depth charges.
 (exposed): 1–2½ pdr on poop.

Pendant Nos.	Name	Launched	Builder—Fate
P.80 (6.19) P.77 (11.19)	HYDERABAD	27. 8.17	Thornycroft. Also CORAL; NICOBAR; S.S.S. 966. Sold 5.20, altered to 1150 TG =LEMNOS.

Notes: HYDERABAD was designed specifically for service as a decoy vessel. She possessed many unique and elaborate features; unusually shallow draught, tilting gun mountings, and collapsible deck structures used to conceal weapons. Twin screws were set in tunnels in the after part of the hull and a false rudder-top that was visible above water suggested a deep draught. Reports of torpedoes passing under her hull indicate that the above-water deception was successful. It was intended that one CMB should be carried. The normal crew was 73 at the time of completion (24.9.17). The number 966 used as an operational name stemmed from the builder's number. After refitting as a depot ship, HYDERABAD served in North Russia during the 1919 campaign. Conversion of GLENMAY (STARMOUNT) to D/S; not completed.

(c) DECOYS LISTED WITH THEIR VARIOUS TYPES

Sloops: BEGONIA, 6 Aubrietia class, 33 Anchusa class.
PC boats: 20 vessels.
Commissioned escort ship: CARRIGAN HEAD.
Armed boarding steamer: ANTWERP as VIENNA.
Fleet messengers: PRINCESS ENA, REDBREAST.
Store carriers: BARALONG, DUNCOMBE as DERWENT, INTABA, LOTHBURY as ARGO, M. J. HEDLEY, WESTPHALIA, WEXFORD COAST, WIRRAL.
Yachts: BROWN MOUSE, LISETTE, MONA.
Trawlers: ASAMA, AUK, COMMISSIONER, COOT, CORMORANT IV, FORT GEORGE, GUNNER, IZAAK WALTON, KING LEAR, KING STEPHEN, OCEANIC II, QUICKLY, ROSSKEEN, SEA KING, SPEEDWELL II, TARANAKI, TENBY CASTLE, WALTER S. BAILEY.
Drifters: BELLONA II, FIZZER as VIOLET, IMPERATOR as IMPREGNABLE, KENT COUNTY, OCEAN FISHER, PRINCIPAL.
Motor drifters: BETSY JAMIESON, EXCEL, FISHER LASSIE II, PASSAWAY, THALIA.
Tug: EARL OF POWIS.
Salvage vessel: LYONS.
Lighter: X.22.

(d) TRAWLER—SUBMARINE DECOYS

C.23 and RATAPIKO, C.24 and TARANAKI, C.26 and WOLSEY, C.27 and PRINCESS LOUISE (ex-Princess Marie Jose* renamed 21.7.15), C.29 and ARIADNE C.33 and MALTA (ex-Weelsby renamed 31.7.15). The submarines C.14, C.16, C.21 and C.34 were also used, but the towing trawler has not been identified.
*See Fishery Trawlers.

DECOY VESSEL OPERATIONAL NAMES INDEX

Name	see under	Name	see under
ABNEY	CONVOLVULUS	BELLMORE	MEROPS
AIRBLAST	SPIRAEA	BEN NEVIS	AUK
ALASTAIR	ARVONIAN	BENDIGO II	ROSSKEEN
ALCALA	PRIVET	BIBBY	DARGLE
ALDEBARAN	ROSSKEEN	BIGOTT	COREOPSIS
ALDWYCH	EGLANTINE	BIRCH	BELLONA II
ALMA	VERA ELIZABETH	BIRD	G & E
ANTIC	AUK	BIRDWOOD	PC.56
AMARIS	MARY B. MITCHELL	BOMBALA	WILLOW BRANCH
ARGO	LOTHBURY	BORGIA	GUNNER
ATHOS	GLEN	BOVERTON	DUNRAVEN
AYRES	SWEETBRIAR	BOY ALFRED	ETHEL & MILLIE
BALFAME	ARVONIAN	BRANGWYN	SWEETBRIAR
BALHAM	SARAH COLEBROOKE	BRIGAND	COWSLIP
BALLANTRAL	GOODWIN	BRINE	MARY B. MITCHELL
BALLISTAN	BRADFORD CITY	BURLINGTON	PC.60
BARYTA	RULE	BURMAH	COOT
BEARDSLEY	COREOPSIS	BYWATER	HEATHER

Name	see under		Name	see under
C. B.	TELESIA		GLEN AFRIC	AUK
CAIRD	CEANOTHUS		GLENDALE	SPEEDWELL II
CALEB	SPIRAEA		GLENMAY	STARMOUNT
CANCALAIS	MARY B. MITCHELL		GOBO	BRIG 11
CAPULET	RESULT		GRABBITT	DARGLE
CAROLINA	QUICKLY		GRANMER	LAGGAN
CASHEL	ANCHUSA		GRAVENY	STARMOUNT
CASSOR	RULE		HARELDA	ACTON
CENTURY	PENHALLOW		HAYLING	WESTPHALIA
CHAGFORD	BRACONDALE		HELGOLAND	BRIG 10
CHAMPION	COMMISSIONER		HEMPSEED	AURICULA
CHAMPNEY	DUNCLUTHA		HESTER	LISETTE
CHARING	PC.43		HICKORY	EGLANTINE
CHARYCE	STOCK FORCE		HILCOLLOW	MARSHFORT
CHEERIO	ENERGIC		HOBBY HAWK	TELESIA
CHERITON	TAY & TYNE		HOPE	AUK
CHESNEY	PC.61		HORLEY	BRIG 10
CHINTZ	PC.67		HUAYNA	MARSHFORT
CHISWELL	MARESFIELD		HUNTER	ROSSKEEN
CHROMIUM	EILIAN		HURTER	PREVALENT
CLAYMORE	AUK		I'LL TRY	G & E
COCKELYTE	PC.51		ILMA	MEROPS
COCKSEDGE	HARMONIC		IMPEY	IMOGENE
COMMODORE	TELESIA		IMPREGNABLE	IMPERATOR
COMPATRIOT	TAMARISK		IMPREST	IMPERATOR
COCKCROFT	BRYONY		IROQUOIS	FRESH HOPE
CORAL	HYDERBAD		ISLAND QUEEN	PRIVET
CRANFORD	VIOLA		J. J. BIBBY	DARGLE
CRAVEN	HYANTHES		JEANETTE	IMOGENE
CULLIST	WESTPHALIA		JEANETTE	MARY B. MITCHELL
CULLODEN	PC.42		JESSOP	BEGONIA
DAG	RESULT		JUGGERNAUT	PC.55
DAMARIS	VIOLA		JUGGLER	WILLOW BRANCH
DANTON	WELLHOLME		JURASSIC	WESTPHALIA
DAVID DAVIES	SPEEDWELL II		KAI	AUBRIETIA
DERWENT	DUNCOMBE		KENTISH KNOCK	KENT COUNTY
DESMOND	SUPERB		KIA ORA	COOT
DEVERILL	POLYANTHUS		KIB	KING LEAR
DHOBY	DIANTHUS		KIDNER	LYNCHIS
DIANA	KING LEAR		KINSNAKE	PC.62
DOLCIS	BEGONIA		KOSTOULA	BRIG 9
DONLEVON	RAVENSTONE		LAMMEROO	REMEMBRANCE
DORA	COOT		LEDGER No. 13	IMPERATOR
DORINDA	ARVONIAN		LEDGER No. 17	KENT COUNTY
DOROTHY	IMOGENE		LEDGER No. 59	OCEAN FISHER
DOWNTON	PC.61		LEDGER No. 778	KING STEPHEN
DUNDREARY	TAY & TYNE		LEDGER No. 897	DREADNOUGHT II
ECHUNGA	BARRANCA		LEDGER No. 898	BAYARD
EDITH E. CUMMINS	FRESH HOPE		LEDGER No. 928	RESULT
ELIXIR	PROBUS		LEDGER No. 928	TAY & TYNE
ELIZABETH	ELEUTHERA		LEDGER No. 929	ETHEL & MILLIE
ELSE	FIRST PRIZE		LEDGER No. 929	G & E
EMELIA C.	BRIG 1		LINKSMAN	CEANOTHUS
ENID	KING LEAR		LODORER	FARNBOROUGH
ETHELWULF II	ROSSKEEN		LORIMER	HYANTHES
EXTIRPATOR	G & E		LORNE	AUK
FAIRFAX	HARTSIDE		LORNE	COOT
FAIRLIGHT	HARMONIC		LYDIA	DUNCOMBE
FAME	REVENGE		LYON	LYONS
FERNRIDGE	TAMARISK		M.105	KEMES
FLASHLIGHT	PC.67		M.135	STRUMBLE
FOAM CREST	G & E		MALLINA	DJERISSA
FRISWELL	PARGUST		MALLORY	PC.42
G. L. M.	GEORGE L. MUIR		MANA	GOBLIN
GAELIC	BRIG 11		MANFORD	PENSHURST
GANDY	ACTON		MANON	IANTHE
GENERAL	ROSSKEEN		MANTON	CONVOLVULUS
GEORGE L. MUNRO	GEORGE L. MUIR		MARACAIBO	MEROPS
GIRDLER	ARVONIAN		MARGARET & ANNIE	BRIG 4
GIRDLER	AUK		MARGIT	THORNHILL

Name	see under	Name	see under
MARIE THERESE	MARY B. MITCHELL	Q.32	QUICKLY
MARY Y. JOSE	MARY B. MITCHELL	Q.33	SPEEDWELL II
MASCOT	ENERGIC	Q.34	ACTON
MASTER	QUICKLY	Q.35	RULE
MAY FLOWER	W. S. BAILEY	Q.36	PEVERIL
MEREDITH	PC.60	Q.500	BRIG 9
MERYL	SARAH COLEBROOKE	QS.9	BRIG 9
METHYL	PC.55	READY	PROBUS
MILFOIL	PC.65	RECORDER	COMMISSIONER
MITCHELL	MARY B. MITCHELL	REMEXO	SEA KING
MODERLEY	GOODWIN	REMO	AMBER
MOERAKI	PERUGIA	RENTOUL	RESOLUTE
MOPSWORTH	PC.51	RESTITUO	LAGGAN
MORNINGTON	PC.62	ROBINA	FORT GEORGE
MORTMAIN	PC.44	ROCHFORT	MONTBRETIA
NADINE	CORMORANT IV	ROGER	SPEEDWELL II
NAKERBY	PC.68	ROLASK	PC.44
NELSON	G & E	ROLLER	COMMISSIONER
NEPTUN	MARY B. MITCHELL	ROSINA FERRARA	BRIG 2
NEW COMET	ROSSKEEN	S.1	ENERGIC
NICOBAR	HYDERABAD	S.2	EARLY BLOSSO
NYROCA	MAVIS	S.3	ETHEL & MILLIE
OLIVE	CYMRIC	S.3	G & E
OOMA	HYANTHES	S.4	TELESIA
ORRISROOT	PC.63	S.5	DORANDO PIETRI
OUSE	RULE	S.6	CHILDREN'S FRIEND
PADRE	GEORGE L. MUIR	S.7	BREADWINNER
PALETTE	HIBISCUS	S. ANNA	BRIG 3
PAMBLA	RESOLUTE	S.S.S. 966	HYDERABAD
PANACHE	PC.56	ST. GOTHARD	AUK
PANGLOSS	PARGUST	SALOMEA K.	BRIG 5
PAVITT	CANDYTUFT	SANDYFORD	FARNBOROUGH
PAXTON	LADY PATRICIA	SANTEE	ARVONIAN
PEGGY	DARGLE	SARAH JONES	MARGARET MURRAY
PLADDA	LAGGAN	SAROS	BRADFORD CITY
PLANUDES	GUNNER	SARUSAN	LOTHBURY
PRIM	WESTPHALIA	SCATLIFF	TUBEROSE
PRIZE	FIRST PRIZE	SCOTIA	SEA KING
PUMA	PEVERIL	SEAGULL	BREADWINNER
Q.1	PERUGIA	SEETRUS	HEATHER
Q.2	INTABA	SENLEY	MARSHFORT
Q.3	BARRANCA	SEQUAX	MARESFIELD
Q.4	CARRIGAN HEAD	SIDNEY	GLEN
Q.5	FARNBOROUGH	SIEUX	BARON ROSE
Q.6	ZYLPHA	SINTON	QUICKLY
Q.7	PENSHURST	SNAIL	PARGUST
Q.8	VALA	SOLAX	DJERISSA
Q.9	MARY B. MITCHELL	SPIKA	AUK
Q.10	BEGONIA	SPINOZA	BROWN MOUSE
Q.11	TAMARISK	SPRIGG	ARBUTUS
Q.12	TULIP	STAMFORD	DUNCLUTHA
Q.13	AUBRIETIA	STEAD	LOTHBURY
Q.14	VIOLA	STEADY	MEROPS
Q.15	SALVIA	STEPHENSON	PEVERIL
Q.16	HEATHER	STONECROP	GLENFOYLE
Q.17	BRIG 10	STORE CARRIER 80	WEXFORD COAST
Q.18	LADY OLIVE	STORE CARRIER 85	WIRRAL
Q.19	PRIVET	STORE CARRIER 89	M. J. HEDLEY
Q.20	BAYARD	STRATHALLAN	SUNSHINE
Q.21	FIRST PRIZE	STRATHEARN	WILD ROSE
Q.22	BRIG 11	SUPERB	SUPERIOR
Q.23	RESULT	SWIFT	QUICKLY
Q.24	LAGGAN	SWISHER	PRIVET
Q.25	LADY PATRICIA	SYREN	BAYARD
Q.26	MAVIS	TELFORD	PC.68
Q.27	WARNER	THALES	THALIA
Q.28	MEROPS	THIRZA	PROBUS
Q.29	DARGLE	TOOFA	MEROPS
Q.30	PROBUS	TOSCA SVERIGE	LADY PATRICIA
Q.31	GUNNER	TREGO	PC.43

Name	see under		Name	see under
TRICORD	HARMONIC		WAITOMO	INTABA
TRING	STARMOUNT		WELLHOLME	THORNHILL
TRIOA	HARTSIDE		WERRIBEE	THORNHILL
UNDERWING	GOODWIN		WILANGIL	LYCHNIS
UNION II	UNION		WINSTREE	ANCHUSA
VANDA	SPEEDWELL II		WINTON	AUBRIETIA
VASSILIKI	BRIG 12		WOFFINGTON	ACTON
VERA	BRIG 4		WOKING	DJERISSA
VEREKER	VIOLA		WONGANELLA	THORNHILL
VIENNA	ANTWERP		WONGANELLA	WELLHOLME
VINETROE	WIILOW BRANCH		WYANDRA	BARALONG
VIOLETTA	VIOLA		ZEBAL	AUBRIETIA
VITTORIA	PARGUST		ZEUS	MONA

DUMMY BATTLESHIPS
(armament: nil)

No.	Dummy	Name	TG/Yr	Service—Fate
1	"ST. VINCENT"	CITY OF OXFORD	4026/82	Purchased 28.10.14; =Kite balloon ship (qv) 17.7.15.
2	"COLLINGWOOD"	MICHIGAN	4935/87	Purchased 28.10.14; expended 1.1.16 as blockship at Mudros.
3	"IRON DUKE"	MONTEZUMA	8360/99	Hired 2.11.14; purchased 7.7.15 =oiler ABADOL (qv).
4	"KING GEORGE V"	RUTHENIA	7394/00	(ex-*Lake Champlain*) Hired 1.11.14; purchased 1.16 = water carrier, later = oiler (qv).
5	"CENTURION"	TYROLIA	7535/00	(ex-*Lake Erie*) Hired 10.14; purchased 6.16, =oiler SAXOL (qv).
6	"ORION"	ORUBA	5971/89	Purchased 28.10.14; expended 1.1.16 as blockship at Kephalo Bay.
7	"MARLBOROUGH"	MOUNT ROYAL	7998/98	Hired 28.10.14; purchased 10.7.16, =oiler RANGOL (qv).
8	"AUDACIOUS"	MONTCALM	5505/97	Hired 28.10.14; purchased 29.1.16, =oiler (qv).
9	"AJAX"	KRONPRINZESSEN CECILIE =PRINCESS 1915	8689/05	Detained vessel, taken up 1.11.14; =AMC (qv) 9.1.16.
10	"VANGUARD"	PERTHSHIRE	5881/93	Hired 28.10.14; purchased 1915, =water carrier 4.9.15, later oiler (qv).

DUMMY BATTLECRUISERS
(armament: 1–3 pdr)

No.	Dummy	Name	TG/Yr	Service—Fate
11	"QUEEN MARY"	CEVIC	8301/94	Hired 1.12.14; purchased 1915, paid off 8.9.15; =oiler BAYOL (qv).
12	"INDOMITABLE"	MANIPUR	7654/06	Hired 11.14; purchased 1915, =repair ship SANDHURST (qv).
13	"INVINCIBLE"	PATRICIAN	7474/01	Hired 30.11.14; purchased 1915, =oiler TEAKOL (qv).
14	"TIGER"	MERION	11621/02	Hired 1.12.14; purchased 30.5.15; sunk 30.5.15 by UB.8 off Strati Island, Aegean Sea.

Notes: Conversion of the first 10 was ordered 21.10.14; the last four ordered in late 11.14. All were converted at Belfast by Harland & Wolff, who completed ships 1 and 2 by 4.12.14 and the last of 14 during 3.15. Superstructures and dummy guns were built of wood and canvas to resemble the real ships as much as possible and the ships were then ballasted heavily to give the impression of great length and acceptable proportions. They masqueraded as heavy fleet units until diverted to other uses as the shortage of shipping became more acute.

Nos 1, 2 and 6 were based at Scapa Flow 1.15 to 10.15 while the others patrolled the North Atlantic from Loch Ewe; Nos 11, 13 and 14 were in the Aegean from 2.15 to 6.15. The purchase date for No. 14 was probably "nominal" only. All survivors had been paid off in the UK by 10.15 Nos 2 and 6 going to the Aegean as blockships in 12.15.

MOTOR BOATS

The Motor Boat Reserve, formed in January 1914, consisted of motor-powered pleasure craft ranging in size from 3 to 65 tons. They were added to the RN from 8.14 and others joined until late 1915 when ML deliveries began. Motor boats flew the white ensign and were manned by RNVR personnel with yachting backgrounds. Although armed only with rifles and lighter small arms, they performed varied and useful local and harbour patrol functions. Capable of high speed in good weather but lacking in sea-keeping qualities, they were reduced in number until mid 1916, leaving few to serve during the later phases of the war. Each of the original armed patrol units included four motor boats until the patrol zones were extended further seaward and larger vessels became available to take their place.

This series of 203 numbers was not associated with the earlier Admiralty MB series which was used to identify craft normally carried aboard large warships. Some MB numbers were re-used and in the following list *, **, and *** is used to denote the successive assignments. Certain motor fishing vessels assigned MB numbers are included with motor drifters. After 6.18 remaining motor boats and motor drifters used Fishery flag superior numbers 4301–4328 to eliminate confusion existing between Admiralty and MB numbers. Some MBs had no recorded number.

The Motor Boat Reserve was incorporated into the yacht patrol organisation 1.10.15.

MB	Name	MB	Name
105	ALLEGRO	116	EVADNE
56	AMAZON	140	EXCALIBUR
136	AMICE	78	FEDERATION
112	ANACAPA		FIONGHALL
119*	ANGUS	23	FLORA
	ANZAC	191	FLOUNDER=4321
85	APTERA	29**	FOREST FLY
55*	ARABIAN	110*	FRANCIS
138	ARIEL	5	GABRIELLE
68	ARMIDA	15*	GENESTA
70	AUK	115	GRETA II
37*	BABY	106	GRIFFIN
114	BABY V	163*	GUDEAVON
48	BAL GAL	130	GWAUN MAID
2	BRAEMAR	14	HATASOO
65*	BURRASTOW	142	HIKIBYDO
134	CALIFORNIA	3	HILARY
124**	CALIFORNIA II	131	HONOLULU
53	CATRIONA	135	IAN
59	CERISE	124*	IDA
39	CLARA	122*	IMP
86	CLIO	104*	INANDA
198	COLLEEN II	123*	IRENE
82	COLONSAY	109	IRIS
64	CURLEW	81	ISLANDER
132	CYNTHIA	125*	JAMES TATE
27	DAPHNE	96	JANA
50**	DAUNTLESS	19	JEAN
31	DAWN	61	KAMI NO MICHI
101*	DEGANWY	28	KESTREL
55**	DOLORES	66	KIA ORA
67	DORA	42	KIWI
89	DOREEN	45	KONATSU
203	DOROTHEA	72	KOROOMA
113	DOROTHY MAY	93*	LADY DORA
21*	DRAGONFLY	62	LADY LEL
7	DRANOEL	95	LALLA II
84	DUNIRA	20	LAXFORD
121*	ELEKTRA	50*	LLYS HELIG
93**	ELIDA		LUCY M.
102	EMERALD	16	MADGETTE
144**	EOTHEN	121**	MAGA
15**	ESPOIR	6	MAIA
137	ESTRELLA	91	MAID OF GUERNSEY
52	EUN MARA	25	MAJOR

MB	Name	MB	Name
41*	MANSURA		=RESOURCE
44	MARGOT		=RESOURCEFUL
94	MARGUERITE	126*	ROKA
98	MARY ROSE II	133	ROLYATINA
202	MARY ROSE III=4328	129	RONALIN
1	MAYFAIR	29*	ROSMAR
80	MAYMIE	57	RUBY
128	MEA	104**	ST. BENEDICT
147	MEGALEEP	117	ST. JOLES
141	MEMPHIS	190	SAKKARA
	MENZIES II	9	SALEE ROVER
126**	MIMIC	192	SALMON=4322
11	MINNEHAHA		=HALYCON II 3.19
35	MINOU	47	SEA GULL
99	MOLLA	90	SEABIRD
43	MOLLY	46	SENORA
146	MORANDY	38	SHAMROCK
73	MORNA	40	SHEARWATER
49*	MORWENNA	148**	SINHALEE
139	MURIEL	144*	SPARROW
36	MY LADY MOLLY	199	SPHINX
8	MYNONIE	26	SPLASH
120*	NAIDIA	119**	SPRING FLOWER
13	NEVA	97	SPROUT
120**	NINA D'ASTY	101**	SUNBEAM
149	NITA PITA	122**	SWEETHEART
17	NOAH	32	TALAWA
34	NORD EST	145	TANTRUM
	NOVICE	69	TARA
63	NYATA	110**	TARBES
75	OLIVE	195	TAUTOG=4325
182	OLIVETTE=4310	51	TERRIER
100	OLIVIA	74	TORTOISE
58	OMBAH	123**	TRIDENT
24	OOMALA	196	TROUT=4326
54	ORCHID	194	TUNA=4324
22	OSPREY	88	TYROL
79	OTTAWA	41**	ULEX
60	PAPAKURA	127*	UTILITY
65**	PEARL II	87	VALERIE
201	PENELOPE=4327	148*	VALKYRIE II
37**	PENGUIN	71	VANDORA
193	PERCH=4323	143	VELSA
125**	PERIWINKLE	77	VERA III
118	PERLONA=4320	186	VICTORY
4	PLATYPUS		=VICAR 1918
92	PLEIONE	127**	VIMONO
197	POPPY	33	WEENIE
108	PUFFIN II	10	WHAT NEXT
12	PUP	30	WHITE SLAVE
33	RAMONA	21**	YAQUI
49***	RAZORBILL	76	YEHONALA
1**	RED LICHTIE	18	YTENE
107	RESOLUTE	103	YVONNE

War losses: DOROTHEA, 21.7.15 by fire in E. Mediterranean; DOLORES, 28.8.15 by fire at Douglas, IOM; NITA PITA, 2.12.15 by fire at Poole; ALLEGRO, DOREEN, and GRIFFIN—all three aboard SS ACHAIA torpedoed 8.9.16 off Oran; and SEAGULL, mined 26.2.17 off Folkestone.

MOTOR LAUNCHES

Fifty wooden-hull motor launches were ordered 9.4.15 to be built in America by Elco of Bayonne, New Jersey. The original order for ML.1–50, placed through Canadian Vickers acting on behalf of the Admiralty was followed on 8.6.15 by an additional order for 500 vessels (ML.51–550) of slightly increased size. Delivery of the first 25 was promised by 30.11.15, followed by 200 more by 31.5.16 and 50 per month thereafter. The last of the 550 boats was delivered by 3.11.16. The MLs were sent to Montreal where they were assembled. Too small to cross the Atlantic on their own, they were then shipped to Britain as deck cargo, four aboard each ship. A final 30 (ML.551–580) were ordered during 7.17, the last of which was delivered by 2.18.

It was intended that all MLs should carry modified army 13 pdr guns but when the defensive arming of merchant ships was acclerated the supply of these guns was diverted and a 3 pdr gun was substituted and later vessels were completed with 3 pdrs.

In the Auxiliary Patrol they were manned by RNVR personnel, including many who had formerly been in MBs. At least 82 ML patrol units were formed (Units 500–581) each consisting of six vessels. In addition to replacing the MBs, the MLs were actively employed in the patrol as scouts, anti-submarine craft, inshore minesweepers, smokescreen generators and hydrophone vessels. They sometimes served at considerable distances from their bases. Their larger size gave them improved seaworthiness as compared with the MBs, but they still had limitations, also their design was not entirely without defect. The fire hazard involved with their petrol engines was great and overheating brought about the decision in mid 1916 to use a fuel mixture of one part petrol to two parts paraffin thereafter. Rapid production of a very large number of these craft, provided when the need for them was greatest, more than offset any deficiencies which were encountered.

Forty boats (ML.114–117, 388, 390, 392, 394, 396, 400, 402, 404, 442, 444, 446, 448–454, 456, 458–460, 462, 464, 469–472, 489, 491–493, 543, 544, 547 and 548) were delivered to the French and became part of their V.1–73 series.

From late 1919 surviving boats were sold in large lots. On 31.12.19 M. Eugene Bloch bought 200 for £55000, on 23.1.20 W. J. O'Loghlen bought 95 for £25000. and 32 went to A. E. Cree at Malta for £1600, all bargain prices. The first 550 MLs had cost £4735000 excluding armaments, but their services rendered certainly justified this expense. Vessels remaining on foreign stations were normally disposed of by local sales. By 5.24 only ML.8, 287, 291, 307, 339, 473, 519 and 542 remained and all were gone by 1927.

ML.1–50: 34 tons; 39 tons gross. 75×12×4 ft. Petrol 440 bhp=19 kts.
1–13 pdr (later 1–3 pdr instead), depth charges. Crew of 8.

ML.51–580: 37 tons; 46 tons gross. 80×12½×4 ft. Petrol 440 bhp=19 kts.

War Losses: ML.19 by fire 31.1.16 at Harwich; ML.40 by fire 18.5.16, Suez Canal; ML.52 by fire 29.11.17 in Sandown Bay; ML.55 by fire 28.1.18 at Sittingbourne; ML.64 by fire 10.6.18 in Granton Harbour; ML.110 and ML.424 in action 23.4.18 off Zeebrugge; ML.149 by fire 10.9.16 at Taranto; ML.197 wrecked 31.1.17 near Ballincourty Light House; ML.230, ML.253, and ML.255 all lost 14.9.16 aboard SS INVERBERVIE torpedoed in Gulf of Squillace; ML.247 wrecked 29.9.18 on Oar Rock near St. Ives; ML.254 sunk to avoid capture 10.5.18 off Ostend; ML.278 wrecked 15.1.18 on Dunkirk Pier; ML.356 sunk after collision 11.4.18 off Dover; ML.403 destroyed 22.8.18 while attempting to salve a German torpedo in Runswick Bay; ML.421 sunk after collision 6.4.18 off Whitby; ML.431 by fire 22.4.17 at Poole; ML.474 destroyed by fire after shell hit 23.7.17 near Chios; ML.534 by fire 13.4.17 at Taranto; ML.540 and ML.541 aboard SS HUNSTRICK torpedoed 8.6.17 by S/M off Algiers; and ML.561 mined 21.10.18 off Ostend.

Losses after the Armistice: ML.18, ML.62, ML.191 all lost 29.9.19 on passage from Norway; ML.98 lost, cause unknown; ML.121 by collision 22.12.18 off Seine Bank; ML.152 grounded 2.1.20 on Southern Oland, Sweden; ML.196 caught fire and sank; ML.434 by fire on the Danube; ML.521 caught fire and sank at Portsmouth; ML.566 swamped 22.12.18 off Cape Barfleur. In addition, ML.97, ML.127 and ML.229 were sold in damaged condition.

COASTAL MOTOR BOATS

Admiralty specifications for a torpedo-carrying motor craft of very light weight and capable of high speed were met by Thornycroft who had considerable experience building boats possessing both features. Utilising test information taken from the hydroplanes MIRANDA IV and CARENA, they produced the 40 foot CMB design. The torpedo was carried in a trough and pushed off stern-first while the boat was converging on the target at high speed. Then the boat was required to outpace the torpedo in order that it could turn and escape to safety. Earlier attempts using Admiralty pinnaces as torpedo carriers had failed because the boats had insufficient speed. All CMB contracts were placed with Thornycroft who produced the subsequent designs and subcontracted among eight other boat builders for production of nearly half the total number of hulls. The first twelve 40 footers were ordered in 1.16 and all of these were delivered by 15.8.16. Additional orders included the 55 footer in mid 1916 and the 70 foot minelayers in 1.18. The 55 and 70 footers were given letter suffixes denoting variations in engines and armament. The boats were assigned both Admiralty MB and CMB numbers, but operationally they were known by the CMB numbers. Pendant numbers consisted of V flag superior to CMB number and letter suffix.

40 FOOT CLASS

5 tons. 45 (oa), 40 (pp) $\times 8\frac{1}{2} \times 2\frac{1}{2}$ to 3 ft. Crew: 2 or 3 men.
Armament: 1–18 in torpedo (in trough), 2 to 4 Lewis MG.
Hull: Mahogany (CMB.1–12), cedar (CMB.112) and double mahogany for all others.
Engines: CMB.1–13   1-Thornycroft V.8 or V.12   250 bhp = 24.8 kts.
(petrol) CMB.40–61   1-Fiat   275 bhp = 35.13 kts.
         CMB.112   1-Thornycroft V.12   = 37.25 kts.
         CMB.121–123 1-Green 12   275 bhp = 37.79 kts.

Built by Thornycroft, Hampton:

Name	MB No.	Completed	Fate
CMB.1	(781)	1916	Lost 19.6.17 in action off Ostend.
CMB.2	(782)	1916	Lost 9.7.18 by fire at Portsmouth.
CMB.3	(783)	1916	=DCB.3 in 7.18; sold 19.5.21 J. Woodcraft.
CMB.4	(784)	1916	Loaned 1921–28 to Imperial War Museum; later preserved at Hampton.
CMB.5	(785)	1916	Sunk 1922.
CMB.6	(786)	1916	Sunk 1925 as target.
CMB.7	(787)	1916	Deleted from list 1921.
CMB.8	(788)	1916	Sunk 27.9.17 to avoid capture off the Belgian coast.
CMB.9	(789)	1916	=DCB.1 in 7.18; deleted 1935.
CMB.10	(790)	1916	Lost 7.5.18 by fire at Dover.
CMB.13	(793)	1916	=DCB.2 in 7.18; sold 10.2.20 John I. Thornycroft.
CMB.40	(1213)	1918	Sunk 11.8.18 by A/C off Terschelling.
CMB.41	(1214)	1918	Sold 9.3.22 John I. Thornycroft.
CMB.42	(1215)	1918	Sunk 11.8.18 by A/C off Terschelling.
CMB.47	(1216)	1918	Caught fire and sank 11.8.18 after A/C action off Terschelling.
CMB.48	(1217)	1918	Sold 9.3.22 John I. Thornycroft.
CMB.50	(1218)	1918	Scuttled 19.7.18 in Heligoland Bight.
CMB.55	(1219)	1918	Sold 9.3.22 John I. Thornycroft.
CMB.56	(1220)	1918	Deleted 1921.
CMB.112	(1632)	1919	Deleted 1928.
CMB.121	(1689)	1921	Deleted 1929.
CMB.122	(1690)	1921	Deleted 1929.
CMB.123	(1691)	1921	Sold 1928 Netherlands Navy.

Built by Tom Bunn, Rotherhithe:

Name	MB No.	Completed	Fate
CMB.11	(791)	1916	Lost 2.11.17 by fire after collision off Dover.
CMB.12	(792)	1916	Deleted 1935.

Built by Taylor & Bates, Chertsey:

Name	MB No.	Completed	Fate
CMB.43	(1228)	1918	Sold 9.3.22 John I. Thornycroft.
CMB.49	(1229)	1918	Deleted 1928.

Built by J. W. Brooke, Lowestoft:

Name	MB No.	Completed	Fate
CMB.44	(1221)	1918	Sold 9.3.22 John I. Thornycroft.
CMB.45	(1230)	1918	Deleted 1921.
CMB.59	(1232)	1918	Deleted 1928.

Built by Frank Maynard, Chiswick:

Name	MB No.	Completed	Fate
CMB.46	(1222)	1918	Deleted 1921.
CMB.53	(1223)	1918	Deleted 1920.
CMB.54	(1224)	1918	Deleted 1921.

Built by Salter Brothers, Oxford:

CMB.51	(1225)	1918	Deleted 1921.
CMB.52	(1226)	1918	Deleted 1921.
CMB.60	(1227)	1918	Sold 1920 = ONWARD IV.
CMB.61	(1231)	1918	Deleted 1921.

Built by Wills & Packham, Sittingbourne:

CMB.57	(1211)	1918	Deleted 1921.
CMB.58	(1212)	1918	Deleted 1921.

Notes: CMB.40 was nominal D/S OSEA from 6.18. Sixteen additional CMBs (MB.1693–1708) of the CMB.121 type were cancelled. Two other 40 footers were built (MB.1571 and builder's No. **917**) but not added to the RN. Five became DCB (Distant Controlled Boats) which were wireless controlled to be expended against enemy targets while carrying explosives. In addition to DCB.1–3 already noted, DCB.4 (ex-*MB.1143*) and DCB.5 (ex-*MB.1256*) designated 7.18 were other conversions. In 1918 the cruiser DIAMOND was converted to carry six 40 foot CMBs. In common with certain other small craft, CMBs were simply omitted from the Navy List without much other disposal information. CMBs 55, 44 and 41 became Thornycroft's 1840–42 and were reconditioned for the Spanish Monopoly along with others built to prevent smuggling.

55 FOOT CLASS

11 tons. 60 (oa), 55 (pp) × 11 × 3 ft. Crew: 3 to 5 men.
Armament: 1 or 2–18 in torpedoes (in troughs), 4 Lewis MG, 4 depth charges.
Hulls: Double or 3 skin mahogany.
Engines: Twin-screw petrol motors 750 to 900 bhp = 34 to 42 kts (see suffixes).

Built by Thornycroft, Hampton:

CMB.14A	(988)	1917	Sold 8.5.23 Ocean Salvage Co Ltd.
CMB.15A	(989)	1917	Sold 28.9.21 F. H. Parry.
CMB.16A	(990)	1917	Deleted 1922.
CMB.17A	(991)	1917	Sold 7.10.21 S. W. Wigglesworth.
CMB.18A	(993)	1917	Lost 12.4.18 in collision off the Belgian coast.
CMB.21B	(992)	1917	Deleted 1924.
CMB.24A	(1001)	1918	Lost 18.8.19 in attack on Bolshevik fleet at Kronstadt.
CMB.25BD	(1004)	1918	Deleted 1921.
CMB.26B	(1002)	1918	Deleted 1920.
CMB.27A	(1003)	1918	Deleted 1922.
CMB.28A	(1006)	1918	Deleted 1921.
CMB.31BD	(1005)	1918	Deleted 1924.
CMB.33A	(1007)	1918	Sunk 12.4.18 in action off Ostend.
CMB.34A	(1008)	1918	Deleted 1924.
CMB.36A	(1009)	1918	Deleted 1924.
CMB.65A	(1011)	1918	Deleted 1921.
CMB.76A	(1013)	1918	Deleted 1921.
CMB.78E	(1012)	1918	Deleted 1921.
CMB.80C	(1010)	1918	Deleted after 7.28, before 10.32.
CMB.82C	(1015)	1918	Deleted 1923, sank on passage to Portsmouth.
CMB.83CE	(1041)	1918	Deleted 1932.
CMB.87B	(1014)	1918	Deleted 1922.
CMB.93E	(1042)	1918	Deleted 1928.
CMB.94E	(1048)	1918	Deleted 1928.
CMB.95E	(1049)	1918	Deleted 1928.
CMB.96E	(1050)	1918	Deleted 1924.
CMB.97E	(1233)		Deleted 1928.
CMB.113CK	(1175)		Deleted 1925.
CKB.120F	( )		Deleted 1925.

Built by Taylor & Bates, Chertsey:

Name	MB No.	Completed	Fate
CMB.19A	(1028)	1918	Deleted 1924.
CMB.68B	(1029)	1918	Sold 8.10.21 J. A. Taylor.
CMB.73B	(1030)	1918	Sold 2.23 J. A. Taylor.
CMB.74B	(1031)	1918	Deleted 1924.
CMB.84C	(1040)	1918	Deleted 1932.
CMB.86BD	(1039)	1918	Deleted 1921.
CMB.114D	(1243)	1919	Caught fire and sank 4.23 off the Nab.
CMB.115DE	(1244)	1919	Deleted 1930.

Built by Camper & Nicholson, Gosport:

Name	MB No.	Completed	Fate
CMB.20A	(1016)	1918	Deleted 1924.
CMB.37A	(1018)	1918	Sold 8.10.21 J. A. Taylor.
CMB.39B	(1017)	1918	Lost 28.4.18 by fire at Dunkirk.
CMB.69A	(1019)	1918	Deleted 1924.
CMB.70A	(1023)	1918	Deleted 1921.
CMB.72A	(1020)	1918	Deleted 1921.
CMB.75B	(1024)	1918	Deleted 1928.
CMB.77A	(1022)	1918	Deleted 1921.
CMB.79A	(1025)	1918	Lost 18.9.19 in attack on Bolshevik fleet at Kronstadt.
CMB.81C	(1021)	1918	Deleted 1932.
CMB.98ED	(1241)	1919	Deleted 1928.
CMB.99ED	(1242)	1919	Lost 1920 by fire at Portsmouth.
CMB.118D	(1562)	1920	Deleted c1932.
CMB.119D	(1563)	1920	Deleted 1932.

Built by Wills & Packham, Sittingbourne:

Name	MB No.	Completed	Fate
CMB.22B	(1032)	1918	Deleted 1924.
CMB.30B	(1033)	1918	Deleted 1928.
CMB.638D	(1043)	1918	Deleted 1921.
CMB.64BD	(1034)	1918	Deleted 1921.
CMB.116D	(1239)	1919	Deleted c1932.
CMB.117D	(1240)	1919	Deleted c1932.

Built by Salter Brothers, Oxford:

Name	MB No.	Completed	Fate
CMB.23B	(1035)	1918	Deleted 1928.
CMB.62BD	(1044)	1918	Lost 18.8.19 in attack on Bolshevik fleet, Kronstadt.
CMB.67A	(1036)	1918	Lost 18.8.19 in attack on Bolshevik fleet, Kronstadt.

Built by Rowhedge Iron Works, Rowhedge:

Name	MB No.	Completed	Fate
CMB.29A	(1037)	1918	Deleted 1922.
CMB.35A	(1038)	1918	Deleted 1921.
CMB.90BD	(1235)	1919	Sunk 1923 as target.
CMB.91BD	(1234)	1919	Deleted 1928.
CMB.92BD	(1236)	1919	Deleted 1928.

Built by Frank Maynard, Chiswick:

Name	MB No.	Completed	Fate
CMB.32A	(1026)	1918	Deleted 1924.
CMB.38B	(1027)	1918	Deleted 1928.
CMB.66BD	(1046)	1918	Deleted 1921.
CMB.71A	(1047)	1918	Missing 15.10.18, believed foundered after collision off the Belgian coast.
CMB.85C	(1238)	1919	Deleted 1932.
CMB.88BD	(1237)	1919	Deleted 1921.

Builder not known

Name	MB No.	Completed	Fate
CMB.89BD	(1045)	1918	Deleted 1928.

Suffixes for 55 foot CMB variations:

A	2-Thornycroft V.12	each 250 bhp=35.25 kts	1 torpedo
B	2-Green 12	each 275 bhp=37.06 kts	1 torpedo
C	2-Sunbeam	each 450 bhp=41.19 kts	1 torpedo
D	2-Green 18	each 450 bhp	1 torpedo
E	2-Thornycroft Y.12	each 350 bhp=40.96 kts	1 torpedo
F	2-		1 torpedo
BD	2-Green 12	each 275 bhp=35.10 kts	2 torpedoes
CE	2-		2 torpedoes
CK	2-		2 torpedoes
DE	2-Green 18	each 450 bhp=40.67 kts	2 torpedoes
ED	2-Thornycroft Y.12	each 350 bhp	2 torpedoes

Notes: In 1917 at least 21 CMBs were used as minelayers. Eleven additional boats numbered between MB.1536 and 1562 were probably cancelled 55 footers. CMB.7 (40 foot class) along with CMBs 24A, 28A, 62BD, 72A, 79A and 86BD all served in the Baltic 1919. The 55 foot CMBs were intended to perform anti-submarine functions in addition to attacks on surface vessels.

70 FOOT CLASS

24 tons. 72½ (oa), 70 (pp) × 14 × 3½ ft.
Armament: 6 Lewis MG, 4 depth charges, 7 sinker mines (in troughs).
Hulls: 3 skin mahogany.
Engines: M suffix   2-Thornycroft Y.12   each 375 bhp=25.96 kts.
(petrol) MT suffix 2-Thornycroft Y.24   each   bhp=36.6 kts.

Built by Thornycroft, Hampton:

CMB.100M	(1267)	1919	Deleted 1921.
CMB.102MT	(1268)	1919	=HORNET 1923; in service WW II.

Begun by Thornycroft, Woolston; completed at Portsmouth DY:

CMB.101M	(1264)	1919	Sold 9.2.20 A. E. Guiness.

Built by Camper & Nicholson, Gosport:

CMB.103MT	(1257)	1920	Deleted 1928; in service 1942–44; =relic at Gosport.
CMB.104MT	(1258)	1920	Laid up 1928; in service WW II.

Notes: The design dates from 11.17, twelve boats designed as minelayers were ordered 1.18. Six torpedoes could be carried in lieu of 4 sinker mines. Seven were cancelled; CMBs 105–111 (MB.1259–1263, 1265–1266). MB.1265 building at Woolston was also reported to have been completed at Pembroke DY. Another 70 footer, MB.1535, building at Hampton with triple troughs for 18 in torpedoes, 3 twin Lewis MG, 4 depth charges and powered by Green 24 cylinder motors does not appear to have been completed for the RN. A 45 foot CMB, Thornycroft's number 1622, built to similar designs as the naval CMBs was also not used by the RN. The CMBs with their high speed and torpedoes caused the enemy great concern and led worldwide development of the motor torpedo boat. In the postwar years many similar craft were built by Thornycroft for foreign governments obviously intended as test vehicles and prototypes. Some changes in boat suffixes occurred in the 1920s as a result of alterations and refits, only the original letters are recorded here.

THE AUXILIARY PATROL

Early experiments using fishing trawlers for sweeping moored mines began when the similarity between trawl fishing and minesweeping principles was first noticed. Admiral Lord Beresford, after an inspection at Grimsby, caused two Grimsby trawlers, ALGOMA and ANDES, to be hired in late 1907 and sent to Portland for tests. The results, although not wholly successful, served to indicate worthwhile potential use of such vessels for this purpose. The first trawlers purchased by the Admiralty were added in April 1909. These few, along with the recent torpedo gunboat conversions, participated in the development of minesweeping rigs, methods and conducted periodic training exercises. The use of mines in recent wars had created interest and had shown what results could be achieved at a comparatively moderate cost and with limited effort. The full impact of this knowledge was not realised until later, by which time it had become very apparent that an impending mine offensive would accompany the expected European war.

The Royal Naval Reserve (RNR) Trawler Section organisation began in late 1911, at first including only trawlers from Grimsby and Aberdeen. Trawlers from all of the larger fishing ports were later included. Although development of the minesweeping trawler reserve proceeded according to plan, a more realistic assessment of the numbers required stemmed from as late as January 1914. Thereafter a more ambitious approach was taken and the number of trawlers earmarked for service multiplied.

Another organisation which became fully associated with what became the Auxiliary Patrol was the Motor Boat Reserve. Formed in late 1912 with the idea of naval patrol service, this reserve became directly associated with the Royal Naval Volunteer Reserve (RNVR) in January 1914. The motor boats were slated for use as picket vessels and service in estuaries and other sheltered waters.

In August 1914 the 80-odd trawlers of the ready reserve were quickly taken up; by 8.8.14 at least 94 trawlers were in service or fitting-out. Within the next two weeks another 100 trawlers were requisitioned and sent to Lowestoft for flitting-out. Lowestoft became the chief depot for minesweepers; very large quantities of sweep gear and assorted stores were maintained there. The other principal fishing ports also became fitting-out bases, but to a lesser degree than Lowestoft. The trawler minesweepers were employed firstly sweeping areas along the East Coast. Soon thereafter protection of the Grand Fleet and its bases received top priority so special flotillas were formed and sent north for this purpose. The total of requisitioned vessels increased rapidly as minelaying operations by the German surface minelayers became known. Later this minelaying was carried on mostly by U-boats specially built for the purpose.

The organisation of what shortly emerged as the Auxiliary Patrol favoured the Scapa Flow area to begin with and as vessels became available, the coverage was extended completely around the British Isles. The post of Admiral of Patrols was created in July 1914 and soon became an important command. Before the war's conclusion there were several thousand vessels in the Patrol. As well as circling the home islands, the patrols were extended further seaward, and in addition, hundreds of the little ships went to the Mediterranean, Aegean and the White Sea. Colonial governments participated in organising their own patrol forces according to their needs and capabilities.

At first the number of mines swept were few, the ratio between those swept and struck by ships was 1 to 1. Much later, after most of the mine areas had been located, and under more favourable conditions in general (with improved efficiency and a larger number of sweepers in action), at least 85 mines were destroyed for every one causing ship damage or loss. The presence of enemy minefields usually became known when several victims fouled them, but others remained undetected (principally those laid by submarines) until after the war.

Repeated requests by fleet and area commanders for more small craft within their commands best illustrated the need for them and caused in-service totals to soar. As the submarine menace grew, the armed patrol and anti-submarine vessels were accordingly added to the Patrol. Duties soon included watching for minelaying, patrolling swept channels, smoke screen generation, examination service, escort work and a multitude of others. The trawlers were joined by yachts, drifters, motor boats, whalers, screw and paddle steamers and a wide variety of other types. Later, as the war construction programme began to bear fruit over 1500 newly-built, Admiralty-owned vessels were added.

The armed patrol units formed in 1914 usually consisted of one yacht, four trawlers or drifters, and several motor boats. The armed yacht was unit leader, fitted with wireless equipment, and if large enough in size, armed with two guns; the yacht number originally was that of the unit number also. All vessels were armed as the supply of small weapons (3 in and smaller) permitted, though the small motor boats were given rifles only. Progressive improvement of the armaments was made as the quantity of heavier guns and newly-developed equipment became available. The 3 pounder guns removed from trawlers were re-mounted in drifters and the trawlers then received either 6 or 12 pounders. Later armaments are indicated in ship lists. Anti-submarine bomb-throwers (or howitzers), 2 pdr AA machine guns (pom-poms), depth charges and listening hydrophones were later added. Some comparison of light guns carried can be made from following table indicating approximate equals:

12 pdr gun, with 8 or 12 cwt mountings of 28 or 40 calibre; similar to 3 in and 76 mm. (with variations in ammunition weight, the 12 to 15 pounders were all of about 3 inch bore).

6 pdr gun, with 6 cwt, 42.3 calibre mountings (Nordenfelt type) or
with 8 cwt, 40 calibre mountings (Hotchkiss type); similar to 57 mm, with a 2.24 inch bore.

3 pdr gun, with 4 cwt, 45.4 calibre mountings (Nordenfelt type) or
with 5 cwt, 40 calibre mountings (Hotchkiss type); similar to 47 mm, with a 1.85 inch bore.

By 1917 there were 150 numbered A/P units, most of them consisting of one yacht (or large trawler, in lieu of a yacht) and six trawlers. Most of the A/P trawlers were fitted for minesweeping and a large number carried wireless equipment. One of the trawlers was fitted as a leader, another was designated second-leader, making flagships alternate to the yacht. Other vessels employed simply as minesweepers carried only 3 pounders or remained unarmed throughout their naval career.

Drifters were sometimes used as A/P vessels, on examination service, or as minesweepers. One special A/P flotilla of drifters at the Downs contained individuals identified by "naval letters" (A to I, and K to U), later on numbers were used. By early 1915 hundreds of them had been requisitioned as net vessels to form anti-submarine barriers using special wire nets. Working together in large groups, they were capable of creating a net barrier many miles in length. Each net drifter could stream 500 yards of buoyed wire netting that extended down about 16 fathoms. The two best known areas where these barriers were used were in the Dover and Otranto Straits, operating against German and Austrian U-boats respectively. Their net barriers served to hamper rather than prevent U-boat traffic and on several occasions the exposed drifter lines suffered heavily when attacked by enemy cruisers and destroyers. In the closing months of the war many drifters became minesweepers and the net barrages were replaced by far more effective barriers formed by deeply moored mines.

Few vessels remained to be requisitioned by 1917 and from then on the Admiralty trawlers and drifters made up nearly all of the fishing craft types subsequently added to the Patrol. In the early part of the war some Admiralty numbers were changed when ships were reassigned to a new unit or area, but this practice was discontinued and the final number listed was soon in effect. All auxiliary warships assigned Admiralty numbers in the 1–4504 series (not all numbers used) were in commission while carrying a number. A number of vessels later serving on boom defence and comparable duties had their numbers rescinded when no longer on white ensign commission. Fishing numbers served as identity numbers for non-commissioned (red ensign) craft. Admiralty numbers were frequently reassigned to new vessels after the first vessel went to non-commissioned status or was struck off the list. Various Y flag plus pendant superiors designated types from 16.3.15; namely Y+Equal Speed pendant superior for yachts and A/P vessels; Y+ Interrogative pendant superior for trawler and paddle minesweepers; and Y+Guard pendant superior for net drifters. Sometime after April 1917 and by January 1918, the Fishery flag superior became effective for all of the Admiralty 1–4504 series.

The Boom Defence Service included many hundreds of fishing vessels and others who served almost exclusively in red ensign status (non-commissioned) while performing harbour protection functions of no less importance than the auxiliary fighting vessels. Some of these craft were armed and generally speaking they used older vessels for this purpose. As previously indicated, they used their fishing numbers while in the navy; commissioned ships (A/P vessels, etc.) of the Auxiliary Patrol at times used either or both numbers. The several thousand vessels of these two auxiliary services contributed considerably to the over-all success of the naval effort, they provided protection for the fleet and its anchorages as well as control of coastal waters in spite of severe opposition from the enemy and natural elements.

The preliminary order outlining demobilisation principles was issued 15.7.18, followed by the first issue of complete instructions 10.12.18. By the middle of February 1919 the demobilisation process was in full operation and essentially completed by August 1919. A few vessels remained to assist the Admiralty-owned ships in the clearance of both enemy and friendly minefields. By the autumn of 1919 the commercial craft had un-shipped their guns and equipment and had returned to their former peacetime occupations. By 30.4.20 the trawler section had been completely demobilised.

AUXILIARY PATROL AREAS

Sufficient numbers of patrol vessels were available by December 1914 to provide coastal patrols of moderate strength surrounding the home islands. Areas received numeral designations which were first listed 19.12.14. These designated areas remained effective until the 1919 demobilisation period. The summer of 1915 saw the patrol organisation approaching maturity, by this time basically similar to the charts indicating area status and strength for January 1917. Alterations after January 1917 included combining areas II and III, combining areas VI and VII, the addition of new area XIIIa (Devonport) from 1.4.17 created from within areas XIII and XIV. Original area XIX (Killybegs) became new area XIXa with altered boundaries in May 1918. Area XX (Galway Bay) was reduced in size and re-numbered to become new area XIX; the remaining southernmost portion made up new area XX (Berehaven). The limits of each area necessarily more clearly defined as the organisation grew and operations extended farther from land.

Assignment of vessels and armed patrols within each area was dictated by the war threat to which it was exposed and as the operational range of enemy submarines was increased, re-alignment of defensive measures became necessary. Extension of the patrol activities into the Mediterranean began when trawler-minesweepers were used in the first attempts to force the Dardanelles. Later they were used to establish a firmer grip on the entire Mediterranean area, thusly making new demands on the ships and men of the fishing fleet. Another notable concentration of smallcraft developed when net drifters were attached to the Taranto (Italian) zone. The Mediterranean Sea was divided into patrol zones dividing responsibility between the British, French and Italian navies.

The charts dated 3.1.17 best illustrate the final number and extent of operational areas at the height of the sea war. Numbers in the patrol service are given for the first Red list issued in January of each year from 1915 to 1919. Since totals were under constant revision all during this period these figures represent the minimal strength of the Patrol; even the official sources differed slightly with regards to the precise numbers and some of the less prominent types were occasionally overlooked. In the following list of areas and zones which is keyed to the two charts for 3.1.17, parent ships are also given. Since command of several areas were sometimes under the same admiral, there are fewer parent ships than patrol areas. The limits of each area were normally taken from lines extended from light houses, buoys or prominent land features, all of which were easily seen. Naturally the coastline served as the inner limits, but the outer extremes were defined as "as far as necessary".

Area:	I	Stornoway	Parent ship:	IOLAIRE
	II	Shetland Islands		BRILLIANT
	III	Orkney Islands		ZARIA
	IV	Cromarty		THALIA
	V	Peterhead		THALIA
	VI	Granton		GUNNER
	VII	Granton		GUNNER
	VIII	Tyne		SATELLITE
	IX	Humber		WALLINGTON
	X	Yarmouth		KINGFISHER
	Harwich local area			GANGES
	Nore local area			ACTAEON
	XI	Dover and the Downs		ATTENTIVE III and CETO
	XII	Portsmouth		HERMIONE
	XIII	Portland		RESEARCH
	XIV	Falmouth		DREEL CASTLE
	Bristol Channel area			LONGSET
	XV	Milford Haven		IDAHO
	XVI	Kingstown		BOADICEA II
	Liverpool local area			EAGLE
	XVII	Lough Larne		THETIS
	Clyde local area			PACTOLUS
	XVIII	Lough Swilly		COLLEEN
	XIX	Killybegs		COLLEEN
	XX	Galway Bay		COLLEEN
	XXI	Queenstown		COLLEEN
	XXII	Holyhead		AMETHYST III
Zone:	I	Gibraltar	Parent ship:	COMORANT
	V	Malta		EGMONT
	VI	Taranto (Italian)		ADMIRABLE
	VIII	Aegean Sea		OSIRIS II
	X	Egypt		HANNIBAL
	West Indies			LEVIATHAN
	White Sea			VINDICTIVE

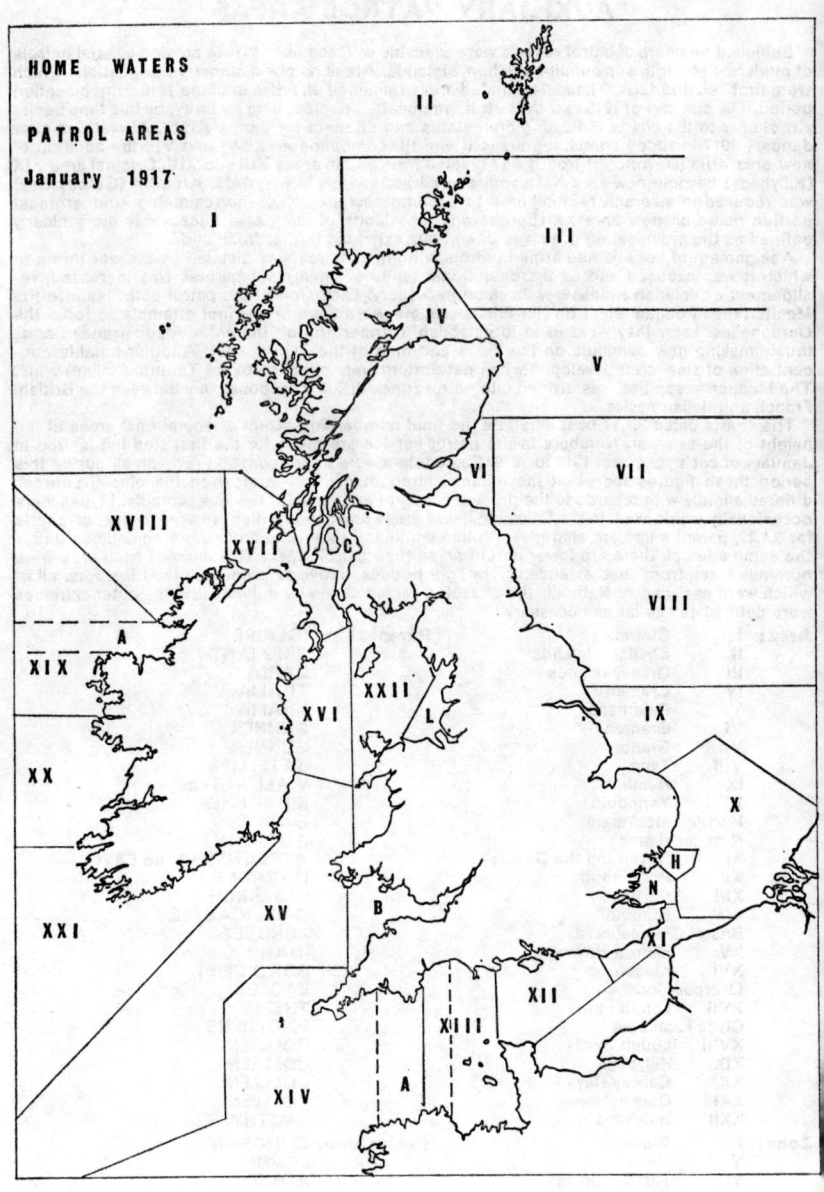

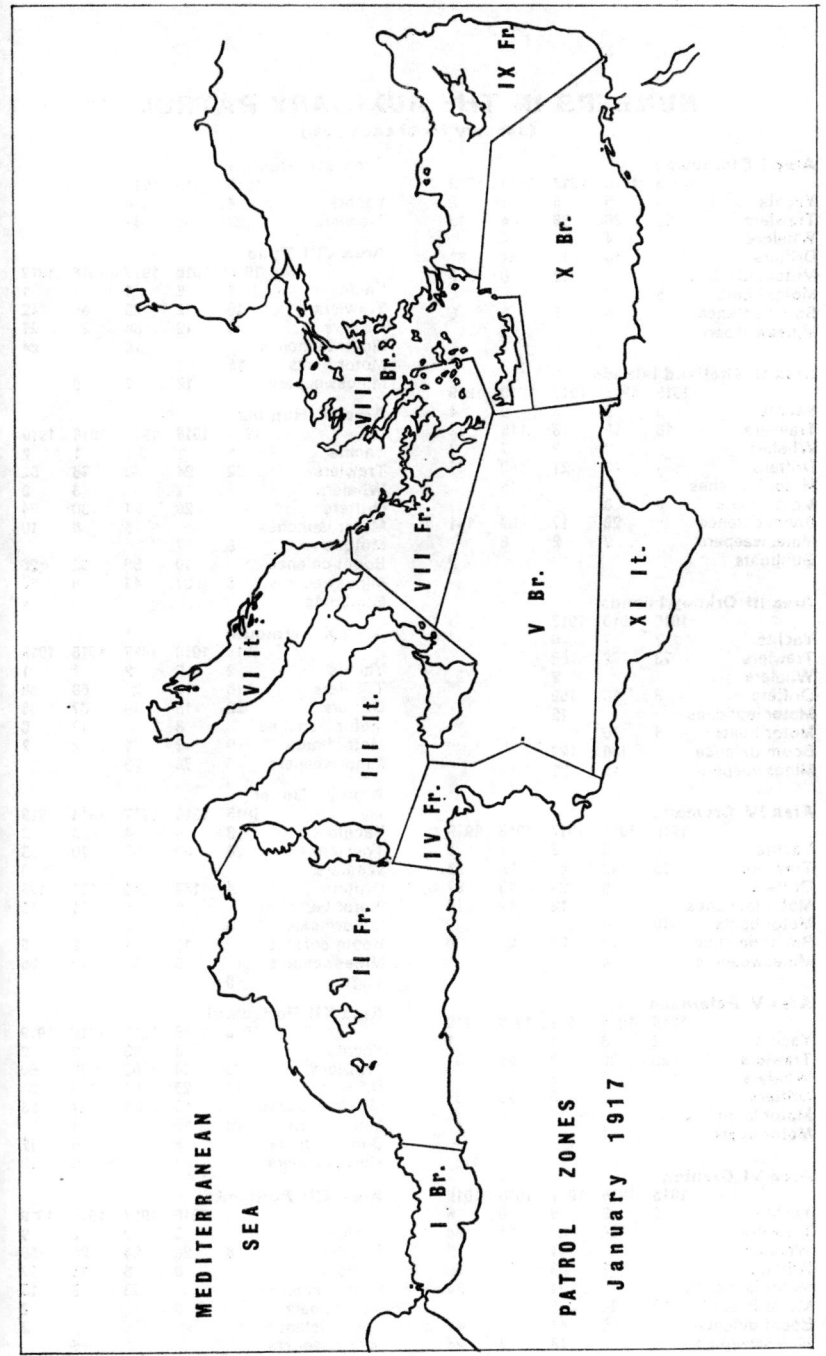

NUMBERS IN THE AUXILIARY PATROL
(January 1st of each year)

Area I Stornoway

	1915	1916	1917	1918	1919
Yachts	5	5	5	5	2
Trawlers	20	36	36	44	13
Whalers			4	4	4
Drifters		15	17	31	31
Motor launches			12	6	5
Motor boats	5	9			
Boom defence		6	5	6	6
Minesweepers				3	

Area II Shetland Islands

	1915	1916	1917	1918	1919
Yachts	3	3	3	6	4
Trawlers	18	18	18	115	82
Whalers		2	2	7	3
Drifters		42	21	190	181
Motor launches				15	
Motor boats	9	3			
Boom defence		20	17	89	141
Minesweepers		2	2	8	
Gunboats					9

Area III Orkney Islands

	1915	1916	1917
Yachts	7	7	6
Trawlers	73	72	68
Whalers			2
Drifters	8	58	169
Motor launches			12
Motor boats	8	10	
Boom defence		138	129
Minesweepers		15	25

Area IV Cromarty

	1915	1916	1917	1918	1919
Yachts	3	2	3	1	1
Trawlers	35	42	43	28	23
Drifters		6	20	13	37
Motor launches			12	12	14
Motor boats	10	14			
Boom defence		19	22	25	20
Minesweepers		4			

Area V Peterhead

	1915	1916	1917	1918	1919
Yachts	2	3	1	1	1
Trawlers	23	26	30	26	31
Whalers		8	8		
Drifters		4	5	20	39
Motor launches			12	8	4
Motor boats		1			

Area VI Granton

	1915	1916	1917	1918	1919
Yachts	3	3	5	6	6
Trawlers	35	24	25	51	94
Whalers			1	1	2
Drifters		7	33	37	56
Motor launches			24	24	24
Motor boats	13	24	1		
Boom defence		5	45	43	41
Minesweepers			18	13	24

Area VII Granton

	1915	1916	1917
Yachts	4	4	4
Trawlers	23	45	47

Area VIII Tyne

	1915	1916	1917	1918	1919
Yachts	1	2	1	1	1
Trawlers	16	12	25	52	42
Drifters	4	12	36	29	27
Motor launches			18	16	24
Motor boats	15	8			
Minesweepers		12	12	9	

Area IX Humber

	1915	1916	1917	1918	1919
Yachts	1	1	1	1	2
Trawlers	32	24	30	96	52
Whalers				3	2
Drifters		20	24	30	64
Motor launches			16	6	10
Motor boats	5	7			
Boom defence		10	35	32	26
Minesweepers	6	37	44	8	13
Gunboats					4

Area X Yarmouth

	1915	1916	1917	1918	1919
Yachts	2	2	2	1	1
Trawlers	116	18	20	68	56
Drifters	20	18	49	37	38
Motor launches		3	18	12	6
Motor boats	9	8	1	2	2
Minesweepers		78	73		

Area XI Dover

	1915	1916	1917	1918	1919
Yachts	3	4	4	3	2
Trawlers	20	80	83	70	83
Whalers					3
Drifters	4	159	140	131	173
Motor launches		6	24	31	19
Motor boats	8	8	2		
Boom defence		16	4	2	6
Minesweepers		6	17	19	36
Tugs	9				

Area XII Portsmouth

	1915	1916	1917	1918	1919
Yachts		3	3	2	2
Trawlers	26	44	62	73	60
Drifters	19	26	84	108	83
Motor launches		10	33	37	28
Motor boats	25	15	3	1	
Boom defence		8	8	10	12
Minesweepers				6	12

Area XIII Portland

	1915	1916	1917	1918	1919
Yachts		3	2	2	9
Trawlers	8	26	24	28	156
Drifters		8	8	15	17
Motor launches			18	9	15
Motor boats		6			2
Boom defence					2
Minesweepers				5	

Area XIIIA Devonport

	1918	1919
Trawlers	54	46
Whalers		2
Drifters	19	25
Motor launches	21	17
Boom defence	1	1
Minesweepers		4

Area XIV Falmouth

	1915	1916	1917	1918	1919
Yachts		3	3	2	2
Trawlers	8	53	54	44	60
Drifters	8	83	53		41
Motor launches			12	14	13
Motor boats	1	2			
Boom defence				2	2
Gunboats					2

Area XV Milford Haven

	1915	1916	1917	1918	1919
Yachts	1	3	3	3	3
Trawlers	11	35	36	47	20
Drifters	8	122	100	61	35
Motor launches			12	8	
Motor boats	4				
Boom defence		5	4	3	4

Area XVI Kingstown

	1915	1916	1917	1918	1919
Yachts		3	2	3	3
Trawlers		12	12	19	19
Drifters		12	12	14	20
Motor launches			12	12	12
Motor boats		1			
Boom defence				1	1
Minesweepers					1

Area XVII Lough Larne

	1915	1916	1917	1918	1919
Yachts	2	1	2	3	3
Trawlers	28	18	17	26	33
Drifters	3	107	95	69	45
Motor launches			18	12	5
Motor boats	4	3			
Boom defence				1	1
Minesweepers				4	5

Area XVIII Lough Swilly

	1915	1916	1917	1918	1919
Yachts	1				
Trawlers		13	20	28	26
Drifters	4	2	3	15	17
Boom defence		7	4	4	4
Minesweepers	7				

Area XIX Killybegs = Area XIXA 5.18

	1915	1916	1917	1918	1919
Trawlers		7	7		3

Area XX Galway Bay = Area XIX 5.18

	1915	1916	1917	1918	1919
Yachts	1				
Trawlers		7	7	6	6
Motor launches				8	9

Area XX Berehaven

	1915	1916	1917	1918	1919
Yachts	1				
Trawlers	2			8	13
Drifters	2			4	5
Motor launches				6	6
Boom defence				1	4

Area XXI Queenstown

	1915	1916	1917	1918	1919
Yachts	1	4	4	1	
Trawlers	10	24	24	15	11
Drifters	2	9	10	17	17
Motor launches			24	16	15
Motor boats	4	5			
Boom defence		3	5	5	5
Minesweepers				7	4

Area XXII Holyhead

	1915	1916	1917	1918	1919
Yachts		1	2	1	1
Trawlers		12	12	13	10
Drifters		12	12	14	14
Motor launches			6	6	6
Motor boats		2			

Harwich local area

	1915	1916	1917	1918	1919
Yachts					1
Trawlers	17	21	26	30	30
Whalers					2
Drifters	2		24	30	30
Motor launches		6	5	6	23
Motor boats	4	2			
Boom defence		5	9		21
Minesweepers			5	7	24

Nore local area

	1915	1916	1917	1918	1919
Yachts		1	1	1	2
Trawlers	24	28	31	29	24
Drifters		50	43	42	39
Motor launches			24	33	25
Motor boats	7	9			
Boom defence		10	9	16	20
Minesweepers		4	12	9	23

Bristol local area

	1915	1916	1917	1918	1919
Trawlers		6	6	6	10
Drifters				6	8
Motor launches			12	6	9
Minesweepers				5	

Liverpool local area

	1915	1916	1917	1918	1919
Yachts		1	1		
Trawlers		12	2	11	19
Drifters	4	12	12	21	34
Motor launches			6	6	
Minesweepers				5	9

Clyde local area

	1915	1916	1917	1918	1919
Yachts	2	1	1	1	
Trawlers	4	6	6	13	14
Drifters		12	12	31	36
Motor launches			6	6	10
Motor boats	1				
Boom defence			6	6	6
Minesweepers		2			

Zone 1 Gibraltar

	1916	1917	1918	1919
Yachts	8	8	7	
Trawlers	9	9	9	15
Drifters				12
Motor launches		18	19	19
Patrol paddlers				1

Zone 5 Malta

	1916	1917	1918	1919
Yachts	1	1	1	1
Trawlers	41	53	51	42
Drifters				14
Motor launches		18	18	31
Boom defence			4	
Minesweepers	6			
Patrol paddlers		5	5	4

Italian Zone 6 Taranto

	1916	1917	1918	1919
Yachts		1	1	
Trawlers			12	17
Drifters	76	113	116	37
Motor launches		36	42	19

Zone 8 Aegean Sea

	1916	1917	1918	1919
Yachts		1	2	3
Trawlers		70	61	90
Drifters	18	58	24	64
Motor launches		42	21	41
Boom defence		4	4	4
Minesweepers				8

Zone 10 Egypt

	1916	1917	1918	1919
Yachts		1	1	
Trawlers	14	48	47	37
Drifters			6	14
Motor launches		17	17	14
Motor boats	11	2		
Boom defence				2
Patrol paddlers		5	5	5

Africa

	1916	1917	1918	1919
Whalers	11	8	14	14
Drifters				4
Boom defence				1

Dardanelles

	1916
Yachts	2
Trawlers	25
Drifters	31
Motor boats	5
Boom defence	3
Minesweepers	47

White Sea

	1916	1917	1918	1919
Yachts			2	1

	1916	1917	1918	1919
Trawlers			14	16
Drifters			4	4
Boom defence			2	
Minesweepers	3	17		

West Indies

	1917	1918	1919
Yachts		2	2
Drifters			6
Motor launches	12	12	12
Miscellaneous			4

On Special Service

	1916	1917	1918	1919
Yachts	7	6	1	
Trawlers		7	2	2
Drifters		3		
Motor launches			11	
Motor boats	2		7	7

On Passage or Fitting-out

	1916	1917	1918	1919
Yachts	5	1		14
Trawlers	48	9		17
Drifters	5			2
Motor launches	21	19		
Motor boats	19			

At Southampton depot

	1917	1918	1919
Motor launches		15	62
Motor boats		9	7

Canada

	1919
Trawlers	36
Drifters	39

East Indies

	1919
Trawlers	6
Motor launches	12

On the Rhine

	1919
Motor launches	12

Grand totals:
- 1.1.15   827 vessels
- 3.1.16   2595 vessels
- 3.1.17   3259 vessels
- 2.1.18   3301 vessels
- 1.1.19   3773 vessels

HIRED YACHTS

Pendant Nos.	Name	TM*	TG/Yr	Armament—Service—Fate
044	ADVENTURESS	362	342/13	2–12 pdr M/S. 23.11.14–18.3.19; =ANGLIA in WW II.
082	AEGUSA	1242	1057/96	(*ex-Erin*) 2–3 in. 3.7.15– mined 28.4.16 near Malta.
N.92 (9.18)	AEROLITE	84	61/80	(*ex-Garland*) Tug 10.17– purchased 4.18; sold 29.8.19; =in WW II.
013	AGATHA	450	353/05	1–12 pdr, 1–6 pdrAA. 28.9.14–15.3.19.
YA.9	ALBION	1346	1116/05	Hospital ship 9.14– =A/P yacht 2–12 pdr, 1–6 pdrAA 22.2.15–11.3.19.
054	=ALBION III 4.15			
	ALVINIA	579	597/01	(*ex-Sokolitza*) Seized 3.8.18– returned 16.7.19 to Russia.
065	AMALTHAEA =IOLAIRE 11.18	634	415/81	(*ex-Iolanthe*) 2–3 in. 14.3.15– wrecked 1.1.19 on Biatan Holm at entrance to Stornoway.
066	AMETHYST =AMETHYST III 3.15	330	201/77	(*ex-Nellie II*) 2–6 pdr. 14.9.14–30.9.14 and 30.3.15–15.2.17.
081	AMY	416	288/77	(*ex-Jason*) 1–12 pdr, 1–6 pdrAA. 7.7.15–30.3.19.
053	ARIANE	630	492/98	(*ex-Sheelah*) 1–12 pdr, 2–6 pdr. 23.2.15– transferred 25.2.16 to France.
05	ARIES	263	201/80	2–3 pdr. 12.9.14– mined 31.10.15 off Leathercoat.
/ (9.18)	ASSEGAI	82	76/76	(*ex-Assagai*) purchased 1915; Tug 3.18 at Portsmouth; sold 2.11.21.
027	ASTER =ASTER II 6.15	249	201/83	2–3 pdr. 25.9.14–5.10.16.
020	ATALANTA	1398	1303/03	(*ex-Lorena*) 2–3 in. 5.6.15–21.2.19.
047	BACCHANTE II	973	759/91	(*ex-Zaria*) 2–12 pdr. 1.2.15– transferred 25.2.16 to France.
032	BERYL	1363	1042/93	(*ex-Princess Alice*) 2–3 in. 11.1.15–15.3.19.
072	BOADICEA II	447	305/82	1–12 pdr, 1–6 pdr. 10.5.15–15.3.19; =SEA-FLOWER in WW II.
080	BRANWEN	151	131/05	2–6 pdr SSV. 4.1.15–12.3.17.
	BROWN MOUSE	75	43/08	Q trawler-yacht (BM.276) also SPINOZA. 23.12.16– burned 28.2.18, total loss.
	CAEROLITE		/	Misc service. 1918–1920.
043	CALANTHE	429	370/98	2–6 pdr. 19.11.14– =Misc yacht (not commissioned) 24.5.17–8.5.19; =in WW II.
014	CALISTA	265	229/02	2–3 pdr. 10.9.14–6.12.17.
07	CATANIA	668	589/95	2–12 pdr. 7.9.14–21.2.19.
03	CETO =CETO II 3.18	185	140/88	1–6 pdrAA, 1–3 pdr. 4.9.14–11.3.18.
	CEYLON	534	311/91	(*ex-Lady Ina*) Misc vessel. 23.3.15–14.7.16.
	CLAYMORE II	66	59/88	Exam tender. Purchased 28.8.17– sold 6.12.19; =ALOMA in WW II.
08	CLEMENTINA	625	469/87	(*ex-Sultana*) 2–6 pdr. 22.9.14– beached 5.8.15 after collision off Tor Point.
025				
051	CONQUEROR II	526	407/89	2–6 pdr. 1.2.15– sunk 26.9.16 by U.52 in Fair Island Channel.
030	CORYCIA	250	196/96	(*ex-Christine*) 1–6 pdr, 1–3 pdr. 25.9.14– purchased 24.11.17 as salvage vessel; sold 1.6.20.
010	DIANE	259	194/02	(*ex-Vanessa*) 2–3 pdr. 16.9.14–23.11.17.
Y4.3	DON RODERIC	56	37/84	Presented 1914 as fleet messenger, paid off 28.5.15.
	DORADE	87	69/05	(*ex-Sparkle*) 1918–1920; =in WW II.
	DOTTER	214	165/87	(*ex-Dotterel*) Attached to A/S division 20.4.18– purchased 1919; sold 7.6.22.
	DRAMA		/	ABS 1915– purchased 1916; sold 1.5.19 G Tumno & Co
04	EILEEN	1022	910/10	(*ex-Doris*) 2–12 pdr 4.11.14–30.4.19
016	ELLIDA	360	265/94	2–6 pdr 9.14–29.8.18.
078	ERISKA	347	285/02	1–12 pdr, 1–6 pdrAA. 3.6.15–25.3.19.
040	EUN MARA	251	210/06	(*ex-Monique*) 2.2.15–4.5.16.

Pendant Nos.	Name	TM*	TG/Yr	Afrmament—Service—Fate
04 033	EVENING STAR	270	191/94	(ex-*The Evening Star*) 2–6 pdr. 6.9.14–9.2.17.
	FOAM	39	33/02	1–.45 in Maxim. 5.9.14–24.4.18.
	FRANKLIN (RAN)		288/06	(ex-*Adele*) T/S purchased 1912; listed to 1924.
	GAEL	115	101/04	1.10.17–5.3.19; =in WW II.
086	GOISSA	1023	882/93	(ex-*Sapphire*) 2–12 pdr, 1–6 pdrAA. 19.2.16– mined 15.11.18 in the Dardanelles.
023	GRETA	393	292/98	1–12 pdr. 8.10.14–25.3.19.
	GRIANAIG	439	351/04	1914–14.11.14; =LADY SHAHRAZAD in WW II.
029	HECATE	471	424/03	1–12 pdr, 1–6 pdr. 15.10.14–30.3.19; =AARLA in WW II.
064	HELGA	323	323/08	2–12 pdr. 12.3.15– purchased 12.3.19; sold 1922 =MUIRCHU.
02	HERSILIA	454	330/95	2–6 pdr. 11.9.14– wrecked 6.1.16 on Eilean Chuai, Hebrides.
068	IDAHO	58	43/10	1–1 pdr SSV. 12.4.15–2.2.19; =tug 3.17; =in WW II.
018	ILEX	131	120/96	(ex-*Anemone*) 2–3 pdr. 16.9.14–20.7.15.
	ILIONA	109	81/86	(ex-*Cassandra*) Exam. 25.3.18–4.2.19.
056	IOLAIRE =AMALTHAEA 11.18	999	862/02	2–3 in, 1–3 pdrAA. 1.3.15–12.2.19; =IOLAIRE in WW II.
031	IOLANDA	1822	1647/08	2–3 in. 21.5.15–5.2.19; =WHITE BEAR in WW II.
	IRIS		/	Tug. 3.18– purchased; sold 8.8.19.
N.83 (9.18)	IRONSIDES		/	6.18–3.20.
	ISLE OF MAY	138	119/96	22.7.18–9.5.19; =in WW II.
017 079	JAMES FLETCHER	330	264/07	2–6 pdrAA, 1–2 pdr. 25.9.14–27.2.19; =MURAENA in WW II.
076	JASON II	702	561/12	2–12 pdr. 1.2.15–15.2.19; =CYNARA in WW II.
042	JEANETTE =JEANETTE II 11.15	1023	921/11	2–12 pdr. 18.1.15–17.2.19.
092	JOSEPHINE	897	974/99	(ex-*Gorislava*) 2–4 in, 2–2 pdr. Seized 3.8.18– returned 21.4.19 to Russia.
	KATHLEEN	316	214/69	Accom. 16.6.17–14.4.19; =tug from 3.17.
	KATHLEEN	70	63/99	At Archangel 8.18–1919.
012	KETHAILES	611	625/03	2–6 pdr. 23.9.14– sunk 11.10.17 in collision off Blackwater LV.
063	LADY BLANCHE	405	360/07	1–12 pdr, 1–6 pdr. 7.3.15–20.3.19; =in'WW II.
	LAPWING =PEEWIT II 2.18	62	57/97	HS tender; =tug 3.18. 9.17– purchased; sold 13.12.22.
	LETO		/	A/P in Mediterranean. 1.9.18–18.1.19.
YA.10	LIBERTY =LIBERTY IV 10.18	1571	1607/07	(ex-*Curityba*) Hospital ship; =A/P yacht 1.9.15. In service 8.14–1919; =Hospital transport 1917–1919.
024	LORNA	484	427/04	(ex-*Beryl*) 2–6 pdr. 30.9.14–2.2.19; =in WW II.
092	LYSISTRATA	2089	1942/00	(ex-*Yaroslava*) 2–4 in. Seized 14.8.18; returned to Russia 28.8.18.
067	MAID OF HONOUR	487	419/07	2–12 pdr. 12.4.15–10.2.19; =SYLVANA in WW II.
099	MAIRI	65	59/11	1–3 pdr S/M depot. 19.8.14– purchased; =tug 3.18; sold 8.8.19.
	MANAGEM	205	206/04	(ex-*Hildegarde*) 1–12 pdr. 15.1.17–1.19.
MI.25 (1.16)	MARCELLA	160	127/87	(ex-*Marchesa*) ABS. 6.7.15– sunk 24.3.16 in collision off the Downs.
017	MARYNTHEA	900	854/11	2–12 pdr. 4.2.15–8.2.19; =CONQUEROR in WW II.
Y4.67	MAVIS	260	218/03	Ferry at Scapa. 9.7.17–26.5.19; =tug from 1918.
	MAY BABY		65/11	(ex-*Bolinders*) 11.14–1915.
049	MEDUSA =MEDUSA II 6.15	627	598/06	1–12 pdr, 1–6 pdrAA. 12.1.15–22.3.19; =MOLLUSC in WW II.
070	MEKONG	899	903/06	(ex-*Maud*) 2–3 in. 14.4.15– wrecked 12.3.16 north of Filey Brigg.
	MELISANDE	367	264/83	(ex-*Monarch*) SSV. 8.8.18–6.8.19; =in WW II.

Pendant Nos.	Name	TM*	TG/Yr	Armament—Service—Fate
045	MERA	293	219/86	1–12 pdr. 1–6 pdrAA. 8.12.14–25.3.19.
041	MINGARY	639	591/99	2–6 pdr. 29.1.15–23.3.19.
011	MINONA	249	199/06	2–6 pdr, 1–6 pdrAA. 7.10.14–6.6.19; =Misc vessel 24.7.18; =in WW II.
048	MIRANDA =MIRANDA II 2.15	942	793/09	2–12 pdr. 9.1.15–25.2.19.
	MIRIEL	65	57/98	(ex-Avis) Exam. 13.8.17–4.2.19.
	MLADA =ALACRITY 7.19	1797	1792/00	(ex-Semiramis) ABS. 16.9.18– purchased 3.19; sold 1926; =ALACRITY in WW II.
075	MONSOON	437	366/97	(ex-Latharna) 2–12 pdr. 10.5.15–13.2.19.
3 (1.18)	MORDRED	195	181/97	(ex-Merlin) 22.4.17–2.5.19; =MERLIN in WW II.
	MUSTARD	137	112/87	(ex-Oberon) Torpedo range vessel, Weymouth. 25.3.18–19.2.19.
069	NAIRN	489	437/13	(ex-St. Serf) 2–12 pdr, 1–6 pdrAA. 15.4.15–2.19; =TIERCEL in WW II.
050	NARCISSUS =NARCISSUS II 9.15	816	661/05	2–12 pdr. 13.1.15–27.2.19; =GRIVE in WW II.
084	NORTH STAR II	924	819/93	(ex-Cherokee) 2–3 in. 28.10.15–4.3.19.
	NYKR	31	30/93	Hydrophone tender. 1916–12.3.20.
	OLIVIA	105	84/83	(ex-Lola) 5.15– purchased 1917; =Tug 3.18; sold 28.12.18.
021	OMBRA	275	236/02	2–3 pdrAA. 8.9.14–10.3.19; =Misc vessel 13.2.18; =in WW II.
	ORANSAY	52	49/04	2.6.18–29.4.19.
019	ORIANA =ORIANA II 12.15	172	122/96	2–3 pdr. 22.9.14–29.11.17.
	OTTER	154	146/03	1916– Purchased 1917; =Tug 3.17; sold 31.7.19; =HINBA in WW II.
089	PAULINA	317	264/94	(ex-The Queen Mother) 2–6 pdrAA. 11.7.16–4.5.19; =MARIA JOAO in WW II.
085	PIONEER II	399	366/14	1–12 pdr, 2–6 pdr. 21.10.15–14.3.19.
026	PORTIA =PORTIA II 12.15	527	433/06	1–12 pdr, 1–6 pdrAA. 8.10.14–1.4.19.
053	PRISCILLA	273	179/88	(ex-Garland) A/P, later tug. 1.8.17– purchased; sold 31.7.19.
YA.15	QUEEN ALEXANDRA		267/02	Hospital ship. 3.15–1919.
098	RESOURCE II	**1000	734/65	(ex-Enchantress; ex-ENCHANTRESS; ex-HELICON) MB depot ship 1.10.15– burned 12.11.15 at Southampton.
011 055	RHIANNON	137	126/14	2–3 pdr. 15.9.14– mined 20.7.15 off the Longsands.
022	RHOUMA	337	279/02	(ex-Triton) 1–6 pdr, 1–6 pdrAA. 1.10.14–2.4.19; =HINIESTA in WW II.
	ROMA	62	49/88	(ex-Icicle) Gunnery T/S. 5.12.17–24.12.18.
061	ROSABELLE	614	526/02	2–6 pdrAA. 28.1.15–17.3.19; =in WW II.
N.95 (9.18)	ROSITA	119	93/00	Tug. Purchased 3.18; sold 14.8.20.
071	ROVENSKA	693	625/04	2–12 pdr. 14.4.15–30.3.19.
	RUNA	95	80/04	(ex-Einna) 18.7.18–14.5.19.
036	SABRINA =SABRINA II 12.15	513	379/99	1–12 pdr, 1–6 pdr. 5.2.15–23.3.19.
055	SAFA EL BAHR	669	487/94	2–3 in. 23.8.15–22.4.19.
01	SAGITTA	756	744/08	2–12 pdr, 1–6 pdrAA. 5.12.14–16.2.18; =in WW II.
058 091 N.76 (9.18)	ST. GEORGE =ORIFLAMME 6.18 =WALLINGTON 9.18 =ST. GEORGE 3.19	871	641/90	1–3 pdrAA SSV. 3.3.15–26.1.16 and 22.4.18–29.3.19.
060	SALVATOR	766	684/03	(ex-Katoomba) 2–12 pdr. 5.3.15–29.3.19; =HELIOPOLIS in WW II.
073	SANDA	351	300/06	(ex. St. Serf) 2–6 pdr. 26.1.15– sunk 25.9.15 by shore batteries off the Belgian coast.
052	SAPPHIRE =SAPPHIRE II 2.15	1421	1207/12	2–12 pdr. 8.1.15–20.2.19; =BREDA in WW II.
035	SAYONARA	581	480/80	(ex-Goizeko Izarra) 2–3 in. 25.6.15–11.10.18.
689 046 074	SCADAUN	157	108/12	1–6 pdrAA. 7.10.14–2.3.19.

Pendant	Name	TM*	TG/Yr	Armament—Service—Fate
039	SEA FAY	210	164/02	2–6 pdr. 26.9.14–3.2.19.
	SEAHORSE II	106	86/91	Exam. 1.7.17–24.5.19.
YA.11	SHEELAH	679	466/02	Hospital ship. 1914–1919.
	SHEILA	80	71/04	Purchased c1918; sold 7.7.20; =in WW II.
06	SHEMARA	588	477/99	(ex-Victoria) 1–12 pdr, 1–6 pdr. 13.9.14–5.3.19.
047	SIMOUN	308	204/97	ABS. 30.5.16–10.3.19; later =DRAGON.
N.94 (9.18)	=SIGISMUND 4.18			
	SLEUTH (RAN)	104	65/01	(ex-Ena) 1–3 pdr. 1915–1920.
035	SORCERESS	328	222/87	(ex-Enchantress) 17.12.14–26.2.15.
	STADACONA (RCN)	682	780/93	(ex-Columbia) 1–4 in, 1–12 pdr Base ship at Halifax. Purchased 3.16–4.20. Sold =same name =KUYAKUZMT.
057	SURF	560	496/02	2–12 pdr. 25.2.15–4.4.19; =in WW II.
	SURPRISE	1322	1144/96	(ex-Razsvet) Seized 24.9.18; =despatch vessel 6.3.20; sold 4.6.23; =in WW II.
	TAURUS	373	229/80	(ex-Aline) HS. 10.14–15.10.17.
031	THISTLE	544	369/81	A/P. 10.10.14–11.6.15.
N.88 (1919)	TRIAD	1413	1212/09	2–12 pdr HQ ship. 19.2.15– purchased 19.6.19; =SSV 1.1.20; sold 5.33.
	VACUNA	48	43/98	7.5.18–23.10.19.
08	VAGRANT	484	440/03	1–12 pdr, 1–6 pdr. 25.9.14–1.2.19; =LADY VAGRANT in WW II.
088	VALHALLA =VALHALLA II 2.17	1490	1219/92	4–12 pdr. 20.6.16–9.9.19; =Repair ship 1917; =in WW II.
038	VALIANT =VALIANT II 2.15	2184	1855/93	4–12 pdr. 18.11.14–6.2.19; =VALIANT II 1919.
083	VANADIS	333	207/80	2–6 pdr. 12.6.15–27.10.17.
036	VANDUARA	450	337/86	S/M depot ship. 21.9.14–12.2.15.
028	VANESSA =VANESSA II 2.17	445	356/99	(ex-Golden Eagle) 2–6 pdr. 15.10.14–5.3.19; =CARINA in WW II.
Y4.1 037	VENETIA =VENETIA II 2.17	569	577/05	A/P depot 7.8.14– =A/P yacht 1–6 pdr, 2–1 pdr; returned 22.2.19; =in WW II.
077	VERGEMERE	496	316/03	A/P. 1.6.15–20.12.15.
034	VERONA	437	331/90	(ex-Tighnamara) 2–6 pdr. 7.11.14– mined 24.2.17 off Portmahomack.
090	WARRIOR	1266	1098/04	(ex-Wayfarer) 2–12 pdr SSV. 2.17–29.12.18; =WARRIOR II in WW II.
020	WINTONIA	233	168/94	(ex-Ladye Maisry) 3.11.14–6.4.15.
059	YARTA	357	271/98	2–3 pdr. 3.7.15–3.4.19; =in WW II.
087	ZAIDA	350	255/00	2–6 pdr. 26.5.16– sunk 17.8.16 by U.38 off Alexandria.
062	ZARA	516	422/95	2–3 in. 6.3.15–27.3.19.
01 046	ZAREFAH	279	235/05	(ex-Maretanza V) 2–3 pdr. 20.8.14– purchased 26.5.16; mined 8.5.17 off Mull Head, Deer Ness.
015	ZAZA	455	423/05	1–12 pdr, 2–6 pdrAA. 28.9.14–30.3.19; =in WW II.
Y4.2	ZINAIDA	84	62/82	(ex-Caroline) Non-commissioned Misc vessel 8.14–2.2.16.
09	ZORAIDE	549	532/94	(ex-Sylvabelle) 1–12 pdr, 1–6 pdrAA. 12.9.14–1.3.19.

*Thames measurement tonnage. **Navy-list displacement.
Notes: LYSISTRATA had pendant Fy.092; later assigned to JOSEPHINE. Two small yachts, LYTTON and MAUD, were in RIM service. Two small yachts reported serving in the Bahamas were CORALLINE and RANGER; auxiliary sail yachts of only 10 tons gross. The New Zealand-owned government yacht HINEMOA 542/76 was also in existence during WW I. SURPRISE may have used the name RAZSVET before becoming SURPRISE. Some yachts such as SCADAUN, JAMES FLETCHER, ZAREFAH, etc. had several changes of pendant numbers when first in service as organisational changes were made, but the final number shown was quickly put in effect. The motor yacht YEHONALA listed with MBs also appeared in yacht lists until 1919; she served as HILDEGARD in WW II. Most yachts served as A/P group leaders and carried wireless equipment; others were formed into special yacht squadrons and served in home waters and in the Mediterranean.

ADMIRALTY TRAWLERS
PURCHASED VESSELS

Adty No.	Name	TG/Yr	Builder—Armament—Fate
57	DRIVER =NAIRN 6.19	207/10	Duthie. 1–6 pdrAA M/S. Purchased 1910—sold 1920 =NAIRN.
53	ROSE	243/07	Smiths Dock. (ex-*Nizam*) 1–6 pdrAA M/S. Purchased 1910—sold 1921 =ABY.
1	SEAFLOWER =SEA ROVER 1.20	275/08	Goole SB. (ex-*Osprey II*) 1–12 pdrAA M/S. Purchased 4.09—sold 1920 =HEINRICH BEERMAN.
2	SEAMEW =NUNTHORPE HALL 1.20	248/09	Smiths Dock. (ex-*Nunthorpe Hall*) 1–12 pdr M/S. Purchased 4.09—sold 5.20 =NUNTHORPE HALL.
58	SPARROW =JOSEPHINE I 1.20	266/08	Goole SB. (ex-*Josephine I*) 1–12 pdr M/S. Purchased 4.09—sold 5.20 =ORION.
54?	SPIDER	256/08	Cochrane. (ex-*Assyrian*) M/S. Purchased 4.09—wrecked 21.11.14 off Lowestoft.
12	ALNMOUTH	236/12	Cochrane. 1–6 pdrAA M/S. Purchased 7.14—sold 1919.
163	DANIEL STROUD	209/12	Hall. 1–12 pdr M/S. Purchased 7.14—sold 1919; =LOCH ESK in WW II.
372	JACKDAW =EXCELLENT 2.17 =JACKDAW 2.19	250/03	Goole SB. 1–12 pdr M/S. Purchased 10.14—sold 1919.
167	JANUS =KILDA 1.20	243/11	Goole SB. (ex-*Kilda*) 1–12 pdr M/S. Purchased 5.14—sold 5.20 =TUBAL CAIN.
164	JASPER	221/12	Smiths Dock. (ex-*Rayvernol*) M/S. Purchased 1914—mined 26.8.15 in Moray Firth.
21	JAVELIN	205/13	Hall. (ex-*Braconlea*) M/S. Purchased 1914—mined 17.10.15 off the Longsands.
1498 1499	KINGFISHER =ADELE 6.18	304/15	(ex-*Alcyon*) 1–6 pdr, 1–7.5 in BT Hydro. Purchased 4.15—sold 1919 =ALCYON.
3	OSBORNE STROUD	209/12	Hall. 1–6 pdrAA M/S. Purchased 7.14—sold 1920; =BEATHWOOD in WW II.
17	XYLOPIA	262/11	Cochrane. 1–12 pdrAA M/S. Purchased 7.14—sold 1919.

Notes: Except for the survey vessels DAISY and ESTHER (qv) also fitted for minesweeping, this group includes all trawlers which were Admiralty property at the start of the war. The first six vessels were employed as M/S training ships used to train crews of the fishery reserve which later became the nucleus of the Auxiliary Patrol. DRIVER and ROSE were based at Devonport in 1914; SEAFLOWER and SEAMEW at Chatham or Sheerness; SPARROW and SPIDER at Portsmouth. The other trawlers purchased by 7.14 had been mainly used for towing targets (some had previously been hired for this purpose). From 8.14 all, including the survey trawlers, became minesweepers and were included in the patrol organisation.

KINGFISHER and the hired drifter ADELE (qv), both used as nominal parent ships (carried numerous other small craft on their muster books), traded names and numbers on 15.6.18.

MILITARY CLASS

303 tons gross.   130 (pp) ×24 × 13¼ (dhd) ft.   TE

Adty No.	Name	Launched	Builder—Armament—Fate
1517	BOMBARDIER	1. 4.15	Smiths Dock. 1–12 pdr M/S. Sold 4.5.20 =BOMBARDIER.
1530	BRIGADIER =BUGLER 1.20	1. 4.15	Smiths Dock. 1–12 pdr M/S. Sold 4.5.20 =BUGLER.

276 tons gross.   130 (pp) ×23½ × 12¾ (dhd) ft.   TE

Adty No.	Name	Launched	Builder—Armament—Fate
1164	CARBINEER	15. 2.15	Smiths Dock. 1–3 pdr M/S. Wrecked 18.5.16 on Crebawethan Point.
1152	DRAGOON =DRUMMER 1.20	16. 1.15	Smiths Dock. 1–12 pdr, 1–7.5 in BT. Sold 26.2.20, same name; =DRUMMER in WW II.
1163	FUSILIER =CARBINEER II 3.20	1. 2.15	Smiths Dock. 1–12 pdr M/S. Sold 1920, same name; =CARBINEER II in WW II.
1153	GUNNER	16. 1.15	Smiths Dock. 1–4 in, 2–12 pdr, 2–6 pdr, 2–14 in TT. =Q ship 2.15, also BORGIA, PLANUDES, Q.31. Sold 1920 =TEMEHANI; =MILLIMUMUL 1926.
1151	LANCER =LANCER II 7.17	17.12.14	Smiths Dock. 1–3 pdr. Sunk 18.7.18 in collision off the Brighton LV.
1162	SAPPER	1. 2.15	Smiths Dock. 1–12 pdr. Foundered 29.12.17 off Owers LV.

239 tons gross.   118 (pp) ×22½ × 12½ (dhd) ft.   TE

Adty No.	Name	Launched	Builder—Armament—Fate
1526	HIGHLANDER	29. 4.15	Smiths Dock. 1–6 pdrAA M/S. Sold 1921 =FREGATE II.
1541	TROOPER	29. 4.15	Smiths Dock. 1–6 pdrAA. Sold 25.10.20 =EIDER II; =ALMA in WW II.

Notes: All purchased while building; six by order 11.12.14 and four by order 14.4.15 for a total of £93800. The first completions were DRAGOON, GUNNER and LANCER all on 27.2.15 while the last vessel, TROOPER, was completed 22.6.15.

EX-PORTUGUESE

Adty No.	Name	TG/Yr	Builder—Armament—Etc.
180	ACHERNAR	256/08	Duthie. (ex-Chire; ex-Hebden) 1–6 pdr. Sold 17.5.19 =RIO GUADIANA.
176	ALGENIB	321/07	Goole SB. (ex-Neptuno; ex-Vinca) 1–6 pdr, 1–7.5 in BT. Sold 17.5.19 =RIO DOURO.
179	ALGOL	213/01	Mackie & Thomson. (ex-Maria Amalia; ex-Caithness-shire) 1–6 pdr. Sold 17.5.19 =RIO LIMA.
178	ALTAIR =ALTAIR II 10.17	257/07	Duthie. (ex-Victoria Laura; ex-Star of Freedom) 1–6 pdr, 1–7.5 in BT. Sold 17.5.19 Cruz Bros.
177	ANTARES =ANTARES II 10.17	218/06	Duthie. (ex-Cabo Verde; ex-Ben Alligin) 1–3 pdr. Sunk 2.5.18 by gunfire after collision off Gibraltar.
175	ARCTURUS =ARCTURUS II 6.18	337/10	Cook, W & G. (ex-Rio Tejo; ex-Alberia) 1–6 pdr, 1–7.5 in BT. Sold 17.5.19 Cruz Bros.
173	CORVI	216/09	Mackie & Thomson. (ex-Mindello II; ex-Baron Ruzette) 1–6 pdr. Sold 17.5.19 =RIO ZEZERE.
172	CRUCIS	243/11	Goole SB. (ex-Bicalho; ex-Lucida) 1–6 pdr, 1–7.5 in BT. Sold 17.5.19 =RIO MINHO.
174	CYGNI	207/03	Hall. (ex-Monchique; ex-Loch Laggan) 1–6 pdr, 1–7.5 in BT. Sold 17.5.19 =RIO VOUGA

Notes: All British-built, they were an assortment of vessels purchased 9.15 for a total of £80788. Intended as M/S, they appear to have been used only as A/P trawlers. The surviving eight were sold 17.5.19 to Cruz Brothers, Gibraltar and most of them returned to Portuguese ownership shortly thereafter.

STRATH, CASTLE AND MERSEY CLASS

During the first 18 months of the war sufficient numbers of trawlers for the Auxiliary Patrol were obtained by drawing heavily from the fishing fleet. Expansion of the patrol continued on such a large scale, that by mid 1916, further acquisition of fishing trawlers was neither adequate nor prudent Since it was unacceptable that the commercial fishing fleet should be diminished further, it became necessary to build trawlers for use in the patrols. Replacement tonnage had for some time fallen far short of making good the losses due to war causes. Commercial trawler orders placed with ship builders since 1914 had been on a steady decline because of the threat of naval requisition.

In order to provide both wartime patrol vessels and suitable post war fishing fleet replacements, the Admiralty began its own trawler building programme. Additionally, it was intended that such a programme should serve to rejuvenate the trawler-building industry for the benefit of all concerned.

Three prototypes were selected to serve as the standard plans for the Admiralty vessels; namely Hall Russell's "Strath", Smith's Dock "Castle" and Cochrane's "Mersey" types, all of which were recently built for commercial registry and had proven to be successful designs. STRATHLOCHY, RAGLAN CASTLE and LORD MERSEY were respective standard vessels built to these plans and soon thereafter taken into the Navy. These three varied enough in size to provide acceptable choice for most fishing requirements.

During 11.16 approval was given and 250 trawlers were ordered to be built, in 1917 another 150 (from an original 250) were ordered, and a final 140 during 1918. The names selected for these trawlers were taken from the rosters of the 100 gun ships VICTORY and ROYAL SOVEREIGN at the time of the Battle of Trafalgar. Some variation in the names is evident in official orders and publications, the more accepted renditions have been included in the class lists. Note the progression of the Admiralty numbers, which closely follows the sequence in which contracts were placed. Surnames are generally grouped together beginning with the same letter within these blocs. A large number of contracts were assigned at first, followed by a series of repeat orders in accord with progress of work and within the capabilities of each builder.

Certain trawlers already in the course of construction in 11.16 whose advanced state made cancellation unwise, were allowed to be completed and were included as part of the orders. These were termed "Non-Standard" units and were included in the class whose dimensions they most closely approximated.

Trawlers completed during the war were employed in the Auxiliary Patrol and along with later completions served in the post war Mine Clearance Service. 20 trawler M/S were taken over by the USN in the summer of 1919 to participate in sweeping the North Sea mine barrage.

Production: 285 vessels were completed by 11.11.18, another 40 completed as unarmed minesweepers 11.18–1919, 133 completed as fishing vessels (F) including 105 sold directly by the builders There were 82 contracts cancelled, a few reassignments, and at least 16 projected vessels not built Some of the cancelled vessels were completed and sold commercially.

	Strath	Castle	Mersey	
Delivered by 11.11.18	89	127	69	285
Unarmed M/S	14	18	8	40
Completed as (F)	46	52	35	133
Cancelled	18	20	44	82
Totals:	167	217	156	540

The normal wartime complement was 15; up to 18 with wireless aboard. Their armaments varied but usually consisted of a 12 pdr gun and a bomb thrower. Two vessels, GEORGE IRELAND and HENRY JENNINGS, were fitted with experimental water-jet propulsion which greatly delayed their delivery (25.10.19 and 22.7.19 respectively) and was not successful so they were given conventional systems. Pendant numbers consisted of Fishery Flag superior to their Admiralty number. Later their names were painted up in lieu of the number. River names were given in 9.20 to a number of vessels that were to be retained in the peacetime establishment, while many others, still Admiralty property were given LO (London) fishing numbers and registered commercially with official numbers.

The average cost per vessel for hull and machinery was £18000 for a Strath, £21000 for a Castle, and £22000 for a Mersey. Numerous trawlers were sold at auction during 1920 and others individually. In spite of a market suddenly flooded with trawlers, the government usually recovered over half their original cost.

STRATH CLASS

215 tons gross.   123 (oa), 115½ (pp) ×22×12 (dhd) ft.
311 tons displacement. (429 deep)   TE 430 ihp=10½ kts.

Adty No.	Name	Launched	Builder—Armament—Fate
	Non-Standard Units:		
3658	CORNELIUS CARROLL	19. 3.18*	Hall. 1–12 pdr Hydro. Sold 1922 =BOYNE BRAES.
3660	GEORGE COULSTON	27. 4.18	Hall. 1–12 pdr, 1–3.5 in BT Hydro. Sold 1922 =DOONIE BRAES; =DOONIE BRAES in WW II.
3617	ISRAEL ALDCROFT	20. 6.17	Duthie. 1–12 pdr T/S. Sold 1921 =GEORGE R. PURDY; =GEORGE R. PURDY in WW II.
3614	JAMES ALDRIDGE	10. 4.17	Duthie. 1–12 pdr M/S. Sold 1921, same name; =SYLVERDYKE in WW II.
3615	JAMES ARCHIBALD	24. 4.17	Duthie. 1–12 pdr M/S. Sold 1921; =NISUS 1928.
3618	JOHN ABBOTT =JOHN MASON 5.20	7. 8.17	Duthie. 1–12 pdr M/S Hydro. Sold 1921 =CHRISTANIA T. PURDY; =CHRISTANIA T. PURDY in WW II.
3647	JOHN BRADFORD	25. 4.17	Hall Russell. 1–12 pdr Hydro. Sold 15.7.20 =DORILEEN; =BEN ARDNA in WW II.
3657	JOHN CLAY	16.11.17	Hall. 1–12 pdr. Loaned to USN 5.19–8.19. Sold 1921 =BRACONASH.
3754	JOHN FITZGERALD	14.12.17	Duthie. 1–12 pdr. Loaned to USN 5.19–8.19. Sold 1921, same name; =in WW II.
3619	JOSEPH ANNISON	19. 9.17	Duthie. 1–12 pdr M/S. Sold 1922, same name; =WILLIAM STEPHEN in WW II.
3655	MATTHEW CROOKE	2.10.17	Hall. 1–12 pdr. Sold 1921 =FORTROSE; =FORTROSE in WW II.
3649	RICHARD BENNETT	17. 5.17	Hall Russell. 1–12 pdr, 1–7.5 in BT M/S. Sold 1921, same name; =in SAN WW II.
3650	SAMUEL BAKER	7. 6.17	Hall Russell. 1–12 pdr M/S. Sold 1921 =BRACONMOOR.
3616	THOMAS ANSELL	21. 5.17	Duthie. 1–12 pdr. Sold 1921, same name; =in WW II.
3620	WILLIAM ASHTON =CITY OF PERTH 9.19	1.11.17	Duthie. 1–12 pdr. Loaned to USN 1919. Sold 1922 =WILLIAM ASHTON.
3646	WILLIAM BARLOW	25. 4.17	Hall Russell. 1–12 pdr Hydro. Sold 15.7.20 =BEN ARDNA; =DORILEEN in WW II.
3648	WILLIAM BROWNING	17.5.17	Hall Russell. 1–12 pdr Hydro. Sold 1919 =MADDEN; =MADDEN in WW II.
3656	WILLIAM CASTLE	18.10.17	Hall Russell. 1–12 pdr. Sold 1921, same name.
3659	WILLIAM COGSWELL	10. 1.18	Hall. 1–12 pdr Hydro. Sold 1921 =STRUAN.
3755	WILLIAM FERRINS	3. 5.18*	Duthie. 1–12 pdr. Sold 1921, same name.
	Standard Units:		
3773	AARON HUBERT	19. 2.19*	Fullerton. (F) Sold 1919 =GRAFFOE.
3817	ARTHUR HERWIN	19.12.19	Fleming & Ferguson. (F) Sold 10.11.19; delivered 23.1.20 =RIVER LOSSIE; =RIVER LOSSIE in WW II.
3642	BARNARD BOYLE	13. 6.18	Hall Russell. 1–12 pdr AA. Sold 3.11.21 =DULCIBELLE; =DULCIBELLE in WW II.
3687	BENJAMIN COLEMAN	2.11.17	Fleming & Ferguson. 1–12 pdr. Sold 16.11.21, same name; =in WW II.
3631	BRAZIL BRASBY	31.10.17	Hall Russell. 1–12 pdr, 1–3.5 in BT Hydr. Sold 17.5.19 =TYRWHITT.
4424	CHARLES BLIGHT	13.3.19	Hall Russell. (F) Sold 1919 =JACK JOHNSON; mined 9.20.
3690	CHARLES CARROLL	11. 4.18	Montrose SB. 1–12 pdr. Sold 1919 =RIVER AYR.
4495	CHARLES DOYLE	21.11.19*	Rennie Forrestt. (F) Sold 1921 =SABINA; =SABINA in WW II.,
3734	DANIEL DIZMONT	19. 8.19*	Montrose SB. (F) Sold 1920 =PATRICIA SCULLION; =French AD.146 IBIS in WW II.
3825	DANIEL HILLIER	18. 3.19*	Hawthorns. (F) Sold 1919 =OCEAN FISHER; =OCEAN FISHER in WW II.
3643	DAVID BLAKE	13. 6.18	Hall Russell. 1–12 pdr AA. Sold 1921, same name.
3639	DAVID BUCHAN	9. 4.18	Hall Russell. 1–12 pdr AA. Sold 10.11.19 =RIVER NESS; =RIVER NESS in WW II.
3691	DAVID CONN	13. 7.18	Montrose SB. 1–12 pdr. Sold 15.11.19 =RIVER SPEY; =RIVER SPEY in WW II.

Adty No.	Name	Launched	Builder—Armament—Fate
4420	EDWARD BARKER	21.11.18	Hall Russell. 1–12 pdr M/S. Sold 1921 =MIRABELLE; =MIRABELLE in WW II.
3769	EDWARD GREY	29.11.20*	Ritchie G & M. (F) Sold 1921 =SUZETTE; =SUZETTE in WW II.
3621	GEORGE BORTHWICK	21. 6.17	Hall Russell. 1–12 pdr, 1–3.5 in BT M/S Hydro. Sold 1921 =ANNABELLE; =ANNABELLE in WW II.
3633	GEORGE BURTON	8.12.17	Hall Russell. 1–12 pdr M/S. Lent to USN 5.19–8.19. Sold 1922 =BERVIE BRAES; =BERVIE BRAES in WW II.
4482	GEORGE CASTLE	25. 8.19*	Williamson. (F) Sold 1919 =Lord Tennyson 1928; =RIVER ANNAN in WW II.
4469	GEORGE CLINES	13. 6.19*	Hawthorns. (F) Sold 1920 =SKIRBECK; =French AD.119 ROCHE FRANCOISE in WW II.
3747	GEORGE FRENCH	10. 6.18*	Murdoch & Murray. 1–12 pdr Hydro. Sold 1921 =ARLETTE; =ARLETTE in WW II.
3820	GEORGE HODGES	20. 6.18*	Hawthorns. 1–12 pdr. Sold 1919 =HOOD.
3846	GEORGE IRELAND =TEVIOT 9.20	25.10.19*	Rennie Forrestt. Sold 1923 =FIRSBY.
4230	GEORGE LANE	19. 6.19*	Scott, Bowling. (F) Sold 1919 =RIVER KELVIN.
3638	HENRY BUTCHER	26. 3.18	Hall Russell. 1–12 pdrAA. Sold 1919 =RIVER TAY.
4470	HENRY COLBY	10. 7.19*	Hawthorns. (F) Sold 1920 =FREISTON; =French AD.144 ROCHE GRISE in WW II.
3758	HENRY FLIGHT	2.10.18*	Abdela Mitchell. 1–12 pdr. Sold 1922 =YESSO; =YESSO in WW II.
3822	HENRY HARDING	2.12.18*	Hawthorns. 1–12 pdr. Sold 1920 =OCEAN CLIPPER.
3848	HENRY JENNINGS =URE 9.20	22. 7.19*	Rennie Forrestt. Sold 1922 =ABY 1924; =MORAY in WW II.
3733	ISAAC DOBSON	23. 4.19*	Montrose SB. (F) Sold 1919 =HOLLAND; =LIDDOCK in WW II.
3826	ISAAC HARRIS	12. 4.19*	Hawthorns. (F) Sold 1919 =POCHARD II.
4429	JAMES BASHFORD	12. 6.19	Hall Russell. (F) Sold 1919 =STRATHRANNOCH; =STRATHRANNOCH in WW II.
3630	JAMES BEAGAN	9.10.17	Hall Russell. 1–12 pdr. Sold 1921 =LOCH BLAIR; =LOCH BLAIR in WW II.
3622	JAMES BENTOLE	21. 6.17	Hall Russell. 1–12 pdr. M/S Hydro. Sold 1922 =FORT ROBERT; =FORT ROBERT in WW II.
4419	JAMES BRODIGAN	21.11.18	Hall Russell. Sold 1920 same name; =WOODS in WW II.
3708	JAMES CURRY	20.11.17	Murdoch & Murray. 1–12 pdr. Sold 1921 =ADY; =French AD.34 GENEVIEVE in WW II.
3731	JAMES EVANS	31. 8.18*	Abdela Mitchell. Sold 1923 same name.
3760	JAMES FEAGAN	17.12.19*	Montrose SB. (F) Sold 1919 =RIVER EARN.
3753	JAMES FENNELL	9. 7.18*	Fullerton. 1–12 pdr. Wrecked 16.1.20 at Blacknor Point, Portland.
3761	JAMES GARRICK	16. 2.20*	Montrose SB. (F) Sold 1920 =RIVER FINDHORN.
3693	JAMES HARTWELL	11.11.18*	Ouse SB. 1–12 pdr. Sold 1921 =GEORGETTE; =GEORGETTE in WW II.
3827	JAMES HINES	13. 5.19*	Hawthorns. (F) Sold 1919 =NORTHWARD HO; =NORTHWARD HO in WW II.
3624	JOHN BARRY	24. 7.17	Hall Russell. 1–12 pdr M/S. Sold 1921 =CHRISTABELLE.
3635	JOHN BELL	12. 2.18	Hall Russell. 1–12 pdrAA Hydro. Sold 1923 =JOHN SMART.
3637	JOHN BOWLER	12. 2.18	Hall Russell. 1–12 pdrAA Hydro. Sold 1922 =KARABIGHA.
3627	JOHN BRASKET	13. 9.17	Hall Russell. 1–12 pdrAA, 1–7.5 in BT M/S. Sold 1921 same name; wrecked 11.21.
4427	JOHN BRITTON	2. 5.19	Hall Russell. (F) Sold 1920 =ELSIE JESSOP.
4416	JOHN BULLER	11. 9.18	Hall Russell. Sold 1920, later =SAN PEDRO.
3707	JOHN CALLAGHAN	7.10.17	Murdoch & Murray. 1–12 pdr. Sold 1921 same name; =STAR OF LIBERTY in WW II.
4476	JOHN CONN	30. 5.19	Hawthorns. (F) Sold 1921 =BRACONBUSH.
3692	JOHN COPE	19.11.18*	Rennie Forrestt. 1–12 pdr. Sold 1919 =RIVER GARRY; =RIVER GARRY in WW II.

Adty No.	Name	Launched	Builder—Armament—Fate
3685	JOHN CORWARDER	20. 9.17	Fleming & Ferguson. 1–12 pdr MS. Sold 1919 =RIVER NITH.
3688	JOHN CURRAN	8. 6.18*	Montrose SB. 1–12 pdr Hydro. Sold 1921 =COMMANDANT GAMAS.
3727	JOHN DUNKIN =PEKIN 3.19 =JOHN DUNKIN 5.19	6. 8.18	Fleming & Ferguson. 1–12 pdr. Lent to USN 5.19–8.19. Sold 1921, same name.
3732	JOHN DUPUIS	3. 7.18*	Abdela Mitchell. 1–12 pdr Hydro T/S. Sold 1924 =RAVENNA.
3744	JOHN EDSWORTH	3. 6.18*	Fullerton. 1–12 pdr Hydro. Sold 1919 =RIVER LEVEN; =RIVER LEVEN in WW II.
3750	JOHN FAIRMAN	28. 6.18*	Rennie Forrestt. 1–12 pdr Hydro. Sold 1920 =OCEAN VICTOR; =OCEAN VICTOR in WW II
3752	JOHN FISSER	27. 9.18*	Ritchie G & M. 1–12 pdr Hydro T/S. Sold 1920 =JOULE; =MARY CAM in RAN WW II.
3748	JOHN FRANCOIS	9. 8.18*	Murdoch & Murray. 1–6 pdrAA. Sold 1923 =EDITH M. PURDY; =EDITH M. PURDY in WW II.
3763	JOHN GRAY	11. 4. 18	Scott, Bowling. 1–12 pdr Hydro. Sold 1920, same name; =FORT RONA 1932.
3819	JOHN HAILE	9. 5.18*	Hawthorns. 1–12 pdr Hydro. Sold 1924 =TUMBY; =TUMBY in WW II.
3757	JOHN HEATH	14. 6.19*	Ouse SB. (F) Sold 1919 =KUVERA; =KUVERA in WW II.
4203	JOHN HOWARD	22. 7.19*	Rennie Forrestt. (F) Sold 1921 =EVELINA; =EVELINA in WW II.
3774	JOHN HUNS =JOHN MOSS 1919	4. 4.19*	Fullerton. (F) Sold 1919 =LORD ALLENBY; =SARAH A. PURDY in WW II.
3777	JOHN HUNTER	5. 2.19*	Rennie Forrestt. Sold 1921 =DELILA; =DELILA in WW II.
3847	JOHN JACKSON	10. 9.18*	Rennie Forrestt. 1–12 pdr M/S. Sold 1921, same name; =INCHGOWER in WW II.
3853	JOHN KENNEDY	1. 7.19*	Abdela Mitchell. (F) Sold 1919; =JOHN ELLIOTT; =GILLIAN in WW II.
3850	JOHN KENTALL	20. 9.18*	Williamson. 1–12 pdr. Sold 1920 =WHEATSTONE.
4229	JOHN LANGSHAW	20. 3.19	Scott, Bowling. (F) Sold 1919 =ETHEL CRAWFORD.
4421	JONATHAN BAZINO	29. 1.19	Hall Russell. (F) Sold 1919 =PITSTRUAN.
4471	JONATHAN CREIG	16. 9.19*	Hawthorns. (F) Sold 1919, same name; =STRATHGLASS 1928.
3772	JONATHAN HARDY	7.11.18*	Fullerton. 1–12 pdr. Sold 1921 =ROCHE BLEUE; =French AD.170 ROCHE BLEUE in WW II.
3636	JOSEPH BURGIN	12. 2.18	Hall Russell. 1–12 pdr. Sold 1920, same name.
3709	JOSEPH COATES	3. 5.18*	Murdoch & Murray. 1–12 pdr, 1–3.5 in BT Hydro. Sold 1921 =AIGRETTE.
4425	JOSHUA BUDGET	11. 4.19	Hall Russell. (F) Sold 1919 =MARY CROWTHER; =OLDEN TIMES in WW II.
4201	LAWRENCE HUGHSON	21. 3.19*	Rennie Forrestt. (F) Sold 1919 =ELLOE.
4202	MATTHEW HARTLEY	6. 5.19*	Rennie Forrestt. (F) Sold 1919 =WYBERTON.
4430	MICHAEL BRION	12. 6.19	Hall Russell. (F) Sold 1919 =STURDEE; =STURDEE in WW II.
3860	PAT CAHARTY	8.10.18*	Rennie Forrestt. 1–12 pdr. Lent to USN 1919. Sold 1922 =KIRBY; =BUCHANS II in WW II.
3689	PATRICK BORROW	3. 7.18*	Montrose SB. 1–12 pdr, 1–3.5 in BT Hydro. Sold 1919 =RIVER DON.
4496	PATRICK DEVINE	11.12.19*	Rennie Forrestt. (F) Sold 1921 =YOLANDA; =SEDOCK in WW II.
4423	PETER BARRINGTON	13. 3.19	Hall Russell. (F) Sold 1920 =CARIAMA II.
3729	PETER DOBBIN	23. 2.18*	Williamson. 1–12 pdr. Sold 1921 =PHILIPPE; =PHILIPPE in WW II.
4426	RICHARD BOWDEN	11. 4.19	Hall Russell. (F) Sold 1919 =CISSIE SCATCHARD; =French AD.233 AIGRETTE in WW II.
4418	RICHARD BRISCOLL	9.10.18	Hall Russell. M/S T/S. Sold 1921 =BRACONBURN; =BRACONBURN in WW II.
3771	RICHARD HEAVER	7.10.18*	Fullerton. 1–12 pdr. Sold 1920 =FORTH VALE.
3759	ROBERT FARECLOTH	11. 1.19*	Abdela Mitchell. 1–12 pdr. Sold 1920 =Humphrey; =HUMPHREY in RNZN WW II.
3762	ROBERT GIBSON	12. 2.18	Scott, Bowling. 1–12 pdr, 1–3.5 in BT Hydro. Sold 1920, same name; =CORENNIE 1933.

Adty No.	Name	Launched	Builder—Armament—Fate
3823	ROBERT HARDING	19. 2.19*	Hawthorns. 1–12 pdr. Sold 1921 =HENRIETTE; =HENRIETTE later ARTEGAL in WW II.
3628	SAMUEL BARKAS	13. 9.17	Hall Russell. 1–12 pdrAA. Sold 1920, same name; =INVERNEILL 1926.
3645	SAMUEL BENBOW	9. 7.18	Hall Russell. 1–12 pdr, 1–6 pdrAA. Sold 1921, same name; =in RAN WW II.
3768	SAMUEL GASBY	24. 9.20*	Ritchie G & M. (F) Sold 1921 =SOUBRETTE; =SOUBRETTE in WW II.
3775	SAMUEL HAMPTON	18. 9.19*	Ouse SB. (F) Sold 1919 =BOSTONIAN; went missing 10.11.20.
3852	STEPHEN KENNEDY	3. 4.19*	Abdela Mitchell. (F) Sold 1919 =WITHAM; =WITHAM in WW II.
4417	THOMAS BARCLAY	9.10.18	Hall Russell. Sold 1921 =JOHN MORRICE.
4428	THOMAS BILLINCOLE	2. 5.19	Hall Russell. (F) Sold 1919 =SALTAIRE.
3623	THOMAS BIRD	24. 7.17	Hall Russell. 1–12 pdr. Sold 1919 =RIVER TWEED.
3625	THOMAS BRYAN	16. 8.17	Hall Russell. 1–12 pdr M/S Hydro. Sold 1921, same name.
4415	THOMAS BURNHAM	9. 9.18	Hall Russell. 1–12 pdr. Sold 1921 =FLORIBELLE.
3686	THOMAS COLLARD	11. 7.17	Fleming & Ferguson. 1–12 pdr, 1–7.5 in BT. Sunk 1.3.18 by S/M North of Rathlin Island.
4475	THOMAS COWELL	27.11.19*	Hawthorns. (F) Sold 1920 =DUDLEY, N. B.; =SOUTHWARD HO in WW II.
4481	THOMAS CURRELL	8. 5.19*	Williamson. (F) Sold 1919; later =ENRICO; =THOMAS CURRELL in RNZN WW II.
3730	THOMAS DEAR	3. 5.18*	Williamson. 1–12 pdr. Sold 1921, same name; later =NINETTE.
3728	THOMAS DENNISON	27.10.19	Fleming & Ferguson. (F) Sold 1919 =THE TOWER; =THE TOWER in WW II.
3743	THOMAS EVISON	12. 4.18*	Fullerton. 1–12 pdr Hydro. Sold 1922 =JEANIE M. ROBERTSON; =AVONDEE in WW II.
3751	THOMAS FOLEY	3. 8.18*	Ritchie G & M. 1–12 pdr, 1–3.5 in BT Hydro. Sold 1919 =RIVER TUMMEL; =BELTON in WW II.
3767	THOMAS GOODCHILD	31.10.19*	Ritchie G & M. (F) Sold 1921 =CHANDOS; =CHANDOS in WW II.
3764	THOMAS GRAHAM	6. 6.18	Scott, Bowling. 1–12 pdr M/S. Loaned to USN 1919. Sold 1921, same name; =SUNLIGHT in WW II.
3756	THOMAS HAGGERTY =ITCHEN 9.20	18.12.18*	Ouse SB. M/S. Sold 1926 =RIVER ENDRICK; =MARY A. PURDY in WW II.
3821	THOMAS HENRIX	13. 8.18*	Hawthorns. 1–12 pdr. Lent to USN 1919. Sold 1921 =CREVETTE; =CREVETTE in WW II.
3641	TIMOTHY BRANNON	30. 4.18	Hall Russell. 1–12 pdrAA, 1–3.5 in BT Hydro. Sold 1919 =KEYES.
3632	WILLIAM BARNETT	8.12.17	Hall Russell. 1–12 pdr. Sold 1919 =VALERIE W.; =French AD.355 ROCHE NOIRE in WW II.
3640	WILLIAM BARROW	30. 4.18	Hall Russell. 1–12 pdr, 1–3.5 in BT. Sold 1921 =CLARIBELLE; =CLARIBELLE in WW II.
3644	WILLIAM BEAUMONT	9. 7.18	Hall Russell. 1–12 pdrAA. Sold 1920, same name; =STAR OF SCOTLAND 1928.
4422	WILLIAM BENTLEY	30. 1.19	Hall Russell. (F) Sold 1919 =BRACONHILL; =BRACONHILL in WW II.
3626	WILLIAM BIGGS	16. 8.17	Hall Russell. 1–12 pdr M/S. Sold 1920, same name; =KINGSCOURT in WW II.
3634	WILLIAM BOND	10. 1.18	Hall Russell. 1–12 pdrAA Hydro. Sold 1919 =RIVER ESK; =RIVER ESK in WW II.
3629	WILLIAM BUTLER	18.10.17	Hall Russell. 1–12 pdrAA. Sold 1921, same name.
4472	WILLIAM CHALMERS	30. 8.19*	Hawthorns. (F) Sold 1919 =CRADOCK.
3749	WILLIAM FALL	29. 5.18*	Rennie Forrestt. 1–12 pdr Hydro. Sold 3.20 =AVONDALE.
3770	WILLIAM GIBBONS	14. 8.18*	Fullerton. 1–12 pdr. Sold 1921 =NORDZEE I.
3766	WILLIAM GILLETT	5.11.19*	Ritchie G & M. (F) Sold 1925 =ADASTRAL; =ADASTRAL in WW II.
3765	WILLIAM GRIFFIN	27.11.18*	Scott, Bowling. 1–12 pdr. Sold 1921, same name; =TYNEMOUTH CASTLE 1928.
3776	WILLIAM HALLETT	7. 1.19*	Rennie Forrestt. Sold 1920, same name; =in WW II.
3824	WILLIAM HANBURY	30.10.18*	Hawthorns. 1–12 pdr. Sold 1921, same name; =in WW II.
4204	WILLIAM HARRISON	27. 8.19*	Rennie Forrestt. (F) Sold 1921 =FLAVIA.

Adty No.	Name	Launched	Builder—Armament—Fate
3816	WILLIAM HARVEY	10.11.19	Fleming & Ferguson. (F) Sold 1919 =RIVER ORCHY; =FLIXTON in WW II.
3818	WILLIAM HUTCHINSON	4. 4.18*	Hawthorns. 1–12 pdr Hydro. Sold 1921 =ROCHE VELEN; =ROCHE VELEN in WW II.
3849	WILLIAM IVEY	14. 8.18*	Rennie Forrestt. 1–12 pdr. Sold 1920, same name.
3851	WILLIAM KING	18.12.18*	Williamson. 1–12 pdr. Sold 1921, same name.

*Denotes delivery date in launch column.

Notes: The non-standard units varied between 194 and 237 TG; dimensions (pp) varied between 115 and 122¾ ft, by 22 to 22½ ft beam. Delivery of the first standard ship, GEORGE BORTHWICK, occurred on 3.8.17. 18 Straths were cancelled after 11.18;

Hall Russell:
4436 CHARLES BARBER   4443 JONATHAN COLLIS
4432 FREDERICK BOYCE   4434 PIERCY BRETT
4433 HENRY BATTERSBY   4444 SAMUEL CUNNINGHAM
4440 JOHN CONDON   4438 THOMAS BRAUND
4442 JOHN CORBETT   4441 THOMAS COPSEY
4435 JONATHAN BENJAMIN   4439 THOMAS CURR
4431 JONATHAN BRONTON   4437 WILLIAM BOREHAM

Hawthorns:
4473 CHARLES COUCHER   4477 THOMAS CALTRAFFE
4474 JOSHUA CARRETTS   4478 THOMAS CLAYTON

In addition, Yarwood had two cancellations, these were probably completed by Rennie Forrestt. Since builders' numbers were given in Admiralty Orders very shortly after the contracts had been assigned, it was not here necessary, that the vessel should be laid down before receiving a number. Three of Rennie Forrestt's trawlers; JOHN COPE, WILLIAM HALLETT and JOHN HUNTER were very likely reassignments that were effected very shortly after the original orders had been placed.

CASTLE CLASS

275 tons gross.
360 tons displacement. (547 deep).
134 (oa), 125½ (pp) × 23½ × 12¾ (dhd) ft.
TE 480 ihp =10½ kts.

Adty No.	Name	Launched	Builder—Armament—Fate
	Non-Standard Units:		
3505	DANIEL HARRINGTON	8. 2.17	Smiths Dock. 1–12 pdr M/S. Sold 1920 =START POINT; =LUCIENNE JEANNE in WW II.
3503	DANIEL HENLEY	24. 1.17	Smiths Dock. 1–12 pdr. Solid 4.5.20 =KILGERRAN CASTLE.
3501	FESTING GRINDALL =PEKIN 5.19	9. 1.17	Smiths Dock. 1–12 pdr M/S. Sold 11.5.20. =FESTING GRINDALL.
3611	GEORGE AUNGER	20. 9.17	Cook, W & G. 1–12 pdr. Sold 1922, same name.
3602	HUGH BLACK	10. 5.17	Cook, W & G. 1–12 pdr M/S. Sold 1923 =MACBETH; =OGANO in WW II.
3603	JAMES BERRY	10. 5.17	Cook, W & G. 1–12 pdr Escort. Sold 1922 =MONTANO; =MONTANO in WW II.
3504	JAMES HUNNIFORD	24. 1.17	Smiths Dock. 1–12 pdr. Sold 1920 =CREMLYN; =ETHEL TAYLOR in WW II.
3506	JAMES JOHNSON =THOMAS DEAS 12.19	8. 2.17	Smiths Dock. 1–12 pdr, 1–7.5 in BT M/S. Sold 1922 =THOMAS DEAS.
3610	JOHN ANDERSON =CHARLES DORAN 12.19	20. 9.17	Cook, W & G. 1–12 pdr Hydro. Sold 1922 =CHARLES DORAN; =CHARLES DORAN in WW II.
3609	JOHN BRENNAN	4. 9.17	Cook, W & G. 1–12 pdr. Sold 1922 =IOLITE; =OSAKO in WW II.
3608	JOHN BRICE =DERWENT 9.20	22. 8.17	Cook, W & G. 1–12 pdr. Sold 1924 =BEAULNE VERNEUIL; =BEAULNE VERNEUIL in WW II.
3605	JOHN BROOKER	9. 6.17	Cook, W & G. 1–12 pdr. Sold 1921 =OBSIDIAN; =LOCH PARK in WW II.
3600	JOHN BURLINGHAM	21. 4.17	Cook, W & G. (*ex-Rehearo*) 1–12 pdr, 1–7.5 in BT M/S. Sold 1920 =REHEARO; =REHEARO in WW II.
3502	JOHN GILLMAN	9. 1.17	Smiths Dock. 1–12 pdr, 1.7–5 in BT M/S. Sold 1920, same name.
3604	RICHARD BAGLEY	9. 6.17	Cook, W & G. 1–12 pdr. Sold 1921 =MALACOLITE; =MALACOLITE in WW II.
3601	ROBERT BETSON	21. 4.17	Cook, W & G. (*ex-Remillo*) 1–12 pdr. Sold 1920 =REMILLO; =REMILLO in WW II.

Adty No.	Name	Launched	Builder—Armament—Fate
3606	THOMAS BLACKTHORN	7. 7.17	Cook, W & G. 1–12 pdr M/S. Loaned to USN 1919 Sold 1922 =ALEXANDRITE; wrecked 1923.
3607	THOMAS BUCKLEY	7. 7.17	Cook, W & G. 1–12 pdr M/S. Loaned to USN 1919. Sold 1922 =CEYLONITE; =CEYLONITE in WW II.

Standard Units:

Adty No.	Name	Launched	Builder—Armament—Fate
3517	ALEXANDER PALMER =NESS 9.20	21. 5.17	Smiths Dock. 1–12 pdr M/S. Sold 1922 to Spain =UAD LUCAS.
3530	ALEXANDER SCOTT	3. 8.17	Smiths Dock. 1–12 pdr. Sold 4.5.20, same name; =in WW II.
4405	ANDREW ANDERSON	15. 8.19	Cook, W & G. (F) Sold 13.2.22 =NORMANBY.
4298	ANDREW APSLEY	2. 6.19	Cook, W & G. (F) Sold 13.10.19, delivered 9.12.19 =CALLANCROFT; =MILFORD EARL in WW II.
3523	ANDREW SACK	5. 7.17	Smiths Dock. 1–12 pdr M/S. Sold 1924 =ALEXANDRITE; =NORTH NESS in WW II.
3677	ARTHUR CAVANAGH	28. 5.18*	Bow McLachlan. 1–12 pdr, 1–3.5 in BT Hydro. Sold 1925, same name; =in WW II.
3510	ARTHUR LESSIMORE	9. 3.17	Smiths Dock. 1–12 pdr M/S, Escort. Sold 1924 =AVANTURINA; =IRVANA in WW II.
3667	BENJAMIN COOKE	1.11.17*	Bow McLachlan. 1–12 pdr. Sold 1922 =EMIEL VANDERVELDE; =NAMUR in WW II.
3522	BENJAMIN STEVENSON	19. 6.17	Smiths Dock. 1–12 pdr. Sunk 18.8.17 by S/M gunfire 40 miles E. of Fetlar, Shetlands.
4401	CHARLES ANTRAM	18. 6.19	Cook, W & G. (F) Sold 1922 =EDMOND VAN BEVERN; =FLANDERS in WW II.
3593	CHARLES BOYES	14. 2.18	Cook, W & G. 1–12 pdr, 1–3.5 in BT Hydro. Sold 1921, same name; =in WW II.
3662	CHARLES CHAPPELL	19. 6.17	Bow McLachlan. 1–12 pdr Hydro. Sold 1922 =S. NICOLA.
3679	CHARLES DONELLY	12. 7.18*	Bow McLachlan. 1–12 pdr Hydro. Sold 4.5.20 =CALYDAVIA; =PELAGOS in WW II.
4213	CHARLES LEGG	20. 1.19*	J. P. Rennoldson. Sold 1923 =RODERIGO; =MILFORD COUNTESS in WW II.
4446	DANIEL CLOWDEN	13.11.19*	George Brown. (F) Sold 8.8.19 while building =HANNAH WOODBRIDGE; =DANIEL CLOWDEN in WW II.
4488	DANIEL DICK	25. 8.20*	J. P. Rennoldson. (F) Sold 1921 =AGATE; =CLYTH NESS in WW II.
4221	DANIEL LEARY	9. 7.20*	C. Rennoldson. (F) Sold 1923 =STRATO.
4484	DAVID DILLON	28. 7.19*	J. P. Rennoldson. (F) Sold 28.7.19. =EDOUARD NIERINCK; =EDWARD WALMSLEY in WW II.
3514	DAVID OGILVIE	7. 5.17	Smiths Dock. Sold 1919, same name; =in WW II.
3711	DENIS CASEY	19. 3.18*	Ailsa, Ayr. 1–12 pdr M/S. Sold 7.20 =CARDIGAN CASTLE.
4296	DOMINICK ADDISON	2. 4.19	Cook, W & G. (F) Sold 1919 =TENEDOS; =GADFLY in WW II.
3726	DOMINICK DUBINE	15. 5.18*	J. P. Rennoldson. 1–12 pdr, 1–3.5 in BT Hydro. Sold 4.5.20, same name; later =EMILDOR; =French AD.52 FRUCTIDOR in WW II.
3793	DOMQUE GENTILE	5. 8.18	Ailsa, Ayr. 1–12 pdr. Sold 1921 =HAGNABY; later =SANTIAGO RUSINOL.
4459	EDWARD CATTELLY	17. 3.19	Ailsa, Ayr. (F) Sold 1919, same name; =LOCH NAVER in WW II.
3675	EDWARD COLLINGWOOD	26. 4.18*	Bow McLachlan. 1–12 pdr. Sold 1922 =MUMBY; =T. R. FERENS in WW II.
4216	EDWARD GALLAGHER	14. 2.19	C. Rennoldson. (F) Sold 1919 =EBOR DOWNS; =CARDIFF CASTLE in WW II.
4294	EGILIAS AKERMAN	18. 3.19	Cook, W & G. (F) Sold 1919 =KESTEVEN; =COMPUTATOR in WW II.
3717	EMMANUEL CAMELAIRE	25. 4.18	Ailsa, Troon. 1–12 pdr M/S. Sold 1921 =PRESIDENT FRANCQUI; =BRABANT in WW II.
4458	FRANCIS CONLIN	21. 1.19	Ailsa, Troon. (F) Sold 1919 =INVERYTHAN.
3594	FREDERICK BUSH	14. 3.18	Cook, W & G. 1–12 pdr Hydro. Sold 1922 =CAWDOR.

Adty No.	Name	Launched	Builder—Armament—Fate
4402	GEORGE ADGELL	18. 6.19	Cook, W & G. (F) Sold 1920, same name; =in WW II.
4291	GEORGE AIKEN =CECIL COOMBES 11.19	19.12.18	Cook, W & G. (F) Sold 1919 =HIGHBRIDGE.
3714	GEORGE CLARK	2.10.17	J. P. Rennoldson. 1–12 pdr M/S. Loaned to USN 1919. Sold 1923 =TRANIO; =LADY STANLEY in WW II.
3721	GEORGE COCHRAN	28. 6.18	Cook, W & G. 1–12 pdr. Loaned to USN 1919. Sold 1920, same name.
3697	GEORGE CORTEN	6. 2.19*	Cox. Sold 1921 =ZENCON; =ZIRCON 1921; =NORTHCOATES in WW II.
4461	GEORGE COUSINS	13. 6.19	Ailsa, Ayr. (F) Sold 1919, same name; =in WW II.
3681	GEORGE DARBY	21.10.18*	Bow McLachlan. 1–12 pdr. Sold 1923 =BULBY.
3790	GEORGE GREAVES	12. 5.19*	George Brown. (F) Sold 1919 =RAGLAN CASTLE; =RAGLAN CASTLE in WW II.
3787	GEORGE GREENFIELD	15.10.18*	George Brown. 1–12 pdr Escort. Sold 1921; =RIO MESA 1922.
3854	GEORGE HARRIS	12.12.18*	Hepple. 1–6 pdr. Sold 11.5.20; =KARACHI 1921; =LAXMI in RIN WW II.
3792	GIOVANNI GUINTI =IDAHO 1.19	31. 5.18	Ailsa, Ayr. 1–4 in Escort. Sold 1920 =CYMREA.
3780	GRIFFITH GRIFFITH	27. 8.18	Cook, W & G. Sold 11.5.20; =KILINDINI 1921.
3673	HENRY CHEVALLIER	3. 4.18*	Bow McLachlan. 1–12 pdr. Sold 1922 =ALBERT =LIGNY in WW II.
3698	HENRY CORY	28. 5.19*	Cox. (F) Sold 1919 =CALIBAN; =CALIBAN in WW II.
4297	ISAAC ARTHAN	1. 5.19	Cook, W & G. (F) Sold 1921 =AMBER; =LOCH BUIE in WW II.
3829	ISAAC HEATH	21. 8.18*	J. P. Rennoldson. 1–12 pdr. Sold 1920, same name; later =RYLSTON; =TEROMA in WW II.
3653	JAMES BURGESS	31. 8.17	C. Rennoldson. Escort. Sold 1920 =BEAUMARIS CASTLE; =BEAUMARIS CASTLE in WW II.
3718	JAMES CEPELL	29. 3.18	George Brown. 1–12 pdr. Sold 1925 =CLIXBY; =ANTIOCHE II in WW II.
3694	JAMES CHAPMAN	8. 9.17	George Brown. 1–12 pdr. Sold 1923 =DUNSBY.
3715	JAMES CHRISTOPHER	27. 3.18*	J. P. Rennoldson 1–12 pdr. Sold 1923, same name; =MARSONA in WW II.
3700	JAMES CONNOR =WAVENEY 9.20	19. 7.17	Harkness. 1–12 pdr. Sold 1922 to Spain =UAD MULUYA.
3716	JAMES COSGROVE	5. 3.18	Ailsa, Ayr. 1–12 pdr. Sold 1919, same name; =in RNZN WW II.
3678	JAMES DINTON	29. 5.18*	Bow McLachlan. 1–12 pdr Hydro. Sold 1922 =SCAWBY; =MILFORD DUKE in WW II.
4217	JAMES GILL	17. 2.19	C. Rennoldson. (F) Sold 1919 =PIERRE FRANCOIS DESWARTE; =MILFORD DUCHESS in WW II.
3537	JAMES GREEN	3.10.17	Smiths Dock. 1–12 pdr M/S. Sold 1922, same name; later =E. & F.; =LAVEROCK in WW II.
4215	JAMES LAVENEY	30.10.19*	Chambers. (F) Sold 1925 =KELBY; =French AD.186 LA BLANCHE II in WW II.
4222	JAMES LAY	4.11.18*	Fletcher & Fearnall. 1–12 pdr. Sold 1920, same name; =in WW II.
3540	JAMES PEAKE	17.10.17	Smiths Dock. 1–12 pdr Hydro. Sold 1923; =ARRAGONITE 1924.
3515	JAMES POND	21. 5.17	Smiths Dock. Sunk 15.2.18 by German destroyers in the Dover Straits.
3159	JAMES ROBERTSON	6. 6.17	Smiths Dock. 1–12 pdr Hydro. Sold 1922 =CAPSTONE; =CAPSTONE in WW II.
3526	JAMES SECKAR	20. 7.17	Smiths Dock. Foundered 25.9.17 in the Atlantic, last seen at 46.30N, 12.00W.
3525	JAMES SIBBALD	20. 7.17	Smiths Dock. Escort. Sold 1919 =KIRKLAND; =OUR BAIRNS in WW II.
4292	JOHN AIKENHEAD	19.12.18	Cook, W & G. (F) Sold 1919 =POLLY JOHNSON; =POLLY JOHNSON in WW II.
4293	JOHN ASHLEY	18. 3.19	Cook, W & G. (F) Sold 1919 =LIMESLADE.

Adty No.	Name	Launched	Builder—Armament—Fate
3596	JOHN BAPTISH	29. 4.18	Cook, W & G. 1–12 pdr. Sold 1921, same name; =in WW II.
3599	JOHN BATEMAN	29. 4.18	Cook, W & G. 1–2 pdr. Sold 1922 =ANDERBY.
3597	JOHN BOMKWORTH =WEAR 9.20	29. 5.18	Cook, W & G. 1–6 pdr, 1–7.5 in BT M/S. Sold 1922 to Spain =UAD RAS.
3651	JOHN BULLOCK	9. 7.17	C. Rennoldson. 1–12 pdr. Sold 1921, =FILIEP COENEN 1922; =FLYING ADMIRAL in WW II.
3695	JOHN CAMPBELL =GEORGE DIXON 12.19	1.11.17	George Brown. 1–12 pdr. Sold 1923 =LUSHBY.
3713	JOHN CASEWELL	3.10.17	Ailsa, Troon. 1–12 pdr, 1–3.5 in BT M/S. Sold 4.5.20, same name; lost 1921.
3676	JOHN CATTLING	29. 4.18*	Bow McLachlan. 1–12 pdr, 1–3.5 in BT Hydro. Sold 4.5.20, same name; =in WW II.
3671	JOHN CHIVERS =ERNE 9.20	17.12.17	Bow McLachlan. 1–12 pdr M/S. Sold 1922 to Spain =UAD MARTIN.
3668	JOHN CHURCH	16.10.17	Bow McLachlan. Escort. Sold 1920, same name; later =ANTARES.
4480	JOHN CLAVELL	18.10.20*	Hepple. (F) Sold 1921, same name; later =DENIS.
3712	JOHN COLLINS	19.11.17	Ailsa, Troon. 1–12 pdr M/S. Loaned to USN 1919. Sold 1920 =JANERA.
3699	JOHN COOPER	5. 7.17	Harkess. 1–12 pdr. Sold 1922 =PENFRET.
3682	JOHN DAVIS	22.10.18*	Bow McLachlan. 1–12 pdr. Sold 1922 =CESAR DE PAEPE.
4485	JOHN DORMOND	15.10.19*	J. P. Rennoldson. (F) Sold 1922, same name; later =AMETHYST.
3779	JOHN GAUNTLET	12. 8.18	Cook, W & G. Sold 11.5.20, same name; =NAIROBI 1921; lost 1922.
3794	JOHN GEOGHAN	9.10.18	Ailsa, Troon. 1–12 pdr. Sold 1921, same name; =CONGRE in WW II.
3778	JOHN GRAHAM	27. 7.18	Cook, W & G. Loaned to USN 1919. Sold 1921 =RUBY; =EASTCOATES in WW II.
3789	JOHN GREGORY	2. 5.19*	George Brown. (F) Sold 1919 =INVERDEE; =French AD.57 NADINE in WW II.
3782	JOHN GULIPSTER	24. 9.18	Cook, W & G. (F) Sold 1919 =BETTY JOHNSON; =COMITATUS in WW II.
3508	JOHN KIDD	20. 2.17	Smiths Dock. 1–12 pdr M/S. Sold 11.5.20 =ROTHERSLADE; =ROTHERSLADE in WW II.
4219	JOHN LEWIS =JOHN EVANS 1.20	30. 3.20*	C. Rennoldson. (F) Sold 1921 =HARRY MELLING; =HARRY MELLING in WW II.
3511	JOHN LYONS	23. 3.17	Smiths Dock. 1–12 pdr, 1–3.5 in BT Hydro. Sold 1922 =LES ILLATES.
3516	JOHN POLLARD	21. 5.17	Smiths Dock. 1–12 pdr, 1–7.5 in BT M/S. Sold 4.5.20 =GROSMONT CASTLE; =GROSMONT CASTLE in WW II.
3527	JOHN THORLING	20. 7.17	Smiths Dock. 1–12 pdr M/S. Sold 1925 =RIVER KENT; =CONCERTATOR in WW II.
3586	JOSEPH BARRATT	2.11.17	Cook, W & G. 1–12 pdr. Sold 1920, same name; later =LOCH MORAR; =TILBURY NESS in WW II.
3584	JOSEPH BUTTON	17.12.17	Cook, W & G. 1–12 pdr. Sold 1920, same name; =in WW II.
3696	JOSEPH CONNELL	20.12.17	George Brown. 1–12 pdr. Sold 1922 =HOURTIN.
3786	JOSEPH GIDDICE	12.12.18*	George Brown. 1–12 pdr. Sold 1922 =OSEBY.
3785	JOSEPH GORDON	29. 6.18	George Brown. 1–12 pdr, 1–3.5 in BT Hydro T/S. Sold 1922 =GROUIN-DU-COU; =French GROUIN DU COU in WW II.
3855	JOSEPH HODGKINS	20. 6.19*	Hepple. (F) Sold 1919, same name; lost 1921.
4299	JOSHUA ARABIN	1. 5.19	Cook, W & G. (F) Sold 1920 =RIVER FORTH; =DE LA POLE in WW II.
4457	MATTHEW CASSADY	18.12.18	Ailsa, Troon. (F) Sold 1919 =INVERDON.
3745	MATTHEW FLYNN	23. 2.18*	Hepple. 1–12 pdr. Sold 1921 =AMIRAL MARQUER; =COMMILES in WW II.
3784	MICHAEL GING	11. 5.18	George Brown. 1–12 pdr. Sold 1922, same name.
3781	MICHAEL GRIFFITH	5. 9.18	Cook, W & G. Sold 1921, same name; =in WW II.
3513	MICHAEL MALONEY	7. 5.17	Smiths Dock. 1–12 pdr. Stranded 19.2.20 at Egersund, Norway.

Adty No.	Name	Launched	Builder—Armament—Fate
3845	MORGAN JONES	10. 3.18	Fletcher & Fearnall. 1–12 pdr. Sold 1920, same name; =in WW II.
3507	NATHANIEL COLE	20. 2.17	Smiths Dock. Foundered 6.2.18 off Buncrana Lough Swilly.
3524	NEIL SMITH	5. 7.17	Smiths Dock. Sold 1921, same name; =ir WW II.
3518	OLIVER PICKIN	21. 5.17	Smiths Dock 1–12 pdr. Sold 1922 =FERMO =DAMITO in WW II.
3591	PATRICK BOWE =TEST 9.20	17. 1.18	Cook, W & G. 1–12 pdr Hydro. Sold 1922 to Spair =UAD TARGA.
4460	PATRICK CULLEN	31. 3.19	Ailsa, Ayr. (F) Sold 1919 =BRIARLYN.
4487	PATRICK DONOVAN	20. 6.20*	J. P. Rennoldson. Sold (F) 1922 =LOCH NEVIS
3583	PETER BLUMBERRY	18.10.17	Cook, W & G. M/S, Escort. Sold 1921 =INGOUVILLE.
4445	PETER CAREY	25. 6.19	George Brown. (F) Sold 1919 =CICELY BLANCHE; =PETER CAREY in WW II.
3795	PETER HALL	6.11.18	Ailsa, Ayr. 1–12 pdr. Sold 1922 =TRANSPORT UNION; =ALVIS in WW II.
4207	PETER KILLEN	31. 3.19*	Duthie. (F) Sold 1919, same name; later =CRAONNE BEAURIEUX; =SIR JOHN LISTER in WW II.
3509	PETER LOVETT	9. 3.17	Smiths Dock. 1–12 pdr. Sold 1922, same name; =LOWDOCK 1934.
3783	PHILIP GODBY	24. 9.18	Cook, W & G. (F) Sold 1919, same name; =CISNELL 1924.
3588	PHINEAS BEARD	17.11.17	Cook, W & G. 1–12 pdr. Sold 1920, same name; =in WW II.
3587	RICHARD BACON	2.11.17	Cook, W & G. 1–12 pdr. Sold 1922 =HAGNABY; =COMMODATOR in WW II.
3720	RICHARD CROFTS	13. 6.18	Cook, W & G. 1–12 pdr. Sold 1921, same name; =in WW II.
4462	RICHARD CUNDY	12. 8.19	Ailsa, Ayr. (F) Sold 1920 =RIVER CLYDE; =RIVER CLYDE in WW II.
3520	RICHARD ROBERTS	6. 6.17	Smiths Dock. 1–12 pdr M/S, Escort. Sold 11.5.20, same name; lost 1922.
3595	ROBERT BOWEN	14. 3.18	Cook, W & G. 1–12 pdr Hydro. Sold 1920, same name; =in WW II.
3672	ROBERT CLOUGHTON =CORONET 1933	18.12.17	Bow McLachlan. =BDV 1933; BU 1953 Pollock Brown, Northam.
3725	ROBERT DAVIDSON	30.11.17	C. Rennoldson. 1–12 pdr M/S. Sold 1921 =AUGUSTINE ISABELLE.
4486	SAMUEL DAWSON	5. 2.20*	J. P. Rennoldson. (F) Sold 1922, same name; later =SAN JUAN.
3683	SAMUEL DRAKE	26.11.18*	Bow McLachlan. 1–12 pdr. Sold 1924 =RHODOLITE; =SOUTHCOATES in WW II.
3791	SAMUEL GREEN	30. 4.19	George Brown. (F) Sold 1919 =OCEAN ROVER; later =ARIES; =OCEAN ROVER in WW II.
3533	SAMUEL SPENCER	17. 9.17	Smiths Dock. 1–12 pdr, 1–7.5 in BT M/S. Sold 1921 =FLASH.
3684	SIAM DUFFY	27.11.18*	Bow McLachlan. 1–12 pdr. Loaned to USN 1919. Sold 1922 =EDOUARD ANSEELE; =FONTENOY in WW II.
4295	THOMAS ADNEY	2. 4.19	Cook, W & G. (F) Sold 1919 =LINDSEY; lost 8.9.20.
4404	THOMAS ALEXANDER	18. 7.19	Cook, W & G. (F) Sold 1920 =ETOILE POLAIRE II; =BEN DEARG in WW II.
4403	THOMAS ALLEN	18. 7.19	Cook, W & G. (F) Sold 1922 =THEOPHILE MASSART; =MILFORD PRINCE in WW II.
4300	THOMAS ALTOFT	2. 6.19	Cook, W & G. (F) Sold 1920, same name; =in WW II.
3598	THOMAS BARTLETT	29. 5.18	Cook, W & G. 1–6 pdrAA. Sold 11.5.20, same name; =in WW II.
3592	THOMAS BOOTH	14. 2.18	Cook, W & G. 1–12 pdr Hydro. Sold 1920, same name.
4406	THOMAS BOUDIGE	15. 8.19	Cook, W & G. (F) Sold 1921 =JADE; =DARNETT NESS in WW II.
3670	THOMAS CHAMBERS	1.12.17	Bow McLachlan. 1–12 pdr, 1–3.5 in BT M/S. Sold 1922 =PROSPER; =LORRAINE in WW II.

Adty No.	Name	Launched	Builder—Armament—Fate
3589	THOMAS CONNOLLY	29.11.17	Cook, W & G. 1–12 pdr. Sold 1920, same name; =in WW II.
3661	THOMAS CROFTON	18. 6.17	Bow McLachlan. 1–12 pdr Hydro. Sold 4.5.20, same name; =REVESBY 1929; =GWMAHO in WW II.
3680	THOMAS DANIELS	12. 8.18*	Bow McLachlan. 1–12 pdr, 1–3.5 in BT Hydro. Sold 1922 =JAN VOLDERS.
3724	THOMAS DOWDING	16.11.17	C. Rennoldson. 1–12 pdr M/S. Sold 1923 =LEONATO; =BEN BHEULA in WW II.
3539	THOMAS GOBLE	17.10.17	Smiths Dock. 1–12 pdr M/S. Sold 1922 =COTSMUIR; =COTSMUIR in WW II.
4218	THOMAS GREEN	28. 5.19	C. Rennoldson. (F) Sold 1920 =EBOR ELECT; =CAERPHILLY CASTLE in WW II.
3828	THOMAS HANKINS	19. 6.18*	J. P. Rennoldson. 1–12 pdr M/S. Sold 11.5.20, same name.
4212	THOMAS LAUNDRY	27.11.18*	J. P. Rennoldson. Loaned to USN 1919. Sold 11.5.20 =TEESBAY.
4214	THOMAS LAWRIE	1.10.19*	Chambers. (F) Sold 1925 =SOMERSBY.
4210	THOMAS LEEDS	12. 9.19*	Duthie. (F) Sold 1919, same name; later =SAINT GABRIEL; =THOMAS LEEDS in WW II.
3531	THOMAS ROBINS	3. 9.17	Smiths Dock. 1–12 pdr. Sold 4.5.20 =CHERITON.
3528	THOMAS TWINEY	20. 7.17	Smiths Dock. 1–12 pdr. M/S. Sold 1922 =CLYRO.
3710	TIMOTHY CRAWLEY	4.10.17	Ailsa, Troon. 1–12 pdr Escort. Sold 11.5.20 =LOCH LONG; =LOCH LONG in WW II.
3654	VALENTINE BOWER	1.10.17	C. Rennoldson. 1–12 pdr M/S. Sold 1923 =MALVOLIO; =MILFORD KING in WW II.
3532	WALTER BURKE	3. 9.17	Smiths Dock. 1–12 pdr Hydro. Sold 1922, same name; =GONERBY 1924.
3534	WILLIAM BEATTY	17. 9.17	Smiths Dock. 1–12 pdr. 1–7.5 in BT. Sold 4.5.20 =CRESSWELL.
3652	WILLIAM BEETON	20. 7.17	C. Rennoldson. 1–12 pdr. To Maltese Government 1921 =GIROLAMO CASSAR.
3590	WILLIAM BELL	17. 1.18	Cook, W & G. 1–12 pdr Hydro. Sold 1920, same name; =in WW II.
3585	WILLIAM BRADY	17.12.17	Cook, W & G. 1–12 pdr, 1–3.5 in BT Hydro. Sold 1920, same name; =in WW II.
3582	WILLIAM BROWIS	18.10.17	Cook, W & G. 1–12 pdr. Sold 1922 =GONERBY; =JOHN 1923; =MILFORD QUEEN in WW II.
3538	WILLIAM BUNCE	3.10.17	Smiths Dock. 1–12 pdr, 1–3.5 in BT M/S. Sold 1920, same name; =in WW II.
3719	WILLIAM CALDWELL	12. 6.18	Cook, W & G. 1–12 pdr. Loaned to USN 1919. Sold 11.5.20, same name; =in WW II.
3666	WILLIAM CALE	19. 9.17	Bow McLachlan. 1–12 pdr. Sold 1922, same name; =in WW II.
4479	WILLIAM CARBERRY	13.12.19*	Hepple. (F) Sold 1919, same name; later =MICAELA DE C.
3674	WILLIAM CARR	4. 4.18*	Bow McLachlan. 1–12 pdr. Sold 1921, same name; later =JACQUES II; =NAZARETH in WW II.
3665	WILLIAM CARRICK	18. 9.17	Bow McLachlan. 1–12 pdr. To Indian Government 1920, same name.
3529	WILLIAM CHASEMAN	3. 3.17	Smiths Dock. 1–12 pdr. Sold 4.5.20 =RADNOR CASTLE; =RADNOR CASTLE in WW II.
3664	WILLIAM COBURNE	24. 7.17	Bow McLachlan. Escort. Sold 1920 =CARNARVON CASTLE.
3663	WILLIAM COWLING	23. 7.17	Bow McLachlan. Sold 1922 =ASTERBY; =NOTRE DAME DE LOURDES in WW II.
3669	WILLIAM CUMMINS	17.11.17	Bow McLachlan. 1–12 pdr M/S. Sold 1925 =ERNEST SOLVAY; =NIBLICK in WW II.
3722	WILLIAM DARNOLD	11. 7.18	Cook, W & G. 1–12 pdr. Loaned to USN 1919. Sold 11.5.20 =CAPE HATTERAS.
3723	WILLIAM DOWNES	5.11.17	C. Rennoldson. 1–12 pdr. Sold 1921, same name.
4483	WILLIAM DRAKE	19. 5.19*	J. P. Rennoldson. (F) Sold 1919 =EBOR COURT
3746	WILLIAM FLEMMING	18. 5.18*	Hepple. 1–12 pdr, 1–3.5 in BT Hydro. Sold 4.5.20 =TRAWLER PRINCE; =TRANIO in WW II.
3788	WILLIAM GRIFFTHS	21. 2.19*	George Brown. (F) Sold 1919 =INVERSPEY.

Adty No.	Name	Launched	Builder—Armament—Fate
4206	WILLIAM HANNAM	20. 2.19*	Duthie. Sold 1920, same name; =in WW II.
4205	WILLIAM HUMPHRIES	24.12.18*	Duthie. Sold 1921, same name.
4208	WILLIAM KNIGHT	19. 6.19*	Duthie. (F) Sold 1919 =HENRICUS; =COBBERS in WW II.
4209	WILLIAM LAMBKIN	16. 7.19*	Duthie. (F) Sold 1919 =NELLIE CRAWFORD.
4211	WILLIAM LEEK	10.10.18*	J. P. Rennoldson. 1–12 pdr Escort. Sold 11.5.20 =CAVENDISH; =HILDINA in WW II.
4220	WILLIAM LOFT	30. 8.19	C. Rennoldson. (F) Sold 1923 =TAMORA; =TAMORA in WW II.
3512	WILLIAM MANNELL	23. 3.17	Smiths Dock. 1–12 pdr Escort. Sold 11.5.20, same name; =in WW II.
3521	WILLIAM SPENCER	19. 6.17	Smiths Dock. Sold 1924 =NORMANBY; =ASTROS in WW II.
3535	WILLIAM SYMONS	1.10.17	Smiths Dock. 1–12 pdr M/S. Sold 1922 =RAYVERNOL; =LEPHRETO in WW II.
3536	WILLIAM WILMOT	1.10.17	Smiths Dock. 1–12 pdr. Sunk 9.20 in collision with SS MEISSONIER in the Irish Sea.

*Delivery dates in launch column.

Notes: The non-standard ships included in this class varied between 236 and 276 TG; dimensions (pp) varied between 117½ and 125½ ft, by between 22 and 23½ ft beam. The first standard vessel was delivered on 4.5.17 (NATHANIEL COLE). Sixteen projected Castles were cancelled in 1917 to enable Smiths Dock to concentrate on gunboat production. 20 trawlers of this class were cancelled after 11.18 but some of these vessels were actually completed for commercial service.

George Brown:
- 4455 ALEXANDER COLVILLE
- 4451 COLLIN CRAIG
- 4454 JAMES COILE
- 4447 JOHN CHATWAY
- 4453 JOHN COOMBE
- 4449 JOHN CREIGHTON
- 4448 JOSEPH CROWELL
- 4456 WALTER CANE
- 4450 WILLIAM CABLE
- 4452 WILLIAM CORAN

Cook, W & G:
- 4407 EPHRAIM BRIGHT =MAI.
- 4411 JAMES BAIRD =IJUIN; =IJUIN in WW II.
- 4414 JAMES BOYLE
- 4409 JOHN BENSON =KARI SOLMUNDARSON.
- 4412 MATTHEW BERRYMAN =RIGHTO; =RIGHTO in WW II.
- 4410 RICHARD BANE =KYOTO.
- 4408 WILLIAM BENNETT =NJORDUR.
- 4413 WILLIAM BURTE =REBOUNDO; =REBOUNDO in WW II.

Hepple:
- 4493 ALEXANDER DUNBAR
- 4494 JOSEPH DOE

MERSEY CLASS

324 tons gross.
438 tons displacement. (665 deep).
148 (oa), 138½ (pp) =23¾ × 12¾ (dhd) ft.
TE 600 ihp=11 kts.

Adty No.	Name	Launched	Builder—Armament—Fate
	Non-Standard Units:		
3579	ANTHONY ASLETT =ROTHER 9.20	22. 2.17	Cochrane. 1–12 pdr. 1–7.5 in BT M/S. Sold 1922 to Spain =UAD QUERT.
3578	CHARLES ASTIE	25. 1.17	Cochrane. 1–12 pdr. Mined 26.6.17 off Lough Swilly.
3581	CORNELIUS BUCKLEY	24. 2.17	Cochrane. 1–12 pdr M/S. Sold 1922 =SAVARIA.
3612	JOHN APPLEBY	30. 1.17	Cook, W & G. (ex-*Corinthia*) 1–12 pdr Hydro. Sold 1923 =LOIS; =LOIS in WW II.
3613	JOHN ARTHUR	10. 2.17	Cook, W & G. (ex-*Sannyrion*) 1–12 pdr Hydro. Sold 1922 =GLADYS; =GLADYS in WW II.
3580	WILLIAM ABRAHAMS	24. 2.17	Cochrane. 1–12 pdr M/S. Sold 1922 =SANTINI.
3577	WILLIAM WESTENBURGH	25. 1.17	Cochrane. 2–12 pdr M/S. Sold 1921 =LORD TALBOT; =STAR OF THE REALM in WW II.

Adty No.	Name	Launched	Builder—Armament—Fate
	Standard Units:		
3549	ALEXANDER HILLS =MOY 9.20	22. 5.17	Cochrane. 1–12 pdr. Sold 1.46; =CORAL ISLAND 1947.
4241	ALEXANDER MACBETH	14. 7.19*	Cochrane. (F) Sold 1919 =JOHN W. JOHNSON.
3844	ANDREW JEWER =NITH 9.20 =EXCELLENT 6.22	4.12.18*	Cochrane. 1–12 pdr. Gunnery tender. Sold 1946 =MALVERN.
3545	ANDREW KING =OUSE 9.20	19. 4.17	Cochrane. 1–12 pdr M/S Hydro. Mined 20.2.41 off Tobruk.
3858	BENJAMIN HAWKINS	7. 2.20*	Goole SB. (F) Sold 17.10.19, delivered 2.20 =FROBISHER; purchased 6.33 as BDV =FASTNET.
3551	CHARLES ADAIR	7. 6.17	Cochrane. 1–12 pdrAA Hydro. Sold 1923; =SLEAFORD 1924; =French SAINT BENOIT in WW II.
3830	CHARLES HAMMOND	26. 3.18*	Cochrane. 1–12 pdr. Sunk 2.11.18 in collision with MARKSMAN off Kirkcaldy.
3563	CHRISTOPHER DIXON	4. 9.17	Cochrane. 1–12 pdr. To Irish Government 1922, same name; =LORD GAINFORD in WW II.
3571	DANIEL FEARALL =STOUR 9.20 =PEMBROKE 9.22 =STOUR 1939	2.11.17	Cochrane. 1–12 pdr, 1–7.5 in BT T/S. Sold 7.46; =STORESSE 1947.
4242	DANIEL MCPHERSON	16. 8.19*	Cochrane. (F) Sold 1919 =LORD HALIFAX.
4239	DANIEL MUNRO	20. 6.19*	Cochrane. (F) Sold 1919 =ESTRELLA DO NORTE; =ESTRELLA DO NORTE in WW II.
4237	DEGARA LEROSA	6. 6.19*	Cochrane. (F) Sold 1919 =JAMES JOHNSON; =Greek AXIOS in WW II.
3736	EDWARD DRUCE	30. 7.18*	Goole SB. 1–12 pdr Hydro. Sold 1920 =GIRARD; =GIRARD in WW II.
4251	EDWARD MCGUIRE	17. 5.19	Cochrane. (F) Sold 1920 =CAPE ST. VINCENT; =KOROWA in RAN WW II.
3547	EDWARD WILLIAMS	8. 5.17	Cochrane. 1–12 pdr, 1–7.5 in BT M/S. Sold 1922; =CAPE TRAFALGAR 1923; =CAPE TRAFALGAR in WW II.
3567	FRASER EAVES =DOON 9.20	2.10.17	Cochrane. 1–4 in, 1–12 pdrAA, 1–7.5 in BT. Sold 1946 =DONESSE.
3556	GEORGE ANDREW	23. 7.17	Cochrane. 1–12 pdrAA M/S. Sold 1921 =LORD ASTOR; =CRANEFLY in WW II.
3542	GEORGE BLIGH	24. 3.17	Cochrane. 1–12 pdr, 1–7.5 in BT. Bold 1921, same name; =in WW II.
3548	GEORGE BROWN =WILLIAM DOGHERTY 12.19	10. 5.17	Cochrane. 1–12 pdr. Sold 1922 =ROSEDALE WYKE.
3568	GEORGE FENWICK	10. 1.18*	Cochrane. 1–12 pdr. Sold 1923 =CAPE OTWAY; =Greek STRYMON in WW II.
3575	GEORGE WESTPHALL	7. 3.18*	Cochrane. 1–12 pdr. Sold 1921 =ESTELLE YVONNE; lost 1923.
3705	HENRY CRAMWELL	24.12.18*	Lobnitz. 1–12 pdr M/S. Sold 1922 to Spain =XAUEN.
3569	HENRY FORD =BOADICEA II 2.19 =HENRY FORD 2.20	18.10.17	Cochrane. 1–12 pdrAA M/S. Sold 1921 =DUPERRE; =French DUPERRE in WW II.
4231	HENRY LANCASTER	8. 4.19*	Cochrane. Mark buoy vessel. Sold 8.21, same name; =LONGTOW in WW II.
4253	HENRY MARSH	31. 5.19	Cochrane. (F) Sold 1920 =SPRINGBOK.
3704	ISAAC CHANT =COLNE 9.20	1.10.18*	Lobnitz. 1–12 pdr M/S. Sold 1949.
3555	JAMES ADAMS	7. 7.17	Cochrane. 1–12 pdrAA, 1–7.5 in BT. Sold 1920 =PILOTE 5; Belgian PILOTE 5 in WW II.
3565	JAMES BUCHANAN	18. 9.17	Cochrane. 1–12 pdrAA M/S Hydro. Sold 1922 =STONEFERRY; =FORCE in WW II.
3703	JAMES CATON	26. 8.18	Lobnitz. 1–12 pdr. Sold 1921 =EMILIE PIERRE; =French ST. PIERRE D'ALCANTARA in WW II.
3859	JAMES HAYES	27. 6.19*	Goole SB. (F) Sold 1919 =VISCOUNT GREY; stranded 11.3.20, total loss.

Adty No.	Name	Launched	Builder—Armament—Fate
3799	JAMES HULBERT	9. 9.19*	Lobnitz. (F) Sold 1919 =M. J. REID; =JEAN FREDERIC in WW II.
3842	JAMES JONES =CHERWELL 9.20	9.11.18*	Cochrane. 1–12 pdr. Sold 1946 =CHERWELL.
4235	JAMES YOUNG	8. 5.19*	Cochrane. (F) Sold 1919, same name.
4232	JAMES LUDFORD	1. 5.19*	Cochrane. Mark buoy vessel. Mined 14.12.39 off the Tyne.
4238	JAMES MANSELL	26. 6.19*	Cochrane. (F) Sold 1919 =SNORRI STURLUSON; =JAMES MANSELL 1922.
4244	JAMES MCDONALD	9. 9.19*	Cochrane. (F) Sold 1919 =GRAND FLEET; =BARBARA ROBERTSON in WW II.
4250	JAMES MCLAUGHLIN	1. 5.19	Cochrane. (F) Sold 1919 =GENERAL BIRDWOOD; =GENERAL BIRDWOOD in WW II.
3576	JAMES WRIGHT	15. 3.18*	Cochrane. 1–12 pdr. Sold 1921 =LORD ANCASTER; =LOCH MOIDART in WW II.
4234	JEREMIAH LEWIS	25. 3.18*	Cochrane. Sold 1920 =FIELD MARSHAL ROBERTSON.
3562	JOHN CORMACK	4. 9.17	Cochrane. 1–12 pdrAA. Sold 1922 =LORD PIRRIE; =CHILTERN in WW II.
4463	JOHN COTTRELL	1.11.19*	Goole SB. (F) Sold 1919 =ST. ENDELLION; =BLIGHTY in WW II.
3741	JOHN DUNN	27. 3.18	Ferguson. 1–12 pdr Hydro. Sold 1923, same name; =FLORENCE BRIERLEY in WW II.
3739	JOHN DUTTON	17. 1.18	Ferguson. 1–12 pdr. Sold 1921; later =KARLSEFNI.
3566	JOHN EBBS	2.10.17	Cochrane. 1–12 pdr, 1–3.5 in BT Hydro. Sold 1920. =PILOTE 4; =Belgian PILOTE 4 in WW II.
3738	JOHN EDMUND =FOYLE 9.20	22.10.18*	Goole SB. 1–12 pdr. Loaned as SONNEBLOM, SAN 9.21 to 6.34; sold 1946 =CRAMOND ISLAND.
3570	JOHN FELTON	1.11.17	Cochrane. 1–12 pdrAA, 1–6 in BT. Sold 1920, same name.
3797	JOHN HIGHLAND	23. 9.18	Ferguson. 1–12 pdr. Sold 1920 =OCEAN ENSIGN.
3833	JOHN JACOBS	15. 4.18*	Cochrane. 1–12 pdr. Sold 1922 =CASTLENAU; =CASTLENAU in WW II.
3834	JOHN JEFFERSON	23. 4.18*	Cochrane. 1–12 pdr, 1–3.5 in BT Hydro. Sold 1920 =ST. AMANT; =LADY ENID in WW II.
3832	JOHN JOHNSON	19. 4.18*	Cochrane. 1–12 pdr. Sold 1922 =CLOUGHTON WYKE; =CLOUGHTON WYKE in WW II.
4245	JOHN MANN	6. 9.19*	Cochrane. (F) Sold 1920 =EARL HAIG; purchased 1933 =BARNET; sold 1947.
3544	JOHN PASCO	19. 4.17	Cochrane. 1–12 pdr Escort. Sold 1922 =ARINBJORN HERSIR.
3541	JOHN QUILLIAM	12. 3.17	Cochrane. 1–12 pdrAA Hydro. Sold 1921 =DANA.
3573	JOHN WELSTEAD	15. 2.18*	Cochrane. 1–12 pdr. Sold 1922 =LORD HAREWOOD; =MYRLAND in WW II.
3543	JOHN YULE	24. 3.17	Cochrane. 1–12 pdr Hydro. Sold 1921 =NOTRE DAME DE LORETTE.
4465	JONATHAN CLARKE	24. 3.20*	Goole SB. (F) Sold 1920 =ST. KEVERNE.
4464	JONATHAN COLLINS	26.11.19*	Goole SB. (F) Sold 1919 =ST. MINVER; =ST. MINVER in WW II.
4243	LANGDON MACKENNON	21.10.19*	Cochrane. (F) Sold 1919 =DOUGLAS H. SMITH; lost 1921.
4240	LEWIS MACKENZIE	26. 6.19*	Cochrane. (F) Sold 1919 =FLORENCE JOHNSON.
3553	LEWIS REEVES	23. 6.17	Cochrane. 1–12 pdrAA, 1–7.5 in BT. Sold 1922 =LORD HAWKE; lost 1922.
3554	LEWIS ROATLEY	7. 7.17	Cochrane. 1–12 pdrAA M/S. Sold 1922 =STALWART.
3561	MICHAEL CLEMENTS	21. 8.17	Cochrane. 1–12 pdrAA M/S. Sunk 8.8.18 in collision off St. Catherines Point.
4252	MICHAEL MCDONALD	17. 5.19	Cochrane. (F) Sold 1919 =KANUCK.
4236	NICHOLAS COUTEUR	20. 5.19*	Cochrane. (F) Sold 1919 =MARY A. JOHNSON; lost 11.20.

Adty No.	Name	Launched	Builder—Armament—Fate
3740	NICHOLAS DEAN	11. 3.18	Ferguson. 1–12 pdr, 1–3.5 in BT Hydro. Sold 1921 =NOTRE DAME DE FRANCE.
4248	PATRICK MITCHELL	16. 4.19	Cochrane. (F) Sold 1919 =KELVIN.
3798	PETER HOFFMAN	8. 7.19*	Lobnitz. (F) Sold 1919 =K. M. HARDY; =French IMBRIN in WW II.
4249	PETER MAGEE	1. 5.19	Cochrane. (F) Sold 1919 =LORD ERNLE.
3560	RICHARD BULKELEY	21. 8.17	Cochrane. 1–12 pdr. Mined 12.7.19 in the North Sea while on loan to USN.
3701	RICHARD COLLIVER	26. 2.18*	Lobnitz. 1–12 pdr. Sold 1922 =LAURETTE.
3836	RICHARD JEWELL	6. 8.18	Cochrane. 1–6 pdrAA. Sold 1922 =LORD KNARESBOROUGH; =FAIRWAY in WW II.
3559	ROBERT BARTON	28. 8.17	Cochrane. 1–12 pdr M/S. Sold 1922 =HAYBURN WYKE; =HAYBURN WYKE in WW II.
3557	ROBERT BOOKLESS	23. 7.17	Cochrane. 1–12 pdr M/S. Sold 1921 =GRIZ NEZ; =German M.4005 in WW II.
4468	ROBERT CAHILL	13. 4.21*	Goole SB. (F) Sold 1921 =PIERRE ANDRE; =PIERRE ANDRE/in WW II.
3735	ROBERT DOUBLE	5. 6.18	Goole SB. 1–12 pdr Hydro. Sold 1922, same name; =WOLBOROUGH 1925.
3742	ROBERT DRUMMOND	4. 5.18	Ferguson. 1–12 pdr. Sold 1922, same name; =SALMONBY 1924; lost 23.3.26.
3857	ROBERT FINLAY	23. 5.19*	Goole SB. (F) Sold 1919 =VISCOUNT ALLENBY.
4256	ROBERT MURRAY	30. 6.19	Cochrane. (F) Sold 1923, same name; =NORTHLYN in WW II.
3564	SAMUEL DOWDEN	18. 9.17	Cochrane. 1–12 pdr, 1–3.5 in BT Hydro. Sold 1922 =ROYAL REGIMENT; =SEA MIST in WW II.
3839	SAMUEL JAMESON =ETTRICK 9.20	10.10.18*	Cochrane. 1–12 pdr. Sold 1926 =LOUGHRIGG; =PHYLLISIA in WW II.
4255	SAMUEL MARTIN	28. 6.19	Cochrane. (F) Sold 1920 =FIELD MARSHAL PLUMER.
4254	SIMEON MOON	31. 5.19	Cochrane. (F) Sold 1920 =GENERAL RAWLINSON.
3546	THOMAS ATKINSON	8. 5.17	Cochrane. 1–12 pdr M/S. Sold 1923 =CAVENDISH; =ERITH in WW II.
3558	THOMAS BAILEY	4. 8.17	Cochrane. 1–12 pdr M/S. Sold 1922 =PAMXON.
3702	THOMAS CORNWALL	10. 6.18*	Lobnitz. 1–12 pdr, 1–3.5 in BT. Sunk 29.10.18 in collision off Flamborough Head.
3706	THOMAS CRUIZE	30. 1.19*	Lobnitz. (F) Sold 1919 =CELERINA; lost 11.12.22.
3835	THOMAS JAGO	31. 7.18	Cochrane. 1–4 in Escort. Sold 1922 =ST. VALERY; =LADY ELEANOR in WW II.
3840	THOMAS JARVIS =EXE 9.20	24.10.18*	Cochrane. 1–12 pdr SSV. Sold 1928 =JAN VOLDERS.
3837	THOMAS JOHNS =EDEN 9.20	3. 9.18*	Cochrane. 1–12 pdr. =IMMORTELLE in SAN 1921–34; sold 1945.
4247	THOMAS MALONEY	14. 6.19	Cochrane. (F) Sold 1919 =ST. NEOTS; =ADAM in WW II.
4246	THOMAS MATTHEWS	6.10.19*	Cochrane. (F) Sold 1919 =EARL BEATTY.
3572	THOMAS THRESHER	9. 2.18*	Cochrane. 1–12 pdr M/S. Sold 1922, same name; =SYRIAN in WW II.
3574	THOMAS WHIPPLE	4. 3.18*	Cochrane. 1–12 pdr. Sold 1922 =LORD LASCELLES.
4467	WILLIAM CHATWOOD	24. 3.21*	Goole SB. (F) Sold 1921 =BLANC NEZ.
4466	WILLIAM COURTNEY	2. 2.21*	Goole SB. (F) Sold 1921 =TERNOISE.
3737	WILLIAM DOAK	23. 9.18*	Goole SB. 1–12 pdr Hydro. Sold 1922 to Spain =ARCILA.
3856	WILLIAM FORBES	25. 5.19*	Goole SB. (F) Sold 1919 =SYRIAN.
3796	WILLIAM HONNOR	26. 8.18	Ferguson. 1–12 pdr Escort. Sold 1922 =GRIMURKAMBAN.
3841	WILLIAM INWOOD =BLACKWATER 9.20	30.10.18*	Cochrane. 1–12 pdr. Sold 1946 =SPLEIS.
3831	WILLLIAM JACKSON	29. 3.18*	Cochrane. 1–12 pdr. Sold 1921 =LORD BYNG; =EVELYN ROSE in WW II.
3843	WILLIAM JOHNSON	22.11.18*	Cochrane. 1–12 pdr. Loaned to USN 1919. Sold 1921 =LORD BIRKENHEAD.

Adty No.	Name	Launched	Builder—Armament—Fate
3838	WILLIAM JONES =BOYNE 9.20	8. 9.18*	Cochrane. 1–12 pdr M/S. Sold 1946 =NYPU-BERG.
4233	WILLIAM LEECH =EXCELLENT 2.19	12. 3.19*	Cochrane. Sold 1922 =WILLIAM LEECH =French EXCELLENT in WW II.
3550	WILLIAM RAM	7. 6.17	Cochrane. 1–12 pdr Escort. Sold 1921 =LORD CARSON; =WELBECK in WW II.
3552	WILLIAM RIVERS	9. 6.17	Cochrane. 1–12 pdr M/S. Sold 1921 =MONT CASSEL; =French MONT CASSEL in WW II.

*Denotes delivery date in launch column.

Notes: The smallest of the non-standard ships measured 248 TG with dimensions (pp) of 120½ and a 22 ft beam. WILLIAM WESTENBURGH, the largest of the seven, had particulars identical to the standard ships. JOHN QUILLIAM, delivered 30.6.17, was the first of the standard completions. Contracts for 44 more vessels of this class were cancelled after 11.18:

Cochrane:
- 4273 ALEXANDER MCDOWELL
- 4280 ALEXANDER MURRAY
- 4270 ANDREW MCWILLIAM
- 4279 ANGUS MCDONALD
- 4285 BERNARD FLYNN
- 4266 DAVID MIFFON
- 4288 EDWARD FLINN
- 4277 EDWARD MARR
- 4276 EDWARD MOONEY
- 4290 EZEKIEL JOHNSON
- 4286 FRANCIS FRENCH
- 4257 GEORGE MARTIN
- 4283 JOHN DIXON
- 4262 JOHN MARSHALL
- 4260 JOHN MASON
- 4271 JOHN MCCONNELL
- 4263 JOHN MELEBURY
- 4259 JOHN MINUTE
- 4268 JOHN MONDAY
- 4264 JOHN MORRIS
- 4272 JOHN MOSS
- 4281 JOHN MURPHY
- 4274 JOSEPH MURRAY
- 4258 OWEN MCMANNERS
- 4278 PAT MERRYGAN
- 4289 PETER JONES
- 4282 ROBERT DARBY
- 4287 STEPHEN FOLEY
- 4284 WILLIAM FORD
- 4269 WILLIAM MAINLAND
- 4267 WILLIAM MARSHALL
- 4261 WILLIAM MORRIS
- 4275 WILLIAM MORTON
- 4265 WILLIAM MUCK

Goole SB:
- 4489 JOHN DETHERIDGE
- 4491 JOHN DOWNIE
- 4492 RICHARD DORROWDALE
- 4490 WILLIAM DONALDS

John Lewis:
- 4226 CHARLES LOWRANE
- 4225 JAMES LENHAM
- 4223 JOHN LEMON
- 4227 JOHN LEVER
- 4224 SAMUEL LOVITT
- 4228 THOMAS LAVERICKS

CANADIAN-BUILT NAVAL TRAWLERS

320 tons gross. 130 (pp) ×23½×13½ (dhd) ft. TE 480 ihp=10½ kts. Armament: 1–12 pdr (designed for 2–12 pdr).

Name	Launched	Builder—Fate
FESTUBERT	2. 8.17	Polson Iron Works. Sold 1946; =INVERLEIGH 1947.
MESSINES	6. 6.17	Polson Iron Works. To Canadian Dept of Marine & Fisheries 1920 =Lightship No. 3.
ST. ELOI	2. 8.17	Polson Iron Works. To Canadian Dept of Marine & Fisheries 1920 =Lightship No. 20.
ST. JULIEN	6. 6.17	Polson Iron Works. To Canadian Dept of Marine & Fisheries 1920 =Lightship No. 22.
VIMY	6. 6.17	Polson Iron Works. To Canadian Dept of Marine & Fisheries 1920 =Lightship No. 5.
YPRES	6. 6.17	Polson Iron Works. Sunk 12.4.40, rammed by REVENGE at Halifax.

Notes: These six trawlers and the Armentieres group were ordered 1.17 to be built for patrol work along the Atlantic coast. All twelve were manned by the RCN. Polson's vessels were built of iron, the others of steel. Construction of these vessels and also the TRs and CDs were supervised by the manager of the Canada Steamship Line at Montreal under the general direction of the Naval Dept. All six were in naval hands 13.11.17.

357 tons gross. 130 (pp) × 25 × 13 (dhd) ft. TE 480 ihp = 10½ kts.
Armament: 1–12 pdr.

Name	Launched	Commission	Builder—Fate
ARLEUX	1918	5. 6.18	Canadian Vickers. Sold 1966, same name; sunk 26.8.49 by internal explosion.
ARMENTIERES	1918	17. 6.18	Canadian Vickers. Sold 1946; =A. G. GARRISH 1947.
ARRAS	1918	8. 7.18	Canadian Vickers. BU 12.57.
GIVENCHY	1918	22. 6.18	Canadian Vickers. Sold 22.9.52 and BU in USA.
LOOS	1918	1. 8.18	Kingston SB. BU 1949.
THIEPVAL	1918	24. 7.18	Kingston SB. Wrecked 27.2.30 in Barclay Sound, Vancouver.

Notes: LOOS and THIEPVAL were originally assigned to Canadian Vickers. Names were first reported 24.9.17.

CANADIAN-BUILT CASTLE CLASS TRAWLERS

Built by Port Arthur SB:

Name	Completed	Paid off	Armament—Disposal—Etc.
TR.1	17.10.17	8.19	1–12 pdr M/S. Sold 1920 Captain Munro; to RNZN =WAKAKURA 1925; sold 1947 Tasman SS Co, same name.
TR.2	21.11.17	8.19	M/S. Sold 1920.
TR.3	16. 5.18	8.19	M/S. Sold 1920.
TR.4	24. 5.18	3.19	M/S. Sold 1920; =CARTAGENA 1926.
TR.5	30. 5.18	31. 1.19	M/S. Sold 1919 Brazilian navy =COMMANDANTE LORETTI.
TR.6	27. 5.18	8.19	M/S. Sold 1920.
TR.37	1.11.18	21. 1.19	Loaned to USN as CT.37; sold 1919; =THEIR MERIT 1925; =THEIR MERIT in WW II.
TR.38	20. 8.18	21.12.18	Sold 1919; later =ALCATRAZ.
TR.39	1.11.18	15. 8.19	Loaned to USN as CT.39; sold 1920; =CHANDBALI 1930; =CHANDBALI in RIN WW II.
TR.40	1.11.18	15. 8.19	Loaned to USN as CT.40; sold 1920; =MARIE YETTE 1921; =French navy AD.157 in WW II.
TR.41	5. 5.19	not cmd	Sold 1920 =MARIE SIMONE; =French AD.110 in WW II.
TR.42	5. 5.19	not cmd	Sold 1920 =MARIE GILBERTE; =French AD.158 in WW II.
TR.43	12. 5.19	not cmd	Sold 1920 =MARIE ANNE; =French navy in WW II.
TR.44	12. 5.19	not cmd	Sold 1919 Anglo Newfoundland Development Co =TR.44; =FLORENCIA 1920.

Built by Collingwood SB:

Name	Completed	Paid off	Armament—Disposal—Etc.
TR.7	27. 5.18	31. 1.19	M/S. Sold 1920 Captain Munro; =SANTANDER 1926.
TR.8	26. 6.18	2.19	M/S. Sold 1920.
TR.9	16. 5.18	2.19	M/S. Sold 1920.
TR.10	16. 5.18	8.19	M/S. Sold 1920 Captain Munro.
TR.11	28. 6.18	8.19	Sold 1920 Captain Munro; =SAN SEBASTIAN 1926.
TR.12	25. 8.18	2.19	Sold 1920.

Built by Thor Iron Works, Toronto:

Name	Completed	Paid off	Armament—Disposal—Etc.
TR.13	15. 6.18	8.19	Sold 1920 Captain Munro; =MALAGA 1926.
TR.14	10. 6.18	7.1.19	Sold 1920 Captain Munro; =PASAGES 1926.

Built by Polson Iron Works:

Name	Completed	Paid off	Armament—Disposal—Etc.
TR.15	21. 6.18	31. 1.19	Sold 1920 =JACQUELINE.
TR.16	22. 6.18	14. 1.19	Sold 1920.
TR.17	28. 8.18	21. 1.19	Sold 1920 =JEANNE.
TR.18	1. 8.18	31. 1.19	Sold 1920 Captain Munro; later =MARIE LOUISE.

Begun by Kingston SB; transferred to Collingwood SB:

Name	Completed	Paid off	Armament—Disposal—Etc.
TR.19	25. 8.18	7. 1.19	Sold 1920; =ALMERIA 1926; =GOOLGWAI in WW II.
TR.20	31. 8.18	14. 1.19	Sold 1920; =SEVILLE 1926; =DURRAWEEN in WW II.

Built by Canadian Vickers, Montreal:

TR.21	31. 5.18	19.12.18	Sold 1920; later =SACIP.
TR.22	21. 5.18	19.12.18	Sold 1920.
TR.23	1. 8.18	31. 1.19	Sold 1920; =FONTENAY 1926.
TR.24	16.11.17	10. 1.19	Sold 1920 =GOSSE; =French AD.278 in WW II.
TR.25	1. 6.18	14. 1.19	Sold 1920 =YVONNE CLAUDE.
TR.26	22. 5.18	19.12.18	Sold 1920.
TR.27	17. 5.18	22. 1.19	Sold 1920 =GALOPIN; =French AD.164 in WW II.
TR.28	30. 5.18	31. 1.19	Sold 1920; =WELLVALE 1926.
TR.29	30. 5.18	19.12.18	Sold 1920 =FERNANDO DE C.
TR.30	28. 5.18	22. 1.19	Sold 1920 =BLANCA DE C.
TR.31	20. 5.18	10. 1.19	Sold 1920 =JOSE IGNACIO DE C.

Built by Government Shipyard, Sorel:

TR.32	16. 5.18	22. 1.19	Sold 1920; =AUTHORPE 1926.
TR.33	4. 6.18	22. 1.19	Sold 1920; =WINDROOS 1927.
TR.34	28. 7.18	14. 1.19	Sold 1919 =VALENTIA; =French ETOILE DU NORD AD.1 in WW II.
TR.51	20.11.18	23. 7.19	Loaned to USN as CT.51; sold 1919 =MARIE CAROLINE.
TR.52	11.18	23. 7.19	Sold 1919 =MARIE MAD; =French AD.148 in WW II.
TR.53	11.18	9.19	Sold 1920 Captain Munro; later =MARIE THERESE II; =French AD.149 in WW II.

Built by Davie SB & R, Levis:

TR.35	5. 6.18	31. 1.19	Sold 1920.
TR.36	5. 6.18	7. 1.19	Sold 1920; =FERROL 1926.
TR.45	12. 5.19	not cmd	Sold 1919 Gulf of St. Lawrence Shipping & Trading Co; later to Dept of Transport =LABRADOR, then =MARDEP and later =BERNIER.
TR.46	12. 5.19	4.10.19	Sold 1920; =ALGOA BAY 1926; =ALGOA BAY in WW II.
TR.47	12. 5.19	14.10.19	Sold 1919 =HERON.
TR.48	12. 5.19	25. 9.19	Sold 1919 =DRAGON VERT; =MIQUELON in WW II.
TR.49	12. 5.19	25. 9.19	Sold 1919 =JOSELLE.
TR.50	12. 5.19	not cmd	Sold 1920 =COLONEL ROCKWELL.

Built by Kingston SB:

TR.54	30. 9.18	8.19	Sold 1920; =TABLE BAY 1925.
TR.55	8.11.18	25. 7.19	Loaned to USN as CT.55; sold 1920 =MARIE JACQUELINE.
TR.56	22.11.18	15. 8.19	Loaned to USN as CT.56; sold 1920; =ROMANITA 1921.
TR.57	10.19	not cmd	Sold 1920 =COLONEL ROOSEVELT; =TEXAS in WW II.

Built by Tidewater SB, Trois Rivieres:

TR.58	21.11.18	23. 7.19	Loaned to USN as CT.58; wrecked 20.11.20 in Barra Sound.
TR.59	21.11.18	15. 8.19	Loaned to USN as CT.59; sold 1920 =PILOTE GIRONDE I.
TR.60	25.11.18	15. 8.19	Loaned to USN as CT.60; sold 1919 =DAVID HAIGH; =DAVID HAIGH in SAN WW II.

Notes: 36 vessels were ordered 1.17 as Admiralty trawlers of the same design as the Castle class. An additional 24 trawlers were ordered 7.17. Upon completion they were manned by the RCN or in the case of nine vessels, by the USN who used them for mine clearance work post-war. TR.52 was also allocated for USN use but not taken over. By 1.1.18 TR.1 and 2 were at Halifax, TR.3, 4, 7–9, 13, 24–28, 32, 33 were completed but still on the St. Lawrence awaiting re-opening of navigation in the spring, all others were completing, fitting-out or still on the stocks. The dates given in the listing indicate when the completed vessel was first in naval hands and the 1.1.18 status shows that most of them were still builder's responsibility then. The TR.37–60 group was reported 28.1.18 designated as such and with the builders indicated. Lloyds gives different builders for a few vessels. Vessels of this class whose original name is not known include BONTHORPE, SOMERSBY (of TR.8–10, 12 group); Marie Evelynne (either TR.22 or 26); also 6 vessels sold to the Mexican navy 1920 as COBARRIBAS, GUAYMAS, MAZATLAN, SALINAS, TAMPICO and VERA CRUZ.

For the vessels sold to Captain Munro, see the note following the "CD" drifters.

INDIAN TRAWLERS

German mine-laying activity in the Colombo area had been successfully dealt with by two harbour tugs used as minesweepers until 1917, when risking concern over an increased number of mine reports led local authorities to ask for additional M/S vessels. The heavy world-wide demand for trawlers had caused the Italians to purchase vessels in Japan because they were not available more closely at hand. Five trawlers were reported to have been purchased by the Italians 5.3.17, and following special negotiations, they agreed to lend three of these for a period of one month to sweep the Colombo minefields provided that they would be returned by 20.5.17 at the very latest. The trio loaned 8.3.17 were ONO MARU No. 11 221/12, WADA MARU 255/12 and KORYO MARU No. 5 232/11. They were returned 4.17 to become the Italian G.45, G.46 and G.47 respectively.

PURCHASED TRAWLERS (ALL M/S)

Name	TG/Yr	Other names
KUMARIHAMI	259/13	(ex-*Minato Maru No. 3*) =KUMARIHAMI 1920.
LAKSHMI	249/13	(ex-*Daitoku Maru*) =LILLA 1920.
LANKDYS	255/11	(ex-*Nishiso Maru No. 1*) =LANKA 1920.
PARVATI	208/12	(ex-*Naniwa Maru*) =PARVATI 1920.
RANMENIKA	224/13	(ex-*Nishiso Maru No. 2*).
SARASVATI II	204/11	(ex-*Chokai Maru*) =SARASVATI 1920.

Notes: LANKDYS was also known as LANKA in some official reports. Three were purchased 10.3.17 and another three 14.3.17. These vessels, all of Japanese origin, replaced the vessels which were on temporary loan and were all disposed of in 1920. Some went to Ceylon government service.

*WAR CONSTRUCTION TRAWLERS

265 tons gross. 125 (pp) ×33½×12 ft. TE 480 ihp=10¼ kts.
588 tons (deep). Armament: 1–12 pdr (in BOMBAY, CALCUTTA, KIDDERPORE and SEALDAH only).

Name	Launched	Builder—Fate
BOMBAY	21. 9.19	Bombay DY. Listed to 4.32.
CALCUTTA	1919	Burn & Co, Howrah, Calcutta. Listed to 4.32.
COLOMBO	1919	Burn & Co. Listed to 4.32.
JUBBULPORE		Bombay DY. Probably cancelled.
KENNERY	1919	Bombay DY. Listed to 4.32.
KIDDERPORE	1919	Bombay DY. Listed to 4.32.
MADRAS	1919	Burn & Co. =TANJORE 1.42; lost by stranding 6.42.
SALSETTE	1919	Bombay DY. =Light vessel by 1928.
SEALDAH	1919	Bombay DY. Listed to 4.32.

Notes: In 1917 arrangements were made to build nine "Castle" type trawlers in India under the supervision of the Munitions Board. They were of composite construction (teak planking over steel frames), three to be built by Burn & Co at Calcutta and six by Bombay Dockyard. In a report 12.2.19 construction was still in progress and six were to complete as unarmed M/S and three as ordinary fishing vessels; however, four were later listed with a gun. This programme originated when the need for M/S existed. At first 20 wooden drifters had been suggested in 8.17, but since the engines would have had to have been shipped from the UK, it was not carried out. By early 1919 there were no mines left in the area to be swept so the purpose for their completion was no longer valid.

MADRAS seems to have been the only vessel to have been commissioned.

PRIZE TRAWLERS

Adty No.	Name	TG/Yr	Builder—Former name—Fate
1937	CABALSIN	218/04	Tecklenborg, Geestemunde. (ex-Burhave) 1–6 pdr. Captured 30.9.15 by ARETHUSA; added 10.15– sold 16.3.20; =STAR OF THE ORIENT 1921.
1932	CACHOSIN	218/12	Seebeck, Geestemunde. (ex-Doktor Krugler) 1–12 pdr. Captured 7.10.15 by UNDAUNTED; added 10.15– sold 16.3.20 =CAIRNRIGH.
1949	CAERSIN	133/92	Wencke, Bremerhaven. (ex-Dora) 1–6 pdrAA. Captured 30.9.15 by PENELOPE; added 10.15– sold 17.3.20 =CAERSIN.
1917	CALLSIN	136/96	Tecklenborg, Geestemunde. (ex-Mond) 1–6 pdrAA, 1–3 pdr. Captured 7.8.15 by CONQUEST; added 10.15– sold 7.4.21 =CALLSIN.
1935	CALUMSIN	224/02	Seebeck, Geestemunde. (ex-Wurzburg) 1–12 pdr. Captured 7.10.15 by British warship; added 10.15– sold 13.12.21; =BRIDGE OF EARN 1922.
1946	CAMBRISIN	158/91	Wencke, Bremerhaven. (ex-Orion) 1–6 pdrAA M/S. Captured 30.9.15 by CLEOPATRA; added 10.15– sold 17.3.20 =CAMBRISIN.
856	CAMPSIN	133/94	Tecklenborg, Geestemunde. (ex-Adjudant) 1–6 pdrAA M/S. Captured 30.9.15 by AURORA; added 10.15– sold 18.2.20 =CAMPSIN.
1936	CANOSSIN	153/94	Seebeck, Geestemunde. (ex-Paul) 1–6 pdr. Captured 7.10.15 by CLEOPATRA; added 10.15– sold 16.3.20 =CANOSSIN.
1947	CARBOSIN	158/96	Bremer Vulcan, Vegesack. (ex-Darmstadt) 1–6 pdrAA M/S. Captured 30.9.15 by CLEOPATRA; added 10.15– sold 5.10.20 =KEITH HALL; lost 27.11.21.
857	CENSIN	145/94	Seebeck, Geestemunde. (ex-Burgermeister Smidt) 1–6 pdrAA M/S. Captured 30.9.15 by CONQUEST; added 10.15– sold 11.5.20 =KEELBY.
1931	CHARLSIN	241/07	Eiderwerft, Tonning. (ex-Esteburg) Captured 5.9.15 by S/M E.4; added 9.15– sunk 30.9.17 by UC.74 eight miles N of Marseh Matruh.
1941	CHECKSIN	140/95	Bremer Vulkan, Vegesack. (ex-Wulsdorf) 1–6 pdrAA. Captured 7.10.15 by British warship; added 10.15– sold 11.5.20; =GEORGE TURNER 1921.
812	CHIRSIN	218/12	Unterweser, Lehe. (ex-Else Kunkel) 1–6 pdrAA M/S. Detained 4.8.14 at Aberdeen; added 12.14– sold 16.3.20; =STAR OF ENGLAND 1922.
1943	CHURCHSIN	142/00	Smiths Dock. (ex-St. Georg; ex-Northmoor) 1–6 pdr M/S. Captured 30.9.15 by CONQUEST; added 10.15– sold 11.5.20 =BANKS O'DEE.
1942	CLAROSIN	159/97	Bremer Vulkan, Vegesack. (ex-President Rose; ex-Dueren) 1–6 pdr. Captured 7.10.15 by CONQUEST; added 10.15– sold 18.2.20 =BLACKHALL.
1934	CLASSIN	182/89	Wencke, Bremerhaven. (ex-Sophie) 1–3 pdr M/S. Captured 30.9.15 by ARETHUSA; added 10.15– sold 17.3.20 =M. KANGO.
858	CLEARSIN	155/91	Wencke, Bremerhaven. (ex-Resie) 1–6 pdrAA M/S, mark vessel. Captured 7.10.15 by AURORA; added 10.15– sold 18.2.20 =CLEARSIN.
813	CLONSIN	202/11	Seebeck, Geestemunde. (ex-Dr. Robitzsch) 1–6 pdrAA M/S. Detained 4.8.14 at Aberdeen; added 12.14– sold 3.20 =BIRKHALL.
859	COALSIN	130/92	Tecklenborg, Geestemunde. (ex-Toni) 1–6 pdrAA M/S mark vessel. Captured 7.10.15 by MENTOR; added 10.15– sold 5.10.20; =LACEBY 1922.
860	COOKSIN	149/96	Seebeck, Geestemunde. (ex-Herbert) 1–6 pdrAA M/S mark vessel. Captured 7.10.15 by British warship; added 10.15– sold 17.3.20 =LOWHAR.

Adty No.	Name		Builder—Former name—Fate
1933	COOMASIN =CINCERIA 9.19 =COOMASIN 12.19	170/97	Neptun, Rostock. (ex-Heppens) 1–6 pdr. Captured 7.10.15 by ARETHUSA; added 10.15– sold 11.5.20; =CONOVIUM 1921.
1940	CORINSIN	159/96	Bremer Vulkan, Vegesack. (ex-Jutlandia; ex-Stuttgart) 1–6 pdr. Captured 30.9.15 by ARETHUSA; added 10.15– sold 18.2.20 =CORINSIN.
	CORTASIN	156/91	Mackie & Thomson. (ex-Sonntag; ex-Rover) Captured 7.10.15 by British warship; fitting for service 11.15– released 17.12.15 =SKERNE; later taken over as FT (qv).
1945	CRADOSIN	133/95	Tecklenborg, Geestemunde. (ex-Elma) 1–12 pdr. Captured 7.10.15 by ARETHUSA; added 10.15– sold 5.10.20; =JEANNIE ANNETTE 1925.
861	CRAIGSIN	141/95	Bremer Vulkan, Vegesack. (ex-Blumenthal) 1–6 pdrAA M/S. Captured 7.10.15 by British warship; added 10.15– sold 5.10.20; =FLORIC 1921.
1881	CROMSIN	138/95	Cook, W & G. (ex-Ost; ex-Alderney) 1–6 pdrAA M/S. Captured 24.6.15 by S/M S.1; added 6.15– sold 11.5.20 =ARO.
1950	CROWNSIN	137/95	Tecklenborg, Geestemunde. (ex-Varel) Captured 7.10.15 by ARETHUSA; added 10.15– mined 4.5.16 off Malta.
1944	CUDWOSIN	112/07	Neptun, Rostock. (ex-West) 1–6 pdr. Captured 7.10.15 by MANLY; added 10.15– sold 16.3.20 =CUDWOSIN; =KARL GRAMMERSDORF I 1921.
1948	CULBASIN	133/93	Tecklenborg, Geestemunde. (ex-Nereus) 1–6 pdrAA. Captured 7.10.15 by British warship; added 10.15– sold 5.10.20; =LEITH HALL 1921.

Notes: They were former German fishing vessels, 27 of which were captured at sea, mostly during cruiser and destroyer sweeps in the North Sea. It is uncertain which warship took possession of some of them due to the large number of high speed ships that took part in the operations. Many other trawlers were sunk because they were short of coal. Most of them were sent to Grimsby and later assigned to Mediterranean service with the Patrol. All vessels originally had "SIT" suffixes until 8.11.15 when the suffixes became "SIN". What inspired the built-up names is still undetermined. They were referred to as "PTs" (prize trawlers) in the Red Lists.

AXE CLASS EX-RUSSIAN TRAWLERS

520 tons. 138¾ (oa), 130 (pp) ×23½ ×12 ft. TE 490 ihp=10¼ kts.
296 tons gross.

Adty No.	Name	Launched	Builder—Former names—Fate
4333	BATTLEAXE =DEE 9.20	19. 6.16	Smiths Dock. (ex-T.16) 1–75 mm. Sold 1946 =SAFIR.
4331	GOLDAXE =GARRY 9.20	1. 6.16	Smiths Dock. (ex-T.13) 1–75 mm M/S. Sold 1946 and BU.
4334	ICEAXE =KENNET 9.20	17. 7.16	Smiths Dock. (ex-T.17) 1–75 mm. Sold 1946 and BU.
4337	IRONAXE	31. 8.16	Smiths Dock. (ex-T.22) 1–12 pdr. To French navy 12.18 =COMMANDANT VERGOIGNAN; =IRONAXE 1922; =IRONAXE in WW II.
4332	STONEAXE =LIFFEY 9.20	1. 6.16	Smiths Dock. (ex-T.14) 1–75 mm M/S. Sold 1947.
4336	WOODAXE	3. 8.16	Smiths Dock. (ex-T.20) 1–75 mm. To French navy 12.18.

540 tons. 135¼ (pp) ×23½ ×12½ ft. TE 500 ihp=11 kts.
304 tons gross.

Adty No.			
4335	POLEAXE	8.17	Cochrane. (ex-T.19ii) 1–12 pdr M/S. Sold 22.7.21 =DORBIE.

Adty No.	Name	TG/Yr	Builder—Former names—Fate
4343	BONEAXE	/	(ex-T) Added 11.9.18– sold 1920.
4339	BRONZEAXE	/	(ex-T) Added 11.9.18– sold 1920.
4346	COALAXE	263/10	Hall Russell. (ex-T.36; ex-Seis) Sold 11.5.20; =CALICUT 1921.
4341	DREADAXE	/	(ex-T) Added 11.9.18– sold 18.5.20.

Adty. No.	Name	TG/Yr.	Builder—Former names—Fate
4345	FIRMAXE	270/08	Hall Russell. (*ex-T.34; ex-Cuatro*) Sold 11.5.20; =CANNANORE 1921.
4347	FROSTAXE	191/99	Edwards, North Shields. (*ex-T.41; ex-Atlas*) Sunk 30.4.19 in collision with SS EPIROS off Newhaven.
4340	GREATAXE	187/99	Aitken & Scott, Glasgow. (*ex-T.6; ex-Wostock; ex-Alcyon; ex-Windsor Castle*) Sold 11.5.20 =GREATAXE; =ROSLIN 1925.
4338	SILVERAXE	272/08	Hall Russell. (*ex-T.33; ex-Tres*) 1–12 pdr M/S. Sold 11.5.20 =SILVERAXE; =FINMARK 1925.
4342	STEAMAXE	332/08	Goole SB. (*ex-T.12; ex-Zapad; ex-Sapad; ex-River Dart*) Wrecked 1.11.19 near Inchkeith, raised 1921 and BU.
4344	SUREAXE	195/07	Hall Russell. (*ex-T.31; ex-Uno*) Sold 11.5.20; =SUREAXE; =SUREAXE in WW II.

Notes: All 17 trawlers were reported seized 3.8.18 in the White Sea according to British accounts, but it seems that eight of them were handed over by "White" Russian authority and T.20 (WOODAXE) was captured 5.8.18 by the French AMIRAL AUBE. IRONAXE and WOODAXE perhaps had French crews from 8.18, although listed with RN vessels.

Six vessels came from the T.13–24 group built during 1916, another was built 1917 (as a replacement for T.19 i, which had been wrecked 3.10.16 before acceptance by the Russians) and 10 older vessels were part of a number purchased into the Russian service. Vessels of the T.30–40 series were formerly owned by the Argentines. The war-built vessels from Smiths Dock had prominent forecastles, bows specially strengthened for navigation in ice with the forefront sharply cut-away below the waterline. BONEAXE, BRONZEAXE and DREADAXE whose former identity has not been determined, could have been three of the vessels also claimed to have been later in Russian hands, but their movements in RN lists indicate that the British had control of them for a considerable length of time.

TOP: The destroyer SEABEAR. 'S' class (note 14in TT) /Imperial War Museum
CENTRE: The destroyer WITHERINGTON. Modified 'W' class
/National Maritime Museum
ABOVE: The torpedo boat No 042 /National Maritime Museum

TOP: The torpedo boat No 3   /*National Maritime Museum*
CENTRE: The submarine C.5   /*National Maritime Museum*
ABOVE: The submarine E.8   /*National Maritime Museum*

TOP: The submarine S.1 on trials /*Imperial War Museum*
CENTRE: The submarine V.3 /*Imperial War Museum*
ABOVE: The submarine G.10 /*National Maritime Museum*

TOP: The submarine H.32 /*Kestins*
CENTRE: The submarine K.22, with bulbous bows /*Vicary*
ABOVE: The submarine M.2—post-war /*National Maritime Museum*

TOP: The submarine L.54 'L.50' class   /*Kestins*/
CENTRE: The submarine R.10   /*Kestins*/
ABOVE: The 1st class gunboat BRAMBLE.   'Bramble' class   /*Imperial War Museum*/

TOP: The sloop VESTAL. 'Condor' class—as gunnery tender
/*National Maritime Museum*/
CENTRE: The sloop PRIMULA. 'Arabis' type /*Imperial War Museum*/
ABOVE: The convoy sloop COREOPSIS. 'Anchusa' type—guns concealed
/*Imperial War Museum*/

TOP: The sloop BEND OR. '24' class   /*National Maritime Museum*
CENTRE: The patrol boat P.40. 'P' class   /*Kestins*
ABOVE: The patrol gunboat KILKEEL. 'Kil' class   /*National Maritime Museum*

TOP: The river monitor **HUMBER**.   'Humber' class   /*Ministry of Defence*
CENTRE: The coastal monitor M.19.   'M' class   /*Imperial War Museum*
ABOVE: The river gunboat **MANTIS**.   'Insect' class   /*Imperial War Museum*

TOP: The monitor **ABERCROMBIE**. 'Abercrombie' class   /*Imperial War Museum*
CENTRE: The monitor **PRINCE RUPERT**. 'Lord Clive' class   /*Imperial War Museum*
ABOVE: The monitor **MARSHAL NEY**. 'Marshal Ney' class   /*Imperial War Museum*

TOP: The monitor **TERROR**.　'Erebus' class　　/*Imperial War Museum*
CENTRE: The gunboat **KITE**.　'Ant' class　　/*National Maritime Museum*
ABOVE: The torpedo gunboat **HALCYON**.　'Dryad' class

TOP: DUCHESS OF ROTHESAY. Hired paddle minesweeper /*Imperial War Museum*
CENTRE: Paddle minesweeper ERIDGE. 'Ascot' class /*National Maritime Museum*
ABOVE: Minesweeper CROOME. Early 'Hunt' class /*National Maritime Museum*

TOP: The minesweeper CRAIGIE. Later 'Hunt' class /*National Maritime Museum*
CENTRE: The minelayer NAIAD. Ex-'Apollo' class cruiser
ABOVE: WAHINE. Hired minelayer /*Imperial War Museum*

TOP: SHACKLETON. Hired trawler minelayer   /*Imperial War Museum*
CENTRE: COLUMBELLA.   Hired armed merchant cruiser   /*Imperial War Museum*
ABOVE: AVENGER.   Hired armed merchant cruiser   /*Vicary*

TOP: CORONADO. Hired escort ship /*Imperial War Museum*
CENTRE: ROWAN. Hired armed boarding steamer /*Imperial War Museum*
ABOVE: The coastguard vessel WATCHFUL /*Imperial War Museum*

TOP: GOODWIN (as UNDERWING).   Q ship   /*Imperial War Museum*
CENTRE: PATRICIAN as dummy INVINCIBLE   /*Imperial War Museum*
ABOVE: The motor launch ML.123   /*Imperial War Museum*

TOP: The coastal motor boat CMB.95E.   55 foot class   /*National Maritime Museum*
CENTRE: ADVENTURESS.   Hired yacht   /*National Maritime Museum*
ABOVE: NILLA.   Hired patrol vessel   /*Imperial War Museum*

HIRED TRAWLERS AND DRIFTERS
PORT IDENTIFICATION LETTERS

A	Aberdeen	GW	Glasgow	PD	Peterhead
AH	Arbroath	GY	Grimsby	PE	Poole
AR	Ayr	H	Hull	PH	Plymouth
BCK	Buckie	HL	West Hartlepool	PN	Preston
BE	Barnstaple	INS	Inverness	PW	Padstow
BF	Banff	KY	Kirkcaldy	RE	Reykjavik
BK	Berwick	LH	Leith	SA	Swansea
BL	Bristol	LK	Lerwick	SD	Sunderland
BM	Brixham	LL	Liverpool	SH	Scarborough
BN	Boston	LO	London	SM	Shoreham
CE	Coleraine	LT	Lowestoft	SN	North Shields
CF	Cardiff	LY	Londonderry	SS	St Ives
D	Dublin	M	Milford Haven	SSS	South Shields
DE	Dundee	ME	Montrose	SY	Stornoway
FD	Fleetwood	ML	Methil	WK	Wick
FR	Fraserburgh	O	Ostend	WY	Whitby
GN	Granton	P	Portsmouth	YH	Yarmouth

HIRED TRAWLERS

Adty No.	Port No.	Name	TG/Yr	Armament, Fate, etc.	Service
113	A.357	A. SPENCE MACDONALD	195/11	1–6 pdrAA M/S	8.14–1919
151	M.17	ABELARD	187/09	1–6 pdr M/S Wrecked 24.12.16 off Plymouth.	8.14–12.16
639	GY.129	ABERDEEN	163/96	1–6 pdr	10.14–1919
1598	A.391	ABERGELDIE	200/15	1–6 pdr	7.15–1919
65	A.183	ABOYNE	233/08	1–6 pdrAA M/S =LIBRA in WW II.	8.14–1919
704	GY.112	ABRONIA	242/06	1–12 pdr M/S =in WW II.	11.14–1919
293	GY.182	ACHILLES =ACHILLES II 12.15	225/06	1–6 pdr M/S Mined 26.6.18 off Shipwash LV.	8.14–6.18
2768	PD.361	ACTIVE =ACTIVE IV 8.15	185/99	1–6 pdrAA	6.15–11.18
820	GY.1185	ADRIAN	199/00	1–6 pdrAA M/S Sunk in collision 13.3.18 off Harwich.	12.14–3.18
2771	FD.154	ADVENTURE II	184/06	1–6 pdrAA M/S	6.15–1919
19	GY.187	AGAMEMNON =AGAMEMNON II 2.15	225/07	M/S Mined 15.7.15 off the Shipwash.	8.14–7.15
1635	H.2	AGATE	248/14	1–6 pdr M/S Mined 14.3.18 off R. Sovereign LV.	5.15–3.18
803	GY.107	AGATHA II	137/96	1–3 pdr M/S	11.14–1920
697	GY.263	AGILE	246/07	M/S Mined 27.4.17 off Harwich.	12.14–4.17
105	SN.187	AGNES H. HASTIE	210/12	1–6 pdr M/S	8.14–1919
3041	A.743	AGNES H. WETHERLY	229/17	1–6 pdrAA M/S =in WW II.	5-17–1919
	A.215	AGNES NUTTEN	183/15	BDV =in WW II.	6.15–1920
125	FD.32	AGNES WICKFIELD	219/09	(ex-*Solva*) 1–6 pdr M/S =in WW II.	8.14–1919
	FD.133	AKRANES	184/99	BDV	6.15–1919
728	GY.477	ALASKA	135/98	1–6 pdr M/S	12.14–1919
919	PH.17	ALBATROSS =ALBATROSS II 2.15	220/06	1–6 pdr M/S	11.14–1919
772	H.277	ALBATROSS =ALBATROSS III 5.15	151/95	1–12 pdr M/S	12.14–9.18
768	GY.588	ALBERIA	286/10	1–12 pdr M/S =ALBERIC in WW II.	12.14–1919

Adty No.	Port No.	Name	TG/Yr	Armament, Fate, etc.	Service
7	GY.212	ALBERTA	209/07	M/S Mined 14.4.16 off Grimsby.	8.14–4.16
139	M.219	ALBION =ALBION II 2.15	240/07	M/S Mined 13.1.16 off St Catherine's Point.	8.14–1.16
1457	SN.56	ALEX HASTIE	206/14	1–6 pdr M/S =in WW II.	4.15–1919
316	SN.81	ALEXANDRA	182/04	1–6 pdr M/S	8.14–1919
1977	FD.192	ALIDA	270/15	1–6 pdr =in WW II.	12.15–1919
	A.356	ALLAN RAMSAY	210/11	1–3 pdr BDV	6.15–1919
1131	LO.24	ALPHA	274/00	1–12 pdr M/S	3.15–1920
524	BN.73	ALSATIAN =ALSATIAN MINOR 12.14	191/00	1–6 pdr =FT ALSATIAN.	12.14–10.16
922	PH.8	AMADAVAT	171/99	1–6 pdr =FT; Mined 12.12.17.	11.14–11.15
38	GY.397	AMEER	216/08	1–6 pdr M/S Mined 18.3.16 off Felixstowe.	8.14–3.16
1214	H.401	AMETHYST =AMETHYST II 2.15	172/98	1–3 pdr M/S =FT AMETHYST.	1.15–10.15
1982	GY.789	AMPLIFY	342/16	1–6 pdr M/S Wrecked 17.1.17 at Skeirascape, Castlebay.	2.16–1.17
59	GY.949	AMPULLA	248/13	1–6 pdrAA M/S =in WW II.	9.14–1919
2665	SA.8	AMROTH CASTLE	255/13	1–12 pdr, 1–6 pdr M/S =in WW II.	5.15–1919
334	FD.39	AMY	223/05	M/S Mined 11.4.17 off Le Havre.	8.14–4.17
1180	H.466	ANDREW MARVEL	285/12	1–12 pdr M/S	2.15–1919
1629	GY.19	ANGELUS	304/14	1–12 pdr M/S Mined 28.2.16 off Dover.	5.15–2.16
526	BN.92	ANGERTON	186/01	1–6 pdr M/S	11.14–1919
1367	M.225	ANGLE	222/08	1–12 pdr M/S	4.15–1919
3059	FD.299	ANIDA	270/17	1–12 pdr Hydro	9.17–1919
1347	A.365	ANN FORD MELVILLE	212/11	1–6 pdr M/S =SHIELBURN in WW II.	4.15–1919
2985	A.621	ANN LEWIS	216/16	1–6 pdr AA M/S =JEAN EDMONDS in WW II.	12.16–1919
1596	A.254	ANN MELVILLE	201/09	1–6 pdr M/S =in WW II.	6.15–1919
1593	PN.61	ANNIE MELLING	221/06	1–6 pdr M/S	4.15–12.18
1090	GY.47	ANSON =ANSON II 3.17	211/05	1–6 pdrAA M/S =in WW II.	2.15–1920
1380	H.1006	ANTHONY HOPE	288/13	1–3 pdr Mined 16.11.16 off Le Havre.	4.15–11.16
1158	GN.29	ANWOTH	211/15	1–6 pdrAA M/S Hydro	2.15–1919
3305	H.487	ANZAC =ANZAC II 3.17	317/16	1–6 pdr, 1–7.5 in BT M/S	8.16–1919
143	M.226	APLEY	222/08	1–3 pdr M/S Mined 6.12.17 off Worthing.	8.14–12.17
1843	H.356	AQUAMARINE	333/11	1–6 pdr, 1–7.5 in BT M/S	8.15–1919
	GY.76	AQUARIUS	187/05	=FT.	6.15–8.15
	A.209	ARABIAN	180/99	1–3 pdr M/S; BDV	6.15–1919
514	GY.355	ARACARI	245/08	1–12 pdr, 1–6 pdrAA M/S =in WW II.	9.14–1919
1470	SN.169	ARCTIC PRINCE	194/15	1–12 pdr M/S =CLIFTON in WW II.	4.15–1919
1798	M.222	ARDENT =ARDENT II 3.17	228/08	1–6 pdr M/S	6.15–1919
134	M.223	ARFON	227/08	1–6 pdrAA M/S Mined 30.4.17 off St. Alban's Head.	8.14–4.17
1540	SA.48	ARGON =ARGON II 5.17	226/07	1–6 pdrAA M/S	6.15–1919

Adty No.	Port No.	Name	TG/Yr	Armament, Fate, etc.	Service
349	GY.173	ARIADNE =ARIADNE II 2.15	225/06	1–6 pdrAA M/S	8.14–11.18
1404	GY.584	ARIAN	221/10	M/S	3.15–1919
616	H.843	ARIEL =ARIEL II 2.15	174/05	1–6 pdrAA M/S	9.14–1919
28	GY.131	ARIES =ARIES II 2.15	250/06	1–12 pdrAA M/S =SORANUS in WW II.	9.14–1919
591	FD.44	ARLEY	304/14	1–12 pdr, 1–6 pdr, 1–7.5 in BT M/S =in WW II.	10.14–1919
1748	H.319	ARMAGEDDON	323/15	1–6 pdr M/S =DHOON in WW II.	9.15–1919
	CF.12	ASAMA	284/14	Q ship Sunk 16.7.17 by S/M 160 miles SW of Fastnet.	1.17–7.17
191	FD.1	ASHLYN	304/14	1–6 pdr M/S =BERNADETTE in WW II.	11.14–1919
640	GY.123	ASHTON	144/96	1–3 pdr	10.14–9.18
652	H.829	ASIA	309/05	1–3 pdr M/S Mined 12.9.17 off Bressay.	10.14–9.17
1996	GY.793	ASPASIA	342/16	1–12 pdr M/S	4.16–1919
343	GY.648	ATHELSTAN	202/11	1–6 pdrAA M/S =in WW II.	8.14–1919
648	H.441	AUCKLAND	155/99	1–6 pdr M/S	10.14–1919
	GY.117	AUCUBA	211/06	1–3 pdr BDV	12.14–1919
422	H.755	AUK =ANTIC 4.18	168/03	1–13 pdr, 1–6 pdr M/S =Q ship 3.17; 1–12 pdr, 1–7.5 in BT (BEN NEVIS, CLAYMORE, GIRDLER, GLEN AFRIC, HOPE, LORNE, ST GOTHARD, SPIKA)	11.14–11.18
	A.482	AUK	183/01	1–3 pdr BDV	6.15–1919
3066	FD.300	AUREA	270/17	1–12 pdr, 1–3.5 in BT Hydro	9.17–1920
345	GY.172	AURORA =AURORA II 2.15	225/06	1–6 pdrAA M/S	8.14–1919
	H.1328	AUSTRALIA =BENDIGO 4.18	238/82	1–6 pdrAA BDV	8.16–1919
705	GY.340	AVON =AVON II 7.16	250/07	1–12 pdr M/S =in WW II.	12.14–1919
963	BL.4	AVONMOUTH	139/90	1–3 pdr =FT.	1.15–4.15
1228	H.432	BALFOUR	285/12	1–3 pdr M/S Sunk 13.5.18 in collision with the ROYAL SOVEREIGN LV.	2.15–5.18
350	A.113	BALMEDIE	205/06	M/S Sunk 27.4.15 in collision in the Dardanelles.	8.14–4.15
3043	GY.1001	BALMORAL II	222/16	1–6 pdrAA M/S =AVALANCHE in WW II.	6.17–1919
	A.510	BALMORAL CASTLE	145/90	BDV	6.15–1919
967	GY.186	BALTIC	154/88	1–3 pdr	1.15–6.15
544	H.938	BARBADOS =BABS 4.18	183/07	1–6 pdr AA M/S	10.14–1919
	GY.71	BARBADOS	211/05	BDV =in WW II.	12.14–1919
1862	GY.78	BARLE	283/14	1–6 pdrAA, 1–3.5 in BT M/S	9.15–1919
717	GY.125	BARNSLEY	144/96	M/S =Mercantile loss 13.2.17.	10.14–5.15
513	LH.296	BASS ROCK	169/07	M/S	9.14–1919
309	H.372	BASSANIO	270/04	1–12 pdr M/S	8.14–1919
621	H.922	BEATRICE	173/06	1–12 pdr	9.14–1919
362	M.212	BEATRICE =BEATRICE II 12.14	239/07	1–3 pdr M/S =BERGEN in WW II.	8.14–1919
353	GN.80	BEDOUIN	188/02	M/S Mined 13.2.15 off Tory Island.	8.14–2.15
	GY.779	BEECHWOLD	129/95	=Mercantile loss 23.9.16.	8.14–9.14

Adty No.	Port No.	Name	TG/Yr	Armament, Fate, etc.	Service
923	FD.233	BEGA	318/14	1-12 pdr Sunk 18.6.17 by S/M 40 miles N of Muckle Flugga.	11.14-6.17
1985	RE.161	BELGAUM	337/16	1-6 pdrAA M/S	3.16-1919
5 168	GY.335	BELLEROPHON =BELLEROPHON II 2.15	184/07	1-12 pdr M/S	8.14-1919
23	GY.336	BELLONA =BELLONA III 5.15	184/07	1-6 pdr M/S =in WW II	8.14-1919
3248	FD.64	BELMONT	209/06	1-6 pdrAA M/S	6.15-1919
1369	H.19	BEMPTON	226/14	1-12 pdr M/S	4.15-1919
	A.16	BEN ALDER	151/99	1-3 pdr BDV	6.15-1919
289	A.517	BEN ARDNA	197/12	M/S Mined 8.8.15 near Elbow Buoy.	8.14-8.15
	A.473	BEN ASDALE	197/12	BDV	6.15-1919
	A.168	BEN ATTOW	156/00	BDV	8.16-1919
	A.111	BEN BARVAS	198/14	BDV =in WW II.	6.15-1920
2951	A.704	BEN BHRACKIE	235/16	1-6 pdr AA M/S =in WW II.	8.16-1919
2953	A.705	BEN BREAC	235/16	1-12 pdr M/S =in WW II.	8.16-1919
83	A.40	BEN CHOURN	197/14	1-3 pdr M/S	8.14-1919
	A.178	BEN DORAN	155/00	BDV	9.15-1920
3309	SN.312	BEN EARN	235/16	1-12 pdr, 1-7.5 in BT M/S =in WW II.	10.16-1919
3314	A.738	BEN GAIRN	204/16	1-12 pdr, 1-7.5 in BT M/S =in WW II.	11.16-1919
1494	SN.110	BEN GLAMAIR	198/14	M/S	5.15-1919
3039	SN.336	BEN GLAS	234/17	1-6 pdr AA M/S =in WW II.	5.17-1919
1344	A.118	BEN GULVAIN	197/14	1-6 pdr AA M/S =in WW II.	3.15-1919
97	A.470	BEN HEILEM	196/12	1-12 pdr, 1-6 pdr AA M/S Wrecked 8.10.17 off Berwick.	8.14-10.17
84	A.38	BEN HOLDEN	197/14	1-3 pdr M/S	8.14-1919
94	A.602	BEN IVER	197/14	1-6 pdrAA M/S	8.14-1919
472	A.311	BEN LAWERS	176/00	1-12 pdr, 1-6 pdr AA M/S	11.14-1919
303	SN.269	BEN LORA	197/13	1-6 pdr AA M/S	8.14-1919
279	A.500	BEN LOYAL	183/01	(ex-Columbia) 1-3 pdr M/S	8.14-1919
	A.185	BEN LUI	155/00	(ex-Iris) BDV	6.15-1919
3036	SN.340	BEN MEIDIE	234/17	1-6 pdrAA M/S =in WW II.	4.17-1919
	A.488	BEN RINNES =BEN DEARG 6.18	183/01	1-6 pdr BDV	9.15-1920
	A.121	BEN SCREEL	197/14	BDV	6.15-1919
2657	A.109	BEN STROME	198/14	1-6 pdr M/S	4.15-1919
	A.476	BEN TARBERT	197/12	BDV =in WW II.	6.15-1919
1571	A.604	BEN TORC	199/14	1-6 pdrAA M/S	5.15-1919
3325	A.739	BEN URIE	234/16	1-6 pdrAA M/S =in WW II.	1.17-1919
1497	SN.113	BEN VURIE	200/14	M/S	5.15-1919
1203	H.287	BENGAL	149/96	1-6 pdrAA =in WW II.	12.14-11.18
1150	GY.103	BENGAL =BENGAL II 3.15	211/05	1-6 pdr M/S	2.15-1919
1972	SA.1	BENTON CASTLE	283/14	1-6 pdr Mined 10.11.16 off Dartmouth.	9.15-11.16
995	GY.398	BERKSHIRE	133/97	Sunk 15.5.15 in collision in Red Bay.	12.14-5.15
712	GY.56	BERMUDA	211/05	1-6 pdr M/S	12.14-1920
30 50 1772	GY.611	BERU	195/11	1-3 pdr M/S =in WW II.	11.14-1919
1139	H.31	BERYL =BERYL II 3.15	248/14	2-6 pdrAA M/S =RAN BERYL II in WW II.	12.14-1919

Adty No.	Port No.	Name	TG/Yr	Armament, Fate, etc.	Service
600	H.845	BIANCA	174/05	1–3 pdr M/S	9.14–1919
1129	GY.677	BIRCH	215/12	M/S Mined 23.8.16 off Yarmouth.	2.15–8.16
432	GY.1278	BITTERN =BITTERN II 2.15	207/03	1–6 pdr M/S	12.14–1919
X.01 X.09		BLACKSTONE	148/15	Water carrier	10.15–4.21
1044	GY.1162	BLAKE =BLAKEDOWN 2.15	207/00	Wrecked 19.2.15 at Crudensgeir.	1.15–2.15
1768	H.928	BLANCHE	173/07	1–6 pdr M/S	5.15–1919
	A.533	BLOODHOUND	150/90	1–3 pdr BDV	6.15–1919
728 479	GW.5	BLUEBELL =BLUEBELL III 8.15	169/04	1–6 pdr.	11.14–11.18
1890	GY.247	BOMBAY	229/07	1–3 pdr, 1–2 pdr. =in WW II.	9.15–1919
458	GY.429	BONA DEA	322/15	1–12 pdr M/S; Escort	2.15–1919
510	A.231	BONACCORD	214/08	1–6 pdrAA M/S	9.14–1919
1223	H.437	BONAR LAW	285/12	1–3 pdr M/S Sunk 27.10.15 in collision off the South Goodwins.	2.15–10.15
165	GY.338	BOREAS	184/07	1–6 pdr M/S =CUCKOO in WW II.	8.14–1919
809	GY.115	BORNEO	211/06	1–6 pdr M/S Mined 18.6.17 off Beachy Head.	11.14–6.17
1761	FD.70	BOSCOBEL	225/06	1–6 pdr M/S	5.15–1919
670	BN.74	BOSTONIAN =BASTION 8.17	192/00	1–6 pdr M/S	11.14–11.18
377	H.51	BOVIC	162/96	1–3 pdr M/S Sunk 5.8.17 in collision off Souter Point.	11.14–8.17
667	FD.2	BRACKLYN	303/14	M/S Mined 11.5.17 off Yarmouth.	12.14–5.17
	A.631	BRACONDALE	189/03	1–3 pdr BDV	9.14–1919
3261	A.615	BRACONDENE	235/16	1–6 pdrAA M/S =in WW II.	2.16–1919
114	A.95	BRACONHEATH	201/06	1–12 pdr M/S = WW II.	8.14–1919
86	A.584	BRACONLYNN	206/13	1–6 pdrAA M/S =in WW II.	8.14–1919
829	GY.132	BRADFORD	163/96	1–6 pdr Foundered 28.10.16 near the Old Head of Kinsale.	11.14–10,16
	FD.215	BRAEMAR	197/00	1–12 pdr BDV	6.15–1919
104	A.331	BRAES O'MAR	227/15	1–6 pdrAA M/S =in WW II.	9.15–1919
1989	SA.36	BRECON CASTLE	274/16	1–6 pdrAA, 1–5 in BT M/S =in WW II.	3.16–1919
826	GY.410	BRITANNIA =BRITANNIA III 5.15	138/91	Stores & Water carrier =Sunk 23.9.16.	1.15–9.15
1170	A.101	BRITON	196/06	Mined 21.7.15 off the Longsands.	2.15–7.15
927	FD.47	BROCK	304/14	1–6 pdr =in WW II.	11.14–1919
3203	GY.113	BROMELIA	242/06	1–12 pdr M/S Hydro	6.15–1919
79	H.893	BRUTUS	311/06	1–3 pdr M/S	11.14–1919
297	GY.339	BUCENTAUR	184/07	M/S =in WW II.	8.14–1919
1597	GY.52	BUFFALO =BUFFALO II 12.15	230/05	1–6 pdr M/S	7.15–1919
	H.86	BURMAH	168/92	M/S; =FT.	10.14–11.14
3277	FD.242	BURNLEY	276/16	1–12 pdr M/S Mined 25.11.16 off Orford Ness.	5.16–11.16
2667	M.227	BUSH	221/08	1–12 pdr =in WW II.	5.15–1920
549	H.971	BUZZARD	199/07	1–6 pdrAA M/S	10.14–1919

Adty No.	Port No.	Name	TG/Yr	Armament, Fate, etc.	Service
253	GY.69	BY GEORGE	225/14	1–3 pdr M/S Mined 7.9.17 in the Gulf of Ruphani, Aegean Sea.	8.14–9.17
3055	GY.1072	CADORNA	255/17	1–12 pdr =in WW II.	7.17–1919
539	H.874	CAESAR =CAESAR II 2.15.	311/06	2–6 pdr M/S	10.14–1919
635	H.550	CAIRO	172/02	1–6 pdr M/S	10.14–1919
1372	M.228	CALDY	222/08	1–12 pdr M/S =in WW II.	4.15–1919
	GN.34	CALEDONIA	161/06	Special Service Sunk 17.3.17 by S/M off Newton, Northumberland on passage to fit out.	3.17–3.17
133	M.197	CALIPH	226/06	1–6 pdrAA, 1–3.5 in BT M/S Hydro	8.14–1919
367	M.214	CALLIOPE =CALLIOPE II 6.15	240/07	1–3 pdr M/S Sunk 5.3.16 in collision off the Butt of Lewis.	8.14–3.16
852	GY.476	CALVIA	304/15	1–12 pdr, 1–7.5 in BT M/S Hydro	5.15–1919
734	GY.559	CALVINIA	191/01	(ex-Svendborg) 1–6 pdrAA M/S =in WW II.	1.15–1919
1521	GY.597	CAMBODIA	284/11	1–6 pdrAA, 1–3 pdr	5.15–1920
154 1358	M.92	CAMBRIA	206/05	1–12 pdr M/S	9.14–1919
662	BN.75	CAMBRIAN =CAMBRIAN II 2.15	191/00	1–6 pdrAA M/S	11.14–1919
1216	H.394	CAMEO	172/98	1–12 pdr M/S	2.15–9.18
	H.1	CANADA =CANADA II 2.17	231/86	1–6 pdrAA BDV	11.16–1919
2957	GY.918	CANCER =INVERTAY in WW II.	230/16	1–6 pdr M/S	8,16–1919
91	GN.31	CANDIDATE	161/06	1–12 pdr M/S	8.14–1919
3205	GY.469	CANTATRICE	302/15	M/S Mined 5.11.16 near Yarmouth.	7.15–11.16
1264	GY.1022	CAPRICORNUS	219/17	1–6 pdrAA M/S =in WW II.	4.17–1919
1656	GY.1108	CAPTAIN POLLEN	275/17	1–12 pdr M/S =AVONGLEN in WW II.	12.17–1919
1648	GY.1100	CARBILL	242/17	1–12 pdr, 1–6 pdrAA M/S =HOVERFLY in WW II.	8.17–1919
638	SA.44	CARDIFF CASTLE	255/07	1–12 pdr, 1–7.5 in BT M/S	11.14–1919
1576	H.584	CARDINAL	309/12	1–12 pdr	5.15–1920
2984	GY.956	CARENCY	233/16	1–6 pdrAA M/S =in WW II.	12.16–1919
2671	SA.106	CAREW CASTLE	256/12	1–12 pdr M/S Mined 12.6.17 off Hartland Pt.	5.15–6.17
1751	GY.908	CARIEDA	225/13	1–12 pdr M/S =in WW II.	4.15–1919
21	GY.692	CARILON	226/15	1–3 pdr M/S Mined 24.12.15 off Margate.	11.15–12.15
1965	GY.270	CARLTON	267/07	1–3 pdr M/S Mined 21.2.16 off Folkestone.	12.15–2.16
3221 N.1A N.19	GY.268	CARMANIA II	250/07	1–6 pdrAA M/L, M/S	5.15–1919
1533	M.32	CARYSFORT II	243/15	1–6 pdr, 1–7.5 in BT M/S	6.15–1919
808	GY.567	CASORIA	185/97	(ex Delfinen) 1–6 pdrAA M/S	11.14–1919
1767	H.848	CASSANDRA =CASSANDRA II 7.17	174/05	1–3 pdr M/S	5.15–1919
806	GY.634	CASSOWARY	222/08	1–6 pdr M/S	11.14–1919
2960	GY.963	CASTOR =CASTOR II 3.17	209/16	1–12 pdr M/S	9.16–1919
3323	SA.70	CASWELL	276/17	1–6 pdrAA M/S =in WW II.	1.17–1919
3201	GY.792	CAULONIA	296/12	1–6 pdrAA, 1–7.5 in BT M/S =in WW II.	5.15–1919
389	H.463	CAVE	247/02	1–12 pdr, 1–6 pdrAA M/S	11.14–1919

Adty No.	Port No.	Name	TG/Yr	Armament, Fate, etc.	Service
3085	GY.645	CAYRIAN	216/11	BDV =in WW II.	11.16–1919
1229	GY.480	CEDAR	219/09	1–6 pdrAA M/S	3.15–1919
	GN.6	CENTURION	156/04	1–3 pdr BDV	10.15–1919
674	GY.549	CEREALIA	220/05	(ex-Gudrun) 1–3 pdr	12.14–1919
194	FD.26	CERESIA	284/14	1–12 pdr, 1–7.5 in BT M/S =CHORLEY in WW II.	11.14–1919
346	H.341	CHALCEDONY	333/11	1–6 pdr M/S	8.14–1919
3336	GN.19	CHAMBERLAIN	161/05	1–6 pdr AA M/S =RIVER YTHAN in WW II.	3.17–1919
	A.367	CHAMPION	150/94	1–3 pdr BDV	5.15–1919
	GN.7	CHANCELLOR	156/04	BDV Accom.	6.15–1919
921	PH.402	CHANTICLEER	173/94	1–6 pdr M/S	11.14–11.18
366	BL.14	CHARMOUTH	195/10	1–6 pdrAA M/S	8.14–1919
629	GY.148	CHESTER =CHESTER II 5.15	143/96	1–3 pdr M/S Sunk 29.2.16 in collision in the Firth of Forth.	10.14–2.16
945	H.847	CHIEFTAIN	278/05	1–12 pdr, 1–7.5 in BT M/S	1.15–1919
67	GY.364	CHIKARA	250/08	1–12 pdr M/S	10.14–1919
946	GY.557	CHINA	190/93	1–6 pdrAA M/S	1.15–1919
476	GN.16	CHOICE	165/05	1–6 pdr M/S	11.14–1919
1502	H.207	CHRISTOPHER	316/11	1–12 pdr M/S Mined 30.3.17 off Southwold.	5.15–3.17
626	GY.745	CHRYSEA	210/12	1–6 pdr M/S =in WW II.	9.14–1919
2982	H.513	CHRYSOLITE	251/16	1–6 pdrAA M/S =in WW II.	12.16–1919
149	H.931	CICERO =CICERO II 11.17	173/07	1–12 pdr M/S =BARNSNESS in WW II.	9.14–1919
1205	H.58	CITY OF CARLISLE	208/99	1–6 pdr M/S	1.15–1919
678	FD.4	CITY OF DUNDEE	269/14	A/P Sunk 14.9.15 in collision off Folkestone.	11.14–9.15
338 1359	FD.185	CITY OF EDINBURGH II	300/08	1–6 pdrAA M/S	8.14–1919
	FD.197	CITY OF LIVERPOOL	179/00	BDV	6.15–8.18
	FD.201	CITY OF LONDON	195/01	BDV	6.15–1919
	FD.193	CITY OF MANCHESTER	189/00	BDV	6.15–8.18
193	FD.8	CITY OF SELBY	284/14	1–12 pdr M/S; Escort =WESTLYN in WW II.	11.14–1919
	FD.16	CITY OF YORK	202/04	1–12 pdr BDV	6.15–1920
1466	GY.318	CLAIRE	219/07	1–6 pdrAA M/S	4.15–1919
1175	A.900	CLEMENTINA II	200/03	1–6 pdr M/S	3.15–1919
1514	GY.240	CLEON	266/07	1–3 pdr M/S Mined 1.2.18 off Folkestone.	5.15–2.18
140	M.213	CLEOPATRA =CLEOPATRA II, 12.14	240/07	1–6 pdrAA M/S =TEAZER in WW II.	8.14–1919
657	H.860	CLEOPATRA =CLEOPATRA III 4.15	311/06	1–12 pdr, 1–5 in BT M/S	10.14–1919
954	GY.116	CLIFTON	242/06	1–12 pdr Mined 18.2.17 off Daunt LV.	12.14–2.17
924	FD.232	CLOTILDE	289/13	1–6 pdr M/S =in WW II.	11.14–1919
971	GY.317	CLYDE	146/91	1–3 pdr M/S Sunk 14.10.17 in collision off Sidmouth.	2.15–10.17
137	SA.43	CLYNE CASTLE	252/07	1–6 pdr M/S	9.14–1919
1415	GN.41	COADJUTOR	207/15	1–6 pdr M/S	3.15–1919
802	GY.610	COCKATRICE =COCKATRICE II 2.15	115/94	M/S =Mercantile loss 23.9.16.	11.14–6.15
1631	GN.53	COLLEAGUE	207/15	1–6 pdrAA M/S	5.15–1919
1585	FD.115	COLLENA	293/15	1–6 pdrAA M/S =in WW II.	5.15–1919
344	H.973	COLTMAN	312/07	1–12 pdr M/S Hydro	8.14–1919
	GN.43	COLUMBA	138/93	1–3 pdr BDV Mined 10.3.18 off May Island.	5.16–3.18

Adty No.	Port No.	Name	TG/Yr	Armament, Fate, etc.	Service
200	H.42	COLUMBIA	266/86	A/P Sunk 1.5.15 by German TB off Thornton Ridge, Foreness.	9.14–5.15
1440	GN.36	COMMANDANT	207/15	M/S Mined 2.4.16 off Sunk LV.	4.15–4.16
3063	H.286	COMMANDER FULLERTON	227/15	A/P Sunk 12.12.17 by SMS EMDEN and destroyers in the North Sea.	9.17–12.17
1968	H.385	COMMANDER NASMITH	243/15	1–6 pdr, 1–7.5 in BT M/S =in WW II.	9.15–1919
1690	GN.18	COMMISSIONER	161/05	2–12 pdr, 1–3 pdr, 1–7.5 in BT Q ship (1–12 pdr, 1–6 pdr) (CHAMPION, RECORDER, ROLLER)	3.17–1919
3012	GN.23	COMPANION	163/03	1–6 pdrAA =T/S	3.17–1919
1500	GN.30	COMRADE	161/06	1–12 pdr	5.15–1919
722	GY.95	CONCORD =CONCORD III 12.15	235/05	1–12 pdr M/S	12.14–1919
	GY.85	CONDOR	227/05	1–6 pdr Mined or Foundered 22.11.14 off Lowestoft.	11.14–11.14
920	PH.15	CONDOR	191/00	1–6 pdr M/S	11.14–1919
	GN.21	CONDUCTOR	163/03	BDV	10.15–1919
317	GN.81	CONFEDERATE	202/13	1–6 pdr M/S	8.14–1919
822	GY.274	CONGO	152/97	1–3 pdr =FT.	11.14–1.17
34	BN.119	CONINGSBY	257/06	1–6 pdr M/S	9.14–1919
	FD.194	CONNIE	198/00	BDV	6.15–1919
1612	GY.498	CONSORT	181/09	1–12 pdr M/S	4.15–1919
298	GN.79	CONTROLLER	201/13	1–3 pdr M/S =in WW II.	8.14–1919
1532	GY.1288	CONWAY	228/04	1–6 pdrAA M/S =in WW II.	6.15–1919
1987	SA.35	CONWAY CASTLE	274/16	1–6 pdrAA M/S =in WW II.	3.16–1919
420	H.897	COOT	172/06	2–12 pdr, 1–7.5 in BT M/S =Q ship (1–12 pdr, 1–6 pdr) 3.17–11.18 (BURMAH, DORA, KIA ORA, LORNE).	11.14–1920
	A.390	COQUET	174/01	BDV	6.15–1919
278	GY.63	CORCYRA	225/14	M/S Stranded 20.2.15 off Bacton, later salved. =in WW II.	8.14–2.15
952	GY.281	CORELLA	243/07	(ex-Renown) 1–3 pdr	12.14–1919
1149	GY.552	CORIENTES	280/10	1–6 pdr M/S Mined 23.6.17 off Malin Head.	2.15–6.17
831	GY.345	CORMORANT IV	162/97	1–6 pdrAA M/S =Q ship (1–6 pdr) (NADINE). =ADRIAN in WW II.	11.14–1919
3067	H.575	CORNELIAN	262/17	1–12 pdr M/S =FORFEIT in WW II.	9.17–1919
1137	GY.684	CORONA	212/12	1–6 pdr, 1–2 pdr Mined 23.3.16 near Ramsgate.	2.15–3.16
323	SN.337	CORONATIA	185/02	1–12 pdr M/S =in WW II.	8.14–1919
3218	GY.635	CORRIE ROY	327/15	1–12 pdr, 1–7.5 in BT	11.15–1919
1621	GY.862	CORTINA	213/13	1–6 pdr M/S =in WW II.	4.15–1919
456	GY.553	CORYTHAIX	280/10	M/S =BDV	2.15–1920
1537	M.15	COTSMUIR	243/15	1–6 pdrAA M/S Disappeared 2.2.17 between the Tyne and Humber	6.15–2.17
	GY.79	COURSER	227/05	BDV =in WW II.	10.16–1920
449	GY.564	COURTIER	181/10	M/S Mined 6.1.16 off Kilnsea.	1.15–1.16
1075	LH.17	CRAIG ISLAND	210/14	1–6 pdr M/S	1.15–1919

Adty No.	Port No.	Name	TG/Yr	Armament, Fate, etc.	Service
	A.51	CRAIGENDARROCH	198/10	(ex-John C. Meikle) BDV	6.15–1919
88	PD.551	CRAIGEWAN	204/10	1–12 pdr M/S	8.14–1919
1647	A.860	CRAIGMILLAR	112/96	1–6 pdrAA M/S	8.17–1920
3294	HL.83	CRAIGMORE	210/16	M/S	6.16–1919
1471	FD.134	CRAIK	219/15	1–12 pdr M/S =in WW II.	4.15–1919
1495	LH.114	CRAMOND ISLAND	180/10	1–12 pdr, 1–6 pdrAA M/S =in WW II.	5.15–1919
106	A.350	CRATHIE	210/11	M/S Mined 27.8.14 off the Tyne.	8.14–8.14
2980	A.713	CRATHIE	225/16	1–6 pdrAA M/S Wrecked 16.12.16 on Nizam Point, Barra Head.	11.16–12.16
709	GY.49	CROTON	149/98	1–12 pdr, 1–6 pdrAA M/S	11.14–1919
27	GY.271	CROUPIER	302/14	1–12 pdrAA M/S	9.14–1919
1632	GY.642	CROXBY	215/11	1–6 pdrAA M/S	5.15–1919
388	H.309	CUCKOO =NIGHTJAR 5.18	156/96	1–12 pdr M/S	11.14–1919
851	GY.436	CUIRASS	321/15	1–6 pdrAA M/S =in WW II.	5.15–1919
108	A.339	CULBLEAN	210/11	1–6 pdrAA M/S	8.14–1919
975	M.138	CYELSE	237/12	1–12 pdr, 1–7.5 in BT M/S =in WW II.	2.15–1919
126	FD.110	CYGNET =CYGNET II 3.17	300/07	1–6 pdr M/S	8.15–1919
1528	GY.80	CYRANO	214/05	1–12 pdr M/S	6.15–1919
863	A.629	D. W. FITZGERALD	235/16	1–6 pdrAA M/S =in WW II.	4.16–1919
3202	GY.957	DAGON	250/14	1–12 pdr Sunk 8.12.16 by S/M off Dover.	6.15–12.16
731	GY.223	DAHLIA =DAHLIA II 10.15	154/89	1–6 pdr	1.15–7.18
260	H.167	DAIMLER	257/10	(ex-S. L. Haldane) M/S	8.14–1920
823	GY.1133	DALE	198/00	A/P =Mercantile loss 12.2.17.	12.14–6.15
976	SA.99	DALE CASTLE	246/09	1–3 pdr M/S =in WW II.	2.15–1919
656	BN.83	DALMATIAN	186/00	A/P =Mercantile loss 15.4.17.	1.15–2.15
1265	GY.1032	DANDINI	212/17	1–6 pdrAA M/S	4.17–1919
1446	GY.947	DANE	265/13	A/P Mined 28.8.15 off Aldeburgh.	4.15–8.15
1370	H.227	DANE =DANE II 6.15	346/11	1–6 pdr =in WW II.	4.15–1919
	A.245	DANESTON	239/15	BDV	6.15–1920
1491	GY.191	DAROGAH	221/14	1–6 pdrAA M/S =in WW II.	5.15–1920
770	H.138	DARRACQ	256/10	(ex-H. A. L. Russell) 1–4 in, 1–6 pdrAA M/S	12.14–1919
523	FD.152	DAVARA	291/12	1–6 pdrAA M/S	11.14–1919
1636	H.377	DE LA POLE	255/11	1–47 mm M/S Wrecked 4.2.16 on the Goodwin Sands.	5.15–2.16
1619	GY.958	DELPHINE	250/14	1–6 pdrAA M/S	5.15–1919
624	GY.981	DELPHINUS	257/06	(ex-Amelia) 1–12 pdr, 1–6 pdrAA M/S =in WW II.	9.14–1919
610	GY.344	DENTARIA	259/08	1–12 pdr, 1–7.5 inBT M/S	9.14–1920
1779	GY.153	DERBY =DEBENEY 10.18	144/96	1–6 pdr M/S	5.15–1919
251	GY.788	DESIREE	213/12	1–6 pdr M/S =in WW II.	8.14–1919
1587	GY.307	DESTINN	226/14	1–6 pdr M/S =in WW II.	5.15–1919
129	A.458	DEVANHA	196/01	1–6 pdr BDV	8.15–1919
695	GY.96	DEVERON	233/05	1–6 pdrAA, 1–7.5 in BT M/S	11.14–1919
2664	M.220	DEWSLAND	236/07	1.12 pdr M/S	5.15—1919

Adty No.	Port No.	Name	TG/Yr	Armament, Fate, etc.	Service
2959	FD.244	DHOON	275/16	1–3 pdr M/S Mined 24.11.16 near Newarp LV.	9.16–11.16
1376	H.665	DIAMOND =DIAMOND II 6.15.	289/13	1–6 pdrAA M/S	4.15–1919
	FD.135	DIANA	172/99	2–12 pdr BDV Collier	6.15–1920
155	M.19	DINAS	219/09	1–6 pdrAA M/S	8.14–1919
288	A.505	DINORAH	192/03	(ex-Picton Castle) 1–3 pdr M/S	8.14–1919
594	GY.1205	DIVER	207/00	A/P =FT.	12.14–12.15
1582	H.50	DOCTOR LEE	307/14	1–12 pdr =in WW II.	5.15–1919
	H.673	DOGGER BANK	274/13	BDV	8.16–1920
	A.443	DON	168/98	2–3 pdr BDV	6.15–1919
1760	GY.149	DONALDA	226/14	1–6 pdr M/S	5.15–1919
1981	GY.237	DONNA NOOK	307/15	1–12 pdr, 1–3 pdrAA, 1–7.5 in BT M/S =in WW II.	2.16–1919
268	A.155	DONSIDE	182/00	M/S Mined 7.1.17 off Lowestoft.	8.14–1.17
824	GY.844	DORANDO	139/95	1–6 pdrAA M/S	12.14–7.18
14	H.925	DORCAS	173/06	1–6 pdrAA M/S	8.14–1919
	SD.130	DOREEN	194/03	(ex-Braconhill) BDV =T/S	5.16–1919
3003	FD.198	DORINDA	270/17	1–12 pdr Escort =in WW II.	2.17–1919
96	PD.533	DOROTHY GRAY	199/08	1–6 pdr M/S =in WW II.	8.14–1919
390	H.279	DOVE =DOVE II 2.15	168/97	1–3 pdr M/S	11.14–1919
630	GY.142	DOVER	163/96	1–3 pdr M/S	10.14–12.18
3040	PD.277	DOWNIEHILLS	227/17	1–6 pdrAA	5.17–1919
	GY.842	DRACO	139/95	BDV	1.15–1919
428	GY.201	DRAGON =DRAGON II 3.17	214/06	1–6 pdr M/S	11.14–1919
817	GY.1163	DRAKE =DRAKE II 2.15	207/00	1–3 pdr Wrecked 3.7.17 in the Kenmare River, Ireland.	11.14–7.17
2992	A.144	DREADNOUGHT II	150/07	1–6 pdrAA	2.17–1919
467	A.133	DRUMBLADE	195/00	M/S =BDV	9.14–1919
2969	GY.964	DRUMMER BOY	209/16	1–12 pdr M/S =in WW II.	9.16–1919
342	A.516	DRUMOAK	208/02	M/S Mined 5.10.14 off the Belgian Coast.	8.14–10.14
357	A.403	DRUMTOCHTY	211/15	1–3 pdr M/S Mined 29.1.18 off Dover.	10.15–1.18
36	GY.951	DRUSILLA	250/14	1–10 pdr M/S	5.15–1919
1753	H.375	DRYPOOL	331/11	1–12 pdr	4.15–1919
3004	H.77	DUNNET	205/14	1–6 pdrAA M/S	2.17–1919
3045	SA.69	DUNRAVEN CASTLE	276/17	1–12 pdr, 1–3.5 in BT M/S Hydro =in WW II.	6.17–1919
1209	H.378	DURBAN	152/97	A/P =FT.	12.14–10.15
300	GY.612	DURGA	216/11	1–6 pdrAA M/S	8.14–1919
421	H.267	DUSTER	192/11	1–6 pdrAA M/S Wrecked 17.12.17 near Portreath.	11.14–12.17
393	H.454	EAGLE =EAGLET 2.15 =OWLET 4.18	168/99	1–6 pdr M/S	12.14–1919
292	GY.48	EARL ESSEX	225/14	1–12 pdr M/S =in WW II.	8.14–1920
2653	GY.449	EARL GRANARD	211/04	(ex-Pauline) 1–6 pdrAA M/S =CASTLETON in WW II.	4.15–1919
1907	H.345	EARL KITCHENER	348/15	1–12 pdr M/S =in WW II.	10.15–1920
1441	GY.367	EARL LENNOX	226/14	1–6 pdr M/S Mined 23.10.17 off Sound of Islay.	4.15–10.17
3292	PD.242	EARL OF BUCHAN	227/16	1–6 pdrAA M/S	6.16–1919
2652	GY.446	EARL OF WARWICK	208/05	(ex-Thora) 1–12 pdr M/S	3.15–1919
1172	A.122	EAST COAST	202/07	(ex-Horace Stroud) 1–12 pdr M/S =in WW II.	2.15–1919

Adty No.	Port No.	Name	TG/Yr	Armament, Fate, etc.	Service
1766	H.765	EASTELLA	183/03	1–3 pdr M/S	5.15–1919
1217	H.415	EASTWARD HO	162/98	1–3 pdr M/S	2.15–12.18
998	GY.743	EBRO =EBRO II 6.15	175/98	1–3 pdr	12.14–1921
3334	H.376	ECCLESHILL	226/11	1–6 pdrAA, 1–3.5 in BT M/S =in WW II.	3.17–1919
	H.367	ECHO	165/97	BDV	9.15–1921
	GY.1285	EDINBURGH CASTLE	241/99	(ex-*Magnific*) BDV	6.15–1919
395	H.430	EDISON	196/98	M/S Wrecked 6.7.15 on Isle of Lewis.	12.14–7.15
398	H.442	EDITOR	169/99	1–12 pdr M/S =FT.	12.14–9.18
22	M.196	EDWARD VII	231/06	1–6 pdrAA M/S =Cable repairs	8.14–1919
1453	GY.704	EDWARDIAN	295/12	1–12 pdr, 1–7.5 in BT M/S	4.15–1919
1919	FD.205	EDWINA	267/15	1–12 pdr M/S =in WW II.	10.15–1919
8 404	H.459	EIDER	168/99	1–6 pdrAA M/S	8.14–1919
508	LL.36	EILEEN DUNCAN	223/10	1–6 pdrAA M/S =in WW II.	1.15–1919
622	GN.68	ELCHO	155/08	1–3 pdr M/S	9.14–1919
1743	H.661	ELECTRA =ELECTRA II 8.15	269/04	1–6 pdrAA M/S =ELECTRA II in WW II.	7.15–1919
3019	H.1012	ELF KING	289/13	1–12 pdr, 1–7.5 in BT	2.17–1919
1622	PD.164	ELISE	239/07	1–6 pdr M/S Sunk, presumed torpedoed, 22.9.18 off St. Mary's Light House near Blyth.	6.15–9.18
150	H.714	ELITE	180/02	1–6 pdr M/S	9.14–1919
380	H.440	ELK	169/98	1–6 pdrAA M/S	11.14–1919
706	GY.1235	ELK II	181/02	1–3 pdr M/S =in WW II.	12.14–7.18
1275	H.767	ELLESMERE	183/03	1–6 pdrAA M/S =HYAENA in WW II.	3.17–1919
397	H.23	ELM	168/99	1–12 pdr M/S	12.14–1920
1603	GY.969	ELMIRA	197/14	1–6 pdr AA M/S	3.15–1919
944	H.320	ELSIE	184/96	1–6 pdr M/S	1.15–1919
1535	FD.78	ELSWICK	215/06	1–6 pdr M/S	7.15–1919
701	GY.238	ELVINA	201/14	1–12 pdr, 1–7.5 in BT M/S	11.14–1919
1777	H.770	ELY	183/03	1–3 pdr M/S	5.15–1919
3206	GY.661	ELYSIAN	214/12	1–6 pdrAA M/S =P & Y in WW II.	1.15–1919
1579	H.910	EMERALD	289/13	1–12 pdr M/S =CAMPINA in WW II.	11.14–1919
1613	GY.243	EMILION	201/14	1–12 pdr M/S =in WW II.	4.15–1919
665	H.384	EMLEY	223/11	1–12 pdr M/S Mined 28.4.18 off May Island.	10.14–4.18
552	H.741	EMPEROR	181/03	M/S =FT	9.14–2.15
9	GY.209	EMPYREAN	215/14	1–6 pdrAA, 1–7.5 in BT M/S =in WW II.	9.14–1920
1765	H.516	EMU	164/00	1–3 pdr A/P; later BDV.	5.15–1919
	A.403	ENDEAVOUR	156/94	BDV Sunk 10.3.18 in collision off Kirkwall.	6.15–3.18
1371	H.161	ENDON	235/14	1–6 pdrAA M/S	4.15–1919
229	YH.80	ENGLISH ROSE	188/14	1–6 pdrAA M/S =Net trawler	9.14–1919
379	H.386	EPWORTH	223/12	1–3 pdr M/S Sunk 22.5.17 in collision off the East Coast.	11.14–5.17
836	H.463	EQUATOR	168/99	1–6 pdr M/S	12.14–11.18
3353	GY.461	EQUINOX	198/99	(ex-*Catulus*) 1–3 pdr =Mercantile loss 25.8.16.	6.15–8.15
408	H.461	ERA	168/99	1–3 pdr M/S Sunk 11.7.16 by gunfire of U.46, U.49, U.52, and U.69 off Aberdeen.	10.14–7.16
184	A.90	ERIC STROUD	213/14	1–6 pdr, 1–7.5 in BT M/S	3.15–1919

Adty No.	Port No.	Name	TG/Yr	Armament, Fate, etc.	Service
1403	GY.234	ERILLUS	201/14	1–6 pdr M/S =in WW II.	3.15–1919
381	H.757	ERIN =ERIN II 2.15	181/03	M/S Mined 19.10.15 off the Nab.	9.14–10.15
1776	H.753	ERMINE	181/03	1–3 pdr	5.15–1919
1586	FD.158	ERNA	330/15	1–6 pdrAA M/L, M/S =in WW II.	5.15–1920
405	H.465	ERNE	168/99	1–3 pdr M/S	10.14–11.18
294	GY.35	EROICAN	225/14	1–3 pdr M/S =in WW II.	8.14–1920
698	GY.284	EROS	286/07	M/S Mined 5.9.17 off Felixstowe.	12.14–9.17
43	GY.631	ESCALLONIA	285/11	1–12 pdr M/S	3.15–1919
	H.33	ESCORT	165/97	BDV	9.15–1921
1754	H.163	ESHER	235/14	1–3 pdr	4.15–1919
1225	H.859	ESKE	290/06	1–6 pdrAA, 1–7.5 in BT M/S	2.15–1920
142	M.193	ESSEX =ESSEX II 2.15	220/06	1–6 pdrAA M/S	8.14–1919
3329	H.762	ESSEX =ESSEX III 4.15	183/03	1–6 pdrAA M/S	3.17–1919
1595	FD.173	ETHEL	278/07	1–6 pdr M/S	6.15–1919
3333	GN.59	ETHEL NUTTEN	182/06	1–6 pdrAA M/S	3.17–1919
286	SN.344	ETHELWULF	185/03	M/S =Mercantile loss 1.12.18.	8.14–1.15
1276	H.940	ETNA	189/07	1–6 pdrAA	3.17–12.18
1402		ETOILE POLAIRE	278/15	1–3 pdr Mined 3.12.15 off S. Goodwin LV.	3.15–12.15
	H.380	ETON	165/97	1–6 pdr BDV	9.15–1920
669	BN.85	ETRURIAN	186/00	1–6 pdrAA M/S =in WW II.	11.14–1919
1882	GY.939	ETRUSCAN	202/13	1–6 pdrAA M/S =in WW II.	9.15–1919
	H.373	EUREKA	165/97	1–6 pdrAA BDV	9.15–1921
1740	H.959	EURIPIDES	307/07	2–6 pdr Escort	7.15–1919
1589	FD.67	EUSTON	209/06	1–3 pdr M/S Mined 12.2.17 off Hartlepool.	6.15–2.17
966	FD.85	EVA WALES	251/15	1–12 pdr M/S Hydro =AVONSTREAM in WW II.	1.15–1919
148	H.945	EVADNE	189/07	1–3 pdr M/S Mined 27.2.17 off Owers LV.	9.14–2.17
1408	GY.970	EVANGEL	197/14	1–6 pdr M/S Mined 25.3.17 off Milford Haven.	3.15–3.17
1581	A.286	EVELINE NUTTEN	183/15	1–6 pdrAA M/S	5.15–1919
121	FD.59	EVELYN	235/06	1–6 pdr M/S	8.14–1919
43 656 385	H.942	EVEREST	189/07	1–6 pdr, 1–7.5 in BT	9.14–1919
1515	H.297	EVERTON	239/15	1–6 pdrAA M/S =in WW II.	5.15–1919
1544	H.306	EVESHAM	239/15	1–6 pdrAA =in WW II.	6.15–1919
146	BL.16	EXMOUTH =EXMOUTH II 2.15	236/12	1–3 pdr M/S =M/S T/S	8.14–1919
	A.521	EXPERT	156/94	BDV	9.14–1919
264	GY.150	EXYAHNE	226/14	1–12 pdr M/S =in WW II.	9.14–1919
263 3033	GN.70 GY.820	FAIR ISLE =FAIR ISLE II 5.17	192/09	1–6 pdr M/S =1–6 pdrAA M/S Wrecked 26.12.14 in Sinclair Bay, salved and re-acquired 4.17.	8.14–1920
266	GN.71	FAIR VIEW	187/09	2–6 pdr M/S	8.14–1919
769	GY.428	FALMOUTH =FALMOUTH II 2.15	165/97	1–6 pdr	12.14–1919
152	BL.12	FALMOUTH =FALMOUTH III 4.15	198/09	M/S Mined 19.11.15 off Deal.	8.14–11.15
1795	H.917	FALSTAFF	173/06	1–3 pdr M/S	10.15–1919
132	FD.94	FANE	269/07	1–6 pdrAA M/S	8.14–1919

Adty No.	Port No.	Name	TG/Yr	Armament, Fate, etc.	Service
3312	H.490	FARADAY	322/16	1–12 pdr M/S =in WW II.	11.16–1919
1655	GY.1039	FAVORITA	314–16	1–12 pdr M/S	12.17–1919
448	GY.804	FENTONIAN	221/13	1–6 pdrAA M/S =in WW II.	3.15–1919
1349	H.629	FERRIBY	324/13	1–12 pdr M/S =RNZN SOUTH SEA in WW II.	5.15–1919
1278	A.706	FEUGH	227/16	1–6 pdrAA M/S =BERENGA in WW II.	6.17–1919
1362	GY.444	FEZENTA	228/14	1–6 pdr M/S =in WW II.	3.15–1919
1658	GY.1040	FIAT	314/16	1–12 pdr M/S	1.18–1919
1279	GY.1038	FIFINELLA	314/16	1–6 pdr M/S	7.17–1919
1363 3826	H.8	FILEY	226/14	1–12 pdr Wrecked 2.10.16 at Camusmore Bay, Tory Island, salved and re-acquired 7.18.	3.15–1920
969	LO.209	FISHERGATE	205/05	1–6 pdrAA M/S	2.15–1919
522	BN.94	FISHTOFT	188/01	1–6 pdr M/S	11.14–1919
853	GY.598	FLANDRE	226/15	M/S =in WW II.	9.15–12.18
413	H.334	FLICKER	192/11	1–3 pdr Mined 4.3.16 off Dover.	11.14–3.16
3315	SA.66	FLINT CASTLE	275/16	1–6 pdrAA M/S	12.16–1919
3287	GY.875	FLINTSHIRE	215/16	1–6 pdrAA, 1–11 in BT, 1–7.5 in BT Purchased; sold 5.1.26. =TAIPO in WW II.	4.16–1.26
	FD.196	FLORENCE DOMBEY	182/00	(ex-Wyre) BDV =FT.	9.15–9.18
1653	GY.1042	FLORIO	314/16	1–12 pdr M/S =in WW II.	10.17–1919
1958	GY.690	FLYING WING	226/15	1–6 pdrAA M/S =In WW II.	11.15–1919
273	A.71	FORT ALBERT	193/06	1–6 pdrAA M/S	8.14–1919
2654	A.180	FORT EDWARD	208/08	1–6 pdr M/S	4.15–1919
	GN.77	FORT GEORGE	180/02	1–6 pdr Q ship (ROBINA) =FT.	3.17–11.18
1409	GY.98	FORWARD =FORWARD II 5.15	250/06	1–6 pdr M/S	4.15–1919
1560	H.331	FORWARD HO	269/15	1–6 pdr M/S	7.15–1919
35	BN.149	FOSDYKE	245/08	1–6 pdrAA M/S	8.14–1919
3278	FD.243	FOSS	275/16	1–12 pdr M/S =in WW II.	5.16–1919
1270	GY.1041	FRANC TIREUR	314/16	1–12 pdr M/S, Escort =in WW II.	6.17–1919
49	GY.315	FRASCATI	220/14	1–12 pdr M/S	11.14–1919
1379	H.951	FRASER	310/07	1–3 pdr M/S Mined 17.6.17 near Boulogne.	4.15–6.17
716	GY.633	FREESIA	285/11	1–12 pdr, 1–7.5 in BT M/S	12.14–1919
	GY.459	FRIESLAND	268/99	(ex-Balmoral Castle) 1–12 pdr BDV	12.14–1919
2661	CF.40	FUJI	255/12	1–12 pdr M/S =GERBERDINA JOHANNA in WW II.	5.15–1919
1756	GY.470	FULMAR	231/99	1–3 pdr Mined 17.1.16 in the Gulf of Sollum.	5.15–1.16
308	M.47	G. M.	225/10	1–6 pdr M/S	8.14–1919
1486	GY.497	GABIR	219/09	M/S Mined 24.5.18 off Lowestoft.	5.15–5.18
1467	GY.485	GADRA	219/09	1–6 pdr M/S =in WW II.	4.15–1919
	GY.245	GAELIC	159/90	A/P =FT.	1.15–2.15
908	LL.116	GALLINULE	238/07	1–6 pdrAA M/S =in WW II.	1.15–1919
1263	GY.992	GAMBRI	274/16	1–6 pdr M/S Mined 18.1.18 off the Royal Sovereign LV.	4.17–1.18

Adty No.	Port No.	Name	TG/Yr	Armament, Fate, etc.	Service
419	H.810	GAMECOCK	171/05	1–6 pdr M/S	11.14–1919
1524	H.110	GANTON	330/14	1–12 pdr M/S	5.15–1919
723	GY.402	GARDENIA	146/91	1–6 pdrAA M/S	12.14–11.18
810	GY.1165	GARMO	203/00	A/P Mined 20.12.14 off Scarborough.	11.14–12.14
3001	H.495	GARNET	251/16	1–6 pdrAA M/S =LOUISE ET MARIE in WW II.	2.17–1919
457	GY.679	GAROLA	249/12	1–6 pdr M/S =in WW II.	2.15–12.18
1601	GY.644	GARU	215/11	1–3 pdr M/S	3.15–1919
733	H.761	GAUL	270/05	1–12 pdr, 1–7.5 in BT M/S	2.15–1920
1995	FD.236	GAVINA	289/15	1–12 pdrAA M/S	4.16–1919
3258	GY.869	GELSINA	226/15	1–3 pdrAA M/S Mined 25.6.17 off Girdle Ness.	2.16–6.17
3316	A.709	GENERAL BOTHA =ISLAND PRINCE 3.19	245/16	1–6 pdrAA M/S =in WW II.	12.16–1919
3331	H.844	GENERAL GORDON	267/05	1–6 pdr M/S	3.17–1920
1455	SN.123	GENERAL JOFFRE	194/14	1–6 pdr M/S	4.15–1919
116	A.387	GEORGE D. IRVIN	194/11	1–6 pdrAA M/S =in WW II.	8.14–1919
2952	SN.274	GEORGE H. HASTIE	229/16	1–6 pdrAA M/S	8.16–1919
3301	A.634	GEORGE MILBURN	235/16	1–6 pdrAA M/S Mined 12.7.17 off Dunmore.	7.16–7.17
3262	SN.270	GEORGE SCOTT	209/16	1–6 pdrAA M/S	3.16–1919
359	A.64	GEORGE STROUD	202/06	(ex-Loch Earn) 1–6 pdr M/S	8.14–1919
	HL.74	GERTRUDE CAPPLEMAN	195/15	BDV	6.15–1920
968	LO.231	GILLYGATE	207/05	1–12 pdr	2.15–1919
482	GW.12	GLAMIS CASTLE	203/02	1–12 pdr M/S	12.14–1919
821	GY.866	GLATIAN	220/13	1–6 pdr M/S =in WW II.	11.14–1919
438	GW.14	GLENBERVIE	224/15	1–12 pdr M/S =CONQUISTADOR in WW II.	11.15–1919
289	GW.10	GLENBOYNE	224/15	1–6 pdrAA M/S Mined 4.1.19 off N. Foreland.	9.15–1.19
301	GW.18	GLENESK	226/07	1–6 pdrAA M/S	8.14–1919
	GW.8	GLENOGIL	203/02	BDV	8.15–1919
315	GW.20	GLENPROSEN	224/07	M/S Mined 3.11.16 off Cross Sand LV.	8.14–11.16
595	GY.817	GLENROY	137/95	1–6 pdr M/S	12.14–1919
2673	M.215	GLORIA	264/07	1–6 pdr	6.15–1919
275	A.135	GLORIA =GLORIA II 7.15	187/07	1–6 pdr M/S =in WW II.	8.14–1919
1194	LL.2	GOELAND II	245/15	1–6 pdr AA M/S =NEW COMET in WW II.	3.15–1919
2578	H.892	GONZALO	173/06	1–3 pdr M/S	6.15–1919
355	H.722	GOOD HOPE	256/03	1–12 pdr, 1–6 pdrAA M/S	8.14–1921
1342	H.497	GOOD LUCK	294/12	1–12 pdr M/S, Escort =TRANQUIL in WW II.	4.15–1919
910	LL.118	GOOSANDER	238/08	1–6 pdr M/S =in WW II.	1.15–1919
430	GY.1194	GOSHAWK =GOSHAWK II 5.15	208/00	1–6 pdr M/S	12.14–1919
477	GW.9	GOWAN	173/05	1–12 pdr M/S	12.14–1920
644	H.545	GOZO	172/02	1–6 pdrAA M/S	10.14–1919
3337	A.744	GRACE WETHERLY	270/17	1–6 pdrAA M/S =in WW II.	3.17–1919
1218	H.224	GRACKLE	191/15	1–6 pdr M/S	1.15–1919
2512	GY.683	GRAND DUKE	327/15	1–12 pdr M/S =NIGHT RIDER in WW II.	11.15–1919
290	GN.78	GRANTON, N. B.	180/12	1–6 pdrAA M/S =PANORAMA in WW II.	8.14–1919
474	A.265	GRANUWEAL	174/09	1–6 pdr M/S	11.14–1919
1208	GY.15	GRECIAN	119/96	1–3 pdr =Mercantile loss 20.4.17.	1.15–7.15
792	H.479	GRECIAN EMPIRE	195/99	1–12 pdr M/S	1.15–1919
3035	A.730	GREG NESS	240/17	1–6 pdrAA, 1–7.5 in BT M/S	4.17–1919

Adty No.	Port No.	Name	TG/Yr	Armament, Fate, etc.	Service
402	H.947	GRENADA	183/07	1-6 pdrAA M/S	10.14-1919
714	GY.323	GRENADIER	219/07	(ex-Grenada) 1-6 pdrAA M/S	12.14-1919
119	FD.79	GRETA =GRETA II 5.15	273/06	1-6 pdr M/S	8.14-1919
	GY.9	GRIMENCO	153/99	(ex-Alroy) BDV	4.17-1919
951	GY.168	GRIMSBY	163/96	1-3 pdr	1.15-7.18
660	H.108	GROSBEAK	192/10	1-12 pdr M/S	10-14/1919
371	H.100	GROUSE	167/97	1-12 pdr M/S	10.14-1919
730	GY.1198	GUILLEMOT	208/00	1-6 pdr M/S	12.14-1919
409	H.241	GULL	166/97	1-3 pdr M/S	10.14-1919
663	GY.39	GURTH	226/05	1-12 pdr M/S	10.14-1919
354	M.70	GWENLLIAN	220/11	1-3 pdr M/S =in WW II.	8.14-1919
1346	A.270	H. E. STROUD	214/15	1-6 pdrAA M/S	4.15-1919
80	H.867	HAMLET	311/06	1-6 pdr M/S	11.14-1919
1990	SA.42	HARLECH CASTLE	275/16	1-6 pdrAA M/S, Escort =in WW II.	4.16-1919
	A.453	HARRY ROSS	183/01	BDV	6.15-1919
2662	CF.39	HATANO	255/12	1-6 pdrAA M/S	5.15-1919
690	H.238	HAWK	243/97	2-3 pdr M/S Sunk 17.2.17 by S/M off Malta.	11.14-2.17
958	GY.152	HELCIA	230/06	1-6 pdr	1.15-1919
696	GY.965	HELGIAN	220/14	1-3 pdr M/S Mined 6.9.17 in the Gulf of Ruphani, Aegean Sea.	12.14-9.17
953	GY.784	HELIOS	201/03	A/P =FT.	4.15-5.15
1266	GY.1026	HELVETIA	261/17	1-12 pdr Hydro =in WW II.	4.17-1919
1975	SA.33	HENE CASTLE	274/15	1-12 pdr M/S Hydro	12.15-1919
	D.86	HENRY GRATTAN	212/03	(ex-Diadem) 1-12 pdr BDV	6.15-1919
63	HL.57	HEORTNESSE	198/11	1-6 pdr AA M/S	9.14-1919
431	GY.811	HERCULES II	165/98	1-6 pdrAA	12.14-1919
3	A.562	HERCULES =HERCULES III 3.15	238/06	1-6 pdr M/S =ROLLS ROYCE in WW II.	12.14-1919
1361	FD.172	HERCULES IV	261/03	1-12 pdr M/S	3.15-1919
355	GY.1153	HERMIA	216/00	1-6 pdrAA M/S	6.15-1919
156	M.218	HERO =HEROINE in WW II.	226/07	1-6 pdrAA M/L, M/S	8.14-1920
715	GY.1230	HERON =FOAMCREST in WW II.	223/02	1-12 pdr M/S	12.14-1919
1480	HL.64	HEUGH	200/14	1-6 pdr, 1-6 pdrAA M/S	5.15-1919
141	LO.266	HIBERNIA =HIBERNIA II 5.15	216/07	1-6 pdrAA M/S	8.14-1919
3280	CF.44	HIROSE	274/15	1-3 pdr Mined 29.6.16 off Aldborough Napes.	6.16-6.16
	H.555	HOBART	172/02	BDV	9.15-1919
437	FD.161	HOLDENE	274/15	1-13 pdr, 1-3 pdrAA Mined 2.2.17 off Orford Ness.	9.15-2.17
438	GY.90	HOLYROOD	210/14	1-12 pdr M/S =in WW II.	4.15-1919
6	GY.701	HONDO	229/12	1-6 pdrAA	8.14-1919
	CF.48	HONJO	275/17	1-12 pdr M/S	1.18-1.18
280	A.324	HORACE STROUD =DANDOLO in WW II.	207/10	1-6 pdr M/S	8.14-1919
15	H.877	HORATIO	174/06	1-12 pdr M/S	9.14-1919
	H.485	HORNSEA	305/00	1-6 pdrAA BDV	8.16-1920
	GY.292	HORTENSIA =in WW II.	244/07	(ex-Conquest) BDV	8.16-10.18
618	GY.650	HOUBARA	293/11	1-12 pdr M/S	4.15-1919
24	GY.26	HOWE =HOWE II 3.17	134/96	1-6 pdrAA	12.14-7.18
25	BN.89	HUNGARIAN	186/00	1-6 pdr M/S	11.14-1919
0	GN.74	HUNTER	185/03	M/S =BDV 9.15	8.14-1919
531	GY.536	HUXLEY	191/99	(ex-Khedive) 1-6 pdrAA	6.15-1919
918	GY.196	HYDRA =HYDRA II 7.16	214/06	1-6 pdrAA, 1-7,5 in BT M/S	10.15-1919

Adty No.	Port No.	Name	TG/Yr	Armament, Fate, etc.	Service
1364	H.963	IAGO	206/07	1–3 pdr M/S	3.15–1919
410	H.764	IBIS	168/03	1–12 pdr, 1–6 pdrAA M/S	10.14–1919
3308		ICELAND	312/16	1–6 pdrAA M/S, Escort	10.16–12.18
252	GY.58	IDA ADAMS	275/07	(*ex-Ruby*) 1–4 in, 1–7.5 in BT M/S	8.14–1919
3332	FD.288	IDENA	270/17	1–12 pdr M/S Abandoned and scuttled 5.2.18 (sunk by gunfire) off Tromso.	3.17–2.18
2669	CF.35	IJUIN	257/11	1–6 pdr Sunk 22.7.18 by S/M gunfire.	5.15–7.18
53 1221	GY.127	ILUSTRA	448/14	1–4 in, 1–6 pdr M/S	8.14–1919
519	FD.13	IMELDA	251/14	1–6 pdrAA M/S =in WW II.	9.14–1919
620	GY.758	IMPERIA	213/12	1–6 pdrAA =in WW II.	9.14–1919
1348	H.193	IMPERIAL QUEEN	246/14	1–12 pdr, 1–7.5 in BT M/S Hydro	5.15–1919
2658	GY.872	INAWILLIAM	337/13	1–12 pdr M/S Mined 30.5.17 off Berehaven.	4.15–5.17
3338	A.755	INCHGARTH	226/17	1–6 pdrAA M/S =STAR OF FREEDOM in WW II.	3.17–1919
481	LH.106	INCHKEITH	174/06	1–6 pdr M/S	12.14–1919
798	H.957	INDIAN EMPIRE	289/07	1–12 pdr, 1–7.5 inBT M/S	12.14–1919
429	GY.178	IPSWICH	161/96	1–6 pdrAA M/S	12.14–1919
1604	GY.728	IRANIAN	202/13	1–6 pdrAA M/S =in WW II.	3.15–1919
270	H.941	IRAWADI	238/06	(*ex-Hector*) M/S Wrecked 10.8.16 on Tigani Rocks, Eastern Mediterranean.	8.14–8.16
1456	HL.73	IRENE WRAY	216/14	1–6 pdrAA M/S =MARIA R. OMMERING in WW II.	5.15–1919
473	A.418	ISABELLA FOWLIE	196/11	1–12 pdr, 1–6 pdrAA M/S	11.14–1919
1746	GY.164	ISERNIA	198/99	1–6 pdrAA, 1–7.5 in BT M/S	7.15–1920
62	SN.148	ISLAND PRINCE	205/11	1–6 pdrAA M/S	8.14–1919
651	H.826	ISLE OF MAN	176/05	1–12 pdr M/S	10.14–1919
543	H.852	ISLE OF WIGHT	176/05	1–6 pdrAA, 1–7.5 in BT M/S	10.14–1919
720	GY.92	ITALY	145/96	1–6 pdr Sunk 3.9.16 in collision off Sunderland.	12.14–9.16
1980	GY.108	ITONIAN	288/14	1–6 pdrAA, 1–7.7 in BT M/S	1.16–1919
664	GY.902	IVANHOE	190/98	A/P Wrecked 3.11.14 in the Firth of Forth.	10.14–11.14
661	SA.47	IZAAK WALTON	252/07	1–4 in, 1–6 pdrAA M/S =Q ship 7.18–11.18.	11.14–1919
1592	LL.3	JABOO II	236/15	1–6 pdrAA M/S	5.15–1919
1207	GY.649	JACAMAR	293/11	1–12 pdr M/S Sunk 28.1.17 in collision off Folkestone LV.	5.15–1.17
1976	FD.235	JACINTA	289/15	1–6 pdr, 1–7.5 in BT M/S =in WW II.	12.15–1920
1226	H.33	JACINTH	248/14	1–12 pdr, 1–6 pdrAA M/S =INVERFORTH in WW II.	2.15–1919
1666	H.216	JAMAICA	205/14	Hydro tender =ALL HALLOWS in WW II.	2.17–1919
64	HL.9	JAMES B. GRAHAM	198/14	1–3 pdr M/S	9.14–1919
85	SN.172	JAMES PITCHERS	197/11	1–3 pdr M/S	8.14–1919
516	A.392	JAMES S. MELVILLE	211/11	1–12 pdr, 1–7.5 in BT M/S	9.14–1919
3351	A.454	JANE ROSS	184/01	1–12 pdr M/S	6.15–1919
325	GY.64	JANUS =JANUS II 12.14	240/05	1–3 pdr M/S	8.14–1920
42	GY.28	JAPAN	205/04	M/S Mined 16.8.15 off the Shipwash.	8.14–8.15
10	SN.76	JASON	176/98	M/S =Mercantile loss 1.4.15.	8.14–9.14
375	H.534	JAY	166/97	1–6 pdrAA M/S Torpedoed 11.8.17 off Southwold.	10.14–8.17

Adty No.	Port No.	Name	TG/Yr	Armament, Fate, etc.	Service
282	HL.82	JEANIE STEWART	210/16	1–6 pdr AA, 1–3.5 in BT M/S Hydro	6.16–1919
546	GY.522	JELLICOE =RUSHCOE 7.15	338/15	1–4 in, 1–12 pdr, 1–3 pdr =CERESIO in WW II.	7.15–1919
319	GY.985	JERIA	344/16	1–6 pdr M/S	12.16–12.17
577	H.310	JERICHO	351/14	(ex-Sir John Jellicoe) 1–12 pdr =KOPANES in WW II.	5.15–1920
3	H.870	JESSICA	173/06	1–6 pdr AA M/S	8.14–1919
312	A.243	JESSIE NUTTEN	187/08	M/S Mined 4.9.16 off Lowestoft.	8.14–9.16
796	H.711	JOHANNESBURG	181/03	1–3 pdr M/S	10.15–1919
436	SN.70	JOHN C. MEIKLE	194/14	1–3 pdr M/S	11.14–1919
435	SN.52	JOHN DONOVAN	206/14	1–3 pdr M/S	12.14–1919
321	A.354	JOHN E. LEWIS	253/11	1–3 pdr M/S Mined 16.1.18 off the Cork LV, Harwich	8.14–1.18
427	A.327	JOHN G. WATSON	196/10	1–6 pdr M/S Sunk 31.10.15 in collision near Stornoway.	11.14–10.15
322	SN.305	JOHN G. WATSON	235/16	1–6 pdr AA M/S, Escort	1.17–1919
	A.593	JOHN H. IRVIN	199/13	BDV	6.15–1919
252	SN.233	JOHN HIGH	228/15	1–6 pdr AA M/S Mined 7.8.16 off Mount Sozonova, White Sea.	1.16–8.16
315	H.644	JOHN SHERBURN	244/02	A/P Wrecked 6.3.15 near Dover.	12.14–3.15
467	HL.69	JOHN T. GRAHAM	198/12	1–6 pdr AA M/S	10.14–1919
132	LO.175	JOSEPH & SARAH MILES	272/02	1–12 pdr M/S	4.15–1920
45	H.880	JULIET	173/06	1–6 pdr AA M/S	9.14–1919
657	H.587	JUNCO	191/17	1–12 pdr M/S	1.18–1919
778	GY.572	KALMIA	189/94	1–6 pdr Damaged by Fire 7.10.18 at Stavros, repaired. =AMOS in WW II.	5.15–10.18
91	M.142	KALMIA =KALMIA II 8.25	184/98	1–6 pdr AA M/S	1.15–1919
64	FD.188	KAPHREDA	245/11	(ex-A. G.) M/S Mined 8.6.16 near Corton LV.	8.14–6.16
324	GY.1017	KASTORIA	307/17	1–12 pdr M/S, Escort =in WW II.	1.17–1919
975	A.620	KATE LEWIS	207/16	1–6 pdr AA M/L, M/S Purchased; sold 1939	8.16–1939
469	HL.30	KATHLEEN BURTON	197/14	M/S	5.15–1919
974	H.357	KELVIN	322/15	1–6 pdr AA M/S Mined 7.7.17 off Harwich.	11.15–7.17
	A.332	KENNET	167/99	BDV	6.15–1919
373	GY.38	KENNYMORE	225/14	1–12 pdr, 1–7.5 in BT M/S =in WW II.	4.15–1919
87	GY.1156	KENSINGTON	172/00	1–3 pdr, 1–2 pdr	11.14–1919
41	SA.40	KIDWELLY CASTLE	259/07	1–6 pdr AA M/S	4.15–1919
87	H.1014	KILLDEER	192/13	1–6 pdr AA M/S	11.14–1919
1	GY.167	KIMBERLEY	190/02	1–12 pdr M/S =in WW II.	8.14–1919
05	A.83	KINALDIE	197/14	1–6 pdr M/S	11.14–1919
	A.263	KINCORTH	148/09	Special service, Mine duties	2.17–1920
042	A.813	KINELLAR	216/17	1–6 pdr M/S	6.17–1919
354	GY.11	KING ARTHUR	159/99	1–3 pdr M/S	6.15–1920
	GY.1195	KING EDWARD	163/00	1–6 pdr BDV	1.15–1919
576	GY.97	KING EGBERT	159/99	1–3 pdr M/S	6.15–1920
220	H.202	KING EMPEROR	246/14	1–3 pdr M/L, M/S =in WW II.	5.15–1919
J.5A N.66					
368	GY.474	KING ERIK	228/99	1–3 pdr M/S	4.15–1919
659	GY.482	KING FREDERICK	260/09	(ex-King Frederick III) 1–12 pdr M/S =GLACIER in WW II.	5.15–1919

Adty No.	Port No.	Name	TG/Yr	Armament, Fate, etc.	Service
78	H.871	KING LEAR	311/06	1–12 pdr, 1–7.5 in BT M/S =Q ship 5.17–4.18 (DIANA, ENID, KIB).	11.14–1919
1775	GY.1181	KING RICHARD	162/00	1–3 pdr M/S	10.15–1920
	GY.1174	KING STEPHEN	162/00	Q ship (LEDGER No. 778) Sunk 25.4.16 by S/M in the North Sea.	2.16–4.16
1628	GY.486	KING'S GREY	338/15	1–10 pdr M/S =in WW II.	5.15–1919
2575	GY.206	KINGSTON	161/97	1–3 pdr M/S	6.15–1919
	GY.37	KINGSWAY	211/05	1–3 pdr BDV =in WW II.	12.14–1919
360	LO.282	KIRKLAND	224/08	M/S Mined 20.8.17 off Fugla Skerry Papastour, Shetlands.	8.14–8.17
3272	SN.236	KIRKLINTON	227/16	1–6 pdrAA M/S	4.16–1919
	GN.42	KIRTON	125/86	1–3 pdr BDV	5.16–1919
415	H.773	KITE =KITE II 2.15	168/03	1–6 pdrAA M/S	11.14–1919
647	H.420	KLONDYKE	155/98	M/S Sunk 4.6.16 in collision near Owers LV.	10.14–6.16
683	H.784	KNOT	168/03	1–3 pdr M/S Wrecked 5.11.16 on North Caer Rock.	11.14–11.16
2668	CF.34	KODAMA	257/11	1–12 pdr M/S	5.15–1919
324	M.120	KOORAH	227/12	1–3 pdr M/S	8.14–1919
3273	A.617	KOSMOS	231/16	1–6 pdrAA M/S	4.16–1919
1343	A.374	KUDOS	207/11	1–6 pdr M/S	4.15–1919
128	FD.176	KUMU	315/13	1–6 pdr M/S	9.14–1919
3343	CF.46	KUNISHI	268/17	1–12 pdr M/S Hydro =NORINA in WW II.	7.17–1919
655	CF.8	KUROKI	248/09	1–6 pdr M/S =in WW II.	11.14–1919
970	GY.421	KYMRIC	126/91	1–3 pdr M/S	2.15–1919
625	GY.641	LACERTA	270/11	1–12 pdr M/S =in WW II.	9.14–1919
4	GY.183	LADYSMITH	254/06	1–12 pdrAA M/S	8.14–1920
3254	FD.292	LANERCOST	227/16	1–12 pdr M/S =DARWEN in WW II.	1.16–1919
3311	GY.930	LAPAGERIA	274/16	1–12 pdr M/S =in WW II.	10.16–1919
1206	H.258	LAPWING =LAPWING II 2.15	152/94	1–6 pdrAA M/S	1.15–10.18
39	GY.24	LAPWING =LAPWING III 5.15	217/04	1–6 pdrAA M/S =in WW II.	8.14–1919
480	GY.322	LARK =LARK II 2.15	280/07	1–12 pdr, 1–6 pdrAA M/S	12.14–1919
708	GY.275	LAUREL =LAUREL II 2.15	138/97	1–3 pdr	11.14–11.18
1797	GY.1177	LAVINIA	198/00	1–3 pdr BDV	5.15–1919
1357	SA.52	LAWRENNY CASTLE	256/08	1–12 pdr M/S	3.15–1919
2995	FD.290	LEAM	236/17	A/P =BELLDOCK in WW. II.	1.17–1919
18	GY.260	LEANDER =LEANDROS 2.15	276/07	M/S Mined 6.8.15 off North Knock.	8.14–8.15
469	GN.22	LEITH, N. B.	203/14	1–12 pdr M/S	12.14.–1919
1547	GY.374	LEMBERG	275/14	1–12 pdr	7.15–1919
3223	FD.189	LENA MELLING	274/15	1–3 pdr M/S Mined 23.4.16 near Elbow Light Buoy off Broadstairs.	11.15–4.16
37	GY.20	LEONORA	217/04	1–6 pdr AA M/S =in WW II.	8.14–1920
	A.103	LEUKOS	216/14	BDV	6.15–1919
	A.447	LEVEN	168/00	BDV	6.15–1919
3026	FD.291	LEYLAND	236/17	1–6 pdrAA M/S	3.17–1919
3330	GY.1023	LEYS	222/16	1–6 pdrAA M/S	3.17–1919

Adty No.	Port No.	Name	TG/Yr	Armament, Fate, etc.	Service
26	GY.159	LIBERIA	250/06	1–3 pdr =in WW II.	8.14–1919
29	GY.687	LIBRA	211/12	1–3 pdr M/S =TOCSIN in WW II.	9.14–1919
127	GY.938	LIBYAN	202/13	1–6 pdr M/S =in WW II.	2.15–1919
400	FD.222	LILY MELLING	246/08	1–6 pdr M/S	12.14–1919
771	GY.1125	LIMEWOLD	189/98	(ex-*Derwent*) 1–6 pdr M/S	12.14–1919
513	A.338	LINN O'DEE	227/15	1–6 pdrAA M/S =OCEAN BRINE in WW II.	11.15–1919
	A.43	LINNET	142/87	(ex-*Her Majesty*) BDV =FT	6.15–7.18
256	H.496	LIVINGSTONE	213/00	1–3 pdr M/S Sunk 12.12.17 by SMS EMDEN and destroyers in the North Sea.	8.14–12.17
432	FD.156	LIZZIE	278/07	1–12 pdr M/S	8.14–1920
2511	PN.45	LIZZIE MELLING	207/04	1–6 pdr M/S	6.15–1919
974	M.147	LOBELIA =LOBELIA II 12.15	184/98	1–3 pdr Mined 19.4.17 off Fanad Point, Lough Swilly.	4.15–4.17
830	A.503	LOCH ARD	225/12	M/S Mined 10.9.17 off Lowestoft.	8.14–9.17
198	A.321	LOCH ASSATER	210/10	1–3 pdr M/S =in WW II.	4.15–1919
341	A.274	LOCH AWE	216/09	1–6 pdr M/S	4.15–1919
326	A.141	LOCH BROOM	197/07	1–3 pdr M/S Hydro	8.14–1919
3263	A.761	LOCH BUIE	221/15	1–12 pdr M/S	3.16–1919
271	A.161	LOCH DOON	193/07	1–6 pdrAA M/S	8.14–1919
840	A.241	LOCH ESK	215/08	1–3 pdr M/S	8.14–1920
2965	A.693	LOCH EYE	225/16	1–6 pdr M/S Mined 20.4.17 off Dunmore.	9.16–4.17
	HL.32	LOCH GARRY	176/03	A/P Foundered 14.9.16 off Kirkwall.	1.16–9.16
173	A.502	LOCH HOURN	209/12	1–12 pdr M/S Hydro	2.15–1919
107	A.163	LOCH KILDONAN	211/J7	1–3 pdr M/S	8.14–1919
190	A.325	LOCH LEE	210/10	1–6 pdr	3.15–1919
76	A.132	LOCH LOYAL	196/07	1–6 pdrAA M/S	8.14–1919
298	A.649	LOCH LYON	225/16	1–12 pdr M/S	7.16–1919
339	A.312	LOCH MAREE	215/10	1–6 pdrAA M/S	4.15–1919
272	A.501	LOCH MORAR	228/12	1–6 pdrAA M/S	8.14–1919
179	A.45	LOCH NAVER	216/06	1–6 pdr Mined 13.5.18 in Aegean Sea.	2.15–5.18
	A.475	LOCH RANNOCH	178/01	BDV	9.16–1919
572	A.273	LOCH SHIEL	216/09	1–3 pdr Mined 26.9.16 off Milford Haven.	4.15–9.16
178	A.494	LOCH TUMMEL	228/12	1–6 pdr Foundered 14.7.18 in the Mediterranean.	4.15–7.18
222	A.457	LOCH WASDALE	210/15	1–12 pdrAA M/S	10.15–1919
461	FD.113	LOIS	310/10	1–12 pdr M/S	1.15–1919
611	GY.478	LOMBARD	272/09	1–12 pdr M/S, Escort =in WW II.	4.15–1920
503	GY.376	LONGSET	275/14	1–6 pdr Mined 6.2.17 off Wells Point.	5.15–2.17
06	H.119	LOON	191/14	1–12 pdr M/S =in WW II.	10.14–1919
47	GY.910	LORD AIREDALE	215/11	1–3 pdr Mined 29.11.16 off Sunk LV.	2.15–11.16
351	GY.891	LORD ALLENDALE	215/11	1–12 pdr M/S	2.15–1919
4047	GY.1059	LORD ALVERSTONE	247/17	1–6 pdrAA M/S Sunk 12.12.17 by SMS EMDEN and destroyers in the North Sea.	6.17–12.17
234	GY.909	LORD ASHBY	215/11	1–3 pdr M/S	3.15–1919
000	GY.768	LORD CECIL	228/16	1–12 pdr M/S =in WW II.	7.16–1919
144	GY.911	LORD DE RAMSEY	215/11	1–6 pdr M/S	2.15–1919

Adty No.	Port No.	Name	TG/Yr	Armament, Fate, etc.	Service
1525	H.118	LORD DENMAN	309/14	1-12 pdr M/S Sunk 22.10.15 in collision in the White Sea.	6.15-10.15
460	GY.879	LORD DURHAM	215/11	1-6 pdrAA M/S	2.15-1919
688	GY.83	LORD GEORGE	229/05	(ex-*St. George*) 1-6 pdrAA M/S =CEDRIC in WW II.	2.15-1919
1605	GY.904	LORD GREY	215/11	1-6 pdrAA M/S Wrecked 2.12.17 on La Barrier Shoal, Cape Gris Nez.	3.15-12.17
2993	GY.1013	LORD HARDINGE	212/17	1-6 pdrAA M/S Sunk 9.4.18 in collision off Daunt LV.	1.17-4.18
1140	H.27	LORD HENEAGE	324/09	1-12 pdr, 1-7.5 in BT M/S	2.15-1919
1177	H.327	LORD KNOLLYS	285/11	1-12 pdr Hydro	3.15-1919
3020	H.1004	LORD LANSDOWNE	289/13	1-12 pdr, 1-7.5 in BT M/S	2.17-1919
1568	H.484	LORD LISTER	285/12	1-12 pdr, 1-7.5 in BT M/S	5.15-1919
1991	H.427	LORD MERSEY	326/16	1-12 pdr, 1-7.5 in BT M/S	4.16-1919
1516	H.105	LORD MINTO	295/14	1-12 pdr M/S	5.15-1919
3260	GY.759	LORD NORTHCLIFFE	228/16	1-6 pdr M/S, Escort =in WW II.	3.16-1919
1609	GY.898	LORD PERCY	215/11	1-6 pdr M/S	3.15-1920
1994	H.429	LORD READING	326/16	1-12 pdr, 1-7.5 in BT M/S	4.16-1919
850	GY.900	LORD RIDLEY	215/11	M/S Mined 10.5.17 off Whitby.	2.15-5.17
545	H.955	LORD ROBERTS	293/07	1-12 pdr, 1-3 pdr Mined 26.10.16 off the Shipwash.	11.14-10.16
1212	H.323	LORD SALISBURY	285/11	1-12 pdr M/S Mined 4.5.17 off Eros Island, Salonika.	1.15-5.17
1652	GY.1058	LORD SELBORNE	247/17	1-12 pdr M/S, Escort =in WW II.	10.17-1919
2961	GY.931	LORD STANHOPE	212/16	1-12 pdr M/S =SANSONNET in WW II.	9.16-1919
703	GY.916	LORD WIMBORNE	215/11	1-12 pdr M/S	11.14-1919
1235	GY.917	LORD WOLMER	215/11	1-3 pdr M/S	3.15-1919
1519	H.264	LORDSHIP	351/15	(ex-*Lord Fisher*) 1-12 pdr, 1-6 pdr, 1-7.5 in BT M/S	5.15-1919
603	H.865	LORENZO	173/06	A/P Wrecked 17.12.14 in Hoy Sound.	9.14-12.14
1588	GY.830	LOROONE	214/13	1-6 pdrAA M/S =CALVERTON in WW II.	6.15-1919
471	A.112	LOTOS	216/14	1-12 pdr M/S	11.14-1919
3289	GY.396	LOUIS BOTHA	226/16	1-6 pdrAA M/S =in WW II.	6.16-1919
144	SA.50	LOUISE	270/07	1-6 pdr M/S	8.14-1920
965					
51	SN.244	LOYAL PRINCE	208/13	1-6 pdrAA	8.14-1919
925	FD.20	LUCIDA	251/14	1-12 pdr, 1-7.5 in BT M/S	11.14-1919
649	H.739	LUCKNOW	171/03	1-3 pdr M/S Mined 18.5.17 off Portsmouth.	10.14-5.17
	A.259	LUNAN BAY	126/88	(ex-*Maggie Walker*) 1-3 pdr BDV	6.15-1919
1791	H.993	LUNDY	188/08	1-3 pdr Sunk 16.8.15 in collision at Suvla Bay.	5.15-8.15
	GY.1143	LUNE	197/00	BDV	1.15-1919
926	FD.230	LUNEDA	288/12	1-12 pdr, 1-7.5 in BT M/S	11.14-1919
162	M.232	LYDIAN	244/08	A/P Mined 18.9.15 off S. Foreland.	8.14-9.15
964	BL.5	LYNMOUTH	140/92	1-12 pdr	1.15-1919
31	GY.133	LYNX =LYNX II 2.15	250/06	1-6 pdrAA M/S	9.14-1919
255	H.800	LYSANDER =LYSANDER II 2.15	264/03	2-6 pdr M/S	8.14-1919
2660	GY.473	LYSANDER =LYSANDER III 6.15	173/98	(ex-*Karsivina*) 1-3 pdr	5.15-11.18
	SN.152	M. A. DODDS	150/92	BDV	6.15-8.18

Adty No.	Port No.	Name	TG/Yr	Armament, Fate, etc.	Service
45	M.18	MACAW	187/09	1–6 pdr AA M/S =in WW II.	8.14–1919
69	H.869	MACBETH	311/06	1–12 pdr, 1–3 pdr M/S	10.14–1919
577	H.894	MACDUFF =MACDUFF II 9.17	179/06	1–3 pdr M/S	6.15–1919
220	H.997	MACFARLANE	284/08	1–6 pdrAA M/S	2.15–1919
36	H.349	MACKENZIE	335/11	1–6 pdrAA M/S	8.14–1919
327	H.1022	MACLEAY	317/13	1–12 pdr, 1–7.5 in BT	2.17–1919
37	H.716	MAFEKING	181/03	1–12 pdr, 1–7.5 in BT M/S	10.14–1919
970	H.354	MAGNETA	322/15	1–12 pdr, 1–7.5 in BT M/S	9.15–1919
741	GY.226	MAGNOLIA =MAGNOLIA II 7.15	213/97	1–6 pdr AA, 1–2 pdr	1.15–1919
90	M.146	MAGNOLIA =MAGNOLIA III 8.15	184/98	1–6 pdr M/S	7.15–1919
80	H.802	MAGPIE =MAGPIE II 8.15	278/04	1–6 pdrAA M/S	11.14–1919
00	GY.325	MALTA	138/97	A/P Mined 1.9.15 off the North Shipwash Buoy.	11.14–9.15
99	FD.174	MANOR	314/13	1–12 pdr M/S =in WW II.	8.14–1919
	A.439	MANORBIER CASTLE	153/98	BDV Accom.	6.15–1920
	GY.665	MANX ADMIRAL	219/12	1–6 pdr BDV	12.14–1919
39	GY.585	MANX HERO	221/10	(ex-Berian) M/S Mined 10.3.15 in the Kephez minefield, Dardanelles.	8.14–3.15
291	GY.883	MANX HERO	235/16	1–6 pdrAA M/S =ROTTERDAM in WW II.	7.16–1919
274	GY.881	MANX KING	235/16	1–6 pdrAA M/S	4.16–1919
11	GY.542	MANX PRINCE	220/10	1–6 pdr M/S =in WW II.	8.14–1919
529	GY.491	MANX QUEEN	234/15	1–6 pdr M/S Wrecked 1.3.16 on Filey Brig.	6.15–3.16
304	H.488	MARCONI	322/16	1–12 pdr M/S =in WW II.	8.16–1919
93	LL.123	MARGARET DUNCAN	224/13	1–6 pdr =LUDA LORD in WW II.	12.14–1919
	A.344	MARGARET WETHERLY	211/11	BDV Accom.	6.15–1920
18	GY.218	MARGATE	161/97	1–6 pdrAA Sunk 24.4.17 by S/M off Severn Point.	11.14–4.17
0	DE.14	MARION	128/91	1–3 pdr M/S Mined 23.2.18 off Malta.	8.14–2.18
978	M.14	MARISTO	287/14	1–12 pdr M/S	12.15–1919
	GY.306	MARLBOROUGH	213/07	BDV =in WW II.	12.14–1919
5	M.76	MARLOES	220/11	1–6 pdrAA M/S	8.14–1919
365	H.231	MARNE =MARNE II 1.16	257/15	1–6 pdrAA M/S	4.15–1919
14	H.187	MARTIN =MARTIN II 2.15	242/97	1–12 pdr M/S	11.14–11.16
	GY.505	MARTINETA	279/09	BDV	10.16–1920
590	FD.38	MARTON	232/05	1–6 pdrAA M/S	6.15–1919
61	FD.84	MARY	256/06	M/S Mined 5.11.14 off Yarmouth.	8.14–11.14
345	A.159	MARY WETHERLY	221/07	1–6 pdr M/S	4.15–1919
34	H.981	MASTWING	199/08	1–6 pdr M/S	11.14–1919
22	FD.81	MAUN	271/06	1–6 pdr M/S	8.14–1919
049	H.563	MAX PEMBERTON	334/17	1–12 pdr M/S Hydro experiments	6.17–1919
97	GY.973	MAXIMUS	236/98	(ex-Ulleswater) 1–6 pdrAA	12.14–1919
09	A.483	MEDIATOR	178/12	A/P Mined 2.1.16 off Hornsea.	9.14–1.16
47 53	GY.210	MENA	234/14	M/S =LUDA LADY in WW II.	2.15–1920
27	FD.153	MERISIA	291/12	1–6 pdr M/S	9.14–1919
794	GY.190	MERLIN	186/99	1–3 pdr M/S	5.15–1920
74	H.924	MERLIN =MERLIN II 8.15	172/06	1–6 pdrAA M/S	10.14–1919

Adty No.	Port No.	Name	TG/Yr	Armament, Fate, etc.	Service
685	GY.94	MEROR	250/05	(ex-Emperor) 1–3 pdr, 1–2 pdr =in WW II.	11.14–1920
1759	FD.77	MERRYDALE	225/06	1–6 pdr M/S	5.15–1919
980	FD.62	MERSE	296/14	1–12 pdr M/S Mined 22.5.17 off Garroch Head, Bute.	2.15–5.17
1993	SA.34	MEWSLADE	275/16	1–6 pdr M/S =in WW II.	4.16–1919
1510	H.324	MICHAEL ANGELO	285/11	1–12 pdr M/S	5.15–1919
1222	H.823	MIKADO	265/05	1–6 pdrAA M/S	2.15–1919
1771	CF.41	MIKASA	255/13	1–6 pdr, 1–7.5 in BT	5.15–1919
1886	H.366	MILETUS	313/15	1–12 pdr =LOWTHER in WW II.	9.15–1919
33	BN.148	MININGSBY	245/08	1–3 pdr M/S	9.14–1919
416	H.799	MINO	168/03	1–6 pdr M/S	11.14–1919
348	GY.484	MINORU =MINORU II 11.17	260/09	1–12 pdr M/S	8.14–1920
601	H.875	MIRANDA =MIRANDA III 2.15	173/06	1–3 pdr M/S Wrecked 14.1.18 in Pelwick Bay.	9.14–1.18
461	HL.10	MIRIAM STEWART	197/14	1–3 pdr M/S	9.14–1919
3078	GY.1105	MITRES	261/17	A/P =in WW II.	12.17–1919
979	CF.36	MIURA	257/11	1–3 pdr Mined 23.8.15 off Yarmouth.	2.15–8.15
3302	CF.45	MIURA	275/15	1–12 pdr, 1–6 pdr M/S Hydro	8.16–1919
1599	GY.29	MONARCH =MONARCH III 8.15	234/04	1–12 pdr, 1–7.5 in BT M/S	7.15–1919
1606	H.966	MOPSA	206/07	1–6 pdr AA M/S	3.15–1919
1272	GY.1018	MORAVIA	206/17	1–12 pdr M/S =in WW II.	6.17–1919
1630	GN.55	MORAY	201/15	1–6 pdrAA M/S	5.15–1919
	SH.61	MORNING STAR	145/00	BDV	6.16–1919
2656	A.238	MOROCOCALA	265/15	1–6 pdr Mined 19.11.17 off Daunt LV.	4.15–11.17
2769	A.567	MORVEN	198/02	1–6 pdrAA M/S	6.15–1919
1439	GY.300	MORVINA	226/14	1–6 pdr M/S	4.15–1919
1174	H.379	MYNA	333/12	1–6 pdrAA, 1–7.5 in BT M/S =BORTIND in WW II.	2.15–1919
693	GY.138	NADINE	150/98	(ex-Niobe) A/P. Mined 1.9.15 off the North Shipwash Buoy.	11.14–9.15
3269	0.144	NAIADE	240/07	(ex-St. Clear) 1–6 pdrAA M/S	3.16–1919
2513	M.238	NAIRANA =NAIRANA II 3.17	225/13 =in WW II.	1–6 pdr M/S	11.15–1919
1360	FD.133	NANCY HAGUE	299/11	1–6 pdrAA M/S =in WW II.	3.15–1919
3268	0.141	NARVAL	211/10	1–12 pdr M/S Disappeared 26.11.16 between Grimsby and Harwich.	3.16–11.16
305	GY.1277	NATAL =NATAL II 2.15	208/03	1–3 pdr =in WW II.	8.14–1919
3267	0.128	NAUTILUS =NAUTILUS II 7.16	257/05	1–6 pdrAA M/S	3.16–1919
1763	SA.6	NEATH CASTLE	225/13	1–3 pdr Sunk 14.8.16 in collision off the Orkneys.	5.15–8.16
2981	SA.65	NEATH CASTLE	275/16	1–12 pdr M/S	11.16–1919
161	GY.624	NEIL GOW	255/11	1–12 pdr, 1–3 pdr, 1–7.5 in BT M/S	8.14–1920
521	FD.175	NELLIE BRADDOCK	314/13	1–12 pdr M/S	11.14–1919
426	SN.159	NELLIE DODDS	220/11	1–12 pdr M/S =EBOR ABBEY in WW II.	11.14–1919
81	GN.89	NELLIE NUTTEN	184/01	1–3 pdr M/S Sunk 11.7.16 gunfire of U.46, U.49, U.52 and U.69 off Aberdeen.	8.14–7.16
1523	H.626	NEPTUNIAN	315/13	1–6 pdr M/S Sunk 27.10.18 in collision near Albacarry Light House.	5.15–10.18

Adty No.	Port No.	Name	TG/Yr	Armament, Fate, etc.	Service
3266	O.143	NEREE	230/09	(ex-Athalia) 1–6 pdrAA M/S, Special Service	3.16–1919
1793	H.879	NERISSA =NERISSA II 12.15	173/06	1–6 pdr Wrecked 28.2.18 off Lemnos.	8.15–2.18
1496	GN.75	NEW COMET	177/10	M/S Mined 20.1.17 off Orford Ness.	5.15–1.17
	H.413	NEW ZEALAND =HOKIANGA 4.18	290/98	BDV	8.16–1920
963	FD.55	NEWBRIDGE	228/06	1–3 pdr M/S Sunk 19.11.17 in collision off Prawle Point.	5.15–11.17
82	GN.72	NEWHAVEN, N. B.	182/09	1–6 pdr M/S =in WW II.	8.14–1919
942	H.713	NEWLAND	245/03	1–12 pdr, 1–7.5 in BT M/S Hydro =in WW II.	1.15–1919
57	GY.643	NIGHT HAWK	287/11	M/S Mined 25.12.14 off Scarborough.	8.14–12.14
1936	GY.822	NIGHT HAWK	307/16	1–6 pdrAA M/S, Escort =in WW II.	3.16–1919
	FD.11	NILE	196/98	BDV	6.15–1919
1536	GY.700	NINUS	292/12	2–12 pdr, 1–7.5 in BT Hydro =LOVANIA in WW II.	6.15–1919
1356	CF.37	NODZU	257/11	1–12 pdr Wrecked 1.1.19 off Nash Point, Bristol Channel; salved. =CLARINET in WW II.	3.15–1.19
192	CF.24	NOGI	257/08	1–6 pdr M/S	11.14–1919
2663	M.9	NOOGANA	237/14	1–3 pdr =ST. OLIVE in WW II.	5.15–1919
1374	FD.30	NORBRECK	201/05	1–3 pdr =CRAIGMILLAR in WW II.	4.15–1919
1575	H.249	NORMAN =NORMAN II 12.15	346/11	1–6 pdr, 1–7.5 in BT M/S Escort =DERVISH in WW II.	5.15–1919
1314	PD.502	NORMAN =NORMAN III 7.16	120/94	1–6 pdr Net	6.15–1919
1352	FD.72	NORSE	279/14	1–12 pdr, 1–7.5 in BT M/S	3.15–1919
512	A.86	NORTH KING	194/06	1–12 pdr M/S	9.14–1919
304	H.882	NORTH KING =NORTH KING II 12.14	271/06	1–6 pdrAA M/S	8.14–1919
681	A.78	NORTH QUEEN	195/06	1–3 pdr, 1–2 pdr =FINTRAY in WW II.	11.14–1919
267	A.172	NORTH STAR =NORTH STAR III 12.15	188/07	1–6 pdr M/S	8.14–1919
257	SN.282	NORTHERN PRINCE	208/13	1–6 pdrAA M/S	8.14–1919
327	A.414	NORTHMAN	197/11	1–6 pdr M/S =in WW II.	8.14–1919
623	GY.169	NORTHUMBRIA	211/06	1–12 pdr M/S Mined 3.3.17 near May Island.	9.14–3.17
807	GY.110	NORTHWARD	204/06	1–6 pdr M/S =in WW II.	11.14–1919
3279	GY.889	NOVELLI	226/16	1–12 pdr, 1–7 in BT M/S	5.16–1919
3270	O.127	NUMITOR	242/03	1–12 pdrAA, 1–6 pdrAA M/S Mined 20.4.18 off Orford Ness.	3.16–4.18
1488	GY.363	NYLGHAU	261/08	1–12 pdr M/S	5.15–1919
959	GY.948	OAKWOLD	129/95	A/P	1.15–11.15
160	YH.405	OCEAN COMRADE	133/92	(ex-Pesha) M/S, Net =FT.	8.14–3.18
	A.576	OCEAN PRINCE	203/02	BDV	9.14–1920
111	A.580	OCEAN PRINCESS	203/02	1–6 pdrAA, 1–7.5 in BT M/S	8.14–1919
546	H.856	OCEAN QUEEN	284/06	1–6 pdrAA M/S	11.14–1919
1555	A.362	OCEAN SCOUT I	200/15	1–6 pdrAA Sunk 21.12.17 in collision off Western Ireland.	7.15–12.17
391	H.449	OCEANIC =OCEANIC II 2.15	168/95	1–12 pdr =Q ship.	11.14–1919
1431	HL.68	OCTOROON	195/14	1–6 pdrAA M/S	4.15–1919
1406	GY.975	OFFA =OFFA II 12.15	313/13	1–12 pdr, 1–7.5 in BT	3.15–1919

Adty No.	Port No.	Name	TG/Yr	Armament, Fate, etc.	Service
285	GY.4	OKINO	241/14	M/S Mined 8.3.15 near Yeni Cale, Dardanelles.	8.14–3.15
3051	GY.1060	OKINO	311/17	1–12 pdr, 1–7.5 in BT M/S, Escort =in WW II.	7.17–1919
1355	CF.25	OKU	248/09	1–12 pdr, 1–6 pdrAA M/S	3.15–1919
825	GY.538	OLDHAM	165/98	1–12 pdr	12.14–1919
1211	H.849	OLIVINE	289/05	1–12 pdrAA M/S	1.15–1919
3064	GY.1080	OLYMPIA	261/17	1–12 pdr, 1–3.5 in BT Hydro =in WW II.	9.17–1919
283	A.592	ONETOS	217/13	M/S =in WW II.	8.14–1919
274	GY.213	ONTARIO	208/07	1–6 pdrAA M/S	8.14–1919
399	H.980	ONWARD	266/08	1–12 pdr M/S Sunk 11.7.16 by gunfire of U.46, U.49, U.52 and U.69 off Aberdeen.	12.14–7.16
1186	H.1029	ONYX =ONYX II 5.15	248/13	1–6 pdr, 1–7.5 in BT Escort =AMSTERDAM in WW II.	4.15–1919
351	GY.171	OPHIR =OPHIR II 2.15	213/06	1–6 pdrAA M/S	8.14–1919
1204	H.725	OPHIR =OPHIR III 2.15	230/03	1–12 pdr, 1–6 pdrAA, 1–7.5 in BT M/S =LADYLOVE in WW II.	1.15–1919
40	GY.640	ORCADES	270/11	M/S Mined 14.4.16 off Grimsby.	8.14–4.16
99	GY.291	ORIANDA	273/14	M/S Mined 19.12.14 off Scarborough.	9.14–12.14
636	H.926	ORIOLE =ORIOLE II 12.15	172/07	1–6 pdr M/S	10.14–1919
	GY.356	ORIZABA	233/08	1–6 pdr BDV =in WW II.	12.14–1919
365	GY.248	ORLANDO	276/07	M/S Wrecked 14.3.15 at Stornoway.	8.14–3.15
147	GY.162	ORMONDE =ORMONDE II 11.17	250/06	1–6 pdrAA M/S =in WW II.	8.14–1919
711	GY.358	OROPESA =OROPESA II 6.15	324/14	1–6 pdr M/S =DUSK in WW II.	11.14–1919
956	FD.119	ORPHESIA	273/07	1–6 pdr M/S Struck a wreck and sank 22.7.17 off Alexandria.	12.14–7.17
41	GY.74	ORPHEUS =ORPHEUS II 12.15	228/05	1–6 pdrAA M/S =in WW II.	8.14–1919
602	H.864	ORSINO	172/06	1–3 pdr Torpedoed 28.9.16 by S/M between Loch Eribol and Stromness.	9.14–9.16
282	A.591	ORTHOS	218/13	M/S Mined 9.4.17 off Lowestoft.	8.14–4.17
2962	GY.897	ORVICTO	226/16	1–6 pdrAA, 1–7.5 in BT M/S =in WW II.	9.16–1919
1354	FD.129	OSPRAY II	295/11	1–12 pdr M/S	3.15–1919
1591	FD.106	OSTA	230/15	1–6 pdrAA M/L, M/S =in WW II.	5.15–1920
1750	H.729	OSTRICH =OSTRICH II 10.15	244/03	1–6 pdrAA M/L, M/S	9.15–1920
1651	GY.1104	OSWALDIAN	261/17	1–12 pdr M/S =in WW II.	9.17–1919
619	GY.333	OTHELLO	201/07	1–6 pdr =in WW II.	9.14–1919
1193	H.956	OTHELLO II	206/07	1–6 pdr Mined 31.10.15 off Leathercoat.	3.15–10.15
940	M.24	OTHONNA	180/99	1–12 pdr, 1–6 pdrAA M/S Mined 20.4.17 off Fife Ness.	1.15–4.17
1757	GY.144	OTTILIE	226/14	1–6 pdrAA M/S	5.15–1919
	GW.15	OUSE	167/00	BDV	2.16–1919
373	H.801	OWL =OWL II 2.15	169/04	1–6 pdrAA M/S	10.14–1919
144	SA.46	OXWICH CASTLE	252/07	1–6 pdrAA M/S	1.15–1919

Adty No.	Port No.	Name	TG/Yr	Armament, Fate, etc.	Service
628	CF.23	OYAMA	257/08	1–12 pdr, 1–7.5 in BT M/S	10.14–1919
3060	SA.4	OYSTERMOUTH CASTLE	283/14	1–6 pdr =in WW II.	8.17–1919
1816	A.349	P. FANNON	211/15	1–6 pdr M/S	7.15–1919
164	HL.76	PARKMORE	199/15	1–6 pdrAA M/S =BEN TORC in WW II.	10.15–1919
679	H.445	PARRAMATTA	168/91	1–6 pdr M/S =FT.	12.14–9.15
814 328	GY.646	PARTHIAN =PARTHIAN II 12.15	202/11	1–6 pdr M/S =in WW II.	8.14–1919
58	GY.877	PASSING	459/13	1–12 pdr M/S	8.14–1920
1542 56	GY.716	PAVLOVA	342/12	1–6 pdr M/S =MARGARET ROSE in WW II.	8.14–1919
830	GY.1121	PEARL	198/99	1–6 pdr M/S	11.14–1919
306	H.883	PEARL =PEARL II 2.15	289/13	1–12 pdr M/S Hydro =CADELLA in WW II.	8.14–1919
1350	H.1016	PEARY	289/13	1–12 pdrAA M/S	5.15–1919
3068	GY.1101	PEGAS	219/17	(ex-Pegasus) 1–12 pdr M/S	12.17–1920
1171	A.170	PEGGY NUTTEN	193/07	1–6 pdrAA M/S =in WW II.	4.15–1919
24	GY.354	PEKEN	228/08	1–6 pdrAA M/S =in WW II.	8.14–1919
3295	A.623	PELAGOS	231/16	1–6 pdrAA, 1–7.5 in BT M/S	7.16–1919
527	PH.98	PELICAN I	248/08	1–12 pdr M/S =CEVIC in WW II.	11.14–1919
3265	GY.91	PELICAN II	205/05	1–12 pdr M/S =ERIDANUS in WW II.	7.16–1920
528	PH.178	PENGUIN	190/02	1–6 pdr M/S	11.14–1919
138	SA.38	PENNARD CASTLE	259/07	1–6 pdr M/S	9.14–1919
1799	SA.7	PENRICE CASTLE	255/13	1–3 pdr	6.15–1919
733	H.234	PERIDOT	214/94	A/P =Mercantile loss 10.7.17.	12.14–1.15
608	GY.197	PERIHELION	215/14	1–6 pdr =INVERCLYDE in WW II.	9.14–1920
799	H.476	PERSIAN EMPIRE	195/99	1–6 pdr, 1–7.5 in BT M/S	12.14–1919
302	GY.126	PERSIMON	255/11	A/P =Mercantile loss 5.6.15.	8.14–1.15
631	GY.244	PETERBOROUGH	161/97	1–6 pdrAA M/S	10.14–1919
333	SD.5	PETREL	151/93	M/S =Mercantile loss 30.3.17.	8.14–11.14
941	M.23	PETUNIA =PETUNIA II 12.15	180/99	1–6 pdrAA, 1–7.5 in BT M/S	1.15–1919
44	H.881	PHOEBE =PHOEBE II 12.15	178/06	1–6 pdrAA, 1–7.5 in BT M/S	9.14–1919
520	FD.142	PHRONTIS	288/11	1–12 pdr M/S =in WW II.	9.14–1919
1545	A.298	PHYLLIS BELMAN	211/15	1–6 pdrAA M/S	6.15–1919
2672	SA.107	PICTON CASTLE	245/11	1–3 pdr M/S Mined 19.2.17 off Dartmouth.	5.15–2.17
378	H.155	PIGEON =PIGEON II 12.15	166/97	1–6 pdrAA M/S	11.14–1919
382	H.982	PINTAIL	199/08	1–12 pdr, 1–6 pdrAA M/S	10.14–1919
2976	PD.241	PITFOUR	227/16	1–6 pdrAA, 1–7.5 in BT M/L, M/S	10.16–1919
89	A.585	PITSTRUAN	206/13	1–3 pdr M/S Mined 13.4.17 off Noss Head Light House.	8.14–4.17
468	A.545	PLETHOS	210/13	1–12 pdr, 1–6 pdrAA M/S Mined 23.4.18 off Montrose.	9.14–4.18
1273	H.25	PLYM	193/04	1–6 pdrAA M/S	3.17–1919
1196	A.57	POINTER	198/06	1–6 pdrAA, 1–7.5 in BT M/S =in WW II.	3.15–1919
2666	SA.5	POINTZ CASTLE	283/14	1–12 pdr Hydro =in WW II.	5.15–1919
95	SN.171	POLAR PRINCE	194/15	M/S	9.15–1919
401	H.462	POMONA	161/99	1–12 pdr	10.14–12.18

Adty No.	Port No.	Name	TG/Yr	Armament, Fate, etc.	Service
530 550	H.737	POONAH	171/03	1-3 pdr M/S Sunk 18.8.15 in collision near Stromness.	11.14-8.15
800	BL.10	PORTSMOUTH	178/03	1-12 pdr M/S	1.15-1919
3318	SA.68	POWIS CASTLE	275/16	1-6 pdr M/S =in WW II.	12.16-1919
1984	GY.737	PREFECT	302/16	1-4 in, 1-12 pdr, 1-7.5 in BT M/S =NORLAND in WW II.	3.16-1919
514 848	GY.385	PREMIER	253/08	1-6 pdrAA M/S	9.14-1919
721	GY.762	PRESIDENT =PRESIDENCY 2.15	257/07	1-12 pdr	12.14-1919
368	H.701	PRETORIA	180/02	1-6 pdr M/S	10.14-1920
32	GY.180	PRETORIA =PRETORIA II 5.15	283/06	M/S =Mercantile loss 10.7.17.	3.15-9.15
1634	GY.920	PRINCE LEO	218/13	1-6 pdrAA M/S =in WW II.	5.15-1919
341	H.95	PRINCE PALATINE	256/14	1-12 pdrAA M/S Hydro =LORD DARLING in WW II.	8.14-1919
1442	GY.569	PRINCE VICTOR	207/10	1-6 pdr M/S =in WW II.	4.15-1919
1504	GY.636	PRINCEPS	264/11	1-6 pdr	8.14-1919
2655	SN.15	PRINCESS ALICE	225/14	1-6 pdr Sunk 6.3.18 in collision off Alexandria.	4.15-3.18
287	SN.202	PRINCESS BEATRICE	214/12	M/S Mined 5.10.14 off the Belgian Coast.	8.14-10.14
199	H.824	PRINCESS JULIANA	266/05	(ex-Lord Curzon) 1-6 pdr M/S	11.14-1919
1176	H.140	PRINCESS LOUISE =PRINCESS LOUISE II 3.15	289/05	1-6 pdr M/S	2.15-1919
1770	H.242	PRINCESS MARIE JOSE	274/15	1-12 pdr, 1-7.5 in BT M/S =LOCH HOPE IN WW II.	5.15-1919
1181	SN.27	PRINCESS MARY	225/14	1-12 pdr Hydro =in WW II.	3.15-1919
322	A.440	PRINCESS MELTON	224/01	1-6 pdr AA M/S	8.14-1919
3031	SN.326	PRINCESS OLGA	245/16	1-6 pdr AA M/S Mined 14.6.18 off Le Havre.	4.17-6.18
518	SN.209	PRINCESS ROYAL =PRINCESS ROYAL II 2.15	213/13	1-6 pdrAA M/S	9.14-1919
1971	H.766	PRINCESS VICTORIA	272/03	1-3 pdr Sunk 7.11.15 in collision off Ushant.	9.15-11.15
3320	SN.321	PRINCESS VICTORIA	245/16	1-6 pdrAA M/S =MARANO in WW II.	1.17-1919
	A.899	PROCYON	195/03	(ex-Strathmartin) 1-3 pdr BDV	6.15-1919
659	H.974	PUFFIN	199/07	1-12 pdr M/S	10.14-1919
645	H.236	QUAIL =QUAIL II 2.15	162/97	2-3 pdr M/S Sunk 23.6.15 in collision off Portland.	11.14-6.15
691	GY.1197	QUEEN =QUEEN II 2.15 =QUEST 6.17	161/00	1-6 pdr M/S	11.14-1920
446	GY.680	QUERCIA	288/12	1-12 pdr M/S, Escort =in WW II.	12.14-1919
675	H.99	QUICKLY	242/97	(ex-Swift) 2-12 pdr, 1-6 pdrAA M/S =Q ship 7.15-11.18 (CAROLINA, MASTER, Q.32, SINTON, SWIFT).	10.14-1919
3296	HL.79	R. H. DAVISON	210/16	1-6 pdrAA M/S =TRITELIA in WW II.	7.16-1919
52	SN.246	R. IRVIN	208/13	1-6 pdrAA M/S	8.14-1919
241	YH.245	R. R. S.	159/13	1-6 pdrAA, 1-2 pdr	9.14-1919
1232	GY.707	RAETIA	295/12	1-12 pdr M/S =in WW II.	3.15-1919
1957	SA.30	RAGLAN CASTLE	274/15	1-12 pdr M/S, M/L experiments	11.15-1919

Adty No.	Port No.	Name	TG/Yr	Armament, Fate, etc.	Service
1574	A.69	RAINBOW	176/06	1–3 pdr =DOLORES in WW II.	4.15–1919
117	A.434	RAINDROP	167/12	1–6 pdrAA M/S	9.14–1919
694	GY.3	RAJAH	172/99	1–6 pdrAA M/S	11.14–9.18
672	GY.663	RALCO	228/12	1–6 pdr AA M/S =in WW II.	11.14–12.18
	H.399	RAMBLER	162/98	1–6 pdrAA BDV	11.15–1920
347	A.446	RATAPIKO	247/12	1–12 pdr, 1–6 pdrAA M/S =in WW II.	8.14–1919
357	SN.104	RATTRAY	182/00	M/S =FT	8.14–8.15
407	H.858	RAVEN =RAVEN II 2.15 =RAVEN III 8.15	172/06	1–12 pdr M/S	10.14–1919
2967	GY.895	RAYMONT	226/16	1–6 pdr M/S =in WW II.	9.16–1919
47	GY.254	RECEPTO	245/14	M/S Mined 16.2.17 in Tees Bay.	11.14–2.17
1988	GY.625	RECONO	248/16	1–6 pdrAA M/S, Escort =in WW II.	3.16–1920
1128	GY.507	RECORDO	230/10	1–3 pdr M/S =in WW II.	2.15–1920
411	H.692	REDCAP	199/07	1–3 pdr M/S =Mercantile loss 1.3.17.	11.14–12.15
423	H.846	REEVE	172/05	1–6 pdrAA M/S	11.14–1919
3053	GY.1063	REFUNDO	258/17	1–6 pdrAA, 1–7.5 in BT M/S Hydro =in WW II.	7.17–1919
1539	GY.158	REGAL	212/06	1–6 pdrAA M/S	6.15–1919
1963	GY.623	REGARDO	248/15	1–12 pdrAA M/S =in WW II.	12.15–1919
816	GY.1236	REINDEER =REINDEER II 1.15	192/02	1–6 pdrAA M/S	11.14–1920
1615	GY.670	RELEVO	176/12	1–12 pdr Wrecked 30.12.16 off El Arijh.	4.15–12.16
999	GY.30	RELIANCE =RELIANCE II 2.15	203/04	1–6 pdr M/S	12.14–1919
1614	GY.229	RELONZO	245/14	1–12 pdr Hydro =in WW II.	4.15–1920
1487	GY.843	REMAGIO	174/13	1–3 pdr M/S	5.15–1919
1489	GY.228	REMARKO	245/14	M/S Mined 3.12.16 off Lowestoft.	5.15–12.16
1136	GY.721	REMEXO	231/12	1–4 in, 1–7.5 in BT M/S =in WW II.	2.15–1920
3065	GY.1089	REMINDO	258/17	1–12 pdr Hydro Lost 2.2.18 off Portland.	9.17–2.18
948	GY.1206	REMO	169/00	1–6 pdr M/S	1.15–1920
1043	GY.868	RENARRO	230/13	1–3 pdr M/S Mined 10.11.18 in the Dardanelles.	2.15–11.18
1130	GY.512	RENCO	230/10	1–6 pdr M/S	2.15–1919
198	GY.826	RENZO	230/13	1–6 pdr M/S =in WW II.	11.14–1919
	GY.298	REPERIO	233/07	BDV	1.15–12.18
455	GY.380	REPORTO	230/08	1–6 pdrAA M/S =in WW II.	2.15–1919
1138	GY.510	REPRO	230/10	1–12 pdr Mined 26.4.17 off Tod Head.	2.15–4.17
3081	GY.1103	RESERCHO	258/17	1–12 pdr M/S	1.18–1919
3021	GY.1029	RESMILO	258/17	1–12 pdr, 1–3.5 in BT M/S Hydro =in WW II.	3.17–1920
459	GY.942	RESOLVO	231/13	1–6 pdrAA M/S =in WW II.	2.15–1920
1042	GY.508	RESONO	230/10	A/P Mined 26.12.15 near Sunk LV.	1.15–12.15
2958	GY.926	RESPARKO	248/16	1–12 pdr M/S, Escort =in WW II.	9.16–1919

Adty No.	Port No.	Name	TG/Yr	Armament, Fate, etc.	Service
196	GY.666	RESPONSO	228/12	1–3 pdr Wrecked 31.12.15 near Sanday Island.	1.14–12.15
1041	GY.379	RESTLESS	125/91	A/P =Mercantile loss 23.9.16.	1.15–12.15
48	GY.265	RESTRIVO	245/14	1–3 pdr M/S =in WW II.	11.14–1919
1608	GY.253	RETAKO	245/14	1–12 pdr =in WW II.	4.15–1919
1623	GY.952	RETRUDO	178/13	1–6 pdr M/S	4.15–1920
1602	GY.264	RETURNO	245/14	1–6 pdrAA M/S =in WW II.	3.15–1919
673	GY.373	REVELLO	230/08	1–3 pdr =in WW II.	11.14–1919
	BN.50	REVESBY	194/98	BDV	11.16–1919
1215	H.443	RHODESIA	155/99	A/P Wrecked 19.4.15 near Stornoway.	1.15–4.15
658	GY.521	RHONE	117/93	1–3 pdr	12.14–7.18
1045	GY.360	RIALTO	139/97	1–6 pdrAA	1.15–1919
671	GY.181	RIANO	212/06	1–6 pdr M/S = WW II.	11.14–1919
1274	H.255	RIBBLE	193/04	1–6 pdrAA M/S	1.18–1919
957	GY.1159	RIBBLE II	197/00	1–6 pdr M/S	2.15–1919
	GY.594	RIBY	214/10	1–12 pdr BDV	6.15–1919
258	SN.60	RICHMOND CASTLE	178/01	(ex-Loch Leven) 1–6 pdrAA M/S	8.14–1919
726	GY.185	RIGOLETTO	212/06	1–12 pdr M/S =in WW II.	12.14–1919
3340	GY.1046	RILETTE	212/17	1–12 pdr, 1–7.5 in BT M/S Hydro	5.17–1919
686	GY.1199	RINALDO =RINALDO II 2.15	166/00	1–6 pdr M/S, BDV	11.14–1920
434	GY.1146	RINTO	169/00	1–6 pdrAA M/S	11.14–1919
1236	GY.870	RIPARVO	230/13	1–3 pdr Sunk 2.11.18 in collision North of Benghazi.	3.15–11.18
3281	GY.914	RISKATO	248/16	1–6 pdrAA M/S =in WW II.	5.16–1919
819	GY.946	RISTANGO	178/13	1–6 pdrAA M/S =in WW II.	11.14–1919
1261	GY.893	RIVIERE	226/16	1–6 pdrAA M/S =in WW II.	5.16–1919
643	SN.189	ROBERT HASTIE	210/12	1–6 pdrAA M/S =in WW II.	11.14–1919
1737	A.353	ROBERT SMITH	211/15	1–12 pdr, 1–6 pdr Disappeared 20.7.17 NW of the Hebrides.	7.15–7.17
376	H.4	ROBIN =ROBIN II 2.15	169/04	1–6 pdrAA M/S	10.14–1919
1353	SA.105	ROCHE CASTLE	241/10	1–12 pdr M/S	3.15–1919
642	GY.671	ROCHESTER	165/98	1–3 pdr M/S	10.14–1919
1230	GY.836	RODINO	230/13	1–12 pdr M/S =in WW II.	3.15–1920
953	GY.195	RODNEY =RODNEY III 3.17	246/06	1–12 pdr, 1–7.5 in BT M/S	5.15–1919
1490	GY.839	RODOSTO	174/13	1–12 pdr	5.15–1920
1046	GY.65	ROLANDO	120/96	1–6pdrAA	1.15–1919
1468	GY.399	ROLULU	170/09	A/P Wrecked 27.5.15 on Obb Rock, Isle of Lewis.	4.15–5.15
832	H.431	ROMAN EMPIRE	182/98	1–6 pdrAA M/S	4.15–1919
2651	GY.81	ROMILLY	214/05	1–12 pdr M/S	3.15–1919
	FD.128	ROMULUS	159/85	BDV	10.15–1919
666	GY.528	RONDO	117/93	A/P Wrecked 3.3.15 in the Shetlands.	11.14–3.15
1594	GY.865	RONONIA	213/13	1–6 pdr	6.15–1919
862	GY.605	RONSO	248/15	1–6 pdr M/S =in WW II.	1.16–1920
973	M.16	ROSA	242/04	1–3 pdr M/S	1.15–1919

Adty No.	Port No.	Name	TG/Yr	Armament, Fate, etc.	Service
1780	H.839	ROSALIND =ROSALIND II 12.15	174/05	1–3 pdr M/S	10.15–1919
592	GY.312	ROSE =ROSE II 2.15	213/07	1–6 pdr M/S Mined 23.4.17 in Belfast Lough.	12.14–4.17
1183	GW.26	ROSE =ROSE IV 5.15	218/11	1–12 pdr M/S Hydro =ROSETTE in WW II.	4.15–1919
507	LL.6	ROSE OF ENGLAND	223/09	1–6 pdrAA M/S =in WW II.	1.15–1919
2340	FD.100	ROSETTA	236/07	1–3 pdr Net	4.15–1919
633	GN.14	ROSSKEEN	196/07	1–4 in, 1–12 pdr M/S =Q ship 1–4 in, 1–12 pdr, 1–6 pdr 3.17–11.18 (ALDEBARAN, BENDIGO II, ETHELWULF II, GENERAL, HUNTER, NEW COMET).	10.14–1919
2770	SH.59	ROSY MORN	181/14	1–6 pdr Mined 13.1.16 near Dogger Bank.	5.15–1.16
947	GY.22	ROTO	170/04	1–6 pdr, 1–7.5 in BT M/S	1.15–1920
1665	H.410	ROWSAY	207/12	Hydro tender	2.17–1919
1610	GY.751	ROWSLEY	213/12	1–6 pdr M/S	4.15–1919
718	GY.320	ROXANO	228/07	1–3 pdr =in WW II.	12.14–1920
1145	GY.313	ROYALLIEU	211/07	1–12 pdr, 1–6 pdr M/S =in WW II.	2.15–1919
2955	GY.941	ROYALO	248/16	1–6 pdrAA M/S =in WW II.	8.16–1919
1742	GY.1136	RUBY	198/99	1–3 pdr Wrecked 24.11.15 in Grandes Bay.	7.15–11.15
2970	H.494	RUBY	251/16	1–12 pdr M/S Torpedoed 17.10.17 off Ushant.	9.16–10.17
676	H.34	RUFF	169/04	1–6 pdr M/S	11.14–1919
2979	GY.994	RUGBY =RUGBY II 11.17	274/16	1–6 pdrAA, 1–7.5 in BT M/S =in WW II.	11.16–1919
433	GY.463	RUPERT	114/92	1–6 pdr =Mercantile loss 6.2.17.	11.14–6.15
N.3A N.87	GY.192	RUSSELL II	246/06	1–6 pdrAA M/L	5.15–1920
3317	SA.67	RUTHIN CASTLE	275/16	1–6 pdr M/S Mined 21.4.17 off Skinningrove, Yorkshire.	12.16–4.17
2964	GY.932	SABREUR	188/16	1–6 pdrAA M/S =BADINAGE in WW II.	9.16–1919
296	SN.88	ST. AGNES No. 1	205/08	M/S	8.14–1919
1844	H.803	ST. CLAIR	255/04	1–6 pdr, 1–3 pdr M/S =in WW II.	8.15–1919
1992	GY.824	ST. CUTHBERT	311/16	1–12 pdr, 1–7.5 in BT M/S	4.16–1919
1527	H.257	ST. CYR	315/15	1–12 pdr M/S	6.15–1919
3326	H.228	ST. DENIS	294/15	1–12 pdr =MASONA in WW II.	2.17–1920
1583	H.3	ST. ELMO	314/14	1–12 pdr, 1–5 in BT M/S	5.15–1919
552	H.929	ST. GERMAIN	307/07	(ex-Golden City) 1–6 pdrAA M/S	2.15–1919
3306	H.493	ST. HUBERT	349/16	1–12 pdr M/S	9.16–1919
1192	H.11	ST. IVES	325/09	A/P Mined 21.12.16 off St. Anthony Falmouth.	3.15–12.16
1906	H.18	ST. JOHNS	208/10	1–3 pdr Sunk 3.6.18 by S/M gunfire 45 miles N of Tory Island.	10.15–6.18
291	GY.1131	ST. LAWRENCE	196/99	A/P =Mercantile loss 22.4.15.	10.14–11.14
454	GY.799	ST. LEONARD	296/12	1–6 pdr M/S =FINESSE in WW II.	2.15–1919
462	SN.217	ST. LEONARD No. 1	210/13	M/S =ST. LEONARD in WW II.	8.14–1919
1202	H.503	ST. LOUIS	233/00	1–6 pdr M/S	12.14–1919

Adty No.	Port No.	Name	TG/Yr	Armament, Fate, etc.	Service
1375	H.371	ST. MALO	335/11	1–12 pdr =WARDOUR in WW II.	4.15–1919
551	H.715	ST. MAURICE	251/03	1–6 pdrAA, 1–7.5 in BT M/L, M/S	9.14–1920
369	H.993	ST. VINCENT =ST. VINCENT II 2.15	186/07	1–12 pdr M/S	10.14–1919
2670	M.230	SALOME	252/08	1–12 pdr	5.15–1919
3283	GY.892	SALVINI	226/16	1–6 pdrAA M/S =in WW II.	6.16–1919
1443	GY.175	SAMURAI	221/14	1–6 pdrAA M/S	8.15–1920
	GY.59	SANDRINGHAM	179/05	1–12 pdr BDV	12.14–1919
2997	GY.996	SANSERIT	212/16	1–6 pdrAA	2.17–1919
1863	GY.295	SANSON	231/07	1–6 pdrAA, 1–7.5 in BT M/S =in WW II.	9.15–1919
3077	H.580	SAPLER	262/17	(ex-*Sapphire*) 1–12 pdr M/S =INVERCAULD in WW II.	12.17–1919
277	A.889	SAPPHIRE =SAPPHIRE III 2.15	156/03	M/S	8.14–11.18
329	FD.140	SARAH ALICE	299/11	1–3 pdr M/S Sunk 26.9.16 by S/M near Fair Island Channel.	8.14–9.16
928	FD.177	SARBA	315/13	1–12 pdr, 1–7.5 in BT M/S =in WW II.	11.14–1919
727	H.197	SARDIUS	213/92	1–12 pdr	12.14–11.18
3357	GY.1140	SARDIUS =SARDIUS II 8.15	206/00	1–3 pdr M/S Wrecked 13.2.18 in Pendower Cove, near Tolpeden, Penwith.	6.15–2.18
702	GY.858	SARGON	297/13	1–6 pdrAA M/S =in WW II.	12.14–1919
2998	GY.984	SARPEDON =SARPEDON II 3.17	344/16	1–12 pdr M/S =in WW II.	1.17–1919
3050	GY.1071	SARRAIL	255/17	1–12 pdr M/S =BILSDEAN in WW II.	7.17–1919
1773	CF.42	SASEBO	255/13	1–12 pdr M/S =AVOLA in WW II.	6.15–1919
2971	GY.976	SATURN	230/16	1–6 pdrAA M/S =in WW II.	9.16–1919
3293	GY.901	SAURIAN	219/16	1–12 pdr M/S =in WW II	7.16–1919
1271	GY.1028	SAVITRI	212/17	1–6 pdrAA, 1–7.5 in BT M/L, M/S	6.17–1919
627	CF.31	SAXON	239/07	1–12 pdr, 1–7.5 in BT M/S	9.14–1919
732	GY.722	SAXON II	119/94	1–6 pdr	1.15–10.18
262	SN.58	SAXON PRINCE	237/07	1–3 pdr M/S Disappeared 28.3.16 in storm off Dover.	8.14–3.16
632	GY.266	SCARBOROUGH	161/97	1–6 pdr M/S	10.14–1919
1864	GY.935	SCARRON	296/13	1–12 pdr, 1–6 pdrAA, 1–5 in BT M/S =in WW II.	9.15–1919
352	A.905	SCHIEHALLION	198/03	M/S Mined 9.6.15 in Mediterranean.	8.14–6.15
2990	A.727	SCHIEHALLION	225/16	1–6 pdrAA M/S	12.16–1919
1749	H.308	SCHIPPERKE	331/11	1–12 pdr, 1–7.5 in BT	9.15–1919
445	FD.98	SCOMBER	321/14	1–6 pdr AA M/S =in WW II.	12.14–1919
1745	GY.1155	SCOOPER	195/00	(ex-*Kastoria*) 1–6 pdr AA BDV	7.15–1919
1580	A.179	SCOT	202/07	1–6 pdr, 1–7.5 in BT M/S	5.15–1919
3218 N.2A	H.968	SCOTT	238/13	M/L	4.15–10.15
	A.512	SCOTTISH BELLE	145/90	Mined 22.10.15 off the Tongue. BDV	6.15–1919
1600	GY.1180	SCOUTER	195/00	(ex-*Moravia*) 1–6 pdr M/S	7.15–1919
3321	H.531	SEA KING	321/16	1–12 pdr M/S =Q ship, REMEXO; =in WW II.	1.17–1919
259	H.542	SEA LION	231/02	2–6 pdr M/S	8.14–1919

Adty No.	Port No.	Name	TG/Yr	Armament, Fate, etc.	Service
1983	H.411	SEA MONARCH	329/15	1–12 pdr, 1–7.5 in BT M/S = in WW II.	2.16–1919
1219	H.188	SEA RANGER	263/14	1–12 pdr, 1–6 pdrAA M/S = DUNGENESS in WW II.	2.15–1919
1187	H.148	SEA SEARCHER	263/14	1–6 pdr M/S, Escort	3.15–1919
1979	A.409	SEA SWEEPER	329/15	1–12 pdr M/S Hydro	1.16–1919
1213	H.407	SEALARK = SEALARK II 2.15	182/98	(ex-Sea Lark) 1–6 pdrAA M/S Sunk 30.9.18 in collision off St. John's Point.	1.15–9.18
1512	H.312	SEAWARD HO = ATTENTIVE III 5.18	331/15	1–12 pdr, 1–7.5 in BT M/S	5.15–1919
3313	GY.991	SEDDON	296/16	1–6 pdrAA M/S = in WW II.	11.16–1919
358	GY.324	SEMIRAMIS	246/07	1–12 pdr, 1–7.5 in BT M/S Hydro	8.14–1919
1195	A.18	SEMNOS	216/14	1–3 pdr M/S = in WW II.	3.15–1920
295	GY.61	SENATOR	211/05	1–3 pdr M/S Mined 21.5.17 off Tory Island.	8.14–5.17
3034	H.536	SERFIB	210/17	1–6 pdr M/S	4.17–1919
	GY.504	SERIEMA	279/09	1–6 pdr BDV	6.16–1919
1998	GY.894	SESOSTRIS	293/16	1–12 pdr, 1–3.5 in BT M/S Hydro	5.16–1919
3310	GY.928	SETHON	295/16	1–6 pdrAA, 1–7.5 in BT M/S = in WW II.	10.16–1919
729	A.139	SETTER = SETTER II 12.15	171/99	1–6 pdr = FT.	12.14–7.18
650	CF.38	SETTSU	231/12	1–6 pdr, 1–7.5 in BT M/S	10.14–1919
3219	H.1003	SHACKLETON	288/13	1–3 pdr M/L	5.15–1920
N.0A N.93					
3083	H.641	SHAMA	191/18	1–12 pdr M/S = in WW II.	4.18–1919
509	A.448	SHANDWICK	166/12	1–6 pdr AA M/S = in WW II.	9.14–1919
1407	GY.696	SHELDON	288/12	1–6 pdr, 1–7.5 in BT M/S = in WW II.	3.15–1919
804	A.466	SHELOMI	175/12	1–6 pdr M/S Hydro	11.14–1919
1659	GY.230	SHERATON	283/07	1–6 pdr BDV = in WW II.	6.16–1919
1617	GY.179	SHIKARI = SHIKARI II 2.18	221/14	1–12 pdr M/S	4.15–1919
1660	GY.780	SIALKOT	308/12	1–6 pdrAA BDV = 1–12 pdr M/S 3.18	12.14–1919
30	GY.163	SICYON	283/06	1–6 pdrAA M/S	9.14–1919
123	BL.1	SIDMOUTH	220/06	1–6 pdr M/S	8.14–1919
949	GY.1284	SILANION	199/03	1–6 pdr M/S	2.15–1919
60	GY.809	SILICIA	250/13	1–6 pdrAA M/S = in WW II.	9.14–1919
1447	GY.960	SIMERSON	248/13	1–12 pdr M/S = in WW II.	5.15–1919
1269	GY.1024	SIMPSON	260/17	1–6 pdrAA M/S = in WW II.	5.17–1919
1887	H.32	SIR JAMES RECKITT	324/09	1–12 pdr, 1–7.5 in BT M/S Hydro = SUNBURST in WW II.	9.15–1919
1501	H.262	SIR JOHN FRENCH	351/14	1–12 pdr Hydro	5.15–1919
1513	H.43	SIR MARK SYKES	307/14	1–12 pdr, 1–3.5 in BT M/S Hydro	5.15–1919
1951	A.459	SISTERS MELVILLE	260/15	M/S Mined 13.2.17 near Aldeburgh.	11.15–2.17
197	FD.49	SITVEL	290/14	(ex-Velia) 1–12 pdr, 1–7.5 in BT = VELIA in WW II.	12.14–1919
1744	GY.1167	SLASHER	195/00	(ex-Sethon) 1–6 pdr M/S	7.15–1919
1758	M.229	SLEBECH	222/08	1–6 pdrAA M/S = in WW II.	5.15–1919
1201	LL.11	SMEW	223/07	(ex-Atlanta) 1–6 pdr M/S	1.15–1919
384	H.133	SNIPE	166/97	1–3 pdr BDV	11.14–1920
1620	FD.155	SOAR	219/15	1–12 pdr M/S	4.15–1919
284	SN.277	SOLDIER PRINCE	156/00	1–3 pdr M/S	8.14–1920
55	GY.714	SOLON	295/12	1–6 pdrAA M/S	8.14–1919

Adty No.	Port No.	Name	TG/Yr	Armament, Fate, etc.	Service
1185	A.22	SOPHOS	217/14	1–3 pdr M/S	3.15–1919
725	GY.1270	SOPHRON	195/03	1–6 pdrAA M/S Mined 22.8.17 off Firth of Tay.	12.14–8.17
392	H.481	SPEEDWELL =SPEEDWELL II 2.15	273/99	2–12 pdr, 1–6 pdrAA M/S =Q ship 4.16 (GLENDALE, Q.33, ROGER, VANDA) Ran ashore 15.7.18 in Mounts Bay and BU.	11.14–7.18
1908	H.104	SPEETON	205/13	1–3 pdr Mined 31.12.15 off Lowestoft.	10.15–12.15
1378	H.914	SPIDER	271/06	1–12 pdr M/S	4.15–1919
3341	FD.297	SPRINGWELL	286/17	1–12 pdr M/S, Escort	5.17–1919
1838	GY.496	STALKER	197/99	(ex-Jeria) 1–6 pdr, 1–7.5 in BT M/S =CHOICE in WW II.	7.15–1919
2999	H.213	STALWART =STALWART II 2.18	333/14	1–12 pdr M/S, 1–7.5 in BT M/S	3.17–1919
1210	H.1005	STANLEY WEYMAN	288/13	1–12 pdr, 1–7.5 in BT M/S	1.15–1919
465	A.239	STAR OF BRITAIN	228/08	M/S =in WW II.	9.14–1920
955	FD.200	STAR OF FREEDOM	258/11	1–12 pdr M/S Mined 19.4.17 off Trevose Head.	1.15–4.17
1952	A.481	STAR OF PEACE	220/15	1–6 pdr M/S =STAR OF DEVERON in WW II.	11.15–1919
331	A.464	STAR OF THE EAST	218/12	1–6 pdr M/S	8.14–1919
318	A.509	STAR OF THE EMPIRE	219/12	1–3 pdr M/S	8.14–1919
319	A.452	STAR OF THE ISLES	217/12	1–6 pdrAA M/S	8.14–1919
118	A.633	STAR OF THE NORTH	192/03	1–6 pdrAA M/S	9.14–1919
	A.901	STAR OF THE OCEAN	203/03	BDV	6.15–1919
67 510 1956	A.913	STAR OF THE WAVE	205/04	1–6 pdrAA, 1–7.5 in BT M/S	9.14–1919
710	GY.350	STAUNTON	283/08	1–6 pdr M/S =in WW II.	11.14–1920
517	GW.27	STEWART BOYLE	197/11	1–6 pdrAA M/S	10.14–1920
1792	H.83	STORNOWAY	208/10	1–6 pdr M/S	6.15–1919
109	A.551	STRATHAFTON	209/13	1–12 pdr M/S	8.14–1919
1168	A.39	STRATHAIRLIE	193/05	1–6 pdrAA M/S	2.15–1919
950	A.189	STRATHALLADALE	199/08	1–12 pdr M/S =in WW II.	2.15–1919
3005	A.757	STRATHALVA	215/17	2–6 pdrAA	2.17–1919
100	A.477	STRATHATHOLL	209/12	1–12 pdr M/S	8.14–1919
333	A.96	STRATHAVON	202/06	M/S =in WW II.	8.14–1919
	A.431	STRATHBLANE	186/01	BDV	6.15–1919
3259	A.536	STRATHBRAN	212/15	1–6 pdrAA M/S	2.16–1919
98	A.552	STRATHCARRON	209/13	1–12 pdr M/S	8.14–1919
66	A.587	STRATHCLOVA	210/13	1–6 pdrAA M/S	8.14–1919
1199	A.583	STRATHCLUNIE	211/13	1–6 pdrAA M/S	4.15–1919
2991	A.751	STRATHCOE =VERNON 1923 =STRATHCOE 1938.	215/16	1–6 pdrAA M/L, M/S Purchased 8.18; sold 4.46.	1.17–4.46
1197	A.60	STRATHDEE	193/06	1–6 pdrAA M/S	3.15–1919
95	A.401	STRATHDERRY	193/11	1–3 pdr BDV Accom. =in WW II.	8.14–1919
1960	A.539	STRATHDEVON	212/15	1–3 pdr, 7–7.5 in BT M/S =in WW II.	11.15–1919
	A.59	STRATHEBRIE	210/14	1–6 pdr BDV	6.15–1919
1189	A.108	STRATHEDEN	201/06	1–6 pdr	3.15–1919
101	A.586	STRATHELLA	210/13	1–12 pdr M/S =in WW II.	8.14–1919
1182	A.46	STRATHELLIOT	211/15	1–6 pdr M/S =WW II.	3.15–1919
417	A.105	STRATHERRICK	201/06	1–6 pdrAA, 1–7.5 in BT M/S	11.14–1919
466	A.341	STRATHFINELLA	192/11	1–12 pdr M/S =in WW II.	9.14–1919
1366	A.251	STRATHGAIRN	211/15	1–6 pdrAA M/S	3.15–1919
	A.97	STRATHGARRY	202/06	BDV Sunk 6.7.15 in collision at Scapa.	6.15–7.15
87	A.399	STRATHGELDIE	192/11	1–3 pdr M/S	8.14–1919

Adty No.	Port No.	Name	TG/Yr	Armament, Fate, etc.	Service
130	GY.987	STRATHISLA	193/06	1–6 pdr BDV =BURNBANKS in WW II.	5.17–1919
3339	A.756	STRATHLEE	215/17	1–6 pdrAA M/S	5.17–1920
	A.340	STRATHLETHEN	192/11	1–3 pdr BDV Accom.	6.15–1919
3249	A.596	STRATHLOCHY	221/16	1–6 pdrAA M/S	1.16–1919
92	A.316	STRATHLOSSIE	193/10	1–6 pdr M/S	8.14–1919
1578	A.191	STRATHLUI	199/08	1–12 pdr, 1–7.5 in BT M/S	8.14–1919
	A.72	STRATHMAREE	210/14	BDV	6.15–1920
1573	A.79	STRATHMARTIN	210/14	1–6 pdrAA M/S =in WW II.	4.15–1919
335	A.480	STRATHMORAY	209/12	M/S	8.14–1919
112	A.582	STRATHNETHY	211/13	1–6 pdrAA M/S	8.14–1919
102	A.54	STRATHORD	195/06	1–3 pdr M/S	8.14–1919
2994	A.752	STRATHRANNOCH	215/17	1–6 pdrAA M/S Mined 6.4.17 off St. Abbs Head.	1.17–4.17
3253	A.599	STRATHRYE	212/16	1–12 pdr M/S	1.16–1919
1169	A.92	STRATHSPEY	202/06	1–6 pdrAA M/S =in WW II.	2.15–1919
511	A.402	STRATHTUMMEL	210/11	1–6 pdrAA M/S	9.14–1919
1570	A.61	STRATHUGIE	210/14	1–3 pdr =in WW II.	4.15–1919
115	A.403	STRATHURIE	210/11	1–3 pdr M/S	8.14–1919
1233	GY.810	STREPHON	250/13	1–12 pdr Hydro =in WW II.	3.15–1919
1969	H.387	STRONSAY	207/11	1–6 pdrAA M/S	9.15–1919
1842	GY.912	STRYMON	198/99	1–12 pdr M/S Mined 27.10.17 off Shipwash LV.	8.15–10.17
2972	GY.979	SUCCESSION	212/16	1–6 pdrAA M/S	9.16–1919
131	FD.87	SULBY	287/09	1–6 pdrAA M/S	8.14–1919
611	GY.753	SUNCLOUD	213/12	1–6 pdr AA M/S	9.14–1919
3002	GY.1012	SUSARION	260/17	1–12 pdr M/S =in WW II.	2.17–1919
654	H.97	SWALLOW	243/97	1–3 pdr M/S Sunk 29.3.18 in collision off Whitby.	10.14–3.18
261	A.76	SWALLOW =SWALLOW II 12.14	204/06	1–6 pdrAA M/S	8.14–1919
811	H.700	SWAN =SWAN II 2.15	239/09	1–6 pdr M/S =SWAN II in WW II.	12.14–1919
136	FD.116	SWAN =SWAN III 12.15	270/07	1–6 pdr M/S	8.14–1919
54 1224	GY.853	SWEEPER	395/13	1–6 pdr, 1–6 pdrAA, 1–7.5 in BT M/S =NORDHAV II in WW II.	8.14–1919
	H.439	SYLVIA	213/98	BDV	6.15–8.18
269	M.21	SYRINGA =SYRINGA II 3.17	243/05	1–13 pdr M/S	8.14–1919
1518	H.1027	T. R. FERENS	307/13	1–12 pdr, 1–7.5 in BT M/S	5.15–1919
783	M.36	TACSONIA	243/05	1–6 pdrAA M/S	1.15–1919
451	GY.744	TAGALIE	210/12	1–6 pdrAA M/S	9.14–1919
1627	GY.415	TAIPO	247/14	1–12 pdr M/S Mined 24.6.17 off the Royal Sovereign LV.	5.15–6.17
1973	H.522	TALLY HO	216/00	1–6 pdr M/S, T/S	10.15–1919
3046	CF.47	TAMURA	268/17	1–6 pdrAA M/S	6.17–1919
386	H.134	TANAGER	192/10	1–3 pdr M/S	11.14–1919
634	H.759	TANJORE	168/03	1–6 pdr M/S	10.14–1919
337	A.445	TARANAKI	247/12	1–12 pdr, 1–6 pdrAA M/S =Q ship	8.14–1919
1607	GY.723	TARTAN	202/12	1–6 pdrAA M/S =in WW II.	4.15–1919
418	H.90	TEAL	165/97	1–6 pdr M/S Wrecked 2.1.17 off Buckie.	11.14–1.17
2579	M.161	TENBY	215/13	1–12 pdr M/S Hydro =EWALD in WW II.	6.15–1919
977	SA.53	TENBY CASTLE	256/08	1–12 pdr, 1–7.55 in BT M/S =Q ship 6.15–1917	2.15–1919
548	H.961	TERN	199/07	A/P Wrecked 23.2.15 in Loch Eriboll.	10.14–2.15

Adty No.	Port No.	Name	TG/Yr	Armament, Fate, etc.	Service
356	A.34	TERRIER	179/05	1–12 pdr M/S	8.14–1919
3204	GY.10	TERVANI	457/14	2–12 pdr, 1–2 pdr Mined 5.12.16 off Orford Ness.	5.15–12.16
1538	FD.43	TETTENHALL	227/05	M/S Mined 23.5.17 off Lowestoft.	6.15–5.17
780	GY.795	TEUTON =FT ANGOLIAN 6.18	141/98	1–6 pdr	1.15–1.18
	H.459	THANET	172/02	BDV	9.15–1919
450	GY.128	THE BANYERS	448/14	M/S Mined 6.1.15 off Scarborough.	12.14–1.15
1762	CF.30	THE NORMAN	225/08	1–6 pdrAA, 1–7.5 in BT M/L, M/S	5.15–1919
195	CF.29	THE ROMAN	224/09	1–6 pdr M/S =in WW II.	11.14–1919
254	GY.945	THE TETRARCH	225/13	1–3 pdr M/S	8.14–1919
617	GY.937	THEBAN	202/13	1–3 pdr	9.14–12.18
1311	GW.3	THERESA BOYLE	224/15	1–3 pdr M/S	9.15–1919
517	SN.311	THISTLE	158/01	M/S =1–3 pdr BDV 3.16	9.14–12.14 3.16–1919
	GW.2	THISTLE	178/04	1–3 pdr BDV	10.15–1919
909	LL.64	THISTLE =THISTLE IV 4.16	228/06	1–3 pdr M/S	2.15–1919
3000	H.116	THOMAS STRATTEN	309/14	1–12 pdr Mined 20.10.17 off Butt of Lewis.	3.17–10.17
3276	HL.80	THOMAS SUTTON	211/16	1–6 pdrAA M/S	5.16–1919
61	A.421	THOMAS W. IRVIN	201/11	M/S Mined 27.8.14 off the Tyne.	8.14–8.14
3257	SN.265	THOMAS W. IRVIN	209/16	1–6 pdrAA M/S	2.16–1919
1143	SN.67	THOMAS YOUNG	194/14	1–12 pdr, 1–6 pdrAA M/S	2.15–1919
1764	FD.41	THORNTON	225/05	1–6 pdr	5.15–1919
547	H.703	THRUSH →THRUSH II 2.15	166/02	1–6 pdr M/S =AMBITION in WW II.	11.14–1920
1755	GY.907	THUNDERSTONE	225/13	1–3 pdr =in WW II.	4.15–1919
1624	GY.855	THURINGIA	297/13	1–3 pdr M/S Sunk 11.11.17 off Youghal, presumed torpedoed.	4.15–11.17
1200	A.333	TINA NUTTEN	187/11	1–6 pdrAA M/S	4.15–1919
313	H.954	TOKIO	295/07	1–3 pdr M/S Sunk 12.12.17 by SMS EMDEN and destroyers in the North Sea.	8.14–12.17
25	GY.157	TOKIO =TOKIO II 12.14	221/06	1–6 pdr M/S =TOKIO II in WW II.	8.14–1919
	D.216	TOM MOORE	194/03	(ex-Clan Grant) 1–3 pdr BDV	6.15–1919
424	H.35	TOM TIT	169/04	A/P Wrecked 26.12.14 off Peterhead.	11.14–12.14
1262	H.511	TOPAZ	251/16	1–6 pdrAA M/S =VALDORA in WW II.	11.16–1919
3335	H.218	TORONTO	204/15	1–6 pdrAA M/S	3.17–1919
46	H.934	TOUCHSTONE	173/06	1–6 pdr M/S	9.14–11.18
609	GY.347	TOURACO	245/03	1–6 pdrAA, 1–7.5 in BT M/S	9.14–1920
1231	H.850	TOURMALINE	289/05	1–6 pdr M/S	3.15–1919
370	H.987	TOWHEE	199/08	1–3 pdr M/S Disappeared 15.6.17 in the English Channel.	10.14–6.17
3307	GY.953	TRANSVAAL	250/16	1–12 pdr, 1–6 pdrAA M/S =in WW II.	9.16–1919
120	FD.12	TRENT =TRENT II 3.17	218/04	1–6 pdr M/S	8.14–1919
1847	GY.837	TRIBUNE =TRIBUNE II 2.18	293/13	1–6 pdrAA, 1–7.5 in BT M/S	9.15–1920
1377	H.153	TRIER	324/10	1–12 pdr	4.15–1919
470	GN.24	TRINITY, N. B.	203/14	1–12 pdr, 1–6 pdrAA M/S	12.14–1919
1769	SA.61	TRITON	230/07	1–6 pdr M/S =in WW II.	5.15–1919
677	H.949	TROGON	182/07	1–12 pdr, 1–6 pdrAA M/S	11.14–1919

Adty No.	Port No.	Name	TG/Yr	Armament, Fate, etc.	Service
782	GY.848	TROJAN =TROJAN II 12.18	140/98	1–6 pdr M/S =in WW II.	12.14–1919
403	H.1020	TRUMPETER	192/13	1–6 pdrAA M/S	10.14–1919
978	FD.221	TRYGON	289/08	A/P Sunk 30.3.15 in collision in the Clyde.	2.15–3.15
1817	H.521	TUGELA	233/00	1–3 pdr Mined 26.6.16 off Lowestoft.	7.15–6.16
93	SN.97	TYNE PRINCE	206/09	1–12 pdr, 1–6 pdrAA M/S	8.14–1919
	PD.85	UGIEBANK	205/13	BDV	6.15–1919
124	M.200	UHDEA	191/06	M/S =BDV 9.15	8.14–1919
	A.337	ULSTER	185/97	BDV	9.15–1919
1047	GY.198	ULYSSES =ULYSSES II 7.16	165/89	1–6 pdr	1.15–11.18
2196	INS.249	UNICORN	134/95	1–3 pdr Net	6.15–1920
699	GY.924	UNITIA	296/13	1–6 pdrAA M/S =PORTIA in WW II.	12.14–1919
425	FD.73	URANA	308/14	1–6 pdrAA M/S, Escort	11.14–1919
960	AR.1	URANIA	226/07	1–6 pdr M/S	12.14–1919
1267	A.754	URIE	226/17	1–6 pdrAA =CRAFTSMAN in WW II.	5.17–1919
3328	FD.289	URKA	249/17	1–12 pdr M/S	3.17–1919
515	A.192	VALE OF CLYDE	223/08	1–12 pdr, 1–6 pdrAA M/S	9.14–1919
3275	A.542	VALE OF FORTH	226/16	1–6 pdrAA M/S =VIKING DEEPS in WW II.	4.16–1919
3250	A.546	VALE OF FRUIN	211/15	1–6 pdr M/S =SANGARIUS in WW II.	12.16–1919
991	LH.264	VALE OF LENNOX	233/09	(ex-Gardar Landnemi) 1–12 pdr, 1–7.5 in BT M/S	12.14–1919
1188	A.177	VALE OF LEVEN	223/07	1–6 pdr M/S Sunk 10.7.17 in collision off Worthing.	3.15–7.17
2963	GY.915	VALESCA	188/16	1–6 pdrAA, 1–7.5 in BT M/S =in WW II.	9.16–1919
864	GY.885	VALMONT	245/16	M/S =in WW II.	5.16–12.18
1543	FD.160	VALPA	230/15	1–12 pdr Mined 19.3.16 off Spurn Head.	6.15–3.16
1280	GY.1082	VAMBERY	316/17	1–6 pdr, 1–7.5 in BT M/S, Escort =SARONTA in WW II.	7.17–1920
5	GY.511	VARANIS	258/10	1–6 pdrAA M/S =in WW II.	8.14–1919
1584	A.260	VASCO DA GAMA	265/10	1–6 pdr M/S	5.15–1919
1520	GY.827	VENATOR	293/13	1–6 pdrAA	5.15–1919
1654	GY.1098	VENOSTA	316/17	1–12 pdr, 1–3.5 in BT M/S Hydro =in RCN WW II.	10.17–1919
692	GY.66	VENTURE	193/05	1–12 pdr M/S =in WW II.	11.14–1919
1569	H.960	VERA	333/07	1–12 pdr, 1–7.5 in BT M/S	5.15–1919
135	FD.211	VERA GRACE	232/08	1–6 pdrAA M/S	8.14–1919
827	GY.176	VERBENA =VERBENA II 12.15	152/97	1–3 pdr	4.15–10.18
1616	GY.483	VERESIS	302/15	1–6 pdr =WYOMING in WW II.	4.15–1921
1340	GY.156	VESPER =VESPER II 2.17	264/06	1–12 pdr M/S	8.14–1919
828	GY.57	VESTA	240/05	1–6 pdr M/S	11.14–1919
	A.511	VICTOR	193/97	BDV	6.15–1919
110	PD.75	VICTOR =VICTOR II 2.15	201/06	1–3 pdr M/S	8.14–1919
1752	M.117	VICTORIA =VICTORIA II 6.15	221/12	1–6 pdr M/S	4.15–1920
320	A.590	VICTORIA REGINA	146/97	M/S	8.14–11.18
1841	GY.1189	VICTORIAN II	195/00	1–6 pdrAA M/S	8.15–1920
	SN.242	VICTORIAN PRINCE	126/97	BDV =FT.	6.15–7.18
972	GY.499	VICTRIX	164/98	(ex-Victory) 1–3 pdr (M/S)	2.15–11.15
834	GY.54	VIDETTE =VIDETTE II 2.17	240/05	(ex-Ulverston) 1–12 pdr M/S =OUTPOST in WW II.	11.14–1919

Adty No.	Port No.	Name	TG/Yr	Armament, Fate, etc.	Service
10	GY.257	VIDONIA	276/07	1–12 pdr M/S =in WW II.	12.14–1919
1505	GY.297	VIERNOE	273/14	1–6 pdrAA, 1–3.5 in BT M/S =RCN WW II.	5.15–1919
396	H.232	VIGILANT =VIGILANT II 2.15	279/04	1–12 pdr	11.14–1919
452	GY.452	VINDELICIA	248/13	1–6 pdrAA M/S =in WW II.	9.14–1919
6	GY.67	VIOLA =VIOLA II 12.14	228/05	1–12 pdr M/S =ELENA in WW II.	8.14–1920
614	H.868	VIOLA =VIOLA III 11.15	173/06	1–12 pdr M/S	9.14–1919
383	H.446	VIREO	192/12	1–6 pdrAA M/S =in WW II.	10.14–1919
618	GY.211	VIRGINIAN =VIRGINIAN II 2.15	211/06	1–3 pdr M/S	9.14–1919
1481	SH.63	VITALITY	202/14	M/S Mined 20.10.17 off Orford Ness.	5.15–10.17
3264	GY.878	VIVANTI	226/15	1–12 pdr M/S Foundered 7.3.17 off Fairlight, Hastings.	3.16–3.17
713	GY.235	VOLANTE	255/07	M/S	1.15–1919
1454	GY.851	VOLESUS	293/13	1–6 pdrAA, 1–7.5 in BT M/S, Escort =EN AVANT in WW II.	4.15–1920
310	H.470	VULTURE =VULTURE II 2.15	190/99	1–3 pdr M/S Sunk 16.3.18 in collision in Loch Eriboll.	8.14–3.18
154	M.1	W. H. PODD	225/14	1–6 pdrAA M/S	2.15–1919
3037	HL.86	W. S. BURTON	234/17	1–6 pdrAA M/S =STAR OF THE WAVE in WW II.	4.17–1919
854	GY.927	WALDORF	293/13	1–6 pdrAA M/S =ALFREDIAN in WW II.	5.15–1919
907	GY.12	WALLENA	225/14	1–3 pdr M/S =in WW II.	1.15–1919
1659	GY.599	WALLINGTON =ORIFLAMME 9.18	259/11	1–6 pdrAA BDV =1–12 pdr M/S 9.18	12.14–1919
1625	GY.269	WALPOLE =WALPOLE II 2.18	302/14	1–6 pdr, 1–7.5 in BT	5.15–1919
265	H.546	WALTER S. BAILEY	244/02	1–12 pdr, 1–6 pdrAA M/S =Q ship 1–4 in, 1–12 pdr, 1–3.5 in BT 10.17–11.18 (MAY FLOWER, W. S. BAILEY)	8.14–1919
689	GY.303	WALTHAM	162/97	1–6 pdr M/S Disappeared 10.10.17 off Isle of Man, Presumed sunk by S/M.	12.14–10.17
1774	SA.9	WALWYNS CASTLE	255/13	1–12 pdr, 1–7.5 in BT M/S =in WW II.	6.15–1919
1268	GY.1037	WAR DUKE	246/17	1–12 pdr M/S =in WW II.	5.17–1919
3342	GY.1033	WAR GREY	246/17	1–12 pdr M/S Hydro	7.17–1919
3286	GY.857	WAR WING	226/14	1–6 pdrAA M/S =in WW II.	6.16–1919
412	H.507	WARBLER	192/12	1–3 pdr M/S	11.14–1919
1626	GY.819	WARLAND	214/13	1–6 pdrAA, 1–7.5 in BT M/S =in WW II.	5.15–1919
1444	GY.341	WARLORD	226/14	1–6 pdr M/S	4.15–1919
1048	GY.944	WARRIOR II	236/98	1–12 pdr	2.15–1919
1633	GY.73	WARSTAR	225/14	1–6 pdrAA M/S	8.15–1919
653	H.811	WARTER PRIORY	299/06	1–12 pdr, 1–6 pdrAA, 1–7.5 in BT M/S	10.14–1919
833	GY.468	WASHINGTON	209/09	1–12 pdr M/S =in WW II.	12.14–1919
153	M.96	WEIGELIA	262/11	1–3 pdr M/S Mined 28.2.16 off Dover.	8.14–2.16
N.4A N.8A	GY.455	WELBECK	302/15	1–6 pdrAA M/L =OHM in WW II.	5.15–1920

Adty No.	Port No.	Name	TG/Yr	Armament, Fate, etc.	Service
475	GN.28	WEMYSS	167/05	1–12 pdr, 1–6 pdr AA M/S	11.14–1919
1277	H.390	WESTRAY	207/12	1–6 pdrAA M/S	2.17–1919
394	H.347	WESTWARD HO =WESTWARD HO II 5.15	146/97	1–6 pdr M/S	12.14–1919
939	BL.11	WEYMOUTH II	178/03	1–6 pdr M/S	2.15–1919
542	H.129	WHITE EAR	191/14	1–6 pdrAA M/S	10.14–1919
1191	H.866	WHITEFRIARS	286/06	1–12 pdr M/S	3.15–1919
668	FD.15	WHOOPER	302/14	M/S Mined 30.6.16 off Lowestoft.	12.14–6.16
1997	FD.241	WIGAN	275/16	1–12 pdr M/S =in WW II.	5.16–1919
314	SN.325	WILD ROSE	156/02	M/S	8.14–11.18
646	H.976	WILLET	199/08	1–6 pdrAA M/S	10.14–1919
719	A.165	WILLIAM ALLAN	203/14	1–13 pdr, 1–7.5 in BT M/S	1.15–1919
1999	SN.283	WILLIAM H. HASTIE	229/16	1–12 pdr M/S Hydro =in WW II.	7.16–1919
3217	A.355	WILLIAM MORRISON	211/15	1–3 pdr M/S Mined 28.11.15 near Sunk Head Buoy.	9.15–11.15
801	SN.92	WILLIAM PURDY	194/14	1–3 pdr M/S	11.14–1919
	A.107	WILLIAM STROUD	214/14	BDV =in WW II.	6.15–1919
1747	GY.544	WILLONYX	327/15	1–6 pdr, 1–5 in BT M/S	8.15–1919
2956	GY.923	WIMPOLE	320/16	1–12 pdr M/S, Escort =ANDANES in WW II.	8.16–1919
2988	GY.998	WINDSOR =WINDSOR II 2.18	222/16	1–6 pdrAA M/S	12.16–1919
735	GY.302	WISTARIA =WISTARIA II 12.15	143/91	(ex-Lynton) 1–6 pdr M/S	1.15–1919
	GY.814	WORSLEY	309/13	1–3 pdr A/P Mined 14.8.15 off Aldeburgh.	7.15–8.15
682	H.215	WREN =WHITETHROAT 7.18	166/97	1–6 pdrAA	11.14–1919
1534	FD.80	WRENTHORPE	225/06	1–6 pdrAA M/S	6.15–1919
3303	GY.930	WYNDHAM	303/16	1–12 pdr, 1–5 in BT M/S	8.16–1919
962	FD.132	WYRE	295/11	1–12 pdr M/S Hydro =in WW II.	4.15–1919
641	GY.330	XANIA	161/97	1–6 pdrAA M/S	10.14–1919
835	SA.55	XERXES	243/08	1–6 pdr M/S Sunk 16.11.15 in collision off Girdle Ness.	12.14–11.15
281	BL.9	YARMOUTH =YARMOUTH II 2.15	235/07	1–3 pdr, 1–7.5 in BT M/S	8.14–1919
166	GY.600	YESSO	229/11	1–6 pdr M/S Mined 9.2.17 off Aberdeen.	8.14–2.17
1227	H.20	YOKOHAMA	291/09	1–12 pdr M/S	2.15–1919
307	M.159	YUCCA	193/12	M/S Mined 24.5.18 off Lowestoft.	8.14–5.18
540	SA.112	ZENA DARE	242/09	1–3 pdr M/S	12.14–1919
707	GY.227	ZONIA	150/98	(ex-Apollo) 1–6 pdrAA M/L, M/S	11.14–1919

* N pendants for M/L (minelayers) date from 9.15 and 1.18. For vessels having more than one Admiralty number, subsequent numbers appear below the first number. All Admiralty number changes occurred early and the final number given was effective for nearly all of the period of service.

Note: The trawler ICELAND had been laid down for Icelandic owners (original name not recorded); in 1919 she became Icelandic EGILL SKALLAGRIMSSON.

FISHERY TRAWLERS

In February 1917 a special assessment of the commercial fishing trawler fleet was made, the results of which confirmed the opinion that without immediate measures being taken to conserve remaining vessels, it would soon cease to exist. The fleet had been severely reduced in both numbers and effectiveness by enemy action, accidents, fishing restrictions, and by wholesale diversion of trawlers to the naval patrols. Over 1400 of the existing 1900 trawlers under British registry had been requisitioned by the Admiralty and were serving with the Auxiliary Patrol. War losses continually reduced the number of vessels available to provide the national fish supply. Since 1914 only a few new trawlers had been added to the fishing fleet and the average age of the vessels had increased while the average size of each had sharply decreased. The price of fish had risen to an unprecedented high and the quantity of fish available was at its ebb. Due to the effects of the war, the productivity per vessel engaged in fishing had decreased.

It was suggested to the Admiralty that considerable advantage and economy could be taken by requisitioning all remaining fishing craft and placing them under direct government control. The proposal was taken under consideration for several months and various approaches were taken in an effort to provide a workable system of management. War order N.67028 dated 29.5.17 placed all remaining steam vessels engaged in trawl fishing under immediate requisition. Nearly all of the 400-odd vessels affected by this order were conventional trawlers, but certain other craft fitted for trawling were also included. The requisition order was compulsory for all British fishing trawlers, but foreign-owned vessels based in Britain at the time could only be taken up with the consent of the owners. Most of the foreign fishing vessels were Belgian.

A special Fishery Reserve of the Trawler Section was created for these vessels placed in commission under the white ensign. A nominal payment of one shilling per vessel and one shilling per crew member per month of hire was paid by the government during their naval service. All other expenses resulting from their operation were paid from their commercial fishing incomes. Thusly, they conducted their fishing operations under the control of their owners while in a status of being an HM ship. Personnel were paid on a RNR (Trawler Section), plus five per cent profit bonus from their fishing income. It was planned that they should fish in fleets of 20 vessels, of which one fourth were to be given guns as soon as they became available.

The purpose of the take-over was to effect an increase in the fish supply, protect the remaining vessels more adequately from the enemy, and to reduce both fish prices and profits. The average yearly profit per trawler before 1914 was £6000–7000; by 1917 it had risen to £30000–40000 per annum. All vessels were released during the immediate post war demobilisation period when the Auxiliary Patrol was being paid off. Although release occurred during the same period, the Fishery Trawlers nevertheless were not at any time part of the Patrol. While on naval service, the FTs were given unrestricted fishing rights.

It was also under consideration to include all remaining sailing trawlers (smacks), and steam drifters. Although attacks on the smacks in particular had been extremely heavy and their losses high, sailing vessels, by nature of their fishing methods, would have been difficult to concentrate effectively in fleets and provide protection for them. Drifters were not taken up because their fishing grounds were closer to shore and in the past they had suffered far less from the enemy.

Following is a list of essentially all such trawlers, with an additional list of smaller craft that represented the remainder of the fleet. As indicated earlier many old and very few modern vessels are included along with trawlers denoted * who had previously been used in the patrol organisation but later released as being no longer suitable.

Port No.	Name	TG/Yr.	Port No.	Name	TG/Yr.
H.103	ADMIRAL CRADOCK	295/14	GY.795	ANGOLIAN*	141/98
A.114	AFRICAN PRINCE	125/96	LH.195	ANNIE WALKER	123/90
GY.143	AGAMI	186/99	H.990	ANTONIO	202/08
H.243	AISNE	315/15	GY.76	AQUARIUS*	187/05
CF.22	ALERT IV	150/96	GY.371	ARALIA	229/99
O.35	ALFRED EDITH	262/08	A.554	ARGO	174/03
GY.6	ALGOMA	169/99	A.295	ARIES II	159/99
H.887	ALONSO	172/06	DE.126	ATLANTIC	167/98
BN.73	ALSATIAN*	191/00	H.854	AUDREY	186/06
DE.3	AMBASSADOR	149/99	M.54	AVONMOUTH*	139/90
H.398	AMBER	172/98	SN.72	AYACANORA	147/94
GY.481	AMENITY	212/08	A.614	BALGOWNIE	185/02
H.401	AMETHYST*	172/98	O.120	BARON RUZETTE	214/10
H.169	AMPERE	154/91	A.285	BEN HOPE	160/00
GY.5	ANDES	169/99	A.847	BEN LEDI	149/98
SD.9	ANDROMEDA	130/99	H.855	BONA	186/06
LO.186	ANGLIA	196/04		=in WW II.	

Port No.	Name	TG/Yr
GY.922	BRAERIACH	199/02
A.305	BRAVO	137/96
GN.32	BREADALBANE	112/91
A.62	BRENT	142/92
H.1009	BRIDLINGTON	205/13
A.791	BRILLIANT STAR	125/96
GY.1281	BRISBANE	207/03
GN.10	BRUCE	103/83
DE.5	BRUCKLAY	182/00
GN.27	BUCCLEUCH	146/03
GY.1096	BUCKINGHAM	172/99
GY.576	BULL DOG	148/92
H.86	BURMAH*	168/92
GY.825	BUZZARD II =in WW II.	181/98
H.210	CADET =LADY ESTELLE in WW II.	323/15
A.198	CAIRNWELL	141/95
A.93	CALEDONIA II	144/98
M.168	CALYPSO	187/01
H.998	CAPE TOWN II =in WW II.	188/08
GN.50	CAPTAIN	134/98
GY.755	CASPIAN	150/95
A.667	CECIL RHODES	112/91
M.216	CELTIA =in WW II.	239/07
GY.440	CEPHEUS	155/91
GY.548	CETUS	139/93
FD.186	CEVIC	151/95
GN.49	CHALLENGER	146/97
A.423	CHANCELLOR	168/01
A.237	CHIEFTAIN II	149/99
H.383	CITY OF ABERDEEN =in WW II.	194/98
GY.301	CITY OF LONDON	225/97
GY.1223	COLLINGWOOD =in WW II.	172/02
H.223	COMMANDER HOLBROOK =in WW II.	227/15
H.233	COMMANDER HORTON	227/15
GN.33	COMMODORE	137/91
O.55	COMTE HORACE VAN DER BURGH	200/07
H.240	CONAN DOYLE	314/15
GY.274	CONGO*	152/97
A.360	CONQUEROR II	148/99
LH.	CONSTANCE	166/02
GY.63	CORCYRA* =in WW II.	225/14
M.46	CORNET	191/99
GY.550	CORVUS	140/93
GN.17	COUNCILLOR	116/85
A.820	CRAIG GOWAN	126/97
SN.266	CRAIGELLACHIE	112/96
A.782	CRAIGIEVAR	112/96
GY.111	CRATER	132/96
H.303	CRYSTAL	149/95
LT.689	CUCKOO	135/94
A.906	CURLEW	125/97
A.435	CYGNET III	138/93
GY.346	CYNTHIA	167/97
LO.187	DANIA	196/04
M.80	DARTMOUTH	139/90
GY.513	DEE	151/93
DE.112	DEFENDER	128/99
H.742	DELHI	171/03

Port No.	Name	TG/Yr
O.170	DELTA A. sunk 21.4.18.	241/08
GY.525	DERWENT	151/93
GY.603	DIAMOND III	150/94
GY.1205	DIVER*	207/00
GY.1132	DOON	199/99
H.364	DORIS	174/97
GY.310	DOURO	152/97
A.130	DRUMBLAIR	196/00
H.378	DURBAN*	152/97
SA.3	DYNEVOR CASTLE	283/14
GY.378	EAGLE	146/91
GY.155	EASTBOURNE	163/96
H.360	EBOR	165/97
PD.364	ECLIPSE sunk 1.7.17.	185/99
H.368	EDDYSTONE	165/97
H.442	EDITOR*	169/99
GY.1084	EGRET	224/99
H.21	EGRET sunk 1.6.18.	169/99
A.75	EIDER II	142/92
H.358	ELBE	165/97
H.710	ELDORADO =in WW II.	180/02
WY.105	ELEAZAR sunk 12.8.17.	111/95
H.438	ELECTOR	169/98
GY.236	ELECTRIC	183/90
H.362	ELF	165/97
GY.1235	ELK*	181/02
H.320	ELSIE*	184/96
GY.613	EMERALD III	150/94
H.741	EMPEROR*	181/05
GY.1	EMU	154/95
H.468	EMULATOR	168/99
H.523	ENCORE	164/00
H.519	ENDYMION	164/00
H.769	ENNERDALE	183/03
A.507	ENVOY	150/94
H.315	EQUITY	158/96
H.768	EROS sunk 8.6.18.	181/03
H.747	ESMERALDA	181/03
A.205	EUDOCIA	147/91
GY.285	EUTHAMIA sunk 22.9.18	142/90
H.718	EVERGREEN	180/02
GY.426	EXETER	165/97
A.55	FAITH	135/91
GY.798	FALCON	154/95
GY.1008	FAWN	201/98
GY.773	FERMO	175/98
H.177	FIDELIA =in WW II.	147/91
A.419	FLEETWING II	119/96
GY.166	FLEETWOOD	163/96
FD.196	FLORENCE DOMBEY*	182/00
FD.166	FLY	158/90
GN.77	FORT GEORGE*	180/02
GY.712	FORT WILLIAM	178/03
GY.140	FORTUNA =in WW II.	259/06
A.769	FRIGATE BIRD II	99/95
O.182	GABY	210/09
GY.245	GAELIC*	159/90
A.173	GENERAL	191/98
GY.1120	GILDEROY	153/99

Port No.	Name	TG/Yr
GW.13	GLEN CLOVA	161/94
GY.871	GOLDEN GLEAM	191/95
GY.733	GREAT ADMIRAL =in WW II.	284/08
GY.219	GREBE	265/06
SN.4	GRECIAN PRINCE mined 15.12.18.	126/99
GY.1240	GRIFFIN	183/03
A.514	HALCYON II	141/93
GY.442	HALIFAX	165/97
GY.1228	HAWTHORN II	179/02
GW.9	HEATHER	179/04
GY.784	HELIOS	201/03
GY.698	HILARIA	207/98
O.75	IBIS V	196/08
GY.450	ILFRACOMBE	165/97
A.146	IMPERIAL PRINCE	128/99
GY.833	INDIA	190/94
GY.32	INGOMAR =CONISTON in WW II.	217/04
H.709	IONA	187/04
GY.256	IONIC	159/90
GY.1176	IRWELL =SAXONIA in WW II.	197/00
O.81	ISA	217/12
H.878	ISABEL	174/06
GY.75	ISIS	175/99
H.406	J. BAELS MAURICX	211/06
H.176	JASPER	156/91
O.131	JOHN	221/10
SN.111	JOHN M. SMART sunk 12.12.17.	113/91
GY.391	JONQUIL	143/91
GY.725	KALSO	179/99
SN.63	KIELDER CASTLE	129/00
GY.1124	KING CANUTE	195/99
GY.1214	KING GEORGE	164/01
GY.479	KING HARALD	227/99
GY.1169	KING HENRY =in WW II.	162/00
A.469	KITTIWAKE	153/91
A.819	KITTY	135/97
SA.110	LABORE ET HONOUR	150/93
GY.281	LADAS	172/98
A.424	LAPWING V	124/96
GY.68	LARCHWOLD	129/96
FD.29	LAURA	280/05
SN.237	LAUREATE	194/98
GY.275	LAUREL*	138/97
GY.207	LEEDS	161/97
GY.36	LEO =in WW II.	181/05
H.41	LEONATO	213/09
FD.118	LINCOLNIA	138/96
A.43	LINNET*	142/87
GY.703	LITTLE EMMA	167/90
A.857	LOCH LOMOND	145/98
GY.867	LOCH STROM	176/03
LT.427	LOLIST	180/14
GY.718	LORD ROTHSCHILD	174/06
GY.392	LORD SELBORNE	167/97
GY.395	LORD SHREWSBURY	168/98
GN.5	LOTHIAN	131/04
GY.1202	LUCERNE	198/00
O.153	LUCIENNE JEANNE	223/07
GY.434	LYRIC	126/91
GY.1010	MAGPIE III	156/96
GY.682	MAJESTIC	159/94
FD.178	MANDA	150/98
A.526	MANNOFIELD	206/05
GY.460	MANSFIELD	165/95
A.594	MARGUERITE	151/95
O.97	MARIE LOUISE	140/00
LO.235	MARION II	256/06
O.43	MARTHE =CRAIG ISLAND in WW II.	234/13
FD.107	MEUSE	217/04
H.	MINERVA III	222/00
GY.732	MINERVA IV	142/00
GY.654	MOLLYMAWK =REFORMO in WW II.	242/99
A.35	MONARCH IV	130/95
GY.806	MONS	163/96
A.773	MORNING STAR VI	120/95
O.151	NADINE	198/10
GY.232	NEWHAVEN II	161/97
GY.520	NIBLICK	154/91
FR.239	NORTH CAPE	122/89
A.478	NORTH WEST	123/90
GY.1275	NUBIA	196/03
YH.405	OCEAN COMRADE*	133/92
GY.863	OCEANIC IV	235/98
H.876	OCTAVIA	173/06
GY.986	OSIRIS III	173/98
GY.200	OSTERO	138/97
GY.311	OSTRICH	146/91
HL.61	OSTRICH III	148/89
FD.180	OTTOMAN EMPIRE	162/94
A.618	OWL III	117/96
H.445	PARRAMATTA*	168/91
SD.6	PAULINE	133/99
A.531	PEMBROKE CASTLE	153/93
SH.225	PENGUIN II	151/95
H.131	PERICLES	208/10
GY.710	PETUNIA III	209/99
SH.274	PHALAROPE	124/96
FD.121	PHOEBE III	278/07
GY.177	PINEWOLD	141/98
A.250	POCHARD sunk 28.6.18.	146/89
FD.6	PORT JACKSON	197/04
GY.828	PORTIA III	178/95
O.85	PRESIDENT STEVENS	212/05
SN.245	PRETORIA	159/00
O.36	PRINCE CHARLES	226/04
GY.1036	PRINCE CONSORT	154/90
O.38	PRINCESS MARIE JOSE	222/13
GY.215	QUAIL	265/06
GY.1141	QUASSIA	207/99
H.530	QUEEN ALEXANDRA =in WW II.	231/01
GY.982	QUIXOTIC	197/98
GY.1157	RANEE	194/00
FD.199	RATTLER	149/91
GY.720	RATTRAY*	182/00
O.130	RAYMOND	221/10
A.425	REDWING	119/96
A.202	REGINA	125/91
GY.23	RENOVO	170/04
GY.1019	RESPONDO	209/05
GY.255	RICHMOND	161/97
GY.1003	ROBINA	168/03
GY.1147	ROBINIA	208/00
GY.1208	RODRIGO	169/00
A.876	ROLAND	159/99
GY.647	ROLLO	167/99
GY.639	ROMANOFF	178/00
GY.1233	ROSARENO	166/02

Port No.	Name	TG/Yr
GY.1232	ROSCO	166/02
GN.8	ROSEBERY	103/83
GY.1090	ROYALIST	183/98
A.865	SABINE	118/88
GY.856	ST. CLOUD	189/99
GN.46	ST. GOTHARD	156/94
H.355	ST. KILDA	187/04
SN.102	ST. LAWRENCE No. 1	211/09
H.937	ST. LUCIA	186/07
GY.55	SALACON	211/05
SN.40	SARAH	135/99
GW.25	SARK	145/95
GY.467	SCORPIO	145/88
SH.182	SCORPION	155/91
LH.68	SCOTIA	149/91
H.348	SCOTLAND	152/97
GN.37	SEA HAWK	169/98
GY.1011	SEA HORSE III	229/01
GY.1154	SERAPION =in WW II.	195/00
A.139	SETTER*	171/99
H.483	SHAMROCK	184/99
GY.801	SILURIA =CORYPHENE in WW II.	207/07
H.505	SINGAPORE	159/00
H.453	SKERNE*	156/91
GY.301	SOMERVILLE	149/91
GY.288	SOUTHWARD	225/07
GN.63	SPARTAN	120/93
H.460	STANDARD	162/99
A.411	STAR OF HOPE	124/96
GY.676	STAR OF THE SOUTH	182/03
H.405	STORM COCK	151/92
GN.76	STRATHALLAN	175/00
GY.997	STRATHDON	155/91
GN.40	STRATHEARN	152/98
GN.11	STRATHISLA II	154/94
GY.694	STRATON sunk 8.2.18.	197/99
GY.546	STROMO	142/92
CF.2	SUMA	284/14
DE.13	SUNBEAM IV	133/91
A.766	SUNLIGHT	168/94
A.648	SUNRISE	167/91
GN.1144	SWALLOW	200/00
SA.108	SWANSEA CASTLE =in WW II.	256/12
A.737	TASMANIA	146/91
A.655	TAURUS	128/83
A.54	TAYMOUTH	137/91
A.156	TAYSIDE	137/99
GY.1055	THRUSH IV	134/93
H.482	TOBAGO	159/99
A.866	TORFRIDA	120/81
H.335	TURQUOISE	164/96
GY.82	TUSCAN	178/05
LL.375	TYNDRUM	192/02
A.	TYNE WAVE sunk 23.4.18.	121/91
A.49	UNDAUNTED	141/95
GY.1190	UVULARIA	207/00
GY.568	VALENTIA	164/98
GY.818	VALERIA	189/98
GY.1127	VENETIA III	201/99
SN.242	VICTORIAN PRINCE	126/97
A.534	VIGILANT	139/02
GY.1051	VIOLET CAIE	141/89
H.111	VOLTA	157/90
SSS.8	VOLUNTEER	112/91
GN.12	WALLACE	100/83
GY.746	WAYNFLETE	157/01
GY.524	WHITBY	164/98
SN.345	WOLSELEY	159/03
H.49	YORICK	213/09
GY.348	YULAN	144/91
GY.337	ZENNOR	161/97
GY.760	ZETLAND	165/98
GY.151	ZODIAC II	149/90

SMALLER FISHING VESSELS

Port No.	Name	TG/Yr
LT.570	ADVANCE	62/05
SN.268	BADEN POWELL II	93/00
YH.616	BERRY CASTLE	59/01
YH.285	BERRY HEAD	58/01
KY.14	BETTY INGLIS =in WW II.	104/95
YH.170	CHARM	62/07
LT.118	CHIMAERA	107/07
YH.380	CLAUDIAN	63/99
YH.514	COUNTY OF FIFE	114/96
LT.274	DIADEM	55/01
LT.372	EARLY MORN*	58/01
SN.198	EVELYN JOYCE	93/12
YH.376	FANCY	53/99
SN.73	FELICIA	75/08
YH.707	FORTUNATUS	53/02
LT.324	HAWTHORNDALE	60/09
CS.	HECLA	65/96
BF.965	KIMBERLEY IV	102/07
LT.1182	LAVEROCK	58/01
LT.149	LORD ROBERTS	72/00
YH.178	MON AMI	77/10
LT.877	NEVER CAN TELL	62/05
PD.485	NORTH AMERICAN	97/94
LT.471	PRIDE	62/04
LT.418	PROLIFIC	60/06
LT.54	PROSPECT*	58/02
SN.247	RAMBLER	92/98
SN.300	RANTER	99/01
SN.2	REAPER II	91/99
LT.360	RECORD	67/04
SN.297	REDVERS BULLER	99/01
LT.629	REQUEST	56/01
LT.1754	ROSE	96/95
LT.529	ROSE OF SHARON	59/02
LT.738	ST. ABBS	92/95
WY.96	ST. MARY	99/98
YH.270	SPRAY	61/06
LT.1104	ZEALOT	60/07

Notes: Included are some vessels described as Fishery Drifters. A dozen or so additional names appear in navy lists but they are not in registers.

ADMIRALTY WHALERS

237 tons gross. 132¾ (oa), 125 (pp) × 25 × 8½ ft. TE 1200 ihp = 13 kts.
336 tons displacement.
Armament: 1–12 pdr (ZEDWHALE 1–12 pdr, 1–6 pdrAA).

Adty No.	Name	Launched	Fate
878	ARCTIC WHALE (Z.15)	7.10.15	Sold 20.4.20, same name; =BERMUDIAN 1923; =BERMUDIAN in WW II.
865	BALENA (Z.2)	29. 5.15	Sold 20.4.20 A. J. Ashwin; =BEECHWIN.
866	BELUGA (Z.3)	26. 6.15	Sold 20.4.20 A. J. Ashwin, same name.
868	BLACKWHALE (Z.5)	28. 6.15	Mined 3.1.18 off Fife Ness.
867	BOWHEAD (Z.4)	26. 6.15	Sold 20.4.20 A. J. Ashwin, same name.
869	BULLWHALE (Z.6)	28. 6.15	Sold 6.3.20 Allen Adams & Co, same name; later =RIO CASMA.
870	CACHALOT (Z.7)	28. 7.15	Sold 1933 =GLADIATOR.
871	COWWHALE (Z.8)	28. 7.15	Sold 6.3.20 =RASIT.
876	FINWHALE (Z.13)	24. 9.15	Sold 6.3.20 =HOPKINS BROS; later =CANADIAN NATIONAL No. 1.
872	HUMPBACK (Z.9)	12. 8.15	Sold 6.3.20.
875	ICEWHALE (Z.12) =OSPREY 3.24	10. 9.15	Sold 15.10.28 Plymouth & Devon S Bkg Co.
1790	MEG (Z.1) =ZEDWHALE 1.16	29. 5.15	Sold 12.2.20, same name; later =TSAR DUSHAN.
877	PILOTWHALE (Z.14)	24. 9.15	Sold 20.4.20, same name.
874	RIGHTWHALE (Z.11)	10. 9.15	Sold 6.3.20 =RIO TAMBO.
873	RORQUAL (Z.10)	12. 8.15	Sold 6.3.20.

Notes: Ordered 15.3.15; all built by Smiths Dock Co using designs prepared for whalers to be built for the Russian government. The expected manoeuvrability of these vessels made them suitable as anti-submarine escorts in coastal waters. They were originally numbered Z.1–15, the names came a little later. The first vessel was completed in 7.15. Their performance in heavy weather was inferior to trawlers of the same tonnage and the design was therefore not repeated in later orders. In addition, post-war demand would be far lower than standard fishing types. From 1915–18 they formed three squadrons, respectively based at Stornoway, Shetlands and Peterhead or the Humber.

WHALERS

(a) GERMAN VESSELS SEIZED IN SOUTH AFRICA

Name	TG/Yr	Former name—Service—Fate
AFRIKANDER	126/83	(ex-*Bismarck*; ex *Victoria*) Base ship at Simonstown 11.14–2.19; Sold, =VICTORIA 1922.
FLY	167/13	(ex-*Sturmvogel*) 1–12 pdr, 2–3 pdr. In service 3.15–1919.
PICKLE	167/13	(ex-*Seeadler*) 1–12 pdr, 2–3 pdr. In service 3.15–1919.

(b) HIRED VESSELS

Adty No.	Port No.	Name	TG/Yr	Armament—Service—Fate
2017	LH.157	HIRPA	110/11	1–6 pdr. 1.15– Wrecked 2.1.18 near Buckie.
2018	LH.366	RAMNA	108/08	1–6 pdr AA. 1.15– Purchased; Sold 13.11.19.

(c) PURCHASED VESSELS

Name	TG/Yr	Service—Fate
CHARON	165/08	(ex-*Eclair*) 1–12 pdr, 2–3 pdr. Purchased 4.15– Sold 6.3.19 Irvin & Johnson =ECLAIR.
CHILDERS	182/12	(ex-*Norvegia*) 1–12 pdr. Purchased 1.15– Sold 1919.
ECHO	182/12	(ex-*Barrowby*) 1–12 pdr, 2–3 pdr. Purchased 1.15– Sold 6.3.19 Irvin & Johnson =BARROWBY.
FAIR HELGA	175/12	M/S. 3.8.17–13.3.19; Sold 1921 Premier Whaling Co, same name.
FAIR MAGDA	175/12	M/S. 3.8.17–13.3.19; Sold 1921 Premier Whaling Co, same name.
NIVONIA	175/12	3.8.17–26.5.19; Sold 1919 Eastern Whaling Co, same name.
NOBLE NORA	160/12	25.6.17–13.3.19; Sold 3.19 Premier Whaling Co, same name; =in WW II.
SALAMANDER	174/12	(ex-*Krabben*) 1–12 pdr. Purchased 4.15– Sold 6.3.19 Irvin & Johnson =KRABBEN.
SILESIA	175/12	3.8.17–26.5.19; Sold 1920 Eastern Whaling Co, same name.
SPLINT =RATTLER 6.15 =PRATTLER 7.16	136/12	Purchased 4.15– in service 26.5.15– Sold 6.3.19 Premier Whaling Co =SPLINT.
STYX	165/03	(ex-*Etoile*) 1–12 pdr. Purchased 4.15– Sold 6.3.19 Premier Whaling Co =ETOILE.
TRANSVAALIA	160/12	6.17– Sold 3.19 Eastern Whaling Co, same name; =in WW II.

Notes: Another small whaler of 14 tons net, BJORN, was purchased and in service 26.1.18–23.9.19 as a store vessel at Scapa. CHARON, CHILDERS, ECHO, FLY, PICKLE, SALAMANDER and STYX served in East Africa; NIVONIA and SILESIA in West Africa; HIRPA and RAMNA in home waters and the others at the Cape Station.

ADMIRALTY DRIFTERS

The Admiralty decision to augment the Auxiliary Patrol with additional vessels of this type necessitated a drifter construction programme because insufficient numbers of commercial vessels remained to be requisitioned. The building programme began in May 1917 when 115 contracts were placed in lieu of a projected 50 trawler orders. The scheduled delivery of these drifters was by 1.5.18 when it was intended to redeploy larger vessels as the drifters became available for harbour and coastal patrol duties.

A standard design for vessels to be built of wood was prepared while a similar design was prepared for vessels to be built of steel. Chambers' BOY ROY was used as the wooden prototype and "Ocean" type drifters built just prior to the war served as the steel prototype. Numerous builders not accustomed to building larger vessels were selected for this purpose, but the initial orders were placed with well established firms who were traditional drifter builders. Some steel ship-builders were diverted from trawler construction in an attempt to deliver large quantities of the smaller vessels at an earlier date. Approval of a standard design that was acceptable to all of the builders concerned caused considerable delay in production in view of opposition and limitations of the builders who favoured their own designs.

Later in 1917, 60 more drifters were contracted for (also in lieu of 50 trawlers), and by May 1918 when contracts for the final order of 160 vessels were being let there were 37 builders engaged in the production of hulls. Contracts for 96 of these vessels were distributed among the seven traditional builders while the remaining 20 contracts went to 9 smaller firms. 64 companies were under consideration before the 9 small firms received the contracts. Of the 335 vessels authorised, 292 were contracted for; of these 118 were completed for service, 105 completed as commercial fishing vessels and 69 were cancelled. 84 vessels were completed by 11.11.18 and a further 34 were later completed as minesweepers. 25 of the fishing vessels were sold as soon as they became available.

Receiving natural phenomenon or meteorological names, this class failed to reach the planned production schedule. Many drifters were forced to lie idle for months before machinery delivery permitted them to be completed.

War service was very limited due to their late inception and production difficulties. As they were completed they were incorporated into the Auxiliary Patrol and later many became mine sweepers and fleet tenders. Most of these craft were sold in the early twenties for commercial fishing by various government agencies who took over many of them from the Admiralty. The vessels which were retained as tenders, etc. survived in most instances to serve in World War II and were joined by numerous sisters requisitioned from commercial registry.

The average cost of a wood drifter for both hull and machinery was £11500 while the average for a steel drifter was £10800. Note that the Admiralty numbers which were part of Fishery flag superior run in sequence agreeable with the order in which contracts were placed. 42 drifters were under construction when the first orders were placed; some of these were included as non-standard units while others were allowed to be completed and then requisitioned as hired vessels.

ADMIRALTY WOOD DRIFTERS

94 tons gross. 94½ (oa), 86½ (pp) × 20 × 10 (dhd) ft.
179 tons displacement. (deep). TE 270 ihp = 9 kts.

Adty No.	Name	Launched	Builder—Armament—Fate
	Non-Standard Units:		
3883	DARKNESS =COLUMBINE 11.19	15. 6.18*	Fellows. 1–6 pdr M/S. Sold 1925; =SEA HOLLY 1927; =SEA HOLLY in WW II.
3890	FLAT CALM	3. 6.18*	Forbes. 1–6 pdr M/S. Sold 1920 =ROWAN TREE; =ROWAN TREE in WW II.
3889	FOGBOW	3. 6.18*	Forbes. 1–6 pdr M/S. Sold 1923; =FERTILE VALE 1924; =FERTILE VALE in WW II.
3913	IRIDESCENCE	21.12.17*	Innes. 1–6 pdr. Sold 1926, same name; =in WW II.
3930	MIDNIGHT SUN	1. 5.18*	Richards. 1–6 pdr M/S. BU 1929.
3931	NADIR	29. 5.18*	Richards. 1–6 pdr. Sold 1921=SALPA; =SALPA in WW II.
3932	NIGHTFALL	4. 7.18	Richards. 1–6 pdr M/S. Sold 1921, same name.
3933	NIMBUS	27. 8.18*	Richards. 1–6 pdr M/S. To MA & F 1921; =GIRL BELLA 1921; =JETSAM 1923; lost 28.7.24.
3945	RAY	9.10.18*	Stephen, Banff. 1–6 pdr M/S. Sold 14.10.27 =MARGARET & FRANCIS.
3972	SHOOTING STAR	5. 6.18*	Colby. 1–6 pdr. Sold 1929; =SHOOTING STARS 1930.

Adty No.	Name	Launched	Builder—Armament—Fate
	Standard Units:		
3863	AFTERGLOW	7.10.18*	Chambers. 1–6 pdr M/S. Sold 1921 =PORT RICHARD; =AFTERGLOW in WW II.
3866	AIRPOCKET =AMBITIOUS 8.19	8. 9.18*	Chambers. 1–6 pdr AA. To FBS 14.10.20; =CINERARIA 1921; =CINERARIA in WW II.
3865	ANTICYCLONE	2.12.18*	Chambers. 1–6 pdr AA. Sold 9.31, same name; =in WW II.
3864	ASTRAL	17. 8.18*	Chambers. 1–6 pdr. Sold 6.10.21; foundered 10.21 on delivery passage.
3862	ATMOSPHERE	6. 7.18*	Chambers. 1–6 pdr M/S. To MA & F 2.8.21; same name; lost 6.12.29.
3861	AVALANCHE	2. 7.18*	Chambers. 1–6 pdr M/S. Sold 1926 =LOCHALSH.
3869	BACKWASH	19. 7.18*	Colby. 1–6 pdr M/S. To MA & F 4.8.21; =WILLIAM C. FARROW 1922; =MORVEN HILL in WW II.
3871	BLACK FROST =COLUMBINE 1925	2. 9.18*	Colby. 1–6 pdr AA. Sold 1929 =TIMOR; =MILL WATER in WW II.
3872	BLACK NIGHT	14.11.18*	Colby. 1–6 pdr Experiments. To MA & F 3.10.21; =BLACKNIGHT 1921.
3867	BLUE SKY	19. 6.18*	Colby. 1–6 pdr M/S. Foundered 12.6.22 off the Thames estuary.
3868	BOREALIS	5. 7.18*	Colby. 1–6 pdr M/S. To MA & F 1921; =BRASH 1921.
3873	CIRRUS	9. 9.18*	Colby. 1–6 pdr PB. Sold 1926 =TRAVELLER'S JOY.
3874	CUMULUS	19. 9.18*	Colby. 1–6 pdr. To MA & F 2.10.20; =BOY JERMYN 1920; =BOY JERMYN in WW II.
3884	DAYLIGHT	12. 7.18*	Fellows. 1–6 pdr M/S. Sold 5.21 =TRADEWIND; =TRADEWIND in WW II.
4138	DOLDRUM	22. 1.20*	Smith, Rye. (F) Sold 1920 =BEATRICE EVES; =GLOAMIN in WW II.
3885	ETESIAN	31.10.18*	Fellows. 1–6 pdr M/S. To MA & F 19.11.20; same name; =M. H. STEPHEN in WW II.
3891	FAIR WEATHER	25. 3.18	Forbes. 1–6 pdr M/S. To FBS 19.8.20; same name; =in WW II.
3893	FIERY CROSS	9. 8.18*	Forbes. 1–6 pdr M/S. Sold 1930 =FIRCROFT.
3888	FIREBALL	30. 1.20*	Fellows. (F) To FBS 28.4.20; =MAVISTON 1920; =HOLLYDALE in WW II.
4154	FIRELIGHT	7.11.19*	Chambers. (F) To MA & F 3.2.20; =JUST REWARD 1921.
3895	FIRMAMENT	28.11.18*	Forbes. 1–6 pdr Experiments. To FBS 28.8.20; =FOXGLOVE 1921.
3894	FLAME	10.10.18*	Forbes. 1–6 pdr M/S. To FBS 13.10.20; =UBEROUS 1921; =UBEROUS in WW II.
4155	FLECK	1.10.19*	Chambers. (F) To MA & F 2.10.19; same name.
4157	FLOTSAM	1.10.19*	Chambers. (F) To MA & F 2.10.19; same name.
4158	FLURRY	9. 3.20*	Chambers. (F) To FBS 28.4.20; same name; =GLEAM ON in WW II.
4504	FLUSH	12. 3.20*	Wood, Lossiemouth. (F) To FBS 29.4.20; same name; =in WW II.
4160	FOGBANK	4. 3.20*	Clapson. (F) To FBS 7.10.20; =DYKER LASSIE 1921.
4161	FOUNTAIN	3. 6.20*	Clapson. (F) To FBS 14.12.20; =WHITENIGHT 1922.
3892	FULL MOON	25. 3.18	Forbes. 1–6 pdr M/S. Sold 1929 =ROSE HAUGH; =ROSE HAUGH in WW II.
3898	GLACIER	15.12.18*	Forbes. (F) To FBS 18.12.19; =GIRL JOEY 1921; =SILVER SKY in WW II.
3896	GLEAM	10. 5.19*	Forbes. Sold 1921; =DOUGALS 1922; =REIDS in WW II.
3899	GLINT	26.11.19*	Forbes. (F) To FBS 20.12.19; =PROSPECTS AHEAD 1921; =PROSPECTS AHEAD in WW II.
3897	GLOAMING	17. 6.19*	Forbes. Stranded 4.3.21 near the Lizard.
3901	GREEK FIRE	17. 6.20*	Forbes. (F) To FBS 17.6.20; same name; =PARADIGM in WW II.
3900	GREY SKY	3. 7.20*	Forbes. (F) To FBS 30.8.20; same name; =STAR OF BUCHAN 1929.

Adty No.	Name	Launched	Builder—Armament—Fate
3982	HAILSTORM	22.10.18*	Richards. 1–6 pdr. To MA & F 2.10.20; =GIRL LIZZIE 1923; =GIRL LIZZIE in WW II.
3983	HEAT WAVE	6.12.18*	Richards. For experiments. To MA & F 1921; same name.
3984	HURRICANE	5. 4.19*	Richards. (F) Sold 1919, same name; =CHARDE in WW II.
3915	ICEBLINK	14. 2.20*	Jones, Buckie. (F) To FBS 11.5.20; =STAR DIVINE 1920.
3914	IMBAT	23.11.18*	Jones, Buckie. 1–6 pdr Experiments. To FBS 2.9.20; same name; =in WW II.
4170	LOP	15. 1.20*	Courtney. (F) To FBS 6.7.20; =GREYNIGHT 1922.
3928	MACKEREL SKY	24. 4.19*	Noble. To FBS 21.10.20; =DRAINIE 1921; =DRAINIE in WW II.
4171	MAELSTROM	11. 3.20*	Courtney. (F) To FBS 16.6.20; same name; =FAIR HAVEN in WW II.
3929	MILKY WAY	11. 5.20*	Noble. (F) To FBS 11.5.20; same name.
3985	MISTRAL	29. 7.19*	Richards. (F) Sold 1919 =GOLDEN LINE; =GOLDEN LINE in WW II.
3933	PACKICE	22.10.18*	Smith, Buckie. 1–6 pdr. To FBS 5.7.20; MURRAY CLAN 1921; =UTILISE in WW II.
3939	PHASE	26. 1.20*	Smith, Buckie. (F) To FBS 26.1.20; same name; =in WW II.
3992	RAINSTORM	18.10.18*	Colby. To MA & F 1920; same name.
3941	RED SKY	26.11.18*	Stephen, Banff. 1–6 pdr Experiments. To FBS 31.7.20; same name; =in WW II.
3942	REFRACTION	19. 6.19*	Stephen, Banff. (F) To FBS 17.12.19; same name; =in WW II.
	REVERBERATION	5. 4.19*	Colby. (F) Sold 1919, same name; =in WW II.
3940	RIFT	17.12.20*	Smith, Buckie. (F) To FBS 17.12.20; =DOORIE BRAE 1921; =DOORIE BRAE in WW II.
3943	RIME	4.12.19*	Stephen, Banff. (F) To FBS 18.12.19; same name; =in WW II.
3993	RISING SEA	31.10.18*	Colby. To MA & F 1921; same name; =in WW II.
3994	RUNNEL	9.12.18*	Colby. To MA & F 12.10.20; same name.
3957	ST. ELMO'S LIGHT	24.11.19*	Innes. (F) To FBS 22.12.19; =SWEET PROMISE 1920; =SWEET PROMISE in WW II.
3995	SCEND	11. 3.19*	Colby. To MA & F 26.10.20; =GIRL HAZEL 1920; =W. WOOLLVEN 1922; lost 31.8.25.
3996	SCOUR	4. 1.19*	Colby. To MA & F 26.11.20; =CHEVIOTDALE 1922.
	SCUD	23. 5.19*	Colby. (F) Sold 1920 =FLEURBAIX.
	SETWEATHER	22.10.19*	Colby. (F) Sold 1919; same name.
	SHADE	27. 1.20*	Colby. (F) To FBS 1920; same name.
3947	SHADOW	3.11.18*	Stevenson & Asher. 1–6 pdr. To FBS 20.10.20; =PILOT US 1921; =PILOT US in WW II.
3956	SHEET LIGHTNING	26.10.18*	Innes. 1–6 pdr. To FBS 29.10.20; =ROSEACRE 1921; =ROSEACRE in WW II.
3997	SHIMMER	6. 3.19*	Colby. To MA & F 1921; same name.
3870	SILHOUETTE	3. 8.18*	Colby. 1–6 pdr. Sold 3.31 =HONORA EVELYN.
3960	SILT	13. 1.19*	Herd & Mackenzie. To FBS 3.9.20; =ROSEVALLEY 1921; =ROSEVALLEY in WW II.
	SIROCCO =DOUBLETIDE 1920	11. 6.20*	Colby. (F) To FBS 1921; =CAT'S EYE 1921.
3959	SOLSTICE	3.10.18*	Herd & Mackenzie. 1–6 pdr M/S. To FBS 5.7.20; same name; =in WW II.
4000	SPATE	26. 7.19*	Dunston. (F) Sold 1919, same name; =MARGUERITA in WW II.
4101	SPLASH =SPACE 1920	8.10.20*	Dunston. (F) To MA & F 1920; same name.
4105	SQUALL	5.10.18*	Chambers. Sold 1920, same name; =GOLDEN FEATHER 1925.
3948	STARLIGHT	25. 2.19*	Stevenson & Asher. To FBS 17.9.20; =STARLIGHT RAYS 1921; =STARLIGHT RAYS in WW II.
4106	STORMCENTRE	21.11.18*	Chambers. For experiments. To MA & F 1922; same name; =NORTH HAVEN in WW II.
3946	STORMWRACK	7. 8.18*	Stevenson & Asher. Sold 1927, same name; =PERILIA in WW II.

Adty No.	Name	Launched	Builder—Armament—Fate
4107	SUNLIGHT	16. 1.19*	Chambers. To MA & F 26.11.20; =HANNAH TAYLOR 1920.
3949	SUNRISE	3.10.19*	Stevenson & Asher. (F) To MA & F 10.10.19; =TAAL HINA 1921; =TILLYDUFF in WW II.
3961	SUNSPOT	19.11.20*	Herd & Mackenzie. (F) To FBS 24.11.20; same name.
4108	SURGE	19. 5.19*	Chambers. (F) Sold 1919 =RESURGE; =RESURGE in WW II.
4186	SWELL	23. 6.20*	Routh & Waddingham. (F) To FBS 14.12.20; =SILVERNIGHT 1922.
4109	SWIRL	1. 2.19*	Chambers. For experiments. To MA & F 1921; same name.
3963	THAW	16. 3.20*	Rose Street Foundry. (F) To FBS 22.4.20; same name; =in WW II.
3958	THUNDERBOLT	1. 4.20*	Innes. (F) To FBS 21.4.20; =INA ADAM 1920; =MIDNIGHT SUN 1922; =GREEN PASTURES in WW II.
	TIDAL RANGE	13. 4.20*	Colby. (F) To FBS 1921; same name.
4110	TIDERIP	19. 5.19*	Chambers. (F) Sold 1919 =KENTISH BELLE; lost 18.2.23 in collision.
3962	TROPIC	22. 3.19*	Rose Street Foundry. Fleet tender. Sold 1922 =JOHN PLENDERLEATH.
	TWINKLE	8. 8.20*	Colby. (F) Sold 8.21 =CLOUDARCH; =CLOUDARCH in WW II.
4139	VAPOUR	24. 8.20*	Smith, Rye. (F) Sold 1920, same name; =XMAS EVE in WW II.
3964	WILL O' THE WISP	21.10.20*	Kitto. (F) Sold 1920 =WATERWAY; =T. R. B. 1921.

* Delivery dates in launch column.

Notes: RAY, at 86 TG, was the smallest non-standard vessel; the others averaged 95 TG. Admiralty drifters laid down after 9.18 included many who were never given numbers, by the time they were delivered the Patrol was being demobilised. Many drifters of both wood and steel hulls were transferred to the Ministry of Agriculture and Fisheries (MA & F) or to the Fishery Board for Scotland (FBS) on the dates indicated, for disposal with special consideration to be given ex-service fisherman buyers. Soon thereafter they were taken up in commercial registry. A total of 21 wood drifters were cancelled. 17 named drifters were reported to have been cancelled 17.12.18. FLUTTER, Fellows No. 299, and SPRING TIDE for a short time intended to complete as (F) but these contracts were cancelled very soon after. In the cancellations list below many vessels were completed for commercial service:

Builder	Adty No.	Name	Fate
Chambers:	4156	FLOODTIDE	=MARJORIE GRACE 1920.
	4159	FLUTTER	=GOLDEN SUNBEAM 1921; =GOLDEN SUNBEAM in WW II.
Colby:		VOLUME	=GO AHEAD 1919; =GO AHEAD in WW II.
		WINDHOWL	=HARNSER 1919.
		WINDWAIL	=PLUMER 1919; =PLUMER in WW II.
		No. 75	=SILVER WAVE 1920; later CADIZ.
		No. 76	=launched, never completed; BU c1956.
Fellows:		No. 299	=BELLE VUE 1922; =BELLE VUE in WW II.
		No. 300	
Forbes:	3902	GLARE	
	3903	HAZE	
	3904	HOARFROST	
Herd & Mackenzie:	4102	SPOONDRIFT	
Kitto:	3965	ZENITH	
Richards:	3986	MOONLIGHT	=CARRY ON 1919; =CARRY ON in WW II.
	3987	MOONRISE	=ASCENDANT 1920.
Rose Street Fdy:	4111	BORA	
Routh & Waddingham:	4187	TIDERACE	
Smith, Buckie:	4103	SPRING TIDE	
Stephen, Banff:	3944	REFLECTION	
Stevenson & Asher:	4104	SPUME	

CANADIAN-BUILT ADMIRALTY WOOD DRIFTERS

99 tons gross. 84 (pp) ×19¼×10 (dhd) ft.
150 tons displacement. Compound engines 24 nominal hp=9 kts.
Armament (designed): 1–6 pdr.

Built by Davie SB & R, Levis:

Name	Commission	Paid off	Armament—Disposal—Etc.
CD.1	4. 9.17	1946	=EBBTIDE 11.24; Sold 1946 Northern S Bkg Co.
CD.2	16.10.17	1921	Sold 1921; =WESTBY 1922; resold 25.9.22 to Spain.
CD.3	29. 9.17	31. 1.19	Sold 1921 Puerto Monte Agency, Peru; =CORCOVADO.
CD.4	3.10.17	31. 1.19	Sold 1921 Puerto Monte Agency, Peru.
CD.5	11.10.17	31. 1.19	Sold 1921 Empresa Maritima de Cuba.
CD.6	8.10.17	31. 1.19	Sold 1921 =BAY QUEEN; foundered 1925 off Nova Scotia.
CD.7	15.10.17	1920	Sold 1921; =UTTERBY 1922; resold 1.10.24 to France.
CD.8	16.10.17	1920	Sold 12.20.
CD.9	17.10.17	12.18	1–6 pdr. Sold 1920 Captain D. J. Munro.
CD.10	20.10.17	12.18	1–6 pdr. Sold 1920 Captain Munro; engines to COLEUS 1922 and hull BU.
CD.11	22.10.17	12.18	Sold 1921; =RAUCEBY 1922; =PONTOISE 1925.
CD.12	23.10.17	1920	1–6 pdr. Sold 12.20.
CD.13	29.10.17	12.18	1–6 pdr. Sold 1920 Captain Munro; =EWERBY 1923; =LOCQUELTAS 1925.
CD.14	30.10.17	1.19	1–6 pdr. Sold 1921; =GILBY 1922; resold 21.10.26 to France.
CD.15	31.10.17	12.18	1–6 pdr. Sold 1921; =BRETONIA 1922.
CD.16	31.10.17	12.18	1–6 pdr. Sold 1920.
CD.17	8.11.17	2.19	1–6 pdr. Sold 1921 Captain Munro; =yacht STANSGATE 1925.
CD.18	7.11.17	8.19	1–6 pdr. Sold 1921; engines to ABELIA 1922 and hull BU.
CD.19	10.11.17	12.18	1–6 pdr. Sold 1921; engines to TELIA 1922 and hull BU.
CD.20	10.11.17	2.19	1–6 pdr. =GUELPH base ship 1918; Sold 1921 Captain Munro.
CD.21	6. 9.17	8.19	1–6 pdr. Sold 1920 Captain Munro; engines to FORSYTHIA 1922 and hull BU.
CD.22	12.11.17	4.19	1–6 pdr. Sold 1921; =GUNBY 1922; resold 25.9.22 to Spain.
CD.23	14.11.17	1919	1–6 pdr. Sold 1921; =BLAIRMORE I 1924; resold 1927 to USA.
CD.24	17.11.17	12.18	1–6 pdr. Sold 1920 Captain Munro; engines to BIOTA 1922, converted to motor =DARON 1924; BU c1924.
CD.25	17.11.17	2.19	1–6 pdr. Sold 1921 Captain Munro; =FENBY 1923; resold 13.6.25 to France.
CD.26	19.11.17	12.18	1–6 pdr. Sold 1921; =MOON 1924; sank 1927.
CD.27	19.11.17	2.19	1–6 pdr. Loaned to Dr Grenfell (Labrador Mission) 7.20; =WOP 1921.
CD.28	21.11.17	12.18	1–6 pdr. Sold 1920 Captain Munro; =GRABY 1922; =MAS-SABIELLE 1923.
CD.29	21.11.17	1919	1–6 pdr. Sold 1920 Captain Munro; resold 1921 W. N. Macdonald.
CD.30	14. 7.18	9. 7.19	Loaned to USN. Sold 10.9.19 Empresa de Pesca Vianese L'tada, Portugal.
CD.31	14. 7.18	23. 7.19	Loaned to USN. Sold 1920 Captain Munro; =SWABY 1923; resold 1925 to Spain.
CD.32	12. 7.18	12.18	1–6 pdr. Sold 1920 Captain Munro.
CD.33	12. 7.18	12.18	1–6 pdr. Sold 1920 Captain Munro; resold 1921 W. & T. Macdonald of Sydney, NS.
CD.34	17. 7.18	12.18	1–6 pdr. Sold 1920 Captain Munro; engines to MYRICA 1922 and hull BU.
CD.35	17. 7.18	2.19	1–6 pdr. Sold 20.5.19 Wm. Smith & Co; =H. A. WALKER 1920.
CD.36	14. 7.18	9. 7.19	Loaned to USN. Sold 1920 W. N. Macdonald =MARGARET MAC.
CD.37	17. 7.18	12.18	1–6 pdr. Sold 11.20; last noted 27.12.20 refloated off Magilligan Point.
CD.38	17. 7.18	12.18	1–6 pdr. Sold 1920; engines to COLUTEA 1922 and hull BU.
CD.39	12. 7.18	12.18	1–6 pdr. Sold 1920; engines to DEUTZIA 1922 and hull BU.

Name	Commission	Paid off	Armament—Disposal—Etc.
CD.40	12. 7.18	12.18	1–6 pdr. Sold 1920 Captain Munro.
CD.41	14. 7.18	9. 7.19	Loaned to USN. Sold 1920 T. Hogan & Co, Halifax, NS.
CD.42	15. 7.18	12.18	1–6 pdr. Sold 1920 Captain Munro; engines to EXTENSION 1922 and hull BU.
CD.43	1. 9.18	8.19	Sold 1920 Captain Munro; wrecked 1921.
CD.44	19. 8.18	8.19	1–6 pdr. Sold 1920 Captain Munro; =RANBY 1922; resold 25.7.22 to France.
CD.45	19. 8.18	8.19	Sold 4.8.19 Georges Latil, Cette, France.
CD.46	14. 7.18	23. 7.19	Loaned to USN. Sold 10.9.19 Empresa de Pesca Vianese L'tada, Portugal.
CD.47	28. 8.18	1919	Sold 4.8.19 Georges Latil, Cette, France.
CD.48	19. 7.18	12.18	1–6 pdr. Sold 1920; engines to OLEARIA 1922 and hull BU.
CD.49	10. 7.18	12.18	1–6 pdr. Sold 1920 Captain Munro.
CD.50	14. 7.18	9. 7.19	Loaned to USN. Transferred 9.19 to Dept of Marine & Fisheries =No. 21.

Built by Government Shipyard, Sorel:

Name	Commission	Paid off	Armament—Disposal—Etc.
CD.51	1. 9.18	1920	1–6 pdr. Sold 1921; =TEALBY 1922; =LOCMARIA 1925.
CD.52	1. 9.18	7.19	Sold 1920 Captain Munro; =ROXBY 1922.
CD.53	12.11.17	12.18	1–6 pdr. Sold 1920 Captain Munro; =KARRIER 1922.

Built by Sorel SB & Coal Co, Sorel:

Name	Commission	Paid off	Armament—Disposal—Etc.
CD.54	1. 9.18	8.19	Foundered 4.10.20 on passage to the UK.
CD.55	1. 9.18	8.19	Sold 1920 Captain Munro; =LUSBY 1923; missing 12.2.24.
CD.56	1. 9.18	8.19	Sold 1920 Captain Munro; =BULBY 1923; =FANION 1924.
CD.57	1918		Lost at sea before 8.20.
CD.58	14.10.18	3. 9.19	Loaned to USN. Sold 11.20 =MARY CURRIE.
CD.59	14.10.18	16. 8.19	Loaned to USN. Sold 1920 T. Kirkwood =TWO ROSES.

Built by H. H. Sheppard & Sons, Sorel:

Name	Commission	Paid off	Armament—Disposal—Etc.
CD.60	19. 8.18	8.19	Sold 1920; =WELBY 1923; resold 30.10.24 to France.
CD.61	14.10.18	2. 9.19	Loaned to USN. Sold 1920 T. Kirkwood, Montreal; =LAURA A.1 1928; =FOUNDATION MARGARET 1930.
CD.68	12.11.17	12.18	1–6 pdr. Sold 1920 Captain Munro.
CD.69	20.10.17	1920	1–6 pdr. Sold 1920; =EWERBY 1921; =ALINE 1921; BU 1929.
CD.70	1. 9.18	7.19	Sold 1920 Captain Alex Smith =MARY SMITH.

Built by LeClaire & Sons, Sorel:

Name	Commission	Paid off	Armament—Disposal—Etc.
CD.62	1. 9.18	7.19	Sold 1920 Captain Munro; =OSEBY 1923; resold 9.3.23 to France.
CD.63	1. 9.18	7.19	Sold 1920 Captain Munro; =DRIBY 1922; =YVONNE GASTON 1924.
CD.64	1. 9.18	7.19	Sold 1920 Captain Munro.
CD.65	28. 8.18	16. 8.19	Loaned to USN. Sold 1920 T. Kirkwood =METAK.
CD.66	1. 9.18	7.19	Sold 1920 Captain Munro; =SAXBY 1922; resold 25.9.22 to Spain.
CD.67	14.10.18	16. 7.19	Loaned to USN. Sold 1920.

Built by Canadian Vickers, Montreal:

Name	Commission	Paid off	Armament—Disposal—Etc.
CD.71	22.10.17		1–6 pdr. =EVENTIDE 1923; Sold c1926.
CD.72	23.10.17		1–6 pdr. =FLOODTIDE 1923; Sold c1926.
CD.73	5.11.17	1.19	1–6 pdr. Sold 1920 Captain Munro; =CLIXBY 1923; =FOI 1925.
CD.74	17.10.17	2.19	1–6 pdr. =SEAGULL 1921; Sold 1921.
CD.75	19.10.17	1926	1–6 pdr. Sold 1926.
CD.76	19. 8.18	8.19	Sold 1920; engines to SILENE 1922 and hull BU.
CD.77	19. 8.18	7.19	Sold 1920 Captain Munro; =KELBY 1923; resold 6.12.24 to Spain.
CD.78	14.10.18	3. 9.19	Loaned to USN. Sold 11.20 W. & T. Maconald.
CD.79	17. 7.18	12.18	Sold 1920.
CD.80	19. 8.18	7.19	Sold 1920 Captain Munro; =RISBY 1922.
CD.81	5. 8.18	1919	Sold 1920 =DONNA.
CD.82	19. 8.18	1946	=ONYX 7.19; foundered 21.3.47.
CD.83	1. 8.18	7.19	Sold 1920; =NORMAN MAC 1921.

Name	Commission	Paid off	Armament—Disposal—Etc.
CD.84	12. 8.18	7.19	1–6 pdr exam. Sold 1920 Captain Munro; =INGOLDB 1923.
CD.85	17. 7.18	12.18	1–6 pdr. Sold 1920 Captain Munro; engines to AREA 192 and hull BU.
CD.86	19. 8.18	7.19	Foundered 11.10.20 on passage to the UK.
CD.87	10.11.17	12.18	1–6 pdr. Foundered 12.10.20 on passage to the UK.
CD.88	1. 9.18	7.19	Foundered 25.7.20 on passage to the UK.
CD.89	19. 8.18	1919	Sold 1920 Job Brothers, St. John, NFL.
CD.90	19. 8.18	1919	Sold 1920 Salaverry Agencies, Peru; later =GOUVENEUF D'ANGEAC.
CD.91	12. 8.18	7.19	1–6 pdr exam. Sold 1920.
CD.92	19. 8.18	.19	Sold 1920 Salaverry Agencies, Peru.
CD.93	19. 8.18	10.19	Foundered 27.8.20 on passage to the UK.
CD.94	5. 8.18	16. 9.19	Loaned USN. Sold 11.20.
CD.95	1. 9.18	7.19	Sold 1920 Captain Alex Smith =ALICE L. SMITH; san 1921; still extant 1924 as a hulk.
CD.96	14.10.18	16. 9.19	Loaned USN. Sold 1920 =MARY PATRICIA 1921.

Built by Harbour Commissioners, Montreal:

CD.97	14.10.18	16. 9.19	Loaned USN. Sold 1920 =GRACE HANKINSON; los 25.1.30.
CD.98	14.10.18	3. 9.19	Loaned USN. Sold 1920 =CD.98; =PEARL CANN 1921.
CD.99	14.10.18	2. 9.19	Loaned USN. Sold 1920 T Kirkwood =MARY FRANCIS WHALEN; =DONNELLY 1925.
CD.100	14.10.18	16. 9.19	Loaned USN. Sold 1920 =ARICHAT 1921.

Notes: Built to the same general design as the UK-built wood drifters. They were ordered 1.17 and all 100 were launched during 1917. Production of 50 hulls by one firm and 26 by another contributed to a remarkable achievement in shipbuilding. CD.60–61 were originally to have been buil by Sorel SB & Coal Co and were still so assigned as late as 5.17. Boilers and engines were produced by 15 manufacturers, including four American companies who contributed 47½ sets. Goldie & McCulloch of Galt Ontario was the leading engineer, supplying 38 units.

By 31.12.17 CD.1–29, 51–53, 63–69, 71–75 and 87 were complete and at Halifax. 24 others were completed but could not be delivered until navigation re-opened on the St Lawrence River in the spring. All others were completing or fitting out at this time.

18 vessels were loaned to the USN from completion. CD.1, 12, 44, 51, 60, 69, 71, 72, 75–77, 80, 88 and 93 served at Gibraltar 1918–19; CD.45, 47, 81, 82, 90 and 92 at Bermuda 1918–19; and CD.2, 7, 8 and 11 in West Africa 1918–19.

Numerous TRs and CDs indicated as "sold" were in fact taken over in 1920 by Captain D J Munro on behalf of the Rose Street Foundry, Inverness and sailed from Canada in three groups in July and August 1920. After arriving at Inverness they were reconditioned then put up for sale; al this was done by Admiralty Order. CD.88 lost en route, was part of Munro's first delivery.

The boilers and engines of 12 CDs were reconditioned and installed 1922 in newly-built steel hulls At least five other sets were used in BERBERIS, C K WELTON, RIBES, W J COOK and WILLIAM GEMMELL also built 1922–23. DANTE, ERITHIAN, MARIE ODILE, SADIE MAC VRAI PASTEUR (of CD.1–50 group); ETENARD, ORIFLAMME (CD.60 & 68), HARRY MATHERS (CD.64 or 67); JEAN MAC, JOVEN LUIS, MAC HINERY, MARTHE & MARGUERITE, SALVATOR and WALTER KENNEDY (CD.75–94 group) were vessels that originated from this class.

ADMIRALTY STEEL DRIFTERS

84 tons gross. 93¼ (oa), 86 (pp) ×18½×9¼ (dhd) ft.
199 tons displacement (deep) TE 270 ihp = 9 kts.

Adty No.	Name	Launched	Builder—Armament—Fate
	Non-Standard Units:		
3882	DAYSPRING	19.12.17*	Fellows. 1–6 pdr. To MA & F 10.8.20;=CASTLEBAY 1921; =CASTLEBAY in WW II.
3886	ELEPHANTA	16. 1.20*	Fellows. (F) Sold 1920 =BYNG; =BYNG in WW II.
	Standard Units:		
4140	BLARE	29. 4.19*	Brooke. (F) Sold 1919 =MAY BIRD.
3971	BLIZZARD	30. 7.18*	Colby. 1–6 pdr. Sold 1921 =SATINSTONE; =HARVEST GLEANER in WW II.
4144	BLUE HAZE	6. 6.19*	Brooke. (F) Sold 14.7.19, same name; =in WW II.
4142	BOW WAVE	29. 7.19*	Brooke. (F) Sold 26.6.19, same name; =in WW II.
4143	BREAKER	16. 9.19*	Brooke. (F) Sold 1919 =KATHLEEN; =KATHLEEN in WW II.
3966	BRINE	17. 5.18	Ouse SB. 1–6 pdr. To FBS 28.7.20; same name; =in WW II.
4144	BROIL	8.10.19*	Brooke. (F) To MA & F8.10.19; same name; =M A WEST in WW II.
4145	BUBBLE	30.10.19*	Brooke. (F) To MA & F 2.12.19; same name; =UNICITY in WW II.
3877	CALM	9. 5.18	Duthie. 1–6 pdr. To MA & F 10.8.20; =JOHN HEDLEY 1920; =PRE-EMINENT in WW II.
3967	CASCADE	3. 7.18	Ouse SB. 1–6 pdr M/S. Sold 1945; =ILLUSTRIOUS 1946.
3968	CATSPAW	6. 8.18	Ouse SB. 1–6 pdr. Foundered 28.12.19 in the Kattegat while enroute from Reval to Copenhagen.
4146	CHIMERA	16. 7.20*	Brown's DD, Hull. (F) To FBS 21.9.20; =J. R. MITCHELL 1920; =TWINKLING STAR in WW II.
	CLEARING	14.11.19*	Ailsa, Troon. (F) Sold 17.3.21 =VERNAL; =VERNAL in WW II.
3876	CLOUD	11. 4.18	Duthie. 1–6 pdr. Sold 1946; =CORNUCOPIA 1947.
3875	COLD SNAP	28. 1.18	Duthie. 1–6 pdr. Sold 1945; =WHITEHILL 1948.
	COLDBLAST	19.11.19	Ailsa, Troon. (F) Sold 17.3.21 =ELSIE BRUCE.
4200	CONFLAGRATION	25. 9.19*	Watson. (F) To MA & F 3.9.20; same name; =MADELEINE JEANNE 1927.
3878	CRESCENT MOON	27. 5.18	Duthie. 1–6 pdr M/S. To WD 30.4.46.
4148	CURRENT	3.12.19*	Chambers. (F) To MA & F 29.9.20; =COPIOUS 1923; =COPIOUS in WW II.
4501	CYCLONE	21.10.19*	Watson. (F) To MA & F 5.12.19; =BLUSTER 1920.
3879	DAWN =EXPANSE 1919	11. 6.18	Duthie. 1–6 pdr M/S. To FBS 13.11.19; same name; =JANE WRIGHT 1922.
3880	DAYBREAK	9. 7.18	Duthie. 1–6 pdr. To MA & F 24.8.20; =RALPH HALL CAINE 1920; =ALLOCHY in WW II.
3969	DEW	6. 9.18*	Ouse SB. 1–6 pdr. To FBS 24.6.20; same name; =MOYRA 1923; =OLIVE TREE in WW II.
4149	DISTANCE	20. 1.20*	Chambers. (F) To MA & F 24.9.20; =LEONARD BOYLE 1920; =DUNDARG in WW II.
4150	DRIZZLE	10. 2.20*	Chambers. (F) To FBS 8.5.20; same name; =PILOT STAR in WW II.
3881	DUSK	9. 8.18	Duthie. 1–6 pdr. To MA & F 23.6.20; same name; =COSMEA in WW II.
3973	EDDY	6. 8.18	Hall. M/S. Mined 26.5.42 off Malta.
3974	FAIR WIND =ATTENTIVE II 5.19	6. 8.18	Hall. 1–6 pdrAA. To FBS 21.6.20; =HAWTHORN-BANK 1920; =HAWTHORNBANK in WW II.
3975	FALLING STAR	20. 8.18	Hall. 1–6 pdr. To MA & F 8.11.19; =BETTY BODIE 1921; =BETTY BODIE in WW II.
4502	FLAFF	2. 1.20*	Watson. (F) To FBS 30.1.20; =RIVER UGIE 1921; =NELLIE GARDINER 1921.
3970	FLASH	16. 2.18	Colby. 1–6 pdr. To MA & F 17.11.20; =A. J. A. 1920.
3976	FLICKER	21. 8.18	Hall. Sold 1935 =MARY WATT; =MARY WATT in WW II.

Adty No	Name	Launched	Builder—Armament—Fate
4503	FLOW	31. 3.20*	Watson. To FBS 19.8.20; same name; =in WW II.
	FOAM	1.10.20*	Abdela Mitchell. (F) To FBS 7.1.21; =STARWOF 1921; =PLOUGH in WW II.
	FOGBREAK	21.12.20*	Abdela Mitchell. To FBS 7.1.21; =CRAIGHAI 1921; =SPES AUREA in WW II.
4112	FORK LIGHTNING	22.11.18*	Brooke. 1–6 pdr M/S. To MA & F 20.8.20; same nam =RAMSEY BAY 1921.
3977	FRESHET	21.10.18*	Hall. 1–6 pdr M/S. To FBS 24.7.20; =JEAN PATE SON 1920; =XMAS ROSE in WW II.
3978	FROTH	25.10.18*	Hall. M/S. To MA & F 1920; =FLORENCE PRI CHARD 1921; =EUNICE & NELLIE in WW II.
4162	FUMAROLE	11. 1.19*	Colby. Sold 1947, same name.
4163	FUME	4. 6.19*	Colby. (F) Sold 1920, same name; later =SAIN PIERRE.
4164	GALAXY	29. 4.19*	Colby. (F) Sold 1919, same name.
4125	GALE	6. 6.19*	Hall. (F) Sold 5.19, delivered 6.19 =OCEAN LOVE =OCEAN LOVER in WW II.
3979	GLITTER =RALEIGH 1930	8.10.18	Hall. M/S. Sold 1946 =OCEAN RALEIGH.
4165	GLOSS	8. 8.19*	Colby. (F) Sold 1919, same name; later =MURIELL
3980	GLOW	21.11.18*	Hall. M/S. To MA & F 13.11.19, same name; = WW II.
4166	GREEN SEA	13. 4.20*	Colby. (F) To FBS 21.12.20; =GLADYS & VIOLI 1920; =RIANT in WW II.
4113	GREY SEA	13. 1.19*	Brooke. To MA & F 1.9.20; same name; =ROSEBA 1930; =PYRAMUS in WW II.
4137	GROUNDSWELL	17. 5.19	Ouse SB. (F) To FBS 19.11.20; =ELIE NESS 192 =TRUSTY STAR in WW II.
4167	GULF STREAM	10. 9.19*	Colby. (F) To MA & F 24.8.20; =JENNY IRVIN 192 =JENNY IRVIN in WW II.
3981	GUST	6.12.18*	Hall. M/S. To MA & F 12.10.20; same name; =BUR HAVEN 1922; =BURNHAVEN in WW II.
3908	HALO	4. 5.18*	Hall. 1–6 pdr M/S. Sold 1946, same name.
3906	HARMATTAN	17. 4.18*	Hall. 1–6 pdr M/S. Sold 1946, same name; =WE SPRING 1948.
4168	HIGH TIDE	28.10.19*	Colby. (F) To MA & F 28.11.19; same nam =French AD.75 HIGH TIDE, later RN in WW II.
3905	HORIZON	30. 3.18*	Hall. 1–6 pdr. Sold 1945; =HAMNAVOE 1947.
3910	ICEBERG	1. 7.18*	Hall. 1–6 pdr M/S. To MA & F 13.11.19; =MARIGOL 1921; =MARIGOLD II in WW II.
4136	ICEFIELD	5. 4.19	Ouse SB. (F) To FBS 2.9.20; =JESSIE WATSC 1920.
3909	ICEFLOE	28. 6.18*	Hall. 1–6 pdr M/S. To MA & F 15.12.19; same nam =SUNNY BIRD 1923; =SUNNY BIRD in WW II.
3911	ICEPACK	12. 6.18	Hall. 1–6 pdr. Sold 1922 =ACCORD; =ACCORD WW II.
3912	ICICLE	25. 6.18	Hall. 1–6 pdr M/S. To MA & F 8.7.20; =MILDRED RAWSON 1922; =JUNE ROSE in WW II.
3916	INDIAN SUMMER	8. 2.18*	Lewis. 1–6 pdr. Sold 1947, same name.
4169	LANDBREEZE	11. 2.20*	Colby. (F) To FBS 17.4.20; same name.
3921	LANDFALL	15. 6.18	Lewis. 1–6 pdr. For disposal 1946 at Alexandr
4130	LASHER	9. 2.20*	Hall. (F) To FBS 10.2.20; same name; =in WW II.
3917	LEEWARD	20. 2.18*	Lewis. 1–6 pdr. Sold 1947 =BETTY DUTHIE.
4118	LEVANTER	14.12.18*	Hall. M/S. Sold 9.27 after stranding 13.10.26 ne Peterhead.
	LOW TIDE	3.12.19*	Brooke. (F) To MA & F 25.1.20; =SEAWARD 192 =LOYAL FRIEND in WW II.
3919	LULL	9. 4.18*	Lewis. 1–6 pdr. Sold 1921, same name; =EUNELM 1924.
3920	LUNAR BOW	15. 6.18	Lewis. 1–6 pdr M/S. Sold 1945, same name.
4172	MELODY	4. 2.21*	Crichton Thompson. (F) To FBS 4.2.21; =RO: DUNCAN 1921.
3926	MIRAGE	16.12.18*	Lewis. 1–6 pdr. To FBS 6.7.20; =THORNTREE 192
3927	MIST	21.11.18	Lewis. 1–6 pdr M/S. To WD 1943; =JAMES JOH STON 1947.
3922	MOONBEAM	4. 9.18	Lewis. 1–6 pdr M/S. Sold 1922 =SKIMMER.
	MOONSET	10. 2.20*	Brooke. (F) To FBS 20.10.20; =FLORA TAYLC 1920.

Adty No.	Name	Launched	Builder—Armament—Fate
923	MOONSHINE	4. 9.18	Lewis. 1–6 pdr M/S. Sold 1924; same name.
173	MORN	17. 3.21*	Crichton Thompson. (F) To FBS 1921; same name; =HOMEFINDER 1922; =DEFENSOR in WW II.
925	MURK	13.11.18*	Lewis. 1–6 pdr. To MA & F 16.10.20; =GIRLS FRIEND 1922; =TRUST in WW II.
174	NEAPTIDE	21. 8.20*	Ouse SB. (F) To FBS 19.11.20; same name; =SMILING THRU' 1923; Stranded 20.4.24.
934	NEBULA	19.11.18*	Rose Street Foundry. 1–6 pdr. To FBS 20.8.20; =NACRE 1920; =CALLIOPSIS in WW II.
936	NEW MOON	27. 1.20*	Rose Street Foundry. (F) To FBS 27.1.20; =THE MILNES 1920; =UGIEVALE in WW II.
988	NODE	18.10.18*	Colby. Sold 1922 =TIGER'S EYE; =GOLDEN VIEW in WW II.
989	NOONTIDE	11. 6.18	Colby. 1–6 pdr. Sold 11.6.48, same name.
935	NORTHERN LIGHTS	16. 4.19*	Rose Street Foundry. (F) Sold 1919 =SUNNYSIDE GIRL; =SUNNYSIDE GIRL in WW II.
990	OVERFALL	29.10.18*	Colby. M/S. Sold 1921, same name; =in WW II.
937	OZONE	30. 3.20*	Rose Street Foundry. (F) To FBS 3.5.20; =GIRL GEORGIA 1920.
133	PAMPERO	1.11.19*	Hall. (F) Sold 10.19, delivered 11.19 =EDALBA; =ACORN in WW II.
122	PHOSPHOROUS	21. 2.19*	Hall. (F) Sold 1919 =OCEAN SPRITE; =OCEAN SPRITE in WW II.
991	QUICKSAND	6. 3.19*	Colby. To FBS 4.8.20; same name; =EPHRATAH in WW II.
176	RADIATION	18.11.20*	Ouse SB. (F) To FBS 26.11.20; same name; =AGNES GARDNER 1922; =AGNES GARDNER in WW II.
175	RAINBAND	17. 6.19	Ouse SB. (F) To FBS 15.12.20; =CRAIGLEA 1922.
907	SANDSTORM	31. 5.18*	Hall. 1–6 pdr. To FBS 12.7.20; =GLENBRECK 1920; =RIVER EYE 1924.
177	SCINTILLA	25.11.20*	Ouse SB. (F) To FBS 7.12.20; =ASPARAGUS 1921; =MARY SWANSTON in WW II.
952	SEA FOG	18.12.18*	Webster & Bickerton. 1–6 pdr M/S. To MA & F 15.11.19; same name; =SELIMUS 1921; =PRIMORDIAL in WW II.
119	SEABREEZE	22.11.18	Hall. M/S Sold 1946; =SAPPHIRE STONE 1947.
955	SHEEN	11. 5.18	Brooke. 1–6 pdr. Sold 1946 =GOOD TIDINGS.
998	SHOWER	30. 9.18*	Brooke. Sold 1946, same name.
999	SLEET	6.11.18*	Brooke. To MA & F 20.8.20; same name; =EYEDALE 1924; =CONSOLATION in WW II.
918	SNOWDRIFT	3. 4.18*	Lewis. 1–6 pdr. To FBS 12.10.20; =FIFE NESS 1921; =GEORGE G. BAIRD in WW II.
953	SNOWFLAKE	2.12.19*	WEBSTER & BICKERTON. (F) To MA & F 28.8.20; =C. S. D. 1920; =MARY HERD in WW II.
954	SPECTRUM	27. 3.18	Brooke. 1–6 pdr M/S. To MA & F 29.9.20; same name; =in WW II.
184	SPURT	16. 1.20*	Pimblott. (F) To FBS 15.9.20; =CRAIGENTINNY 1920; =CRAIGENTINNY in WW II.
185	STERN WAVE	27. 3.20*	Pimblott. (F) To FBS 25.8.20; =CRAIGLEITH 1920; =SUMMER ROSE in WW II.
924	SUNBURST	11.11.18*	Lewis. 1–6 pdr. Sold 1921 =BOY ANDREW; =BOY ANDREW in WW II.
120	SUNDOWN	22.11.18	Hall. M/S. Wrecked 30.8.39 on Sullom Voe, Shetlands
950	SUNSET	22. 6.18*	Webster & Bickerton. 1–6 pdr. Total loss 1.4.42 by air attack at Malta; BU 7.43.
951	SUNSHINE =BILLOW 1918	26. 9.18*	Webster & Bickerton. 1–6 pdr. Sold 1935; =CRAIGROY 1936; =CRAIGROY in WW II.
123	THUNDERCLAP	2. 6.19*	Hall. (F) Sold 1919 =ZENA & ELLA; =MACE in WW II.
126	TIDAL WAVE	8. 3.19	Hall. (F) To FBS 11.12.19; =SOPHIA S. SUMMERS 1920; =NORMAN WILSON 1923; =NORMAN WILSON in WW II.
124	TYPHOON	22. 5.19*	Hall. (F) Sold 1919 =OCEAN LASSIE; =OCEAN LASSIE in WW II.
190	UNDERTOW	7. 8.19*	Scott, Bowling. (F) To FBS 5.1.20; same name; =SPES MELIOR in WW II.

Adty No.	Name	Launched	Builder—Armament—Fate
4191	WAFT	11. 9.19*	Scott, Bowling. (F) To FBS 9.1.20; =GENIUS 1921 =GENIUS in WW II.
4132	WATERFALL	16. 9.19*	Hall. (F) Sold 1919 =HOMOCEA.
4127	WATERSHED	18.10.19*	Hall. (F) To MA & F 24.10.19; same name; late =SALVIAN; =CONVALLARIA in WW II.
4131	WATERSMEET	16. 9.19*	Hall. (F) Sold 1919, same name; =GEORGE BAKER 1922; =GEORGE BAKER in WW II.
4121	WAVELET	21. 2.19*	Hall. (F) Sold 1919 =OCEAN DAWN.
	WHIRLBLAST	31. 7.20*	Lea SB. (F) To FBS 31.7.20; =STELLA AURORA 1921; =JACKEVE in WW II.
4129	WHIRLPOOL	10.10.19	Hall. Tender. Sold 1947, same name.
4128	WHITE HORSES	29.10 19*	Hall. (F) To FBS 30.4.20; =BENACHIE 1920; =BENACHIE in WW II.
	WHITECLOUD	25. 8.20*	Lea SB. (F) To FBS 9.12.20; same name; =ADMIRAL STARTIN 1922; =FISHER LAD in WW II.
	WILLIWAW	29. 1.20*	Brooke. (F) To MA & F 3.9.20; same name; =MORAY ROSE in WW II.
4135	WINDFALL	10. 5.20*	Hall. (F) To FBS 10.5.20; same name.
4196	WINDRISE	31. 8.20*	Warren. (F) To FBS 26.11.20, same name; =CAS SIOPEA in WW II.
4197	WINDSHIFT	23.10.20*	Warren. (F) To FBS 22.12.20, same name; =QUIE" WATERS 1922.
4134	WINDWARD	4.12.19*	Hall. (F) To FBS 16.12.19, same name; =COULI" HEAD 1921; =SCARLET THREAD in WW II.

* Delivery dates in launch column.

Notes: The two non-standard vessels measured 108 TG and 107 TG respectively and were of slightly larger dimensions that the standards. Steel drifters were disposed of in larg numbers to government departments for resale in the same manner as the wood-hulled vessels A total of 48 steel contracts were cancelled; SKYLINE disappeared from Red Lists about 8.18 while the remainder were reported cancelled by an order dated 17.12.18. In the list of cancelle contracts below some are identified only by builders' numbers and commercial completions ar noted:

Builder	No.	Name	Fate
Abela Mitchell:		FULMINATION	
		HERTZIAN RAY	
		INUNDATION	
		LONGSWELL	
Ailsa:		DROUGHT	
		DOUBLETIDE	
		EXPANSE	
		EQUINOX	
		Nos. 363–366	
Brooke:		OCEAN SWELL	=OCEAN SWELL 1920; =in WW II.
		OUTLINE	=OUTLINE 1920; =NORBREEZE in WW II
		PUFF	=PUFF 1920; =GOWANHILL in WW II.
Brown's DD, Hull:	4147	CLOUDBURST	
Chambers:	4151	EBBTIDE	
	4152	EVENTIDE	
	4153	FALLING SEA	
Duthie:		WINDWHISTLE	
		BURN	
		STREAM	
		SHEMAL	
		GREGALI	
		BRASH	
		CLOUDARCH	
		BREAKING SEA	
		Nos. 461–462	
Fellows:	3887	SKYLINE	=PLIOSAURUS 1923.
Ouse SB:	4178	SCOTCH MIST	
	4179	SEA MIST	
	4180	SMOKE CLOUD	
	4181	SNOWSTORM	
	4182	SPARK	
	4183	SPACE	
T. H. Scarr, Howden:	4188	TIDESET	
	4189	TRADEWIND	

Scott, Bowling:	4192	WATERWAY	
	4193	WAVECREST	
	4194	WHISK	
	4195	WHITE FROST	
Thomas, Amlwch:	4193	BLUSH	
	4199	BLUSTER	
Webster & Bickerton:	4114	CLOUDBANK	=ARABIS 1922.
	4115	CROSSTIDE	
	4116	DARK NIGHT	
	4117	DOWNPOUR	

HIRED DRIFTERS

Adty. No.	Port No.	Name	TG/Yr	Armament, Fate, etc.	Service
	PD.492	A. M. LEASK	79/03	BDV	9.15–1919
1307	FR.274	ABERDOUR	93/08	1–3 pdr PB =in WW II.	9.15–1919
M 1299	LT.1125	ACCEPTABLE	82/11	1–6 pdr PB, M/S	12.14–1919
3237	LT.1184	ACCUMULATOR	85/12	1–6 pdrAA Net =in WW II.	12.15–1920
212	LT.87	ACHIEVABLE	89/13	1–3 pdr PB, M/S, Escort	9.14–1919
	FR.582	ACQUISITION	83/13	1–3 pdr Stores and Water carrier =in WW II.	12.14–1919
1086	LT.520	ACTIVE II	65/06	1–6 pdrAA Net	2.15–1919
2486	BF.771	ACTIVE =ACTIVE III 5.15	81/07	1–3 pdr Net Mined 15.10.17 off Milford Haven.	4.15–10.17
1499	YH.473	ADELE	99/15	1–6 pdrAA Net	3.15–1919
1498		=KINGFISHER 6.18		=ADELE in WW II.	
2234	BCK.203	ADMIRABLE	90/14	1–3 pdrAA Net Sunk 15.5.17 by Austrian cruisers off Fano Island, Adriatic Sea.	2.15–5.17
	INS.99	ADMIRATION	77/14	BDV Water carrier	7.15–1919
2051	INS.518	ADMIRE	93/08	1–6 pdr Exam =in WW II.	1.16–1919
	BF.425	ADORATION	93/12	BDV =in WW II.	6.15–1919
2763	BK.328	AGNES & JANET	91/14	1–6 pdrAA Net, HS	4.15–1919
1802	INS.325	AIVERN	72/10	Net Foundered 8.2.17 in the English Channel.	4.15–2.17
1069	LT.340	AJAX =AJAX II 2.15	81/09	Net Sunk 27.10.16 by German destroyers in the Dover Straits.	1.15–10.16
744	WY.169	ALABURN	85/12	1–6 pdrAA Net	1.15–1919
	FR.478	ALBATROSS	76/03	BDV Lost 15.2.19, accidental.	7.15–2.19
2428	FR.226	ALBATROSS =ALBATROSS IV 8.15	86/07	1–3 pdr Net	5.15–1919
2418	PD.131	ALERT II	83/07	1–6 pdr Net	6.15–1919
2199	PD.506	ALERT =ALERT III 7.15	96/07	Net	4.15–1920
943	FR.586	ALEX WATT	86/13	1–6 pdr M/S =in WW II.	1.15–1919
1036	LT.1053	ALFRED	96/07	1–6 pdr Net, M/S	1.15–1920
73	KY.210	ALICES	84/07	1–6 pdr Hydro T/S	5.15–1919
1818	LT.751	ALL'S WELL	87/10	M/S	8.15–1919
2177	INS.559	ALPHA =ALPHA II 8.15	92/03	1–3 pdr Net, M/S	5.15–1919
215	LT.519	AMBITIOUS =AMBITIOUS II 8.19	90/10	1–3 pdr PB, M/S	9.14–1921
755	YH.554	AMIABLE	72/10	1–6 pdrAA Net =in WW II.	1.15–1919
2551	BF.929	AMITY	82/07	1–6 pdrAA Net	2.15–1919
2376	FR.214	ANCHOR OF HOPE	95/07	1–3 pdr Net, M/S	2.15–1919
2295	PD.484	ANCHOR OF HOPE =ANCHOR OF HOPE II 5.15	79/03	1–3 pdr Net	2.15–1920
2718	LT.127	ANCHOR STAR	82/08	Net	12.15–1920
2132	KY.134	ANDRINA	92/11	1–3 pdr Net =ROSSARD in WW II.	4.15–1920
1850	LT.69	ANGELINA	86/08	1–3 pdrAA Net	9.15–1919
3076	YH.622	ANIMATE	88/17	1–6 pdr =in WW II.	12.17–1919
2118	FR.420	ANNIE	94/07	1–3 pdr Net Destroyed 19.12 17 after grounding off Enos.	1.15–12.17

Adty No.	Port No.	Name	TG/Yr	Armament, Fate, etc.	Service
2377	FR.536	ANNIE CUMINE	80/13	1–6 pdrAA Net =MARY J. MASSON in WW II.	2.15–1919
2413	INS.422	ANNIE SMITH	84/07	1–3 pdr Net Sunk 9.4.18 in collision off Lundy Island.	4.15–4.18
2510	BCK.124	ANT	61/03	Net, Stores & Water carrier	6.15–1920
B 1290	LT.741	ARCADY	85/10	1–6 pdr PB, M/S =in WW II.	12.14–1919
	YH.720	ARCHIMEDES	83/11	Misc. Service =in WW II.	10.15–1919
2036	FR.44	ARDLAW	94/09	Net, HS	8.15–1919
1122	LT.1084	ARIMATHEA	87/07	1–6 pdr Net	4.15–1919
564	INS.500	ARNDILLY CASTLE	78/08	1–6 pdrAA Net	1.15–1919
1025	YH.402	ARTHUR H. JOHNSON	99/13	1–6 pdr Net	1.15–1919
1312	PD.510	ASPIRANT	81/09	1–3 pdr Net	6.15–1919
2478	BF.941.	ASPIRE	87/07	1–6 pdrAA Net	2.15–1919
2452	BF.57	ASTRUM SPEI	82/14	Net Sunk 9.7.16 by Austrian cruiser off Brindisi.	2.15–7.16
	BCK.165	ATALANTA	60/03	BDV tender	5.15–1919
763	LT.364	AU FAIT	83/09	Net Sunk 25.4.16 by German destroyer off Zeebrugge.	1.15–4.16
2407	LT.550	AU RETOUR	73/06	1–6 pdr Net	4.15–1919
2380	FR.74	AUCHMEDDEN	82/14	1–3 pdr Net, M/S	2.15–1919
1097	LT.496	AULD LANG SYNE	75/06	1–3 pdr Net	2.15–1919
	BF.387	AURORA II	74/06	BDV =in WW II.	2.15–1920
2114	BF.311	AVONDALE	80/11	1–57 mm Net Sunk 15.5.17 by Austrian cruisers off Fano Island, Adriatic Sea.	1.15–5.17
565	KY.169	AZARAEL	94/07	1–6 pdr, 1–2 pdr Net	2.15–1919
2053	BCK.214	B. SUTHERLAND	96/15	Fleet duties =LORD CAVAN in WW II.	1.16–1919
1553	LT.1153	B. T. B.	89/11	1–12 pdrAA, 1–6 pdr Net =in WW II.	8.15–1919
1448	LT.152	BADEN POWELL	72/00	Net, HS	4.15–1920
2509	BCK.43	BARBARA COWIE	82/09	1–6 pdr Net	4.15–1919
3112	BF.365	BARLEY STALK	91/17	1–6 pdr M/S	7.17–1919
1135	LT.318	BARNARDO	77/09	1–6 pdr Net	3.15–1919
2259	BCK.32	BARTONIA	82/08	1–6 pdr Net	3.15–1919
	LT.770	BEACON STAR	99/11	1–3 pdr BDV workshop	9.15–1920
1425	LT.389	BEATRICE =BEATRICE II 5.15 =BEATRICE III 6.15	62/05	1–3 pdr AA Net	4.15–1919
1393	INS.319	BEGONIA =BEGONIA II 10.15	91/07	1–6 pdrAA Net	3.15–1919
2370	INS.256	BELLE O'MORAY	83/11	1–3 pdr Net, M/S =WW II.	1.15–1919
2002	INS.403	BELLONA II	82/07	1–6 pdr Net	1.15–1920
1939	YH.515	BELOS	68/00	ABS, Misc. Service	10.15–3.18
1902	LT.714	BEN & LUCY	83/10	1–6 pdr Net, M/S =in WW II.	9.15–1919
2135	INS.158	BEN BUI	73/10	1–3 pdr, 1–57 mm Net	5.15–1920
2134	FR.195	BENEFICENT	80/07	Net Sunk 1.6.16 by gunfire near Saruichey LV, Adriatic Sea.	5.15–6.16
2481 2574	BF.1114	BERRIE BRAES	82/08	1–3 pdr Net, M/S	3.15–1919
	BCK.46	BERYL II	88/09	BDV =in WW II.	9.15–1919
2165	INS.353	BERYL =BERYL III 11.15	81/07	1–3 pdrAA Net	5.15–1919
	WK.605	BESSIE =CROSSBOW 8.18	79/03	Misc. Service	7.15–1920
2494	PD.472	BETSY	86/03	1–6 pdr Net	3.15–1919
2408	BF.390	BETSY SLATER	84/11	1–6 pdr Net, M/S =In WW II.	5.15–1919

Adty No.	Port No.	Name	TG/Yr	Armament, Fate, etc.	Service
3243	LT.631	BIEN VENU	77/10	1–6 pdr AA Net	1.16–1919
1493	YH.828	BLACKTHORN	79/04	1–6 pdr AA Net	5.15–1919
2554	BCK.16	BLITHESOME	81/08	1–3 pdr Net	2.15–1919
2042	BCK.151	BLOEMFONTEIN	82/03	1–3 pdr Net	8.15–1919
2167	BF.933	BLOOM	87/07	1–6 pdr AA Net	5.15–1919
	BF.218	BLOOMFIELD =BUDLEIA 8.18	83/06	Misc. Service	12.15–1920
2572	BF.922	BLOSSOM	86/07	1–3 pdr Net	4.15–1919
2719	D.223	BLOSSOM II	58/00	1–6 pdr AA Net, HS	10.15–1919
777	PD.363	BLUEBELL II	94/07	1–.45 in MG M/S	1.15–1919
1840	LT.1044	BLUEBELL IV	88/07	1–6 pdr Net	8.15–1919
1507	YH.664	BOADICEA II =BOADICEA III 6.15	59/02	Net	6.15–7.15
1938	LT.2	BOB READ	95/13	1–6 pdr AA PB	11.15–1919
	INS.609	BON AMI	76/08	BDV Water carrier	3.15–1919
1251	LT.641	BON AVENIR	67/10	Net	5.15–1919
	BCK.17	BON CHIEF	83/08	Misc. Service	1.16–1919
1156 566	LT.109	BON ESPOIR	86/08	1–57 mm Net	3.15–1919
1445	YH.331	BONO	70/08	1–57 mm Net	6.15–1919
2755	BK.72	BORDER KING	92/14	1–6 pdr Net, M/S =in WW II.	4.15–1919
2759	BK.5	BORDER LADS	86/14	1–6 pdr Net Sunk 25.3.18 off the Tyne, probably torpedoed.	4.15–3.18
1424	LT.164	BOUNTEOUS SEA	56/00	1–3 pdr AA Net =in WW II.	3.15–1919
1554 2218	LT.1151	BOUNTIFUL	91/11	1–6 pdr AA Net	7.15–1919
1110 2375	LT.331	BOY ALAN	109/14	1–6 pdr Net =in WW II.	2.15–1919
2014	FR.286	BOY ALEX	75/08	1–6 pdr Net, M/S =in WW II.	3.15–1919
	WK.10	BOY ARCHIE	58/01	Minefield tender	1.16–1919
3214	PD.1	BOY ARTHUR	90/07	1–3 pdr AA Net, M/S	8.15–1919
1079	LT.212	BOY BEN	84/06	Net, Exam	1.15–1919
1472	YH.850	BOY BILLY	70/04	1–6 pdr Net	5.15–1920
3288	YH.667	BOY BOB =ELSIE & NELLIE in WW II.	101/16	1–6 pdr Net, M/S	7.16–1919
1883	YH.368	BOY CHARLES	86/13	1–6 pdr AA Net	9.15–1919
211	LT.1067	BOY CHARLEY	83/07	1–3 pdr PB, M/S	9.14–1919
1040	LT.29	BOY CHY	78/08	1–6 pdr Net, Hydro	1.15–1919
2128	SM.325	BOY DANIEL	83/12	1–3 pdr Net	4.15–1919
1147	YH.157	BOY EDDIE	59/09	1–57 mm Net	3.15–1919
3242	LT.413	BOY EDWARD	80/09	1–6 pdr AA Net	1.16–1920
1967	SN.34	BOY ERNEST	56/02	1–3 pdr Net	12.15–1919
1464	YH.517	BOY FRED	58/00	Net	4.15–4.15
2290	BCK.55	BOY GEORGE	84/06	1–3 pdr AA Net	3.15–1919
1801	PD.146	BOY GEORGE =BOY GEORGE II 6.15	70/03	1–6 pdr AA Net	4.15–1919
1927	LT.441	BOY GEORGE III	83/06	1–6 pdr Net	10.15–1920
2708	LT.1127	BOY HAROLD	74/11	Net Mined 3.3.16 off Brindisi.	10.15–3.16
1248	LT.963	BOY HECTOR	81/03	1–6 pdr AA Net	5.15–1919
2761	BK.326	BOY JACOB	62/06	Net	4.15–1919
1003	FR.550	BOY JOE	85/13	Stores and Water carrier, 1–6 pdr M/S	12.14–1919
209	LT.1167	BOY ROY	95/11	1–6 pdr AA PB =in WW II.	9.14–1919
210	LT.17	BOY SCOUT	80/13	1–6 pdr PB =in WW II.	9.14–1919
2502	FR.486	BOY WILLIE	81/07	1–6 pdr Net	3.15–1919
2746	PD.87	BOY WILLIE =WILLIAM II 7.17 =RAMESES 12.17	66/04	Net	6.16–1919
2011	BF.231	BOYNDIE BURN	73/10	1–6 pdr Net	1.15–1919
3210	YH.827	BRACKEN	66/03	1–3 pdr AA Net	8.15–1919

Adty No.	Port No.	Name	TG/Yr	Armament, Fate, etc.	Service
3297	LT.695	BRACKENDALE	88/16	1–6 pdr Net =in WW II.	5.16–1919
2117	FR.491	BRACODEN	81/12	1–6 pdr Net, Exam	1.15–1919
2043	INS.36	BRAE LOSSIE	77/01	(ex-Se/enteen)Net	8.15–1920
	INS.61	BRAEHEAD	85/14	BDV	7.15–1920
	BCK.69	BRAES O'BUCKIE	84/10	BDV =in WW II.	7.15–1920
	BCK.207	BRAES O'ENZIE	87/15	BDV repair tender	7.15–1920
2187	BCK.137	BRAMBLE =BRAMBLE II 8.15	91/08	1–6 pdr Net	6.15–1919
606	PD.516	BRANCH	93/08	1–3 pdr Net, M/S =in WW II	9.14–1919
2010	INS.207	BRANDENBURGH	79/11	1–3 pdr Net	1.15–1919
2192	KY.253	BREADWINNER	88/07	1–6 pdr Net =in WW II.	4.15–1919
2359	BF.9	BREADWINNER =BREADWINNER II 8.15	93/07	1–6 pdr Net	1.15–1919
762	LT.101	BRESSAY	81/08	1–3 pdrAA Net	1.15–1919
2808	BF.59	BRIGHTER HOPE	53/09	1–3 pdr Net	4.15–1920
2133	INS.194	BRIGHTON =BRIGHTON II 8.15	75/06	1–6 pdr Net	5.15–1919
	INS.382	BRIGHTON O'TH'NORTH	98/14	Misc Service	9.18–1920
2055	PD.357	BRITANNIA II	94/07	Transport	1.15–1919
2184	INS.47	BRITANNIA IV	63/02	1–3 pdr Net	6.15–1920
2115	BF.545	BRITISH CROWN	85/13	1–3 pdr Net =in WW II.	1.15–1919
1437	LT.889	BRITISH MONARCH	57/02	Net, Exam	4.15–1919
2717	LT.1017	BRITON	79/06	1–6 pdrAA Net	10.15–1920
1070	YH.718	BROADLAND	76/13	1–6 pdrAA Net =in WW II.	1.15–1919
2120	FR.308	BROCH	90/08	1–3 pdrAA Net	3.15–1919
2291	INS.254	BROCH HEAD	85/11	1–57 mm Net	3.15–1920
1124	LT.216	BROTHERS	65/03	Net, Exam	3.15–1919
2739 2857	FR.241	BROTHERS GEM	96/07	1–6 pdr Net, M/S	5.15–1919
	BF.753	BRUCES	92/07	BDV	7.15–1919
2498	FR.254	BUCHAN	81/08	1–3 pdr Net =in WW II.	3.15–1919
F 1294	LT.756	BUCKLER	81/11	1–6 pdrAA PB, M/S =in WW II.	12.14–1919
	BF.39	BUDDING ROSE	88/14	BDV	7.15–1919
1953	YH.972	BULRUSH	90/07	1–6 pdr PB	3.15–1919
2166	BF.1465	BURD	83/04	1–3 pdr Net	5.15–1919
2487	BCK.205	BUSY BEE	84/07	1–6 pdr Net	3.15–1919
	PD.479	BUSY BEE	92/03	BDV	12.15–1919
162	PD.352	BYDAND	90/17	1–6 pdr M/S	10.17–1919
1889	YH.637	C. & E. W.	81/11	1–6 pdr Net	9.15–1920
	FR.224	CAIRNBULG	104/07	Misc Service	1.16–1919
1414	YH.42	CAISTER CASTLE	109/14	1–3 pdr Net	3.15–1919
562	KY.267	CALCEOLARIA	92/08	1–3 pdrAA Net Mined 27.10.18 off Elbow Light Buoy, Downs.	2.15–10.18
2710	INS.174	CALEDONIA =CALEDONIA II 9.17	87/06	1–6 pdr Net	9.15–1919
2728	LY.852	CALISTOGA	72/10	1–57 mm Net	10.15–1919
2854	KY.143	CAMELLIA =CAMELLIA II 10.15	85/07	1–3 pdrAA Net	5.15–1919
2568	BCK.98	CAMPANIA =CAMPANIA II 8.15	90/07	1–3 pdr Net Disappeared 5.3.17 in gale off St. Abb's Head.	4.15–3.17
N 1300	LT.102	CAMPANULA =CAMPANULA II 12.15	95/13	1–6 pdrAA PB, M/S	12.14–1919
2136	KY.150	CAMPERDOW N	97/07	1–3 pdr Net	4.15–1919
2497	FR.525	CAPE COLONY	82/08	1–6 pdrAA Net Mined 8.1.17 off Harwich.	3.15–1.17
2723	DE.31	CAPELLA	111/92	1–6 pdr Net	10.15–1920
1013	LT.76	CAPETOWN =CAPO 9.18	83/08	1–3 pdr Net, M/S	1.15–1919

Adty No.	Port No.	Name	TG/Yr	Armament, Fate, etc.	Service
3073	YH.277	CAPTAIN FRYATT	87/17	1-6 pdrAA Net	12.17-1919
2122	KY.300	CARMI III	88/08	1-3 pdr Net =J. T. HENDRY in WW II.	2.15-1919
2725	INS.120	CAROL & DOROTHY	89/05	1-6 pdr Net, M/S	10.15-1920
2061	LY.921	CARRIGART	84/12	1-6 pdr Net, Misc Service	8.15-1919
	INS.610	CAWDOR CASTLE	84/08	(ex-Cawdor Castle II) BDV	7.15-1920
	BF.253	CEDAR LEAF	76/11	Misc Service	1.16-1919
	BF.991	CEDRON	84/07	Tender, Exam	1.16-1919
1387	BF.316	CELANDINE =CELANDINE II 12.15	73/06	1-3 pdr Net	5.15-1919
2169	BF.1056	CELOSIA	87/08	1-3 pdr Net	11.14-1920
2748	ME.38	CELURCA	94/16	Hydro Experiments =INVERCAIRN in WW II.	6.16-1919
	LT.49	CENWULF =GREYWOLF 4.18	93/12	BDV	8.15-5.18
1388	INS.155	CHAMPION II	71/06	1-3 pdr Net	8.15-1919
	WK.270	CHANCE	92/08	Fleet duries Sunk 26.1.16 in collision in the Orkneys.	12.15-1.16
	INS.40	CHARITY	102/01	Net Disappeared 24.10.15 between Great Yarmouth and Poole.	10.15-10.15
3103	PD.474	CHARITY	65/03	1-3 pdr Net	11.16-1919
2253	INS.470	CHARLES HAY	75/09	1-3 pdrAA Net, M/S	3.15-1919
1463	YH.737	CHATTERENO	58/02	(ex-Girl Kathleen) Net, Misc	6.15-1920
3058	YH.257	CHEERIO LADS	103/17	1-6 pdr M/S	8.17-1919
	YH.6	CHESTNUT	107/14	Misc Service =MAIDA in WW II.	11.18-1920
2088	LT.358	CHILDREN'S HOPE	83/09	BDV, M/S	9.15-1920
2436	FR.200	CHILDREN'S TRUST	95/07	1-6 pdrAA Net	5.15-1919
3082	YH.571	CHOICE LASS	75/17	1-6 pdr Control vessel =LORD HOWE in WW II.	2.18-1919
740	SN.118	CHRIS	81/10	1-6 pdrAA Net =in WW II.	2.15-1919
2438	FR.26	CHRISOBEL	84/04	1-3 pdr Net, M/S	5.15-1919
2752	BK.271	CHRISTINA CRAIG	86/12	1-3 pdr Net Sunk 15.2.18 by German destroyers in the Dover Straits.	4.15-2.18
2265	ML.123	CHRISTINA MAYES	82/08	Net, BDV	2.15-1919
2213	BF.850	CHRYSANTHEMUM =CHRYSANTHEMUM II 10.17	82/07	1-6 pdrAA, 1-2 pdr Net	4.15-1919
	BF.32	CINCERIA	75/11	BDV	7.15-1919
2028	SN.294	CISSY	60/01	Water carrier	7.15-1919
2395	FR.439	CITRON	78/11	1-3 pdrAA Net =in WW II.	3.15-1919
1329	YH.208	CITY OF BELFAST =CITY OF BELFAST II 11.15	88/07	1-3 pdrAA Net	11.14-1919
U 1306	YH.311	CITY OF EDINBURGH	88/07	1-6 pdr PB, M/S	11.14-1919
P 1302	YH.204	CITY OF GLASGOW	88/07	1-3 pdr PB, Eacort	12.14-1919
1330	YH.185	CITY OF HULL	88/07	1-3 pdrAA Net	4.15-1919
0 1301	YH.244	CITY OF LIVERPOOL	88/07	1-6 pdr PB Mined 31.7.18 off S. Foreland.	11.14-7.18
1331	YH.301	CITY OF LONDON	88/07	1-3 pdrAA Net	4.15-1919
1332	YH.203	CITY OF PERTH =EMBLEM 7.19	88/07	1-3 pdrAA Net	4.15-1920
2215	BCK.152	CLACH-NA-CUDIN	78/08	1-57 mm Net	4.15-1920
918	BF.191	CLANS	89/15	1-6 pdr PB =in WW II.	6.15-1919
1821	LT.456	CLARA & ALICE	79/09	1-57 mm Net Foundered 26.5.18 off Palermo.	8.15-5.18
3069	HL.88	CLARA SUTTON	102/17	1-6 pdr AA =in WW II.	8.17-1919
3107	BF.284	CLARA WOOD	88/16	1-6 pdr M/S =GILT EDGE in WW II.	2.17-1919
2456	FR.271	CLARION	100/08	1-6 pdrAA Net	2.15-1919

Adty No.	Port No.	Name	TG/Yr	Armament, Fate, etc.	Service
2278	BCK.93	CLAVIS	87/11	Net Sunk 9.7.16 by Austrian cruiser off Brindisi.	1.15–7.16
4329	BF.323	CLOVER =NAIRN 1.19 =CLOVER 6.19	83/11	1–3 pdr Stores and Water carrier. Purchased 1916, sold 1921.	1.15–1921
750	A.379	CLOVER BANK	78/12	1–6 pdr Net Mined 24.4.16 in British minefield off Zeebrugge.	1.15–4.16
561	A.731	CLOVER BANK	92/17	1–6 pdrAA Net Sunk 15.2.18 by German destroyers in the Dover Straits.	5.17–2.18
2476	BF.71	CLUNY	83/08	1–6 pdr Net	2.15–1920
2400	INS.9	CLUNY HILL	86/09	1–6 pdrAA Net	2.15–1920
2447	INS.310	CLUPEA	83/07	1–3 pdr Net, Fleet tender	5.15–1920
2013	BF.866	CLYDE =CLYDE II 5.15	97/07	1–3 pdr Net	3.15–1920
2745	LT.678	COLEUS	102/16	1–3 pdr Net Mined 4.10.18 off Dover.	5.16–10.18
1067	LT.71	COLONIAL	84/08	1–6 pdr Net =EASTERN DAWN in WW II.	1.15–1919
2387	PD.539	COMELY	95/07	1–3 pdr Net	3.15–1919
2279	A.31	COMELY BANK	87/14	1–6 pdr Net =in WW II.	2.15–1919
2138	LY.44	COMET STAR	60/06	1–6 pdrAA Net	5.15–1919
	INS.544	COMMODORE	88/03	BDV	7.15–1920
3247	LT.990	COMRADES	63/03	Net Mined 18.10.17 off Cape Antifer.	1.16–10.17
1784	BCK.45	CON-AMORE	88/09	1–6 pdr Net	3.15–1919
439	PD.507	CONCORD =CONNARD 10.17	65/03	1–6 pdr Net, HS	12.16–1919
2020	BF.162	CONCORD II	81/06	1–3 pdr Net	7.15–1919
	BF.615	CONCORDIA	91/13	Misc Service =in WW II.	1.16–1920
	BF.528	CONDOR =RAWLINSON 8.18	84/07	Tender, Exam	2.16–1919
1087	LT.338	CONDOR =CONDOR II 4.15	63/05	1–6 pdrAA Net	2.15–1919
761	LT.658	CONFIER	69/10	1–6 pdr Net	1.15–1919
	BF.93	CONIE	85/07	BDV Water carrier	6.15–1919
2907	BCK.197	CONNAGE	77/01	(ex-Nine) 1–6 pdr Net, M/S	5.15–1919
2766	LT.596	CONSOLATION	70/06	1–6 pdrAA Net	6.15–1919
2039	BF.373	CONSTANCY	63/03	(ex-Commerce) 1–3 pdr Net, M/S	8.15–1919
1834	LT.1172	CONSTANT FRIEND	92/12	1–6 pdr Net, Hydro =in WW II.	8.15–1919
1564	LT.32	CONSTANT HOPE	86/13	1–6 pdrAA Net =in WW II.	7.15–1919
	LT.1158	CONSTANT STAR	98/11	BDV =in WW II.	8.15–1919
1819	LT.1123	CONTRIVE	95/11	1–6 pdr Net, Hydro =in WW II.	8.15–1919
2394	BF.169	CONVALLARIA	77/10	1–3 pdr Net	1.15–1919
752	A.48	CORAL BANK	85/14	1–6 pdrAA Net =in WW II.	1.15–1919
2112	FR.566	CORAL HAVEN	82/13	1–57 mm Net Sink 15.5.17 by Austrian cruisers off Fano Island, Adriatic.	1.15–5.17
1809	INS.230	CORAL HILL	56/11	1–3 pdrAA Net	4.15–1919
2363	KY.116	COREOPSIS =COREOPSIS II 11.17	88/11	1–6 pdr Net =OLIVINE in WW II.	1.15–1919
2108	BF.765	CORMORANT =CORMORANT III 4.15	94/07	1–3 pdr Net	1.15–1920
	BCK.83	CORN RIG	97/11	BDV =in WW II.	7.15–1920
3106	BF.309	CORNSTALK	73/16	1–3 pdr Net, M/S	12.16–1919
	BF.208	CORONA	76/06	Misc Service	2.15–1919

Adty No.	Port No.	Name	TG/Yr	Armament, Fate, etc.	Service
2023	BF.397	CORONARIA	81/11	1–3 pdr Net, Tender	7.15–1919
2809	BF.465	CORONATA	83/12	1–6 pdrAA Net, M/S	4.15–1919
	BF.66	CORONATION	58/02	BDV, Aircraft tender	7.15–1920
	PD.125	CORONET	79/03	BDV	8.15–7.16
	INS.558	CORYPHAENA	92/03	Hospital carrier	1.16–1920
1435	LT.477	COSMOS	91/14	1–3 pdrAA Net Sunk 15.2.18 by German destroyers in the Dover Straits.	4.15–2.18
1385	BCK.144	COULARD BANK	88/10	1–6 pdr Net	4.15–1919
2445	INS.551	COULARD HILL	86/08	1–6 pdrAA Net, M/S	5.15–1920
	INS.355	COUNTY OF INVERNESS	84/13	BDV	7.15–1919
2446	INS.461	COUNTY OF NAIRN	81/07	1–6 pdrAA Net	5.15–1919
2105	BF.449	COURAGE	88/12	1–6 pdrAA Net	1.15–1919
767	LT.21	COURONNE	83/08	PB, Hydro tender	1.15–1919
1029	YH.851	COVENT GARDEN	84/12	1–6 pdrAA Net	1.15–1919
	INS.21	COVESEA	94/09	Misc Service =in WW II.	1.16–1919
	BF.45	CRAIG-ALVAH	80/09	Stores and Water carrier =in WW II.	12.14–1920
2496	BCK.50	CRAIG-BO	94/09	1–6 pdrAA Net =WW II.	3.15–1920
2137	FR.95	CRAIGHAUGH	89/14	1–6 pdr Net, M/S	5.15–1919
	INS.549	CRAIGHEAD	93/08	BDV	7.15–1920
2417	BCK.47	CRAIGMIN	74/09	1–3 pdr Net	4.15–1919
2493	INS.57	CRAIGMOUNT	80/14	1–6 pdr Net	3.15–1919
2270	BF.93	CRAIGNEEN	90/14	1–6 pdrAA Net	4.15–1920
2271	KY.279	CRAIGNOON	77/08	1–57 mm Net Sunk 15.5.17 by Austrian cruisers off Fano Island, Adriatic.	2.15–5.17
1855	LT.147	CRESCENT	63/02	1–3 pdrAA Net	9.15–1919
2459	KY.73	CROMORNA	85/10	1–6 pdr Net, M/S =LEMNOS in WW II.	2.15–1919
2056	INS.229	CUDWEED	68/11	1–3 pdr Transport	4.15–1919
2810	BF.122	CULLYKHAN	75/10	1–6 pdr Net, M/S	4.15–1919
1848	LT.1136	CYCLAMEN =CYCLAMEN II 12.15	94/11	1–3 pdrAA Net	9.15–1919
1923	LT.469	D. H. S.	100/15	1–3 pdrAA Net =DEWY ROSE in WW II.	10.15–1919
	BF.1463	DAFFODIL	74/04	BDV	7.15–1919
2397	PD.362	DAFFODIL =DAFFODIL II 10.15	94/07	1–3 pdr Net, M/S =CLARICE in WW II.	4.15–1919
1849	LT.269	DAILY BREAD	56/01	1–6 pdr Net	9.15–1920
2297	INS.124	DAIRLIE	79/10	1–3 pdr Net, M/S	3.15–1919
2391	FR.270	DAISY =DAISY II 2.15	100/08	1–3 pdr Net, M/S =in WW II.	11.14–1919
2057	PD.334	DAISY III	54/00	PB, Water carrier	2.15–1920
2463	BF.1016	DAISY =DAISY IV 4.15	92/07	1–6 pdr Net	3.15–1919
2130	KY.105	DAISY =DAISY V 5.15	77/04	1–6 pdr Net	4.15–1919
2905	BF.306	DAISY VI	85/06	1–6 pdr Net, M/S	5.15–1919
2569	BF.393	DAISY BANK	84/11	1–3 pdr Net =in WW II.	3.15–1919
	INS.212	DAISY ROCK	76/11	BDV repair vessel	7.15–1920
915	BF.332	DAISY WOOD	72/11	1–3 pdr Net, M/S	5.15–1919
3105	PD.260	DAN O'CONNELL	52/11	Net	2.17–1919
	BCK.99	DARDA	99/11	BDV =in WW II.	7.15–1919
1083	YH.713	DASHING SPRAY	69/11	1–3 pdr Net, Pilot service	2.15–1919
1001	LT.503	DATUM	90/10	Net Sunk 27.10.16 by destroyers in the Dover Straits.	1.15–10.16
3157	PD.20	DAVID B. SUMMERS	61/11	1–6 pdr Net	5.15–1919
	BCK.112	DAVID FLETT	84/12	Misc Service =in WW II.	1.16–1919

Adty No.	Port No.	Name	TG/Yr	Armament, Fate, etc.	Service
2561	BF.151	DELIVERER	79/10	1–6 pdrAA Net Disappeared 3.11.17 outside Dublin Bay, presumed sunk by S/M.	2.15–11.17
	BCK.191	DENFORD	77/01	(ex-*Fourteen*) BDV Collier	7.15–1920
	FR.496	DENNYDUFF	80/12	Stores and Water carrier, HS	1.15–1919
1398	BCK.27	DESIRE	83/08	1–6 pdr Net =ROSA in WW II.	4.15–1919
2106	BF.82	DEVERONSIDE	89/14	1–3 pdr Net, M/S	1.15–1919
1066	LT.526	DEVON COUNTY	86/10	(ex-*Scadaun*) 1–6 pdr Net =in WW II.	1.15–1919
	INS.127	DEVOTION	88/10	Tender =in WW II.	1.16–1919
K 1297	LT.59	DEWEY	84/08	1–6 pdr PB Sunk 12.8.17 in collision off the ROYAL SOVEREIGN LV.	11.14–8.17
3213	BF.1117	DEXTERITY	87/08	1–6 pdrAA Net	8.15–1919
1905	YH.377	DIADEM II	75/04	1–6 pdr Net	10.15–1919
213	LT.61	DICK WHITTINGTON	80/13	1–6 pdr PB =in WW II.	9.14–1919
2806	KY.164	DILIGENCE =DILIGENCE II 9.15.	85/05	1–6 pdr Net	4.15–1919
	BF.1138	DILIGENT =DIGIT 6.18	80/02	(ex-*Thirty Seven*) Tender =in WW II.	1.16–1920
598	PD.50	DIRECT ME	71/12	1–6 pdrAA	12.14–1919
2968	SH.242	DIXON	104/16	1–6 pdr Net	9.16–1919
2372	INS.214	DO WELL	71/11	1–6 pdr Net =ELOQUENT in WW II.	1.15–1919
	BCK.70	DOCILE III	82/10	Misc Service	1.16–1920
1896	LT.746	DOLLAR PRINCESS	74/11	1–6 pdrAA Net	9.15–1919
1078	LT.890	DORIS II	79/02	Net, Exam	3.15–1919
2715	YH.702	DORIS MAUD	79/14	1–57 mm Net	10.15–1920
1959	YH.	DOROTHY F. =KINGFISHER 2.19	107/15	1–6 pdrAA Net	1.16–1919
1822	LT.692	DOROTHY ROSE	74/10	1–6 pdr Net, Hydro	8.15–1919
2480	BF.871	DOVE	81/07	1–3 pdr Net	3.15–1919
2573		=DOVE III 4.15			
1921	LT.1068	DRAKE III	89/07	1–6 pdrAA Net, M/S	10.15–1919
2251	KY.71	DREEL CASTLE	97/08	(ex-*Terfrid*) 1–6 pdrAA Net	1.15–1919
2553		=MARA SMITH 2.18		=DREEL CASTLE in WW II.	
3271	LT.45	DRIFT FISHER	96/16	1–3 pdr PB	6.16–1919
1926	LT.277	DULCIE DORIS	80/13	1–57 mm Net	10.15–1920
2495	BF.175	DUNEDIN	78/10	1–6 pdr Net =in WW II.	4.15–1919
1829	LT.1139	DUSTY MILLER	73/11	1–3 pdr Net, M/S	8.15–1919
2378	FR.106	DUTHIES	89/14	1–3 pdr Net =in WW II.	2.15–1919
778	PD.322	DUTIFUL	98/07	1–.45 in MG PB, M/S	11.14–1919
1027	YH.137	E. A. B.	67/10	1–2 pdr Net	1.15–1919
1120	LT.309	E. B. C.	60/09	Net =ROLETTA in WW II.	3.15–1919
1028	YH.740	E. E. S.	91/11	1–6 pdrAA Net	1.15–1919
2462	PD.97	E. J. M.	72/10	1–6 pdr Net, M/S	2.15–1919
1872	LT.1124	E. W. B.	95/11	1–3 pdr Net	9.15–1919
743	YH.228	EADWINE	96/14	1–6 pdrAA Net, BDV =in WW II.	2.15–1919
202	LT.1166	EAGER	102/12	1–6 pdr AA PB =in WW II.	8.14–1919
1428	LT.372	EARLY MORN	58/01	Net	4.15–7.16
	BF.1402	EARN	80/03	BDV	7.15–1920
1017	LT.328	EAST ANGLIA	83/09	1–6 pdrAA Net	1.15–1919
1483	LT.447	EAST BRITON	88/15	1–6 pdrAA Net	5.15–1919
2217					
1002	LT.1169	EAST HOLME	75/12	1–3 pdrAA Net	1.15–1919
	BCK.2	EASTER MORN	81/07	Minefields tender	1.16–1920
775	A.278	EASTERN DAWN	91/09	1–.45 in MG M/S	11.14–1919
2294	BF.355	EBENEZER	83/06	1–3 pdr Net =HALL MARK in WW II.	3.15–1919

Adty No.	Port No.	Name	TG/Yr	Armament, Fate, etc.	Service
2471	BCK.173	ECONOMY	79/06	1-57 mm Net	2.15-1919
3104	PD.99	EDITH	67/01	1-3 pdrAA Net	11.15-1919
1104	LT.1043	EFFORT =LAVATERA 1.19	82/07	1-3 pdr Net, Pilot service	2.15-1919
794	FR.481	EGBERT	84/10	1-6 pdr M/S	12.14-1919
2492	BF.860	EGLANTINE =GULLWING 9.17	95/07	1-6 pdrAA Net	3.15-1919
2566	BCK.180	EGLISE	99/14	1-3 pdr Net	3.15-1919
1846	LT.342	EILEEN EMMA	102/14	1-3 pdr PB =in WW II.	8.15-1919
2453	BF.303	ELEGANT	84/11	1-6 pdr Net, M/S	2.15-1919
1451	YH.558	ELEVEN	77/01	1-57 mm Net	4.15-1919
2389	PD.386	ELGAR	94/07	(ex-Vivid) 1-3 pdr Net. M/S	2.15-1919
	BCK.210	ELIBANK	96/15	BDV Water carrier	7.15-1919
	PD.470	ELLA	92/03	BDV	2.16-1919
	WK.709	ELLA =GUINEVERE 8.18	92/01	Base duties	11.15-1919
1034	YH.272	ELLEN & IRENE	88/14	1-6 pdrAA Net	1.15-1919
2058	A.277	ELYSIAN DAWN	91/09	PB =in WW II.	11.14-1920
	INS.402	EMBRACE	94/07	1-3 pdr BDV =in WW II.	4.15-1920
2472	INS.433	EMBLEM =CITY OF PERTH 6.19	85/07	1-3 pdr Net, M/S	2.15-1919
1417 2742	LT.963	EMILY	63/03	Net, Experiments	3.15-1919
2190	BCK.85	EMILY REAICH	83/04	1-6 pdr Net, Gunnery tender	6.15-1919
2357	INS.111	EMINENT	79/10	1-3 pdr Net, M/S	1.15-1919
2954	LT.703	EMPIRE'S HEROES	89/16	1-3 pdr Net	8.16-1919
1475	YH.349	EMULATE	77/08	1-6 pdrAA Net	5.15-1919
	SH.164	EMULATOR	66/04	BDV, Tender	9.15-1919
914	BCK.190	EN AVANT	90/14	1-6 pdr Net, M/S	1.15-1920
2701	PD.356	ENDEAVOUR =ENDEAVOUR II 8.15	89/07	1-57 mm Net	5.15-1919
2706	FR.69	ENDURANCE	94/07	1-6 pdrAA Net	12.15-1919
2189	BF.324	ENERGY	79/06	1-6 pdrAA Net	6.15-1920
613	PD.368	ENTERPRISE =ENTERTAIN 7.18	100/07	1-6 pdr AA Net	9.14-1919
1063	LT.408	ENTERPRISE =ENTERPRISE II 5.15	84/06	Net Mined 8.3.16 off Brindisi.	1.15-3.16
	BCK.187	ENTERPRISING	98/14	Misc Service =in WW II.	6.18-1919
	BCK.31	ENZIE	93/08	BDV =in WW II.	7.15-1919
2194	PD.360	ERA =ERA II 7.15	94/07	1-3 pdr Net, Tender	6.15-1919
2474	FR.272	ERASTUS	100/08	1-6 pdr Net	2.15-1919
1051	YH.313	ERIN =ERIN III 5.15	81/07	1-3 pdr Net	1.15-1919
747	WY.18	ESKBURN	90/14	Net Sunk 30.11.16 in collision off Dover.	1.15-11.16
2307	LT.46	ESLEA	83/08	1-6 pdrAA Net	1.16-1919
754	SN.227	ETHNEE	86/13	Net Wrecked 15.1.18 on Goodwin Sands near Fork Light.	1.15-1.18
	BCK.21	EUNICE & NELLIE	93/08	BDV =INTER NOS in WW II.	7.15-1919
1253	KY.109	EVA	88/93	1-6 pdrAA Net	5.15-1919
1915	LT.1117	EVENING PRIMROSE	88/11	1-6 pdr Net, M/S =in WW II.	11.15-1919
2131	KY.189	EVENING STAR =EVENING STAR II 5.15	89/07	1-57 mm Net	3.15-1919
2460	INS.30	EVERARD	82/07	Net Sunk 15.1.16 in collision off Tuskar Rock.	2.15-1.16
1134	LT.350	EX FORTIS	90/14	1-3 pdr Net, M/S =in WW II.	3.15-1920

TOP: The M/S trawler SPARROW   /*National Maritime Museum*
CENTRE: The trawler DAVID BLAKE.   'Strath' class   /*National Maritime Museum*
ABOVE: The trawler JOHN DAVIS.   'Castle' class   /*National Maritime Museum*

TOP: The trawler JOHN EDMUND. 'Mersey' class   /*Imperial War Museum*
CENTRE: The trawler ICEAXE (as KENNET).   'Axe' class (post-war)
   /*National Maritime Museum*
ABOVE: RELONZO.   Hired hydrophone trawler   /*Imperial War Museum*

TOP: GUILLEMOT. Hired M/S trawler   /*Imperial War Museum*
CENTRE: IMPERIAL QUEEN.   Hired M/S trawler   /*Vicary*
ABOVE: The whaler MEG.   'Z' class   /*Imperial War Museum*

TOP: The drifter **AIR POCKET**. Wood type /*National Maritime Museum*
CENTRE: The drifter **CRESCENT MOON**. Steel type /*National Maritime Museum*
ABOVE: **COSMOS**. Hired net drifter /*Imperial War Museum*

TOP: EAST BRITON.   Hired net drifter   /Vicary
CENTRE: The target service tug FORTITUDE
ABOVE: The dockyard paddle tug CRACKER.   'Dromedary' class (post-war)

TOP: The dockyard tug ASSURANCE. 'Enterprise' class   /National Maritime Museum
CENTRE: The dockyard tug EGERTON   /National Maritime Museum
ABOVE: The dockyard tug ATLAS.   'Rover' class

TOP: The dockyard paddle tug FIRM. 'Robust' class
CENTRE: The rescue tug JAUNTY. 'Frisky' class   /*National Maritime Museum*/
ABOVE: The rescue tug ROLLICKER. 'Resolve' class   /*National Maritime Museum*/

TOP: The rescue tug ST CLEARS.   'Saint' class
CENTRE: RESCUE.   Hired salvage vessel (with Kite-balloon)   /*Vicary*/
ABOVE: The barrage vessel BV.2   /*National Maritime Museum*/

TOP: The boom defence vessel BD.35   /*Imperial War Museum*
CENTRE: The mooring vessel FIDGET   /*Imperial War Museum*
ABOVE: The mooring vessel MOORDALE.   'Moor' class

TOP: The destroyer depot ship **HECLA**   /*National Maritime Museum*
CENTRE: The depot ship **AQUARIUS**   /*National Maritime Museum*
ABOVE: The destroyer depot ship **DIDO**.   Ex-cruiser   /*National Maritime Museum*

TOP: The fleet repair ship SANDHURST /National Maritime Museum
CENTRE: The oil tanker PETROLEUM
ABOVE: The oil tanker THERMOL /National Maritime Museum

TOP: The oil tanker **FORTOL**. 'Belgol' class   /*National Maritime Museum*
CENTRE: The water tanker **DESPOT** (ex-**DESPATCH**).   'Despatch' class
ABOVE: The fleet messenger **AQUILLA** (store carrier)   /*National Maritime Museum*

TOP: The landing craft X.207 in service as fuel lighter
CENTRE: The tender NETTLE   /*National Maritime Museum*
ABOVE: The ferry HARLEQUIN   /*National Maritime Museum*

TOP: The gunnery tender RAVEN. Ex-gunboat   /*National Maritime Museum*
CENTRE: The trials gunboat EXCELLENT. Ex-DRUDGE   /*Imperial War Museum*
ABOVE: The survey vessel ESTHER

TOP: The hospital ship BERBICE /National Maritime Museum
CENTRE: The harbour service coal hulk C.10. Ex-screw corvette RUBY
/National Maritime Museum
ABOVE: The harbour service coal hulk C.109. Ex-armoured ship AGINCOURT

TOP: The harbour training ship **FOUDROYANT**.   Ex-5th Rate **TRINCOMALEE**
CENTRE: The harbour training ship **TRITON**.   Ex-survey ship
/*National Maritime Museum*
ABOVE: The harbour torpedo-training ship **VESUVIUS**   /*Imperial War Museum*

Adty No.	Port No.	Name	TG/Yr	Armament, Fate, etc.	Service
2300	BF.344	EXCEL	77/06	1–6 pdr AA Net	5.15–1920
	FR.235	EXCEL	103/07	1–3 pdr BDV	8.15–1920
2767	BK.260	EXCEL III	86/07	1–6 pdr Net	4.15–1919
3208	BCK.95	EXCELLENT =EXCELLENCY 8.15	60/04	1–2½ pdr Net	8.15–1920
2182	BF.683	EXCELSIOR	85/07	1–6 pdr AA Net	6.15–1920
	BCK.182	EXCHEQUER	86/14	Tender =in WW II.	1.16–1920
1899	LT.9	EXPECTANT	93/13	1–6 pdr Net, M/S	9.15–1919
2556	PD.127	EXPECTATION	77/10	1–6 pdr Net	3.15–1919
612	PD.138	EXPERT	100/07	1–3 pdr Net	9.14–1919
2404	ML.12	EXPLORATOR	79/09	1–3 pdr Net	4.15–1919
2164	BCK.148	EXUBERANT	79/02	(ex-Thirty One) 1–3 pdr Net	5.15–1919
214	LT.1121	EYRIE	84/11	M/S Mined 2.9.14 off the Outer Dowsing.	9.14–9.14
1558 2202	YH.87	F. & G. G.	85/14	1–3 pdr AA Net. =GEORDIE in WW II.	7.15–1919
1155 569	YH.809	F. H. S.	95/08	1–6 pdr AA Net	3.15–1919
2046	FR.268	FAIR ISLE	97/08	1–6 pdr Net	8.15–1919
	WK.757	FAIRY HILL	84/00	(ex-One) Misc Service	1.16–1919
786	PD.477	FAITHFUL	92/03	1–6 pdr Net, M/S	12.14–1220
3102	BK.426	FAITHFUL =FAITHFUL II 3.17	86/07	1–3 pdr AA Net	10.16–1919
1901	LT.33	FAITHFUL FRIEND	110/13	1–6 pdr Net	9.15–1919
	FR.985	FAITHLIE	79/03	Tender	1.16–1919
	WY.71	FAME	68/01	Net Wrecked 22.10.16 on Hook Sand, Poole.	10.16–10.16
1831	LT.1144	FAMILIAR FRIEND	92/11	1–6 pdr AA Net, M/S	8.15–1919
1478	LT.366	FANCY	84/06	1–6 pdr Net, M/S	4.15–1919
2439	BF.388	FANNY MAIR	84/11	1–3 pdr Net, M/S =CRANNOCK in WW II.	5.15–1919
2195	BF.477	FAVO	77/01	1–6 pdr AA Net	6.15–1919
	INS.530	FAVOUR	93/08	BDV & Accom =in WW II.	7.15–1919
2505	LY.32	FAVOURITE	95/07	1–3 pdr Net	4.15–1919
1460	YH.497	FEAR NOT	60/02	Net	4.15–11.15
2415	BCK.9	FEAR NOT =FEAR NOT II 5.15	101/08	1–6 pdr Net =in WW II.	4.15–1919
760	LT.1081	FEARLESS =FEARLESS II 2.15	81/07	1–6 pdr AA Net	1.15–1919
221	LT.1191	FEASIBLE	103/12	1–6 pdr AA PB, Escort =in WW II.	9.14–1919
1084	LK.1	FELICIA	90/07	1–3 pdr Net, Misc Service	2.15–1919
1399	BCK.75	FELICITAS	67/10	1–57 mm Net Sunk 15.5.17 by Austrian cruisers off Fano Island, Adriatic.	4.15–5.17
1167	YH.94	FENNEW	85/11	1–6 pdr Net, M/S =YOUNG ALFRED in WW II.	3.15–1919
1459	YH.763	FERN	59/02	Net, Misc Service	4.15–1920
1310	BF.679	FERN II	85/07	1–3 pdr PB	9.15–1920
2269	INS.171	FERNDALE	75/10	Net Wrecked 27.12.15 on St. Ann's Head.	2.15–12.15
2507	LY.37	FERTILE	98/07	1–3 pdr Net	4.15–1920
2303	BF.584	FERTILITY	89/07	1–6 pdr Net	5.15–1919
	WK.563	FIDELIA	74/03	Collier & Tender	1.16–1919
2726	LY.872	FINROSS	78/11	1–57 mm Net Wrecked 26.11.16 near Gallipoli.	10.15–11.16
452	LT.334	FISHER BOY	91/14	1–3 pdr AA Net =in WW II.	4.15–1920
2713	LT.77	FISHER GIRL	85/14	1–57 mm Net =in WW II.	10.15–1919
3299	LT.679	FISHER QUEEN	88/16	1–6 pdr AA Net, M/S =in WW II.	8.16–1919

Adty No.	Port No.	Name	TG/Yr	Armament, Fate, etc.	Service
	LK.174	FITFUL HEAD	62/07	(ex-Ocean Spray) Stores and Water carrier	1.16–1919
1050	YH.510	FIVE	84/10	1–3 pdr Net =REGINA STELLA in WW II.	1.15–1920
2293	BF.645	FLEETWING	84/07	1–3 pdr Net	3.15–12.18
3052	SH.325	FLO JOHNSON	117/17	1–6 pdr M/S =ABIDING STAR in WW II.	7.17–1919
748	YH.973	FLOANDI	99/14	1–12 prd Net	1.15–1919
	WK.719	FLORA	92/01	BDV Tender	7.15–1919
2204	BCK.25	FLOREAT	93/08	1–3 pdr Net	6.15–1919
2140	BF.1417	FLOURISH	82/03	1–3 pdr Net	5.15–1920
2412	BCK.4	FLOWER	83/07	1–6 pdr Net =in WW II.	4.15–1919
	BF.376	FLOWER O'MAY	80/11	HS	8.15–1919
	INS.584	FLOWER O'MORAY	84/08	Exam	9.17–1919
	BF.640	FLOWING TIDE	83/13	Chaplain Tender	1.16–1919
	BCK.60	FORELOCK	89/10	BDV	7.15–1919
1892	LT.1160	FORERUNNER	92/11	1–3 pdr Net =in WW II.	9.15–1919
1061	LT.763	FORESIGHT =FORESIGHT II 2.15	87/11	1–57 mm Net =in WW II.	1.15–9.18
2063	BF.536	FORETHOUGHT	86/13	1–6 pdr Net	1.16–1919
2457	BF.81	FORGLEN	80/09	1–6 pdr Net	2.15–1919
3074	LT.100	FORMIDABLE	87/17	1–6 pdrAA =FIDGET in WW II.	12.17–1919
3151	INS.546	FORTITUDE	86/03	1–6 pdr Net	5.15–1919
2298	BF.624	FORWARD =FORWARD III 5.15	89/07	1–6 pdrAA Net Mined 31.3.17 off the Shipwash.	3.15–3.17
2139	BF.608	FORWARD IV	74/05	1–6 pdrAA Net, M/S	7.15–1919
1053	YH.212	FOUR	91/07	1–3 pdr Net	1.15–1920
2558	BF.149	FRAGRANCE	72/10	1–3 pdr Net	3.15–1919
2621	PD.513	FRAGRANT	94/10	1–6 pdrAA Net =in WW II.	10.15–1919
3111	YH.503	FRANK ARNOLD	82/17	1–6 pdr M/S	7.17–1919
1154 982	H.950	FRASERBURGH	83/07	1–6 pdr Net	3.15–1919
1888	YH.665	FRED SALMON	102/12	1–3 pdr Net =STRIVE in WW II.	9.15–1919
2859	BF.619	FREEDOM	90/07	1–6 pdr Net, M/S	5.15–1919
2506	BCK.29	FREUCHNY	84/08	Net Mined 8.1.16 off Brindisi.	4.15–1.16
2094	LK.401	FRIENDLY GIRLS	90/13	M/S, Water carrier =in WW II.	5.15–1919
1121	LT.370	FRIENDLY STAR	58/09	1–6 pdrAA Net	3.15–1919
1562	LT.552	FRIENDS	81/06	1–6 pdr Net	7.15–1919
2276	BCK.68	FRIGATE BIRD	84/05	1–57 mm Net Sunk 11.3.18 in collision off Mars Scirocco, Mediterranean.	2.15–3.18
Q	YH.217	FRONS OLIVAE	98/12	1–3 pdr PB Mined 12.10.15 off Elbow Buoy.	12.14–10.15
3285	YH.217	FRONS OLIVAE	93/16	1–6 pdrAA Net, M/S =in WW II.	6.16–1919
	BCK.194	FRUITFUL	89/04	BDV	7.15–1919
242	YH.723	FURZE	99/11	1–2½ pdr PB =in WW II.	9.14–1919
3290	YH.627	G. A. W.	99/16	1–6 pdr Net, M/S =GEORGE ALBERT in WW II.	7.16–1919
2144	BCK.189	G. C. D.	77/01	(ex-Thirteen) Net	5.15–1920
	SH.201	G. E. S.	60/09		9.18–1920
	INS.50	G. M. B.	93/09	Misc Service	1.16–1919
1093	YH.987	G. M. H.	88/11	1–3 pdr Net, M/S	2.15–1919
1109	LT.1062	G. M. V.	94/07	Net Mined 13.3.15 off Larne.	2.15–3.15
2158	BCK.110	G. S. L.	85/12	1–6 pdr Net, M/S	5.15–1919
2989	YH.487	G. S. P.	100/16	Net Sunk 2.2.17 in collision off Owers LV.	12.16–2.17
563	FR.68	GALILEAN	72/11	1–6 pdrAA Net	1.15–1919

Adty No.	Port No.	Name	TG/Yr	Armament, Fate, etc.	Service
	BF.115	GAMRIE BAY	87/14	BDV	9.15–1919
1924	LT.395	GARRIGILL	99/14	1–6 pdr Net	10.15–1920
1808	BF.144	GAVENEYBRAE	54/10	1–6 pdr AA Net	4.15–1919
2104	BF.92	GAVENWOOD	88/14	Net	1.15–2.16
				Mined 20.2.16 off Brindisi.	
2483	BF.1136	GELLYBURN	86/08	1–6 pdr Net, Hydro =in WW II.	3.15–1919
1421	LT.151	GENERAL WHITE	72/00	1–3 pdrAA Net, Exam	3.15–1919
1088	LT.701	GEORGE V	67/10	Net	4.15–6.17
				Sunk 3.6.17 after EC mine explosion near Dover.	
2489	BF.544	GEORGE A. WEST	86/13	1–3 pdr Net	3.15–1919
2362	FR.511	GEORGE HAY	83/12	1–3 pdr Net	1.15–1919
2416	FR.415	GEORGE WALKER	65/11	1–3 pdr Net	4.15–1919
1082	YH.700	GIRL ANNIE	67/10	1–6 pdrAA Net	1.15–1919
795	FR.579	GIRL EILEEN	82/10	1–6 pdr M/S	12.14–1919
1832	LT.3	GIRL ENA	89/07	1–3 pdr Net =in WW II.	8.15–1919
216	LT.283	GIRL ETHEL	88/14	1–6 pdr PB =in WW II.	9.14–1919
1559 2201	YH.346	GIRL EVA	76/13	Net	7.15–10.16
				Mined 2.10.16 off Elbow Light Buoy.	
	FR.519	GIRL EVELYN	85/11	BDV	9.15–1919
3075	LT.1174	GIRL GLADYS	110/17	1–3 pdr Net =in WW II.	12.17–1919
1869	LT.276	GIRL GRACIE	95/13	Net	9.15–5.17
				Sunk 15.5.17 by Austrian cruisers off Fano Island, Adriatic Sea.	
1833	LT.1040	GIRL HILDA	88/07	1–3 pdr Net	7.15–1919
2974	YH.295	GIRL KATHLEEN	95/13	1–6 pdrAA Net =UNITED BOYS in WW II.	10.16–1919
	BCK.115	GIRL LILY	85/11	(ex-Ocean Reward) Misc Service	1.16–1919
1567	LT.420	GIRL MARGARET	99/14	1–6 pdrAA Net =in WW II.	7.15–1919
1081	YH.866	GIRL MARJORIE	92/12	1–6 pdr Net, M/S	2.15–1919
2906	FR.473	GIRL MAY	81/07	1–3 pdr Net	5.15–1919
1126	YH.167	GIRL NANCY	67/10	1–3 pdrAA Net =in WW II.	2.15–1920
1856	LT.1137	GIRL NORAH	75/11	1–6 pdr Net	9.15–1919
2563	YH.367	GIRL RHODA	86/08	1–6 pdrAA Net	3.15–1919
2714	YH.786	GIRL ROSE	86/11	1–57 mm Net	10.15–5.17
				Sunk 15.5.17 by Austrian cruisers off Fano Island, Adriatic Sea.	
1022	YH.997	GIRL WINIFRED	90/12	1–3 pdr M/S =in WW II.	1.15–1919
	INS.368	GLADYS	75/06	BDV	8.15–1919
3156	BCK.192	GLADYS & ROSE	72/08	1–3 pdr Net	5.15–1919
1060	LT.1033	GLADYS MAY	88/07	1–6 pdrAA Net	1.15–1919
2282	BF.370	GLEAM OF HOPE	72/11	1–6 pdr Net	2.15–1919
1009	LT.1170	GLEANER OF THE SEA	91/12	Net	1.15–10.16
				Sunk 27.10.16 by German destroyers in the Dover Straits.	
781	INS.580	GLEN CORRAN	86/08	1–6 pdr M/S	12.14–1920
1866	LT.62	GLEN HEATHER	95/13	1–6 pdrAA Net =in WW II.	9.15–1919
1397	BF.416	GLENAFTON	72/06	1–6 pdrAA Net	4.15–1919
	BCK.53	GLENALBYN	82/09	1–3 pdr Exam =In WW II.	9.17–1919
	INS.27	GLENERNE	79/09	BDV	7.15–1920
2727	A.207	GLENGARRY	64/00	Net, Exam	12.15–1919
2461	INS.401	GLENGYNACK	96/07	1–6 pdrAA Net	2.15–1919
103	KY.493	GLENOGIL	95/94	PB, Hydro tender	8.14–1919
	GN.45	GLENTILT =GLENEALY 6.18	61/00	Store carrier & Transport	5.15–1919

Adty No.	Port No.	Name	TG/Yr	Armament, Fate, etc.	Service
2383	INS.553	GLENURQUHART	76/08	1-3 pdr Net, M/S	2.15-1919
1096	LT.371	GOLDEN CHANCE	85/14	1-6 pdr Net =in WW II.	2.15-1919
2369	A.559	GOLDEN DAWN	79/13	1-3 pdr Net, M/S	1.15-1919
2912	FR.408	GOLDEN EFFORT	86/14	1-6 pdr Net, M/S Purchased 1915, sold 1921. =in WW II.	7.15-1921
2455	BF.614	GOLDEN FEATHER	88/13	1-3 pdr Net	2.15-1919
1000	LT.1135	GOLDEN GAIN	84/11	1-6 pdrAA Net	1.15-1919
1059	LT.706	GOLDEN GIFT	90/10	1-3 pdrAA Net =in WW II.	1.15-1919
3084	BCK.	GOLDEN GRAIN	94/18	1-6 pdr PB =DARNAWAY in WW II.	6.18-1919
	INS.404	GOLDEN HARP	94/07	Hospital carrier =ACQUIRE in WW II.	1.16-1919
1117	LT.1011	GOLDEN HARVEST	87/14	1-6 pdr Net =in WW II.	2.15-1919
1108	LT.373	GOLDEN NEWS	95/14	1-3 pdr Net =in WW II.	2.15-1919
2571	BF.54	GOLDEN RAY	79/14	1-3 pdr Net, M/S	3.15-1919
1870	LT.593	GOLDEN RING	83/10	1-6 pdrAA Net	9.15-1919
1119	LT.500	GOLDEN RULE	65/05	1-3 pdrAA Net	3.15-1919
2749	BCK.223	GOLDEN SHEAF	95/16	1-6 pdr Net =in WW II.	8.16-1919
2095	YH.97	GOLDEN SPRAY	59/09	Misc Service	2.16-1919
1429	LT.234	GOLDEN SPUR	57/08	Net, M/S	4.15-1919
2288	KY.107	GOLDEN STRAND	69/11	1-6 pdr Net	2.15-1919
	KY.188	GOLDEN SUNRAY	94/06	(ex-Maggie Leask) BDV	9.15-1919
1914	LT.1194	GOLDEN SUNSET	85/13	1-6 pdrAA Net Sunk 4.1.18 in collision off Shambles LV.	10.15-1.18
2361	BF.63	GOLDEN WEST	88/14	1-6 pdr Net, Misc. =in WW II.	1.15-1919
2103	FR.85	GOOD DESIGN II	79/10	1-6 pdr Net	1.15-1919
2211	AH.39	GOOD FRIEND	88/08	1-6 pdrAA Net	4.15-1919
1461	YH.736	GOOD HOPE II	63/02	1-6 pdr Net	5.15-1920
2902	BF.622	GOOD HOPE III	85/07	1-3 pdr Net	5.15-1919
1309	BF.516	GOOD HOPE IV	63/05	1-3 pdr PB	9.15-8.18
2034	PD.182	GOOD TIDINGS	98/07	1-6 pdr Net	8.15-1919
240	YH.724	GORSE	99/11	1-3 pdr PB =in WW II.	9.14-1919
	FR.232	GOWAN	97/07	BDV	9.15-1919
1807	BF.347	GOWAN =GOWAN II 6.15	86/06	1-6 pdr Net	4.15-1920
2427	BCK.3	GOWAN =GOWAN III 6.15	84/07	1-3 pdr Net =in WW II.	5.15-1919
3207	INS.181	GOWAN BRAE	82/06	1-6 pdr AA Net, M/S	8.15-1920
2142	INS.97	GOWAN CRAIG	82/15	1-3 pdr Net, M/S =in WW II.	4.15-1919
2141	BF.193	GOWANBANK	78/10	1-6 pdr Net	4.15-1919
2102	FR.105	GOWANLEA	84/14	1-6 pdr Net	1.15-1919
1115	LT.967	GRACE LILIAN	69/03	1-6 pdrAA Net	3.15-1919
3212	BF.973	GRACIE	83/07	1-6 pdr AA Net Sunk 10.2.17 in collision off Tongue LV.	8.15-2.17
2399	INS.322	GRATEFUL	107/07	Net Wrecked 25.3.16 off Torr Head; salved. =CLOVERDALE in WW II.	2.15-3.16
1420	LT.177	GRATITUDE	60/02	1-3 pdr Net, Exam	3.15-1919
1395	INS.233	GREAT HEART	78/11	Net Sunk 24.9.15 off Dover, probably by own mine.	6.15-9.15
3108	BCK.237	GREEN PASTURES	99/17	1-6 pdr M/S =GERVAIS RENTOUL in WW II.	5.17-1919

Adty No.	Port No.	Name	TG/Yr	Armament, Fate, etc.	Service
2384	A.579	GREY DAWN	84/13	1–3 pdr Net =SUNNY VALE in WW II.	2.15–1919
2287	KY.283	GUERDON	89/08	1–3 pdr Net	2.15–1919
1423	LT.630	GUIDE ME	60/05	1–3 pdrAA Net	3.15–1919
	BF.1410	GUIDE ME	77/03	BDV	7.15–1919
2567	PD.144	GUIDE ME II	100/07	1–6 pdrAA Net Sunk 29.8.18 in collision off the Muglins.	3.15–8.18
2764	BK.247	GUIDE ME III	87/07	1–6 pdrAA Net	6.15–1919
1805	INS.251	GUIDE ME IV	79/01	1–6 pdr Net	6.15–1919
3114	INS.451	GUIDE ON	88/17	1–6 pdrAA Cable repairs =in WW II.	1.18–1919
2030	PD.132	GUIDING STAR	93/06	1–3 pdr Net, M/S	7.15–1919
	LY.937	GWEEDORE	82/13	BDV Water carrier	9.15–1920
1479	YH.485	H. F. E.	58/09	Net	4.15–1919
758	YH.729	HALF MOON	95/11	1–6 pdrAA Net	1.15–1919
2214	BCK.1	HANDSOME	84/07	1–6 pdrAA Net =in WW II.	4.15–1919
1691	BCK.161	HANDY =DANDY 4.18	67/03	1–6 pdr BDV	6.15–1919
1813	LT.185	HAPPY DAYS	101/14	1–6 pdrAA Net =DORIENTA in WW II.	7.15–1919
2730	FR.527	HARRY	60/01	1–6 pdrAA Net	12.15–1919
3072	YH.711	HARRY & LEONARD	92/17	1–6 pdrAA	5.18–1919
2009	BCK.90	HARVEST HOPE	91/11	1–6 pdrAA Net =in WW II.	1.15–1920
1458	YH.853	HARVEST MOON	72/04	(ex-Joe Mudd) 1–6 pdrAA Net, M/S =in WW II.	4.15–1919
2751	BK.355	HARVESTER =HARVESTER II 11.17	95/14	1–6 pdr Net	4.15–1919
1054	YH.93	HASTFEN	77/11	1–2½ pdr Net Mined 24.9.17 off the Longsands.	1.15–9.17
1037	LT.1188	HASTINGS CASTLE	73/12	1–57 mm Net	1.15–1919
2145	BF.923	HAWTHORN	93/07	1–6 pdr Net	5.15–1919
	BF.80	HAWTHORN BUD	81/14	BDV	9.15–1919
2087	BCK.29	HAZAEL	85/08	Misc Service	7.15–1919
72	LH.13	HAZEL BANK	77/08	1–6 pdr Net	1.15–1919
1007	LT.1061	HEARTY =HEARTY II 4.15	83/07	1–6 pdr Net	1.15–1919
2504	BF.1090	HEARTY =CHEERY 5.15	67/03	1–6 pdrAA Net	4.15–1919
	BCK.176	HEATH BANK	75/08	Misc Service	1.16–1919
3080	YH.657	HEATHER	92/17	1–6 pdr	5.18–1919
1930	LT.1122	HEATHER BLOOM	88/11	Net	10.15–1920
1316	BCK.153	HEATHER SPRIG	83/13	1–6 pdr =in WW II	1.17–1920
2396	PD.22	HEATHERBELL	91/04	1–3 pdr Net	2.15–1919
	INS.118	HEATHERY BRAE	90/10	1–3 pdr Exam =in WW II.	1.17–1919
	BCK.256	HELEN ANN	90/15	BDV Mail duties	7.15–1919
3427	BCK.289	HELEN SLATER	102/18	1–6 pdr Control vessel =in WW II.	6.18–1919
1804	BF.466	HELENA	87/06	1–6 pdrAA Net	4.15–1919
2274	BF.662	HELENORA	88/14	1–3 pdr Net Sunk 15.5.17 by Austrian cruisers off Fano Island, Adriatic Sea.	2.15–5.17
765	LT.1181	HELPMATE	76/12	1–6 pdr Net	1.15–1919
2179	BF.908	HERALD	86/07	Fleet duties	5.15–1920
3216	INS.209	HERO II	84/06	1–6 pdrAA Net	8.15–1919
2027	SY.251	HERRING FISHER	76/08	1–6 pdr Net	7.15–1919
3057	YH.273	HERRING GULL	93/17	1–6 pdr Net, M/S	8.17–1919
3038	YH.593	HERRING HO	85/17	Experiments	4.17–1919
1071	YH.714	HERRING QUEEN	72/11	Net, M/S	1.15–1919
1405	YH.51	HERRING SEARCHER	99/14	1–6 pdrAA Net	3.15–1919
2216					
1815	LT.1154	HERRING SEEKER	75/11	1–6 pdrAA Net	7.15–1919
561	KY.276	HIEDRA	78/08	PB	2.15–1919
77					

Adty No.	Port No.	Name	TG/Yr	Armament, Fate, etc.	Service
2178	INS.143	HIGHLAND LASSIE	78/10	Net, Target towing	5.15–1920
2146	INS.313	HIGHLAND LEADER	82/12	1–6 pdr Net	5.15–1920
1410	YH.674	HILARY II	78/02	(ex-*Twenty Four*) 1–3 pdr Net Mined 25.3.16 near Spit Buoy.	5.15–3.16
201	LT.1173	HILDA & ERNEST	102/12	1–3 pdrAA PB =AVAILABLE in WW II.	9.14–1919
776	BF.710	HOLLY	90/07	1–6 pdr M/S	12.14–1919
1031	YH.831	HOLLY =HOLLY II 5.15	79/04	1–3 pdr Net, M/S	1.15–1919
2705	FR.528	HOLLY =HOLLY III 9.15	93/07	1–3 pdr Net Sunk 11.5.18 in collision off Land's End.	8.15–5.18
1141	A.258	HOLLY BANK	78/09	1–57 mm Net	3.15–1919
1873	LT.437	HOLLYDALE	99/14	1–6 pdrAA Net =PECHEUR in WW II.	9.15–1920
2560	INS.372	HOLME ROSE	89/13	1–6 pdrAA Net	3.15–1919
2743	LT.34	HOLMSGARTH	85/08	1–6 pdrAA Net	5.16–1919
	BCK.89	HOME FRIEND	89/11	BDV	8.15–1920
1105	LT.125	HOMELAND	83/08	1–6 pdr Net	2.15–1919
2292	PD.70	HONEY BEE	84/05	1–6 pdrAA Net	3.15–1919
	BCK.96	HONEY DEW	99/11	BDV =in WW II.	7.15–1919
1386	PD.11	HONEYSUCKLE II	62/03	Stores and Water carrier	8.15–1919
2756	BK.22	HONOR	72/13	1–6 pdrAA Net	4.15–1919
	INS.138	HOPE	67/04	BDV Collier	7.15–1920
1004	LT.1075	HOPE =HOPE II 4.15	92/07	1–6 pdrAA Net	1.15–1919
2860	BF.573	HOPE =HOPE III 6.15	79/07	1–3 pdr Net	5.15–1919
2029	PD.96	HOPE IV	90/06	1–3 pdr Net	7.15–1919
2336	PD.504	HOPEFUL	94/07	1–3 pdr Net	3.15–1919
2744	LT.691	HUMOROUS	101/16	1–3 pdr Net	5.16–1919
1068	LT.997	HYACINTH =HYACINTH II 5.15	79/03	1–3 pdr Net Later purchased, sold 1920.	1.15–1920
	BF.1277	HYSSOP	88/03	BDV Workshop	8.15–1919
2735	FR.293	I. & J.	95/16	1–6 pdrAA Net, M/S Wrecked 1.1.19 off Newhaven.	4.16–1.19
751	YH.188	I. F. S.	95/08	(ex-*Tarbat Ness*) 1–6 pdrAA Net	1.15–1919
	PD.407	IDA	94/07	Naval stores tender =STRATHBEG in WW II.	12.14–1919
2987	LT.730	IMPLACABLE =IMPLACABLE II 2.17	88/16	1–6 pdrAA M/S	12.16–1919
219	LT.1118	IMPREGNABLE =IMPREST 2.15 =IMPERATOR 9.16	108/11	1–6 pdrAA PB	9.14–1919
796	INS.167	INCHBROOM	78/10	1–6 pdr M/S	12.14–1919
2054	LT.196	INDOMITABLE II	83/08	1–3 pdr Net	10.15–1919
911	PD.378	INDUSTRY	100/07	1–6 pdr Net, M/S =in WW II.	5.15–1919
3284	LT.795	INFINITIVE	103/16	1–6 pdr Net	6.16–1919
2908	KY.178	INTEGRITY	86/07	1–6 pdr Net, M/S	5.15–1919
2731	PD.51	INTEGRITY =INTEGRITY II 11.15	67/03	1–3 pdr Net	10.15–1919
2198	INS. 32	INTER NOS	90/07	1–3 pdr Net	6.15–1919
2064	BF.322	INVERBOYNDIE	89/10	1–6 pdrAA Net	1.16–1920
	INS.237	INVERNAIRNE	78/10	BDV	7.15–1919
2193	PD.511	INVERUGIE	93/08	1–3 pdr Net, M/S =in WW II.	6.15–1919
2161	BCK.196	IRENE	66/06	1–3 pdr Net, Tender	2.15–1920
2475	BK.23	IRENE =IRENE II 8.15	85/07	1–6 pdr Net, M/S	4.15–1919
741	SN.105	ISA	87/14	1–6 pdrAA Net =BOY JOHN in WW II.	2.15–1919
	BF.1121	ISABELLA FERGUSSON	60/03	BDV Telephone Maintenance	7.15–1919
2355	INS.210	ISCO	100/07	1–3 pdr Net, M/S	1.15–1919
913	BF.1067	IVA	85/08	Net, M/S	1.15–1920
607	PD.183	IVY	94/07	1–57 mm Net	9.14–1919
1111	LT.1071	IVY II	83/07	1–6 pdr Net	2.15–1919

Adty No.	Port No.	Name	TG/Yr	Armament, Fate, etc.	Service
2803	BF.18	IVY III	71/05	1–3 pdr Net	6.15–1919
2485	BCK.23	IVY GREEN	76/08	1–6 pdr Net, M/S	3.15–1919
	BF.286	IVY LEAF	87/11	BDV =RESTORE in WW II.	9.15–1920
2353	INS.110	J. A. C.	79/10	1–3 pdr Net	1.15–1920
2762	BK.304	J. & A.	98/14	1–6 pdr Net Sunk 4.4.18 in collision off Scarborough.	4.15–4.18
2812	INS.2	J. & M. MAIN	89/13	1–6 pdrAA Net	4.15–1919
1877	YH.767	J. C. P.	73/08	Net Sunk 22.3.18 in collision off Green Flash Buoy.	9.15–3.18
2911	INS.367	J. E. C. M.	84/13	1–6 pdrAA PB, M/S	7.15–1919
1557	YH.271	J. H. F.	78/14	1–3 pdr AA Net	7.15–1919
1885	YH.746	J. S.	90/11	1–6 pdr Net	9.15–1919
993	PD.523	J. T. STEPHEN	82/08	1–6 pdrAA M/S	12.14–1919
759	YH.252	JACK GEORGE	98/13	1–6 pdrAA Net =in WW II.	1.15–1919
1023	YH.68	JACK SALMON	99/14	Net, Mine experiments =YOUNG JACOB in WW II.	1.15–1919
1148	YH.176	JACOB GEORGE	67/10	1–6 pdrAA Net	3.15–1919
983					
2738	LT.671	JAMES & WALTER	96/16	1–6 pdrAA Net, M/S	1.17–1919
	BCK.193	JAMES REAICH	78/01	(ex-Fifteen) BDV	9.15–1919
	WK.425	JANE	104/01	Collier	1.16–12.18
2008	BCK.48	JANET GEDDES	88/09	Net, Tender	1.15–1919
2811	ML.126	JANET REEKIE	81/08	1–3 pdr Net	4.15–1919
2041	BF.611	JASPER =JASPER II 8.15	84/07	1–3 pdr Net, M/S	4.15–1920
746	WY.186	JBURN	90/13	1–6 pdrAA Net, Mine experiments.	1.15–1919
2490	FR.238	JEAN	94/07	1–3 pdr Net Mined 17.10.17 off Cape Santa Maria di Leuca, Italy.	3.15–10.17
	BF.877	JEANIE GILCHRIST	92/07	1–3 pdr Exam	1.17–1919
2360	FR.310	JEANIE ROBERTSON	93/08	1–6 pdr Net, M/S =THAINS in WW II.	1.15–1919
2173	BF.1002	JEANNIE	83/07	1–6 pdr Net	5.15–1919
1781	PD.483	JEANNIE II	79/03	1–6 pdr Net	8.15–1919
2559	PD.193	JEANNIE LEASK	95/07	1–6 pdr Net =in WW II.	3.15–1919
	BCK.209	JEANNIE MACKINTOSH	88/15	BDV Water carrier =in WW II.	7.15–1919
989	BF.623	JEANNIE MURRAY	90/07	1–3 pdrAA Net Sunk 15.2.18 by German destroyers in the Dover Straits.	4.15–2.18
1396	BF.859	JEANNIE SIMPSON	90/07	1–6 pdrAA Net	4.15–1920
773	PD.145	JEANNIES	100/07	1–3 pdr M/S =in WW II.	12.14–1919
3054	WY.187	JESBURN	99/17	1–6 pdrAA =in WW II.	8.17–1919
74	FR.148	JESSIE TAIT	84/15	1–6 pdr Net =in WW II.	6.15–1919
1011	LT.19	JESSMAR	86/14	1–6 pdr Net	1.15–1919
E 1293	LT.981	JOE CHAMBERLAIN	79/03	1–3 pdr PB, Escort	12.14–1919
1852	LT.470	JOHN ALFRED	81/09	1–6 pdrAA Net =in WW II.	9.15–1919
1867	LT.203	JOHN & NORAH	95/13	1–6 pdrAA Net =in WW II.	9.15–1919
220	LT.140	JOHN LINCOLN	83/08	1–3 pdr PB, Escort	9.14–1919
1065	LT.211	JOHN MITCHELL	89/13	1–3 pdr Net Sunk 14.11.17 in collision off St. Alban's Head.	2.15–11.17
1035	YH.708	JOHN ROBERT	89/12	1–3 pdrAA Net Lost 1.2.19 enroute Mersina to Alexandretta, presumed mined off Cape Karadash.	1.15–2.19

Adty No.	Port No.	Name	TG/Yr	Armament, Fate, etc.	Service
2147	PD.566	JOHN S. SUMMERS	62/10	1–6 pdr AA Net	5.15–1919
1382	BF.359	JOHN WATT	84/11	1–3 pdr Stores and Water carrier =in WW II.	1.15–1919
2977	HL.85	KATREEN	104/16	1–3 pdr Net, M/S	11.16–1919
203	LT.1129	KENT COUNTY	86/11	PB Mined 8.12.16 off Cross Sand, Lowestoft.	9.14–12.16
1056	LT.210	KESSINGLAND	78/08	1–6 pdr AA Net =REFLECT in WW II.	4.15–1919
1006	LT.442	KESTREL =KESTREL II 4.15	75/06	1–6 pdr AA Net	1.15–1919
1080	YH.766	KIAMA	93/14	1–6 pdr AA Net =GIRL ELLEN in WW II.	2.15–1919
2464	KY.304	KILMANY	88/08	1–6 pdr AA Net	2.15–1919
2107	BF.96	KILNBURN	88/14	1–3 pdr Net, M/S	1.15–1920
1381	BF.965	KIMBERLEY II	102/07	1–6 pdr Net	3.15–1919
2025	PD.168	KING EDWARD	63/01	1–3 pdr Net, PB	7.15–1919
1922	YH.7	KING HERRING	100/09	1–3 pdr AA Net	10.15–1919
	FR.205	KINNAIRD	94/07		1.15–4.15
1106	LT.1111	KIPPER	92/08	1–6 pdr AA Net	2.15–1920
1548	YH.263	KITTY GEORGE	87/13	1–3 pdr AA Net =in WW II.	7.15–1920
3048	YH.247	LA MASCOT	83/17	1–6 pdr M/S	7.17–1919
1835	LT.213	LA PARISIENNE	85/13	1–6 pdr AA Net	8.15–1919
1015	LT.1051	LABURNUM =LABURNUM II 11.15	82/07	1–6 pdr AA Net	1.15–1919
1422	LT.508	LADY AUDREY	62/02	1–3 pdr AA Net	3.15–1919
2180	BF.1528	LADYSMITH	89/04	Net Disappeared 27.12.15 in gale off Milford Haven.	6.15–12.15
2388	INS.31	LAICH O'MORAY	79/09	1–6 pdr Net	2.15–1919
208	LT.1176	LANNER	103/12	1–6 pdr AA PB =in WW II.	9.14–1919
916	BF.888	LAPWING IV	89/07	1–3 pdr Net, M/S	7.15–1919
	BF.236	LASS O'DOUNE	92/10		9.18–1919
2371	BCK.51	LASSIE II	88/09	1–3 pdr Net, M/S	2.15–1919
	INS.135	LASSIE MAIN	84/10	BDV Engine repairs =in WW II.	7.15–1919
1851	LT.344	LAUNCH OUT	67/09	Net Sunk 27.10.16 by German destroyers in the Dover Straits.	9.15–10.16
2863	FR.245	LAUREL III	97/07	1–6 pdr Net	8.15–1919
2482	BCK.178	LAUREL BANK	84/08	1–6 pdr Net	3.15–1919
2050	FR.506	LAUREL CROWN	81/12	Net Mined 2.6.16 west of the Orkneys.	12.14–6.16
2060	WK.127	LAURELIA	96/07	1–6 pdr Misc Service	1.16–1919
917	BF.652	LAVATERA	84/13	1–6 pdr PB =in WW II.	3.15–1920
3029	WY.72	LAVINIA L.	73/17	Net =in WW II.	4.17–1919
2410	BCK.33	LEA RIG	83/08	1–6 pdr Net, M/S =SCOURGE in WW II.	4.15–1919
2858	BF.305	LEAD ME	71/06	1–3 pdr Net	5.15–1919
2031	BF.1338	LEADER	72/03	1–6 pdr AA Net, M/S	7.15–1920
	BF.1531	LEBANON	60/04	BDV Provision tender	8.15–1920
2802	BF.632	LEONARD	89/00	(ex-Two) 1–6 pdr. Lost 8.1.20	5.15–1920
1552	SN.37	LETIRA	79/14	1–6 pdr AA Net, M/S	7.15–1919
1955	YH.747	LERWICK	86/08	Net Wrecked 27.3.16 in Yarmouth Roads.	12.15–3.16
2403	BCK.24	LETTERFOURIE	77/08	1–6 pdr Net	4.15–1919
1102	LT.1055	LIBERTY =LIBERTY II 5.15	88/07	1–6 pdr Net	2.15–1919
2191	BF.1269	LIBERTY III	86/03	1–3 pdr Net =in WW II.	4.15–1920
236	YH.728	LICHEN	99/11	1–3 pdr AA PB, Hydro tender =in WW II.	9.14–1920

Adty No.	Port No.	Name	TG/Yr	Armament, Fate, etc.	Service
2433	FR.260	LIGHT	81/08	1–3 pdr Net	5.15–1919
2148	BF.445	LILACINA	83/12	1–3 pdr Net, M/S	4.15–1919
	WK.687	LILIAN MAUD	57/90	Misc Service	1.16–1919
1313	PD.118	LILIUM	83/13	1–6 pdrAA Net =in WW II.	6.15–1919
1875	YH.502	LILY	61/00	Net	9.15–1919
2465	KY.78	LILY & MAGGIE	87/09	1–6 pdr Net	2.15–1919
1157	LT.1115	LILY JANE	74/11	1–6 pdrAA Net	3.15–1919
2277	BCK.34	LILY OAK	84/08	1–6 pdr Net, M/S =in WW II.	2.15–1919
1430	LT.988	LILY OF THE VALLEY	60/03	Net	4.15–10.15
2296	BCK.11	LILY REAICH	88/08	Net Mined 26.2.16 off Durazzo.	3.15–2.16
2006	BF.345	LILYBANK	83/11	1–3 pdr Net, Exam	1.15–1919
224	LT.322	LINDSDELL	88/14	M/S Mined 3.9.14 off the Outer Dowsing.	9.14–9.14
1785	PD.151	LINUM	77/01	(ex-Seven) 1–3 pdr Net	3.15–1919
2430	FR.549	LIVELIHOOD	84/07	1–6 pdr Net	5.15–1919
2501	BF.262	LIVELY =LIVELY II 5.15	79/03	1–6 pdr Net	4.15–1919
788	BCK.172	LIVONIA	89/04	1–6 pdr M/S	12.14–1919
	LT.545	LIVONIA =GREEN MANTLE 8.18	62/05	Chaplains tender	2.16–1919
	BCK.19	LIZZIE ANNIE	87/08	Misc Service	1.16–1919
2062	BCK.163	LIZZIE BIRRELL	92/13	1–6 pdr M/S =in WW II.	1.16–1920
2402	A.373	LIZZIE BROWN	76/11	1–6 pdr Net	4.15–1919
2116	BCK.87	LIZZIE FLETT	88/11	1–3 pdr Net =in WW II.	1.15–1920
2406	ML.122	LIZZIE HUTT	82/08	Net	4.15–1919
2373	PD.94	LLOYD GEORGE	79/10	1–6 pdrAA Net	2.15–1919
2109	BF.251	LOCH CRAIG	91/10	1–3 pdr Net	1.15–1919
2458	INS.173	LOCH SPYNIE	80/10	1–6 pdr Net, M/S	2.15–1920
3152	INS.112	LOCHNABO	76/10	1–6 pdr Net, M/S	5.15–1919
3246	LT.329	LONDON COUNTY	83/09	1–3 pdrAA Net Lost 28.10.19 off Beadnell.	1.16–1919
2354	BF.301	LONICERA	78/11	1–6 pdrAA Net	1.15–1920
2365	BF.407	LOOK SHARP	83/12	1–6 pdr Net	1.15–1919
2077	SN.287	LORAINE	96/16	1–3 pdr Frozen meat carrier. Purchased 1918, sold 1936.	4.16–1936
Y5.8 S 1304	LT.1046	LORD CHARLES BERESFORD	81/07	1–6 pdr PB, Escort	12.14–1919
H 1296	LT.1047	LORD CLAUD HAMILTON	81/07	1–6 pdr PB, M/S	12.14–1919
C 1291	LT.117	LORD CROMER	84/08	1–6 pdrAA PB, M/S	12.14–1919
3062	LT.7	LORD CURZON	88/17	1–6 pdr M/S =in WW II.	9.17–1919
	LT.1152	LORD DUNWICH	75/11	BDV =in WW II.	9.15–1920
2966	LT.711	LORD FISHER	89/16	PB	4.17–1919
1913	LT.1141	LORD HALDANE	91/11	1–6 pdr Net	9.15–1919
2707	LT.623	LORD LEITRIM	78/10	1–6 pdrAA Net, BDV =WEST NEUK in WW II.	12.15–1919
1561	LT.56	LORD LOVAT	79/13	1–6 pdrAA Net	7.15–1919
738	LT.982	LORD MILNER	79/03	1–3 pdr Net, BDV	1.15–1919
2741 1434	LT.149	LORD ROBERTS II	72/00	Net	5.15–3.17
1057	LT.686	LORD STRADBROKE	79/10	1–6 pdr Net =OUR KATE in WW II.	1.15–1919
1871	LT.1143	LORD WENLOCK	91/11	1–3 pdrAA Net	9.15–1919
3238	LT.777	LORD ZETLAND	89/14	1–6 pdrAA Net	12.15–1919
	WK.15	LOTTIE	71/04	Misc Service	1.16–1920
1072	SN.184	LOTTIE LEASK	94/07	Net Sunk 18.12.15 by S/M gunfire off Saseno Island.	1.15–12.15
2469	BF.654	LOVEDALE	84/14	1–6 pdr Net	2.15–1919

Adty No.	Port No.	Name	TG/Yr	Armament, Fate, etc.	Service
1811	LT.64	LOYAL FRIEND	85/13	1–6 pdr AA Net	7.15–1919
A 1289	LT.111	LOYAL STAR	95/13	1–6 pdr AA PB, M/S	12.14–1919
2398	BCK.59	LUCANIA II	78/10	1–3 pdr Net, M/S	2.15–1919
	INS.66	LUCRATIVE	87/14	1–3 pdr BDV =EASTER ROSE in WW II.	7.15–1920
2853	KY.172	LUCY MACKAY	94/07	(ex-Bruces) 1–6 pdr Net, M/S	5.15–1919
1506	YH.843	LUDHAM CASTLE	66/04	1–6 pdr AA Net	5.15–1919
	BF.905	LUFRA	84/07	Misc Service	1.16–1919
2451	PD.519	LUPINA	88/08	1–6 pdr Net =in WW II.	2.15–1919
2564	BF.526	LUSTRE GEM	82/07	1–3 pdr Net	2.15–1919
2003	BF.195	LUSTRING	71/10	1–3 pdr Net Sunk 3.10.18 in collision off Hellier Holm.	1.15–10.18
2149	BCK.174	LYRE BIRD	80/02	(ex-Twenty-three) 1–6 pdr Net	5.15–1920
3109	PD.325	M. H. BUCHAN =BUCK 6.18	101/17	1–3 pdr Hydro tender =in WW II.	5.17–1919
	BCK.10	M. THOMSON	87/08	BDV	7.15–1920
749	YH.927	MA FREEN	92/13	1–6 pdr AA Net	1.15–1919
	LT.1185	MABEL VERA	98/12	BDV	9.15–1919
2801	ML.125	MACKAYS	83/08	1–6 pdr Net	4.15–1919
1845	LT.577	MADIS	79/09	Net	8.15–4.17
2862	KY.217	MAGDALEN	94/07	1–6 pdr AA Net, M/S	4.15–1919
2162	BF.424	MAGGIE	96/07	1–3 pdr Net	3.15–1919
2437	BCK.94	MAGGIE BRUCE	76/11	1–3 pdr Net, M/S	5.15–1919
2758	BK.334	MAGGIE COWE	91/14	1–6 pdr Net, M/S =RACHEL FLETT in WW II.	4.15–1919
	INS.126	MAGGIE GAULT	91/10	1–3 pdr Exam =in WW II.	1.17–1919
2129	KY.138	MAGGIES	85/07	1–6 pdr AA Net	3.15–1919
	BF.1122	MAGNET	60/03	Mining duties	1.16–1920
797	BCK.40	MAGNET III	92/08	1–3 pdr BDV Repairs vessel	12.14–1919
	INS.538	MAGNIFICENT	68/03	BDV	8.15–1920
	INS.23	MAGNIFICENT III	93/09	BDV =in WW II.	7.15–1919
	INS.224	MAID O'MORAY	84/11	BDV	7.15–1920
166	LK.682	MAID OF THULE	97/17	1–6 pdr M/S	9.17–1919
D 1292	LT.66	MAJESTY	84/08	1–6 pdr AA PB, M/S =in WW II.	12.14–1919
1038	LT.1113	MANZANITA	93/11	Net Wrecked 6.9.16 in the Adriatic.	1.15–9.16
2553	BCK.22	MARA SMITH	88/03	1–6 pdr AA Net	2.15–1920
2251		=DREEL CASTLE 2.18			
2200	ME.156	MARE	92/11	1–3 pdr Net =in WW II.	7.15–1919
1876	YH.717	MARIE	60/05	Net, Exam	9.15–1919
2426	INS.259	MARINER	88/07	1–3 pdr Net, M/S	5.15–1919
2275	BF.715	MARITANA	97/07	1–6 pdr AA Net, M/S	2.15–1919
2565	FR.474	MARVELLOUS	82/08	1–6 pdr AA Net	3.15–1919
1005	LT.650	MARY ADELINE	73/10	Net	1.15–1919
1783	BCK.86	MARY BOWIE	79/11	1–3 pdr Net	3.15–1919
1806	LY.48	MARY COWIE	83/08	1–6 pdr AA Net	4.15–1919
2757	BK.269	MARY MALTMAN	79/08	1–6 pdr AA Net	4.15–1919
2304	BCK.36	MARY REID	77/08	1–3 pdr Net, M/S	5.15–1920
2856	INS.243	MARY SLATER	79/11	1–3 pdr Net	5.15–1919
1390	PD.116	MARY STEPHEN	89/06	1–6 pdr Net	5.15–1919
	BK.357	MARY SWANSTON	109/16	Meat carrier =DEWY EVE in WW II.	3.16–1919
	LT.506	MARYLAND	61/02	Stores and Water carrier.	1.15–1920
2467	BCK.198	MARY'S	82/07	1–6 pdr AA Net	2.15–1919
2429	BF.994	MASCOT =MALAPERT 9.18	66/02	1–6 pdr AA Net	5.15–1920
756	YH.407	MASTERPIECE	82/07	1–3 pdr Net	1.15–1919
1837	LT.540	MAUD EVELYN	73/10	1–3 pdr Net	8.15–1920
4397	SN.360	MAUVEEN	95/18		10.18–1919
	WK.79	MAYBERRY	77/01	(ex-Six) HS	1.16–1920

Adty No.	Port No.	Name	TG/Yr	Armament, Fate, etc.	Service
2570	INS.75	MAYFLOWER	97/07	1–3 pdr Net	3.15–1919
1055	LT.316	MEG =MEG II 8.18	82/06	1–6 pdr Net	1.15–1919
2335	FR.432	MELINKA	77/11	1–3 pdr Net	2.15–1919
1910	LT.136	MICHAELMAS DAISY	99/13	Net Mined 26.11.16 near Cape Santa Maria di Leuca.	9.15–11.16
1107	LT.585	MIDAS	89/10	1–3 pdr Net =in WW II.	2.15–1919
	BF.756	MIGNONETTE	96/07	BDV	12.15–1920
2393	FR.72	MILL BURN	85/14	1–6 pdr Net	2.15–1919
2272	BCK.102	MILL O'BUCKIE	99/14	1–3 pdrAA Net =in WW II.	2.15–1919
	BCK.125	MINT	96/12	BDV =in WW II.	7.15–1919
1879	YH.494	MISHE NAHMA	58/00	Net	9.15–1919
226	YH.333	MISTLETOE	79/04	1–3 pdr PB	9.14–1919
	INS.399	MISTRESS ISA	99/15	BDV =in WW II.	7.15–1920
2037	PD.552	MIZPAH	77/01	(ex-Cato) Net	8.15–1919
2901	BF.581	MONARCH II	82/07	1–6 pdr Net, M/S	5.15–1920
3101	PD.266	MONARDA	108/16	1–6 pdr, 1–2 pdr Net =in WW II.	10.16–1919
	BCK.72	MONITOR	63/06	HS Tender	1.16–1919
	INS.311	MONOLIADH	85/12	Tender Purchased 20.12.14 for Cromarty.	8.14–1920
2555	BF.136	MONTBLETTON	76/10	1–6 pdr Net	2.15–1919
2479	BF.85	MONTCOFFER	53/09	Net, HS	2.15–1919
	INS.206	MORAY GEM	73/11	BDV	7.15–1920
	INS.22	MORAY VIEW	93/09	BDV =in WW II.	7.15–1920
2431	FR.584	MORMOND HILL	93/08	(ex-Kate Baird) 1–6 pdr Net	5.15–1919
2286	FR.237	MORNING STAR	97/07	Net Mined 8.1.16 off Brindisi.	2.15–1.16
2127	KY.128	MORNING STAR II	84/06	1–3 pdr Net	2.15–1919
71	LH.250	MORNING STAR III	90/07	1–6 pdrAA Net	5.15–1919
2903	BCK.201	MORNING STAR IV	84/07	1–6 pdr Net, M/S	5.15–1919
2716	PD.135	MORNING STAR V	68/04	1–47 mm Net, PB	10.15–1919
597	PD.580	MORRISON	80/09	1–6 pdr M/S	12.14–1919
248	YH.734	MOSS	99/11	1–3 pdr PB =GUIDING LIGHT in WW II.	9.14–1920
	INS.117	MOY HALL	71/10	Misc Service	8.17–1920
1827	LT.473	MYRTLE SPRIG	77/10	1–6 pdr Net	8.15–1919
2059	PD.521	NELLIE MCGEE	93/08	Hospital tender Purchased 1915, sold 27.6.22. =in WW II.	11.14–1922
2367	INS.362	NELLIE REID	94/07	1–3 pdrAA Net	1.15–1919
1473	SN.350	NELLY	75/03	1–3 pdr Net	5.15–1919
1018	LT.516	NELSON	71/06	1–6 pdr Net	1.15–1920
2514	LT.1112	NESMAR =NESMAR II 12.17	87/11	1–3 pdr Stores and Water carrier, Net, M/S	1.15–1920
206	LT.271	NETSUKIS	85/13	1–6 pdrAA M/S, Net =in WW II.	9.14–1919
1019	LT.1148	NEVERTHELESS	88/11	1–6 pdrAA Net	1.15–1920
774	A.221	NEW DAWN	93/08	1–.45 in MG M/S Mined 23.3.18 at entrance to the Needles Channel.	11.14–3.18
1146	YH.135	NEW SPRAY	70/12	1–5 pdrAA Net =in WW II.	2.15–1919
570					
3211	BCK.159	NEXUS	86/07	(ex-Roxana) 1–3 pdrAA Net Mined 13.3.18 in the Thames estuary.	8.15–3.18
2709	PD.152	NIGELLA II	77/01	(ex-Eight) 1–6 pdrAA Net, HS	12.15–1919
1094	LT.175	NIL DESPERANDUM	91/03	1–3 pdr Net	2.15–1919
994	PD.497	NINA	83/04	1–3 pdr Sunk 2.8.17 by explosion off Prawle Point.	4.15–8.17
157	LT.608	NINE SISTERS	92/10	1–6 pdrAA PB, Net	11.14–1919

Adty No.	Port No.	Name	TG/Yr	Armament, Fate, etc.	Service
1550	SN.44	NOREEN	79/14	1–6 pdr AA Net, BDV	7.15–1919
2219	LT.103	NORFOLK COUNTY	83/08	1–3 pdr AA Net =in WW II.	9.15–1919
753	YH.45	NORFORD SUFFLING	86/14	1–6 pdr AA Net =in WW II.	1.15–1919
2499	PD.102	NORHAM CASTLE	93/99	1–3 pdr Stores and Water carrier	3.15–1919
2285	BCK.177	NORLAN	90/14	1–3 pdr Net =WW II.	2.15–1920
2425	INS.248	NORTHERN SCOT	90/11	1–3 pdr Net =in WW II.	5.15–1919
2022	ME.244	NORTHESK =NORTHESK II 12.15	100/13	1–12 pdr Net =in WW II.	7.15–1919
3070	YH.610	NULLI SECUNDUS	104/17	1–6 pdr	12.17–1920
249	YH.365	OAK APPLE	98/10	1–2½ pdr PB =in WW II.	9.14–1920
1073	YH.719	OAKLAND	67/10	1–6 pdr AA Net	1.15–1919
2508	BF.471	OBERON =OBERON II 12.15	86/07	1–6 pdr Net	4.15–1919
3113	BCK.355	OBTAIN	105/17	1–6 pdr =in WW II.	12.17–1919
1551	WY.165	OBURN	93/12	1–6 pdr AA Net =GIRL PAMELA in WW II.	7.15–1919
2466	KY.208	OCEAN ANGLER	84/11	1–6 pdr Net, M/S	2.15–1919
231	YH.876	OCEAN CREST	88/11	1–3 pdr PB, Escort	9.14–1919
233	YH.29	OCEAN CREST II	99/14	1–6 pdr AA PB	9.14–1919
245	YH.239	OCEAN FAVOURITE	99/13	1–6 pdr PB	9.14–1919
234	YH.345	OCEAN FISHER	96/13	1–3 pdr PB Mined 16.6.18 off Haddock Bank Buoy.	9.14–6.18
1954	YH.970	OCEAN FOAM	90/11	1–3 pdr PB Sunk 7.10.18 in collision in Penzance Bay.	3.15–10.18
1333	LT.184	OCEAN GAIN	77/15	1–6 pdr =in WW II.	12.17–1919
2557	FR.563	OCEAN GIFT	91/07	1–3 pdr Net	2.15–1919
2012	BF.600	OCEAN GLEANER	86/13	1–3 pdr Net, M/S	1.15–1920
238	YH.24	OCEAN GUIDE	75/14	1–3 pdr PB =in WW II.	9.14–1919
247	YH.305	OCEAN HARVEST	95/13	1–6 pdr PB	9.14–1919
244	YH.732	OCEAN HOPE	81/12	1–3 pdr PB, Escort	9.14–1919
227	YH.325	OCEAN PILOT	95/13	1–3 pdr PB, Escort =in WW II.	9.14–1919
1334	YH.19	OCEAN PIONEER	90/15	1–6 pdr =in WW II.	9.17–1919
250	YH.792	OCEAN PLOUGH	99/12	PB Mined 27.8.16 off Lowestoft.	9.14–8.16
2364	FR.104	OCEAN PRIDE	95/11	1–3 pdr AA Net =in WW II.	1.15–1920
246	YH.725	OCEAN RAMBLER	96/14	1–6 pdr AA PB, Hydro	9.14–1919
232	YH.470	OCEAN REAPER	101/12	1–3 pdr PB, Hydro tender	9.14–1919
239	YH.307	OCEAN RETRIEVER	94/12	1–6 pdr PB =in WW II.	9.14–1919
235	YH.33	OCEAN RETRIEVER II	94/14	1–6 pdr PB	9.14–1920
243	YH.730	OCEAN REWARD	95/12	1–6 pdr AA PB, Hydro =in WW II.	9.14–1919
3044	YH.497	OCEAN ROAMER	90/17	1–6 pdr AA	6.17–1919
	LT.10	OCEAN SCOUT	86/13	Exam =in WW II.	1.16–1920
2261	FR.75	OCEAN SEARCHER	83/12	1–6 pdr Net	2.15–1919
1032	YH.264	OCEAN SPRAY	82/12	1–6 pdr Net =in WW II.	1.15–1920
785	BF.960	OCEAN STAR	92/07	PB Sunk 26.9.17 off the Nab LV, probably mined.	12.14–9.17
228	YH.574	OCEAN TREASURE	92/13	1–6 pdr PB =in WW II.	9.14–1919
	YH.160	OCEAN TRUST	77/14	Misc Service	10.18–1919

Adty No.	Port No.	Name	TG/Yr	Armament, Fate, etc.	Service
789	FR.220	OCEANIC =OCEANIC III 2.15	99/07	1-6 pdr M/S	12.14-1919
2205	PD.122	OLIVE	89/06	1-3 pdr Net, M/S	1.16-1919
3154	BF.1554	OLIVE =OLIVE II 8.15	60/04	Net	5.15-1919
2035	BF.282	OLIVE III	83/06	1-6 pdr Net	8.15-1920
2409	KY.220	OLIVE LEAF	82/07	1-3 pdrAA Net	4.15-1919
2150	BCK.61	OLYMPUS	58/10	1-6 pdrAA Net	4.15-1920
2302	BF.919	ONWARD =ONWARD II 8.15	94/07	1-6 pdrAA Net =ONWARD II in WW II.	5.15-1919
	PD.40	ONWARD III	63/02		7.17-1920
	INS.291	OPTIMISTIC	95/07	BDV	8.15-1919
	INS.148	ORD HILL	90/10	BDV	7.15-1919
1894	LT.859	ORIENT II	93/11	1-57 mm Net	9.15-1919
2280	BF.368	ORION =ORION II 5.15	70/06	1-6 pdrAA Net, M/S	4.15-1919
1860	LT.1076	OSPREY	82/07	1-6 pdrAA Net	9.15-1919
2978	YH.34	OSWY	95/16	1-6 pdrAA Net	11.16-1920
2206	LT.492	OUR ALLIES	91/15	1-57 mm Net	8.15-1920
3239	LT.72	OUR FRIEND	86/13	1-6 pdrAA Net	12.15-1919
1566	LT.1149	PAISIBLE	90/11	1-6 pdrAA Net	7.15-1919
2135 1413	YH.680	PAMELA	79/02	(ex-Twenty Seven) 1-3 pdr Net	3.15-1919
2470	BCK.18	PANOPIA	77/08	1-6 pdr Net	2.15-1920
	WK.578	PANSY =PLUMER 8.18	58/02	Misc Service	7.15-1919
3215	BF.1312	PANSY II	67/03	Net, HS	8.15-1919
2024	ME.203	PANSY III	91/07	Net, Tender	12.15-1919
757	YH.710	PARADOX II	73/10	1-6 pdrAA Net	1.15-1919
2855	BF.500	PARAGON =PARAGON II 3.17	83/06	1-3 pdr Net, M/S =in WW II.	5.15-1919
G 1295	LT.1116	PARAMOUNT	95/11	1-6 pdrAA PB, M/S =in WW II.	12.14-1919
	BCK.162	PAX VOBISCUM	84/13	Exam =SCOTCH THISTLE in WW II.	1.16-1920
1008	LT.1114	PAXTON	92/11	1-6 pdrAA Net =in WW II.	1.15-1919
2484	PD.130	PEACE	83/07	1-6 pdr Net, M/S	3.15-1919
1912	LT.768	PEACEMAKER =in WW II.	89/11	1-6 pdr Net, M/S	10.15-1919
2306	LT.461	PEARL III	72/06	1-57 mm Net	12.15-1919
1824	LT.638	PECHEUR	67/10	Net Sunk 3.4.16 in collision off Smalls Light.	8.15-4.16
1315	PD.149	PEGGY	100/07	1-6 pdr Net	6.15-1919
2722	CE.227	PELAGIA	84/00	(ex-Thirty-four ex-Three) Mined 28.11.16 off the Nab LV.	10.15-11.16
2045	FR.401	PENNAN	64/10	1-3 pdr Net, Exam	8.15-1919
2001	BF.428	PERILIA	83/12	1-6 pdrAA Net	1.15-1919
1003	LT.42	PERSISTIVE	82/08	Net Mined 9.2.16 off Dover.	1.15-2.16
	PD.210	PETERUGIE	81/15	BDV, Mooring tender	9.15-1919
2488	BF.914	PETREL	86/07	1-6 pdrAA Net	3.15-1919
1895	LT.199	PEVENSEY CASTLE	101/13	1-6 pdr Net	9.15-1919
2111	FR.211	PHILORTH	100/07	1-3 pdr Net Foundered 24.2.19 en route from Syra to Malta.	1.15-2.19
599	FR.296	PHINGASK =JULIUS 10.19	97/08	1-6 pdrAA M/S, Depot	12.14-1920
3056	GY.578	PHYLLIS MARY	94/17	1-6 pdr =in WW II.	9.17-1919
1103	LT.353	PILOT ME	83/09	1-6 pdrAA Net	2.15-1919
1830	LT.1060	PILOT STAR	92/07	1-6 pdr Net	8.15-1919
1159	YH.390	PIMPERNEL	88/09	1-6 pdr Net =PHYLLIS ROSE in WW II.	3.15-1919
2724	PD.54	PIONEER III	95/93	1-3 pdr Net, Exam	12.15-1919
	SH.188	PISCATOR	53/99	Gunnery tender	1.17-1919

Adty No.	Port No.	Name	TG/Yr	Armament, Fate, etc.	Service
2760	BK.26	PISCATOR =PISCATOR II 9.17	83/07	1-6 pdrAA Net	4.15-1919
3300	YH.762	PISCATORIAL II	93/16	1-6 pdr Net Disappeared 29.12.17 off Newhaven.	8.16-12.17
	BF.882	PISCES	94/07	Misc Service	1.16-1919
793	INS.357	PITBLAE	93/08	1-3 pdr M/S, BDV =GUIDE US in WW II.	12.14-1919
2449	INS.11	PITGAVENY	88/09	1-6 pdr Net, M/S	5.15-1919
2113	FR.544	PITTENDRUM	84/13	1-3 pdrAA Net	1.15-1919
2390	FR.221	PITULLIE	99/07	1-3 pdr Net, M/S	2.15-1919
1814	LT.553	PLACEO	83/10	1-6 pdrAA Net	7.15-1919
1400	BF.453	PLANTIN	84/12	1-3 pdr Net Mined 26.4.17 off Standfast Point.	4.15-4.17
1898	LT.1079	PLAYMATES	93/07	1-6 pdr Net	9.15-1919
1966	SH.168	PLEASANCE	80/09	1-6 pdrAA Net	12.15-1919
567	YH.350	PLEASANTS	86/13	1-6 pdrAA Net	3.15-1919
2733	FR.489	PLEIADES	90/07	1-6 pdrAA Net	11.15-1920
1909	LT.1177	PLOUGHBOY	102/12	1-3 pdrAA Net =in WW II.	9.15-1920
	BCK.175	POPPY =RECLUSE 8.18	76/02	(ex-*Thirty Six*) Exam	7.15-1920
	BCK.157	POSEIDON	96/13	Misc Service =in WW II.	1.16-1919
2736	SH.152	PREMIER II	71/06	1-6 pdr Net, M/S	5.16-1919
1565	LT.89	PRESENT FRIENDS	89/14	1-6 pdrAA Net =in WW II.	7.15-1919
222	LT.1120	PRESENT HELP	82/11	1-3 pdr M/S, PB =in WW II.	9.14-1919
	LT.323	PRESENTER	106/15	Minefields tender	10.16-1919
2152	BCK.7	PRESS HOME	77/08	Net	5.15-1920
2151	BCK.156	PRESTIGE	81/07	1-6 pdr Net	4.15-1919
76	KY.121	PRESTON	84/06	1-6 pdrAA Net	7.15-1919
2125	KY.218	PRIDE O'FIFE	83/07	1-6 pdr Net, M/S	2.15-1919
2381	PD.529	PRIDE OF BUCHAN	86/08	Net	2.15-1919
2423	BCK.78	PRIDE OF BUCKIE	79/10	1-6 pdr Net	5.15-1919
1249	SH.215	PRIDE OF FILEY	87/07	(ex-*Emulator*) 1-6 pdrAA Net, Exam	5.15-1919
2442	INS.71	PRIDE OF MORAY	50/09	Transport, Water carrier =in WW II.	5.15-1919
2289	BCK.185	PRIME	101/14	1-3 pdr AA Net =in WW II.	2.15-1919
1925	LT.345	PRIMEVERE	100/14	1-3 pdrAA Net =in WW II.	10.15-1920
	LT.1016	PRIMROSE	88/06	BDV, Water carrier	9.15-1920
2123	KY.163	PRIMROSE =PRIMROSE II 8.15	87/07	1-3 pdr Net	2.15-1919
2052	PD.238	PRIMROSE III	89/15	Fleet tender =FAWN in WW II.	12.15-1919
1116	LT.462	PRINCE ALBERT	64/02	Net	3.15-4.15
990	LK.588	PRINCESS OF SANDWICK	50/07	Net	4.15-1919
604	PD.520	PRINCIPAL	91/08	1-6 pdrAA PB, Net, Q ship =in WW II.	9.14-1919
1427	LT.257	PROCEED	64/01	1-3 pdrAA Net, Exam	3.15-1919
2181	BF.257	PRODUCTIVE	73/06	1-6 pdrAA Net	6.15-1920
	BF.508	PROFICIENCY	82/13	BDV	12.15-1920
2421	BF.956	PROGRESS II	84/07	1-3 pdr Net =APPLE TREE in WW II.	8.15-1919
	BCK.15	PROMOTIVE	78/08	HS =in WW II.	9.18-1919
1039	LT.232	PROSIT	77/06	1-6 pdr Net, M/S	1.15-1919
1418	LT.54	PROSPECT	58/02	Net	3.15-8.15
2260	BF.247	PROSPECTIVE	75/10	1-6 pdr Net	3.15-1919
2753	BK.15	PROSPERITY	72/06	1-6 pdr Net	4.15-1919
2160	BF.649	PROSPERITY =PROSPERITY II 8.15	64/01	1-57 mm Net	5.15-1920
1392	BF.511	PROTECT	98/07	1-3 pdrAA Net Mined 16.3.17 off Dover.	4.15-3.17
2379	PD.517	PROTECT ME	88/08	1-3 pdr Net, M/S	2.15-1919

Adty. No.	Port No.	Name	TG/Yr	Armament, Fate, etc.	Service
1859	LT.143	PROTECTOR	58/02	Net	9.15–1919
1904	YH.999	PROVIDER	99/07	1–3 pdrAA Net	1.16–1919
2124	KY.152	PURSUIT	79/07	Net Sunk 22.4.18 in collision off Penzance.	2.15–4.18
2048	FR.532	Q. E. F.	89/07	1–3 pdr Net, PB	8.15–1920
2414	BCK.181	QUARRY KNOWE	98/14	1–57 mm Net Sunk 15.5.17 by Austrian cruisers off Fano Island, Adriatic.	5.15–5.17
2851	FR.169	QUEEN =QUEEN III 6.15	93/06	1–6 pdrAA Net	4.15–1919
2996	LT.914	QUEEN MOTHER	126/16	1–6 pdr M/S	2.17–1920
3061	YH.580	QUEEN OF THE FLEET	96/17	1–6 pdr =in WW II.	9.17–1919
1823	LT.203	QUI SAIT	83/09	1–57 mm Net	8.15–1919
1077	LT.465	QUICK SET	78/09	Net, Exam	1.15–1919
1549	SN.83	QUINTIA	90/14	1–6 pdr =in WW II.	7.15–1919
1074	YH.770	R. MACKAY	73/10	1–6 pdrAA Net	1.15–1919
2702	BF.382	RACER II	84/06	1–6 pdr Net	8.15–1919
2737	INS.321	RADIANT =RADIANT II 3.17	95/07	1–6 pdr Net, M/S	5.16–1919
1142	YH.553	RAMBLING ROSE	59/09	Net	3.15–1919
2448	BCK.122	RANNAS	85/07	(ex-Silver Thyme) Net, Tender	5.15–1919
992	BCK.39	RATHVEN	87/08	1–6 pdr M/S	12.14–1920
1026	LT.1126	REALITY	87/11	1–3 pdr Net	1.15–1919
1024	LT.365	REALIZE	103/14	1–3 pdrAA Net, M/S	1.15–1920
R 1303	LT.1082	REAPER	90/07	1 6 pdrAA PB, Escort	12.14–1919
3116	LT.78	RECEPTIVE	86/13	1–6 pdr Stores carrier =in WW II.	1.16–1919
L 1298	LT.227	RECLAIM	95/13	1–6 pdrAA PB, M/S	12.14–1919
1419	LT.509	RECOMPENSE	58/02	Net	3.15–1919
	BCK.212	RECRUIT	94/15	BDV, HS	8.15–1920
2358	FR.419	REDRIFT	97/08	1–6 pdrAA Net	1.15–1920
205	LT.1171	REDWALD	80/12	1–3 pdr M/S, PB	9.14–1919
230	YH.738	REED	99/11	1–6 pdrAA PB, Hydro =in WW II.	9.14–1919
1839	LT.757	REGAIN	87/14	1–6 pdrAA Net	8.15–1919
	BCK.49	REGENT BIRD	88/09	BDV =in WW II.	12.15–1919
2044	ML.337	REJOICE	83/15	1–3 pdr Net, M/S	8.15–1919
	BF.1524	RELIANCE	75/04	BDV, Mooring tender	7.15–1920
2175	BF.1590	RELIANCE =RELIANCE III 8.15	67/03	1–6 pdrAA Net	5.15–1919
1112	LT.544	REMEMBRANCE	82/10	1–3 pdr Net, M/S	2.15–1919
1556 2203	SN.51	RENE	89/14	Net, Tender =in WW II.	7.15–1919
1058	LT.307	RENOVATE	81/09	1–6 pdrAA Net	1.15–1920
1384	PD.42	RENOWN =RENOWN II 12.15	86/04	1–6 pdr Net	4.15–1919
2356	BF.530	REPLENISH	83/13	1–3 pdr Net	1.15–1919
2212	FR.556	RESOLUTE	90/04	1–3 pdr Net	4.15–1919
	INS.444	RESOLUTE	82/07	BDV	7.15–3.16
	BF.19	RESPLENDENT	100/14	Misc Service	1.16–1919
1021	LT.1200	RESTART	79/12	1–3 pdr Net, HS =in WW II.	1.15–1919
2804	KY.149	RESTLESS WAVE	84/07	1–3 pdr Net =in WW II.	4.15–1919
1826	LT.215	RESTORE	93/14	Net Sunk 12.10.15 by S/M gunfire in Otranto Strait.	8.15–10.15
	BCK.139	RESULT =ALLENBY 8.18	63/03	Tender	1.16–1919
223	LT.1096	RETRIEVER =RETRIEVER II 12.15	90/07	1–6 pdr PB	9.14–1919

Adty No.	Port No.	Name	TG/Yr	Armament, Fate, etc.	Service
1401 981	LT.463	REWARD	78/06	1–3 pdr AA Net	4.15–1919
	BCK.92	RIG	96/11	Tender =in WW II.	1.16–1919
2168	INS.188	RISING SUN	81/06	1–6 pdr Net	5.15–1919
2473	PD.347	RIVAL =RIVAL II 12.15	95/07	1–3 pdr Net =in WW II.	2.15–1920
2450	BF.1321	ROBIN	86/03	1–2½ pdr Net, M/S	5.15–1919
745	WY.137	ROBURN	83/11	Net Sunk 27.10.16 by German destroyers in the Dover Straits.	1.15–10.16
	BCK.162	ROCHOMIE	79/10	BDV =in WW II.	7.15–1919
2807	PD.157	ROCK DAISY	77/01	(ex-*Nineteen*) 1–3 pdr Net	4.15–1919
2754	BK.33	RODNEY II	81/07	1–3 pdr AA Net	5.15–1919
1	LT.53	ROOKE	84/08	1–6 pdr PB Sunk 3.8.16 in collision off Deal.	12.14–8.16
	INS.345	ROOSEVELT	97/07	BDV	9.15–1920
	INS.285	ROSE	81/07	BDV Collier	11.15–1920
1030	YH.971	ROSE III	91/07	1–6 pdr Net	1.15–1919
	BCK.35	ROSE III	88/08	BDV	11.15–1919
2033	PD.389	ROSE V	77/00	BDV Collier, Stores carrier	8.15–1920
3071	YH.875	ROSE & GLADYS	93/17	1–6 pdr AA	12.17–1919
	BF.108	ROSE O'DOUNE	64/10	Submarine depot	1.16–1919
	PD.528	ROSEBINE	72/01	(ex-*Five*) BDV Repair vessel	1.16–1919
779	PD.176	ROSEBUD	100/07	1–3 pdr M/S =in WW II.	11.14–1919
2197	BCK.6	ROSEDALE	93/07	1–6 pdr Net	12.16–1919
2268	FR.71	ROSEHALL	72/09	(ex-*G. A. W.*) 1–6 pdr AA Net	1.15–1919
2266	FR.565	ROSEHEARTY	82/13	1–3 pdr Net, M/S	2.15–1919
1114	LT.1178	ROSEMMA	92/12	1–6 pdr AA Net =in WW II.	2.15–1919
1812	LT.1198	ROSEVINE	100/13	1–3 pdr AA Net Sunk 24.5.17 in collision off Great Yarmouth.	7.15–5.17
988	BF.77	ROSIEBURN	56/09	Net	4.15–1919
2172	BCK.14	ROSIES	84/08	Net Sunk 26.8.16 by A/C bomb in Otranto Strait.	5.15–8.16
	KY.97	ROTHESAY BAY	101/97	BDV	10.15–1.16
1064	LT.1041	ROULETTE	81/07	1–6 pdr AA Net	1.15–1919
	LK.385	ROVA HEAD	58/03	(ex-*Foxglove*) Stores and Water carrier	6.15–6.16
1125	A.363	ROYAL BANK	90/06	(ex-*Nike*) 1–57 mm Net Purchased, sold 1921.	3.15–1921
2477	BF.394	ROYAL BURGH	78/11	1–6 pdr Net	2.15–1919
2038	BF.364	RUBY GEM	76/11	1–6 pdr Net, M/S	7.15–1919
	LT.361	RULER OF THE SEAS	86/09	BDV Tender =KIDDAW in WW II.	9.15–1920
1857	LT.1187	S. D. J.	100/12	1–6 pdr AA, 1–2 pdr Net	9.15–1919
1911	LT.28	SAILOR KING	89/14	1–6 pdr Net, M/S =in WW II.	10.15–1920
2005	INS.86	ST. AETHENS	76/14	1–3 pdr Net, M/S, PB	1.15–1919
1256	KY.122	ST. AYLES	78/06	1–6 pdr AA Net	5.15–1919
2401	FR.298	ST. COMBS	90/08	1–3 pdr Net	2.15–1919
2119	FR.81	ST. COMBS HAVEN	89/14	1–3 pdr Net	1.15–1919
1563	LT.226	SAM RICHARDS	88/13	1–6 pdr AA Net	8.15–1919
1160	YH.837	SANTORA	90/11	1–6 pdr Net	3.15–1919
	INS.391	SAPPHIRE =SHALOT 8.18	95/07	HS	1.15–1919
2049	PD.100	SARA	62/02	Net, Water carrier	10.15–1919
1929	LT.1119	SARAH MARIAN	89/11	1–6 pdr Net	9.15–1919
739	LT.1021	SAREPTA =WELCOME FRIEND 7.18	89/06	1–6 pdr AA Net	1.15–1919
2986	LT.745	SCANIA	88/16	Net Sunk 2.8.18 in collision in the Dover Straits.	12.16–8.18

Adty No.	Port No.	Name	TG/Yr	Armament, Fate, etc.	Service
1257	KY.139	SCOT =SCOT II 6.15	79/03	1–6 pdrAA Net	5.15–1919
987	BCK.67	SCOTCH GIRL	76/10	1–6 pdrAA Net	4.15–1919
2392	INS.430	SCOTSMAN =SCOTSMAN II 2.18	88/07	1–6 pdr Net	1.15–1919
2805	BCK.79	SCOTTISH CHIEF	78/10	1–6 pdr Net, M/S	4.15–1919
1062	LT.522	SEA FLOWER =SEA FLOWER II 3.15	80/06	1–6 pdrAA, 1–2 pdr Net	1.15–1919
1123	LT.290	SEARCHER =SEARCHER II 2.18 =ATTENTIVE II 5.18 =SEARCHER 5.19	59/08	1–3 pdr Net	2.15–1920
158	YH.2	SEDULOUS	100/12	1–47 mm Net =in WW II.	1.15–1920
2711	PD.123	SELBY	75/03	1–57 mm Net Sunk 15.5.17 by Austrian cruisers off Fano Island, Adriatic.	10.15–5.17
1085	YH.577	SELECT	74/10	1–3 pdr Net Sunk 16.4.18 in collision off St. Govan's Light Buoy.	1.15–4.18
1411	YH.117	SELINA	98/07	1–47 mm Net	3.15–1919
2750	LT.664	SENTINEL STAR	102/16	1–3 pdr Net =in WW II.	11.16–1919
2186	BCK.74	SERENE	86/07	(ex-*Sublime*) 1–47 mm Net Sunk 15.5.17 by Austrian cruisers off Fano Island, Adriatic.	6.15–5.17
2301	BF.1108	SERENITY	81/08	1–6 pdrAA Net, M/S	5.15–1920
2424	BF.946	SHEILA	83/07	1–3 pdr Net	5.15–1919
2121	FR.561	SHEPHERD BOY	81/13	1–3 pdr Net, M/S	1.15–1919
1858	H.723	SHETLAND	77/03	1–3 pdrAA Net	5.15–1919
2765	BK.317	SHIELD	96/07	1–6 pdrAA Net	4.15–1919
1880	H.528	SHIELDS	72/01	1–6 pdrAA Net	10.15–1919
1436	LT.1134	SHIPMATES	82/11	1–6 pdr, 1–6 pdrAA Net =in WW II.	4.15–1919
1893	LT.1145	SILVER HERRING	86/11	1–6 pdr Net	9.15–1919
1509	LT.1034	SILVER KING	81/07	1–6 pdrAA Net	5.15–1919
217	LT.1179	SILVER LINE	92/12	1–3 pdr PB, M/S =in WW II.	9.14–1919
3209	BF.327	SILVER PEARL	71/11	1–6 pdr AA Net	8.15–1920
	LT.145	SILVER PRINCE	108/13	BDV Collier =in WW II.	9.15–1919
764	LT.655	SILVER QUEEN	84/10	1–3 pdrAA Net Sunk 15.2.18 by German destroyers in the Dover Straits.	1.15–2.18
1166 985	YH.175	SILVER SPRAY	61/07	Net =in WW II.	3.15–1919
1426	LT.1077	SILVERDALE	62/07	1–3 pdrAA Net, Exam	3.15–1919
	BF.353	SILVERFORD	85/11	BDV Water carrier, Repairs	7.15–1920
69	LH.12	SILVERSCALE	91/11	Net	1.15–1919
2252	A.550	SILVERY DAWN	95/07	(ex-*St. Mungo*) 1–6 pdr Net, M/S	12.14–1920
1476	LT.135	SILVERY HARVEST	86/13	1–3 pdr Net Sunk 16.5.18 in collision off Berry Head.	5.15–5.18
1900	LT.507	SILVERY WAVE	96/15	Net Wrecked 13.11.15 in Crow Sound.	9.15–11.15
2983	LT.681	SINCERE	92/16	1–3 pdr Net, M/S	12.16–1919
1485	YH.596	SIXTEEN	78/01	1–3 pdr Net, BDV	4.15–1919
	INS.160	SKIBO CASTLE	81/10	BDV Stores carrier & PB	7.15–1919
2016	BF.7	SLAINS CASTLE	81/08	1–3 pdr Net, M/S, PB	3.15–1919
3240	LT.594	SMILAX	81/10	1–3 pdr Net	12.15–1920
2422	BF.34	SNOWDROP =SNOWDROP II 8.15	68/05	Net, HS	5.15–1919
1782	PD.501	SNOWDROP =SNOWDROP III 8.15	94/07	1–6 pdr Net	5.15–1919
3251	YH.647	SNOWDROP IV	63/01	1–6 pdrAA Net	1.16–1919

Adty No.	Port No.	Name	TG/Yr	Armament, Fate, etc.	Service
	LT.672	SNOWDROP =SNOWDROP V 9.17	62/05	Exam	4.16–1919
2721	M.60	SOUTH TYNE	79/04	1–3 pdr Net	12.15–1919
2021	ME.195	SOUTHESK	93/12	Net Mined 7.7.17 in Auskerry Sound.	7.15–7.17
2562	PD.120	SPARKLING STAR	90/06	1–6 pdrAA Net	2.15–1919
1099	LT.1110	SPECULATION	83/11	1–6 pdr Net	2.15–1919
	PD.491	SPEEDWELL =GODSPEED 4.18	79/03	BDV	1.16–1919
2154	FR.201	SPEEDWELL =SPEEDWELL III 6.15	96/07	1–6 pdrAA Net =ALTRUIST in WW II.	5.15–1920
2264	BF.328	SPEEDWELL V	92/11	Net Stranded 28.10.16 on Splaugh Rock near Greenore Point.	2.15–10.16
1161	YH.817	SPERANZA	86/11	1–6 pdr Net, M/S =in WW II.	3.15–1919
2015	BF.601	SPEY BAY	86/07	1–3 pdr Net, M/S	3.15–1919
1928	YH.475	SPHINX =SPHINX II 9.17	77/07	1–6 pdrAA Net, Exam	10.15–1920
1089	LT.88	SPOTLESS PRINCE	85/08	Net Sunk 27.10.16 by German destroyers in the Dover Straits.	2.15–10.16
2262	BF.75	SPRIG OF HEATHER	86/14	Net =in WW II.	2.15–1919
1462	YH.735	SPRING FLOWER	59/02	1–3 pdr Net	4.15–1919
787	FR.534	STAR OF BUCHAN	81/13	PB Mined 20.10.15 off the Nab Buoy.	1.15–10.15
2019	PD.222	STAR OF FAITH	94/15	1–3 pdr Net, M/S	7.15–1919
	WK.76	STAR OF HOPE	56/02	Misc Service =in WW II.	3.16–1919
1133	LT.55	STAR OF THULE	91/13	1–3 pdr Net	3.15–1919
2183	BF.1553	STATELY	72/04	1–6 pdrAA Net	5.15–1919
	BCK.65	STERLOCHY	78/10	Misc Service	4.16–1919
	BF.214	STRATHLENE	81/06	Tender	1.16–1920
	INS.239	STRENUOUS	77/11	BDV =in WW II.	9.15–1920
2110	INS.326	SUBLIME	78/07	1–2½ pdr Net, M/S	1.15–1919
2904	BF.446	SUBLIME =SUBLIME II 7.15	86/03	1–6 pdr Net, M/S =in WW II.	4.15–1920
	BF.1399	SUCCEED	77/03	Misc Service	1.16–1919
	BF.1459	SUCCESS	88/04	BDV	7.15–1919
2405	KY.6	SUFFOLK COUNTY	88/07	(ex-*Spearmint*) 1–3 pdr Net	4.15–1919
2093	LK.367	SUMBURGH HEAD	81/06	(ex-*Superb*) Misc, HS	6.15–1919
2440	BCK.126	SUMMERTON	83/12	1–3 pdr Net, M/S	5.15–1919
2163	BF.1551	SUNBEAM	72/04	Exam, Net, Hydro T/S	5.15–1920
	WK.104	SUNBEAM I	75/04	Exam Sunk 16.4.18 in collision at Inchkeith.	1.16–4.18
2973	YH.279	SUNBEAM II	85/16	1–6 pdr Net =in WW II.	10.16–1919
	WK.638	SUNBEAM II =SUNDORA 8.18	79/03	Collier & Tender	1.16–1919
	WK.91	SUNNY DEVON	61/01	Minefields tender	7.15–1919
2185	BF.167	SUNNYSIDE	80/10	1–6 pdr Net, M/S	6.15–1919
2089	SH.234	SUNSHINE =SUNSHINE II 6.17	60/05	BDV	3.15–1919
2500	BF.510	SUNSHINE =SUNSHINE III 10.17	89/07	1–6 pdr Net, M/S	3.15–1919
3244	LT.750	SUPERNAL	83/10	1–3 pdr Net	1.16–1920
	BF.1028	SUPPORT	100/07	BDV	7.15–1919
1118	LT.119	SUPPORTER	88/14	1–6 pdr Net =in WW II.	2.15–1919
	BCK.127	SURMOUNT	96/12	BDV	7.15–1920
2704	BF.637	SUSANNA	83/07	Net Foundered 14.12.15 off Milford Haven.	8.15–12.15

Adty No.	Port No.	Name	TG/Yr	Armament, Fate, etc.	Service
	WK.325	SUSIE ROSS	52/00	Misc Service	1.16–1919
204	LT.63	SUSSEX COUNTY	83/08	1–6 pdr M/S, PB Purchased, sold 1921. =in WW II.	9.14–1921
2443	BF.1539	SWALLOW =SWALLOW III 6.15	87/04	1–3 pdr Net, M/S =in WW II.	5.15–1919
2153	YH.924	SWEET PEA	73/12	1–3 pdrAA Net	4.15–1919
2026	ME.167	SWIFT II	101/07	1–6 pdr Net, M/S	7.15–1919
2420	BF.496	SWIFTWING	98/12	1–6 pdr Net =in WW II.	5.15–1919
2155	FR.212	TAITS	93/07	1–57 mm Net Sunk 15.5.17 by Austrian cruisers off Fano Island, Adriatic.	5.15–5.17
68	SH.1	TARLAIR	80/08	1–3 pdr Misc, Hydro tender	1.15–1919
2267	BF.330	TEA ROSE	84/11	1–6 pdr Net =in WW II.	1.15–1919
1052	YH.511	TEN	84/10	1–3 pdr Net	1.15–1920
1853	LT.339	TERRITORIAL	80/09	1–6 pdrAA Net	9.15–1919
237	YH.769	TESSIE	87/11	1–6 pdrAA PB, Net =in WW II.	9.14–1919
225	LT.1048	TEST =TEST II 2.15	91/07	1–6 pdrAA PB, Net, BDV	9.14–1919
	BCK.183	THAINS	87/14	Misc Service =AURILIA in WW II.	1.16–1919
	LT.1035	THANKFUL	55/07	Exam	2.16–1919
737	LT.476	THE BOYS	92/14	1–6 pdr Net, M/S =in WW II.	1.15–1919
2382	PD.526	THE BRAE	77/08	1–3 pdr Net	2.15–1920
2468	BF.1140	THE COLONEL	80/08	1–6 pdr Net, Stores & Water	2.15–1920
1033	YH.25	THE MAJESTY	99/14	1–6 pdr Net =FELLOWSHIP in WW II.	4.15–1919
1432	YH.878	THE PRINCE	77/04	1–6 pdr Net	4.15–1920
1091	YH.897	THE PRINCESS	77/04	1–3 pdr Net, BDV	2.15–1919
	INS.545	THE PROVOST	93/08	BDV =in WW II.	7.15–1919
1492	YH.879	THE QUEEN	65/04	1–6 pdrAA Net, HS	5.15–1919
1884	YH.234	THE THRONE	99/13	1–6 pdrAA Net	9.15–1919
2352	BF.620	THERMOPYLAE	84/13	1–3 pdr Net =in WW II.	1.15–1919
2075	YH.693	THIRTY	80/02	BDV, Misc Service	9.15–1920
2090	YH.709	THIRTY TWO	80/02	BDV	9.15–1920
2740	LT.495	THISTLE	70/04	Net	5.16–1919
2491	FR.236	THISTLE =THISTLE II 5.15	87/07	1–6 pdrAA Net	3.15–1919
1433	YH.829	THISTLE III	79/04	1–6 pdrAA Net =in WW II.	5.15–1919
2861	INS.163	THISTLE =THISTLE IV 6.15	71/06	Net Sunk 30.6.15 in collision off Great Orme's Head.	5.15–6.15
2032	PD.390	THISTLE V	77/00	BDV	8.15–6.18
	YH.692	THOMAS BEECHING	99/12	BDV, Misc Service	9.15–1919
1101	YH.874	THREE	87/08	1–3 pdr Net	2.15–1919
1014	LT.736	THREE BOYS	84/10	1–3 pdr Net, M/S	1.15–1919
2419	BF.495	THREE KINGS	98/12	1–6 pdr Net =in WW II.	5.15–1919
2273	BF.1461	THRIVE	81/04	1–6 pdrAA Net	2.15–1919
2004	BCK.186	THRUSH =THRUSH III 2.15	92/07	1–6 pdr Net =in WW II.	1.15–1919
3110	LK.663	THULE ROCK	98/17	Hydro tender =LORD HOWARD in WW II.	6.17–1919
2366	INS.113	THYRSUS	75/10	1–6 pdr Net, M/S	1.15–1919
3117	BCK.195	TITANIA =TOTEM 6.18	92/06	1–6 pdr Misc Service	1.16–1919
1016	LT.609	TOGO	76/05	1–3 pdrAA Net	1.15–1919
	BF.103	TOKEN	89/14	Tender =in WW II.	1.16–1919
1854	LT.677	TORBAY II	83/10	1–3 pdr Net =TORBAY II in WW II.	9.15–1919

Adty No.	Port No.	Name	TG/Yr	Armament, Fate, etc.	Service
207	LT.1150	TOUCHWOOD	84/11	(ex-Merry Spinner) 1–3 pdr PB =MARINUS in WW II.	9.14–1919
2434	BF.497	TRANSIT	83/07	1–57 mm Net Sunk 15.5.17 by Austrian cruisers off Fano Island, Adriatic.	5.15–5.17
986	BCK.204	TREASURE	96/07	1–6 pdrAA Net	3.15–1919
2176	INS.603	TREASURE TROVE	83/08	1–6 pdr Net	5.15–1919
2040	BF.1049	TRIDENT =TRIDENT II 12.15	80/02	(ex-Thirty Five) 1–3 pdr Net	8.15–1919
2444	BF.631	TRIUMPH	90/07	Net, Fleet tender	5.15–1920
1412	YH.568	TRIUMPH =TRIUMPH II 5.15	90/07	1–6 pdrAA Net =in WW II.	3.15–1919
2283	INS.261	TROPHY	83/11	1–3 pdr Net =in WW II.	2.15–1919
	BF.543	TROPIC BIRD	96/07	BDV	7.15–1919
2281	FR.559	TROUP HEAD	86/13	1–6 pdrAA Net =in WW II.	2.15–1919
1891	LT.423	TRUE FRIEND	83/09	1–12 pdr Net =in WW II.	9.15–1919
	LT.172	TRUE REWARD	93/13	BDV Tender =in WW II.	9.15–1919
2007	INS.175	TRUST ON	79/11	1–3 pdr Net	1.15–1920
605	PD.177	TRUSTFUL	95/07	1–3 pdrAA PB, Net =in WW II.	9.14–1919
2441	BF.369	TRUSTFUL =TRUSTFUL II 6.15	87/06	Net	5.15–1919
T 1305	LT.1066	TRY AGAIN	97/07	1–6 pdrAA PB, M/S	12.14–1919
1252	SH.226	TRYPHENA	69/06	Net	5.15–1919
3245	LT.355	TUBEROSE	67/09	Net Mined 31.8.16 off Lowestoft.	1.16–8.16
2503	KY.201	TULIP =TULIP II 3.17	88/07	1–3 pdr Net Sunk 23.8.18 in collision off St. Anthony.	5.15–8.18
1484	YH.562	TWELVE	77/01	1–3 pdr Net, BDV	5.15–1919
1450	YH.681	TWENTY EIGHT	79/02	1–3 pdr Net	4.15–1920
1511	YH.691	TWENTY NINE	79/02	1–6 pdrAA Net	6.15–1919
1449	YH.678	TWENTY SIX	80/02	1–6 pdrAA Net, M/S	4.15–1919
1049	YH.211	TWO	91/07	1–6 pdrAA Net	1.15–1920
1508	LT.1157	TWO BOYS	91/11	1–6 pdr Net	5.15–1919
2263	BCK.160	TYNET	97/07	(ex-Commonwealth) 1–6 pdr Net	4.15–1919
596	FR.263	TYRIE	93/08	1–6 pdr =in WW II.	12.14–1919
2432	INS.405	UBEROUS	97/07	Net	5.15–1919
3155	BF.484	UBERTY	93/12	1–3 pdr Net =in WW II.	5.15–1919
2220	PD.231	UGIEBRAE	88/15	1–6 pdrAA, 1–2 pdr Net =in WW II.	9.15–1919
912	BF.395	UNIFLOROUS	78/11	1–3 pdr Net, M/S	1.15–1920
2159	BF.722	UNION	84/07	1–3 pdr Net	5.15–1920
	BCK.163	UNISON	79/10	BDV =in WW II.	7.15–1919
2126	KY.162	UNITY =UNITY II 5.15	80/07	1–6 pdr Net, Stores & Water	1.15–1919
784	BF.1568	UNITY =UNITY III 5.15	88/04	1–3 pdr M/S	12.14–1919
1874	YH.976	UNITY IV	56/02	1–3 pdrAA Net	9.15–1919
1477	SN.343	URSULA =URSULA II 7.16	72/02	1–3 pdr Net	5.15–1919
2720	M.72	VAL	93/09	1–3 pdrAA Net, HS	1.16–1919
1383	INS.240	VALE O'MORAY	89/11	1–6 pdr Net =in WW II.	2.15–1919
2411	BF.618	VALOROUS =VALOROUS II 2.17	84/07	1–3 pdr Net	4.15–1919
75	KY.693	VANGUARD III	83/04	1–3 pdr PB, Hydro tender	6.15–1919
1254	KY.199	VENUS II	87/07	1–6 pdr Net	5.15–1919
1865	LT.758	VERA CREINA	80/11	1–6 pdrAA Net	9.15–1919

Adty No.	Port No.	Name	TG/Yr	Armament, Fate, etc.	Service
1113	LT.685	VERACITY	96/10	1–3 pdr Net Sunk 15.2.18 by German destroyers in the Dover Straits.	2.15–2.18
2712	BF.448	VERDANT	87/06	1–6 pdr Net, M/S	9.15–1920
2188	FR.557	VERDURE	97/08	1–3 pdr Net	6.15–1919
1897	LT.237	VERITY =VERITAS 7.18	100/13	1–3 pdr Net	2.16–1919
1100	LT.94	VESPER STAR	79/04	(ex-*North Tyne*) 1–6 pdr Net, M/S	2.15–1919
2454	PD.560	VETERAN =VETERAN II 1.16	73/10	1–6 pdr Net	2.15–1919
1828	LT.1190	VICTOR & MARY	81/12	1–6 pdr Net	8.15–1919
763	LT.1056	VICTORIA =VICTORIA II 6.15	92/07	1–3 pdr Net	4.15–1919
2435	BCK.147	VICTORPID	91/03	(ex-*Victory*) 1–3 pdrAA Net	6.15–1919
2552	BF.669	VICTORY =VICTORSIT 4.15	82/07	1–3 pdr Net, M/S	3.15–1919
2156	BF.32	VICTORY =VICTORINE 6.15	88/05	Net	5.15–1919
1394	INS.4	VIGILANT III	87/07	1–6 pdrAA Net	4.15–1919
2351	BF.568	VIGOROUS	81/13	1–6 pdr Net Was to rename VIZIER 1.7.18, change cancelled 27.6.18.	1.15–1919
1482	YH.309	VIKING II	62/00	1–6 pdr Net	5.15–1919
2703	BF.886	VINE	95/07	1–3 pdr Net	8.15–1920
	KY.127	VINE =RED ROVER 8.18	77/04	BDV, Gunnery tender =in WW II.	9.15–1919
1803	BF.574	VINTAGE	80/07	1–6 pdrAA Net	4.15–1919
	BF.897	VIOLA =DYKE 8.18	83/07	Misc Service	1.17–1920
2729	BF.968	VIOLA III	86/07	1–57 mm Net	6.15–1919
70	LH.183	VIOLET =FIZZER 3.15	90/07	1–6 pdrAA Net, Q ship	8.14–1919
	BF.1474	VIOLET	86/04	BDV Accom	7.15–1920
	INS.286	VIOLET	82/07	BDV Collier	7.15–1920
568	KY.251	VIOLET II	84/07	1–6 pdrAA Net	2.15–1919
553	PD.133	VIOLET III	88/06	PB	11.15–1919
1920	YH.757	VIOLET & ROSE	92/12	1–6 pdr Net	10.15–1919
2374	PD.148	VIOLET FLOWER	87/14	1–3 pdr, 1–25 mm Net =in WW II.	4.15–1919
1391	FR.476	VIOLET MAY	74/06	1–6 pdrAA Net	4.15–1919
736	LT.1090	W. A. MASSEY	84/07	Net Mercantile loss 11.3.18.	1.15–10.15
1092 1961	YH.423	W. ELLIOTT	60/08	Net Sunk 15.2.18 by German destroyers in the Dover Straits.	2.15–2.18
	PD.473	W. H. LEASK	86/03	BDV	9.15–1919
1389	PD.150	W. J. R.	78/01	(ex-*Eighteen*) 1–3 pdr Net	5.15–1919
1522 2734	YH.174	W. P. G.	94/15	1–6 pdr	5.15–1919
	BCK.84	WALKERDALE	99/11	BDV =in WW II.	7.15–1920
	PD.498	WATCHFUL	88/03	BDV	9.15–1919
2171	BF.595	WATERLILY	82/07	Net Sunk 23.7.15 in collision off St. Alban's Head.	5.15–7.15
1878	YH.745	WAVENEY II	58/02	Net Sank 27.10.16 while in tow to Ramsgate after being disabled by German destroyers in the Dover Straits.	9.15–10.16
	INS.534	WEAL	93/08	BDV	7.15–1920
1012	LT.1039	WEAR =WEAR II 2.15	82/07	1–6 pdrAA Net	1.15–1919
1010	LT.11	WELCOME BOYS	92/08	1–57 mm Net	1.15–1919
1020	LT.375	WELCOME FRIEND =SAREPTA 7.18	94/14	1–3 pdr Net	1.15–1920
1098	LT.402	WELCOME HOME	77/06	1–3 pdr Net	2.15–1919

Adty No.	Port No.	Name	TG/Yr	Armament, Fate, etc.	Service
2170	FR.522	WELCOME STAR	81/07	1–6 pdrAA Net	5.15–1919
	BF.1296	WELFARE	79/03	BDV	7.15–1919
2299	INS.1	WELLAND =WELLAND II 5.15	72/06	1–3 pdr Net	3.15–1919
1903	LT.376	WELWYN	78/14	1–6 pdrAA Net, M/S =in WW II.	9.15–1919
3241	LT.480	WENLOCK	74/10	1–6 pdr Net	12.15–1920
	LT.250	WENSUM	56/01	Exam	2.16–1919
1825	LT.528	WEST ANGLIA	75/10	1–3 pdr Net, M/S	7.15–1919
2255	FR.459	WESTS	78/01	1–3 pdr Net, M/S	1.15–1919
	BF.205	WHEAT STALK =HECLA II 1.19	72/10	Stores & Water carrier =in WW II.	1.15–1919
	INS.149	WHINNIE KNOWE	91/10	BDV	7.15–1919
1255	KY.571	WHITE CROSS	101/96	1–6 pdr Net	5.15–1919
2852	BF.271	WHITE DAISY	79/10	1–3 pdr Net =in WW II.	5.15–1919
2174	BF.1144	WHITE LILAC	83/08	1–6 pdrAA Net	5.15–1920
	BCK.146	WHITE LILY	87/04	BDV	8.15–1919
2101	FR.558	WHITE OAK	75/13	1–6 pdr Net	1.15–1919
1810	BCK.120	WHITE ROSE	79/07	Net Sunk 26.7.16 in collision off Dover.	4.15–7.16
1247	KY.179	WHITE ROSE II	94/00	1–6 pdrAA Net	4.15–1919
2732	PD.232	WHITEHILL	90/15	1–6 pdrAA Net	11.15–1919
1258	KY.472	WILLIAM TENNANT	93/93	1–6 pdrAA Net Sunk 5.3.18 in collision off the Humber.	6.15–3.18
2368	FR.518	WILLOW BANK	80/09	1–6 pdr Net	1.15–1919
	PD.410	WINCHESTER =WINCHESTER II 2.18	94/07	Misc Service	1.15–1919
3153	BF.1805	WINNER	75/05	1–6 pdr Net	5.15–1919
	BF.912	WINSOME	80/07	1–3 pdr Exam	1.17–1919
218	LT.661	WISHFUL	83/10	1–6 pdrAA M/S, Net	9.14–1919
1250	SH.123	WITHAM	76/06	Net, Exam	5.15–1919
1868	LT.336	WIVENHOE	100/13	1–6 pdrAA Net	9.15–1919
3079	WY.225	WYDALE	102/17	1–6 pdr =in WW II.	5.18–1919
1962	WY.14	WYEBURN	94/14	1–6 pdrAA Net, M/S	12.15–1919
2047	BF.552	XERANTHEMUM	79/02	(ex-Twenty Five) Net	8.15–1919
1836	LT.765	XMAS DAISY	88/11	1–57 mm Net	8.15–1919
	BF.102	XMAS MORN	89/14	BDV =in WW II.	7.15–1919
1165 984	YH.291	YOUNG ARCHIE	60/08	Net, BDV	3.15–1919
1861	LT.457	YOUNG CROW	88/15	1–6 pdrAA, 1–2 pdr Net	9.15–1919
2747	A.665	YOUNG DAWN	86/16	1–6 pdr Net	6.16–1919
159	LT.141	YOUNG FISHERMAN	95/14	1–6 pdrAA Net =in WW II.	1.15–1920
1095	LT.717	YOUNG FRED	83/10	1–6 pdr Net	2.15–1919
996	PD.124	YOUNG HENRY	91/10	1–6 pdrAA M/S	12.14–1919
742	YH.479	YOUNG JOHN	100/14	1–6 pdrAA, 1–2 pdr Net =in WW II.	1.15–1919
1076	YH.697	YOUNG KENNETH	67/10	1–3 pdr Net, PB	1.15–1919
1916	LT.1174	YOUNG LINNET	93/12	1–57 mm, 1–25 mm Net Sunk 15.5.17 by Austrian cruisers off Fano Island, Adriatic.	9.15–5.17
1820	LT.1147	YOUNG MUN	87/11	1–6 pdr Net, M/S =in WW II.	7.15–1919
1416	LT.219	YOUNG ROLAND	57/08	1–6 pdr Net	3.15–1919
1474	LT.1175	YOUNG SID	100/12	1–12 pdr Net =in WW II.	5.15–1920
2157	SH.103	ZEBULON	94/14	1–3 pdr Net, M/S	4.15–1919
2305	BF.846	ZODIAC =ZOROASTER 7.18	80/07	1–6 pdrAA Net	5.15–1919
	WK.653	ZOE	65/01	Minefields tender	1.16–1919

MOTOR DRIFTERS

These hired motor fishing vessels were originally numbered in the same series as the smaller, high-speed motor boats, but they remained in service considerably longer. Most of the motor boats were released from service by autumn 1915 and on 22.9.16 the motor fishing vessels became part of the trawler section. Being of smaller size than steam drifters, they were used in more confined waters as harbour tenders and coastal service craft. This type probably stemmed from small sailing craft who were later fitted with motors. Many of these vessels did not have official registry numbers, nor was any gross tonnage figure available to indicate relative size. Some motor drifters did not appear in registers and the first indication of their existence came when they were taken into the navy.

Motor drifters and motor boats in service 1918 had their MB numbers cancelled and replaced by Fishery flag superior numbers 4301–4319 from 9.5.18 and 4320–4328 from 20.6.18 in order that confusion between duplication of numbers 203 and below could be eliminated. Practically all of the motor fishing vessels requisitioned came from Scottish ports.

Adty. No.	Port No.	Name	TG/Yr	Service—Fate
1680	BF.790	ABANA	44/02	M/S and water carrier. 8.17–1919
MB.158	WK.109	ADEQUATE	41/03	11.14– Sunk 2.12.16 in collision off Kirkabista Light.
	GY.368	ADMIRAL JELLICOE	*17/14	BDV. 7.15–1920
	LH..351	AGNES	51/03	2.15–1919
	AH.5	AGNES =ANGELA 5.18	51/03	5.17–1919
2867	ML.50	AGNES IRVINE	52/05	M/S. 4.17–1919
3007	BF.894	ALASKA =ALASKA II 6.17	49/02	1–6 pdr. 3.17–1919
2869	ML.285	ANNIE MATHERS	56/05	M/S. 4.17–1919
MB.159	WK.35	BANFFSHIRE	46/01	1–3 pdr. 11.14–1919
	AH.7	BARBARA BEATTIE		5.18–1919
MB.160	WK.245	BENAIGEN =BENMORE 5.18	57/	(ex-Ben Aigen) 1–6 pdr. 11.14–1919
4301				
MB.153	BK.7	BETSY JAMIESON	45/00	1–6 pdrAA; Q ship. 11.14–1919
4302				
3018	FR.931	BETSY SIM	53/02	1–6 pdr. 3.17– Sunk 18.7.17 in collision near Haisboro' Light House.
	BF.1047	BETTER HOPE		HS. 9.18–1919
	BCK.306	BLANTYRE	*54/	9.18–1919
3027	H.395	BLESSING	52/85	1–6 pdr. 6.16–1919
1684	FR.964	BLOSSOM =BLOSSOM III 9.17	49/03	M/S. 3.17–1919
MB.176	BF.486	BON AMI	36/01	(ex-Bonamie). 1.15–1916
1682	BF.1217	BOUNTEOUS	63/03	9.17– Wrecked 4.12.17 on North Shore, Rhum.
MB.155	BK.50	BREADWINNER	40/01	11.14–1916
MB.166	WK.343	BRIAR	42/00	12.14–1919
4303				Wrecked 29.1.20 off Wick Harbour.
MB.177	BF.1987	CAMPANIA	40/97	1.15–1916
MB.174	BCK.301	CELERITY	58/02	1.15–1916
2868	FR.207	COMELY =COMELY II 6.17	51/04	M/S. 4.17–1919
	BCK.77	CROY	60/05	(ex-William Beardmore). 6.15–1919
MB.162	WK.113	CRYSTAL RIVER	40/02	12.14–1916
3013	FR.691	DAISY =DAISY VII 6.17	46/96	1–6 pdr Hydro. 3.17–1918
	FR.410	DAYSTAR	*43/00	(ex-Dayspring). 8.18–1919
	BM.136	DORELLA	19/15	BDV. 2.16–1919
3016	FR.434	DOVE =DOVE IV 6.17	49/04	1–6 pdr. 3.17–1917
	AH.46	EBENEZER =EBENEZER II 9.17	*48/03	4.17–1918

Adty. No.	Port No.	Name	TG/Yr.	Service—Fate
	FR.7	ENERGY	45/	3.17– Wrecked 5.3.17 in Peterhead Bay while on passage to Lowestoft to fit out.
MB.183	BF.29	EDITH	52/02	2.15–1918
3030	WK.218	EDITH =EDITH II 6.17	62/02	1–6 pdr. 3.17–1918
MB.163	WK.621	ENDEAVOUR	*36/03	12.14–1916
MB.184 4304	BK.188	EXCEL =EXCEL IV 9.17	40/98	Q ship (2.17–3.17). 5.15–1919
3032	BF.1303	EXCELLENT =SPLENDID 9.17 =SPELLBIND 6.18	61/04	3.17–1919
		FALKIRK	56/	(ex-Falcon?) 10.18– Sunk 29.10.18 in collision off Kinnaird Head.
3006	FR.568	FISHER LASS	59/01	1–6 pdr Hydro. 3.17–1919
MB.175	BF.1069	FISHER LASSIE	59/03	1.15–1916
MB.185 4305	BK.114	FISHER LASSIE II	*44/03	1–6 pdrAA; Q ship. 3.15–1919
2910	BM.33	FLOWER OF THE FLEET	*18/14	7.15–1919
	KY.658	FYALLS	*48/	6.18–1919
2143	FR.61 WY.141	GARDNER	54/09	1–6 pdr Net. 7.15–1919
MB.173	BF.1087	GLEANER	58/03	1.15–1916
1685	FR.332	GOOD HOPE =GOOD HOPE V 9.17	63/03	1–2 pdr. 3.17–1919
	BF.1830	GOWAN	*45/	3.17– Sunk 17.3.17 by S/M off Newton, Northumberland while on passage to Lowestoft to fit out.
1686	PD.462	GOWAN =GOWAN IV 9.17	56/03	1–6 pdr. 4.17–1919
	BM.330	HARD LINES	*18/13	BDV. 5.16–1920
1674	BF.976	HARVEST	60/02	1–6 pdr; light tender. 8.17–1919
	ML.444	HAWFINCH	*49/	(ex-Hawthorn). 6.18–1919
2864	FR.970	HEATHER BELL =HEATHER BELL II 6.17	48/03	4.17–1919
1675	PD.301 KY.340	HELEN WILSON	*44/02	4.17– Destroyed by fire 5.12.17 at Oban.
	ML.5	HONEY BEE =HONEY COMB 10.18	*47/	9.18–1919
3023	FR.189	HONOUR BRIGHT	54/02	1–6 pdrAA. 3.17–1918
MB.172	BF.978	HOPEWELL	52/02	1–6 pdr. 1.15–1918
MB.189 4306	BK.250	ISA WILSON	41/07	12.15–1919
MB.178 4316	BK.217	ISOBEL COLVEN	43/02	1–3 pdr PB. 2.15–1919
MB.181	INS.429	IVANHOE	42/03	2.15–1916
MB.161 2066	WK.342	J. D. FLETCHER	56/03	1–3 pdr. 11.14–1917
	BF.1218	JEANNE LOVIE	61/03	4.17–1918
3024	FR.302	KIMBERLEY =KIMBERLEY III 4.17	54/04	1–6 pdr Hydro. 3.17–1919
MB.164 4307	WK.114	LUSTRE GEM =LUSTRE GEM II 9.17	*51/05	12.14–1919
MB.169 4308	BF.430	MAFEKING =SMUTS 5.18	50/00	12.14–1919
3008	BF.1252	MAGGIE =MAGGIE II 6.17	56/04	1–6 pdr. 3.17–1918
3009	FR.397	MAGGIE JESSIE	50/03	1–6 pdr. 3.17–1919
1687	PD.273	MAJESTIC =MAJESTIC III 9.17	53/02	4.17–1919
1669	ML.206	MAJESTIC =MAJESTIC IV 9.17	56/10	4.17–1919
3011	FR.993	MARCONI =MARCONI II 6.17	61/04	1–6 pdr Hydro. 3.17–1919.

Adty No.	Port No.	Name	TG/Yr	Service—Fate
MB.168	WK.201	MARCONI =MARCONI III 9.17	50/03	12.14–1920
1672	KY.1	MARY DUNCAN	45/00	5.17–1919
MB.187		MARY HENDERSON	*13/13	4.15–1916
MB.202 4328		MARY ROSE III	*16/14	12.15–1919
	BF.1139	MASHONA		9.18–1918
MB.171	BF.432	MAY QUEEN	*41/03	12.14–1916
2866	PD.488	MINERVA =MINERVA III 6.17	49/03	5.17–1919
MB.157	BK.102	NELLIE WILSON	53/04	10.14–1916
3015	FR.863	OCEAN'S GIFT =OCEAN'S GIFT II 6.17	50/01	1–6 pdr. Destroyed by fire 30.8.17 off the Wash.
	PD.	OCLEIAN		10.18–1919
MB.182 4310	BCK.135	OLIVETTE	41/04	(ex-Olive). 5.16–1919
1667	LH.373	ORCADIS	*47/04	5.17–1920
MB.179 4317	BK.77	OUR GIRLS THREE	48/01	1–3 pdr PB. 2.15–1919
	BCK.5	PACIFIC	*55/	10.18–1918
MB.170 4311	BF.1091	PASSAWAY	60/03	(ex-Pass Away). 12.14–1919
MB.167	WK.64	PEARL	54/04	1–6 pdr. 12.14–1918
MB.201 4327		PENELOPE	/14	12.14–1920
	PW.37	PERILLA	18/14	9.15–1919
MB.118 4320		PERLONA	57/95	12.14–1919
MB.182	BK.182	PETER & JOHN	*32/98	3.15–6.15
3028	BF.1128	PHALAROPE	58/04	1–6 pdr Hydro. 3.17–1918
1688	PD.423	PROVIDER =PROVIDER II 9.17	*48/01	1–2 pdr. 4.17–1919
MB.156	BK.203	PURSUIT	*29/03	11.14–5.15
	P.	RUBICON	52/98	10.18–1918
MB.188 4312	BK.210	ST. EBBA	38/06	1916–1919
MB.165 4313	WK.90	SISTERS	45/04	12.14–1920
1673	FR.392	SNOWDROP =SNOWDROP VI 9.17	39/02	8.17–1919
MB.119	GY.790	SPRING FLOWER	40/97	5.15–1917
MB.154	BK.178	STATELY	*33/02	10.14–1916
	BF.954	STRATHLENE =STRATHMORE 1918	*46/	4.18– Destroyed by fire 20.8.18 off Buncrana.
MB.180 4319	BK.218	SUBLIME =SUBLIME III 9.17	46/02	1–3 pdr. 2.15–1919
3025	FR.311	SUNBEAM =SUNBEAM III 4.17	52/03	1–6 pdr. 3.17–1918
1671	BF.318 BF.701	SUNNYSIDE =SUNNYSIDE II 9.17	*47/01	8.17–1919
3017	FR.803	SUPERB =SUPERBUS 8.17	*39/00	1–6 pdr. 3.17–1918
2865	INS.199	TENNIE CAMPBELL	40/02	1–6 pdr. 4.17–1919
	H. LT.931	THALIA	32/86	Q ship; also THALES. 8.16–12.17 carried mined nets. Sunk 31.12.18 on mercantile service.
1670	ML.307	TINA WOOD	63/03	4.17–1919
MB.151 4314	BK.231	TREASURE =TREASURE II 9.17	44/03	10.14–1919
	PD.452	TRUELOVE	54/02	8.17–1919
MB.150 4315	BK.272	TWILIGHT =TYRO 5.18	54/03	later =BDV. 11.14–1920

Adty No.	Port No.	Name	TG/Yr	Service—Fate
1679	BF.837	UPHAZ	*51/02	8.17–1918
3010	WK.116	VALKYRIE =VALKYRIE II 6.17	*41/04	1–6 pdr Hydro. 3.17–1919
1689	PD.47	VANGUARD =VANGUARD IV 9.17	*50/04	4.17–1919
1668	BF.798	VANGUARD =VANGUARD V 9.17	47/02	BDV. 8.17–1919
3022	FR.971	VICTORIA =VICTORIA III 4.17	60/03	1–6 pdr. 3.17–1918
MB.186	WK.95	VICTORY =VICAR 9.17	*31/99	1915–1918
3014	FR.398	VINEYARD	*42/01	1–6 pdr Hydro. 3.17–1918
MB.152 4318	BK.185	VIOLET =PIPIN 5.18	45/06	1–3 pdr PB. 10.14–1919
	BF.1235	VIRTUE	*54/03	9.17–1919
	AH.	WHEATEAR		5.18–1919

*Net registered tonnages.
Notes: PETER & JOHN was the first MB.182 assignment, ENDEAVOUR was MB.163 ** and OLIVETTE, MB.182 ** (see MB list).

MOTOR LIFEBOAT

440		PARTICK	(ex-City of Glasgow) 13.6.18–13.9.19

Notes: Renamed 13.6.18 when taken into service. Served on Harwich Station as tender to GANGES; Sold 1.5.20 J. KING & Co.

MISCELLANEOUS PATROL VESSELS

(a) IN HOME WATERS:

Name	TG/Yr	Armament—Service—Fate
DIRK (Fy.1649)	181/09	1–12 pdr, 1–6 pdrAA M/S. 19.9.17– sunk 28.5.18 by S/M off Flamborough Head.
LOCHIEL (Fy.1650)	241/08	1–12 pdr, 1–6 pdr. 19.9.17– sunk 24.7.18 (mined or torpedoed) off Whitby.
ROBINA	306/14	PB and BDV. 21.11.14–6.6.19.
SYRIA	750/98	PB. 24.11.14–29.7.16.

(b) WEST AFRICA

IVY	1131/95	Nigerian Govt yacht 1–12 pdr, 2–6 pdr. 9.14–1919.
PORPOISE		Nigerian paddle tug 2–12 pdr, 1–3 pdr. 9.14–1919.
REMUS	203/13	Nigerian paddle tug 3–12 pdr. 9.14–1919.
SUNDA	120/99	8.14–1919.

Also the following Nigerian Govt vessels in service from 9.14:
ALLIGATOR 100 ft motor launch, 1–MG.   BALBUS Tug, 3–37 mm.
CROCODILE 100 ft motor launch, 1–MG.   MANATEE Motor launch, 1–3 pdr, 1–MG.
MOLE Dredger, 1–6 in.   VAMPIRE 80 ft St. launch, 1–3 pdr.
VIGILANT 80 ft St. launch, 1–3 pdr.
SOKOTO ex-German gunboat captured 9.14 at Duala.
WALRUS ex-German tug captured 9.14 at Duala, 1–3 pdr.

(c) EAST AFRICA AND LAKE NYASSA:

ADJUTANT	231/05	Ex-German tug captured 10.10.14 by DARTMOUTH; 1–3 pdr. Recaptured 6.2.15 after being damaged by gunfire near the Rufiji River and taken to Lake Tanganyika.
DUPLEX	874/72	(ex-Nentwater) 1–3 pdr. 3.11.14–31.8.15.
GUENDOLEN	250/99	River gunboat, Lake Nyassa 2–6 pdr.
HELLMUTH	774/99	Ex-German tug taken into service c11.14–1915; 1–3 pdr.

(d) INDIAN OCEAN:

Patrol and M/S vessels added from mid-1917 included numerous shallow draught steamers and some vessels not found in shipping registers:

ASHMANI   BADORA 279/14 (=WW II)   BAHREIN(RIM) from 5.15.
BALGAY 303/97 M/S.   BAN WHATT HIN 361/85 M/S.   BHAMO(RIM) 255/96 2–MG.
CURLEW 305/76 M/S.   ELEPHANTA(RIM) M/S   GALLIA 1305/04, 1–4.7 in.
GENERAL BRACKENBURY 127/ M/S.
GENERAL ELLES 154/ M/S and patrol off Colombo.
GOLIATH tug 310/02 M/S Colombo.   GUIDE(RIM) 817/
HINDU 770/94   HYE LEONG 494/82, 1–3 pdr patrol at Rangoon 10.17–19.
INDRAVATI 1053/96.   IRRAWADY 338/ , 2–MG.   JATTRA 371/96 M/S.
KAIPAN 300/88 Singapore.   KATORIA 1127/89.   LADY FRASER(RIM) 1669/08.
LADY INCHCAPE 93/11 M/S and patrol off Colombo.   LARK 133/91, at Singapore.
LADY MACKAY 86/10 patrol off Colombo.   LHASA 2195/04.
MAHANADI 1194/92.   MAYO(RIM) 1125/96.   NANCOWRY 70/ .
MEARCHUS(RIM) 925*/14.   NILLA 208/08, 2–3 pdr.   RETRIEVER.
ROSE tug 308/04 M/S.   SAMSON tug 310/02 M/S.   SANDOWAY 291/15
SARASVATI 962/07 M/S.   SATRUNJI 1192/92.   (=WW II).
SHEIKH-BERKHUD 327/91 at Aden from 1.5.17.   SLADEN(RIM) 270*/86, 5–MG.
TAMIL 93/ M/S.   TAROTYUA 133/14.
VIOLET 251/13 exam vessel from 6.14.   YENGYNA 238/14.
ZAHORA 200/ , 1–3 pdr from 10.12.17.

Displacement. These vessels were a mixture of colonial and commercial craft taken up in India; they returned to owners and former duties in about 1919. BAHREIN, BHAMO, IRRAWADY and SLADEN were paddle river steamers.

(e) PERSIAN GULF:

These ships as well as the vessels in section (f) served in shallow water and rivers supporting military operations in Mesopotamia etc. Certain Thames river steamers were sent out from England, other vessels were built and shipped in sections, while the remainder were acquired from local owners.
Shallow draught Thames paddle steamers: (all arrived mid 1916).
BRUNEL 126/05   CARLYLE 129/05   CHRISTOPHER WREN 120/05
EDMUND IRONSIDES 116/05   FITZ AILWIN 116/05
Local river steamers:
BLOSSE LYNCH 2–18 pdr field guns, from 3.12.14.
JULNAR 884/09 commissioned 17.4.16, lost 24.6.16 by capture during an attempt to reprovision Kut.
MASSOUDIEH stern-wheeler, armed for service in 6.15.
MEJIDIEH 463/82, 2–18 pdr field guns, a stern-wheeler from 3.12.14.
Until the arrival from the UK of newly-built river gunboats, these vessels and the small launches were the main naval force available for river service.
    At least twelve shallow draught stern-wheelers were built and numbered P.50–61 (not to be confused with the P boats of the P.11–75 series) for service on the Tigris; described as 'new MEJIDIEHs', they were similar to the vessel of that name. All were built 1916–17 (P.50–51 by Beardmore, P.52–57 by Caird and P.60–61 by Lobnitz; builders of P.58–59 not known). Plans indicate an armament of 2–12 pdr (service armament probably a single 3 pdr each) a displacement tonnage of 500 and dimensions 220 (pp) ×30×6¼ ft. P.50 arrived 9.6.16 and was completed 30.6.16.
    At least eight "Sumana" tugs arrived in the Persian Gulf between 4.16 and 6.16, identified only by War Office "T" numbers.

(f) ARMED LAUNCHES ETC.:

AZERBAIJAN   River steamer (Persian Customs launch) based at Muscat; to RIM 20.10.18, to Persia 31.11.19.
COMET   Paddle launch-tug 144 tons; ex-RIM, was official yacht of British Resident at Baghdad. In service 5.11.14 armed with 1–3 pdr from ESPIEGLE, later 1–6 pdr, 3–3 pdr, 2–MGs. Lost 1.12.15 after grounding in the Tigris.
DUNNEDA   Launch; to RIM 22.8.18.
EDWARD ROSS   Launch; to RIM 14.9.18.
ENTERPRISE   Launch in the East Indies; survey vessel 1916–19.
FLYCATCHER   Motor patrol boat, built 1912 by Thornycroft for Turkey; sunk 9.11.14 by ESPIEGLE at Shatt el Arab; salved and added late 1915 with 1–6 pdr, 1–MG. Sold c1923.
LEWIS PELLY   Yacht, formerly on Govt service = armed launch 2–3 pdr, 1–MG 11.14; disarmed 5.15 = M/S.
MASHONA   Launch-tug, 1–3 pdr 11.14–1.1.15 = tug service.
MINER   Launch-tug 50/80, 1–12 pdr, 1–3 pdr, 1–MG from 11.14.
MOZAFFIR   (also given as MUZAFRI) Ex-Persian stern-wheeler 3.3.15. Later used as tug for a "horseboat armed with 4.7 in gun".
QUANDMERE   Tug; arrived 20.6.16, completed 17.9.16.
SHAITAN   Launch, 1–3 pdr from 1.12.14; later 1–12 pdr. Lost 29.11.15 after grounding in the Tigris near Aziziya.
SHUSAN   Stern-wheeler, 2–3 pdr from 3.3.15, later 1–12 pdr, 1–3 pdr.
SUMANA   Launch-tug, 2–3 pdr from 22.5.15. Left at Kut 12.15; recaptured 26.2.17 = 1–12 pdr, 2–3 pdr.

Notes: Two launch-tugs named GARMSIR and SIRDAR-I-NAPHTI were commonly identified as CARMSIR and SIRDAR; CARMSIR 40/14, 1–3 pdr, in commission 5.11.14–12.11.14 and SIRDAR, also with 1–3 pdr was in commission 7.11.14–13.12.14. These two along with LEWIS PELLY MASHONA and MINER were commissioned by the battleship OCEAN who provided the guns 4 officers and 41 men in order to put them in service. It was common practice for warships to use small craft in this manner on foreign stations in order that naval influence could be extended inland where insufficient depth of water might prevent the big ships from steaming.
    Other armed launches were the 40 ft MIMI and TOUTOU built 1915 by Thornycroft and diverted for use on Lake Tanganyika; armed each with 1–3 pdr and 1–MG they were re-launched 23.12.15 on the lake after a long overland journey. Their action 26.12.15 with the German KINGANI added another vessel to the list, the sunken German vessel after salvage, becoming FIFI in British service with 1–12 pdr gun from 15.1.16.

(g) AUSTRALIAN WATERS:

COOGIE(RAN)	762/87	(ex-*Lancashire Witch*) 1–4.7 in, 2–3 pdr. 5.18–1921.
GANNET(RAN)	208/	(ex-*Penguin*) 1–12 pdr. 7.18–1919.
MOURILYAN(RAN)	1349/	1–4.7 in, 2–3 pdr. 5.18–1921.
NUSA(RAN)	*64/	(ex-German yacht) Seized 13.9.14 by MELBOURNE in the Solomons. Sold 1921.

*Displacement tons. Another vessel, SUMATRA, is lacking details.

(h) CANADIAN WATERS:

PV.I	390/12	(ex-*William B. Murray*) 1–12 pdr M/S. 3.17–4.19.
PV.II	390/12	(ex-*Amagansett*) 1–12 pdr M/S. 3.17–4.19.
PV.III	323/11	(ex-*Herbert N. Edwards*) 1–12 pdr M/S. 3.17–4.19.
PV.IV	308/11	(ex-*Martin J. Marran*) 1–12 pdr M/S. 3.17–4.19.
PV.V	323/11	(ex-*Rollin E. Mason*) 1–12 pdr M/S. 3.17–4.19.
PV.VI	205/03	(ex-*Leander Wilcox*) 1–12 pdr M/S. 4.17–4.19.
PV.VII	247/11	(ex-*Rowland H. Wilcox*) 1–12 pdr M/S. 4.17–4.19.

Vessels listed from 12.14 included:
ACADIA 846/13, 1–4 in, 2–3 pdr.
BALEINE 418/07 1–3 pdr M/S.
CARTIER 556/10 3–12 pdr.
CURLEW 400/92 3–MG.
FALCON.
GALIANO 393/13. Wrecked 30.10.18 near Vancouver Island.
MALASPINA 392/13 1–6 pdr.
NEWINGTON 193/99.
PREMIER 254/07.
SABLE ISLAND 734/14 1–6 pdr.
SPEEDY II 252/96.
ALBACORE.
CANADA 411/04 2–12 pdr, 2–3 pdr.
CONSTANCE 400/91 3–MG.
DELIVERANCE 280/14 1–3 pdr M/S.
FLORENCE 133/83 1–3 pdr.
GLADIATOR 70/64.
GULNARE 262/93 survey vessel.
MARGARET 756/14 2–6 pdr.
PETREL 192/92 1–3 pdr.
RESTLESS 76/06.
SCOTSMAN 265/03.

Later additions to the patrol were:
GOPHER 198/10 1–3 pdr from 10.15. (see also as rescue tug).
GRIB whaler 140/07 1–6 pdr from 5.17.
GRILSE 287/12 2–12 pdr, 1–14 in TT (yacht listed as torpedo boat).
HOCHELAGA (ex-*Waturas*) 628/00 1–12 pdr.
LADY EVELYN (ex-*Deerhound*) 483/01 from 6.17.
LANSDOWNE 680/84 from 4.17.
LAURENTIAN (ex-*King Edward*) 355/02 from 5.17.
MUSQUASH tug 198/10 1–3 pdr from 10.15.
NEREID tug 40/12.
STARLING 193/88 1–6 pdr.
TUNA (ex-*Tarantula*) 124/02 1–3 pdr, 2–14 in TT (listed as torpedo boat).
WILFRED (ex-*Wilfred C.*) tug 99/97 from 1918.
These vessels were a mixture of government vessels and hired craft. PV.I–VII, ex-coasters purchased in America, were often listed as "trawlers".

(i) WEST INDIES:

ARAWANA	152/14	1–13 pdr; at Demerara. 20.3.17–15.1.19.
BELIZE	1498/14	1–12 pdr. 19.2.17– released by 21.2.19.
ESSEQUIBO	202/91	2–13 pdr; at Demerara. 20.3.17–15.1.19.
LADY HAY	75/00	1–6 pdr M/S; at Barbados. 5.3.17– released by 21.2.19.
PARIKA	304/04	2–13 pdr; at Demerara. 20.3.17–31.1.19.
PONEMAH	69/	aux. schooner from Trinidad Customs 1–6 pdr. 19.2.17– released by 21.2.19.
PURUNI	295/05	2–13 pdr; at Demerara. 20.3.17– wrecked 29.8.18 off Mayero Island, Grenadines.
ST. PATRICK	*180/13	1–3 pdr, from Trinidad Govt. 19.2.17– released by 21.2.19.
TOWY	199/14	1–6 pdr. 28.2.17–21.2.19.

*Displacement tonnage.

(j) WHITE SEA:

BORODINO (*ii*)	2–6 pdr. 4.19–25.9.19.

This was a Russian paddle steamer (not in registers), commissioned as Senior Officer's ship for the Dvina River when it was found that the original S.O. ship (HALDON) drew too much water to navigate the river. She was returned to Russian owners two days before the final evacuation of the area.

(k) CASPIAN SEA:

ALADER YOUSSANOFF	2071/05	1–12 pdr. 1.19–8.19.
ORLIONOCH	1406/88	2–4 in. 1918–24.8.19.
DUBLIN CASTLE		2–6 in. 1918–31.7.19.
EDINBURGH CASTLE		1–12 pdr. 1918–31.7.19.
WINDSOR CASTLE		4–4 in. 1918–6.8.19.

Notes: These Russian mercantile vessels, together with some small craft, were armed and commissioned from late 1918 on the Caspian Sea in support of "White" Russian forces. ALADER YOUSSANOFF and ORLIONOCH each carried two seaplanes and WINDSOR CASTLE two CMBs. Original names of the last three ships are not known; all were finally handed over to "White" Russian crews.

TUGS

At the outbreak of war, only three tugs were wearing the white ensign (MAGNET, SEAHORSE and TRAVELLER) though CONFIANCE, EGERTON, FORTITUDE and STORMCOCK hoisted this as the occasion arose; other tugs wore the blue ensign. Many of the hired tugs (qv) flew the red ensign though under full naval control. Tugs were used for a wide assortment of duties, including examination work, patrol, rescue, general towage, dockyard service, and minelaying and minesweeping as well.

FLEET TUGS

670 tons. 168½ (oa), 160 (pp) ×26×10 ft. TE 1100 ihp=12½ kts.
Armament: 2–6 pdr.

1.18	Name	Launched	Builder—Fate
W.72	SEAHORSE	7. 7.80	Laird. Sold 1.5.20 Crichton Thompson.

Notes: Based at Portsmouth 1914–18, was a rescue tug from 1917.

580 tons. 161½ (oa), 155½ (pp) ×25×10 ft. TE 1000 ihp.
Armament: 2–6 pdr.

W.75	STORMCOCK	5.12.77	Laird. Sold 7.3.22 =MORSECOCK.

Notes: Purchased 24.9.82. Based at Queenstown 1914–18.

430 tons. 136 (pp) ×22½×10 ft. TE 520 ihp=12 kts.
Armament: 4–3 pdr.

7	MAGNET	1883	Stevens, Birkenhead. Sold 1.5.20 =SAN ANTONIO.

Notes: Was KNIGHT OF THE CROSS, purchased 22.4.85. Tender to VICTORY.

700 tons. 167 (oa), 160 (pp) ×24¼×12 ft. Compound 1120 ihp=12 kts.
Armament: 4–3 pdr.

W.80	TRAVELLER	28. 9.85	McIntyre, Paisley. Sold 1.5.20 =BULLGER.

Notes: Was STORMCOCK, purchased 22.4.85. Tender to VIVID 1914–18, rescue tug from 1917.

470 tons. 142 (oa), 135½ (pp) ×25×8 ft. TE 1200 ihp.
Armament: nil.

W.30	FORTITUDE	5.96	Barclay Curle. Sold 31.1.23 Carriden S Bkg Co.

Notes: Purchased 1904; named NEPTUNE to 1909. Tender to VIVID, usually on target service.

DOCKYARD TUGS

484 tons. 130 (pp) ×23×10½ ft. (iron). Paddle 2-cyl. 600 ihp=12½ kts.

Name (Base)	Launched	Builder—Fate
TRUSTY (Devonport) =TRUSTFUL 11.17	14. 2.66	Palmer. Sold 8.9.20 W. J. Webb.

505 tons. 120 (pp) ×25 ft. (wood). Paddle 2-cyl. 876 ihp.

GRINDER (Sheerness)	21. 3.68	White. Sold 28.10.19 Multilocular S Bkg Co.

136 tons. 90 (pp) ×17×9 ft. (iron). Paddle 211 ihp.

PROMPT (Malta)	6. 7.67	Napier. Sold 9.22 at Malta.

530 tons. 128 (pp) ×25×10½ ft. (iron). Paddle 850 ihp.

AETNA (Devonport)	1. 9.83	Laird. Sold 19.2.29 Young, Sunderland.
MALTA (Portsmouth, Rosyth) =BENSHIE.	21. 1.71	Laird. Sold 1.21 =BENSHIE.
METEOR (Chatham) =PERSEVERANCE 1914	5. 9.83	Laird. Sold 31.1.23 Carriden S Bkg Co.
SAMPSON (Malta) =ORIENT 7.18	31. 1.77	Laird. Sold 8.6.23 at Malta.

270 tons. 107 (pp) ×19 ft. (iron). 350 ihp.

CONFIANCE (Devonport)	1884	Poden, Northwich. Sold 5.47.

Notes: Was NAVIGATOR, purchased 4.85. Tender to DEFIANCE.

Name (Base)	Launched	Builder—Fate

450 tons. (iron). Paddle 500 ihp.

CARRON (Chatham)	1880	Chambers, Dumbarton. Sold 27.3.23 at Gibraltar.

Notes: Was FLYING EAGLE, purchased 14.3.88.

630 tons. 157¾ (pp) ×25¼×10 ft. (iron). TE 1000 ihp.

ALLIGATOR (Pembroke)	1885	Laird. Sold 1920 =REFLOATER.

Notes: Was STORMCOCK, purchased 1896 as salvage tug and firefloat. Rescue tug 1917–18.

440 tons. 135 (pp) ×24×10 ft. 630 ihp.

CROCODILE (Gibraltar)	3.12.89	McKnight, Ayr. Sold 5.11.24 at Gibraltar.

Notes: Was FLYING VULTURE, purchased 1896.

346 tons. 130 (pp) ×20×8 ft. (iron. Paddle 750 ihp.

BUSTLER (Gibraltar)	1890	Hepple. Sold 11.21 at Gibraltar.

Notes: Was CONQUEROR, purchased 1896.

DROMEDARY CLASS PADDLE TUGS

680 to 700 tons. 150¾ (oa), 144 (pp) ×27½ (50 oa) ×10¼ ft.

Paddle 2-stage oscillating 1250 ihp=12 kts.

Name (Base)	Launched	Builder—Fate
ADVICE (Chatham)	2.10.99	London & Glasgow. Sold 20.10.50 J. Scott, Cork.
CRACKER (Malta)	7.12.99	London & Glasgow. Arrived 16.7.56 Ward, Grays.
DILIGENT (Sheerness)	31. 8.98	Barclay Curle. Sold 9.10.23 Young, Sunderland.
DROMEDARY (Portsmouth, Invergordon)	31. 5.94	Barclay Curle. Sold 28.4.23 J. A. White.
ENERGETIC (Gibraltar)	22. 5.02	John Brown. Sold 15.4.53, BU Shaws, Rainham, Kent.
ESCORT (Devonport, Rosyth)	28. 7.96	Fawcett, Preston. Sold 31.5.22 J. A. White.
INDUSTRIOUS (Devonport)	19. 6.02	Barclay Curle. BU 12.59 in Holland.
RESTLESS (Malta) =RESTIVE 6.16	7. 6.02	Day Summers. Sold 6.37; BU at Spezia.
VOLCANO (Portsmouth) =VOLATILE 12.18	21. 9.99	Barclay Curle. Arrived 16.4.57 Ward, Grays.

ENTERPRISE CLASS

307 tons. 115½ (oa), 110 (pp) ×23×8 ft. 450 ihp.

ASSURANCE (Devonport)	18.12.99	Bow McLachlan. Sold 31.1.23 Carriden S Bkg Co.
ENTERPRISE (Portsmouth) =EMPRISE 12.18	2.10.99	Bow McLachlan. Sold 1947.
TYRIAN (Sheerness, Invergordon) =TYRE 1.18 =SIDONIAN 3.18	15. 3.00	Bow McLachlan. Sold 17.10.25 Cox & Danks.

Notes: TYRIAN was ADVENTURE until 3.04.

140 tons. 182 ihp.

EMILY (Malta)	28.11.01	Seath, Rutherglen. Sold 1.34 at Malta. =in WW II.

Notes: Was purchased 14.11.01.

140 tons. 86½ (oa), 78 (pp) =16½×7 ft. 200 ihp.

EDITH (Chatham, Scapa)	1904	Malta DY. Sold 31.1.23 T. Rigden.
LUCY (Devonport)	18.10.02	Mordey Carney. Sold 6.37 at Malta.
MARCHWOOD (Portsmouth)	23.11.00	Dundee SB. Sold 1948.

245 tons. 80½ (pp) ×17½ ft. Paddle 340 ihp.

VIGILANT (also C.2)	1900	Purchased 21.6.00; sold 22.10.19 in West Indies.

400 tons. 121 (pp) ×24 ft. 775 ihp.

SALVO (also C.61)	1899	Eltringham. Sold 10.22.

Notes: Was purchased 13.3.01.

325 tons. 125 (pp) ×24½×7 ft. 620 ihp=11¼ kts.

PRUDENT (Chatham)	17. 5.05	Bow McLachlan. Sold 7.10.27 Ward.

Name (Base)	Launched Builder—Fate
350 tons. 102 (pp) ×23×12 ft. TE 660 ihp.	
SECURITY (Cromarty, Sheerness)	1904 J. P. Rennoldson. Sold 8.2.27 =SECURITY.

Notes: Was KINGFISHER, purchased 22.3.06 and named DILIGENCE to 3.10.

378 tons. 101 (pp) ×22½×11 ft. Paddle 800 ihp.	
HERCULANEUM (Dover)	1905 Cran. Sold 1927 =FORMBY.

Notes: Purchased 1908.

144 tons. 80 (pp) ×18×9½ ft. 300 ihp=10 kts.	
SWALLOW (Gibraltar)	1892 Fullerton. Sold 3.15 =LEON & TONY.

Notes: Was GENERAL SKINNER, transferred from War Dept 1906.

337 tons. 92 (pp) ×21 ft. Compound 630 ihp=12 kts.	
EGERTON (Portland)	1908 Cran. Sold 2.23 =BENSON.

Notes: Purchased 23.7.08.

SMALL BERTHING TUGS

Name	Tons	Purchased	Fate, etc.
CARBON (also C.150)	185	1900	Sold 1947.
CROCUS =FEN 1920	46	1897	(ex-*York*) Dansey, Teddington. Sold c1924.
ELEPHANT	56	1893	Portsmouth DY. Sold 21.10.20.
GAZELLE	57	4. 6.03	Sold 1924.
HALLGARTH (also C.62)	175	3.00	Lytham SB. Sold c1943.
MAGPIE (also C.63)	40	1902	Sold 1923.
MARMION (also C.112)	100	3.00	Sold 22.7.20.
MISTLETOE (ex-*Laurel*.13)	30	1901	Lewin, Wandsworth (1897). Sold 3.23.
POLLY (also C.410)	150	1916	Bailey, Hong Kong (1904). Sold 5.31.
SCOTSMAN (also C.371)	172	11.01	Gray, Hull. Sold 19.4.21.
SIR WM. JERVAIS (C.409)	120		Built 1900; at Hong Kong 1919.
TERRIER	95	3.13	Sold 1948.
TOXTETH (also C.111)	148	11.01	Jones, Liverpool (1899). Sold 17.10.30 =CLEADON.
TYKE	95	1.12	Sold 1947.
VICTORY (also C.210)	76	1904	Sold 1934.
WELSHMAN (also C.230)	92	1901	Bow McLachlan. Sold c1947.

Notes: The C numbers were borne in addition to the names from about 1920.

ROVER CLASS

620 tons.   153 (oa), 145 (pp) ×29×12¼ ft.   TE 1400 ihp=11 kts.

Pendant Nos.	Name	Launched	Builder—Fate
W.77 (9.18)	ALLIANCE (Sheerness, Scapa)	23. 8.10	Chatham DY. Lost 19.12.41 at the fall of Hong Kong.
	ATLAS (Hong Kong)	2. 9.09	Chatham DY. Sold 19.5.58.
W.62 (1.18)	PILOT (Portsmouth, Portland)	2. 9.09	Chatham DY. Arrived 27.3.60 in Holland to BU.
	ROVER (Devonport) =ROLLICKER 1929 =RECOVERY 3.34	12.10.08	Chatham DY. Arrived 18.9.57 at Haulbowline to BU.

Notes: Were also used as rescue tugs from 1917.

ROBUST CLASS PADDLE TUGS

690 tons. 150¾ (oa), 144 (pp) ×27¼×11 ft. Paddle 1250 ihp=12 kts.

CAMEL (Rosyth)	19.10.14	Bow McLachlan. BU 1962.
FIRM (Dover, Sheerness)	23. 8.10	Chatham DY. Arrived 2.9.60 Belgium to BU.
GRAPPLER (Portsmouth)	4. 9.08	Chatham DY. Arrived 20.5.57 Dover to BU.
HELLESPONT (Haulbowline)	10. 5.10	Earle. Sunk 4.42 by A/C at Malta.
RAMBLER (Gibraltar)	21.12.08	John Brown. BU 1953.
ROBUST (Sheerness)	24. 9.07	Bow McLachlan. Sold c1955.
SPRITE (Portsmouth)	23. 8.15	Fleming & Ferguson. Arrived 27.3.60 Holland to BU.
STRENUOUS (Sheerness) =SANDBOY 1.18	7.12.12	Thornycroft. Sunk 27.6.47 as target off Bermuda.
STURDY (Portsmouth) =SWARTHY 11.17	12.11.12	Thornycroft. Arrived 24.3.61 Haulbowline to BU.
VETERAN (Malta) =ANCIENT 12.18	30. 8.15	Thornycroft. Sold 1954 at Malta.

1023 tons. 178 (oa), 170 (pp) ×36×12 ft. Paddle 2000 ihp=13 kts.

PERT	4. 4.16	Thornycroft. BU 1962.

WAR CONSTRUCTION AND WARTIME PURCHASES

85 tons. 75 (pp) ×16×5 ft. 300 ihp=8½ kts.

JASON =RIVAL 1937	1915	Sold 1947.

Notes: Purchased 5.2.15.

124 tons. 78½ (oa), 75 (pp) ×17×7½ ft. Compound 250 ihp=9 kts.

FLAMER (Rosyth) (also C.108)	1915	Scott, Bowling. =YC.298 1943; sold 6.48 Pounds, Portsmouth.
FRESCO (Rosyth)	1915	Scott, Bowling. Sold 3.23 =HANDMAID.

Notes: FLAMER purchased 3.15; FRESCO also during 1915.

79 tons. 61½ (pp) ×15×5 ft. Compound.

FROLIC (Queenstown)	1915	Bow McLachlan. Sold 5.23 Cork Harbour Commissioners.

Notes: Purchased 3.15.

240 tons. 96 (pp) ×20×8 ft. TE 700 ihp.

1.18	Name	Launched	Builder—Fate
W.16	CONQUERESS (Rosyth)	1913	Hepple. Sold 6.5.53 Pollock & Brown, Northam to BU.

Notes: Hired 22.1.15 and purchased 6.10.15. Rescue tug 1917–18.

244 tons. 100 (oa), 95 (pp) ×22×8 ft. TE 550 ihp=11½ kts.

	STALWART (Lerwick) =SEADOG 1918	1916	Ardrossan SB. Sold 31.12.19 =AGHIOS GEORGIOS; =AGHIOS GEORGIOS in WW II.

Notes: Purchased 1916.

271 tons gross. 110¼ (oa), 104¼ (pp) ×26×10 ft. Compound 900 ihp=10 kts.

W.73	STOBO CASTLE (also C.102)	1917	Cran. Sold 8.63, BU in Belgium.

Notes: Purchased 1917. Rescue tug 1917–18.

386 tons. 118 (oa), 110¼ (pp) ×24×5 ft. Compound 700 ihp=10¼ kts.

HANDY (Mudros)	2. 3.15	Bow McLachlan. Sold 6.20 =ANTONIO AZAMBUJA.

123 tons gross. 100 (pp) ×20 ft. TE.

W.56	MOONFLEET	2.10.17	Edwards, Millwall. Sold 16.8.23 =SALVAGE CHIEF.

Notes: Purchased 3.11.17 from Argentina. Used as a salvage tug.

162 tons gross. 93½ (pp) ×23½ ft. Compound.

MARY TAVY	1918	Philip. Sold 1947 =DANNY.

WEST CLASS

131 to 161 tons gross. 88¼ (pp) ×21×9¼ (deep) ft. Compound 430 ihp=10 kts.

WEST ACRE (also C.9)	1918	Yarwood. Sold 1950 =LAVERNOCK.
WEST BAY	10.10.18	Yarwood. Sold 23.7.53 =LARKSPUR.
WEST COCKER	1919	Philip. Sunk 9.4.42 by A/C at Malta; BU 7.43.
WEST CREEK	24.12.18	Yarwood. Sold 1948 =MARGARET LAMEY.
WEST DEAN	1919	Philip. Sunk 23.4.42 by A/C at Malta.
WEST HEATH	1918	Crabtree. Sold 6.21 Crichton Thompson; =ASTRID =SALVO in WW II.
WEST HILL	1919	Crabtree. Sold 6.21 Crichton Thompson; =DIRECTOR JACK LETZER.
WEST HOPE	1919	Crabtree. Sold 6.21 Crichton Thompson; resold 6.9.29 =BALLINDALLOCH.
WEST HYDE	1919	Crabtree. Sold 1948 =SEASIDER.
WEST WELL	1919	Philip. Sold 10.19 =FRANK DIXON.
WEST WINCH	1919	Payne, Bristol. Sold 24.11.20 Gueret Gait & Co, same name.

Notes: WEST COCKER was spelt WEST COKER (correct) in builder's list, an Admiralty error altered the name. Twelve vessels were included in the 1918 tug-building programme (reported 5.5.18). They were built for the Director of Inland Waterways and intended for cross-channel barge towing work. The majority were loaned to the War Office and later reverted to the Admiralty. 15 vessels were reported completed and two cancelled. Actually six cancellations were noted:
WEST BRAE (Edwards).
WEST LING (Philip) Sold 17.12.19 to builder; =NOVADOR.
WEST MEON (also H. S. 102) (Edwards) Sold 24.11.19 to builder.
WEST MILL (Philip) Sold 17.12.19 to builder; =NAVEGADOR.
WEST PORT (Philip) Sold 17.12.19 to builder; =SIR ALFRED PALMER.
WEST VALE (Edwards) Sold 24.11.19 to builder.

POULTRY CLASS

65 tons gross. 75¼ (pp) ×15×6 ft. Compound 185 ihp=8¼ kts.

ANCONA	2. 4.19	Henry Scarr. Sold 8.22 W. R. Johnson.
CAMPINE	22. 1.19	Yarwood. Sold 8.22 W. R. Johnson, =BRITANNIA.
COCHIN	20. 5.19	Yarwood. Sold c1946.
FAVERHOLE (ex-Bantam)	1919	Henry Scarr. Sold 21.2.22 F. T. Everard.
HOUDAN (ex-Minorca)	1919	Rowhedge IW. Sold 28.4.24 =ERICH.
LEGHORN	26. 8.19	Yarwood. Sold 3.23 J. Maxwell Jones.
ORPINGTON	1919	Rowhedge IW. Sold 8.23 Llanelly Harbour Board.
WYANDOTTE (also W.74)	1919	Rowhedge IW. Sold 1948.

Notes: Ordered for canal and harbour work (1918 programme). Two vessels were reported cancelled after 11.11.18, though all eight were completed. WYANDOTTE assigned W.74 (Department of Works) from 10.23.

BURN CLASS

51 tons gross. 69 (pp) ×16 ft. Compound 200 ihp.

BUCKIE BURN	1919	McGregor, Kirkintilloch. BU 9.58.
RATHVEN BURN	1919	McGregor, Kirkintilloch. Listed to 1946.

Notes: Purchased while building and included as part of the Admiralty programme. Reported on sale list 10.19, but retained by the Admiralty.

POET CLASS

239 tons gross. 105 (pp) ×25 ft. TE 135 (nominal) hp.

POET CHAUCER	8.10.19	Bailey, Hong Kong. Lost 19.12.41 at Hong Kong.
PORT LANGLAND	1919	Bailey, Hong Kong. To Federated Malay States 23.6.20.

Notes: Approval given 30.5.18 to complete as part of the Admiralty programme. To sale list 10.19, but POET CHAUCER retained.

BOARDING TUGS

1914	9.15	1.18	Name	TG/Yr	Former name-Service, etc.
N.62		N.18	CARCASS	128/05	(ex-Java) 8.14–14.5.19.
N.63	**		CERBERUS	337/89	(ex-Oceana) 3.8.14– =rescue tug 1917; stranded 11.10.18 at Scapa.
		W.58	=OCEANA 1916		
N.64		N.20	CEYLON	149/99	(ex-Seaton) 17.11.14–13.3.19.
			CHAR	148/99	(ex-Stranton) 17.11.14– sunk 16.1.15 in collision.
	N.56	N.22	CHARM	156/02	(ex-Sanda, ex-Maretanza) 1915–20.11.19. =COYTOBEE.
N.65		N.23	CHESTER =CHESTER III 1915	150/09	(ex-Badia) 31.7.14–7.9.17 and 20.1.19–23.5.19.
N.66		N.24	CHICHESTER	180/95	(ex-Arcadia) 4.8.14–29.5.19.
N.67		N.25	CHUB	150/09	(ex-Vincia) 30.7.14–15.12.19.
	N.55	N.27	CODFISH	123/15	(ex-Foremost II) 1.6.15–12.1.20.
N.99*		N.28	COMMONWEAL	115/02	(ex-Commonwealth) 30.10.14–7.6.19.
	N.58	N.30	CRUDEN BAY	125/99	=Water boat. 8.1.15–14.1.20.
		N.35	DORIA	150/09	30.7.14–2.1.19. =in WW II.
	N.63*	N.37	DRAGON	153/93	=DY; =rescue tug 1917. 10.3.15–17.1.19.
		W.20	=DRAGE 1918		
		W.03*			
	N.47	N.45	FOREMOST	123/13	1.6.15–20.11.19.
	N.21	N.63	JOANETTA	49/11	11.11.14– purchased 20.12.14–1919.

*Pendants N.99 (reported 2.15, may have been earlier); N.63 (assigned 1.16, pendant ** N.63 for CERBERUS cancelled 1.16); N.37 and W.20 both assigned to DRAGON 1.18; W.03 as DRAGE assigned 9.18.

Notes: Purchased tugs; served with the Downs Boarding Flotilla based at Ramsgate 1914–18. Six were in service from 8.14, given C names. CODFISH is believed to have been renamed CETO 3.18 when the yacht of this name added the numeral II. CETO was one of the two parent ships at Ramsgate. They were unarmed boarding vessels used to maintain a close check on traffic in the Thames approaches.

HIRED PATROL TUGS

Pendant Nos.	Name	TG/Yr	Service, etc.
T.7	ALEXANDRA	168/07	PB 29.10.14–19.12.14; =tug 7.9.15–wrecked 28.10.15.
T.4	BEAVER	154/97	(ex-Lady Lewis) PB 29.10.14–14.11.14; =tug 1918–2.23 sold.
T.1	BLACKCOCK	254/86	PB 23.8.14–11.14; =tug 1915– wrecked 18.1.18 in the White Sea.
P.9A (1.16)			
P.09 (1.18)			
T.9	HARRINGTON	149/03	PB 29.10.14–15.12.14.
T.6	HERCULANEUM	172/09	PB 29.10.14–9.12.14.
T.8	HORNBY	168/09	PB 29.10.14–14.5.16.
T.10	KNIGHT ERRANT	148/05	PB 29.10.14–28.11.14; =tug 16.7.15– =rescue tug 1917; –28.8.20.
T.2	NORTH COCK	149/03	PB 29.10.14–25.11.14.
T.3	OTTER	165/87	(ex-African) PB 29.10.14–5.11.14.
T.11	RALPH BROCKLEBANK	173/03	PB 30.10.14–26.11.14.
T.4	TORFRIDA	133/89	(ex-San Jacinto) PB 3.11.14–25.11.14; =tug 20.5.18–20.2.19.
T.12	W. E. DORRINGTON	175/06	PB 30.10.14–26.11.14.
T.5	WALLASEY	149/03	PB 29.10.14–10.12.14 to War Dept.

Notes: These vessels were taken up as unarmed patrol boats in the Liverpool area. They served for a very short time during late 1914 and were soon used for other purposes. A few were purchased by the Admiralty and one later served as a rescue tug but did not receive a W pendant number.

HIRED SCREW TUGS (70 TG and over)

Name	TG/Yr	Service—Fate
AJAX	273/94	30.7.14–7.8.14 to War Dept.
ANNA LIFFEY	179/04	28.10.18–22.11.18.
ARCHDALE	119/96	(ex-*Vixen*) 26.9.15–24.12.15.
ATHLETE	119/93	26.9.15–6.10.15.
ATLAS	84/72	HS; 17.1.15–3.7.15.
ATTENDANT	317/13	22.4.18–3.2.19.
BENCLUTHA	70/95	10.12.15–12.12.19.
BERTY	73/14	DY; 26.9.14–30.3.20.
BRITISHER	80/02	(ex-*Britannia*) Purchased 1916–2.23 sold.
BRUNO	100/14	17.8.14–10.3.19.
BUNTY	73/14	26.9.14–10.3.19.
BUREAUCRAT	137/16	HS; 15.12.16–26.5.17 and 23.7.17–31.7.17.
CAIRNGARTH	133/13	3.11.17–1919.
CAMPAIGNER	163/11	13.5.15–3.7.17.
CASTOR	70/14	DY; BDV; 21.11.15–21.5.19.
CITY OF YORK	77/88	25.2.18–27.3.19.
CLEVELYS	292/02	3.17–1917.
COMMERCE	103/07	Loaned by Russian Govt 15.11.16–1.6.17.
CONDOR	90/01	2.8.14–1.19.
CRUISER	98/74	HS; 8.7.17–1.9.19.
DAMSON	232/92	(ex-*Samson*) 29.1.18–26.11.19; missing 21.1.20.
DANUBE II	227/10	23.8.14–4.3.20; =NORGROVE in WW II.
DAUNTLESS =MORDAUNT c1917	109/03	6.2.15–21.1.20.
DAVID GILLIES	375/08	10.17– Stranded 5.5.18 in the Mediterranean.
DELUGE	260/08	(ex-*President de Leeuw*) 16.12.14–8.1.10.
DESIRE	135/12	(ex-*President Desire Maas*) DY; 11.12.15– sunk 24.1.18 by S/M off Yorkshire coast.
EAGLE	103/83	HS; 1.8.14–6.3.19.
EARL OF POWIS	116/82	27.8.14–20.1.17 (Was Q ship from 11.5.16).
EGAD	170/98	(ex-*Greville Vernon*) HS; 7.12.17–6.6.19.
EGERTON	272/11	12.8.14–19.5.17.
EILEEN	85/79	HS; 8.12.14–7.7.15.
ENERGIE	73/85	DY; 30.5.15–20.10.19.
ENERGY	79/99	3.10.18–27.11.18 (loaned to USN).
ENTERPRISE	337/90	(ex-*Samaritan*) 27.5.15–1.4.19.
ENTERPRISE II	185/94	12.4.15–9.8.19.
ESTOY	101/70	2.6.17–22.3.19.
EXPERT	100/92	22.3.17–9.4.17.
FALCON	124/92	29.8.18–31.12.18; =in WW II.
FALCONHURST	77/	25.1.18–25.6.19.
FIERY	/	(ex-*Fairy*) 19.1.18–29.1.19.
FINLAY	73/14	BDV; 1916–1918.
FLYING BREEZE	387/13	2.8.14–17.6.19; =in WW II.
FLYING KESTREL	516/13	2.8.14–1.11.19; =in WW II.
FLYING SERPENT	199/11	5.8.14–3.4.20.
FOREMOST III	98/15	(ex-*Charm*, ex-*Fore*) 19.6.15–21.11.16 to War Dept.
FORION	83/00	(ex-*Orion*) 14.8.17–25.4.19.
FRANCE CHERIE	141/91	BDV; 1916–9.19.
FRANK	76/96	19.5.17–3.11.19.
G. R. GRAY	268/17	29.11.17– Stranded 27.10.18 at Farn Island.
GAUNTLET	149/91	(ex-*Goole No. 8*) 15.3.18–28.9.19.
GEORGE ROBINSON	95/96	(ex-*Amedee Visart*) 15.12.14–29.10.19.
GLADSTONE	214/16	31.8.16–19.2.19.
GOLDEN CROWN	184/96	DY; Purchased 1917–6.19 sold.
GOOLE No. 6	108/85	19.12.17–26.3.19.
GOOLE No. 7	184/85	(ex-*Southesk*) 17.4.16–6.6.19.
GOOLE No. 10	169/96	4.12.14–21.1.20.
GRAN CANARIO	151/07	23.3.17–13.4.20.
GUARDSMAN	102/05	DY; 18.12.15–8.11.19; =in WW II.
HAMPDEN	227/10	(ex-*Southampton*) 23.8.14–14.6.19.
HANNAH JOLLIFFE	178/00	12.8.14–20.10.19.
HARRINGTON	367/89	22.8.15–30.9.15; lost 6.16.
HEATHERCOCK	182/03	(ex-*Torbay Scout*) 20.2.18–17.6.19.
HELEN PEELE	133/01	10.8.17–16.4.19.
HERALD	367/07	8.9.14–4.2.19.
HERCULES	234/90	2.9.14–1914.

Name	TG/Yr	Service—Fate
HERCULES	121/10	11.12.14–20.10.19.
HERCULES	225/85	13.3.15–10.4.19.
=HERACLES 12.16		
HIBERNIA	210/84	2.8.14–10.10.19.
=HIBERNIA III		
HOMER	157/15	1.11.15–28.8.19.
HULLMAN	171/14	1.1.17–22.9.19.
IRISHMAN	99/96	HS; =BDV 9.15; 30.7.14–6.7.20.
JACK	360/85	(ex-Jackal, ex-Jackal, ex-Woodcock, ex-William Jolliffe) 1.1.15– stranded 9.8.17 off the Tyne.
JAVA	114/98	DY; 25.5.15–3.11.19.
JIM MCCAUSLAND	262/86	(ex-Flying Serpent) 2.9.14–15.5.19.
JOHN BULL	165/80	16.12.14–5.2.15.
JOSEPH CROSTWAITE	149/96	(ex-Huskisson) HS; 31.8.15–20.9.20.
JUMBO	95/88	BDV; 30.7.14–8.10.19.
KESTREL	70/97	12.12.14–31.12.18.
KINSMAN	119/08	Exam; 3.1.17–9.5.19; =KEVERNE in WW II.
LA FRANCE	775/15	11.10.15–1915.
LADY DUNCANNON	181/14	25.2.18–20.10.19.
LADY WINDSOR	81/91	30.7.14–3.7.19; =IOLAIRE in WW II.
=IOLAIRE 1919		
LANCELOT	71/06	HS; 10.12.17–12.5.19.
LANGTON	157/92	31.8.15–24.3.20.
LETTIE	89/14	BDV; 18.2.16–20.3.19; =in WW II.
LINESMAN	96/11	HS; 13.3.15–6.7.15.
LORD KITCHENER	78/01	HS; 10.7.15–26.6.16.
LUDGATE	165/92	(ex-President Ludwig) 2.9.17– Stranded 15.2.18 in Wigtown Bay.
LYNX	79/05	2.8.14–16.1.20.
MANILA	180/95	13.5.17–29.7.17.
MARKSMAN	78/14	HS; 24.11.15–8.5.20.
=BOATMAN 4.18		
MERCURIUS	90/12	7.2.19–1.8.19.
MEYUN	567/05	In East Indies. 5.3.17–15.7.19.
MOSELLE	71/87	5.11.15–4.2.16.
NORA	99/89	19.7.17–20.9.19.
NORD	104/05	1915–1919.
NORTHUMBRIA	100/94	29.7.15–6.8.15.
ORION	90/12	BDV; 1916–1919.
OUTPOST	/	(ex-hopper).
PEEWIT	245/81	(ex-Plover) 26.9.14–8.3.20.
PLUMGARTH	164/08	HS; 1.6.16–9.12.19.
POLLUX	/14	5.2.15–21.1.20.
PREMIER	83/94	1.6.18–22.1.19.
PRIMROSE	150/92	(ex-St. George) 1916–1918.
PRINCESS ROYAL	105/88	23.6.15–11.8.15 and 23.5.18–1918.
QUEEN OF THE USK	91/85	HS; 29.1.18–26.4.19.
QUESTER	70/99	(ex-Enterprise) HS; 10.2.18–24.2.19.
QUIXOTIC	197/98	1918–1920.
R. NICHOLSON	200/91	(ex-Vulcan) 28.8.14–5.5.19.
RACIA	410/94	(ex-Oceaan) Purchased 1916–23.6.20 sold.
RESOLUTE	71/03	16.9.16–17.9.19.
RIDGWAY	230/14	8.1.15–11.10.15.
ROBIE	89/15	BDV; 8.3.16–14.2.20.
ROMAN	108/06	Exam; 6.1.17–12.3.20; =ROMAN in WW II.
=ROMANCE 5.18		
ROYAL BRITON	99/85	31.5.16–31.8.16.
RUNNER	146/86	(ex-Champion) 30.7.14–27.10.19.
ST. MAWES	80/17	1.6.17–19.7.19; =in WW II.
SAMPHIRE BATTS	174/93	(ex-Sea King) 25.8.14–6.10.19.
SANDU	118/08	22.4.18–19.8.18.
SARAH JOLLIFFE	333/90	8.3.15–13.1.20.
SHARK	163/91	26.10.14– Loaned to USN 30.9.18–6.1.19.
SIMLA	144/98	30.7.14–21.7.15.
SIR BRIAN	146/93	(ex-Knight Templar) 25.3.18–3.3.19.
SIR FRANCIS DRAKE	478/08	30.7.14–14.1.19.
SIR RICHARD GRENVILLE	420/91	30.7.14–14.1.19.
SIR THOMAS	184/98	(ex-Knight Prender) 13.3.18–30.1.19.
SIR WALTER RALEIGH	478/08	30.7.14–14.1.19.
SMEATON	369/83	30.7.14–5.10.20.

Name	TG/Yr	Service—Fate
SOUTER	123/10	22.10.15–10.1.16.
SOUTHERN CROSS	78/96	BDV; 1916–13.8.19.
SPURN	103/07	2.8.14–21.12.14 and BDV 7.15–1919.
STORK	278/05	17.3.17–11.4.19.
SUN III =SUCCOUR 1915	197/09	DY; hired 3.8.14– purchased 1915–1919 sold; =SUN III in WW II.
SUN IV	200/15	15.2.16–16.3.16.
SUNDERLAND	172/14	HS; 4.12.15–22.3.19.
SYMBOL	119/81	(ex-Samson) 25.9.15–2.6.16.
T. A. JOLLIFFE	199/01	12.8.14–15.11.14 and 9.3.15–14.2.20; later =EASTLEIGH.
TALIESIN	79/83	HS; 24.9.14–7.8.19.
TERRIER =TERRIER II	79/83	BDV; 25.8.14–12.9.19.
THE LIBERATOR	93/06	13.3.16–27.10.19.
TRENT =TRANTER	107/84	BDV mooring tug; 1916–10.3.20.
TRIBESMAN =JUPITER 1916	70/16	29.6.16–26.10.16 sold to France.
TUNISIEN II	/09	27.11.16–24.5.17.
VELMAR	122/83	(ex-Nestor) 20.2.18–18.12.18.
VIOLET	141/92	12.7.17–14.2.19.
VULCAN	288/93	30.7.14–8.8.14.
WALFISCH	/14	BDV; 24.12.14–19.2.19.
WAPITI	208/15	7.12.15–23.8.19.
WAPPING	180/94	(ex-Andrew Jolliffe) 26.8.14–25.2.20.
WARSASH	120/15	12.10.15–22.10.19.
WATCHER	583/11	(ex-PLA hopper No. 15) 1.16–1919.
WESTCOCK	138/98	(ex-Lady Jackson) 13.8.15–22.9.15.
WHITE ROSE	125/85	10.10.18–27.11.18.
WILLIAM FINDLEY	87/84	1.4.18–20.11.19.
WILLIAM GRAY	178/11	29.10.14–6.8.19.
WRESTLER =HOTSPUR 1917	192/14	DY; hired 1916– purchased 1918–6.20 sold; =MURIA; =MURIA in WW II.
WYVERN =WICKSTEAD 7.18	215/05	15.3.15–25.2.20; =WICKSTEAD.
ZEALANDIA	128/82	17.11.14–24.11.14.

Notes: One of the JOLLIFFEs became a rescue tug 9.18, assigned pendant W.24. T. A. JOLLIFFE carried pendant P.8A from 1.16, and P.A6 from 1.18 to 6.18. Many of these tugs were used as expeditionary force tugs during part of the war and most of the vessels released from naval service 1917–18 went to similar duties. With very few exceptions, all of these wore the red ensign and were chartered for service as "naval tugs".

HIRED SCREW TUGS (69 TG and under)

Name	TG/Yr	Service	Name	TG/Yr	Service
ACTIVE	58/75	1915–1918	CONTRACT	38/07	6.18–4.20
ADA	21/85	7.18–9.19	CREED	58/81	3.18–2.19
ADDER	54/06	2.18–9.19	(ex-Cruiser)		
ADDIE	44/15	3.18–10.19	DARTMOTHIAN	50/15	10.17–3.19
ADUR (ex-Helene)	57/77	8.14–5.20	=HELLESPONT DASHER	27/83	8.14–10.19
ADUR II	54/12	8.14–3.19	DEERHOUND	30/78	8.14–1918
AILSA	60/06	9.16–6.20	DIAMOND	36/97	8.14–1.20
ALARM	22/62	10.18–11.18	DORA	33/95	8.14–3.19
ALBERT	61/82	8.14–10.19	DRAGON	56/77	8.14–6.15
ALPHA	33/97	8.14–10.19	DUKE OF YORK	51/00	8.14–10.19
APOLLO	52/00	4.15–7.19	ECLIPSE	30/77	10.18–11.18
AQUILA (BDV) (ex-Pendragon)	59/70	8.17–1.20	EDITA (ex-Falaise)	61/96	12.17–2.20
BEAULIEU (BDV)	58/01	8.14–2.20	ELSA PARTISS	42/08	12.14–4.20
BEAUMONT	58/07	7.18–1.20	EMBER	18/08	4.18–12.19
BOARHOUND (ex-Leopold II)	54/82	8.14–10.19	EMPRESS FISH DOCK No. 1	67/97 58/04	9.14–5.19 –3.19
CAWOOD	34/08	4.18–11.19	FRASERVILLE	51/04	11.17–10.19
CENTRAL No. 8	17/13	9.16–3.17	GAMECOCK	50/86	2.15–3.18
CENTRAL No. 10	17/13	3.17–3.19	(ex-Adventuress)		
CONQUEROR	55/01	9.18–9.19	GARTH	45/84	10.16–4.19

Name	TG/Yr	Service	Name	TG/Yr	Service
GLORY	50/03	10.16–6.20	PETRO	34/91	12.17–4.19
GNAT	38/88	8.14–5.19	PICTON	/14	4.16–5.18
(ex-Hero)			PIONEER (BDV)	47/06	1916–7.20
GOOLE No. 2 (BDV)	56/99	7.16–1.20	=TRACKER 4.18		
GOOLE No. 3 (BDV)	56/99	3.16–2.18	PRIMROSE	52/06	8.16–5.19
GOOLE No. 5	69/84	4.18–12.19	PRINCE	45/85	8.14–6.19
HARMONY	51/93	12.17–3.19	PRINCE GEORGE	27/98	8.14–7.19
HINDE II	43/16	8.16–12.19	PRINCESS	63/04	8.14–7.19
(ex-W. E. Hinde)			PRINCESS	20/86	8.16–2.19
HORTON (RCN)	66/06	4.18–10.19	PRINCESS MAY	43/93	8.14–3.19
IONA	48/05	12.14–9.15	(ex-Elisabeth)		
J. C. MILLER	33/10	6.18–11.20	PROGRESS	65/93	8.14–9.14
J. W. BRANKLEY (RCN)	61/14	6.18–12.19	REGIA	50/92	6.16–10.16
			REGINA	40/87	1916–1918
JAMES S. GREGORY (RCN)	53/11	6.18–12.19	REINDEER	21/79	8.14–10.14
			RENOWN	54/79	8.14–8.19
JOHN FOSTER SPENCE	28/98	8.14–9.19	=RENOWN III 2.18		
JOHN O'GAUNT	51/95	1.18–5.20	RESCUE	35/78	8.14–9.14
JUBILEE	36/97	8.14–10.19	RESOLUTE	32/77	8.16–7.19
K.14 (BDV 9.15)	13/14	1.15–8.19	ROBERT FORREST	33/95	10.16–8.19
KATHLEEN	38/92	12.16–11.19	RODNEY	48/87	1917–1919
KENT	35/03	12.15–10.16	ROMULUS	35/83	6.15–3.16
KENTON (RCN)	46/96	–3.19	ROTIFER	48/83	3.18–7.19
(ex-Frederick A.)			ROY	27/07	8.16–7.19
KESTON	22/04	5.18–10.19	SALAMIS	/	1916–1920
KITE	69/02	11.14–12.13	SAN	22/85	4.17–3.18
KROOMAN	61/05	–10.17	SANDWICH	26/92	9.18–12.18
LADY MORGAN	53/88	11.18–12.18	SILVIA	/	4.15–1.16
LEOPOLD	54/81	8.14–8.19	SPEEDWELL (BDV)		1916–1920
LYDFORD	40/80	10.18–4.19	STAG	38/83	6.17–3.20
(ex-Union)			T. BROWN	50/00	5.18–6.20
MARLTON (RCN)	64/14	8.18–1.20	TEDDINGTON	17/17	5.18–9.19
MAUNA LOA	44/07	11.17–2.19	TENACITY	69/14	12.14–5.19
MEDWAY	30/95	11.14–12.18	THAMES	32/97	11.14–2.18
MIDGE	27/61	12.14–6.15	THEMIS (BDV)	54/09	1916–12.19
MILDRED	26/93	8.14–8.19	TRANSPORT	24/03	7.18–9.19
MINAS (BDV)	64/09	1916–7.19	TYRE (BDV)	49/88	6.15–5.19
MYRTLE	32/67	8.16–8.19	(ex-A. H. K.)		
NAB	59/12	9.18–7.19	USEFUL	45/07	1919–1923
NORMAN	24/85	8.16–8.19	VELOX	60/98	9.18–1.20
ORTHONA	69/78	1.18–4.19	VERNE	42/96	8.14–3.15
PERRAN	35/07	8.16–11.19	VIGILANT	44/06	8.14–1919
			WALRUS	39/89	6.17–7.20

Notes: These were limited to harbour and inland service because of their size, being in the berthing and launch type tug category. THAMES foundered 16.2.18 off the east coast of Scotland and was the only wartime loss. A number of tugs chartered for one towing assignment or in service less than a month have been omitted. Most of these short-term charters lasted only a few days before they were released. All of these hired tugs flew the red ensign. Two large tugs built for Argentina were detained 1914 and for a short time were in use by the Admiralty; ONA and QUERANDI (both 345/14), but they were later released. Some twenty to thirty tugs on foreign stations had some association with the navy but were not properly a part of it; in 2.17 one source lists 15 vessels on the South American station. A few tugs used as minesweepers and patrol craft on foreign stations will be found listed with miscellaneous patrol vessels.

HIRED PADDLE TUGS

Name	TG/Yr	Service—Fate
AGUIA	194/62	(ex-Knight of the Cross) DY; purchased 1915–11.3.22 sold.
AID	194/89	DY; hired 30.1.15 purchased 27.7.15–10.19 sold.
ALBERT VICTOR	128/83	(ex-Lass o'Gowrie) HS; 29.7.14–30.6.19; =M/L 8 mines 1918.
ALEXANDER	196/91	Hired 4.17, purchased 1.9.18–10.20 sold.
AMERICA	244/91	HS; 13.9.15–15.5.20; =M/L 8 mines 1918.
BEN LEDI	114/78	1.8.14–25.9.15.
CONQUEROR =QUERY 2.18	224/97	DY; 9.11.16–18.2.19.
DUNDAS	117/85	HS; 2.8.14–29.4.19.
DUNDEE	264/75	HS; 15.2.18–17.3.19.

Name	TG/Yr	Service—Fate
EARL ROBERTS	199/00	(ex-Lord Roberts) M/S; 28.7.16–15.10.17 and 23.9.18–7.3.19 (loaned to USN 9.18–1.19).
ELECTRIC	62/34	29.1.17–22.9.17.
FLYING FISH	163/32	22.9.18–20.2.19.
FLYING FISH =FLYING FISH II 12.15	187/86	DY; 7.12.14–27.10.19; =M/L 8 mines 1918, not completed.
FLYING FOX =FLYING FOX II 6.18	185/85	DY; 30.7.14–4.6.19.
FLYING MIST	148/92	23.6.15–1.9.20.
FLYING SCUD	74/77	6.10.17–27.10.17.
FLYING SPORTSMAN	187/82	30.7.14–30.3.19.
FLYING WITCH	142/91	23.6.15–29.7.20.
FORTH	129/83	(ex-Flying Owl) HS; 1.8.14–24.3.19.
FRENCHMAN	137/92	(ex-Coquet) 26.2.18–6.5.19.
FURLOUGH	105/88	(ex-Princess Royal) HS; 23.6.15–10.5.19.
GAUNT	87/69	(ex-Gauntlet) 21.5.17–1.9.19.
GRANGE	125/80	(ex-Flying Dutchman) 31.1.15–24.3.19.
GRANITE CITY	113/83	1.4.18–20.11.19.
HENDON	130/06	24.6.15–31.3.20.
HEY DAY	99/04	(ex-Hibernia) 5.6.18–21.8.19.
IRELAND	245/91	M/S; 20.3.18–27.4.20; =M/L 10 mines 4.18.
J. P. RENNOLDSON	149/83	17.5.18–16.12.18.
JOHN MCCONNOCHIE	90/79	HS; 1.4.18–20.11.19.
JUMNA	51/84	9.7.18–23.8.19.
JUNO	89/80	6.7.17–27.10.17.
KING EDWARD VII	138/01	HS; 12.10.18–23.8.19.
LINGDALE	174/82	(ex-Lady Vita) 1.4.15–1.2.20.
MARSDEN	131/06	24.6.15– wrecked 31.10.15.
MONARCH	123/83	(ex-Flying Spear) 30.7.14–25.10.19.
NEMEA	145/77	(ex-Hercules) 28.6.15–12.3.19.
NICOLAI	152/70	4.17–31.8.18.
PERO GOMEZ	96/69	30.12.14–28.3.19.
POWERFUL	182/78	(ex-Flying Huntress) 1.5.18–13.5.18.
QUEEN =QUINCE c1917	169/83	29.7.14–14.12.19; =M/L 8 mines 1918.
REBECCA	86/84	4.2.15–4.5.15.
ROYAL NORMAN	144/81	5.7.18–21.2.19.
SIR HUGH BELL	175/13	27.6.15–7.5.20.
SIR JOSEPH PEASE	180/96	DY; 14.7.15–25.8.19.
SOLWAY	103/86	BDV; 1916–17.5.19.
TRANSFER	169/84	(ex-Transit) 12.8.18–24.5.19.
ULYSSES	118/74	HS; 22.5.17–7.7.17.
UNIVERSE	143/75	5.3.18–13.5.19.
WEXFORD	141/88	31.7.15–29.4.16.
WHITBURN	119/05	HS; 30.7.14–1.4.19; =in WW II.

Notes: Employed on harbour and dockyard service, normally flew the red ensign.

RESCUE TUGS

Towards the end of 1916 a special Tug Committee was formed to control the use of naval tugs for emergency rescue activities. The policy of dispatching sea-going tugs to assist damaged vessels into port had been in existence earlier but not on an organised basis. Adjustments were soon made in order to free all suitable tugs from less important harbour and inland duties to serve as rescue tugs. On 18.2.17 it was estimated that 26 more large tugs were needed; 20 of these could be taken up from existing tugs while 6 others were to be built for the purpose (approved 21.2.17). On 1.3.17 a review of tugs on examination service caused some tugs to be replaced by yachts or trawlers thusly providing additional rescue tugs.

The deployment of rescue tugs in 5.17 placed 5 at Portland, 2 at Plymouth, 5 at Falmouth, 5 in the Scillies, 2 at Milford, 4 at Stornoway, 5 at Lough Swilly, 5 at Berehaven and 5 at Queenstown. 14 American tugs were promised for use at Irish ports. The bulk of the rescue tugs were hired (some later purchased) and originally employed on more routine services. These were joined by some Admiralty vessels and by new construction as soon as completed.

HIRED RESCUE TUGS

Pendant Nos.		Name	TG/Yr	Service, etc.
1.18	9.18			
		ALEXANDRA II	215/17	30.1.18–23.1.20.
		ALICE	253/13	(ex-*Vincent Grech*) DY; 1916–9.25 sold.
		ANDROS	274/85	(ex-*Knight of St. Patrick*) DY; 6.15–8.22 sold.
W.00		ATALANTA III	577/07	21.2.15–26.1.20.
	W.01	AUTOCRAT	128/15	16.2.16–4.2.20.
	W.63	BLAZER	283/88	(ex-*The Rose*) Exam; 4.12.14– stranded 9.11.18 at Scilly Islands.
W.04		BRAMLEY MOORE	214/16	15.9.16–8.2.19.
W.09		CARTMEL	304/07	6.17–30.7.19.
W.10		CENTRAL No. 1	136/10	20.11.14–1919.
W.11		CENTRAL No. 2	137/12	20.11.14–1919.
W.12		CORINGA	287/14	25.5.17–17.4.20; =in WW II.
W.17		CRICCIETH	102/05	(ex-*Conqueror*) BDV; 10.2.15–26.3.20.
W.14		CROFT	149/13	10.7.17–4.12.18.
W.19		DIRECTOR GERLING	166/92	5.1.15–11.9.19.
		DORA DUNCAN	126/91	(ex-*Lionel*) 12.8.15–26.5.19.
W.21		DREADFUL	253/12	9.5.17– purchased 9.5.18–29.7.20 sold; =RUMANIA.
W.22		EPIC	268/09	(ex-*Heroic*) 3.5.17–17.5.20.
W.25		FLYING BUZZARD	200/12	DY; 11.8.14–6.2.19.
W.26		FLYING CORMORANT	203/03	DY; 21.6.16–29.4.19.
W.27		FLYING FALCON	184/04	30.6.17–1920.
W.28		FLYING FOAM	217/17	21.2.17–9.10.19.
W.29		FLYING SPRAY	217/17	8.4.17–29.3.19.
W.31		FRANCIS BATEY	151/14	DY; 31.10.14–8.5.19.
W.32		FURNESS	225/98	
W.33		FYLDE	256/04	26.7.17–7.2.19.
W.38		GEORGE V	224/15	DY; 1.5.15–24.11.15; 1917–1919.
W.37		GEORGE DINSDALE	105/13	21.10.14–10.12.19.
	W.94	GOPHER	198/10	(ex-*H.S. 88*) 1918–7.9.20.
		GREAT EMPEROR	171/09	5.17–8.12.17.
W.39		GUIANA	166/86	(ex-*Power*) DY; 7.11.14– sunk 29.1.18 in collision off the East Coast.
W.42		HEROINE	203/09	3.5.17–31.7.20.
	W.69	JOFFRE	260/16	23.11.17–15.3.19.
		JOHN PAYNE	145/09	17.7.15–23.1.20.
W.45		JOSEPH CONSTANTINE	154/13	HS; 2.5.17–15.2.19
W 48		LABOUR	362/16	(ex-*Labourdonnais*) 3.16–13.9.19.
W.49		LADY BRASSEY	362/13	30.7.14–6.10.19; =in WW II.
W.50		LADY CRUNDALL	366/06	2.8.14–1.8.19.
W.52		MARGARET HAM	113/13	BDV; 7.9.15–29.5.19.
W.53		MARSDEN	195/17	1.10.17–11.11.19.
W.54		MERRIMAC	226/18	23.2.18–17.5.19.
W.55		MILEWATER	283/88	(ex-*Susan McCausland*) 11.8.17–23.1.19.
		MOOSE	208/15	2.10.15–8.1.20

Pendant Nos. 1.18	Pendant Nos. 9.18	Name	TG/Yr	Service, etc.
		MUSGRAVE	220/97	17.12.15–1.12.16 and 1917–18
	W 78	NEPTOR	325/15	(ex-Neptuno) purchased 8.11.15–1920 sold
		NERO	177/15	(ex-N. E. R. No. 3) 20.10.15–22.8.19.
W.68		PALADIN =PALADIN II 1917	326/13	BDV; 17.11.14–31.1.19.
	W.65	PLUNGER	173/00	(ex-Triton) 6.3.18–27.1.19.
	W.66	REVENGER	243/05	(ex-Maas) 3.8.14–1919.
		SEA PRINCE	97/85	19.7.15–16.10.19.
		SLIEVE FOY	154/10	21.7.15–17.5.19.
	W.41	SONIA	294/16	(ex-Limburg) 8.11.17–29.8.19.
W.74		STORMBIRD	215/85	(ex-Storm Cock) DY; 13.8.14–9.10.19.
W.75		STORMCOCK	99/84	(ex-Storm Cock) 11.7.17–14.1.20.
W.76		SUN II	197/09	DY; 3.4.14– purchased 1915–4.12.17. =in WW II.
	W.60	SUN VII	202/18	23.2.18–20.12.19. =in WW II.
W.83		VANQUISHER =VANQUISHER II 1917	179/99	(ex-Abeille No. 10) 30.7.14–11.11.19.
	W.64	VICTOR =ICTOR 1918	153/98	6.3.18–8.2.19.
	W.71	VULCAIN	200/03	5.1.15–7.6.15 and 7.10.17–17.1.19.
W.86		WARRIOR	192/95	HS; 7.8.14–27.10.19.
	W.76	WASHINGTON	167/81	21.12.14–23.4.15 and 5.12.17–13.2.19.
		WATO	292/04	26.11.17–1921. =in RAN WW II.
		WESTBOURNE	185/11	31.10.16–23.7.19.
W.87		WILLIAM POULSOM	219/17	1.4.17–24.11.19.
	W.57	WOONDA	305/15	Purchased 1915–11.21 sold.
W.88		WRESTLER =WRESTLER II 2.18	192/15	14.1.16–17.10.19.
		WYOLA	306/12	28.3.18–1920.
W.91		ZAREE	218/04	(ex-Nere Maitea) Purchased 1917–14.7.20 sold.

Notes: Rescue tugs in service before 1917 served as Dockyard tugs (DY), Harbour service (HS) or on general towing work. Note the renamed tugs OCEANA (ex-Cerberus) and DRAGE (ex-Dragon) included with boarding tugs and numerous others (mostly Admiralty owned). Another tug PENTOWER 102/13 (ex-Cleopatra) is listed briefly in 1917 as a rescue tug.

STOIC CLASS RESCUE TUGS

885 tons. 141¾ (pp) × 29 × 16 ft. TE 1200 ihp = 11¼ kts.

Pendant Nos.	Name	Launched	Builder—Fate
W.15 (1.18)	CYNIC	28.10.16	Bow McLachlan, Sold 18.2.22 =URSUS.
W.79 (9.18)	STOIC	3.15	Bow McLachlan. Resold 5.20 Chile =PILOTO SIBBALD.
	DAINTY	1918	Finch. Sold 1922 Irish Government; later =CHERBOURGEOIS No. 2.
W.93 (1919)	DANDY	1919	Finch. Sold 30.6.21 =LAGOS VULCAN.
	SPRY	1918	Livingstone & Cooper. Sold 1.23 =LAGOS ATLAS.

Notes: The first two were ex-Chilean JUAN SOVERNY and PILOTO SIBBALD respectively, purchased on the stocks. The last three were ordered 1.17 for the Department of Transport & Shipping using STOIC as their prototype but not laid down until 10.17. In commercial service they measured 457 to 507 tons gross. STOIC was on boom defence duty at Scapa to 1918. The W flag superior was mostly made up of rescue tugs and some salvage vessels. Later W pendants were assigned to many fleet tug types.

FRISKY CLASS RESCUE TUGS

612 tons gross. 155¼ (pp) × 31 × 15 ft. TE 1200 ihp.

	Name	Launched	Builder—Fate
	FRISKY	8.18	Lewis. Sold 4.25 =GUSTAVO IPLAND; later =FOUNDATION FRANKLIN.
	JAUNTY	1919	Ritchie G. & M. Sold 17.4.30 =RIO TEJO.
	SAUCY	1918	Livingstone & Cooper. Sold 12.4.24 Shanghai Tug & Lighter Co, same name; =in WW II.

Notes: Ordered 1.17 for the Department of Transport & Shipping using the tug RACIA as their prototype. Sometimes referred to as "Racia type".

RESOLVE CLASS RESCUE TUGS

1400 tons.   182 (oa), 175 (pp) × 34 × 15 ft.   TE 2400 ihp = 14 kts.

Pendants Nos.	Name	Launched	Builder—Fate
W.85 (9.18)	RESOLVE	30. 7.18	Ayrshire. Sold c1950.
W.92 (9.18)	RESPOND	21.11.18	Ayrshire. BU 1956 in Italy.
W.84 (9.18)	RETORT	1918	Day Summers. Sold c1958.
W.81 (9.18)	ROLLCALL	2. 8.18	Ferguson. Sold 6.21 and cancelled; resold 16.8.22 = ROMSEY.
W.95 (1919)	ROLLICKER	16. 1.19	Ferguson. Sold 12.5.22 J. & A. Brown; repurchased 3.34; sold 24.6.52, BU Clayton & Davie.
	ROYSTERER	4. 2.19	Thornycroft. Sold 22.12.54. BU at Genoa.

Notes: Also known as "Hunter class' they were ordered 2.17 using the commercial tug SIR DAVID HUNTER (Ferguson 1915) as prototype. Dimensions were made larger than the prototype, the measurement of 622 tons gross was therefore increased to between 739 and 842 tons gross for these vessels.

SAINT CLASS

800 tons.   143 (oa), 135 (pp) × 29 × 12 ft.
440 tons gross.   TE 1250 ihp = 12½ kts.
Armament: 1–12 pdr (designed)

Pendant Nos. 9.18	Name	Launched	Builder—Fate
W.02	ST. ABBS	17.12.18	Ferguson. Sunk 1.6.40 by German A/C off Dunkirk.
W.36	ST. ANNE	15. 4.19	Ferguson. Sold 10.22 R. MacGregor, same name; = in RCN WW II; = CASCAPEDIA 1943.
	ST. ARISTELL	.19	Crabtree. Sold 7.4.26 J. Brown, Newcastle, NSW, same name.
W.05	ST. ARVANS	.19	Day Summers. Sold 25.8.23 J. H. Clarke = OCEAN-EAGLE; = OCEAN EAGLE in RCN WW II.
W.40	ST. ATHAN	.19	Day Summers. Sold 17.11.24 British Tanker Co, same name.
W.18	ST. AUBIN	.18	Harland & Wolff, Govan. Sold 12.4.24 Shanghai Tug & Lighter Co, same name; = in WW II.
W.23	ST. BEES	.18	Harland & Wolff, Govan. Sold 7.22 Moller Towage Ltd = HENRY BURTON.
W.46	ST. BLAZEY	16. 1.19	Cran & Somerville. Condemned 12.7.46; sunk as target off Bermuda.
W.20 (11.19)	ST. BONIFACE (ex-St. Fergus)	16. 6.19	Fleming & Ferguson. To New Zealand Government 18.3.25; = TOIA 4.26; sold 1955.
W.51	ST. BOSWELLS	2. 5.19	Cran & Somerville. Mined 12.6.20 off Terschelling.
W.34	ST. BOTOLPH	.18	Livingstone & Cooper. Sold 29.12.26 George MacLean = KUMAKI.
+	ST. BREOCK (ex-St. James)	10.11.19	Hong Kong and Whampoa. Sunk 14.2.42 by Japanese A/C off Sumatra.
W.44	ST. CATHERINE	3. 6.19	Livingstone & Cooper. Sold 30.4.26 A. H. Reid, Vancouver = CANADIAN NATIONAL No. 2.
	ST. CLAUDE (ex-St. Mary)	.19	Livingstone & Cooper. Sold 10.25 J. Fenwick, Sydney NSW = LINDFIELD.
W.06	ST. CLEARS	.19	Livingstone & Cooper. Sold 1948 Rigdon Beasley, Southampton.
	ST. CLEMENT	21. 8.19	Ferguson. Sold 6.21 Crichton Thompson; resold 11.21 to Spain = CICLOPE.
W.07	ST. COLUMB	22. 9.18	Crichton. Wrecked 16.1.20; wreck sold 30.1.20 V. Grech Ltd.
W.47	ST. CYRUS	5. 4.19	Crichton. Mined 22.1.41 off the Humber.
	ST. DAY	20.11.18	Taikoo, Hong Kong. Sold 9.4.48 = URSUS.
	ST. DOGMAEL	.18	Taikoo, Hong Kong. Sold 10.50.
	ST. DOMINIC	.19	Hong Kong and Whampoa. Sold 12.11.19 Gibb-Livingstone at Hong Kong, same name; = in WW II.
	ST. ENODER (ex-St. Osyth)	.19	Day Summers. Sold 9.6.25 to Denmark = GARM.
	ST. ERTH	28. 2.19	Murdoch & Murray. Sold 9.25 J. Fenwick, Sydney NSW = HEROS; = HEROS in RAN WW II.

Pendant Nos. 9.18	Name	Launched	Builder—Fate
	ST. EWE	1. 4.19	Murdoch & Murray. Sold 11.10.26 H. Gould Page; to Iraq =ALARM; =ALARM in WW II.
	ST. FAGAN	.19	Lytham SB. Sunk 1.6.40 by German A/C off Dunkirk.
	ST. FAITH	.19	Lytham SB. Sold 6.21 Crichton Thompson, same name.
W.22 (11.19)	ST. FINBARR	7. 7.19	Fleming & Ferguson. Sold 6.23 Canadian Government =FRANKLIN.
	ST. FLORENCE	19. 3.19	Crichton. Sold 14.11.24 Canadian Pacific Railway =KYUQUOT.
W.04 (11.19)	ST. GENNY	28. 5.19	Crichton. Foundered 12.1.30 off Ushant.
W.96	ST. GILES	14. 5.19	Ferguson. Sold 7.22 J. & A. Brown =KHALIFA; =ST. GILES in RAN WW II.
W.08 (11.19)	ST. HELIERS	26. 6.19	Ferguson. Sold 23.6.20 Crichton Thompson, same name.
	ST. HILARY	.19	Lytham SB. 7.4.26 Waratah Tug & Salvage Co, same name.
W.25 (11.19)	ST. ISSEY	.18	Napier & Miller. Sunk 28.12.42 by S/M off Benghazi.
W.90	ST. JUST	.18	Napier & Miller. Sunk 11.2.42 by Japanese A/C off Singapore.
	ST. KEYNE	12. 6.19	Murdoch & Murray. Sold 18.6.26 to Brazil =TIMES.
	ST. KITTS	24. 6.19	Murdoch & Murray. Sold 3.2.26 to Adelaide SS Co =UCO.
	ST. MABYN	.19	Livingstone & Cooper. Sold 3.5.26 J. Brown, Newcastle NSW, same name; =CAROLINE MOLLER in WW II.
W.27 (11.19)	ST. MARTIN	.19	Livingstone & Cooper. Sold 11.46.
W.89	ST. MELLONS	.18	Harland & Wolff, Govan. Sold 8.7.49 H. G. Pounds, Portsmouth.
	ST. MINVER	.19	Day Summers. Sold 23.4.25 =ABEILLE No. 22; =ABEILLE 22 in WW II.
	ST. MONANCE	11. 9.19	Hong Kong and Whampoa. Sold 4.48.
	ST. OLAVES	27.12.19	Harland & Wolff, Govan. Sold 12.6.22 J. & A. Brown, same name; =in WW II.
	ST. OMAR	15. 9.19	Ferguson. Sold 4.48 in the Mediterranean.
W.26 (11.19)	ST. SAMPSON	.19	Hong Kong and Whampoa. Sold 4.22 Wheelock & Co, "who defaulted"; resold 6.22, same name; =in WW II.
	ST. TEATH	29. 5.19	Walker. Sold 2.6.26 to Brazil =PARANA.
	ST. TUDY	11.11.19	Walker. Sold 16.7.26 F. P. Barney, later =ST. EILEEN.

Notes: A total of 64 of these rescue tugs were ordered; the first orders were placed in 4.18 and by 8.18 all contracts had been allocated. This class was the largest part of a belated order to make up for the acute shortage of sea-going tugs which were so urgently needed to assist damaged ships into port. As rescue tugs, they were to be armed, fitted with wireless, smoke-generating apparatus, and carry listening hydrophones. By the time they were delivered there was no longer a need for their designed armament and very few (if any) were armed. They proved to be a very handy and useful type in both the Navy and commercial service. Later they were used towing targets and performed as fleet tugs. In an order dated 6.12.18 eighteen tugs were cancelled from this programme:

Crabtree: ST. ROCHE.
Cran & Somerville: ST. AUSTELL, ST. BREOCK, ST. BUDEAUX.
Crichton: ST. BRIDGET, ST. PHILIP.
Day Summers: ST. OWEN, ST. ROLLOX.
Ferguson: ST. BONIFACE, ST. CLAUDE.
Lewis: ST. ALBERT, ST. ENODER, ST. ETIENNE, ST. GERVAIS.
Livingstone & Cooper: ST. FINELLA, ST. GRACE, ST. GREGORY, ST. KEVERNE.

WAR DEPARTMENT TUGS

A large number of small tugs and steam lighters were acquired for the War Office during the war, some being requisitioned and others built during 1917–19. These were designated "AS" (up to No. 41 as lighters and above that number as tugs); "HS" (tugs of 85 (pp) ×22 ft, displacing about 300 tons, averaging 150 tons gross, built 1917–19 and miscellaneous requisitioned vessels); "TT" (tugs—see "Dance" class tunnel tugs).

Apart from the "Dance" class, some 50 of these vessels were transferred to the Admiralty towards the end of the war and were used on dockyard service; most were sold in the 1920s, though six remained to see service in WW II.

The following vessels were given names by the Admiralty:

ACOR 106/97 (ex-HS.69; ex-Penguin)
CLINCHER 368/92 (ex-HS.41)
COR IV 112/12 (ex-HS.72)
CRAIG 69/17 (ex-HS.306; also TT.9)
CRUSOE (ex-HS.70)
FRIDAY (ex-HS.74)
J. O. GRAVEL 197/09 (ex-HS.45)
JULIA C. MORAN 192/02 (ex-HS.44; ex-Harry G. Runkle)
LAVAL 287/14 (ex-HS.43)
LORD BERESFORD 112/09 (ex-HS.71)
M. MORAN 315/12 (ex-HS.42)

MYSTIC 75/99 (ex-HT.12)
PETER PAN 135/18 (ex-HS.84)
PETREL 55/92 (ex-HS.40)
PUNCHER (ex-HT.1)
SAXON 24/83 (ex-AS.315)
SCOTTISH 141/03 (ex-HS.39)
TALBOT (ex-HT.3)
VAPOUR (ex-AS.27)
VETO (ex-AS.33)
WENDY = EARLY 1920 151/19 (ex-HS.85)

Others included:

C.15 (ex-HT.14)
C.66 (ex-AS.41)
C.134 (ex-AS.40)
C.505 (ex-AS.139) = CONTACT

YC.71 (ex-AS.28)
YC.72 (ex-AS.29)
YC.297 (ex-AS.25)

Also note GOPHER (ex-HS.88), listed with rescue tugs. HS.84 was built by Edwards, Millwall and later became COCKSPUR when sold in 7.22. HS.85 also built by Edwards, was sold 4.20 and became FABIA. Two other vessels, HT.10 (ex-Volunteer) 112/91 and HT.61 (ex-Northumbria) 100/94 were sold by the Admiralty in 1920.

FERRO-CONCRETE TUGS

A total of 24 ferro-concrete tugs were ordered by the Admiralty for the Inland Waterway and Dock Department, intended for towing ferro-concrete barges across the Channel. Only 12 of these "Crete" tugs were actually completed; they measured about 267 tons gross. 125 (pp) ×27¼ × 13¼ ft, had TE 750 ihp engines. The vessels completed 1919–20 were: CRETEBLOCK, CRETEBOOM, CRETEBOW, CRETECABLE, CRETEGAFF, CRETEHATCH, CRETEHAWSER, CRETEMAST, CRETEROPE, CRETESTEM, CRETEWHEEL and CRETEYARD. Three of these vessels became early victims of accidents: CRETECABLE (6.20), CRETEROPE (1.2.20) and CRETEWHEEL (lost 14.10.20). Over 50 ferro-concrete barges of 1000 tons deadweight also assigned "Crete" names were built 1919–20.

SALVAGE VESSELS

Pendant No.	Name	TG/Yr	Service—Fate
	BILBROUGH	554/56	Added 11.17– Sold 3.11.19 Cassar Ltd, Malta.
	DALKEITH	741/89	(ex-*Dalhousie*) Tug. Purchased 3.16– Sunk 18.5.18 by S/M at San Pietro Island, Sardinia.
W.82 (9.18)	HUGHLI	513/94	Tug. 23.2.15– Foundered 15.5.19 off Nieuport.
	LA VALLETTE	325/79	(ex-*Polygon*) 11.17–1919.
W.59 (6.18)	LINNET =LINTON 8.16	426/80	31.10.14–1919.
	LYONS =LA NINA 1917	537/85	(ex-*Lyon*) Also Q ship. 5.8.14–17.4.16 and 7.12.17–20.5.19.
	RACER	*970/84	Sloop (Devonport DY 6.8.84) =Salvage vessel 6.17; sold 6.11.28 Hughes Bolckow, Blyth.
W.67 (9.18)	RANGER	409/80	Late gunvessel (Elder 12.2.80; sold 24.9.92); hired 11.14–1919.
4.18	RECLAIMER	296/85	(ex-*Argo*) 20.3.15–26.2.16.
	RESCUE	357/04	Tug. 23.3.15–14.6.19.

*Displacement.

Notes: Other salvage vessels included ETNA and ZEPHYR listed with MFAs (qv); MARINER W.35 9.18), REINDEER (W.70 9.18) and RINGDOVE (ex-*Melita*) with BDVs; MOONFLEET with tugs; MELITA (ex-*Ringdove*) and THRUSH with coastguard vessels.

LIFTING CRAFT

Pendant No.	Name	TG/Yr	Service
	ALLIGATOR =LC.1 3.17	704/97	15.2.16–10.11.20.
	BUFFALO =LC.3 3.17	704/97	15.2.16–8.4.16 and 12.10.16–10.11.20.
	CROCODILE =LC.4 3.17	706/97	15.2.16–8.4.16 and 12.10.16–10.11.20.
	DROMEDARY =LC.2 3.17	706/97	15.2.17–10.11.20.
W.43 (1.18)	HIPPOPOTAMUS =LC.5 1918	703/97	26.2.17– Purchased 9.17; sold 10.11.20.
W.68 (1.18)	RHINOCEROS =LC.6 1918	706/97	26.2.17– Purchased 1917; sold 10.11.20.

Notes: Large dumb barges with horned bows. They were normally used in pairs to effect progressive lifts by ballasting down, tightening cables on a wreck, then after pumping ballast, they were towed by tugs into shallower water. The submarines E.4 and E.41 were salvaged in this manner. Another vessel, LC.7 was the former YC.96, designated in 1918. YC.96 had been built 1913 and displaced 270 tons; sold 9.22 to C. N. Hamblin.

BOOM DEFENCE VESSELS

Defensive booms are one of the oldest forms of harbour defence. By 1914 the booms comprised a barrier formed by 40-foot timber balks secured alongside each other by chains and stretched across a harbour mouth with the intention of barring the entrance to enemy torpedo boats. Openings in the boom could be closed by "gate vessels" and a number of old naval vessels were used for this purpose. By the end of 1914, the booms had anti-submarine nets suspended from them. Little-used harbour entrances, in particular many of those at Scapa Flow, were closed by blockships. Pivot vessels, opening ships, closing ships, and a multitude of tenders, repair vessels, and supply ships were required to maintain the boom barrier to protect harbours and war anchorages. A very large number of trawlers, drifters, tugs, and barges were requisitioned during the war for the Boom Defence Service. Trawlers, drifters and tugs employed as BDVs are listed in their respected "Hired" lists. The anchorage for the Grand Fleet at Scapa Flow had no less than 125 boom defence vessels attached at the end of the war. Other harbours with less exposed frontages were more secure from the enemy and easier to seal their entrances.

Name (base)	Tons	Launched	Builder—Fate
ARGO (Spithead)	1130	3. 8.80	Devonport DY. Sold 25.8.21 W. Thorpe.
AZOV (Spithead)	1130	30. 7.80	Devonport DY. Sold 25.8.21 C. A. Beard.
BULLFROG (Malta) =EGMONT 3.23 =ST. ANGELO 7.33	465	3. 2.81	Pembroke DY. =Base ship at Malta 3.23; sold 1933.
MAGPIE (Solent)	805	15. 3.89	Pembroke DY. =D/S 10.15; sold 29.12.21.
MARINER (Devonport)	970	23. 6.84	Devonport DY. =Salvage vessel 1917; sold 2.29 Hughes Bolckow.
MELITA (Solent) =RINGDOVE 12.15	970	20. 3.88	Malta DY. =Salvage vessel 11.15; sold 9.7.20 =RINGDOVE'S AID.
PIKE (Solent)	254	16.10.70	Campbell & Johnston, North Woolwich. Sold 27.3.20 G. Sharpe.
PLOVER (Gibraltar)	755	18.10.88	Pembroke DY. Sold 27.4.27 at Gibraltar.
REINDEER (Devonport)	970	14.11.83	Devonport DY. =Salvage vessel 1917; sold 12.7.24 Halifax Shipyard Ltd.
WRANGLER (Solent)	465	5.10.80	Vickers. Sold 2.12.19 J. H. Lee.

Notes: These ten old sloops and gunboats were on boom defence in 8.14. ARGO and AZOV were formerly named ESPIEGLE and MUTINE. Most of the dockyard mooring vessels (qv) were also on boom defence work during the war.

WAR CONSTRUCTION

Boom defence vessels ("BD" series): 300 tons. Armament: 1–12 pdrAA.
Barrage vessels ("BV" series):   275 tons. Armament: 2–12 pdrAA.
Both series were: 100 (oa), 96 (pp) ×25 ×8 ft. No propelling machinery; "dumb".

16 built by Workman Clark:

BV.1	(12.11.17) BU c1944.		BV.8	(12.11.17) =SOUTHGATE 6.33; sold 1946 at Singapore.
BV.2	(12.11.17) BU c1944.		BV.9	(1918) Sold 8.4.42 Ward.
BD.3	(1918) Sold 6.24 J. Jackson.		BV.10	(1917) Sold 1945.
BV.4	(28.11.17) =SANDGATE 6.33; scuttled 2.47.		BV.31	(19.4.18) Sold 6.24 Ward.
			BD.32	(23.5.18) Sold 5.23 McLellan.
BV.5	(12.11.17) =PARKGATE 6.33; =BV.5 1940; sold 1945.		BD.33	(23.5.18) Sold 5.23 McLellan.
			BD.34	(25.5.18) Sold 6.24 J. Jackson.
BV.6	(1917) Sold 28.6.27 Ward.		BD.35	(28.5.18) Sold 5.23 McLellan.
BV.7	(12.11.17) =POLEGATE 6.33; =BV.7 1940; sold 1945.		BD.36	(28.5.18) Sold 5.23 McLellan.

6 built by W. Chalmers, Rutherglen:

BD.11 (1917) Sold 5.23 Ward.		BD.14 (12.4.18) Sold 5.23 Ward.
BD.12 (16.11.17) Sold 5.23 Ward.		BD.51 (1918) Sold 5.23 McLellan.
BD.13 (13.12.17) Sold 5.23 Ward.		BD.52 (1918) Sold 5.23 McLellan.

3 Built by Scott, Bowling:

BD.15 (15.11.17) Sold 5.23 Ward.	BD.39 (1918) Sold 5.23 McLellan.
BD.16 (10.12.17) Sold 5.23 Ward.	

4 built by A. W. Robertson, Millwall:

BV.17	(14.3.18)	=WESTGATE 1937; sold 6.8.46 at Malta.	BV.41	(6.9.18)	Sold 10.10.47.
BV.18	(12.4.18)	Sold 28.4.47.	BV.42	(22.10.18)	Lost 22.12.43 by explosion at Leith.

4 built by Manchester DD Co, Ellesmere Port:

BD.19	(17.11.17)	Sold 5.23 Ward.	BD.37	(1918)	Sold 5.23 McLellan.
BD.20	(1917)	Sold 5.23 Ward.	BD.38	(1918)	Sold 9.4.23 Metals & Accessories Ltd.

2 built by Ritchie, Graham & Milne, Whiteinch:

BD.21	(1917)	Sold 5.23 Ward.	BD.22	(1917)	Sold 5.23 McLellan.

4 built by Day Summers:

BD.23	(28.11.17)	Sold 9.4.23 J. McWilliam.	BD.25	(1918)	Sold 9.4.23 J. McWilliam.
BD.24	(1918)	Sold 9.4.23 J. McWilliam	BD.26	(1918)	Sold 9.4.23 J. McWilliam.

2 built by Thornycroft:

BD.27	(13.4.18)	Sold 9.4.23 J. McWilliam.	BD.28	(1918)	Sold 9.4.23 J. McWilliam.

2 built by W. H. Warren, New Holland:

BD.29	(1918)	Sold 9.4.23 J. McWilliam.	BD.30	(21.9.18)	=REIGATE 6.33; sold 1958.

1 built by E. Finch, Chepstow:

BD.43	(1918)	Sold 9.4.23 J. McWilliam.

2 built by Camper & Nicholson:

BD.45	(1918)	Sold 9.4.23 J. McWilliam.	BD.46	(1.10.18)	=ROGATE 6.33; sold 7.47.

2 built by C. H. Walker, Sudbrook, near Chepstow:

BD.47	(1918)	Sold 9.4.23 J. McWilliam.	BD.48	(1918)	Sold 9.4.23 Metals & Accessories.

2 built by Abdela & Mitchell:

BD.49	(1918)	Sold 9.4.23 J. McWilliam.	BD.50	(1918)	Sold 5.23 E. Suren.

Notes: The first 38 vessels were reported on order 6.17; by 9.17 numbers to 52 were building; two (BD.53–54) were begun 12.17; four more in 2.18 and BD.59–60 were on order 19.2.18. By November 1918, 32 vessels (BD and BV) were in service, the BDs being at Cromarty, Granton and the Humber. The BVs had a powerful searchlight atop the bridge, intended to keep net barrages illuminated at night, preventing U-boats from trying to pass on the surface. The BVs were built for the A/S barrage in the Dover Straits, however, they appear in red lists attached to the Harwich Local Area. The deep minefield barrier in the Dover Straits proved to be a far more effective trap for U-boats and the reliance upon net-drifter barriers (and BVs) had greatly been reduced by the end of 1918. Ten BDs were cancelled 12.18; BD.40 (Scott); BD.44 (Finch); BD.53–54 (Warren); BD.55–56 (Walker); and BD.57–60 (Chalmers).

BLOCKSHIPS

PURCHASED 1914–15

Name	Length (pp) ft	For use at—	TG/Yr	Other names
ALMERIA	293	(Scapa)	2418/88	(ex-Wakefield)
ANNADALE*	264½	(Dover)	1521/78	
ARGYLE	241½	(Scapa)	1185/72	
BERKSHIRE	285	(Sunderland)	2285/94	
CHICKLADE	299	(Sunderland)	2410/88	
CLIO	300	(Scapa)	2733/89	
CORDOVA*	294	(Portland)	2387/88	(ex-Jessmore)
DYLE	260	(Scapa)	1510/79	(ex-Widdrington)
ELTON	300	(Scapa)	2461/88	
FERNLANDS	276	(Sunderland)	2042/85	
GADITANO*	400	(Dover)	4750/93	(ex-Barrister)
GARTMORE	270	(Scapa)	1774/79	(ex-Castilla)
GARTSHORE	255	(Portland)	1564/80	(ex-Iberia)
GLENGOIL*	320	(Portland)	2963/82	
GLENMORE*	265	(Portland)	1656/82	
GOBERNADOR BORIES	285½	(Scapa)	2332/82	(ex-Wordsworth)
GOTHLAND	251½	(Portland)	1485/71	
HUBBUCK*	325	(Portland)	2834/86	
LAPLAND	256	(Scapa)	1234/90	(ex-Dauntless)
LIVONIAN	420¼	(Dover)	4017/81	(ex-Ludgate Hill)
LORNE	241½	(Portland)	1186/73	
MAGDA*	290	(Portland)	2351/88	
MONTROSE	365	(Dover)	4452/05	
NEWBRIDGE	342	(Dover)	3737/06	
NUMIDIAN	400		4836/91	
PONTOS	430¾	(Scapa)	5703/00	
REGINALD	240¼	(Scapa)	930/78	
REINFELD	340	(Scapa)	3582/93	(ex-Ramses)
RONDA	274	(in reserve)	1941/81	(ex-Rydal Holme)
ROSEWOOD	259	(Scapa)	1757/89	(ex-Blakemoor)
ROTHERFIELD	320	(Scapa)	2831/89	
SPANISH PRINCE	450	(Dover)	6505/94	(ex-Knight Bachelor)
TEESWOOD	278½	(Scapa)	1589/82	(ex-Westwood)
THAMES	279½		1327/87	
TYNEDALE	320	(Sunderland)	2948/89	(ex-Incharran)

Notes: Vessels marked * were not used as blockships. ALMERIA was originally purchased as accommodation ship; GADITANO became an oil hulk at Sheerness and later sold; NEWBRIDGE went to East Africa for use in the "KONIGSBERG" operations; CORDOVA, MAGDA, GLENMORE, GLENGOIL, GOTHLAND and HUBBUCK became gate vessels.

OTHER BLOCKSHIPS

Name	Length	For use at	TG/Yr	Other names
AORANGI	389	(Scapa)	4268/83	
FIERAMOSCA	170	(Malta)	578/73	(ex-Sophie Jobson)
GARGANO	180	(Malta)	700/84	(ex-Irene)
LUCANO	180¼	(Malta)	709/84	(ex-Ariadne)
PEREGRINE II*	280	(reserve Medway)	1681/92	
TENERIFFE*	301	(reserve Medway)	1800/85	

Notes: FIERAMOSCA was expended 1915 at Suvla. PEREGRINE II became a BDV and TENERIFFE purchased 14.6.18, was sold 7.1.20. The battleship HOOD (qv) was used as a blockship; Admiralty expense accounts indicate that a total of 49 blockships were purchased for the sum of £424,249 during the war.

MOORING VESSELS

735 tons. 152¼ (oa), 135 (pp) ×27½×10 ft. 500 ihp=9¼ kts.

Name	Launched	Builder—Fate
RECOVERY	26. 2.07	Fleming & Ferguson. Sold 25.8.23 J. A. White.
RESOURCE	7. 6.10	Bow McLachlan. Sold 1923 J. A. White.

Notes: On boom defence duty at Scapa and Granton respectively to 1918.

SIX VESSELS PURCHASED 1915

1916	1.18	Name	Tons	TG/Yr	Dimensions—Fate
X.03	X.12	BULLFROG (ex-*Blairstown*)	895	/	131 (pp) ×36 ft. Sold 2.23 Carriden S Bkg Co.
X.30	X.19	DAPPER (ex-*Chapman*)		419/15	124¼ (pp) ×30½ ft. Sold 3.23, same name; =in WW II.
X.20	X.25	FIDGET	837	/	150 (pp) ×28½ ft. Sold 8.21 J. R. Thomson.
X.19	X.30	HOLDFAST (ex-*Commissioner*)	783	403/10	122¼ (pp) ×35¼ ft. Sold 3.23 Carriden S Bkg Co.
X.18	X.39	LIMPET (ex-*Mauch Chunk*)	570	298/12	112 (pp) ×31½ ft. Sold 5.22 =T. I. C. LIMPET.
X.17	X.68	STEADFAST (ex-*Ohio*) =STANDFAST 11.17	625	339/06	118 (pp) ×35 ft. Sold 5.22 Maritime Salvors =STANDFAST.

Notes: On boom defence duty to 1918: BULLFROG, FIDGET and HOLDFAST at Scapa, LIMPET at Cromarty and STANDFAST at Granton.

TRINCULO CLASS

750 tons. 152 (oa), 135 (pp) ×26¾×10½ ft. 500 ihp=9½ kts.

X.35	X.01	ANCHORITE =HERMIT 1944	24. 1.16	Simons. BU 2.48 Metal Ind, Rosyth.
X.42	X.11	BUFFALO	25. 1.16	Bow McLachlan. Mined 4.4.41 off Singapore.
X.41	X.42	MESSENGER	22. 2.16	Bow McLachlan. Sold c1950 at Malta.
X.39	X.69	STEADY	30. 3.16	Simons. Mined 17.7.40 off Newhaven.
X.34	X.44	TRINCULO =MOLLUSC 1.16	20.11.15	Fleming & Ferguson. Sold 12.22 =YANTLETT.
X.38	X.77	VOLUNTEER =VOLENS 3.19	17. 3.16	C. Rennoldson. Sold 1947 Tees Conservancy =VOLENS.

Notes: ANCHORITE was originally PROGRESS. All on boom defence to 1918: ANCHORITE and BUFFALO at Sheerness, MESSENGER at Granton, STEADY at Portsmouth, TRINCULO at Scapa and VOLUNTEER at Devonport.

MOOR CLASS

720 tons. 148 (oa), 137½ (pp) ×29×10½ ft. TE 600 ihp=9 kts.
Armament: 1–12 pdrAA (not mounted).

MOOR	12. 6.19	Bow McLachlan. Mined 8.4.42 off Malta.
MOORDALE	15. 8.19	Bow McLachlan. Sold 1961.
MOORFOWL	11. 9.19	Bow McLachlan. Sold c1963.
MOORHILL	12. 9.19	Bow McLachlan. Sold c1961.
MOORLAKE	10.11.19	Bow McLachlan. Sold 1946 in the East Indies.
MOORSTONE	12.11.19	Bow McLachlan. Sold 1949 at Malta =KURTARAN.
MOORVIEW	.19	Bow McLachlan. Wrecked 21.3.20 on the Runnelstone, Lands End.

DEPOT AND REPAIR SHIPS
(Sea-going)

Our first depot ship was HECLA dating from 1880, she served as a mother ship for torpedo boats and later for destroyers. By 1905 there were four depots for destroyers and three for submarines with ASSISTANCE as a fleet repair ship. As the number of torpedo craft increased, naturally enough there was a corresponding increase in depot ships to support the flotillas. Essentially they were accommodation ships for the Senior Officer of the flotilla, his staff and for off-duty crews. They were equipped with a machine shop for minor repairs and storage space for torpedoes and supplies.

MERCANTILE CONVERSIONS

5600 tons. 391½ (pp) ×39×21½ ft. TE 2400 ihp=13 kts.
Armament: 4–12 pdr. (2–4 in added in 10.16).

1914 1.18		Name	Launched	Builder—Fate
7A	C7	HECLA	7. 3.78	Harland & Wolff. Sold 13.7.26 Ward, Preston.

Notes: Was BRITISH CROWN, purchased on stocks 1878. Served as depot for 4th DF at Scapa 1914–16 and 2nd DF at Belfast 1917–18.

3560 tons. 320 (pp) ×34×18½ ft. TE 1120 ihp=11 kts.
Armament: 4–12 pdr.

N.76	N.0A	TYNE	1878	Armstrong. Foundered 15.11.20 at moorings, Sheerness while on sale list for Stanlee.

Notes: Was MARIOTIS, purchased on stocks 8.3.78. Served as depot for 8th DF in Firth of Forth 1914–18.

9600 tons. 436 (pp) ×53×20 ft. TE 4000 ihp=12 kts.
Armament: 10–3 pdr.

8C	C2	ASSISTANCE	23.12.00	Raylton Dixon. Handed over 11.3.37 to Ward in part payment for MAJESTIC.

Notes: Fleet repair ship, purchased on stocks 19.9.00. Served at Scapa and Cromarty 1914–18.

11300 tons. 460 (pp) ×55×21 ft. TE 3500 ihp=11½ kts.
Armament: 6–4 in.

A1	C5	CYCLOPS	27.10.05	Laing. Arrived 7.47 Cashmore.

Notes: Was INDRABARAH, purchased on stocks 1905. Served with the Grand Fleet as repair ship 1914–18.

3660 tons. 268¼ (pp) ×37¾×16 ft. TE 1100 ihp=10½ kts.
Armament:

N.13	N.06	AQUARIUS	25. 9.00	Austin. Sold 14.5.20.

Notes: Was HAMPSTEAD, purchased 1902 for use as a distillery vessel and completed 6.07 as depot ship. Served 8th DF Forth 1914–15, Mediterranean S/Ms 1915, then became a water carrier and D/S in Mediterranean.

NAVY-ORDER AND WARSHIP CONVERSIONS

6620 tons. 373 (oa), 350 (pp) ×58×22 ft. TE 12000 ihp=20 kts.
Armament: 8–4.7 in, 8–6 pdr. (8–4.7 in removed and 4–3 pdr added 11.15).
Armour: 5 in deck.

1914 1.18		Name	Launched	Builder—Fate
N.70	N.4A	VULCAN =DEFIANCE III 2.31	13. 6.89	Portsmouth DY. =T/S 2.31; sold 9.55; BU in Belgium.

Notes: Built as a carrier for 2nd class torpedo boats. Served as depot to 7th S/M Flotilla at Leith 1914–16, then to S/M flotillas Humber, Berehaven and Blyth.

4300 tons. 300 (pp) × 46 × 20 ft. TE 5500 ihp = 17 kts.
Armament: 2–12 pdr, 6–6 pdr.

1914	9.15	1.18	Name	Launched	Builder—Fate
D.41	N.15	N.68	LEANDER	28.10.82	Napier. Sold 1.7.20 Castle, Plymouth.

Notes: Ex-cruiser, completed 6.04 as D/S. Depot ship for Grand Fleet destroyers 1914–18.

4050 tons. 300 (pp) × 46 × 20 ft. TE 5700 ihp = 17 kts.
Armament: 4–6 pdr.

| D.06 | N.06 | N.47 | FORTH | 23.10.86 | Pembroke DY. Sold 8.11.21 Slough T. C.; BU in Germany. |
| | N.43 | N.97 | THAMES | 3.12.85 | Pembroke DY. Sold 13.11.20 = GENERAL BOTHA T/S; = THAMES D/S in WW II. |

Notes: Ex-cruisers, completed as D/S in 8.04 and 7.03 respectively. FORTH served S/M flotillas at Devonport 1914, Humber 1914–16, Harwich 1916–18. THAMES was depot ship for 5th S/M Flotilla, Harwich 1914; Sheerness 1914–17, then Portsmouth and Campbeltown.

4360 tons. (See "Astraea" class cruisers).
Armament: 2–6 in, 2–6 pdr, 4–3 pdr. (4–3 pdr only 1917).

| N.41 | N.11 | BONAVENTURE | 2.12.92 | Devonport DY. Sold 12.4.20 Forth S Bkg Co, Bo'ness. |

Notes: Ex-cruiser, completed as D/S in 4.07. Depot for the 6th S/M Flotilla 1914–16, then 2nd S/M Flotilla 1916–18.

9000 tons. 399¾ (oa), 375 (pp) × 65 × 25 ft. TE 20000 ihp = 22 kts.
Armament: 4–6 in, 4–4 in, 4–12 pdr.
Armour: 6 in deck.

| C3 | | BLAKE | 23.11.89 | Chatham DY. Sold 9.6.22 Rees, Llanelly. |
| C2 | C4 | BLENHEIM | 5. 7.90 | Thames IW. Sold 13.7.26 Ward, Pembroke Dock. |

Notes: Ex-cruisers, completed as D/S in 8.07 and 5.06 respectively. BLAKE served the 2nd DF, then the 11th DF of the Grand Fleet 1914–18; BLENHEIM was depot ship for Mediterranean destroyers 1914–18.

810 tons. (See "Alarm" class under minesweepers).
Armament: 2–4.7 in, 4–3 pdr (HEBE); (ONYX nil).

1914	9.15	1.18	Name	Launched	Builder—Fate
	N.52	N.58	HEBE	15. 6.92	Sheerness DY. = M/S 1908; = D/S 1909; sold 22.10.19 Ward, Preston.
D.07	N.07	N.75	ONYX = VULCAN II 4.20	7. 9.92	Laird. Sold 8.24 King, Garston; resold 9.10.24 L. Basso, Weymouth.

Notes: Ex-torpedo gunboats converted in 1909 and 1908 respectively. HEBE served the 6th S/M Flotilla 8.14, the 6th on the Tyne 1914–16, the 1st at Leith 1916–17 and the 3rd S/M Flotilla on the Humber 1917–18. ONYX served the 1st S/M Flotilla at Devonport 1914–16, was base ship 1917–18 at Torbay.

7700 tons. (See "Edgar" class cruisers).
Armament: 4–6 in, 8–12 pdr.

| N.31 | N.88 | ST. GEORGE | 23. 6.92 | Earle. Sold 1.7.20 Castle, Plymouth. |

Notes: Ex-cruiser, completed as D/S 3.10. Served the 9th DF Forth 1914, 7th DF Humber 1914–15, was D/S in the Mediterranean 1915–18.

5750 tons. (See "Arrogant" class cruisers).
Armament: nil.

| P.42 | N.08 | ARROGANT | 26. 5.96 | Devonport DY. Sold 13.11.23 Hughes Bolckow. |

Notes: Ex-cruiser, completed as D/S 7.11. Served the 4th S/M Flotilla at Dover 1914–16, the 5th S/M Flotilla at Dover and base flagship 1915–18.

5600 tons. (See "Eclipse" class cruisers).
Armament: reduced to 3–6 in, 5–12 pdr, 1–3 pdrAA in 1916. (1–3 pdrAA only 1917).

| P.05 | P.87 | DIDO | 20. 3.96 | London and Glasgow. Sold 16.12.26 May & Butcher, Maldon. |

Notes: Ex-cruiser, completed as D/S 1913. Served 3rd DF GF 1914, 3rd DF at Harwich 1914–15, 9th DF Harwich 1915–17, 10th DF Harwich 1918.

2135 tons. (See "P" class cruisers).
Armament: nil.

1914	9.15	1.18	Name	Launched	Builder—Fate
D.08	N.08	N.77	PACTOLUS	21.12.96	Armstrong. Sold 25.10.21 Multilocular S Bkg Co, Stranraer.

Notes: Converted 9.12. Served the 9th S/M Flotilla at Ardrossan 1914–18.

980 tons. (See "Condor" class sloops).
Armament: 4–3 pdr.

	ROSARIO	17.12.98	Sheerness DY. Sold 11.11.21 at Hong Kong.

Notes: Converted in 1910. Served as D/S for S/Ms at Hong Kong.

1070 tons. (See "Dryad" class under minesweepers).
Armament: 2–4.7 in, 4–6 pdr.

P.38	P.96	HAZARD	17. 2.94	Pembroke DY. Sunk 28.1.18 in collision with SS WESTERN AUSTRALIA in the Channel.

Notes: Ex-torpedo gunboat, converted in 1901. Served as S/M depot ship at Dover 1914–18.

MERCANTILE CONVERSIONS

7100 tons. 390 (pp) ×46×20 ft. TE 3600 ihp=14 kts.
Armament: 8–4 in.

1914	1.18	Name	Launched	Builder—Fate
P.77	P.88	DILIGENCE	1907	Henderson. Sold 15.10.26 Hughes Bolckow.

Notes: Was TABARISTAN, purchased 29.1.13 and completed 10.13. Served the 12th DF at Scapa 1915–18.

4580 tons. 330 (pp) ×43×16 ft. TE 2200 ihp=11 kts.

N.71	N.78	PANDORA =DOLPHIN 10.24	5. 7.02	Raylton Dixon. Mined 23.11.39 off Blyth on passage for conversion to blockship.

Notes: Was SETI, purchased 9.11.14. Depot for Harwich S/Ms 1915–18.

5805 tons. 367½ (oa), 351 (pp) ×45×18 ft. TE 2750 ihp=12¼ kts.
Armament: 2–3 pdrAA.

P.2A	LUCIA	21.11.07	Furness. Sold 4.9.46 =SINAI.

Notes: Was German mercantile SPREEWALD, captured 9.14 and completed as D/S 8.16. Served the 10th S/M Flotilla, Tees 1916–18.

1141 tons gross. 220 (pp) ×30 ft.

	UPOLU (RAN)	1891	Fleming & Ferguson. Hired 8.14, paid off 9.12.14 and returned.

Notes: Used only while AE.1 and AE.2 were in Australian waters.

11500 tons. 485 (oa), 470 (pp) ×58×20 ft. TE 4000 ihp=10½ kts.
Armament: 4–4 in, 2–6 pdr.

1.16	1.18	Name	Launched	Builder—Fate
A4	C9	SANDHURST	14.12.05	Harland & Wolff. Arrived 4.46 Arnott Young, Dalmuir to BU.

Notes: Ex-dummy INDOMITABLE (qv), ex-Manipur, hired 11.14 and purchased 1915. Completed as fleet repair ship 9.16. Served at Scapa Flow 1916–18.

5250 tons. 350 (oa), 335 (pp) ×46×18 ft. TE 3200 ihp=14½ kts.

7C	AC	TITANIA	4. 3.15	Clyde SB. Arrived 9.49 Faslane to BU.

Notes: Was building 1914 for the R. Hungarian Sea Navigation Co; purchased 1915 and completed as D/S 11.15. Served with S/Ms at Blyth 1915–18.

8600 tons. 402 (oa), 390 (pp) ×52×18½ ft. TE 2500 ihp=11 kts.
Armament: 4–4 in, 2–6 pdr.

1.16	1.18	Name	Launched Builder—Fate
CA	C6	GREENWICH	5. 7.15 Dobson. Sold 11.7.46 =HEMBURY.

Notes: Purchased on stocks and completed 1916 by Swan Hunter. Served the 14th DF at Scapa 1916–18.

6600 tons. 388 (oa), 338 (pp) ×47½×20 ft. TE 6350 ihp=14¼ kts.
Armament: 2–12 pdr.

	C1	AMBROSE =COCHRANE 6.38	31. 3.03 Raylton Dixon. Sold 10.8.46, BU Ward, Inverkeithing.

Notes: Hired 1914 as an armed merchant cruiser (qv) and purchased 10.15 for conversion. Depot ship for S/Ms at Berehaven 1917–18, then at Falmouth 1918. Became a base ship 1938.

NAVY-ORDERS

935 tons. 212 (oa), 190 (pp) ×32½×11 ft. TE 1400 ihp=14 kts.
Armament: 1–4 in (ADAMANT only).

1914	1.18	Name	Launched Builder—Fate
P.37	P.00	ADAMANT	12. 7.11 Cammell Laird. Sold 21.9.32 Rees, Llanelly.
N.35	N.01	ALECTO	29. 8.11 Cammell Laird. Sold 7.7.49, BU at Faslane.

Notes: ADAMANT was depot for the 8th S/M Flotilla at Harwich 1914–15, then for Mediterranean S/Ms. ALECTO was depot for S/Ms at Yarmouth 1914–18.

3600 tons. 355 (oa), 320 (pp) ×45×16 ft. TE 2800 ihp=14 kts.

P.39	P.4A	MAIDSTONE	29. 4.12 Scotts. Sold 31.8.29.

Notes: Served Harwich S/Ms 1914–18.

3380 tons. 360 (oa), 320 (pp) ×40×14½ ft. TE 2600 ihp=13½ kts.
Armament: 4–4 in, 4–12 pdr.

AC	CA	WOOLWICH	5. 9.12 London and Glasgow. Sold 23.7.26 Ward, Hayle.

Notes: Served with destroyers at Harwich 1914 and Rosyth 1915–18.

300 tons. 150¼ (oa), 132 (pp) ×31×3½ ft. Compound 200 ihp=7½ kts.
Armament: (oil fuel).

		SCOTSTOUN	* 8.16 Yarrow. Sold 4.20 at Basra.

Notes: (* sections completed). A stern-wheel river steamer built as depot ship for gunboats in Mesopotamia. Ordered 2.16 and re-erected 10.16 at Abadan. Transferred to Inland Transport, Royal Engineers in late 1918.

3476 tons. 325 (oa), 310 (pp) ×44×15 ft. TE 2650 ihp=14 kts.

	C8	PLATYPUS (RAN) 28.10.16 =PENGUIN 8.29 =PLATYPUS 3.41	John Brown. On sale list 12.57.

Notes: Depot ship for S/Ms at Campbeltown and Killybegs 1917–18.

TORPEDO SUB-DEPOT SHIPS

Name	TG/Yr	Builder—Dimensions—Fate
ARO	3794/98	Raylton Dixon. 351¾ (pp) ×44 ft. (ex-*Albertville*) Purchased 19.10.14; =troopship 14.8.18; sold 1.20 W. R. Davies, =STELLA.
SOBO	3652/99	Barclay Curle. 345 (pp) ×44 ft. Purchased 10.14; sold 12.2.20 W. R. Davies & Co, =JUPITER.
SOKOTO	3092/99	Vickers. 345 (pp) ×42½ ft. Purchased 10.14; sold 18.9.19 =TABLADA.

Notes: ARO carried pendants Y1.2 and Y8.126. All three were formerly managed by Elder Dempster, purchased 10.14 for £55000. ARO was D/S at Rosyth 1915–18, SOBO was D/S at Cromarty from 1915 and SOKOTO served as D/S at Scapa Flow from 1915.

FUEL SHIPS

Although the majority of the ships of the navy in 1914 were coal-burning and coal-burners were still being built in 1918, there was only one collier (MERCEDES) which was Admiralty-owned; none was acquired during the war years, reliance being placed upon the chartered red-ensign ships. Over 2500 red-ensign colliers were chartered and assigned pendants Y3.1 to Y3.2524. 244 of them became war losses.

No distinction was made between an "oiler" which fuelled ships in harbour and a "tanker" which transported oil from its source to storage tanks on shore. All were termed "oilers" by the Admiralty.

In the following list of fuel ships, all are oilers unless otherwise stated. The red-ensign oilers are not included, except in the case of some of the "Leaf" and "War" classes, all of which later wore the blue ensign. Red-ensign oilers were given pendants Y7.1 to Y7.342 and 44 of these became losses.

1455 tons. 185 (pp) × 29 × 15 ft. TE 775 ihp = 13 kts.

Pendant Nos.			Name	Launched	Builder—Fate
1914	1916	1.18			
P.95	X.31	X.34	KHARKI	22.12.99	Irvine SB, Irvine. Sold 7.31 at Hong Kong.

Notes: Was purchased 20.3.00 and was a collier until 1906.

9930 tons. 351 (pp) × 50½ × 27 ft. TE 2350 ihp = 9 kts.

| P.92 | X.28 | Y3.1923 | MERCEDES | 27.11.01 | Northumberland SB. Sold 7.20 = JUAN OLAV-ARRIAGA. |

Notes: Was a collier, purchased 1908.

9900 tons. 381½ (oa), 370 (pp) × 48½ × 23 ft. TE 2000 ihp = 12 kts.
Armament: 1–3 pdr (from, 6.15).

1914	9.15	1.16 1.18	Name	Launched	Builder—Fate
D.99	N.92	X.10 X.51	PETROLEUM	18.11.02	Swan Hunter. Handed over 26.2.37 Ward in part payment for MAJESTIC.

Notes: Purchased 3.05, the first oiler in the RN.

980 tons. 176 (oa), 170 (pp) × 26 × 12 ft. 650 hp = 10 kts.

1914	1916	1.18	Name	Launched	Builder—Fate
P.93	X.29	X.33	ISLA	14. 2.03	Garston SB. Sold 9.9.21 = PASS OF BRANDER.

Notes: Was a petrol carrier, ex-*Thistle* purchased 6.3.07.

3945 tons. 270 (pp) × 36 × 18 ft. TE 1200 ihp = 11 kts.
Armament: 1–3 pdr (from 6.15).

| N.96 | X.14 | | BURMA | 3. 3.11 | Greenock & Grangemouth. Sold 28.6.35 McLellan. |

1935 tons. 210 (oa), 200 (pp) × 34 × 16 ft. TE 700 ihp = 8 kts.

| N.97 | X.15 | X.02 | ATTENDANT | 5. 7.13 | Chatham DY. Sold 1934 = ATTENDANT. |
| N.89 | X.06 | X.63 | SERVITOR | 26. 5.14 | Chatham DY. Sold 9.22 = PULOE BRANI. |

2178 tons. 210 (oa), 200 (pp) × 34 × 17 ft. TE 450 ihp.

| N.98 | X.16 | X.15 | CAROL | 5. 7.13 | Devonport DY. Sold 28.6.35 McLellan. |
| N.88 | X.07 | X.24 | FEROL | 3.10.14 | Devonport DY. Sold 29.1.20 = OSAGE. |

4060 tons. 280 (pp) × 39 × 18 ft. Diesel 1500 bhp = 12 kts.

| N.93 | X.11 | X.73 | TREFOIL | 27.10.13 | Pembroke DY. Sold 28.6.35 McLellan. |
| | X.12 | X.74 | TURMOIL | 7. 3.17 | Pembroke DY. Sold 28.6.35 McLellan. |

7513 tons gross. 460 (oa), 440 (pp) × 54¼ ft. Diesel 2500 bhp = 10 kts.

| P.84 | X.26 | Y7.121 | OLYMPIA | 1916 | Vickers. Launched as SANTA MARGHERITA. |

Notes: Three others of the same programme were OLAF, OLIVIA and OLNA; all cancelled.

10500 tons. 385 (pp) × 50½ × 25 ft. TE = 10 kts.

1914	1916	1.18	Name	Launched	Builder—Fate
	Y7.188		DELPHINULA	1908	Armstrong. Hulked 1938; BU 9.47 in Spain.

Notes: Was BUYO MARU, purchased 1915.

9830 tons. 370 (pp) × 48½ × 24 ft. TE 2400 ihp = 10 kts.

| | Y7.220 | | NUCULA | 1906 | Armstrong. Sold 1938 as hulk. |

Notes: Was SOYO MARU (Y7.73), purchased 1915. On loan to New Zealand Govt in 1936.

2419 tons gross. 285¼ (pp) × 38¾ ft. TE

| | Y7.54 | | ERIVAN | 1893 | Palmer. Sold 2.19. |

Notes: Commissioned 4.16.

4236 and 4145 tons respectively. 270 (pp) × 38½ × 20 ft. TE 1200 ihp = 11 kts.

| X.02 | X.43 | MIXOL | 17. 6.16 | Caledon SB. Sold 1947 = WHITEBROOK. |
| X.45 | X.71 | THERMOL | 29. 4.16 | Greenock & Grangemouth. Sold 1947 = BROCO-DALE H. |

EIGHT EX-SPECIAL SERVICE VESSELS (dummy battleships) CONVERTED 1915–16

8106 tons gross. 485 (pp) × 59 ft. TE = 13 kts.

| Y7.172 | ABADOL = OAKLEAF 2.17 | 11. 7.99 | Stephen. Sunk 25.7.17 by S/M NW of the Butt of Lewis. |

Notes- Ex-dummy IRON DUKE, purchased 7.15 and converted; ex-*Montezuma* hired 10.14.

8455 tons gross. 500 (pp) × 60¼ ft. TE

| Y7.173 | BAYOL = BAYLEAF 1917 | 1893 | Harland & Wolff. Sold 1919 = PYRULA. |

Notes: Ex-dummy QUEEN MARY, purchased 1915; ex-*Cevic* hired 10.14.

5478 tons gross. 445 (pp) × 52½ ft. TE = 13 kts.

| X.04 | MONTCALM | 17. 5.97 | Palmer. Sold 22.10.19 = CRENELLA; = REY ALFONSO 1923. |
| Y7.143 | = CRENELLA 11.16 | | |

Notes: Ex-dummy AUDACIOUS, purchased 29.1.16; ex-*Montcalm* hired 10.14.

9336 tons. 420 (pp) × 54 ft. TE 3000 ihp = 12 kts.
5865 tons gross.

| X.05 | X.48 | PERTHSHIRE | 1893 | Hawthorn Leslie. Sold 26.2.34, BU in Italy. |

Notes: Ex-dummy VANGUARD, purchased 1915; ex-*Perthshire* hired 10.14. Oiler used as water tanker until 3.20, then oiler to 1922, then became a store carrier.

8039 tons gross. 470 (pp) × 56 ft. TE = 13 kts.

| Y7.174 | RANGOL = MAPLELEAF 11.16 | 17. 8.98 | Swan Hunter. Sold 4.10.19 = BRITISH MAPLE. |

Notes: Ex-dummy MARLBOROUGH, purchased 10.7.16; ex-*Mount Royal* hired 10.14.

7394 tons gross. 446 (pp) × 52 ft. TE = 13 kts.

| X.06 | X.60 | RUTHENIA | 31. 3.00 | Barclay Curle. = Oil hulk 3.31; captured 1942 by Japanese = CHORAN MARU; recaptured 1945 = transport; BU 6.49 at Dalmuir. |

Notes: Ex-dummy KING GEORGE V, purchased 1.16; ex-*Ruthenia* hired 11.14. Was a water carrier 1915, oiler 1916.

7535 tons gross. 446 (pp) × 52 ft. TE = 13 kts.

| Y7.170 | SAXOL = ASPENLEAF 10.16 | 21.11.99 | Barclay Curle. Sold 12.9.19 = PRYGONA. |

Notes: Ex-dummy CENTURION, purchased 6.16 (named SAXOL 9.6.16); ex-*Tyrolia* hired 10.14.

7474 tons gross. 470 (pp) × 56¼ ft. TE

Y7.175	X.70 TEAKOL =VINELEAF 1917	1901	Swan Hunter. Sold 12.7.19 =BRITISH VINE.

Notes: Ex-dummy INVINCIBLE, purchased 1915; *ex-Patrician* hired 11.14. The pendant X.70 was assigned to "TEAKOL" 1.18 but the name had been altered by this time.

Name	TG/Yr.	Service
ESTURIA (RAN)	2143/10	12.16–1917.

Notes: A hired blue-ensign vessel.

EX-PLA HOPPERS CONVERTED AND RENAMED 10.16

1st two: 704 tons gross. 190 (pp) × 30 ft. TE 145 nominal hp.
Others: 869 tons gross. 198 (pp) × 32 ft. TE 116 nominal hp.

1.18	Name	Built	Builder	Commissioned
X.04	BARKOL (*ex-PLA No. 3*)	1898	Simons.	1.17
X.05	BATTERSOL (*ex-PLA No. 4*)	1898	Simons.	11.16
X.08	BLACKOL (*ex-PLA No. 5*)	1906	Fleming & Ferguson.	11.16
X.28	GREENOL (*ex-PLA No. 7*)	1907	Fleming & Ferguson.	11.16
X.56	PURFOL (*ex-PLA No. 6*)	1907	Fleming & Ferguson.	10.16
X.64	SILVEROL (*ex-PLA No. 8*)	1907	Fleming & Ferguson.	12.16

Notes: Names use leading part of borough names situated along the Thames. All were returned to the Port of London Authority in 1920.

EX-DREDGER PURCHASED ON STOCKS

7589 tons. 326½ (pp) × 54½ × 18½ ft. TE 2400 ihp = 11 kts.
3999 tons gross.

1.18	Name	Launched	Builder—Fate
X.80	DREDGOL	25. 5.18	Simons. Sold 28.6.35 Arnott Young, Dalmuir.

LEAF CLASS

12300 tons. Avg 405 (pp) × 54½ × 26 ft. TE 6000 ihp = 14 kts.

Pendant	Name	Launched	Builder—Fate
X.32 Y7.178	APPLELEAF (*ex-Texol*)	28.11.16	Workman Clark. Arrived 12.47 Arnott Young, Dalmuir.
Y7.156	ASHLEAF (*ex-Olga*)	12. 9.16	Ropner. Sunk 29.5.17 by S/M 150 miles west of Bishop Rock.
Y7.154	BEECHLEAF (*ex-Olmos*)	26.10.16	Richardson Duck. Sold 1919 =LIMICANA.
Y7.155	BIRCHLEAF (*ex-Oldbury*)	19. 8.16	Short. Sold 1919 =BRITISH BIRCH.
X.50 Y7.182	BRAMBLELEAF (*ex-Rumol*)	28.12.16	Russell. Damaged and beached 6.42; BU 4.53 in Italy.
Y7.151	BRIARLEAF (*ex-Oletta*)	.16	Readhead. Sold 1.8.20 =LACUNA.
X.48 Y7.181	CHERRYLEAF (*ex-Persol*)	9.11.16	Raylton Dixon. Sold 1947 =ALAN CLORE.
Y7.161	DOCKLEAF (*ex-Oleary*)	11.11.16	Bartram. Sold 1919 =LITIOPA.
Y7.157	ELMLEAF (*ex-Olivet*)	.16	Earle. Sold 1919 =MELONA.
Y7.162	FERNLEAF (*ex-Oleander*)	.16	Napier & Miller. Sold 1919 =BRITISH FERN.
Y7.160	HOLLYLEAF (*ex-Oleaster*)	.16	Hamilton. Sold 1919 =BRITISH HOLLY.
Y7.153	LAURELLEAF (*ex-Olalla*)	30. 8.16	Craig Taylor. Sold 1919 =LAMPAS.
X.26 Y7.183	ORANGELEAF (*ex-Bornol*)	26.10.16	J. L. Thompson. Arrived 25.1.48 Ward, Briton Ferry.
Y7.152	PALMLEAF (*ex-Oliphant*)	15. 8.16	Irvine. Sunk 4.2.17 by S/M 230 miles west of Fastnet.
X.57 Y7.180	PEARLEAF (*ex-Gypol*)	12. 9.16	Gray. Arried 23.12.47 Hughes Bolckow.

Pendant	Name	Launched	Builder—Fate
X.63 Y7.179	PLUMLEAF (ex-Trinol)	4. 8.16	Swan Hunter. Sunk 4.4.42 by A/C at Malta; raised and BU 1947.
X.32 Y7.171	ROSELEAF (ex-Califol)	2. 5.16	Raylton Dixon. Sold 15.7.19, same name; =BRITISH ROSE 1921.

Notes: The X pendants were assigned 2.16 while building under original names, later the Y7 pendants replaced them. Dimensions and gross tonnage varied widely among this group. Extremes were 5311 to 5948 tons gross and 370 to 418½ (pp) ft.

7338 tons gross.   450½ (pp) × 58½ ft.   TE 900 nominal hp.

Y7.159	BOXLEAF (ex-Olinda)	1916	Barclay Curle. Sold 1919 = INDIA.
Y7.158	LIMELEAF (ex-Oligarch)	1916	Barclay Curle. Sold 1919 = CALIFORNIA.

CREOSOL CLASS

2200 tons.   210 (pp) × 34¾ × 12 ft.   TE 700 ihp = 12 kts.

1.16*	1.18	Name	Launched	Builder—Fate
	X.07	BIRCHOL	16. 6.17	Barclay Curle. Wrecked 29.11.39 in the Hebrides.
	X.10	BOXOL	12. 7.17	Barclay Curle. Sold 1947 =PORTNALL; repurchased 1952 = oil hulk; arrived 2.9.59 Rees, Llanelly.
N.11	X.18	CREOSOL	5. 2.16	Short. Sunk 7.2.18 by S/M off E. Coast.
X.46	X.20	DISTOL	4. 3.16	Dobson. Sold 1947 = AKHAWI.
	X.22	EBONOL	16.10.17	Clyde SB. Scuttled 20.12.41 at Hong Kong; = Japanese ENOSHIMA MARU; recovered 1946, sold 1948, mined 5.50.
	X.21	ELDEROL	10. 5.17	Swan Hunter. Arrived 1.9.59 Rees, Llanelly.
	X.23	ELMOL	23. 7.17	Swan Hunter. Sold 1961 = tank cleaning vessel.
	X.29	HICKOROL	30.11.17	McMillan. Sold 1948 = HEMSLEY II.
X.47	X.35	KIMMEROL	4. 4.16	Craig Taylor. Sold 1949 = LANKA BAHU.
	X.37	LARCHOL	19. 6.17	Lobnitz. Arrived 23.8.59 Belgium to BU.
	X.38	LIMOL	18.10.17	Lobnitz. Arrived 23.8.59 Ward, Briton Ferry.
X.43	X.53	PHILOL	5. 4.16	Tyne Iron SB. = hulk 1956; sold 1967.
	X.61	SCOTOL	23. 6.16	Tyne Iron SB. Sold 1947 = HEMSLEY I.
N.09	X.75	VISCOL	21. 2.16	Craig Taylor. Sold 1947; later = FRECCIA-MARE.

*The X pendants in this column date from about 4.16.

As Creosol class; except oil engines 640 bhp = 9½ kts.

	X.46	OAKOL	19. 9.17	Gray. Sold 29.1.20 = ORTHIS.
	X.47	PALMOL	14.11.17	Gray. Sold 29.1.20 = INVERCORRIE.
	X.67	SPRUCOL	4. 7.17	Short. Sold 29.1.20 = JUNIATA.
	X.70	TEAKOL	17. 8.17	Short. Sold 29.1.20 = SAN DARIO.

BELGOL CLASS

4900 tons.   355 (oa), 320 (pp) × 41½ × 20 ft.   TE 3375 ihp = 14 kts.

1.18	Name	Launched	Builder—Fate
X.06	BELGOL	23. 4.17	Irvine. Arrived 22.6.58 Charlestown to BU.
X.16	CELEROL	23. 3.17	Short. Arrived 9.7.58 Rosyth to BU.
X.26	FORTOL	21. 5.17	McMillan. Arrived 1958 Rosyth to BU.
X.27	FRANCOL	18.10.17	Earle. Sunk 3.3.42 by Japanese squadron off Java.
X.45	MONTENOL	5. 7.17	Gray. Sank 21.5.42 after being torpedoed in the North Atlantic.
X.55	PRESTOL	4. 9.17	Napier & Miller. Arrived 6.8.58 White, St. Davids.
X.58	RAPIDOL	23. 4.17	Gray. Sold 4.48 = LOUISE MOLLER.
X.62	SERBOL	7. 7.17	Caledon. Arrives 30.6.58 Hughes Bolckow.
X.65	SLAVOL	21. 4.17	Greenock & Grangemouth. Sunk 26.3.42 by U.205 in the Mediterranean.
X.76	VITOL	24. 5.17	Greenock & Grangemouth. Sunk 7.3.18 by U-boat in the Irish Sea.

8350 tons.   378 (oa), 366 (pp) ×45½×22 ft.   TE 2000 ihp=10 kts.
Armament: 3– pdr.

1.18	Name	Launched	Builder—Fate
X.36	KURUMBA (RAN)	14. 9.16	Swan Hunter. Sold 1946 =ANGELIKI.

1024 tons.   164 (oa), 155 (pp) ×28×11½ ft.   TE 500 ihp=9½ kts.

7.17	1.18	Name	Launched	Builder—Fate
X.78	X.49	PETRELLA	16. 2.18	Dunlop Bremner. Sunk 1944 and raised; sold 1946 =CAPTAIN MIKES.
X.77	X.50	PETROBUS	8.11.17	Dunlop Bremner. Arrived 24.2.59 Ward, Grays.

Notes: Petrol carriers; the water carrier PETRONEL was of the same class.

15020 tons.   436 (pp) ×54 ft.   TE

Y.7.304	BRITISH BEACON =OLCADES 1937	1913	Workman Clark. =hulk 1948; arrived 19.4.53 Hughes Bolckow.
Y.7.286	BRITISH LANTERN =OLIGARCH 1937	1918	Workman Clark. Scuttled 14.4.46 with surplus ammunition in the Red Sea.
Y.7.264	BRITISH STAR =OLYNTHUS 1937	1917	Swan Hunter. Sold 1946 =PENSILVANIA.

13690 tons.   420 (pp) ×54 ft.   TE

X.81 Y.7.242	BRITISH LIGHT =OLWEN 1937	1917	Palmer. Sold 1947 =MUSHTARI.

952 tons gross.   217¼ (pp) ×38¼ ft.   260 hp.

6.18	Name	Launched	Builder—Fate
X.81	RED DRAGON	1912	Napier & Miller. =Oil hulk 1919; on sale list 1946.

Notes: Was Y D'DRAIG GOCH, purchased and renamed 4.18 for conversion to fleet oiler.

9200 tons.   382 (oa), 370 (pp) ×54×22 ft.   TE 2300 ihp=11 kts.
Armament: 2–4 in (not mounted).

	BILOELA (RAN)	10. 4.19	Cockatoo DY. Sold 3.31 =WOLLERT.

Notes: A fleet collier.

WAR CLASS

11600 tons avg.   415 (oa), 400 (pp) ×52½×24 ft.   TE 3000 ihp=10 kts.

Pendant	Name	Launched	Builder—Fate
Y.7.337	WAR AFRIDI	11.11.19	Duncan. =hulk 1.49; sold 1958 at Hong Kong to BU.
Y.7.319	WAR BAHADUR	4.11.18	Armstrong. Arrived 9.46 Hughes Bolckow.
Y.7.336	WAR BHARATA	24.11.19	Palmer. Sold 1947 =WOLF ROCK.
Y.7.338	WAR BRAHMIN	28.11.19	Lithgows. =hulk 1949; arrived 5.2.60 at Spezia to BU.
Y.7.333	WAR DIWAN	28. 6.19	Lithgows. Mined 16.12.44 off the Schelde.
	WAR GAEKWAR	28. 8.19	Lithgows. Sold 1921 =CARDITA.
Y.7.321	WAR GHURKA	.18	Irvine. Sold 1921 =CAPRELLA; =ATHELSTANE in WW II.
Y.7.334	WAR HINDOO	30. 9.19	Hamilton. Arrived 9.5.58 Hughes Bolckow.
Y.7.299	WAR JEMADAR	29. 8.18	Laing. Sold 1921 =CLIONA.
Y.7.335	WAR KRISHNA	24.10.19	Swan Hunter. Sold 1948 as hulk.
Y.7.340	WAR MEHTAR	9.10.19	Armstrong. Sunk 20.11.41 by MTB S.104 off Yarmouth.
Y.7.330	WAR NAWAB	13. 6.19	Palmer. =hulk 11.46; arrived 26.7.58 at Troon to BU.
Y.7.303	WAR NIZAM	8.18	Palmer. Sold 1947 =BASINGHALL.
Y.7.326	WAR PATHAN	19. 3.19	Laing. Sold 1947 =BASINGBANK.
Y.7.341	WAR PINDARI	29.12.19	Lithgows. Sold 1947 =DEEPDALE H.

Pendant	Name	Launched	Builder—Fate
Y7.317	WAR RAJAH	5.11.18	Swan Hunter. Sold 1920 = BRITISH SAILOR.
Y7.277	WAR RANEE	.18	Swan Hunter. Sold 1920 = CORBIS.
Y7.322	WAR SEPOY	5.12.18	Gray. Sunk 7.9.40 as blockship at Dover after bomb damage.
Y7.325	WAR SHIKARI	29. 1.19	Lithgows. Sold 1921 = CHITON.
Y7.339	WAR SIRDAR	6.12.19	Laing. Stranded 28.2.42 near Batavia; = Japanese HONAN MARU; sunk 28.3.45 by US S/M.
Y7.288	WAR SUBADAR	26. 6.18	Gray. Sold 1921 = CRENATULA; = MARIT in WW II.
Y7.342	WAR SUDRA	18. 3.20	Palmer. Sold 1948 = GERMAINE.

Notes: Most of this class wore the red ensign until 1920; there were others of this "Z" type, not Admiralty-owned.

WATER TANK VESSELS

234 tons. (iron)   105 (pp) × 18 ft.   90 ihp.

CHESTER (at Malta)	14. 3.61	Laird. Sold 12.25 at Malta.

370 tons. (iron)   115 (pp) × 22 × 8 ft.   220 ihp.

ELIZABETH (Portsmouth)	4. 3.73	Maudslay. Sold 7.1.21 = FAWLEY.

118 tons. (iron)   74 (pp) × 13½ × 6 ft.   163 ihp.

SHAMROCK (Haulbowline) = ST. PATRICK 11.17	11. 8.73	Pearse, Stockton. Transferred 15.5.23 to Irish Government.

150 tons.   72 (pp) × 15 × 6 ft.   100 ihp.

ECHO (Gibraltar)	4.87	Sunderland SB. Sold 5.10.28 Plymouth & Devonport S Bkg Co.

Notes: Was LUDA purchased 4.87. Also used as a tug and wore the white ensign in 1918.

ASP CLASS

330 tons.   115 (pp) × 22 × 7 ft.   300 ihp.

ASP (Sheerness)	15.10.90	Green, Blackwall. Sold 1947.
CHUB (Simonstown)	17. 2.97	Lobnitz. Sold 17.6.32 in South Africa.
MONKEY (Malta)	21.12.96	Lobnitz. Bombed 26.4.42 at Malta and BU in 4.43.
TORTOISE (Portland)	4. 3.97	Lobnitz. On sale list 1946.

MINX CLASS

390 tons (last four 395 tons).   120¼ (oa), 115 (pp) × 21½ × 9 ft.   300 ihp = 9 kts.

AID (Gosport)	10. 9.00	Willoughby, Plymouth. Sold c1948.
BLOSSOM (Gibraltar)	15. 5.01	Bow McLachlan. BU 1961.
CHERUB (Hong Kong)	7.01	Hong Kong and Whampoa. Lost 12.41 at Hong Kong.
CLINKER (Sheerness)	23. 2.01	Willoughby, Plymouth. Sold 1948.
CREOLE (Bermuda)	29. 8.02	Bow McLachlan. Sold 1948.
HESPER (China)	5.01	Hong Kong and Whampoa. Sold 3.23 at Wei Hai Wei.
MINX (Devonport)	13. 6.00	Cox. On sale list 1946.
FAITHFUL (Gosport)	2. 6.03	Bow McLachlan. On sale list 1948.
HELPFUL (Malta)	30. 9.02	Bow McLachlan. Sold 1.9.33.
PROVIDER (Gosport)	10. 2.03	Bow McLachlan. On sale list 1946.
RIPPLE (Australia)	.04	Foster, Balmain NSW. To RAN 7.13; sold after 1925.

Notes: CHERUB and HESPER were launched complete. BLOSSOM, FAITHFUL and PROVIDER wore the white ensign 1915–18.

DESPATCH CLASS

405 tons (URGENT 425, ZEALOUS 415).   115 (pp) × 21 × 10 ft.   TE 300 ihp.

DESPATCH (Devonport) = DESPOT 12.18	29. 2.04	Bow McLachlan. Sold 1946 = DESPOTE.
PELTER (Portsmouth)	19. 3.04	Day Summers. On sale list 1946.
SUPPLY (Devonport)	10. 1.10	Cox. Sold 10.47 = ROSINA M.
URGENT (Sheerness)	19.10.10	Cox. Hulked 1949; sold c1960.
ZEALOUS (Rosyth) = ZEST 12.18 = ZEAL 1945	29. 8.13	Hall Russell. Sold 2.49.

1024 tons.   155 (pp) × 28 × 11½ ft.   TE 500 ihp = 9 kts.

7.17	1.18	Name	Launched	Builder—Fate
X.79	X.52	PETRONEL	27. 4.18	Dunlop Bremner. Sold 6.47 = PASS OF GLENCOE.

PURCHASED 1915

1.18	Name	TG	Launched	Builder—Dimensions—Service
	INNISFREE	96	8. 4.13	McGregor, Kirkintilloch. 66 (pp) × 18½ ft. Purchased 7.9.15; sold 24.11.20 to Norway.
	INNISINVER	127	20. 5.13	Jeffery, Alloa. 74¼ (pp) × 18¾ ft. Purchased 14.8.15; sold 7.20.
	INNISJURA	127	19. 6.13	Jeffery, Alloa. 74¼ (pp) × 18¾ ft. Purchased 2.10.15; sold 1920.
X.32	INNISSHANNON	238	7. 4.13	Chalmers, Rutherglen. 115¾ (pp) × 21½ ft. Purchased 16.9.15; sold 2.21.
	INNISTRAHULL	238	.13	Chalmers, Rutherglen. 115¾ (pp) × 21½ ft. Purchased 15.9.15– Lost 1916.
	INNISULVA	255	16. 4.14	Chalmers, Rutherglen. 115 (pp) × 21½ ft. Purchased 30.9.15; sold 13.3.20.

TWO EX-GERMAN PRIZES

1915	1.16	1.18		TG/Yr	Service
			GIBRALTAR	5832/13	ex-*Schneefels*. 1.6.15–8.16 = POLESCAR.
P.72	X.25	X.54	POLSHANNON	6121/10	ex-*Birkenfels*. 3.9.15– sold 4.7.21 = PINNA.

Notes: Both served in the Mediterranean, GIBRALTAR red-ensign and POLSHANNON blue ensign.

Also used as water carriers were HUNGERFORD, SAN PATRICIO and SUNIK all listed under MFAs; KRINI hired 22.5.15, later purchased and sold 16.10.19, a vessel named PHIDO and SKAAREHOLME 138/99 in service 19.6.18 to 25.7.19 at Falmouth.

STORE CARRIERS

235 tons. 160 (pp) × 24 ft. 275 ihp.

Pendant Nos.	Name	Launched	Builder—Fate
X.28 (3.21)	GROWLER	1890	Edwards, Millwall. Sold 30.11.21 = BRANKSEA.

Notes: Built of iron. Was MARQUESS OF ANGLESEY, transferred from the War Department 10.91.

600 tons. 151½ (oa), 142½ (pp) × 24 × 10½ ft. 366 ihp.
Armament: 1–3 pdr (from 6.15).

Y2.3	UPNOR	30. 3.99	Bow McLachlan. Sold circa 1952.

Notes: Carrier for armament stores.

1460 tons. 196 (pp) × 30 ft. TE 750 ihp = 10 kts.

1.16	1.18	Name	Launched	Builder—Fate
X.24	X.31	INDUSTRY	7. 6.01	Beardmore. Torpedoed 18.10.18 and sold.

Notes: Was laid down as GLASGOW. The Q ship TAY & TYNE (qv) later = INDUSTRY.

766 tons. 173 (oa), 165 (pp) × 26 × 11 ft. TE 500 ihp = 9½ kts.
Armament: 1–3 pdr (from 6.15).

Y2.1	BISON	1.11.02	Mordey Carney. Sold circa 1946.

Notes: Carrier for armament stores.

9220 tons. 469½ (pp) × 58 ft. TE 3250 ihp = 12½ kts.

1914 9.15	1.16	1.18	Name	Launched	Builder—Fate
D.97 N.90	X.09	X.59	RELIANCE	21. 6.10	Connell. Sold 17.12.19 = EMANUELE ACCAME.

Notes: Was KNIGHT COMPANION, purchased 14.11.12. Served in the Mediterranean.

423 tons. 150 (pp) × 25½ × 10½ ft. TE

		ISLEFORD	1913	Ardrossan SB. Sunk 1.42 unknown cause off Wick.

Notes: Carrier for armament stores; purchased on stocks 26.3.13.

4000 tons. 295 (pp) × 44 × 13 ft. TE 900 = 10 kts.
2343 tons gross.

9.15	1.16	1.18	Name	Launched	Builder—Fate
P.66	X.22	X.03	BACCHUS = BACCHUS II	10. 5.15 5.36	Hamilton. Sunk 15.11.38 as target off Alderney.

Notes: Served in the Mediterranean 1915–18, as a water carrier until 1917; then as a store carrier.

MERCANTILE FLEET AUXILIARIES

(a) FLOTILLA SUPPLY SHIPS

Pendant Nos.	Name	TG/Yr	Service—Fate
5 Y9.29 Y6.9	ALBATROSS	1414/84	(c) 3.8.14–23.7.15; =squadron supply 16.1.15; =mine carrier 3.3.15; =collier Y3.1696 from 24.7.15; =mine carrier (c) 27.9.15–1.1.20.
8	BARON HERRIES	1610/07	(c) 15.8.14–16.2.15; =collier Y3.105 from 18.2.16; sunk 22.4.18 by S/M NW of Bishop Rock.
4 Y9.30	INTABA	4832/10	(c) 5.8.14–11.7.17; =squadron supply 21.4.15; =Q ship 12.4.16, also Q.2, WAITOMO.
2 Y4.47	ORTOLAN	2145/02	(c) 4.8.14–14.4.16; =fleet messenger 2.8.15; sunk 14.6.17 by S/M 100 miles WSW of Bishop Rock.
6	PEREGRINE	1681/92	(c) 4.8.14–22.11.15; wrecked c29.12.17.
1	SORRENTO	1899/12	(c) 2.8.14–22.3.15.
9	STORK	2029/04	(c) 16.8.14–18.8.15.
7	SWIFT =DEAN SWIFT 1914	1141/11	(c) 5.8.14–11.8.15.

See also No. 3 GRIVE listed with ABS.

(b) SQUADRON SUPPLY SHIPS

Y9.16	ALCINOUS	6743/00	(c) 3.8.14–19.12.14.
Y9.5	BARALONG	4192/01	(c) 2.8.14–12.11.16; =Q ship, 3–12 pdr, also WYANDRA 3.15–22.10.16; =MANICA 1916.
Y9.8	BARON ARDROSSAN	4319/05	(c) 5.8.14–18.8.16; =collier Y3.1655 from 17.6.17.
	BATTENHALL	2174/01	1.8.14–30.9.14; =CAPELHALL 1916; =collier Y3.1812 from 1.10.17; later =HILLTOWN.
	CHANTALA	4949/13	14.8.14–31.8.14; sunk 5.4.16 by S/M off Cape Bengut.
Y9.3	CHINKOA	5222/13	(ex-Arabistan) 3.8.14–19.12.14.
	CIVILIAN	7871/02	14.8.14–25.8.14; sunk 6.10.17 by S/M off Alexandria.
	CLAN MACGILLIVRAY	5023/11	15.8.14–14.9.14.
	CLAN MACQUARRIE	5060/13	15.8.14–14.9.14.
Y9.15	CROWN OF ARRAGON	4500/05	(c) 3.8.14–24.4.15; sunk 24.6.17 by S/M 124 miles SW of Bishop Rock.
Y9.4	CROWN OF CASTILE	4505/05	(c) 2.8.14–22.2.15; sunk 30.3.15 by S/M 31 miles SW of Bishop Rock.
Y9.6	CROWN OF GALICIA	4821/06	(c) 3.8.14–23.1.15; later =CENTURION.
Y9.28	EGRET	1394/03	16.1.15–24.3.15; =collier Y3.1788 from 26.7.17.
	EMPIRE	4496/02	8.8.14–30.1.15.
Y9.11	FLORIDIAN	4777/13	(c) 3.8.14–9.7.16; sunk 4.2.17 by S/M 200 miles W of Fastnet.
	GLENTURRET	4696/96	14.8.14–26.8.14; =collier Y3.340 from 1914.
Y9.17 Y8.54	HIRONDELLE	1648/90	(c) 4.8.14–7.6.15; =BDV water carrier from 8.6.15; sunk 25.4.17 by S/M SE of Belle Isle.
Y9.7	INDRANI	3640/88	(c) 4.8.14–3.10.14; sunk 27.6.15 by S/M 40 miles W of the Smalls.
Y9.12	INTOMBI	4253/12	(c) 4.8.14–10.3.15.
Y9.24	JABIRU	1703/11	3.12.14–5.5.16; =collier Y3.1671 from 3.7.17.
	LAKONIA	4686/99	15.8.14–4.9.14.
Y9.25	MANCO	2984/08	(c) 10.12.14–10.15; =A/P depot from 4.15.
Y9.9	MURITAI =PORT VICTOR 1914	7280/10	(c) 3.8.14–12.2.15.
Y9.10	NETHERBY HALL	4461/05	(ex-Glenearn) (c) 3.8.14–22.1.15; sunk 10.1.17 by MOWE 300 miles off Pernambuco.
Y9.2	PALMA	7632/03	(c) 2.8.14–5.3.15.
Y9.1	PESHAWUR	7634/05	(c) 3.8.14–2.5.15; sunk 9.10.17 by S/M SE of Ballyquintin Point, County Down.
Y9.13	STATESMAN	6153/95	(c) 4.8.14–7.3.15; sunk 3.11.16 by S/M 200 miles E of Malta.

Pendent Nos.	Name	TG/Yr	Service—Fate
	SWANLEY	4641/03	24.2.15–10.8.16; =ARGALIA 8.16; sunk 6.8.17 by S/M 81 miles NW of Tory Island.
	TORR HEAD	5911/94	15.8.14–14.9.14; sunk 20.4.17 by S/M 160 miles NW of Fastnet.
Y9.21	TRINGA	2154/13	28.11.14–24.6.15; sunk 26.11.15 by S/M off Malta.
Y9.26	UMGENI	2622/98	23.12.14–17.4.16; =armament carrier Y2.107; foundered 9.11.17.
Y9.27 Y8.90	UMTALI	2622/96	(c) 3.1.15–10.4.16; =store carrier; =armament carrier Y2.106.
Y9.19	VANELLUS	1797/12	(c) 7.11.14–8.10.15; mined 1.10.16 off Havre Roads.
Y9.20	WHIMBREL	1655/07	14.11.14–5.5.15.
Y9.18	WILDRAKE =DRAKE 11.14	2267/08	(ex-Drake) 8.10.14–20.5.15; sunk 30.9.17 by S/M gunfire.
Y9.22	ZARIA	3549/04	(c) 26.11.14–30.7.19; =A/P depot at Longhope from 5.15; later =4816 TG.

See also Y9.14 CARRIGAN HEAD with commissioned escort ships and Y9.23 STEPHEN FURNESS with ABS.

(c) FLEET MESSENGERS

Y4.8	ALERT =ANCHOR 1917	195/10	16.10.14–14.10.19; =tug from 5.5.15.
Y4.62	ALEXANDRA	618/04	
Y4.76	AQUILLA	450/07	Store carrier (c) 27.4.18–5.1.20.
Y4.52	ARETHUSA II	477/06	(c) 25.9.15–26.4.20.
Y4.29	ASTERIA	493/91	(c) 20.7.15–22.1.21.
Y4.28	BARRY =BARRYFIELD 9.17	398/07	Paddle(c) 29.6.15–20.11.19; later =WAVERLEY; =SNAEFELL in WW II.
Y4.6	BORODINO	1970/11	Mess stores 1.12.14–28.4.19.
Y4.27	BRIGHTON	566/78	Paddle (c) 29.6.15– purchased 22.5.17; sold 26.4.19.
Y4.60	BROCKLESBY	508/12	Paddle Air Service scout (c) 21.2.16–9.6.17.
Y4.48	C.64	615/	1915– ; =ROSA c1929. Lost 28.4.30.
Y4.49	C.65	615/	1915– ; =NORA c1930. Listed to 1939.
Y4.35	CELTIC PRIDE	456/10	(c) 23.7.15–1.7.20.
Y4.40	CLIFFORD	487/04	(c) 1.8.15– Sunk 16.5.16 by S/M near Crete.
Y4.42	CURRAN	1106/00	(c) 17.7.15–3.11.15; =collier Y3.933 from 4.11.15.
Y4.74	DEVANEY	314/06	(ex-Devonia) (c) 7.11.17–3.10.19; purchased; sold 1919 =LOCHIEL.
Y4.68	EBLANA	808/92	1.7.17–12.6.18.
Y4.65	ELPINIKI	546/80	(ex-Argo) (c) 11.16– Purchased; sold 13.2.20 J. Bowen Rees & Co.
Y4.25	ERMINE	1777/12	(c) 16.7.15– Mined 2.8.17 in the Aegean Sea.
Y4.12	F. A. TAMPLIN	4004/12	=oiler Y7.90 from 1.8.15.
Y4.79	FLORIS	424/12	(ex-Braeneil) (c) 27.2.18–3.4.19.
Y4.41	GRANSHA	1192/01	(ex-collier Y3.258) (c) 16.7.15–21.3.19.
Y4.6	GRONINGEN	988/02	Mess stores 9.9.14–16.11.14; mined 23.9.15 near Sunk Head Buoy.
Y4.24	HUNGERFORD	5811/13	(ex-Lauterfels) Distilling ship (c) 28.7.15–27.2.16; =collier Y3.1687 from 22.6.17; sunk 16.4.18 by S/M off Owers LV.
Y4.10	INVICTA	1680/05	4.4.15– not retained.
Y4.23	ISIS =ISONZO 1.16	1728/98	18.6.15–28.2.16 and (c) 29.2.16–10.3.20; later =GIBEL SARSAR.
Y4.59	KILLINGHOLME	508/12	Paddle Air Service scout (c) 21.2.16–21.4.17; =in WW II.
Y4.38	NUGGET	405/89	(c) 23.7.15– Sunk 31.7.15 by U.28 SW of the Scillies.
Y4.75	OPULENT	469/07	(ex-Ophir) 30.12.17–18.6.19; =OPHIR in WW II.
Y4.61	OSMANIEH	4041/06	(c) 12.5.16– Mined 31.12.17 off Alexandria.
Y4.54	OVERTON	426/11	(c) 26.9.15–16.11.20.
Y4.31	PEBBLE	477/90	(c) 24.7.15– Purchased 23.5.19; sold 8.20.
Y4.7	PETROLEA	202/04	6.10.14–6.10.15; =oiler Y7.105 from 7.10.15.
Y4.22	POLGOWAN	4347/00	(ex-Macedonia) 6.15–2.17; =collier Y3.1499 from 23.2.17.

Pendent Nos.	Name	TG/Yr	Service—Fate
Y4.77	POLLY BRIDGE	403/16	22.3.18–21.12.18.
Y4.36	PORTIA	494/06	(c) 23.7.15– Sunk 2.8.15 by U.28 off the Scillies.
Y4.58	PRINCESS ALBERTA	1586/05	(c) 4.10.15– Mined 21.2.17 enroute Stavros to Mudros.
Y4.57	PRINCESS ENA	1198/06	Q ship 3–12 pdr (c) 30.4.15–6.7.20; =fleet messenger from 4.10.15.
Y4.63	PRINCESS MAUD	1566/02	(c) 5.5.16–4.2.18; sunk 10.6.18 by S/M NE of Blyth.
Y4.30	PRINCESS OF WALES =PADUA 1917	163/96	Paddle 15.6.17–21.4.20.
Y4.9	PRINCESS VICTORIA	1687/12	Seaplane patrol 1914–2.5.15.
Y4.33	RACE FISHER	493/92	(ex-armament carrier Y2.36; ex-collier Y3.586) (c) 29.7.15– wrecked 25.3.19 in the Mediterranean
Y4.26	REDBREAST	1313/08	(c) 17.7.15– =Q ship 20.3.16–16.9.16; sunk 15.7.17 by UC.38 in the Mediterranean.
Y4.34	RIVER FISHER	457/99	(c) 19.7.15–17.9.19.
Y4.39	ROSALEEN	409/08	(c) 22.7.15–10.11.20.
Y4.19	SAN PATRICIO	9712/95	Water carrier 14.5.15–12.1.16; =oiler Y7.115 from 13.1.16.
Y4.73	SAXON	139/95	(ex-*Charlotte*) Pilot vessel and guardship 28.7.17–26.1.19.
Y4.11	SCANDINAVIA	456/05	9.11.14–5.10.19.
Y4.43	SILVERFIELD	426/15	(c) 4.8.15–7.6.20.
Y4.56	SKELWITH FORCE	562/08	(c) 30.9.15–15.7.16.
Y4.55	SPINEL	509/93	(ex-collier Y3.257) (c) 6.10.15–29.6.20.
Y4.4	STAMFORDHAM	921/98	30.9.14–22.3.16; =collier Y3.513 from 23.3.16; sunk 4.8.16 by S/M 8 miles S of Longstone.
Y4.16	SUNIK	5017/15	Water carrier 13.1.15–24.8.16; =oiler Y7.57 from 25.8.16.
Y4.37	SUSETTA	339/04	(ex-*William Rowland*) (c) 19.7.15–31.7.19.
Y4.32	THE VICEROY	477/05	(c) 21.7.15–29.6.16.
Y4.14	TRENT =ICARUS 1918	5541/00	2–12 pdr (c) 6.3.15–20.9.20.
Y4.30	TURQUOISE	486/93	(c) 22.7.15– Sunk 31.7.15 by U.28 SW of the Scillies.
Y4.15	VITRUVIA	4753/13	10.3.15–9.6.15; =oiler Y7.79 from 10.6.15.
Y4.53	WEXFORD COAST	423/15	(c) 25.9.15–28.7.15–; =Q ship 1–4 in, 1–12 pdr
Y8.80			(c) 13.3.18–18.10.19 also STORE CARRIER 80; =BLARNEY 1919.
Y4.45	WHEATBERRY	405/15	(c) 6.8.15–14.9.16.

Other fleet messengers included Y4.1 ALEXANDER (icebreaker); CHALKIS (store carrier); Y4.5 ALOUETTE (ABS); Y4.13 CITY OF ROCHESTER (PMS); Y4.18 RECLAIMER (salvage vessel); Y4.8 AVIATOR (ex-store carrier VICTOR); five kite balloon ships; two minelayers; four yachts and three other store carriers.

(d) STORE CARRIERS

Y8.42	ABERCRAIG	440/02	8.1.15–13.5.15; =collier Y3.712 from 14.5.15.
Y8.16	AIRE	698/86	8.8.14–6.3.15; =collier Y3.584 from 7.3.15.
Y8.53	ARDGARTH	770/13	(ex-collier Y3.603) BDV supply 22.5.15–8.2.17; =collier again 9.2.17.
Y8.92	ARIADNE CHRISTINE	3550/10	(ex-collier Y3.490) 2.8.18– Became CTL 31.8.18; sold 23.8.19 to Norway.
Y8.81	ARLEIA	795/15	30.3.18–2.8.18; =collier Y3.2162.
Y8.76	ARMOURER	724/88	(ex-*Engineer*) 17.3.18–3.4.19.
Y8.37	ARRIVAL	358/04	(ex-armament carrier Y2.14) 13.10.14–13.10.17; =BDV supply from 7.15; later =ELSIE ANNIE.
Y8.83	ASTURIAN	3193/90	(ex-*Capella*) 28.5.18–2.12.18.
Y8.46	BANGARTH	1872/06	(ex-collier Y3.60) BDV water carrier 10.3.15–1.12.15; =collier again from 2.12.15; sunk 13.12.17 by S/M off the Tyne.
Y8.94	BEN NEVIS	3895/05	(ex-armament carrier Y2.228; ex-collier Y3.1649) 3.8.18–30.10.18; =collier again from 31.10.18.
Y8.36	BERNICIA	957/12	1.11.14–4.7.16.
Y8.38	BRAESIDE	407/09	17.7.15–12.8.15; =collier Y3.863 from 13.8.15.

Pendant Nos.	Name	TG/Yr	Service—Fate
Y8.58	BRIXHAM	501/85	(ex-*Captain McClure*) 4.9.15–8.3.16; =collier Y3.2008 from 13.1.18.
Y8.57	BROOK	1436/06	(ex-collier Y3.94) 14.7.15–27.8.15; =collier again from 8.9.15.
Y8.51	BROOMHILL	1392/09	(ex-collier Y3.319) 21.4.15–31.5.16; =collier again 1.6.16; sunk 10.5.17 by S/M off Portland Bill.
Y8.74 Y8.111	BUCCANEER	970/90	(ex-collier Y3.1683; ex-armament carrier Y2.152) 11.8.17–27.9.17 and 14.11.18–13.5.20.
Y8.56	BURRIANA	1359/06	(ex-collier Y3.675) 14.7.15–19.12.16.
Y8.17	CALDER	708/87	8.10.14–26.3.15; =collier Y3.646 from 1915.
Y8.114	CARLSTON	662/01	(ex-collier Y3.106) 16.11.18–20.10.19.
Y8.10	CARNALEA	579/13	30.9.14–27.3.15; =collier Y3.644 from 28.3.15.
Y8.32	CATO	710/14	4.11.14–21.2.15.
Y8.59	CHALKIS	731/78	(ex-*Azalea*) =fleet messenger (c) 1917–21.8.19; later =NAFKRATOUSA.
Y8.71	CHARLES GOODANEW	791/11	(ex-*Levenwood* 29.1.17–17.4.17.
Y8.20 Y4.64	CHESTERFIELD	1013/13	1.12.14–28.6.16; =fleet messenger (c) 29.6.16– sunk 18.5.18 by S/M 42 miles NE of Malta.
Y8.63	CHEVIOT	258/91	28.8.14–10.8.16.
Y8.101	CLAN MACRAE	6469/12	5.9.18–3.12.18; later =BANFFSHIRE.
Y8.15	CLANDEBOYE	614/13	4.10.14–14.2.15; =armament carrier Y2.41 from 14.2.15; =collier Y3.641 from 25.3.15.
Y8.73	CLERMISTON	1282/95	(ex-collier Y3.68) (ex-*King's Town*) 19.6.17–3.1.18.
Y8.115	CLIFTON GROVE	249/83	(ex-collier Y3.2260) 22.1.19–6.3.19; foundered 10.11.19.
Y8.12	CLYDEBURN	553/02	(ex-*Armorvik*) 29.9.14–21.10.14.
Y8.102	CLYDESDALE	394/05	25.6.17–21.12.17.
Y8.113	CORNISHMAN	5749/91	(ex-*Nomadic*) 24.12.18–3.9.19.
Y8.60	CORTES	1275/84	15.9.15–1.12.15; sunk 26.4.17 in collision.
Y8.35	CRAGSIDE	513/92	5.11.14–29.12.15; =collier Y3.556 from 30.12.15.
Y8.121	CUNENE	5898/11	(ex-*Adelaide*) 19.4.19–24.9.19.
Y8.18	DERWENT =DUNCOMBE 1916	830/88	8.8.14–3.3.15; =collier Y3.585 from 4.3.15; =Q ship (c) 10.15–15.8.17 using names DERWENT, DUNCOMBE and LYDIA; =collier again from 9.10.17.
Y8.4	DON	939/92	26.8.14–20.2.15; =collier Y3.561 from 21.2.15; sunk 8.5.15 by S/M off Coquet Island.
Y8.59	DUNVEGAN	304/83	8.9.15–2.10.15.
Y8.33	ECHO	961/91	6.11.14–8.1.15; =collier Y3.1709 from 22.8.17.
Y8.77	EGBA	4989/14	16.3.18–22.11.18.
Y8.72	EMERALD	736/04	(ex-collier Y3.653; ex-armament carrier Y2.9) 14.11.16–4.4.19.
Y8.30	ENDCLIFFE	368/11	3.11.14–29.3.15; =collier Y3.643 from 30.3.15.
Y8.52	EROS	174/00	(ex-*Ceres*) 6.5.15–24.2.16; wrecked previous to 9.6.18.
Y8.66	ESKWOOD	791/11	(ex-collier Y3.222) 8.7.16–2.3.20.
Y8.109	FAIRY	249/02	(ex-collier Y3.1991) 23.11.18–30.12.18.
Y8.31	FARRALINE	1226/03	3.11.14–21.6.15; sunk 2.11.17 by S/M off Ushant.
Y8.95	FERNLEY	3820/01	(ex-collier Y3.768) 22.8.18–12.12.18; =collier again 13.12.18.
Y8.13	FERRYHILL	411/09	4.10.14–28.5.15; =collier Y3.819 from 29.5.15; =store carrier again 7.6.15; =collier again from 19.7.15; sunk 30.1.18 by S/M off Cape Antifer.
Y8.40	GERTIE	341/02	3.12.14–2.2.15; =collier Y3.494 from 3.2.15.
Y8.61 Y4.66	GOSFORTH	1077/98	(ex-collier Y3.168) (ex-*Altona*) 19.11.15–2.2.17; =fleet messenger (c) 3.2.17–3.11.19.
Y8.69	HAMPSHIRE	833/08	25.9.16–21.4.17; =collier Y3.2351 from 10.9.18.
Y8.128	HARMODIUS	3513/92	(ex-*Warrnambool*) 9.11.14–5.1.16 and 17.6.19–24.9.19; later =KUT.
Y8.119	HARPERLEY	3990/06	30.3.19–26.5.19.
Y8.3	HEBBLE	904/91	3.12.14–24.9.15; BDV store carrier from 30.4.15; mined 6.5.17 off Roker Pier, Sunderland. Also carried pendants Y2.27 and Y3.1594.
Y8.49	HELMSMAN	458/03	(ex-armament carrier Y2.4) 31.3.15–8.9.19.
Y8.97	HERMISTON	4483/01	(ex-collier Y3.471) 5.9.18–20.12.18.

Pendant Nos.	Name	TG/Yr	Service—Fate
Y8.45 Y4.80	HODDER	1016/10	18.3.15–8.3.18; =fleet messenger (c) 9.3.18–22.3.19; =in WW II.
Y8.112	HOVA	4264/10	(ex-collier Y3.1321) 6.12.18–18.8.19; later =CRAWFORD CASTLE.
Y8.132	HUNTSCLYDE	2705/04	(ex-collier Y3.1644) (ex-Athena) 18.6.19–5.9.19.
Y8.129	HUNTSCRAFT	5113/13	(ex-Sudmark) 13.7.19–6.11.19; later =CLAN MACKAY.
Y8.133	HUNTSGULF	3185/92	(ex-collier Y3.1748) (ex-Seriphos) 26.6.19–28.10.19.
Y8.50	IMMINGHAM	2083/06	Accom and store carrier 10.14– Sunk 6.6.15 in collision off Mudros.
Y8.108	JUNIN	4536/07	(ex-collier Y3.1313) 26.10.18–3.2.19.
Y8.88	KASSALA	3825/97	(ex-armament carrier Y2.125; ex-collier Y3.542) 27.6.18–21.9.18; =collier again 22.9.18.
Y8.98	LARNE	3808/94	(ex-Aldenham) 2.9.18–1.1.19.
Y8.23	LEICESTER	1001/91	12.10.14– Mined 12.2.16 off Folkestone Pier.
Y8.68	LIBERTY	895/90	(ex-armament carrier Y2.44) 25.7.16–15.4.19.
Y8.107	LORD ANTRIM	4269/02	(ex-collier Y3.748)16.10.18–1.2.19.
Y8.39	LOSSIE	379/96	(ex-Haller) BDV store carrier 1.12.14–12.4.17; reported lost c5.9.17, still listed 1920.
Y8.64	LUCENT	1409/79	15.2.16–16.3.16; =collier Y3.1103 from 17.3.16; sunk 12.2.17 by S/M off the Lizard.
Y8.24	LUTTERWORTH	994/91	12.10.14–22.10.15.
Y8.89	M. J. HEDLEY	449/91	Q ship, also STORE CARRIER 89 (c) 27.6.18– capsized and sank 4.10.18 while coaling in Barry Docks, Cardiff.
Y8.55	MACCLESFIELD	1018/14	12.6.15–25.7.16.
Y8.9	MERSEY	1087/06	17.9.14–20.6.17.
Y8.100	MOORGATE	3813/07	(ex-collier Y3.668) (ex-Arnell) 26.9.18–20.12.18; =collier again 13.1.19; sold, delivered 25.7.19 =TEWKESBURY; total loss about 25.3.20.
Y8.78	NASCOPIE	2475/12	15.3.18–20.6.18 and 7.12.18–6.6.19.
Y8.43	NIDD	996/00	6.2.15–29.3.15; =collier Y3.598 from 30.3.15; =BDV store carrier 3.7.15–29.3.16.
Y8.70	NIGERIA	3755/01	8.11.16– CTL by fire 8.3.17 while serving as D/S at Murmansk.
Y8.6	NORFOLK COAST	782/10	11.9.14–26.10.14; sunk 18.6.18 by S/M off Flamborough Head.
Y8.22	NOTTS	1045/91	(ex-Nottingham) 12.10.14–16.7.16.
Y8.120	OCEAN TRANSPORT	4643/13	(ex-armament carrier Y2.73; ex-collier Y3.769) 17.4.19–28.8.19.
Y8.91	PALM BRANCH	3891/97	(ex-collier Y3.1475) (ex-Rangoon) 18.7.18–31.1.19.
Y8.41	RAYFORD	471/94	(ex-Blanche Rock) 5.1.15–24.3.15; =collier Y3.642 from 25.3.15.
Y8.47	RIEVAULX ABBEY	1166/08	13.3.15–29.5.15; =armament carrier Y2.56 from 27.8.15; mined 3.9.16 near Rosse Spit Buoy, Humber.
Y8.29	SEA SERPENT	902/98	3.11.14–15.4.15; mined 23.3.16 off Folkestone Pier.
Y8.135	SIBIR	2907/03	(ex-collier Y3.1968) (ex-Dovedale) 7.7.19–11.10.19.
Y8.34	SKIPPER	356/04	(ex-armament carrier Y2.7) (ex-Swyn) BDV store carrier 6.11.14–19.5.19.
Y8.134	SOLFELS	5821/13	25.6.19–13.11.19.
Y8.79	SPORTSMAN	572/14	15.3.18–9.2.19.
Y8.25	STAVELEY	1041/91	12.10.14–8.7.16.
Y8.48	STEERSMAN	562/09	(ex-armament carrier Y2.2) 29.9.14–13.3.19.
Y8.82	STEPHEN	4435/10	15.5.18–12.4.19.
Y8.93	SUSQUEHANNA	3711/96	(ex-armament carrier Y2.220; ex-collier Y3.1564) (ex-Mount Sephar) 1.8.18–16.11.18.
Y8.14	TEES	533/11	4.10.14–7.2.15.
Y8.62	TEESSIDER	1184/09	6.1.16–3.6.16.
Y8.87	TELAMON	4509/04	9.6.18–21.9.18.
Y8.65	THESEUS	6724/08	26.2.16–23.4.16; =collier Y3.1746 from 2.9.17.
Y8.104	THESPIS	4343/01	24.9.18–10.7.19.
Y8.96	TRELAWNEY	3877/07	(ex-collier Y3.278) 23.8.18–27.11.18.
Y8.1	TROSTAN	1624/83	(ex-Jersey) 8.14–19.12.14; =armament carrier Y2.31 from 20.12.14.
Y8.26	VICTOR	435/07	16.10.14–31.3.15; =collier Y3.640 from 1.4.15;

Pendent Nos.	Name	TG/Yr	Service—Fate
Y4.81	=AVIATOR 1917		=fleet messenger 10.8.18–21.1.19.
Y8.8	VOLANA	616/13	31.8.14–22.5.20.
Y8.5	VOLHYNIA	617/11	12.9.14–5.11.14; =collier Y3.443 from 6.11.14; =store carrier again 12.1.15–8.2.19; later =GOWER COAST.
Y8.7	VOLTURNUS	615/13	1.9.14–1.11.19; mined 11.19 off the Scottish Coast.
Y8.124	WAR CASTLE	5685/18	(ex-collier Y3.2377) 15.5.19–11.10.19; =BRADCLYDE 1919.
Y8.131	WAR CYPRESS	5167/17	(ex-collier Y3.1883) 22.6.19–3.11.19; sold, delivered 1.12.19 =LEOPOLD L. D.
Y8.116	WAR DOWN	3099/18	(ex-collier Y3.2455) 5.2.19–9.7.19; sold, delivered 27.10.19 =GRAIG.
Y8.122	WAR GASCON	5180/19	9.5.19–28.8.19; sold, delivered 18.9.19 =ZOVETTO.
Y8.118	WAR GRANGE	3110/17	(ex-collier Y3.1898) 11.3.19–31.7.19; sold 9.8.19 =GIGLIO.
Y8.99	WAR LEMUR	5185/18	(ex-collier Y3.2254) 25.9.18–1.1.19; sold, delivered 27.1.19 =VERENTIA.
Y8.137	WAR MAGPIE	5205/18	(ex-collier Y3.2335) 30.7.19–13.11.19; sold, delivered 24.11.19 =ARABISTAN.
Y8.106	WAR MANGO	2499/18	6.10.18–25.1.19; =collier Y3.2359 from 26.1.19; sold, delivered 26.10.19 =WARCUTA.
Y8.136	WAR MUSIC	6498/18	(ex-collier Y3.2441) 7.7.19–3.9.19; sold, delivered 3.9.19 =GLENSPEY.
Y8.127	WAR WOLF	5875/17	(ex-collier Y3.2001) 22.5.19–3.10.19; sold, delivered 17.10.19 =COMMANDANT MAGES.
Y8.28	WATERLAND	494/03	25.10.14–22.3.15; =collier Y3.597 from 23.3.15.
Y8.110	WEARSIDER	597/12	Salvage service 7.11.18–16.1.19.
Y8.123	WELSHMAN	5730/91	25.5.19–5.11.19.
Y8.19	WENNING	787/87	(ex-Emden) 8.10.14–1.2.15; =armament carrier Y2.39 from 2.2.15.
Y8.84	WESTBOROUGH	3811/01	(ex-collier Y3.195) (ex-Beechley) 23.4.18–5.12.18.
Y8.27	WESTPHALIA	1030/13	21.10.14–14.6.16; =Q ship, 1467 TG (c) 7.3.17; purchased 21.11.17; also named CULLIST, HAYLING, JURASSIC and PRIM; sunk 13.2.18 by U-boat in the Irish Sea.
Y8.2	WHARFE	914/90	26.8.14–2.15; =collier Y3.2419 from 14.11.18.
Y8.11	WHINHILL	478/14	Also assigned pendant Y5.7.
Y8.1	WHITE HEAD	1172/80	31.8.14–27.10.14; =SSV (c) 16.7.15– Sunk 15.10.17 by S/M 40 miles NNE of Suda Bay.
Y8.85	WIRRAL	308/90	Q ship; also STORE CARRIER 85 (c) 29.7.18–1.4.19; sold =STRYMON.
Y8.130	YARBOROUGH	3077/00	(ex-collier Y3.1063) 14.6.19–24.9.19.

Another store carrier, Y8.21 WOONAS, remains untraced.

(e) MISCELLANEOUS VESSELS

	Name	TG/Yr	Service—Fate
	ABBASSIEH	2784/89	(ex-Sicilian Prince) Armed storeship. (c) 6.7.15–22.3.16.
	ACCRINGTON	1629/10	T/S at Portsmouth. (c) 17.4.17–29.11.18.
	ALEXIS	235/79	(ex-Alexandra) Paddle ferry at Chatham. 10.9.15–13.2.20.
	ALHAMBRA	127/88	(ex-Alexandra) Paddle. 23.5.18–25.5.19.
	ANNANDALE	1521/78	(ex-blockship) BDV. Purchased; sold 7.1.20.
	ARGO	1102/98	(c) 28.11.14–3.4.15.
	ARGO =LOTHBURY 1917 =ARGO 4.19	854/06	Q ship (c) 9.6.17–10.4.19; purchased 19.12.17; 2–4 in, 1–15 pdr, 2–12 pdr. Also known as ARGO, SARUSAN and STEAD. =store carrier 16.4.19, with pendant X.54 assigned from 9.18; sold c1939.
Y6.8 Y8.67	ARNO	745/94	(ex-armament carrier Y2.42) (ex-Juno) Mine carrier 1915–1.8.16; =store carrier 2.8.16–28.6.17; =ARBEECO 6.17.
	BORDERGLEN	123/13	(ex-Norah James) BDV water tender 1.9.15–22.8.19.

Pendent Nos.	Name	TG/Yr	Service—Fate
	CORDOVA	2387/88	(ex-blockship) (ex-Jessmore) 1–12 pdr BDV gate vessel 7.15– Sold 29.7.19 A. Rappoport =PROGRESS.
Y6.4 Y8.117	COVE	2734/12	Mine carrier (c) 4.8.14–27.2.17 and (c) 9.5.18–2.1.20; 1–12 pdr added 8.18; =store carrier from 14.2.19.
	DAFFODIL	473/06	Ferry assault ship (c) 2.18–6.18; =ROYAL DAFFODIL.
	EDINBURGH CASTLE =HC.8 1919	158/86	Paddle hospital carrier 29.7.16– Purchased 30.7.17; demolished 24.9.19 in North Russia.
	EL KAHIRA	2034/92	Armed storeship (c) 4.6.15–29.5.16; =ABS 1916; later =CITY OF WINDSOR.
Y6.1	ELEANOR	1980/88	Mine carrier (c) 3.8.14– Sunk 12.2.18 by S/M near St. Catherine's.
	ETNA	107/93	BDV salvage vessel at Scapa 6.1.15–24.5.19.
	FORCADOS	397/07	(c) 20.12.15–
	GLENGOIL	2963/82	(ex-blockship) 1–6 pdr AA BDV gate vessel 1915–29.7.19; sold 1919 to Spain.
	GLENMORE	1656/82	(ex-blockship) BDV 1915– Sold 7.1.20.
	GOLDEN EAGLE	793/09	Paddle A/C transport (c) 6.9.18–3.12.18 and (c) 17.11.19–3.6.20. Conversion to M/L begun, not completed. =in WW II.
	GOTHLAND	1485/71	(ex-blockship) BDV 28.10.15–25.2.20; sold 1920 Claud Langdon Ltd.
	HC.9	714/16	(ex-HP.3) Hospital carrier 31.5.19–1920.
	HC.10	714/16	(ex-HP.2) Hospital carrier 31.5.19–1920.
Y6.3	HARDEN	1686/12	Mine carrier (c) 3.8.14–8.3.19; 1–12 pdr added 8.18.
	HAUPIRI	715/85	(ex-Richmond) (c) 26.10.16–31.3.19.
	HUBBUCK	2834/86	(ex-blockship) 1–6 pdr AA BDV gate vessel 28.10.14– Sold 25.3.19 to Spain, delivered 20.2.20.
	IRIS	475/06	Ferry assault ship (c) 2.18–6.18; =ROYAL IRIS.
	ISLE OF SKYE	211/86	(ex-Madge Wildfire) Tender (c) 19.5.16–10.5.19.
	JOHN PENDER	2336/00	Cable ship (c) 30.6.18–14.6.19.
Y6.5	JOHN SANDERSON	3274/89	Mine carrier (c) 3.8.14–26.8.16; =collier Y3.1660 from 3.7.17; =mine carrier 1–12 pdr (c) 2.8.18–19.9.19.
	KING EDWARD =HC.1 1919	551/01	Paddle hospital carrier (c) 13.4.19–19.6.20.
Y6.7	LADY CORY WRIGHT	2516/06	Mine carrier (c) 3.8.14– Sunk 26.3.18 by S/M off the Lizard.
	LAGOS	392/07	(c) 11.4.15–11.12.15.
	LORD MORTON =HC.7 1919	185/83	Paddle hospital carrier 29.7.16– Demolished 24.9.19 in North Russia.
	MAGDA	2351/88	(ex-blockship) 1–12 pdr BDV gate vessel 23.10.14– Sold 29.7.19 Compania Naviera Bidasoa.
	MAYUMBA	2516/90	BDV 10.9.15–19.6.18; purchased, became oil fuel depot at Killingholme.
	MEDLAR	194/91	(ex-The Mermaid) Paddle M/L, 10 mines 19.5.18–28.3.19.
	MINIA	2061/67	Cable ship (c) 11.7.18–10.2.19.
	MONA'S ISLE	1564/82	Paddle netlayer 1–12 pdr, 1–6 pdr. Purchased 28.9.15; sold 6.8.19 Ward, Morecambe.
	NAUTPUR	718/74	(ex-Nautilus) 1–12 pdr BDV gate vessel 26.2.15–30.9.19.
	NIGEL	1400/03	(c) 26.2.15–22.4.15; mined 12.11.15 off Boulogne.
	PEREGRINE II	2514/91	(ex-blockship) (c) 21.5.18–28.2.19; purchased 28.2.19 as store hulk, sold 20.3.22.
	POLISH MONARCH	4292/12	(ex-Polmont; ex-Karpat) Water carrier (c) 13.3.16–15.3.16; =collier Y3.1102 from 30.4.16.
	PRINCE =PRINCETOWN 1.16	6060/02	(ex-Prinz Adalbert) Accom ship at Invergordon (c) 17.12.14–23.12.16.
	PRINCE ABBAS	2030/92	(c) 5.6.15–29.5.16; sunk 9.7.17 by S/M off Fair Island.
	PRINCE EDWARD	1547/87	(ex-Prince of Wales) Paddle netlayer 1–3 pdr. Purchased 28.1.15; sold 12.2.20 T. C. Pas.

Pendant Nos.	Name	TG/Yr	Service—Fate
N.34* N.81**	PRINCESS LOUISE	1986/12	(ex-Princess Royal) SSV (c) 3.3.15–4.1.18; sunk 26.5.18 by S/M off St. Agnes Head.
	QUEEN VICTORIA	1547/87	Paddle netlayer 1–3 pdr 28.1.15– Purchased 8.15; sold 12.5.20 to BU.
Y6.6	RAMILLIES	2935/92	Mine carrier 3.8.14–30.8.16; sunk 21.7.17 by S/M 120 miles WNW of Tory Island.
	REDSTART	904/80	1–6 pdr BDV gate vessel (c) 24.2.15–15.9.19.
	SPEY	470/92	(c) 24.6.15–26.9.16.
	SUNHILL	837/95	(ex-Kennet) Accommodation ship (c) 23.9.15–18.8.20.
	THE LADY CARMICHAEL	376/71	Paddle M/L, 10 mines 16.5.18–14.5.19.
	VICTORIA IV	229/84	Paddle ferry at Devonport 12.4.17–14.12.19.
Y6.2	WHITE SWAN	2173/03	Mine carrier 3.8.14–23.10.14; =collier Y3.421 from 30.10.14; became CTL 12.16.
	WINIFRED	288/94	BDV supply 7.15–1920.
Y2.177	WREXHAM	1414/02	Armament carrier (c) 20.11.16–18.10.17; wrecked 21.6.18.
	ZEPHYR	201/73	BDV salvage vessel at Lerwick 15.1.15–1919.

*Pendant from 9.15; **from 1.18.

Notes: These groups include merchant vessels used for a wide variety of purposes, particularly the fleet messengers (apparently a catch-all classification), though logistic support was most common. The "(c)" signifies periods of commissioned service; some other commissioned service was possible for vessels employed on foreign stations. The full range of MFAs with Y pendant numbers included: Y1.1–2 (flotilla depots); Y2.1–237 (armament carriers); Y3.1–2524 (colliers); Y4.1–81 (fleet messengers); Y5.1–8 (frozen meat ships); Y6.1–9 (mine carriers); Y7.1–342 (oilers and water carriers); Y8.1–138 (store carriers); Y9.1–30 (squadron supply ships) and YA.1–19 (hospital ships). The flotilla supply ships carried numbers 1 to 9 without any letter flag superior. Transfer of mercantile auxiliaries from one service and government authority to another were very frequent, this listing includes the ships more closely associated with the navy. They flew the red ensign, or if commissioned, the white ensign. Most vessels served in several capacities during the 1914–1919 period and when reverting to a former occupation, returned to the appropriate pendant number assigned earlier. Hundreds of other liners, cargo ships, tugs, tankers, etc. were employed by several government authorities separate from the navy and were operated under the Shipping Controller or the War Office conveying supplies and acting in support of the Expeditionary Forces.

Except for Y2, Y3, Y5 and Y7 vessels (not listed), the MFAs are included in sections according to their first, or sometimes more prominent naval use. Loss details for some vessels not in naval service at the time of loss appears, here it must be noted that such losses are not intended to be implied as naval losses.

LANDING CRAFT

"X" LIGHTERS

160 tons. 105¼ (pp) × 21 × 3½ ft. Oil engines 60 bhp (avg).
130 tons gross.
X.1 to X.200. Ordered 2.15 and all launched between 4.15 and 7.15. Delivery of nearly all vessels effected by 8.15.
137 tons. 93 (pp) × 20 × 3½ ft. Oil engines 60 bhp (avg).
120 tons gross.
X.201 to X.225. Ordered 2.16 and all launched between 6.16 and 9.16.
137 tons. 98 (pp) × 20 × 3 ft. Dumb.
DX.1 to DX.25. All launched late 1916. Similar to the X.201 series, but without engines. It was intended that these craft would be towed by the X lighters or other small vessels.
Builders (all three groups):
Ailsa SB, X.201–202; Austin, X.14–18; Beardmore, X.167–169; Blumer, X.181–185; Blyth SB; Bow McLachlan, X.203–204; George Brown, X.179–180, X.205–206; Caledon, X.90–92; Cochrane, X.130–135; Craig Taylor, X.19–26, X.207–208, DX.1–2; Dobson, X.100; Doxford, X.139–153; Eltringham; Harkess, DX.11–12; Head Wrightson, X.5–7, X.199–200; Laing, X.8–13; Northumberland SB; Osbourne Graham, X.39–47, X.216–217, DX.15–16; Ramage & Ferguson, X.93–94; Readhead; Richardson Duck, X.48–53; Ropner, X.1–4, X.197–198; Short, X.69–78, DX.17–20; Simons, X.220–221, DX.21–22; Sunderland SB, X.54–68, X.222–223; Swan Hunter, X.176–178; Teesside Bridge, X.154–155; J. L. Thompson, X.118–123; Robert Thompson, X.191–196, DX.23–25.
Notes: These craft were designed by James Pollock & Sons, who assigned their builder's numbers to well over 100 lighters although none are known to actually have been built by them. All were built primarily for landing operations in the Dardanelles and their production received top priority; they proved to be very successful and versatile craft. A wide variety of oil engines were fitted, ranging from 30 to 92 bhp. Most of them had been sold by 1925, though 32 lasted until the Second World War. At least 17 vessels were reported to have been transferred to the Indian government. One vessel, X.22, was employed as a decoy (Q) ship. X.207 and 223 were later renamed C.83 and C.84 as coal lighters and X.96, 118, 127, 131, and 182 became L.14, L.11, L.9, L.10 and L.1 respectively as water carriers. X.3, 8, 42, 75, 77, 78, 93, 100, 106, 124, 128, 160 and 199 were respectively renamed OYSTER, TANKARD, LOBSTER, MOILER, WINKLE, COCKLE, BEAKER, TOILER, SHRIMP, PITCHER, FLAGON, MUSSEL and PRAWN 1915–16 as oil or water carriers.

'Y' LIGHTERS

4½ tons (avg). 34 (oa) × 11 × 3¼ (dhd) ft. Dumb.
Y.1–60. Ordered from 2.15, all delivered by 4.15.
Y.61–90. All delivered by 6.15.
Notes: These craft were box-like shells intended for carrying troops and equipment to be towed or fitted with special out-board motors. Y.1–29 and Y.61–90 averaged 4½ tons and were built of steel, Y.30–60 were built of wood and averaged 3¾ tons. Another 20 steel barges measuring 71½ (oa) × 20 × 3¼ ft were built for service in Mesopotamia, these vessels were also dumb and were towed by river craft.

LIGHTERS AND BARGES

Name	TG/Yr	Type—Service
ALIBI	151/87	(ex-Albion) Steam lighter BDV 11.6.18–14.11.19.
ANEMONE	/	Misc small craft from J. T. Crampton & Co 24.7.18–10.6.19.
ARAB	56/01	Steam lighter 31.7.17–23.4.19.
=ARABESQUE 4.18		
ARTHUR	/	Dumb barge BDV from Plymouth & Oreston Timber Co 10.7.18–6.8.19.
BEE	*320/80	(ex-Thames) Dockyard store carrier, listed to 1921.
=YC.128 1915		*displacement tonnage.
BERIEN	94/92	(ex-Hibernia) Water boat at Scapa 10.12.17–27.3.19.
BETTY HANSON	63/11	Dumb barge BDV 9.16–1918.
COCKLE	/	(ex-light vessel) BDV gate vessel 7.15–1917.
CORONATION	95/11	BDV water boat 1.2.16–6.3.20.
DAMPER	75/	(ex-No. 14) From Aire & Calder, water boat at Devonport 14.6.18–14.4.19.
DORA	/86	BDV lighter from J. & J. Hay Ltd 13.12.17–3.1.19.
DRAGON	90/14	2.7.15–18.2.16 and at Kirkwall 12.5.18–20.2.19.
=DRONE 5.18		
FAITH	160/90	(ex-pile barge) BDV repair vessel 18.11.15–24.6.20.
FARRIER	102/91	(ex-Faraday) At Rosyth 17.6.18–18.3.19.
FENCIBLE	71/14	Motor barge for BDV stores 25.1.15; purchased 20.10.15; listed to 1923.
GAINSBOROUGH	70/96	Puffer collier for BDV 1.17–1919.
GARVIN	155/91	(ex-George) 28.6.18–21.10.19.
GEORGE	/	Dumb barge BDV from H. & G. Ham 14.10.18–24.7.19.
HOPCAR	583/11	(ex-PLA Hopper No. 14) Tender to CYCLOPS 27.4.18–20.8.20.
HOPTANK	/	(ex-Hopper No. 2) From Charlton & Co; water boat at Scapa 23.4.18–31.1.20.
I	72/86	Steam lighter BDV 3.8.14– Purchased 28.2.15.
L	77/00	Steam lighter BDV 4.8.14– Purchased 31.3.15.
LEVERHULME	108/89	(ex-Sunlight) 22.5.18–17.2.19.
LIFE BUOY	108/94	22.5.18–19.3.19.
MARY & AGNES	104/77	BDV maintenance lighter 12.9.17–16.10.20.
NIPPER	/	(ex-Evelyn) 1917–1918.
NORMAN	85/95	Steam boat tender to CRESCENT 11.9.14–24.11.19.
=NORM 4.18		
OBERON	91/99	Puffer BDV 12.9.17–27.5.20.
OUSTON	84/90	(ex-Ouse) 12.9.17–24.10.19.
QUENCHER	75/	(ex-No. 10) From Aire & Calder, water boat at Portsmouth 5.6.18–14.4.19.
RACHEL	87/92	BDV lighter on the Humber 29.4.15–3.1.17.
SWIFT	59/94	BDV tender to CRESCENT 29.8.17–15.5.19.
=TIT 4.18		
TEAL	131/89	BDV at Milford Haven 15.11.17–4.2.19.
THEODOSIA	90/63	Dumb barge BDV 13.8.15–1916.
THOMAS	120/93	BDV barge tender at Immingham 9.7.17–27.4.18.
TOGO	70/05	Lighter at Immingham 19.8.17–27.4.18 and 31.7.18–18.10.18.
=TONGA 4.18		
W. N.	114/09	BDV lighter 14.9.17–24.12.19.

Notes: Mostly in service as harbour tenders and boom defence craft. Others included: No. 10 (BDV motor boat); No. 21 (light ship used as BDV gate vessel, 1–12 pdr); No. 51 (another light ship BDV gate vessel, 1–12 pdr); No. 135 (BDV motor boat); No. 334 (BDV engine repair vessel and water boat) and five Admiralty yard craft used on boom defence (YC.16, YC.17, YC.94, YC.96 and YC.296).

AIRCRAFT LIGHTERS

(a) SEAPLANE TOWING LIGHTERS

These craft were designed to accommodate a single flying boat of the H.12, F.2 or F.3 types in a special recess that could be entered from the lighter's stern. They were given a rounded bow, a square stern, and were intended to be towed by destroyers and similar warships. Four lighters designated H.1–4 were ordered 1.17 and built by Thornycroft at Woolston. Completion tests began 18.6.17, followed by further tests conducted from 3.9.17. As a result of the first tests, 50 additional craft were ordered during 7.17 to be built of steel by the Royal Engineers at the Government Shipyard, Richborough, Kent. Designated H.5–54, they displaced 24 tons, and measured 58 (oa) × 16 × 7 ft. The first of the H.5 group was completed during 5.18; 31 units were delivered by 11.11.18, five more were to complete later, and 14 lighters were cancelled. In 1918, twelve lighters (including H.3) were fitted with a 2 inch pine deck platform for operating Camel-type aircraft. The lighter was towed at high speed by a destroyer permitting successful take-off and landing by this type of wheeled aircraft.

(b) SEAPLANE DOCKING LIGHTERS

These lighters were built with hulls similar to the towing lighters and in addition to slightly greater dimensions, were given a large shed to protect the seaplane from the elements. Intended for type H.8 seaplanes, when docked, they covered all of the aircraft except wing-tips and the tail section. Docking lighters designated D.1–2 were built 1918 and measured 60 (oa) × 18 ft. D.3–14 were larger, measuring 70 (oa) × 19 ft. Two units were known to have been cancelled. After the war most of these craft were used as dockyard craft and quickly disappeared from lists.

SPECIAL SERVICE VESSELS

Under this heading are grouped, besides the small craft listed as "Special Service Vessels" in the Navy List, navy-owned yachts, ferries, etc.

(a) TENDERS

Name	Tons/Yr	Fate
ADDER (*ex-Burgoyne*) =ATTENTIVE II 7.19	125/86	Sold 31.1.23 Carriden S Bkg Co.
ADELAIDE (*ex-Miner 18*) =ADDA 10.15 =ST. ANGELO 12.33	/04	Sold 6.37 at Malta.
BITER (*ex-Sir William Reid*)	110/89	Sold 5.23 Dover S Bkg Co.
BOUNCER (*ex-Sir Richard Fletcher*)	100/86	Sold 14.5.20 F. Bevis.
ELFIN (*ex-Dundas*)	125/87	Sold 29.2.28 Ward.
ESK (*ex-Sir Francis Head*)	110/89	Sold 6.20 W. P. Jobson.
FIREBRAND (*ex-Lord Heathfield*)	125/85	Sold 10.2.20 Stanlee.
GLEANER (*ex-General Stothard*)	160/01	Sold 2.11.21 M. S. Hilton.
HASTY (*ex-Napier of Magdala*)	144/91	Sold 20.2.32 Reynolds, Torpoint.
HERON (*ex-Empress*)	100/85	Sold 20.9.23 J. Borrow.
NETTLE (*ex-Pennar*)	130/02	Sold 1934 =TOPMAST I.
PELICAN (*ex-Sir James Jones*) =PETULANT 10.16	100/80	Sold 23.5.27 B. Zammitt, Malta.
PIGMY (*ex-Sir Lothian Nicholson*)	100/97	BU 5.38.
REDWING (*ex-Sir Charles Pasley*)	120/93	Sold 1930.
SKYLARK (*ex-General Elliot*)	110/89	Sold 21.10.30 Ward.
STARLING (*ex-Miner 17*)	/04	Sold 14.9.23 T. Round, Sunderland.
WEAZEL (*ex-Sir W. Green*) =STOAT 12.18	110/86	Sold 14.9.23.

Notes: These were all transferred from the War Department 1905–06. ADELAIDE was FIDGET until 1907, HERON was EMPRESS until 11.06 and HASTY was LINNET until 12.13. REDWING was to rename REDSTART by order 23.6.16; cancelled 7.16. All served as tenders to depot ships or training establishments. Except for N.12 assigned 1.18 to BOUNCER and N.74 to NETTLE in the same list, all were included in harbour pendant series (given a single flag or pendant for local identification.)

180 tons. 115 (pp) ×18 ×5 ft. 300 ihp=11 kts.

ELF	1909	Thames IW. Sold 6.24 W. G. Keen.

Notes: Was RAINBOW; purchased in 1911.

545 tons gross. 164½ (pp) × 33 ft.

ANT	23. 7.13	Murdoch & Murray. Sold 12.6.24 G. Nichol, =RANGITOTO.

Notes: Was purchased on stocks 5.13 and known as "ANT (new)" to 1919.

400 tons. 165 (pp) ×26 ×7 ft. 615 ihp=13 kts.

9.15	1.16	1.18	Name	Launched	Builder—Fate
P.91	X.27	X.78	WATERWITCH	17.10.14	Fairfield. Returned to Turkey 1921, =BOSPHORUS No. 71.
N.60		X.79	WAVE =WAYWARD 11.19	.14	Rennie Forrestt. Foundered in tow 11.11.22 off Anatolia.

Notes: They were the Turkish REHID PASHA and BUYAK ADA respectively, seized while building. Served as tenders or despatch vessels in the Mediterranean.

(b) YACHTS

446 tons. 157 (pp) ×23½ ×11 ft. 500 ihp=11 kts.
Armament: 1–2½ pdr.

5	FIREQUEEN	1882	Ramage & Ferguson. To Board of Trade 5.7.20 =FIREBIRD.

Notes: Was CANDACE, purchased on stocks. All yachts were assigned Portsmouth harbour pendants dating from 1914 (except IMOGENE).

460 tons.   184 (oa), 160 (pp) ×24×11 ft.   420 ihp=11 kts.
Armament: nil.

	IMOGENE =JULIUS 2.23	1882	Barclay Curle. Paid off 24.9.23; sold 1924.

Notes: Was JACAMAR, purchased on stocks.

4700 tons.   439½ (oa), 380 (pp) ×50×18 ft.   Turbine 11800 shp=20 kts.
Armament: 2-6 pdr.

2	VICTORIA & ALBERT	9. 5.99	Pembroke DY. =D/S 1939; sold 1954.

Notes: Royal yacht; laid up at Portsmouth during the war.

3470 tons.   320 (pp) ×40×15 ft.   TE 6400 ihp=18 kts.
Armament: 4-3 pdr.

3	ENCHANTRESS	7.11.03	Harland & Wolff. Sold 24.6.35 Dover Industries.

Notes: Admiralty yacht; laid up at Sheerness 1914.

2050 tons.   300 (oa), 275 (pp) ×40×12 ft.   Turbine 4500 shp=18½ kts.
Armament: nil.

4	ALEXANDRA	30. 5.07	Inglis. Sold 5.25 =PRINCE OLAF.

Notes: Royal yacht; laid up at Portsmouth during the war.

(c) FERRY SERVICE VESSELS

160 tons.

	THISTLE	1902	Greenock & Grangemouth. To Irish Government 1921.

Notes: Purchased 9.10.02; on ferry service at Queenstown.

651 tons.   194 (oa), 185 (pp) ×26×6½ ft.   TE 1300 ihp=13 kts.

	NIMBLE	14. 3.06	Hawthorns, Leith. Sold 11.10.48.

Notes: Was ROSLIN CASTLE, purchased 3.08. On ferry service. Chatham-Sheerness 1914-17; prisoner-of-war exchange service at Boston, Mass. 1917-18.

528 tons.   200½ (pp) ×24×6 ft.   Paddle diagonal compound 1000 ihp=16 kts.

838	HARLEQUIN	11. 3.97	Russell. =M/S 5.17 (1-3 pdr); =ferry 5.19; =accom ship 9.42; wrecked 9.42 on passage Chatham to Clyde.

Notes: Was STRATHMORE, purchased 3.08. Ferry service Portsmouth 1914-17; then M/S Bristol Channel 1917-18, M/S at Sheerness 1918. Assigned Fishery flag superior (838) while on M/S duties.

589 tons.   216 (oa), 210 (pp) ×25×6½ ft.   Paddle diag. comp. 1400 ihp=16 kts.

	WANDERER	12. 6.95	McMillan. =M/S (2-6 pdr) 6.17; sold 28.11.21 J. Hall, Rochester to BU.
1237	=WARDEN 6.17		

Notes: Was LIBERTY, renamed 1913; ex-*Lady Margaret* purchased 3.08. On ferry service Chatham-Sheerness 1914-17. Became M/S based on the Tyne 6.17-18 (Fy.1237 pendant); WARDEN later went to ferry service at Chatham. (Navy Lists give this ship as renamed ROAMER 1917, but this name was not used).

(d) MISCELLANEOUS

Ex-Gunboats: 254, 265 and 196 tons respectively.   7 kts speed.

	ARROW	22. 4.71	Rennie, Greenwich. Sold 1.3.22 W. H. Webber.
8	INSOLENT	15. 3.81	Pembroke DY. =BDV 1.15; foundered 1.7.22 in Portsmouth harbour, raised; sold 18.6.25 Pounds.
	PLUCKY =BANTERER 6.15	13. 7.70	Portsmouth DY. Sold 1928.

Notes: All were at Portsmouth 1914-18.

Ex-Gunboats: 363 tons. 110 (pp) ×34×5½ ft. Avg 400 ihp=9 kts.

Answer	SABRINA =SABINE 7.16 =VIVID 1920	3.10.76	Palmer. Sold 7.22 Fryer, Sunderland.
2	SLANEY	28. 4.77	Palmer. Sold 30.8.19 Ward, Grays.
3	SPEY	5.10.76	Palmer. Sold 1923.
Code	TAY	19.10.76	Palmer. Sold 22.10.20 Stanlee.

Notes: SABRINA and TAY were tenders at Devonport; SLANEY at Sheerness; and SPEY at Chatham.

Ex-Gunboat: 465 tons. 125 (pp) ×23½×10 ft. 360 ihp=9½ kts.

	RAVEN	18. 5.82	Samuda, Poplar. Sold 13.3.25.

Notes: Portsmouth Gunnery School 1914; D/S at Portland from 1914.

Trials gunboat: 890 tons. 130 (oa), 125 (pp) ×35×8 ft.
Armament: 1–9.2 in.

	DRUDGE =EXCELLENT 11.16 =DRYAD 1.19	1883	Armstrong. Sold 27.3.20 G. Sharpe.

Notes: Purchased 28.2.01. Served as gunboat based at Dover 1914–15, disarmed by order 5.11.15 and laid up.

THREE EX-RUSSIAN ICEBREAKERS

6000 tons. 281 (oa), 264¼ (pp) ×64×19 ft. TE 7500 ihp=19 kts.
Armament: 1–4 in, 2–12 pdr. (3 screws).

10.19	Name	Launched	Builder—Fate
N.N3	ALEXANDER	12.16	Armstrong. Returned 1921 to Russia =LENIN.

Notes: Was Russian ALEKSANDR NEVSKI seized before completion and commissioned in 9.17. Pendant N.N3 replaced by N.9A on 1.11.19.

3400 tons. 265 (pp) ×47½×18 ft. TE 6000 ihp=17 kts.

	EARL GREY	8.09	Vickers. Returned to Russia =CANADA.

Notes: Was Russian CANADA seized 1918, ex-Canadian Govt EARL GREY sold to Russia in 10.14.

10625 tons. 323 (oa) ×71×26 ft. TE 10000 ihp=15 kts.
Armament: 1–6 in (originally 2–5 in, 2–13 pdr).

10.19	Name	Launched	Builder—Fate
N.N4	SVIATOGOR	1915	Armstrong. Returned 19.11.21 to Russia; later =KRASSIN.

Notes: Seized 3.8.18 when found scuttled at Archangel. Pendant N.N4 replaced by N.A8 on 1.11.19.

SURVEY VESSELS

1300 tons. 212 (pp) ×30×12½ ft. TE 2100 ihp=14½ kts.
Armament: 4–3 pdr.

1914 1.18	Name	Launched Builder—Fate
D.45* N.55	HEARTY	18. 4.85 Thompson, Dundee. Sold 6.11.20 M. S. Hilton.

*Flag superior changed 9.15 to N.
Notes: Laid down as tug INDIRA and purchased on the stocks. On survey service, Nore Command 1914–18.

900 tons. 185½ (pp) ×29×13 ft. TE 500 ihp=11 kts.
Armament: 1–3 pdr.

SEALARK	1878	Greenock. Sold 3.9.19 at Melbourne.

Notes: Was CONSUELO purchased 1903 and named INVESTIGATOR until 1.04. Laid up in Australia during the war.

THREE SLOOPS CONVERTED 1906–07

FANTOME	23. 3.01	Sheerness DY. Sold 30.1.25 at Sydney, NSW.
MERLIN	30.11.01	Sheerness DY. Sold 3.8.23 at Hong Kong.
MUTINE	1. 3.00	Laird. =RNVR drillship 9.25; sold 16.8.32.

Notes: The first two were "Espiegle" class and MUTINE of "Condor" class (qv). FANTOME paid off in Australia until 7.15 when she was rearmed (2–4 in, 4–12 pdr) and commissioned as a sloop (RAN) in the Pacific until 1918. MERLIN and MUTINE also paid off, the former being commissioned as a sloop in China 8.18 and the latter as a depot ship at Bermuda in 12.17.

TWO RIM VESSELS

1185 tons. 254 (pp) ×33×12 ft. TE 1550 ihp=13 kts.

INVESTIGATOR	11. 6.07	Vickers. Sold 1934.

444 tons. 140 (pp) ×24×9 ft. TE 475 ihp=11 kts.

PALINURUS	.07	Cammell Laird. Sold c1930.

TWO EX-TRAWLERS

510 tons. 125 (pp) ×22½×10 ft. TE 500 ihp=10 kts.

N.31 (1.18)	DAISY	.11	Duthie. Sold 3.20 Newfoundland Government.
N.43 (1.18)	ESTHER	22.11.11	Duthie. Transferred to Board of Customs & Excise 25.9.19.

Notes: Purchased on the stocks 14.2.11. They saw survey duty in Nore Command 1914–18 and at Dover 1918. They were also fitted for minesweeping.

1280 tons. 241 (oa), 200 (pp) ×34×12 ft. TE 1100 ihp=13 kts.
Armament: 1–3 pdr.

ENDEAVOUR	30. 3.12	Fairfield. =D/S 1940; sold 30.9.46.

Notes: Survey service at the Nore 1914–15, then to the Mediterranean.

HOSPITAL SHIPS

8785 tons. 404½ (oa), 390 (pp) × 52¾ × 20 ft. TE=12½ kts.

1914	9.15	1.16	Name	Launched	Builder—Fate
D.95	N.95	X.13	MEDIATOR =MAINE 7.14	1906	Henderson. Sold 7.3.16 Harris & Dixon =HELIOPOLIS.

Notes: Was HELIOPOLIS, purchased 7.3.13. An earlier MAINE (*ex-Swansea*), built 1887 and presented 29.6.01, was sold 6.7.14 after stranding. The name MEDIATOR appears in pendant lists to 1916, but this name was borne by the hulk *ex-Indus V*, *ex-Ganges* from 1914 included in harbour service (qv). Wore the blue ensign as an RFA.

HIRED VESSELS

No.	Name	TG/Yr	Dimensions (pp)	Builder—Service
YA.13	AGADIR	2738/07	285 ×41¼ ft.	Laing. 30.11.14–1919.
YA.18	BERBICE	2379/09	300¾×38¼ ft.	Harland & Wolff. 4.12.15–purchased 1919, sold 1923.
YA.6	CHINA	7932/96	500½×54¼ ft.	Harland & Wolff. 4.8.14–1919.
YA.7	DELTA	8089/07	470¼×56½ ft.	Workman Clark. 5.8.14–12.11.14.
YA.3	DRINA	11483/13	500½×62¼ ft.	Harland & Wolff. 4.8.14–10.2.16; sunk 1.3.17 by S/M off Skokholm Is.
YA.2	GARTH CASTLE	7715/10	452½×54¼ ft.	Barclay Curle. 4.11.14–1915.
	GASCON	6298/97	430 ×52¼ ft.	Harland & Wolff. 21.9.14–10.10.14.
YA.8	GRANTALA =FIGUIG c1915	3655/03	350 ×45¼ ft.	Armstrong. 24.12.14–1918 (RAN).
YA.17	KARAPARA	7117/15	425 ×55½ ft.	Swan Hunter. 8.15–1918; =in WW II.
YA.14	MAGIC =MAGIC II 1916 =CLASSIC 6.18	2147/93	311¼×38¼ ft.	Harland & Wolff. 16.11.14–6.5.19.
YA.4	PLASSY	7346/01	450¼×54¼ ft.	Caird. 3.8.14–8.5.18.
YA.12	PRINCE GEORGE	3372/10	306¾×42¼ ft.	Swan Hunter.
YA.5	REWA	7308/06	456×56¼ ft.	Denny. 3.8.14– Sunk 4.1.18 by S/M off Hartland Point.
	ROHILLA	7409/06	460¼×56¼ ft.	Harland & Wolff. 6.8.14– Wrecked 30.10.14 off Whitby.
YA.19	ST. MARGARET OF SCOTLAND	2467/09	300¾×38¼ ft.	Harland & Wolff. (*ex-Balantia*) 25.1.16–1918.
YA.16	SOMALI	6712/10	450¼×52¼ ft.	Caird. 13.2.15–30.4.16.
YA.1	SOUDAN	6696/01	450 ×52¼ ft.	Caird. 3.8.14–1919.

Notes: BERBICE was the only vessel of this group to fly the blue ensign (from 1919), all others were red-ensign naval hospital ships. Many other vessels served the government as military hospital ships and hospital carriers. Other naval hospital included ALBION, LIBERTY, QUEEN ALEXANDRA and SHEELAH included with yachts (qv). MAGIC II was to be renamed MAGICIAN 2.5.18, this order was cancelled 23.5.18 and on 27.6.18 =CLASSIC instead. Y flag, answer pendant superior numbers were assigned this series about 11.14.

HOSPITAL CARRIERS

Ten paddle vessels were converted to hospital carriers for service in the White Sea in 1919; for HC.1 and HC.7–10 see MFA list; for HC.2–6 see paddle minesweepers. While in service as HC.1–10 they carried Y flag+Numeral pendant superior to their HC numbers.

Paddle hospital vessels designated HP.1–11 were built 1916–17 by Ailsa SB, Blyth SB, Beardmore, Bow McLachlan, Caird and Lobnitz for service in Mesopotamia.

TROOPSHIPS (RIM)

3570 tons.   300 (pp) × 45½ × 16 ft.   2300 ihp = 12 kts.
Armament:

| CLIVE | 1882 | Laird. On sale list 1919. |

3300 tons.   285 (pp) × 36 × 16½ ft.   1080 ihp = 10½ kts.
Armament:

| CANNING | 15.11.82 | Inglis. ex-*Golconda*. On sale list 1919. |

1960 tons.   239 (pp) × 36 × 16 ft.   1500 ihp = 14 kts.
Armament: 6–6 pdr.

| DALHOUSIE | 5. 6.86 | Caird. D/S in WW II. |

1154 tons.   212 (pp) × 32 × 17½ ft.   Paddle 1200 ihp = 13 kts.
Armament: 4–4 in.

| LAWRENCE
=CANNING 1919 | 15. 6.86 | Laird. Sold c1922. |

950 tons.   206 (pp) × 28 × 14 ft.   1670 ihp = 14 kts.
Armament: 4–3 pdr.

| ELPHINSTONE | 14.11.87 | Swan Hunter. ex-*Hindoo* purchased. Sale list 1919. |

960 tons.   206 (pp) × 31½ × 12 ft.   TE 1850 ihp = 14 kts.
Armament: 4–3 pdr.

| MINTO | 22. 3.93 | Laird. Sold 1925. |

6520 tons.   423½ (pp) × 51 × 19 ft.   TE 9366 ihp = 19 kts.
Armament: 6–4.7 in, 6–3 pdr.

| HARDINGE | 11. 8.00 | Fairfield. Sold c1930. |

7457 tons.   437 (pp) × 53 × 20 ft.   TE 9800 ihp = 19 kts.
Armament: 8–4 in, 8–3 pdr.

| DUFFERIN | 14. 8.04 | Vickers. =TS 1927; listed 1954. |

5820 tons.   360 (pp) × 52 × 18 ft.   TE 7000 ihp = 16½ kts.
Armament: 6–4.7 in, 6–3 pdr.

| NORTHBROOK | 6. 7.07 | John Brown. Listed to 1924. |

Notes: All of the above named ships served in the East Indies 1914–18; **DALHOUSIE** was transferred to the RN 20.8.14 and later became a D/S at Basra from 1916; she reverted to the RIM in 1919.

HARBOUR SERVICE

Name	Tons/Year	Service status	Sale date
ACTAEON (ex-Ariadne)	4538/1859	Torpedo school, Sheerness.	11.12.22
ACTAEON (ex-Vernon)	2388/1832	Torpedo school, Portsmouth.	14. 9.23
ACTAEON II (ex-Dido)	1760/1869	Torpedo school, Sheerness.	17. 7.22
ALERT	960/1894	D/S in Persian Gulf.	12. 1.26
AMOKURA (ex-Sparrow)	805/1889	T/S, New Zealand.	2.22
ANTELOPE	810/1893	On sale list, then training at Devonport.	27. 5.19
ARETHUSA	3832/1849	T/S, Greenhithe, R. Thames.	.34
BLACK DRAGON (ex-Kobenhavn)	*3400/1914	Oil hulk; =C.600.	9.22
BRITANNIA (ex-Prince of Wales)	6201/1860	Ex-T/S, laid up.	13.11.14
C.8 (ex-Northumberland)	6621/1866	Coal hulk; =C.68 1926.	6.27
C.10 (ex-Ruby)	2120/1876	Coal hulk.	16. 2.21
C.60 (ex-Himalaya)	4690/1853	Coal hulk.	28. 9.20
C.109 (ex-Agincourt)	6621/1865	Coal hulk, Sheerness.	10.60
C.110 (ex-Jumna)	6211/1866	Coal hulk.	7.22
C.115 (ex-Tourmaline)	2120/1875	Coal hulk.	11.20
C.470 (ex-Shah)	6250/1873	Coal hulk, Bermuda.	19. 9.19
CALCUTTA (ex-Hercules) =FISGARD II 4.15	9300/1868	Hulk, Devonport.	7.32
CALLIOPE =HELICON 6.15 =CALLIOPE 10.31	2770/1884	RNVR drillship, Newcastle.	4.10.51
CALYPSO =BRITON 2.16	2770/1883	Drillship, St. Johns, NFL.	7. 4.22
CERBERUS =PLATYPUS II 1921	3480/1868	RAN base ship, Williamstown, NSW; hulk now a breakwater.	23. 4.24
CHALLENGER	2306/1858	Mooring hulk, Chatham.	6. 1.21
CHAMPION	2380/1878	Hulk, Chatham; later T/S.	23. 6.19
CIRCE =IMPREGNABLE IV 10 15	1447/1827	Accommodation, Devonport.	7.22
CLEOPATRA =DEFIANCE III 1.22	2380/1878	Accommodation, Devonport.	7.31
CLIO	2306/1858	T/S at Bangor.	3.10.19
COLLEEN (old) (ex-Hawk) =EMERALD 1918 =CUCKOO 5.18	416/1869	On sale list, Devonport; =Gunnery tender 5.18.	10. 8.22
COLLEEN (ex-Royalist)	1420/1883	Base ship, Queenstown.	19. 2.23
COLUMBINE (ex-Wild Swan) =COLUMBINE (old) 11.19	1130/1876	Base ship, Rosyth.	4. 5.20
CONWAY (ex-Nile)	4375/1839	T/S at Liverpool; stranded 14.4.53, wreck burnt 31.10.56.	(lost)
CORMORANT =ROOKE 7.46	1130/1877	Base ship, Gibraltar.	.49
CORNWALL (ex-Wellesley)	2917/1815	T/S at Purfleet; sunk 24.9.40 by A/C in the Thames.	(lost)
CORNWALLIS =WILDFIRE 3.16	*1809/1813	Jetty at Sheerness; =Base ship 1916.	.57BU
CRUISER (ex-Kingfisher)	1130/1879	On sale list at Malta.	.19
DEFIANCE	5270/1861	Torpedo school, Devonport.	26. 6.31
DOLPHIN	925/1882	S/M base, Portsmouth.	13. 3.25
EAGLE =EAGLET 1918	2340/1804	RNVR drillship, Liverpool; =Base ship 1914; burnt 1926.	4. 1.27
ECLIPSE	1760/1867	Mine depot, Devonport.	.21
EGMONT (old) (ex-Achilles) =EGREMONT 6.16 =PEMBROKE 6.19	9841/1863	Hulk, Chatham; =Accommodation hulk 1916.	26. 1.23
EGMONT (ex-Firefly) =FIREFLY 3.23	455/1877	Base ship, Malta; =Hulk.	5.31
EMPRESS (ex-Revenge)	5260/1859	T/S, Clyde.	31.12.23
EXCELLENT (ex-Handy) =CALCUTTA 12.16 =SNAPPER II 8.17 (N.54)	508/1883	Gunnery school, Portsmouth; =Gunboat at Dover 1914–15; disarmed 10.16.	27. 4.22
FALCON	780/1877	Hulk, Devonport.	28. 6.20

Name	Tons/Year	Service status	Sale date
FISGARD (ex-*Audacious*) =IMPERIEUSE 10.14	6010/1869	T/S, Portsmouth; =Repair hulk 1914. =pendant N.60 from 14.6.18.	15. 3.27
FISGARD II (ex-*Invincible*)	6010/1869	T/S; foundered 17.9.14 off Portland.	(lost)
FISGARD III (ex-*Hindostan*) =HINDOSTAN 8.20	3242/1841	T/S.	10. 5.21
FISGARD IV (ex-*Sultan*) =SULTAN 1932	9290/1870	T/S.	13. 8.46
FLAMINGO	780/1876	Hulk, Plymouth.	25. 5.23
FLORA =INDUS II 4.15	4360/1893	On sale list, Devonport; =T/S 1915.	12.12.22
FLY	"60/1863	Accommodation hulk, Devonport.	.28BU
FOUDROYANT (ex-*Trincomalee*)	1447/1817	T/S; still in service.	
FURIOUS =FORTE 6.15	5750/1896	Laid up; =T/S 1915.	5.23
GANGES II (ex-*Minotaur*)	10690/1863	T/S, Harwich; =Base ship 1914.	30. 1.22
GAYUNDAH	360/1884	RAN T/S.	.21
HELENA	529/1843	Police hulk, Chatham.	6. 1.21
IMPLACABLE (ex-*Duguay Trouin*)	3223/1800	Training; scuttled 2.12.49	(sunk)
IMPREGNABLE (ex-*Howe*) =BULWARK 12.19	6557/1860	T/S, Devonport.	18. 2.21
IMPREGNABLE II (ex-*Inconstant*) =IMPREGNABLE (old) 12.19 =DEFIANCE IV 1.22 =DEFIANCE II 12.30	5782/1868	T/S.	4.56
IMPREGNABLE III (ex-*Black Prince*)	9210/1861	T/S.	21. 2.23
INDEFATIGABLE (ex-*Phaeton*) =CARRICK II 1941	4300/1883	T/S, River Mersey.	1.47
INDUS (ex-*Defence*)	6270/1861	T/S, Devonport.	8. 8.35
INDUS II (ex-*Temeraire*) =AKBAR 10.14	8540/1876	=Repair hulk at Scapa by 1.15.	26. 5.21
INDUS III (ex-*Bellerophon*)	7550/1875	T/S.	12.12.22
INDUS IV (ex-*Triumph*) =ALGIERS 10.14	6640/1870	=Repair hulk at Scapa by 1.15.	7. 1.21
INDUS V (ex-*Ganges*) =MEDIATOR 12.14 =IMPREGNABLE III 10.22	3594/1821	=Hospital hulk 1914.	31. 8.29
MARS	3842/1848	T/S, Dundee.	10. 6.29
MEDUSA	2800/1888	Calibrating vessel, Bantry.	21.10.21
MERCURY	3730/1878	Hulk, Chatham.	9. 7.19
MERCURY (ex-*Gannet*)	1130/1878	Training; still in service, preserved 1971.	
MOUNT EDGCUMBE (ex-*Winchester*)	2300/1822	Training, Devonport.	8. 4.21
NEWCASTLE	4020/1860	Powder hulk, Devonport.	.29
NORTHAMPTON (ex-*Sharpshooter*)	735/1888	Training.	27. 3.22
PEMBROKE (ex-*Trent*) =GANNET 6.17	363/1877	Base ship, Chatham; =Diving tender 6.17.	21. 2.23
PENGUIN	1130/1876	RAN Base ship, Sydney.	.24
POMONE	2135/1897	Training, Dartmouth.	25.10.22
POWERFUL =IMPREGNABLE 11.19	14200/1895	Training, Devonport.	31. 8.29
POWERFUL II (ex-*Andromeda*) =IMPREGNABLE II 11.19 =DEFIANCE 1.31	11000/1897	T/S.	8.56
POWERFUL III (ex-*Caroline*) =IMPREGNABLE IV 11.19	1420/1882	T/S.	31. 8.29
PRESIDENT (ex-*Buzzard*)	1140/1887	RNVR drillship, London.	6. 9.21
PROTECTOR =CERBERUS 1921	920/1884	RAN Gunnery training, Williamstown.	10. 9.24
RAPID =HART 1916	1420/1883	S/M depot, Gibraltar.	.48
RATTLER =DRYAD 9.19	715/1886	Training, Portsmouth.	10.24
READY =DRUDGE 10.16	610/1872	Tank vessel, Bermuda.	25. 2.20
RESEARCH (P.88 from 1914 P.A0 from 1.18)	520/1888	Laid up, Portsmouth; =D/S at Portland 1915–18.	29. 7.20

Name	Tons/Year	Service status	Sale date
SATELLITE	1420/1881	RNVR drillship, North Shields; =Base ship 1914–18.	21.10.47
SPARTAN =DEFIANCE II 8.21	3600/1891	Accommodation, Devonport.	26. 6.31
SPARTIATE =FISGARD 6.15	11000/1898	Training, Portsmouth.	7.32
STORK	465/1882	T/S for boys, Hammersmith.	.50
SWINGER	430/1872	Store hulk, Devonport.	6.24
TBs (2nd class) 45. 47, 48	14/1889	Ferry service, Chatham.	c1918
TAMAR	4650/1863	Base ship, Hong Kong; Scuttled 12.12.41.	(lost)
TERROR (ex-Malabar)	6211/1866	Base ship, Bermuda.	1.18
THALIA	2240/1869	Store hulk, Cromarty; =Base ship 2.15.	16. 9.20
THUNDERBOLT =DAEDALUS 8.17 =THUNDERBOLT 1920	1844/1856	Jetty at Chatham; =D/S 1916–19; rammed and sunk 3.4.48	(lost)
TINGIRA	1800/1912	RAN T/S, Sydney.	c1928
TRITON	410/1882	Laid up. =T/S 6.19 on loan.	.61
UNICORN =CRESSY 11.41 =UNICORN 7.59	1447/1824	RNVR drillship, Dundee; =Base ship 1914–18; drillship 1918, still in service.	
VALIANT (old) =VALIANT III 1.18	6710/1863	Store hulk, Devonport; =Oil hulk 1924.	12.56
VARYAG (Russian cruiser)	6600/1899	Dismantled 1917, Liverpool; =Ammunition hulk 9.18.	c1919 BU
VERNON (ex-Donegal)	5481/1858	Torpedo school, Portsmouth.	18. 5.25
VERNON II (ex-Marlborough)	6300/1855	Torpedo school, Portsmouth; sank 1924 while in tow.	10.24
VERNON III (ex-Warrior)	9210/1860	Torpedo school, Portsmouth; =Oil hulk 3.29; =C.77 c1945; still in service.	
VESUVIUS	245/1874	Training, Portsmouth.	14. 9.23
VICTORY	"2164/1765	Base ship, Portsmouth; still in service.	
VIVID (ex-Cuckoo) =VIVID (old) 1920	254/1873	Base ship, Devonport; =YC.37 hulk by 1923.	.58
WARSPITE (ex-Waterloo)	4579/1833	Marine Society T/S, Greenhithe. Burnt 20.1.18.	(lost)
WILDFIRE (ex-Nymphe) =GANNET 3.16 =PEMBROKE 6.17	1140/1888	Base ship, Sheerness; =Diving tender 1916; =Base ship at Chatham 6.17.	10. 2.20
WIVERN	2750/1863	Repair hulk, Hong Kong.	5.22
WORCESTER (ex-Frederick William)	4725/1860	Thames Marine Officers T/S, Greenhithe.	7.48
YC.20 (ex-Foxhound)	455/1877	Coal lighter, Sheerness.	.20
YC.37 (ex-Dapper)	284/1855	Cooking depot.	10. 5.22
YC.229 (ex-Tickler) =AFRIKANDER 2.19 =AFRIKANDER II 1933	254/1879	Lighter, Simonstown; =Base ship 1919.	.37
YC.230 (ex-Gadfly)	254/1879	Coal lighter, Capetown.	.18
YC.373 (ex-Griper) =FLORA 6.23 =AFRIKANDER 1933	254/1879	Lighter, Capetown; =Base ship 1923.	c1937

*Tons gross, "tons builders measurement.
Notes: This group includes a very wide assortment of obsolete warships from the Victorian period and earlier. Sailing warships and early iron steamships reduced to little more than hulks had been used on harbour service in large numbers from the turn of the century. Many famous names which were prominent during the 19th century appear here, some of which are borne by vessels on long term loan to various institutions.
    The Russian cruiser VARYAG had arrived at Liverpool in 2.17 damaged; she was hulked after being found beyond repair.

HARBOUR IDENTIFICATION PENDANTS
1914-1919

At Portsmouth:
ALEXANDRA	4
AMPHITRITE	Compass (9.15)
ANT	Answer
ASSEGAI	Oblique (9.18)
ECLIPSE	Oblique (3.16)*
ENCHANTRESS	3
FIREQUEEN	5
INSOLENT	8
MAGNET	7
ONYX	Equal speed (3.16)*
ROBINA	Equal speed (9.18)
SEAFLOWER	6
SPARROW	Code
SPIDER	Blue
VERNON	5
VESTAL	Church
VICTORIA & ALBERT	2
VICTORY	9

At Devonport:
CONFIANCE	9
CUCKOO	1 (9.18)
DEFIANCE	2
DRIVER	Church
ECLIPSE	Oblique (1.18)
ELF	6
FORTITUDE	8
HERON	Interrogative
IMPREGNABLE	7 *
INDUS	4 *
INDUS	7 (3.16)
LINNET	Numeral
ONYX	Equal speed (1.18)
PIGMY	1 *
POWERFUL	T (9.15)*
POWERFUL	3 (3.16)
RINALDO	H international
ROSE	3 *
SABRINA	Answer
TAY	Code
TRAVELLER	5 *
VICTORIA IV	5 (6.18)
VIVID	R international (2.15)

At Chatham and Sheerness:
ACTAEON	1
BLAZER	5
BUSTARD	Compass
ELFIN	Answer
FIREBRAND	8
PEMBROKE	3 *
PEMBROKE	4 (4.15)
SEAHORSE	Interrogative
SEAMEW	Numeral
SLANEY	2 *
SLANEY	3 (4.15)
STARLING	9
WEAZEL	7
WILDFIRE	6

At Harwich:
GANGES	0
NAUTPUR	1 (4.15)
REDSTART	2 (4.15)

At Dartmouth:
POMONE	0

At Portland:
MORDRED	3 (1.18)

Notes: These pendants were duplicated from port to port. Many of the single flags and pendants not listed were assigned to shore installations. There were in fact two assignments of flag 5 at Portsmouth; other pendants denoted * were cancelled before used by another vessel. Most of the 1914 pendants lasted until late 1919; other additions after 1914 are dated.

PENDANT MEMBERS OF USN WARSHIPS SERVING WITH THE RN 1918

Battleships:
1A (9.18)	ARKANSAS
98 (4.18)	DELAWARE
99 (4.18)	FLORIDA
2A (9.18)	NEVADA
96 (4.18)	NEW YORK
4A (9.18)	OKLAHOMA
0A (4.18)	TEXAS
3A (9.18)	UTAH
97 (4.18)	WYOMING

Minelayers: (6.18)
Ri.07	AROOSTOOK
Ri.01	BALTIMORE
Ri.09	BLACK HAWK
Ri.04	CANANDAIGUA
Ri.03	CANNONICUS
Ri.10	HOUSATONIC
Ri.05	QUINNEBAUG
Ri.00	ROANOKE
Ri.02	SAN FRANCISCO
Ri.06	SARANAC
Ri.08	SHAWMUT

Depot ships:
C4 (6.18)	BUSHNELL
Hi.14 (1.18)	DIXIE
Hi.25 (1.18)	MELVILLE
Hi.16 (6.18)	

Minesweepers: (6.18)
T.4A	AVOCET
T.5A	BOBOLINK
T.6A	CARDINAL
T.7A	FINCH
T.A3	HERON
T.8A	LAPWING
T.9A	OWL
T.A0	TANAGER
T.A2	TEAL
T.A4	TURKEY
T.A1	WIDGEON
T.A5	WOODCOCK

Tugs: (6.18)
W.08 (9.18)	GENESEE
T.1A	ONTARIO
T.3A	PATAPSCO
T.2A	PATUXENT
T.0A	SONOMA

Destroyers:
1.18 6.18
Hi.00	Hi.10	ALLEN
Hi.01	Hi.41	AMMEN
	Hi.18	AYLWIN
Hi.02		BALCH
	Hi.42	BEALE
Hi.03	Hi.31	BENHAM
Hi.04	Hi.23	BURROWS
	Hi.05	CALDWELL
Hi.06	Hi.25	CASSIN
	Hi.60	CONNER
Hi.07	Hi.33	CONYINGHAM
Hi.08	Hi.06	CUMMINGS
Hi.09		CUSHING
Hi.12	Hi.35	DAVIS
Hi.11	Hi.21	DOWNES
Hi.15	Hi.37	DRAYTON
Hi.16	Hi.11	DUNCAN
Hi.17	Hi.39	ERICSSON
Hi.19	Hi.29	FANNING
	Hi.49	FLUSSER
Hi.20		JACOB JONES
Hi.21	Hi.15	JARVIS
Hi.22	Hi.19	JENKINS
	Hi.57	KIMBERLEY
	Hi.44	LAMSON
	Hi.59	LITTLE
	Hi.50	MACDONOUGH
Hi.23	Hi.30	MANLEY
	Hi.56	MCCALL
Hi.24	Hi.22	MCDOUGAL
	Hi.45	MONAGHAN
Hi.27	Hi.00	NICHOLSON
Hi.28		OBRIEN
Hi.30	Hi.38	PARKER
Hi.31	Hi.20	PATTERSON
Hi.32	Hi.03	PAULDING
Hi.33	Hi.26	PERKINS
Hi.34	Hi.14	PORTER
	Hi.47	PRESTON
	Hi.51	REID
	Hi.46	ROE
Hi.36	Hi.61	ROWAN
Hi.37	Hi.07	SAMPSON
Hi.38	Hi.26	SHAW
	Hi.58	SIGOURNEY
	Hi.53	SMITH
Hi.39	Hi.12	STERETT
	Hi.62	STEVENS
	Hi.48	STEWART
	Hi.40	STOCKTON
	Hi.43	TERRY
Hi.40	Hi.04	TRIPPE
	Hi.52	TRUXTUN
Hi.41	Hi.36	TUCKER
Hi.44	Hi.34	WADSWORTH
Hi.45	Hi.24	WAINWRIGHT
Hi.46	Hi.08	WALKE
Hi.47	Hi.32	WARRINGTON
	Hi.54	WHIPPLE
Hi.48	Hi.17	WILKES
Hi.49	Hi.01	WINSLOW
	Hi.55	WORDEN

Notes: International flags H and R were used for two American flag superiors; other ships fit into RN flag superiors. Many other USN warships operated with the RN in 1918.
Except for submarines given the special prefix "A" (AL.2, etc.) other warships were not assigned RN numbers.

WARSHIP BUILDERS WORLD WAR I

Short form	Longer description
Abdela Mitchell	Isaac J. Abdela and Mitchell Ltd, Queensferry, Chester.
Ailsa SB	Ailsa Shipbuilding Co Ltd, Troon and Ayr.
Ardrossan SB	Ardrossan Dry Dock and Shipbuilding Co Ltd, Ardrossan.
Armstrong	Sir W. G. Armstrong, Whitworth & Co Ltd, Walker on Tyne
Austin	S. P. Austin and Sons Ltd, Sunderland.
Ayrshire	Ayrshire Dockyard Co, Irvine.
Barclay Curle	Barclay Curle & Co Ltd, Whiteinch, Glasgow.
Bartram	Bartram and Sons Ltd, Sunderland.
Beardmore	William Beardmore & Co Ltd, Dalmuir, near Glasgow.
Blumer	John Blumer & Co, Sunderland.
Blyth SB	Blyth Shipbuilding and Dry Dock Co Ltd, Blyth.
Bow McLachlan	Bow, McLachlan & Co Ltd, Paisley.
Brooke	J. W. Brooke & Co Ltd, Lowestoft.
Brown's DD, Hull	Brown's Dry Dock & Shipbuilding Co, Hull.
George Brown	George Brown & Co, Greenock.
John Brown	John Brown & Co Ltd, Clydebank.
Burntisland	Burntisland Shipbuilding Co Ltd, Burntisland, Fife.
Caird	Caird & Co Ltd, Greenock.
Caledon SB	Caledon Shipbuilding & Engineering Co Ltd, Dundee.
Cammell Laird	Cammell Laird & Co Ltd, Birkenhead.
Camper & Nicholson	Camper & Nicholson Ltd, Gosport, Hampshire.
Chalmers	W. Chalmers & Co Ltd, Rutherglen, Glasgow.
Chambers	John Chambers Ltd, Oulton Broad, Lowestoft.
Clapson	Clapson & Sons, Barton on Humber.
Clyde SB	Clyde Shipbuilding & Engineering Co Ltd, Port Glasgow.
Cochrane	Cochrane & Sons Ltd, Selby.
Colby	Colby Brothers, Lowestoft.
Connell	Charles Connell & Co Ltd, Scotstoun.
Cook, W & G	Cook, Welton & Gemmell Ltd, Beverley.
Courtney	Courtney, Lymington. (later Berthon Boat Co Ltd).
Cox	Cox & Co (Engineers Ltd), Falmouth.
Crabtree	Crabtree & Co Ltd, Great Yarmouth.
Craig Taylor	Craig, Taylor & Co Ltd, Stockton on Tees.
Cran	J. Cran & Co, Leith. (later Cran & Somerville).
Crichton	Crichton & Co, South Saltney, Chester.
Crichton Thompson	Crichton Thompson, Kings Lynn. (later Kings Lynn SB Co Ltd).
Crown	John Crown & Sons Ltd, Sunderland.
Day Summers	Day, Summers & Co Ltd, Southampton.
Denny	William Denny & Brothers, Dumbarton.
Dobson	William Dobson & Co, Newcastle on Tyne.
Doxford	W. Doxford & Sons Ltd, Sunderland.
Duncan	R. Duncan & Co Ltd, Port Glasgow.
Dundee SB	Dundee Shipbuilding Co Ltd, Dundee.
Dunlop Bremner	Dunlop Bremner & Co Ltd, Port Glasgow.
Dunston	R. Dunston Ltd, Thorne, near Doncaster.
Duthie	J. Duthie Torry Shipbuilding Co, Aberdeen.
Earle	Earle's Shipbuilding & Engineering Co Ltd, Hull.
Edwards	Edwards & Co Ltd, Millwall.
Elder	John Elder & Co, Govan. (later Fairfield SB Co).
Eltringham	Joseph T. Eltringham & Co, South Shields.
Fairfield	Fairfield Shipbuilding & Engineering Co Ltd, Govan, Glasgow.
Fellows	Fellows & Co Ltd, Great Yarmouth.
Ferguson	Ferguson Brothers, Port Glasgow.
Finch	E. Finch & Co Ltd, Chepstow.
Fleming & Ferguson	Fleming & Ferguson Ltd, Paisley.
Fletcher & Fearnall	Fletcher, Sons & Fearnall, Limehouse.
Forbes	J. & G. Forbes, Sandhaven and Fraserburgh.
Forth SB	Forth Shipbuilding & Engineering Co Ltd, Alloa.
Fullerton	J. Fullerton & Co, Paisley.
Furness	Furness Withy & Co Ltd, West Hartlepool.
Goole SB	Goole Shipbuilding & Repairing Co Ltd, Goole.
Grangemouth	Grangemouth Dockyard Co Ltd, Grangemouth.
Gray	W. Gray & Co Ltd, West Hartlepool.
Greenock & G	Greenock & Grangemouth Dockyard Co, Greenock and Grangemouth.

Short form	Longer description
Hall	Alexander Hall & Co Ltd, Aberdeen.
Hall Russell	Hall, Russell & Co Ltd, Aberdeen.
Hamilton	William Hamilton & Co Ltd, Port Glasgow.
Hanna Donald	Hanna, Donald & Wilson, Paisley.
Harkess	W. Harkess & Sons Ltd, Middlesbrough.
Harland & Wolff	Harland & Wolff Ltd, Belfast and Govan.
Hawthorn Leslie	R. & W. Hawthorn, Leslie & Co Ltd, Hebburn of Tyne.
Hawthorns	Hawthorns & Co Ltd, Leith.
Head Wrightson	Head, Wrightson & Co, Thornaby on Tees.
Henderson	D. & W. Henderson & Co Ltd, Partick, Glasgow.
Hepple	Hepple & Co Ltd, South Shields.
Herd & Mackenzie	Herd & Mackenzie, Findochty.
Hill	Charles Hill & Co, Bristol.
Inglis	A. & J. Inglis, Glasgow.
Innes	G. Innes, Macduff.
Irvine	Irvine's Shipbuilding & Dry Dock Co Ltd, West Hartlepool.
Jones, Buckie	Jones' Buckie Slip & Shipyard Ltd, Buckie.
Kitto	Kitto & Son, Porthleven, Cornwall.
Laing	Sir James Laing & Sons Ltd, Sunderland.
Laird	Laird Brothers, Birkenhead. (later Cammell Laird 1903).
Lea SB	Lea Shipbuilding Co, Canning Town, London.
Lewis	John Lewis & Sons, Aberdeen.
Lithgows	Lithgows Ltd, Port Glasgow. (formerly Russell, from 1917).
Livingstone & Cooper	Livingstone & Cooper, Hessle, near Hull.
Lobnitz	Lobnitz & Co Ltd, Renfrew.
London & Glasgow	London & Glasgow Co Ltd, Glasgow.
Lytham SB	Lytham Shipbuilding & Engineering Co Ltd, Lytham, Lancashire.
Mackie & Thomson	Mackie & Thomson Ltd, Govan, Glasgow.
Manchester DD	Manchester Dry Dock Co Ltd, Ellesmere Port, Cheshire.
Mare	Mare, Blackwall. (later Thames Iron Works).
Maudslay	Maudslay, Sons & Field, Greenwich.
McGregor	McGregor, Kirkintilloch.
McMillan	A. McMillan & Sons Ltd, Dumbarton.
Montrose SB	Montrose Shipbuilding Co Ltd, Montrose.
Mordey Carney	Mordey Carney Ltd, Southampton.
Murdoch & Murray	Murdoch & Murray Ltd, Port Glasgow.
Napier	R. Napier & Sons Ltd, Glasgow.
Napier & Miller	Napier & Miller Ltd, Old Kilpatrick, Glasgow.
Noble	W. Noble & Co, Fraserburgh.
Northumberland SB	Northumberland Shipbuilding Co Ltd, Howdon on Tyne.
Osbourne Graham	Osbourne, Graham & Co Ltd, Sunderland.
Ouse SB	Ouse Shipbuilding Co, Hook, near Goole.
Palmer	Palmers Shipbuilding & Iron Co, Hebburn on Tyne. (formerly at Jarrow).
Payne	John Payne Ltd, Bristol.
Philip	Philip & Son Ltd, Dartmouth.
Pickersgill	W. Pickersgill & Son Ltd, Sunderland.
Pimblott	Isaac Pimblott & Sons, Northwich.
Pollock	James Pollock & Sons, Faversham.
Priestman	J. Priestman & Co, Sunderland.
Ramage & Ferguson	Ramage & Ferguson Ltd, Leith.
Raylton Dixon	Sir Raylton Dixon & Co Ltd, Middlesbrough.
Readhead	J. Readhead & Sons Ltd, South Shields.
Rennie Forrestt	Rennie Forrestt Shipbuilding & Engineering Co Ltd, Wivenhoe.
C. Rennoldson	Charles Rennoldson & Co, South Shields.
J. P. Rennoldson	John P. Rennoldson & Sons Ltd, South Shields.
Richards	Richards Iron Works, Lowestoft.
Richardson Duck	Richardson Duck & Co Ltd, Stockton on Tees.
Ritchie, G & M	Ritchie, Graham & Milne, Whiteinch, Glasgow.
Robertson	A. W. Robertson & Co, Millwall and Canning Town.
Ropner	Ropner & Sons Ltd, Stockton on Tees.
Rose St. Fdy.	Rose Street Foundry & Engineering Co Ltd, Inverness.
Routh & Waddingham	Routh & Waddingham, Wintringham.
Rowhedge	Rowhedge Iron Works, Rowhedge, Essex.
Russell	Russell & Co, Port Glasgow. (became Lithgows 30.11.17).
H. Scarr	Henry Scarr, Hessle, nr. Hull.
T. H. Scarr	Thomas H. Scarr, Howden, York.
Scott, Bowling	Scott & Sons, Bowling, near Glasgow.
Scotts	Scott's Shipbuilding & Engineering Co Ltd, Greenock.
Short	Short Brothers Ltd, Sunderland.
Simons	William Simons & Co Ltd, Renfrew.

Short form	Longer description
Smiths Dock	Smith's Dock Co Ltd, Middlesbrough.
G & T Smith, Rye	G. & T. Smith Co, Rye, Sussex.
Smith, Buckie	G. Smith Jr, Buckie.
Stephen	Alexander Stephen & Sons Ltd, Linthouse, Govan.
Stephen, Banff	W. & G. Stephen, Banff.
Stevenson & Asher	Stevenson & Asher, Banff.
Sunderland SB	Sunderland Shipbuilding Co Ltd, Sunderland.
Swan Hunter	Swan, Hunter & Wigham Richardson Ltd, Wallsend on Tyne. (Wigham Richardson added 1903).
Teesside Bridge	Teesside Bridge & Engineering Works Ltd, Middlesbrough.
Thames IW	Thames Iron Works, Blackwall.
Thomas	W. Thomas & Co, Amlwch, Anglesey.
Thomson	J. & G. Thomson Ltd, Glasgow. (later Clydebank Engineering; became John Brown 1899).
J. L. Thompson	J. L. Thompson & Sons Ltd, Sunderland.
R. Thompson	Robert Thompson & Sons Ltd, Sunderland.
Thornycroft	J. I. Thornycroft & Co Ltd, Chiswick, Hampton & Woolston. (Chiswick from 1864, Woolston from 1904).
Tyne Iron SB	Tyne Iron Shipbuilding Co Ltd, Newcastle.
Vickers	Vickers Ltd, Barrow in Furness.
Walker	C. H. Walker & Co Ltd, Sudbrook, near Chepstow.
Warren	W. H. Warren, New Holland, Lincolnshire.
Watson	J. S. Watson, Gainsborough.
Webster & Bickerton	Webster & Bickerton Ltd, Goole.
White	J. Samuel White & Co Ltd, Cowes.
Williamson	R. Williamson & Sons, Workington.
Willoughby	Willoughby Brothers, Plymouth.
Wood, Lossiemouth	W. Wood & Son, Lossiemouth.
Wood Skinner	Wood, Skinner & Co Ltd, Newcastle.
Workman Clark	Workman Clark & Co Ltd, Belfast.
Yarrow	Yarrow & Co, Poplar & Scotstoun. (Poplar from 1864, Scoutstoun from 1906).
Yarwood	W. J. Yarwood & Sons Ltd, Northwich.

Notes: Armstrong was originally Armstrong, Mitchell & Co, Elswick. Many shipyards were sited in traditional shipbuilding areas that were occupied in this trade for several centuries with numerous alterations of firm names. The Thames had long been the centre of the private shipbuilding industry in the days of wood and sail. The use of iron and steel in construction caused the industrial centre to shift to the Clyde where in 1914 there were at least 30 private firms building ships, the activity on the Thames was very small at this time. The Wear and Tyne areas were very active. Production of a sizeable share of the world's shipping tonnage came from the British yards, therefore their production capabilities during the wartime emergency proved a very valuable asset in supplying the RN and making good a portion of the shipping losses. After 1920, orders became difficult to come by and a large number of these builders ceased operations or were purchased by other firms.

The only Royal dockyards building ships during the war were Portsmouth, Chatham, Devonport and Pembroke Dock; Rosyth, Sheerness and Haulbowline (Cork) were repair yards as were those abroad—Gibraltar, Malta, Hong King, Simonstown and Bermuda.

SHIP BREAKERS (WARSHIPS ONLY, FROM 1919)

Alloa Ship Breaking Co, Rosyth and Charlestown (1922–30). =Metal Industries about 1930.
Arnott Young, Dalmuir (associated with West of Scotland Ship Breaking Co).
H. Auten (1920).
Barking Ship Breaking Co (1920–21).
Batson Syndicate (1922).
C. A. Beard, Upnor (1921–24); Teignmouth (1921).
A. A. Bond (1922).
Brand (1919).
W. & A. T. Burden (1921).
Cardiff Marine Stores (1920).
Cashmore, Newport (1911–date).
S. Castle, Plymouth (1920–35).
Clarkson, Whitby (1919–21).
Cohen, Briton Ferry (from 1897); Felixstowe (1906–10); Swansea (1905–23).
Cornish Salvage Co, Ilfracombe (1920).
Cove & Distinn (1922).
Cox & Danks, Upnor (1922); Queenborough (1922); sold to Metal Industries 1949.
Demmellweek & Redding, Plymouth (1926–date).
Dover Ship Breaking Co (1922–23). (May be modern "Dover Industries").
Ellis, Newcastle (1920–22).
T. E. Evans, Cardiff (1920–22).
Forth Ship Breaking Co, Bo'ness (1906–20). =McLellan (1922–date).
B. Fryer, Sunderland (1921–23, etc.).
Garnham (1903–21).
Granton Ship Breaking Co (1919–26).
Hammond Lane Foundry, Dublin (1920).
Hayes, Porthcawl (1919–date).
A. O. Hill, Dover (1929).
J. Hornby (1923).
J. W. Houston, Montrose (1923).
Hughes, Bolckow, Tyne (1909–23); Blyth (1912–date).
J. Jackson (1919).
W. G. Keen, Bristol (1923).
King, Garston (1899–1926).
J. J. King, Troon (1905–34).

J. H. Lee, Dover (1919–22); Bembridge (1919–20).
Loveridge & Co (1919).
Maden & McKee, Porthcawl (1919).
Marple & Gillott, Saltash (1921–22).
McLellan, B'ness (1922–date).
Metal Industries, Rosyth (1930–date), Charlestown (1935–date).
Multilocular Ship Breaking Co, Stranraer, (1919–22).
E. W. Payne (1920).
Plymouth & Devon Ship Breaking Co, Plymouth (1926).
Pounds, Portsmouth (1925–date)
Purves, Teignmouth (1920).
Rees, Llanelly (1921–date).
Richardson, Westgarth, Saltash (1923).
Riddle & Co.
Rijsdijk (Dutch), Upnor (1909–20).
Rosyth Ship Breaking Co (1922).
T. R. Sales (1919).
G. Sharp (1920).
Ship Breaking Co, Swansea (1922).
Slough Trading Co (an agency for German buyers).
J. Smith, Poole (1922–23).
South Wales Salvage Co (1921).
Stanlee, Dover (1920–24).
J. E. Thomas, Newport (1921).
W. Thomas, Anglesey (1921).
J. W. Towers, Milford Haven (1920).
Unity Ship Breaking Co, Plymouth (1922–23).
Upnor Ship Breaking Co, Upnor (1914–24).
Ward, Barrow (1894–date); Briton Ferry (1906–date); Grays (1919–date); Hayle (1920); Inverkeithing (1923–date); Lelant (1920); Milford Haven (1920–date); Morecambe (1905–date); New Holland (1920); Pembroke Dock (1926–date); Portishead (1921); Preston (1899–date); Rainham (1919–etc.); and Swansea (1909–etc.).
West of Scotland Ship Breaking Co, Troon (1912–date). (Allied to Arnott Young.)
Willoughby, Plymouth (1920).
Montague Yates (1919–20).
Young, Sunderland (1922–23).

Notes: Some of these were agencies who resold vessels to other firms for scrapping. During World War II the "British Iron & Steel Corporation" was formed and most of the ships from then on were sold to this body and allocated to various yards for scrapping.

RENAMED SHIPS—cross reference

New name	Book section	Old name
ADAMANT II	sloop	LILY
ADDA	SSV, tender	ADELAIDE
ADELE	Adty trawler	KINGFISHER
AFRIKANDER	HS	YC.229
AFRIKANDER	HS	YC.373
AKBAR	HS	INDUS II
ALACRITY	hired yacht	MLADA
ALAUNIA	monitor	MARSHAL NEY
ALGIERS	HS	INDUS IV
ALLENBY	hired drifter	RESULT
AMALTHAEA	hired yacht	IOLAIRE
AMBITIOUS	Adty drifter	AIR POCKET
ANCIENT	DY tug	VETERAN
ANGELA	motor drifter	AGNES
ANGOLIAN	hired trawler	TEUTON
ANTIC	hired trawler	AUK
ARABESQUE	lighter	ARAB
ARGON	coastguard	ARGUS
ARTOIS	AMC	DIGBY
ASPENLEAF	oiler	SAXOL
ATTENTIVE II	hired drifter	SEARCHER
ATTENTIVE II	SSV, tender	ADDER
ATTENTIVE II	Adty drifter	FAIR WIND
ATTENTIVE III	hired trawler	SEAWARD HO
AVIATOR	MFA	VICTOR
BABS	hited trawler	BARBADOS
BALUCHI	escort	PC.55
BANTERER	SSV(d)	PLUCKY
BARRYFIELD	MFA	BARRY
BASTION	hired trawler	BOSTONIAN
BAYLEAF	oiler	BAYOL
BEAUFORT	M/S	AMBLESIDE
BEN DEARG	hired trawler	BEN RINNES
BENDIGO	hired trawler	AUSTRALIA
BENMORE	motor drifter	BENAIGEN
BILLOW	Adty drifter	SUNSHINE
BLACKWATER	Adty trawler	WILLIAM INWOOD
BLAKEDOWN	hired trawler	BLAKE
BOADICEA II	Adty trawler	HENRY FORD
BOATMAN	hired tug	MARKSMAN
BOYNE	Adty trawler	WILLIAM JONES
BRITON	HS	CALYPSO
BROKE	destroyer ldr	ROOKE
BUCK	hired drifter	M H BUCHAN
BUDLEIA	hired drifter	BLOOMFIELD
BUGLER	Adty trawler	BRIGADIER
BULWARK	HS	IMPREGNABLE
CALCUTTA	HS	EXCELLENT
CANNING	troopship	LAWRENCE
CAPO	hired drifter	CAPETOWN
CARBINEER II	Adty trawler	FUSILIER
CARRICK	HS	INDEFATIGABLE
CECIL COOMBES	Adty trawler	GEORGE AIKEN
CERBERUS	HS	PROTECTOR
CH.14, CH.15	submarine	H.14, H.15
CHAMPAGNE	AMC	OROPESA
CHAMPLAIN	destroyer	TORBAY
CHARLES DORAN	Adty trawler	JOHN ANDERSON
CHEERY	hired drifter	HEARTY
CHERWELL	Adty trawler	JAMES JONES
CINCERIA	Prize trawler	COOMASIN
CITY OF PERTH	hired drifter	EMBLEM
CITY OF PERTH	Adty trawler	WILLIAM ASHTON
CLASSIC	hospital ship	MAGIC

New name	Book section	Old name
COCHRANE	depot ship	AMBROSE
COLLINSON	M/S	AMERSHAM
COLNE	Adty trawler	ISAAC CHANT
COLUMBINE	Adty drifter	DARKNESS
COLUMBINE	Adty drifter	BLACK FROST
CONNARD	hired drifter	CONCORD
CORNWALLIS	sloop	LYCHNIS
CORONET	Adty trawler	ROBERT CLOUGHTON
CRENELLA	oiler	MONTCALM
CRESCENT	battleship	GLORY
CRESCENT	cruiser	SUTLEJ
CRESSY	HS	UNICORN
CROSSBOW	hired drifter	BESSIE
CROZIER	M/S	VERWOOD
CUCKOO	HS	COLLEEN
DAEDALUS	HS	THUNDERBOLT
DANDY	hired drifter	HANDY
DART	escort	PC.73
DEAN SWIFT	MFA	SWIFT
DEBENEY	hired trawler	DERBY
DEE	Adty trawler	BATTLEAXE
DEFIANCE	HS	POWERFUL II
DEFIANCE II	HS	SPARTAN
DEFIANCE II	HS	IMPREGNABLE II
DEFIANCE III	HS	CLEOPATRA
DEFIANCE III	depot ship	VULCAN
DEFIANCE IV	HS	IMPREGNABLE II
DERWENT	Adty trawler	JOHN BRICE
DIGIT	hired drifter	DILIGENT
DOLPHIN	depot ship	PANDORA
DOON	Adty trawler	FRASER EAVES
DOUBLETIDE	Adty drifter	SIROCCO
DRAGE	boarding tug	DRAGON
DRAKE	MFA	WILDRAKE
DRAKE	monitor	MARSHAL NEY
DREEL CASTLE	hired drifter	MARA SMITH
DRONE	lighter	DRAGON
DRUDGE	HS	READY
DRUMMER	Adty trawler	DRAGOON
DRYAD	SSV (d)	DRUDGE
DRYAD	HS	RATTLER
DUNCOMBE	MFA	DERWENT
DYKE	hired drifter	VIOLA
EAGLET	hired trawler	EAGLE
EAGLET	HS	EAGLE
EAGLET	sloop	SIR BEVIS
EBBTIDE	Adty drifter	CD.1
EDEN	Adty trawler	THOMAS JOHNS
EGMONT	BDV	BULLFROG
EGREMONT	HS	EGMONT
ELPHINSTONE	sloop	CEANOTHUS
EMBLEM	hired drifter	CITY OF PERTH
EMERALD	HS	COLLEEN
EMPRISE	DY tug	ENTERPRISE
ENTERTAIN	hired drifter	ENTERPRISE
ETTRICK	Adty trawler	SAMUEL JAMIESON
EVENTIDE	Adty trawler	CD.71
EXCELLENCY	hired drifter	EXCELLENT
EXCELLENT	SSV (d)	DRUDGE
EXCELLENT	Adty trawler	JACKDAW
EXCELLENT	Adty trawler	WILLIAM LEECH
EXCELLENT	Adty trawler	ANDREW JEWER
EXE	Adty trawler	THOMAS JARVIS
EXPANSE	Adty drifter	DAWN
FEN	DY tug	CROCUS
FIGUIG	hospital ship	GRANTALA
FIREBRAND	sloop	TORCH
FIREFLY	HS	EGMONT
FISGARD	HS	SPARTIATE
FISGARD II	HS	CALCUTTA

New name	Book section	Old name
FISGARD III	cruiser	TERRIBLE
FITZROY	M/S	PINNER
FIZZER	hired drifter	VIOLET
FLINDERS	M/S	RADLEY
FLOODTIDE	Adty drifter	CD.72
FLORA	HS	YC.373
FORTE	HS	FURIOUS
FOYLE	Adty trawler	JOHN EDMUND
GANNET	HS	WILDFIRE
GANNET	HS	PEMBROKE
GARRY	Adty trawler	GOLDAXE
GEORGE DIXON	Adty trawler	JOHN CAMPBELL
GLENEALY	hired drifter	GLENTILT
GODSPEED	hired drifter	SPEEDWELL
GREEN MANTLE	hired drifter	LIVONIA
GREY WOLF	hired drifter	CENWULF
GUINEVERE	hired drifter	ELLA
GULLWING	hired drifter	EGLANTINE
HALCYON II	motor boat	SALMON
HAMADRYAD	M/S, TGB	DRYAD
HARLECH	cruiser	CAMBRIAN
HART	HS	RAPID
HECLA II	hired drifter	WHEAT STALK
HELICON	HS	CALLIOPE
HERACLES	hired tug	HERCULES
HERALD	sloop	MERRY HAMPTON
HERMIT	mooring vessel	ANCHORITE
HINDOSTAN	HS	FISGARD III
HOKIANGA	hired trawler	NEW ZEALAND
HONEY COMB	motor drifter	HONEY BEE
HOTSPUR	hired tug	WRESTLER
HC.1	MFA	KING EDWARD
HC.2	paddle M/S	LONDON BELLE
HC.3	paddle M/S	WALTON BELLE
HC.4	paddle M/S	QUEEN EMPRESS
HC.5	paddle M/S	SLIEVE BEARNAGH
HC.6	paddle M/S	MARCHIONESS OF BUTE
HC.7	MFA	LORD MORTON
HC.8	MFA	EDINBURGH CASTLE
ICARUS	MFA	TRENT
ICTOR	rescue tug	VICTOR
IDAHO	Adty trawler	GIOVANNI GUINTI
IMPERATOR	hired drifter	IMPREGNABLE
IMPERIEUSE	HS	FISGARD
IMPREGNABLE	HS	POWERFUL
IMPREGNABLE II	HS	POWERFUL II
IMPREGNABLE III	HS	INDUS V
IMPREGNABLE IV	HS	CIRCE
IMPREGNABLE IV	HS	POWERFUL III
IMPREST	hired drifter	IMPREGNABLE
INDUS II	HS	FLORA
INDUS II	battleship	VICTORIOUS
INDUSTRY	Q ship	TAY & TYNE
IOLAIRE	hired yacht	AMALTHAEA
IOLAIRE	hired tug	LADY WINDSOR
IRWELL	sloop	SIR BEVIS
IRWELL	M/S	GOOLE
ISLAND PRINCE	hired trawler	GENERAL BOTHA
ISONZO	MFA	ISIS
ITCHEN	Adty trawler	THOMAS HAGGERTY
JOHN EVANS	Adty trawler	JOHN LEWIS
JOHN MASON	Adty trawler	JOHN ABBOTT
JOHN MOSS	Adty trawler	JOHN HUNS
JOSEPHINE I	Adty trawler	SPARROW
JULIUS	hired drifter	PHINGASK
JULIUS	SSV, yacht	IMOGENE
JUPITER	hired tug	TRIBESMAN
KELLETT	M/S	UPPINGHAM
KENNET	Adty trawler	ICEAXE

New name	Book section	Old name
KILDA	Adty trawler	JANUS
KINGFISHER	hired drifter	ADELE
KINGFISHER	hired drifter	DOROTHY F
LAVATERA	hired drifter	EFFORT
LEANDROS	hired trawler	LEANDER
LIFFEY	Adty trawler	STONEAXE
LOTHBURY	MFA	ARGO
MAHRATTA	paddle patrol	EMPEROR OF INDIA II
MAINE	hospital ship	MEDIATOR
MALAPERT	hired drifter	MASCOT
MAPLELEAF	oiler	RANGOL
MARA SMITH	hired drifter	DREEL CASTLE
MEDEA	monitor	M.22
MEDIATOR	HS	INDUS V
MEDUSA	monitor	M.29
MEDWAY II	monitor	M.29
MELITA	coastguard	RINGDOVE
MELPOMENE	monitor	M.31
MENELAUS	monitor	M.31
MINERVA	monitor	M.33
MOLLUSC	mooring vessel	TRINCULO
MORDAUNT	hired tug	DAUNTLESS
MORESBY	sloop	SILVIO
MOY	Adty trawler	ALEXANDER HILLS
N.1	submarine	NAUTILUS
NAIRN	Adty trawler	DRIVER
NAIRN	hired drifter	CLOVER
NESS	Adty trawler	ALEXANDER PALMER
NIGHTJAR	hired trawler	CUCKOO
NITH	Adty trawler	ANDREW JEWER
NORM	lighter	NORMAN
NUNTHORPE HALL	Adty trawler	SEAMEW
OAKLEAF	oiler	ABADOL
OCEANA	boarding tug	CERBERUS
OLCADES	oiler	BRITISH BEACON
OLIGARCH	oiler	BRITISH LANTERN
OLWEN	oiler	BRITISH LIGHT
OLYNTHUS	oiler	BRITISH STAR
ORIENT	DY tug	SAMPSON
ORIFLAMME	hired yacht	ST GEORGE
ORIFLAMME	hired trawler	WALLINGTON
OSPREY	Adty whaler	ICEWHALE
OUSE	Adty trawler	ANDREW KING
OWLET	hired trawler	EAGLE
PADUA	MFA	PRINCESS OF WALES
PARKGATE	BDV	BV.5
PATHAN	escort	PC.69
PEEWIT II	hired yacht	LAPWING
PEGASUS	A/C carrier	ARK ROYAL
PEKIN	Adty trawler	JOHN DUNKIN
PEKIN	Adty trawler	FESTING GRINDALL
PEMBROKE	HS	WILDFIRE
PEMBROKE	HS	EGMONT
PEMBROKE	monitor	PRINCE RUPERT
PEMBROKE	Adty trawler	DANIEL FEARALL
PENGUIN	cruiser	ENCOUNTER
PENGUIN	depot ship	PLATYPUS
PERSEVERANCE	DY tug	METEOR
PETULANT	SSV, tender	PELICAN
PIPIN	motor drifter	VIOLET
PLATYPUS II	HS	CERBERUS
PLUMER	hired drifter	PANSY
POLEGATE	BDV	BV.7
PORT VICTOR	MFA	MURITAI
PRATTLER	Adty whaler	SPLINT
PRESIDENCY	hired trawler	PRESIDENT
PRESIDENT	sloop	SAXIFRAGE
PRINCETOWN	MFA	PRINCE
QUERY	paddle tug	CONQUEROR
QUEST	hired trawler	QUEEN

New name	Book section	Old name
QUINCE	paddle tug	QUEEN
RALEIGH	Adty drifter	GLITTER
RAMESES	hired drifter	BOY WILLIE
RATTLER	Adty whaler	SPLINT
RAVENROCK	A/C carrier	RAVEN II
RAWLINSON	hired drifter	CONDOR
RECLUSE	hired drifter	POPPY
RECOVERY	DY tug	ROVER
REDOUBTABLE	battleship	REVENGE
RED ROVER	hired drifter	VINE
REIGATE	BDV	BD.30
RESOURCE	motor boat	RESOLUTE
RESOURCEFUL	motor boat	RESOLUTE
RESTIVE	DY tug	RESTLESS
RINGDOVE	BDV	MELITA
RIVAL	DY tug	JASON
ROGATE	BDV	BD.46
ROLLICKER	DY tug	ROVER
ROMANCE	hired tug	ROMAN
ROOKE	HS	CORMORANT
ROTHER	Adty trawler	ANTHONY ASLETT
RUSHCOE	hired trawler	JELLICOE
S.1	submarine	SWORDFISH
SABINE	SSV (d)	SABRINA
SABLE	destroyer	SALMON
ST ANGELO	BDV	BULLFROG
ST ANGELO	SSV, tender	ADELAIDE
ST PATRICK	water tanker	SHAMROCK
SANDBOY	DY tug	STRENUOUS
SANDGATE	BDV	BV.4
SAREPTA	hired drifter	WELCOME FRIEND
SEADOG	DY tug	STALWART
SEA ROVER	Adty trawler	SEAFLOWER
SHALOT	hired drifter	SAPPHIRE
SIDONIAN	DY tug	TYRIAN
SIGISMUND	hired yacht	SIMOUN
SMUTS	motor drifter	MAFEKING
SNAPPER	gunboat	MASTIFF
SNAPPER II	HS	EXCELLENT
SOUTHGATE	BDV	BV.8
SPACE	Adty drifter	SPLASH
SPELLBIND	motor drifter	EXCELLENT
SPEY	escort	P.38
SPLENDID	motor drifter	EXCELLENT
STOAT	SSV, tender	WEASEL
STOUR	Adty trawler	DANIEL FEARALL
STRATHMORE	motor drifter	STRATHLENE
SUCCOUR	hired tug	SUN III
SULTAN	HS	FISGARD IV
SUNDORA	hired drifter	SUNBEAM II
SUPERBUS	motor drifter	SUPERB
SURF II	Q ship	VICTORIA
SWARTHY	DY tug	STURDY
TALBOT	monitor	M.29
TEST	Adty trawler	PATRICK BOWE
TEVIOT	Adty trawler	GEORGE IRELAND
THOMAS DEAS	Adty trawler	JAMES JOHNSON
TIT	lighter	SWIFT
TONGA	lighter	TOGO
TOTEM	hired drifter	TITANIA
TRACKER	hired tug	PIONEER
TRANTOR	hired tug	TRENT
TRUSTFUL	DY tug	TRUSTY
TYRE	DY tug	TYRIAN
TYRO	motor drifter	TWILIGHT
URE	Adty trawler	HENRY JENNINGS
VANCOUVER	destroyer	TOREADOR
VERITAS	hired drifter	VERITY
VERNON	hired trawler	STRATHCOE
VICAR	motor drifter	VICTORY

New name	Book section	Old name
VICTORINE	hired drifter	VICTORY
VICTORIOUS II	battleship	PRINCE GEORGE
VICTORSIT	hired drifter	VICTORY
VIMY	destroyer	VANCOUVER
VINELEAF	oiler	TEAKOL
VIVID	SSV (d)	SABRINA
VIVID	cruiser	CAMBRIAN
VIVID	monitor	MARSHAL NEY
VOLATILE	DY tug	VOLCANO
VOLENS	mooring vessel	VOLUNTEER
VULCAN	sloop	LILY
VULCAN II	depot ship	ONYX
WALLINGTON	hired yacht	ST GEORGE
WALLINGTON	cruiser	WALLAROO
WARDEN	SSV, ferry	WANDERER
WAVENEY	Adty trawler	JAMES CONNOR
WAYWARD	SSV, tender	WAVE
WEAR	Adty trawler	JOHN BOMKWORTH
WELCOME FRIEND	hired drifter	SAREPTA
WESTERN QUEEN	paddle M/S	WESTWARD HO
WESTGATE	BDV	BV.17
WHITETHROAT	hired trawler	WREN
WICKSTEAD	hired tug	WYVERN
WILDFIRE	HS	CORNWALLIS
WILLIAM II	hired drifter	BOY WILLIE
WILLIAM DOGHERTY	Adty trawler	GEORGE BROWN
ZEAL	water tanker	ZEALOUS
ZEDWHALE	Adty whaler	MEG
ZEST	water tanker	ZEALOUS
ZOROASTER	hired drifter	ZODIAC